Fourth Edition

Therapeutic Recreation

Fourth Edition

Therapeutic Recreation

A Practical Approach

Marcia Jean Carter
Western Illinois University

Glen E. Van Andel
Professor Emeritus, Calvin College

WAVELAND

PRESS, INC.

Long Grove, Illinois

For information about this book, contact:
Waveland Press, Inc.
4180 IL Route 83, Suite 101
Long Grove, IL 60047-9580
(847) 634-0081
info@waveland.com
www.waveland.com

Cover photos (from top to bottom): Jasmine Townsend, National Ability Center; Jasmine Townsend, National Ability Center; Ramon Zabriskie; Ryan Jensen, National Ability Center.

Chapter photos: Pages 6, 83, 85, 117, 142, 211, 246, 278, 299, 308, Ryan Jensen, National Ability Center; pages 10 (lower left and right), 19, 62, 78, 180, 197, 228, 264, 279, 297, 307, 317, 319, 322, 388, 397, Jasmine Townsend, National Ability Center; pages 30, 32, National Library of Medicine; page 37, from the files of Dr. Bernath Eugene Phillips, used with permission of Charlie Dixon, Therapeutic Recreation Directory; page 43, Jasmine Townsend for Wheelin Jazz Athletes; pages 77, 91, 121, 128, 165, 178, 185, 342, 362, 364, 367, 390, 438, 458, Ramon Zabriskie, Heritage School; page 385, © Barbara Laws/John Birdsall Archive/The Image Works.

Copyright © 2011 by Marcia Jean Carter and Glen E. Van Andel
Copyright © 2003, 1995, 1985 by Marcia Jean Carter, Glen E. Van Andel, and Gary M. Robb.

10-digit ISBN: 1-57766-644-5
13-digit ISBN: 978-1-57766-644-8

Printed in the United States of America

7 6 5 4 3 2

Contents

Preface

The fourth edition of *Therapeutic Recreation: A Practical Approach* reflects the still-evolving nature of this health-care profession and practice in a diverse global world. Social, cultural, demographic, and economic shifts, as well as technological advancements, have created demand for fiscal accountability by informed consumers/clients who expect safe, quality health and human services that are reliable, responsive to their needs, and have proven benefits. Thus our intention is to provide, in a practical, student-oriented fashion, a comprehensive overview of the fundamentals of therapeutic recreation as a health and human service profession and as a career choice. This revised edition is primarily designed for an introductory course in therapeutic recreation at the undergraduate level. Students majoring in health and human service programs or recreation may also find the text useful, particularly if they anticipate careers in health-care settings and agencies that offer inclusionary programs.

As an introductory text, this book (1) examines the primary roles and responsibilities of a "helping practitioner," (2) describes the fundamental tool—the therapeutic recreation process—used in the field, (3) explores the historical and philosophical growth of the profession, (4) introduces students to the theoretical concepts underpinning the practice, (5) outlines essential management tasks in therapeutic recreation, and (6) surveys practice settings and services and the clients with whom therapeutic recreation practitioners interact. Part I introduces students to the fundamentals of the profession and the practice of therapeutic recreation. Part II explores the application of the therapeutic recreation process to a wide array of clients. Each chapter in this section is organized in a similar fashion that describes the nature of the impairment, discusses delivery settings and intervention strategies, and highlights the role of the therapeutic recreation specialist in improving an individual's health status, quality of life, and/or functional capacities.

We believe that the learning process transcends the walls of academia only to be fully realized through meaningful, practical experiences that allow students to apply knowledge and skills they have developed in a wide variety of settings. Each chapter opens with a list of objectives that encourages students to consider both theoretical underpinnings and practical application of the information presented. Within the text, case studies, illustrations, and photographs depict actual situations. Key terms, study questions, and practical exercises at the end of each chapter reinforce key concepts and suggest ways for students to apply the material presented in the chapter and to access up-to-date information. By encouraging students to become active participants in the learning process, we hope to excite them about the practice of the profession. A key to selecting a rewarding career is to be aware of a profession's history and future direction, and to understand the practical tasks undertaken as a professional. This is why we have endeavored to provide students with both a broad orientation to the field as well as the practical information necessary to become successful practitioners.

Acknowledgments

To the students who have and who will share with us their needs and knowledge, we extend our appreciation and encouragement. We also recognize the support of colleagues who reviewed chapters and contributed updated information in this edition:

- Dana Dempsey, MS, CTRS, and the staff of the Therapeutic Recreation Department, Texas Scottish Rite Hospital for Children, Dallas, Texas
- Claire M. Foret, PhD, CTRS, Professor, University of Louisiana at Lafayette
- Sandra K. Negley, MS, MTRS/CTRS Expressive Therapies, University of Utah Neuropsychiatric Institute, Salt Lake City
- Glenda P. Taylor, PhD, CTRS, Professor, Longwood University, Farmville, Virginia
- Ray E. West, MS, LRT/CTRS, Consultant, Chapel Hill, North Carolina
- Ramon B. Zabriskie, PhD, CTRS, Professor, Brigham Young University, Provo, Utah

We also gratefully acknowledge those who contributed photographs and illustrations to this edition:

- Sandra K. Negley, University of Utah Neuropsychiatric Institute
- Carolyn M. Nagle, Executive Director, Fox Valley Special Recreation Association, Aurora, Illinois
- Stephen P. LeConey, Regional Supervisor, Cincinnati Recreation Commission, Cincinnati, Ohio
- Allison B. Donohue, Department of Therapeutic Recreation/Child Life, The Children's Hospital, Aurora, Colorado
- Dana Dempsey, Therapeutic Recreation Department, Texas Scottish Rite Hospital for Children, Dallas, Texas
- Kelly Sigler, CTRS, Therapeutic Recreation Services, Genesis Medical Center, Davenport, Iowa

- Ramon B. Zabriskie, Professor, Brigham Young University, Provo, Utah
- Jasmine A. Townsend, Indiana University, Bloomington, Indiana
- The National Ability Center, Park City, Utah
- Heritage Schools, Therapeutic Recreation Department, Provo, Utah

Special thanks are given to our families, who have given of their spirit and patience: John and Peg Carter, and John, Nancy, Cory, Daniell, Zachary, and Nathan Carter, who have always been there to give and share; Jim and Angeline Van Andel, who have modeled the spirit of helping and serving others, and to Gloria, Patti, Dave, and Mark Van Andel, who continue to be an inspiration and constant source of love and acceptance.

Our contributions to this text and to our profession have been possible through the prayers, support, memory, and encouragement of our families and colleagues.

Marcia Jean Carter
Glen E. Van Andel

AN OVERVIEW OF THE PROFESSION

Therapeutic recreation is one of the oldest yet one of the youngest health and human service professions. Therapeutic activities have been used to care for individuals with illnesses and disabilities since the beginning of time. During the twentieth century the specialized application of recreation experiences became recognized as a component of health care. In the twenty-first century, the profession of therapeutic recreation continues to evolve, grow, and mature, as do those who practice its tenets. With such changes come challenges and newfound expectations. We believe that a proactive philosophy is required of those entering the profession.

As the professional grows, so does the profession. There is a dynamic interrelationship between the professional and the profession. Fundamental to the growth of the student as a future therapeutic recreation specialist is the *self*. The self is the foundation of professional action and of the caregiving, practitioner-client relationship. Students today will make conscious decisions influencing the nature of the profession and their professional relationships with prospective clients.

A therapeutic recreation specialist implements a therapeutic recreation program in an efficient, effective, and safe manner to assist in maintaining or improving a client's health status, quality of life, and/or level of functioning. Program specialists and managers translate theory and evidence into best practices through the APIE (assessment, planning, implementation, evaluation) process. Regardless of employment level, job description, or staff composition, managerial functions such as staffing, budgeting, marketing, and evaluating are present in each position.

In chapter 1 we consider the unique contributions the therapeutic recreation profession makes to health and human services. The holistic influence of therapeutic recreation is discussed in view of global interpretations of health. A conceptual model is used to describe therapeutic recreation's role and function in health and human services. We explore the theoretical underpinnings and nature of therapeutic recreation by studying each phase of the model.

In chapter 2 we challenge you to consider the present status and nature of therapeutic recreation within the context of philosophical perspectives and historical events and circumstances. We use the framework of developmental stages to outline the major influences on the profession as well as to compare the past with the present, ponder the future, and document events and actions leading to professionalization of our practice.

Chapter 3 examines the helping relationship that is established through interpersonal communication. Why do you want to help? "Helping" can either enhance or detract from the significance of the therapeutic recreation process. It is important to develop appropriate facilitation skills to use with selected modalities and techniques to enable client change and progress toward individual objectives.

Chapter 4 looks at each phase of the therapeutic recreation process (APIE)—assessment, planning, implementation, and evaluation. These tasks require balancing individual client objectives with program objectives, and matching safe client care to appropriate services (theory and evidence-based practices) within a reasonable length of stay to assure achievement of client outcomes.

Chapter 5 notes that the effectiveness of therapeutic recreation programs and services is dependent upon the attention given to several management functions. These important functions include the written plan of operation, financial operations, technical operations, and personnel operations. Ultimately, client outcomes are influenced by those who manage the resources that support program delivery. Although each employment setting is unique, entry-level professionals typically balance their time between direct client interventions and management tasks like quality improvement and advocacy.

Becoming a Member of a Profession

After reading this chapter, students will be able to:

✔ Discuss the various factors and perspectives that have contributed to the current definition of therapeutic recreation

✔ Identify the purpose of therapeutic recreation

✔ Identify several different models that have been advanced to help conceptualize the practice of therapeutic recreation

✔ Describe the basic nature of health-care delivery systems

✔ Identify the roles, settings, and responsibilities common to therapeutic recreation

✔ Identify the service goals and outcomes of therapeutic recreation

✔ Describe the basic elements of the humanistic perspective

Becoming a member of a profession requires that you understand the nature of the profession. You also need to develop a perspective or attitude toward important issues associated with the practice of the profession. This chapter provides an orientation to therapeutic recreation and a conceptual framework to enhance your understanding of the process of becoming a therapeutic recreation specialist.

Chapter 1 was revised with contributions from Ramon B. Zabriskie, PhD, CTRS, Brigham Young University, Provo, Utah.

INTRODUCTION

Approaching the study of a profession that is being considered as a career is both exciting and sobering. The excitement stems from the interest we have in the topic and the potential it holds for fulfilling certain needs or dreams. Helping and serving others is indeed a stimulating and challenging career goal, one that should not be approached lightly. It has been said that if you can help someone by what you do, you also have the potential for harming him or her. Therapeutic recreation is a health and human service profession. Therapeutic recreation specialists are in the business of providing certain services to people for the purpose of improving their health, functional abilities, and quality of life. How these services are provided is extremely critical to the ultimate outcome for those we serve. Becoming a professional is no small or insignificant task. It cannot be accomplished by taking a few courses, reading a few books, listening to more than a few lectures, taking a certification exam, or even applying some professional skills in a therapeutic program. We hope that this chapter will help you begin to understand the nature of therapeutic recreation and grasp the importance of becoming a *professional*—not simply a graduate with a degree in therapeutic recreation.

The field of therapeutic recreation is relatively young. Even in its short lifetime it has been affected by many professional and social changes. As you will soon discover, the profession has been challenged to document its unique role and function in health and human services. What is its primary function? How should that function be modified to accommodate continual changes in our society? Although we cannot propose a final answer to these questions, we will begin to define the parameters and thus provide an orientation to the essential elements of the profession.

THE NATURE OF THERAPEUTIC RECREATION

"Therapeutic recreation—what is that?" You will likely encounter this question repeatedly throughout your career. You might respond with, "Oh, it's a profession that provides recreation programs for people with disabilities or those who are in hospitals or other health-care agencies." There was a time when this answer would have been quite acceptable. Historically, therapeutic recreation has been closely linked with (1) the settings in which the recreation activities occur (usually hospitals or institutions), (2) the emphasis on the therapeutic value of recreation, and (3) the nature of the participants or clients; that is, persons with impairments. In light of recent trends, however, these criteria no longer exclusively define therapeutic recreation. In effect, societal changes have forced the profession to reconsider its specific mission or purpose.

Redefining the Profession

Much has changed since the origin of the profession in the middle of the twentieth century. Most of these changes will be discussed in chapter 2, where we outline in detail the history of the profession. For our purposes here, however, we'll concentrate on just a few factors that have influenced our contemporary understanding of therapeutic recreation.

A Redefinition of Recreation

Early in the twentieth century, social reformers recognized the value of recreation as a tool to fight the social decay of inner-city slums. Following World Wars I and II, the popularity of recreation programs grew and their focus shifted from addressing social needs to providing recreational opportunities to the public. Meanwhile, the fledgling therapeutic recreation profession was taking on the role abandoned by the recreation movement; that is, serving the needs of people with social, emotional, physical, cognitive, and behavioral problems, especially those in institutions. The therapeutic value of recreation experiences was emphasized as this new profession defined its unique role in health and human services.

After the 1950s, however, numerous social changes prompted a reassessment of the nature and purpose of recreation. Of major importance was the increase in citizen participation in all levels of government. Society no longer relied on the institutions of government to meet all its needs. We moved toward a self-help society intent on making our own decisions and determining our own fate. American society also began to recognize and accept cultural and ethnic differences. People placed a higher value on the importance of the individual as a unique human being and the diversity of human beings evident throughout the world. From these changes emerged a **humanistic** ethic that stressed the importance of human development, improved processes of human interaction, and the protection and restoration of the natural environment. We began to see ourselves differently, and as a result, our sense of what it means to be human also changed.

In response to these changes, David Gray and Seymour Greben (1974) outlined a new perspective that sought to define the nature of **recreation** in the context of contemporary social and psychological realities. They proposed that recreation be defined in terms of the psychological construct "what happens to people." They suggested the following:

> Recreation is an emotional condition within an individual human being that flows from a feeling of well-being and self-satisfaction. It is characterized by feelings of mastery, achievement, exhilaration, acceptance, success, personal worth, and pleasure. It reinforces a positive self-image. Recreation is a response to aesthetic experience, achievement of personal goals, or positive feedback from others. It is independent of activity, leisure, or social acceptance. (p. 26)

This redefinition clearly describes the therapeutic value of a recreative experience. Recreation activities promote personal development by reinforcing a positive self-image and providing opportunities for self-satisfying experiences and the achievement of personal goals. Recreation experiences in this context become essential to health and quality of life for all people, which means that therapeutic recreation can no longer claim exclusive right as the profession that uses recreation as a health-related medium. All people can experience the therapeutic benefits of recreation, whether part of a therapeutic recreation program or a self-directed leisure experience.

Deinstitutionalization of Individuals with Disabilities

The passage of the Mental Retardation Facilities and Community Mental Health Center Construction Act of 1963, and similar legislation in the following decades, led to the decline of custodial care, the decentralization of state institutions, and the increase

Recreation activities promote personal development by reinforcing a positive self-image and providing opportunities for participants to experience achievement, self-satisfaction, exhilaration, and pleasure.

in individualized programs and community-based treatment. These trends brought many more people with impairments into communities. Many communities responded by developing special recreation programs for these individuals. Since these programs were held in community settings, the "hospital recreation" characterization of therapeutic recreation no longer applied. The only element that seemed to distinguish therapeutic recreation from general recreation, then, appeared to be the participation of people with disabilities or specific needs. However, suggesting that therapeutic recreation is any recreation program that involves people with impairments imposes serious limitations to our humanistic philosophy, since it emphasizes the "differentness" of these individuals and thus tends to isolate them from other members of society. Categorizing individuals by reason of some distinguishing feature such as a disabling condition has been appropriately challenged in the last several decades as dehumanizing and degrading. Changing attitudes toward individuals with disabling conditions is evidence of a movement in our society to recognize and accept the individual as a person, regardless of differences from the "norm."

Changing Attitudes toward Individuals with Disabilities

Pity or fear have been, and still are, common attitudes our society holds toward individuals with disabilities. If we are honest with ourselves we have to admit to some of these same feelings as we consider working closely with such people. What should I say? How will they act? What should I do if . . . ? Such questions are typical. Or we might think, I feel so sorry for him or her . . . I'm going to do all I can to make him or her happy. These attitudes often result from focusing on the impairment rather than seeing the person as a developing human being who has the capacity to learn and to contribute to society. The therapeutic recreation profession has been guilty of categorizing and labeling individuals by describing community recreation programs as "recreation for special populations," or "special recreation," or even "therapeutic recreation," only because the people involved happen to come to the activity in a wheelchair, or have a visual impairment, or have scored two standard deviations below the mean on a scholastic achievement test. The use of the phrase "recreation for special populations," for example, continues the labeling process and results in categorical judgments about individuals' interests, skills, levels of functioning, and previous experience. This practice perpetuates the idea that people with a particular illness or physical or cognitive impairment are, "within their category," alike in all respects, and "distinctly different" from the "non-ill, nondisabled, and nonspecial" in all respects (Meyer, 1977). Although no harm is intended by the use of our professional terminology and practices, we can readily see the potential implications for those whom we categorize. Hutchinson and Lord (1979) effectively describe how a relatively minor physical or mental disability may develop into a much larger social handicap (see exhibit 1.1).

Despite some of these lingering problems, our society is becoming more sensitive to the needs, interests, and abilities of persons with impairments. As recreation therapists, it is imperative that we encourage friends and colleagues to use "people-first" language, and to become advocates for people with disabilities (Bullock, Mahon, & Killingsworth, 2010). Person-first terminology focuses on the person first as a unique human being with the potential to grow and develop; for example, Dave is an adult with an intellectual disability rather than Dave is mentally retarded (Devine, 2008). Future programs must emphasize positive characteristics while de-emphasizing the impairment these individuals might have in common. Thus, in describing general recreation programs that include participants who have an impairment or special abilities, we cannot summarily refer to these programs as "recreation for special populations," "special recreation," or "therapeutic recreation." We must properly call them "general recreation."

A Redefinition of Health

The World Health Organization (WHO) has defined **health** as a state of complete physical, mental, and social well-being, and not merely the absence of disease and infirmity. Although introduced in the 1940s, this holistic perspective has only recently interpreted the term "health" to be similar in meaning to the term "wellness" (Shank & Coyle, 2002). This approach considers health or wellness in the context of one's environment and the choices made as clients take responsibility for achieving balance among physical, social, emotional, cognitive, and spiritual functioning and development. Recognition of the interrelatedness of client health factors and environmental influences, as well as the desire to promote a common framework to describe health worldwide, led to the release in 2001 of the International Classification of Functioning, Disability, and Health (ICF). Subsequently, the WHO introduced a practical tool to aid in the planning and evaluating of client services, the ICF Checklist (WHO, 2003). Professionals may elect to use this checklist in their battery of assessments to document environmental barriers and facilitators to client capacity and performance in life experiences, including recreation and leisure.

Until recently our concept of health has been predicated on disease and rehabilitation. We are now increasingly interested in preventing illness. Health maintenance organizations (HMOs), for example, are providing a popular alternative to traditional health insurance agencies. The basic philosophy of HMOs is to promote healthy lifestyle behaviors that prevent illness and to diagnose and treat illness before it becomes more serious, requiring costly medical care. Traditional approaches, on the other hand, have usually required that a person be critically ill or hospitalized before insurance coverage is initiated.

Exhibit 1.1   The Effect of Negative Attitudes on Persons with Varying Abilities

Problem	Result	Consequences
Negative Attitudes Society's negative role perceptions and low tolerance for individual differences result in the person with a disability being viewed as deviant (differentness that is negatively valued).	*Labeling* The person with a difference that is devalued (e.g., slower at learning) is then labeled (e.g., learning disabled). The problems with a label are (1) we tend to focus on the person's disabilities rather than the abilities, and (2) we make generalizations about the whole person based on misconceptions regarding that label; in other words, a disability tends to have a spread effect in the minds of others. For example, a person who is intellectually disabled may be considered unfeeling. *Segregating* Once people are labeled, they are often segregated with others who have similar (and not so similar) differences. This segregation is usually done in the name of rehabilitation. *Accentuating the Differences* Putting people with disabilities together is a "juxtaposition of differences" that further accentuates those differences. *Rejection* Accentuation of differences makes it difficult for people to be viewed as developing human beings and leads to rejection and further segregation and isolation.	*Major Handicap* A person who may have started out with a relatively minor physical or mental disability now has a major social handicap, which in turn prevents the development of self-confidence and involvement in the community

From Hutchinson, P., and Lord, J. (1979). *Recreation integration: Issues and alternatives in leisure services and community involvement*. Ottawa, Ontario: Leisurability Publications. Used with permission.

Since recreation experiences enhance health and well-being, they become increasingly important to a society that seeks to keep people well. Recreation thus plays a preventive role in health maintenance, and community recreation personnel contribute to health care as they promote recreation experiences. Quality of life is the goal of the new health movement, and recreation experiences contribute to this effort (Sylvester, 1987). Thus, if therapeutic recreation has a unique rehabilitative purpose, it will have to be more than just the natural benefit of a recreation experience.

Defining Therapeutic Recreation

We have explored some of the common myths associated with therapeutic recreation and outlined professional and societal changes that have helped, as well as forced, us to define therapeutic recreation more appropriately. The primary distinction that remains to be made is the difference between general and therapeutic recreation. **Therapeutic recreation** is a holistic process that purposefully uses recreation and experiential interventions to bring about a change—either social, emotional, intellectual, physical, or spiritual—in an effort to maintain and improve health status, functional capacities, and quality of life. This process is not limited to certain categories of individuals or a particular setting. Rather, therapeutic recreation may be applicable to all individuals whose needs and goals would seem to benefit from such an intervention in whatever setting they find themselves.

Meyer (1977) suggests that the "professional who provides organized activities and experiences for people which are conducive to growth, learning, satisfaction, pleasure, achievement, relaxation, and personal and social acceptance" is functioning as a recreator. A therapeutic recreator, to clarify the difference, is "one who uses organized activities and experiences for specific, purposeful interventions in peoples' lives to bring about specific changes in behavior" (p. 8). As we consider these differences between roles, it is clear that the characteristics used in the past to define therapeutic recreation are no longer applicable. In some hospitals or long-term care institutions, for example, the majority of the programs offered are general recreation. This may be the result of an inappropriately large client/staff ratio, a lower level of professional staff preparation, or the philosophy of the institution. For instance, some nursing facilities do not consider rehabilitation to be their primary purpose. At the same time, there are growing numbers of able-bodied consumers, such as retirees, who could benefit from a therapeutic recreation intervention, such as leisure education, that would improve their adjustment to retirement. Therapeutic recreation, therefore, cannot be defined by a particular setting or category of individuals. Instead, it must be characterized as the specific process that uses recreation as a modality to help achieve predetermined goals and objectives related to any of the life domains, and therefore improves health status, functional capabilities, and overall quality of life.

We have briefly reviewed the developmental process involved in defining the current purpose and function of therapeutic recreation, but you should note that this definition is subject to constant change. Just as the current definition has evolved, future definitions will be affected by social and professional modifications. We will consider the roots and historical development of therapeutic recreation in chapter 2 in preparation for and anticipation of factors that will influence the future of our profession.

Scope of Services

Therapeutic recreation services are provided in a wide variety of settings with clients who present many different needs and who participate in all types of programs. Early in the history of the profession, all services were provided in institutions or hospitals. As society slowly recognized the value of returning people with disabilities to their homes and communities, more programs and services developed in community settings. In today's health-care environment, the extremely high cost of hospital care, along with increasing demands for accountability and the global nature of care, has added pressures to limit the length of hospitalizations and provide more health care on an outpatient, day-treatment, or in-home basis. Although the trend is definitely toward community-based services, the majority of the Certified Therapeutic Recreation Specialists (CTRSs) remain employed in health-care facilities such as (1) rehabilitation centers that serve people with physical disabilities, including those with traumatic brain injuries, spinal cord injuries, or strokes; (2) mental health facilities for children, adoles-

Therapeutic recreation occurs in a variety of settings and with clients who present an array of different needs.

cents, and/or adults who are treated for a variety of psychological impairments includ-ing substance abuse, depression, behavioral disorders, eating disorders, trauma resulting from abuse, or mood disorders; (3) long-term facilities like skilled nursing facilities and assisted living centers that serve the elderly and address impairments associated with aging; and (4) residential transitional facilities that care for people with developmental disabilities (National Council for Therapeutic Recreation Certification [NCTRC], 2009). Some therapeutic recreation personnel are also employed by school systems, prison systems, halfway houses, outpatient day-treatment centers, and a variety of com-munity-based recreation programs including park and recreation departments, special-ized adult day centers, nonprofit agencies, and adaptive sport centers where they serve people with a variety of disabilities and needs. In some respects, therapeutic recreation is provided wherever there is a need for services. Students should stay informed about trends in the health-care industry since job opportunities will closely reflect these trends. See exhibit 1.2 for a list of competencies for twenty-first century professionals.

Exhibit 1.2   21 Competencies for the 21st Century

- Embrace a personal ethic of social responsibility and service
- Exhibit ethical behavior in all professional activities
- Provide evidence-based, clinically competent care
- Incorporate the multiple determinants of health in clinical care
- Apply knowledge of the new sciences
- Demonstrate critical thinking, reflection, and problem-solving skills
- Understand the role of primary care
- Rigorously practice preventive health care
- Integrate population-based care and services into practice
- Improve access to health care for those with unmet health needs
- Practice relationship-centered care with individuals and families
- Provide culturally sensitive care to a diverse society
- Partner with communities in health-care decisions
- Use communication and information technology effectively and appropriately
- Work in interdisciplinary teams
- Ensure care that balances individual, professional, system, and societal needs
- Practice leadership
- Take responsibility for quality of care and health outcomes at all levels
- Contribute to continuous improvement of the health care system
- Advocate for public policy that promotes and protects the health of the public
- Continue to learn and help others learn

O'Neil, E. H., & Pew Health Professions Commission (December, 1998). *Recreating health professional practice for a new century: The fourth report of the Pew Health Professions Commission.* San Francisco: Pew Health Professions Commission.

The types of programs provided reflect the needs of people served. Programs for individuals with spinal cord injuries may include developing adaptive leisure skills that prepare them for participating in activities with family members or friends. People who are in treatment for substance abuse may participate in activities designed to increase self-esteem or to express emotions. In chapters 6 through 12 we will examine specific impairments and outline the variety of services used in therapeutic recreation programs.

TODAY'S HEALTH-CARE SYSTEM

While the physical structure of the health-care system has not changed significantly over the years, the functionality and focus certainly have. Advanced technologies, ever-increasing demands for accountability, and new practical tools such as the ICF have propelled the health-care system toward a more global and unified approach, with consistent terminology focused on health, wellness, and broad client needs versus simply treating symptoms of an illness. Traditional **medical** or **clinical** models are becoming less disease-oriented and instead are developing a broader focus that no longer views the patient as a passive participant in the wellness process. Traditional **custodial** models that once simply focused on maintenance and housing are moving toward improved **long-term care** models that provide a variety of interventions that not only improve levels of functioning but also continually address quality of life issues. Whether **milieu** approaches in mental health settings, or therapeutic recreation components in **education** systems or **community-based** programs, today's therapeutic recreation programs are better integrated in the broader health-care system and focus on health, wellness, and overall quality of life for both clients and their families.

Let's look at a scenario that illustrates how the health-care system works today and where therapeutic recreation (TR) professionals fit in the health-care picture. We'll consider the case of Neil, a relatively new TR student in his junior year and a classmate in your Introduction to Therapeutic Recreation course. He has a history of schizophrenia (paranoid type) for which he was diagnosed just a year and a half ago. You certainly would not be aware of this, however, because he is currently well-balanced on his medications and managing his responsibilities. Although his behavior is a little "unusual" at times, you feel he adds to your class and you've enjoyed him as a classmate.

One day after class, Neil was particularly excited about the discussion in class and was somewhat distracted as he entered the crosswalk between two parking lots on campus. Suddenly he heard the loud squealing of tires and looked up just in time to see a car slam into the girl crossing the street just in front of him. The impact unfolded in slow motion as he saw her body ripple in reaction to the force of the collision. Her head shattered the windshield as she was thrown off the car, hitting the pavement and rolling to a complete stop just in front of him. Everything seemed eerily silent as he saw a pool of blood spread in all directions from under her head. When he was finally able to look up he saw people running at him from all directions, cell phones in hand, fingers pointing, and mouths moving. Suddenly, he became aware of the sounds around him—voices seemed to come from everywhere and the wail of sirens could be heard in the background. All he could do was run away.

Now two blocks away, he could still hear the sirens in the distance as the accident slowly replayed over and over in his head, car hitting, body rolling, blood spreading.

He lost awareness of where he was going, he just knew he had to go. He missed his noon meds and began to cycle down and decompensate quickly as he continued to wander the neighborhood. After missing his dinner meds he knew "they" weren't after the girl, they were after him, and he would have to outsmart them again. Later that night, after missing his evening meds, his delusions of grandeur and persecution were fully present. The voices were back as well, some of which whispered top-secret directions while others discredited him and belittled him unceasingly throughout the night. By morning Neil had missed more meds, had fashioned a knife out of the top half of a broken bottle, had cut himself several times in an effort to remove the chip that had been implanted in his body, and was ready to kill himself and anyone else that stood in the way of his mission.

Could this scenario really unfold? Absolutely. What would happen next? What would you do if you saw Neil the next morning walking down the sidewalk, disoriented and bleeding, brandishing a sharp piece of glass, threatening and yelling at those who walked by to "stay away" or he would get them? Someone would call 911 and the first to arrive would be the police. After disarming him they would take him directly to the emergency room to care for his immediate physical injuries. Enter the health-care system. After injecting him with a sedative to calm him down and treating his wounds, hospital staff would send him to the acute psychiatric unit on the third floor. The treatment team on that unit would likely consist of a psychiatrist, psychologist, social worker/therapist, nurse, dietician, the head of the milieu staff, and a recreation therapist. Their initial purpose would be to diagnose as well as stabilize. As they learned of Neil's history and began to get him stabilized and balanced on his medications again, they would begin addressing functional behaviors and other issues related to Neil's quality of life, all working together from their respective disciplines.

After approximately two weeks, Neil would likely have made significant progress, but certainly would not be ready to return to independent living. So he would be sent to a longer term facility like a community-based residential treatment facility. There, he would still have the structure and support of individual and group therapy, nursing services to help with medications, milieu services, and therapeutic recreation services. About four months later we could expect Neil to be doing much better and able to manage a job in the community. He would still return to the residential facility in the evening where he might be a peer mentor for other clients, and would still participate in structured experiences and ongoing interventions as he continued to make progress. After another three to four months Neil would likely be transitioned back into an independent living situation in an apartment with roommates. He would still have outpatient treatment services and might also be referred to the local parks and recreation department, where he would participate in a variety of recreation programs, some of which may be provided by TR professionals. One year after the incident, Neil might find himself back in school, functioning very well and again enjoying his Intro to TR class.

Let's continue this scenario and look at another aspect of the health-care system. The girl who was hit by the car was a classmate named Meredith. The ambulance transported her to the emergency room where she was treated for the immediate life-threatening trauma. Although she had some broken bones and a minor head injury, her primary diagnosis was a T-4 complete spinal cord injury. After necessary surgery for decompression and stabilization of the spine, Meredith was hospitalized in the physical rehabilitation unit for initial recovery and to begin rehabilitation services. Her treatment team consisted of an MD (physiatrist), nurse, social worker, psychologist, occupational therapist, physical therapist, speech therapist, and a recreation therapist. The team would coordinate efforts to help Meredith adjust to her injury; teach her and her family new basic skills and how to access resources; address secondary diagnoses such as depression, anger, and suicide ideations; and begin to promote holistic health and wellness one to four weeks prior to her transfer to a long-term rehabilitation hospital with spinal cord accreditation.

While at the rehab hospital, Meredith might be fitted for a more appropriate wheelchair that reflects her lifestyle needs. The recreation therapist may help her become familiar with sports chairs and other adaptive equipment as she rekindled her passion for sports; and the family would likely be invited on community outings where they would learn to navigate physical and social constraints in their leisure pursuits. After two to four months Meredith may be discharged from the rehab facility to her home. Prior to discharge, transition planning connects her to the local parks and recreation department where the TR professionals offer a variety of adaptive sport programs of interest to her. There might also be other community-based human service programs with TR professionals that provide inclusive programs such as alpine and water skiing, horseback riding, river running, camping, and other outdoor adventures as well as a plethora of other adaptive sports programs.

The scenario involving Neil and Meredith illustrates how recreation therapists coordinate their efforts with professionals from many other disciplines at different stages throughout the health-care system. Their combined efforts promote health, functional wellness, and overall quality of life among clients and their families no matter what the diagnosis or current need might be.

A CONCEPTUAL UNDERSTANDING: THERAPEUTIC RECREATION PRACTICE MODELS

The delivery of therapeutic recreation services is strongly influenced by the underlying philosophy or belief about the nature and purpose of the profession. One way to describe these beliefs is to use a model that becomes a symbolic description of the service philosophy. Although all models have their limitations, they do provide a framework for visualizing the various components of a theory and often give us greater insights into the relationships of these components. In the following sections we will briefly review several models that have been used and proposed since the 1970s for the therapeutic recreation profession. These models are important to the evolution of the profession as they provide both philosophical and pragmatic orientations that advance both the theory and practice of therapeutic recreation (Austin, 2002). Two models by Van Andel, the Therapeutic Recreation Service Delivery model and the Therapeutic Recreation Outcome model, will be presented in more detail as they represent the authors' personal perspectives on therapeutic recreation practice.

Leisure Ability Model

The Leisure Ability model is one of the oldest and perhaps most commonly used contemporary models of therapeutic recreation service delivery (Gunn & Peterson, 1978). The model assumes the primary outcome of therapeutic recreation service is improved independence and satisfying leisure functioning, which in turn directly affect a person's quality of life and happiness. The conceptual basis for the model flows from a theoretical understanding of leisure and includes the concepts of internal locus of control, intrinsic motivation, personal causality, freedom of choice, and flow or optimal experiences (Stumbo & Peterson, 1998). The therapeutic recreation specialist (TRS) uses three service components (functional intervention, leisure education, and recreation participation) to help the client achieve a satisfying leisure lifestyle— "independent functioning of the client in leisure experiences and activities of his or her choice" (Stumbo & Peterson, 2009, p. 33). Functional intervention addresses functional abilities in physical, social, emotional-affective, and/or mental-cognitive domains that are prerequisites to leisure experiences and participation in other areas of life. The TRS uses carefully selected and designed facilitation skills and techniques "to bring about predetermined client behavioral improvement or change" (Stumbo & Peterson, 2009, p. 41). Leisure education, a priority component of this model, focuses on developing attitudes, knowledge, and skills so clients have a broader capacity to participate in leisure of their "choice that positively impacts health, well-being and quality of life" (p. 43). The TRS assumes various roles—counselor, advisor, or instructor—as clients acquire skills and begin to take personal responsibility for intervention outcomes. Recreation participation services provide a structured and organized program that allows the client to practice and apply the knowledge and skills acquired through functional intervention and leisure education. The TRS fills the role of facilitator, leader, or supervisor while clients make most decisions, self-regulate their behaviors, and assume responsibility for participation outcomes.

Health Protection/Health Promotion Model

The Health Protection/Health Promotion model specifies that the purpose of therapeutic recreation is "to assist persons to recover following threats to health (health protection) and to achieve as high a level of health as possible (health promotion)" (Austin, 1998, p. 110). The model presupposes that all people have an inherent drive for health and wellness that can be facilitated by a therapeutic relationship with a TRS through the use of prescriptive activities (structured by therapist), recreation (mutual participation of client and therapist), and leisure (self-directed activity). Austin (1997) suggests the focus of therapeutic recreation services should be to encourage clients to achieve an optimal state of health, rather than just recover from illness. The underlying concepts of Austin's model include the humanistic perspective, high-level wellness, the stabilization and actualization tendencies, and health. "Health encompasses both coping adaptively and growing and becoming. Healthy people can cope with life's stressors. Those who enjoy optimal health have the opportunity to pursue the highest levels of personal growth and development" (Austin, 1998, p. 111). Therefore, according to this model, therapeutic recreation should assist in protecting and promoting health through the proper use of recreation and leisure experiences.

Optimizing Lifelong Health Model (OLH-TR)

The OLH-TR model uses an integrated systems approach to describe therapeutic recreation services. The basic elements of the system include (1) client needs, (2) resources, opportunities, and environments, (3) achieving or maintaining healthy leisure lifestyles, and (4) the scope and quality of the health and human service system available to the client (Wilhite, Keller, & Caldwell, 1999). Any change in one or more of these elements affects the others and requires client adaptations and adjustments to achieve or maintain optimal health, the ultimate goal of TR services according to the model. The role of the TRS is to help clients achieve the goal of health enhancement through (1) selecting or matching environmental demands with the client's capacities, skills, and motivations, (2) optimizing engagement in leisure activities that maximize personal and environmental resources while making it possible for people to pursue their chosen leisure pursuits, (3) supporting psychological, social, and technological compensatory efforts that are adopted when certain behavioral abilities are lost or are reduced below the minimum level required for desired leisure functioning, and (4) evaluating the costs and outcomes that enable people to decide whether continuing certain activities or patterns of leisure involvement is desirable (Wilhite et al., 1999).

Self-Determination and Enjoyment Enhancement Model

This model suggests that therapeutic recreation services contribute to personal growth and well-being through creating environments conducive to enjoyment and self-determination (Dattilo, Kleiber, & Williams, 1998). Its developers note that "creating conditions that help concentration, effort, and a sense of control and competence while promoting freedom of choice and expression of preference is the engineering of enjoyment" (p. 260). Enjoyment is viewed as the optimal leisure experience—also referred to as "flow"—where the participant becomes deeply absorbed in an activity with resultant feelings of satisfaction and contentment. According to the theoretical assumptions of the model, these experiences encourage personal growth and higher levels of self-determination. "As enjoyment reflects control by the individual, it evokes an orientation for making the most of circumstances and can result in improved physical, social, emotional, and cognitive functioning" (Dattilo et al., 1998, p. 260).

Aristotelian Good Life Model (AGL)

The unique contribution of the AGL is its effort to integrate an ethical component into therapeutic recreation service delivery (Widmer & Ellis, 1998). Based on Adler's (1991) interpretation of Aristotelian virtues, the model suggests the goal of TR services is to help the client attain happiness—the "good life"—through promoting both individual freedom and responsibility. The task of the TRS is to "empower clients to overcome constraints that arise from illness, disability, oppression, wrong desires, challenges in following the principle of enough, and focus on apparent goods that lack potential to become real goods" (Widmer & Ellis, p. 291). Thus, the TRS helps clients achieve not only fundamental needs but also outcomes inherent with leisure, learning, and relationships.

Leisure and Well-Being Model (LWM)

One of the most recent additions to the TR service delivery model literature is the Leisure and Well-Being Model (LWM) developed by Hood and Carruthers (Carruthers & Hood, 2007; Hood & Carruthers, 2007). Well-being is defined as "a state of successful, satisfying, and productive engagement with one's life and the realization of one's full physical, cognitive, and social-emotional potential" (Carruthers & Hood, 2007, p. 280). This model is based on the notion that well-being is a valid and desirable outcome for clients receiving therapeutic recreation services, and that TRSs are ideally positioned to support and help clients build a life of satisfaction and meaning. The model incorporates literature from a wide range of disciplines and is consistent with a strengths-based philosophy of practice. In other words, all clients, regardless of limitations or challenges, have strengths with which to begin creating a desired life. The role of the therapist is to support clients as they identify, enhance, and utilize those strengths to achieve personally meaningful goals.

The LWM identifies two major components of therapeutic recreation service delivery, each of which incorporates positive emotion and the development of resources that support well-being as important areas of focus. The first major component is *enhancing leisure experience,* which recognizes that not all leisure experiences give rise to positive emotion, nor do all leisure experiences support the development of capacities and resources. Therefore, TRSs must assist clients to develop skills and abilities that allow them to realize the greatest benefit from leisure involvement. The LWM identifies five specific ways through which the quality of the leisure experience may be enhanced to support well-being, including savoring leisure, authentic leisure, leisure gratifications, mindful leisure, and virtuous leisure (Hood & Carruthers, 2007).

The second component of the LWM is *developing resources.* Resources are defined by Carruthers and Hood (2007) as "sources of support or strengths, that lie inside or outside of the individual, and that can be drawn upon in time of need" (p. 287). Resources may be developed through engagement in meaningful leisure experiences and may also be enhanced directly through targeted psycho-educational interventions. The model identifies five specific resources that are central to well-being and fit well with therapeutic recreation practice; they include psychological, social, cognitive, physical, and environmental resources.

Van Andel's Therapeutic Recreation Outcome and Service Delivery Models

In this section we present two models that Van Andel (1998) developed to describe different aspects of the therapeutic recreation practice. The first model examines the product, or expected **outcomes,** associated with therapeutic recreation interventions, including changes in functional capacities, health status, and quality of life. The second model identifies four therapeutic recreation service components and describes their interaction with the health-care delivery system's focus on diagnosis/needs assessment, treatment/rehabilitation, education, and prevention/health promotion. Therapeutic recreation interventions in one or more of these service areas, if properly planned and initiated, should effect positive outcomes for the client.

Outcome Model

One of the unique characteristics of therapeutic recreation is that it involves an intervention process that is goal or outcome oriented. As participants in the competitive health-care industry, particularly in clinical settings, TRSs are expected to identify specific outcomes or results of their work that relate to (1) the maintenance or improvement of a person's health status, (2) quality of life, and (3) functional capacities (see figure 1.1). Studies have demonstrated the relationship between therapeutic recreation services and a wide variety of client outcomes (Shank, Coyle, Boyd, & Kinney, 1996). While we recognize the need to focus our efforts on these outcomes, we also agree with those who have argued that therapeutic recreation can and should contribute much more to the quality of one's life than improved health or functional capacities (Sylvester, 1987). Health (or optimal functioning) is not *the* standard of happiness (Everett, 1918). There is more. Therapeutic recreation can make the greatest contribution to the essential qualities of human nature and civilization by enhancing the quality of life through meaningful leisure experiences (Sylvester, 1987). Of the three outcome goals, improving the quality of life is clearly one that therapeutic recreation has the most potential to fulfill compared with other health-care services. It is likely the most significant outcome to the people we are called to serve (Seibert, 1991).

Traditionally, **health status** has referred to a continuum determined by physiological measures such as pulse rate, temperature, blood pressure, and other criteria used by medical practitioners to assess physical health. However, the WHO's definition of health—a contemporary health continuum that includes physical health as well as mental, spiritual, emotional, and social health—seems more appropriate because it recognizes the complexities of the human organism. New fields of behavioral medi-

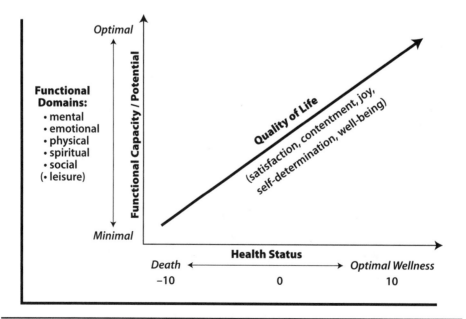

Figure 1.1   Therapeutic Recreation Outcome Model

cine and health psychology confirm the dynamic interrelationship between body, mind, and spirit by reporting, for example, that up to two-thirds of all visits to physicians are stress related (Davison & Neale, 2001; Wallis, 1983). Thus, in addition to tests for physical health, standardized assessments are being used to evaluate each of the other health components—mental, emotional, social, and spiritual—that comprise total health status. Thus, health status is really a composite picture of five *independent* and yet *interdependent* health dimensions that define our relative level of health and well-being.

A term that is often used to describe the integration of body, mind, and spirit is **holistic health** (Williams & Knight, 1994). From this perspective a person with AIDS or a similar terminal illness, for example, may be in poor physical health but could be experiencing a high level of **wellness** within the limitations of the disease process. This means he or she works to maintain an optimal level of fitness given the state of health, has good relationships with others, is able to maintain meaning and purpose in life, expresses emotions appropriately, and is mentally alert. Research indicates that those who are able to achieve this level of integration among life's domains experience a true sense of wellness or well-being, in spite of their circumstances (Dossey, 1993). On our health status continuum this would be rated as a +10, or **optimal wellness.** This quality appears to be more common for religious people who have a strong faith commitment (Gartner, Larson, & Allen, 1991; Heintzman, 1997). Research also has indicated a strong relationship between leisure satisfaction and wellness (Coleman & Iso-Ahola, 1993; Compton & Iso-Ahola, 1994; Iso-Ahola & Weissinger, 1984; Ragheb, 1993). Activities that are meaningful, relaxing, and embody an aesthetic quality tend to contribute substantially to the integration of all life's dimensions. The importance of leisure is summarized by Sylvester (1987), who claims it is an essential component of one's humanity and therefore must be included in a therapeutic recreation program. Facilitating leisure experiences should in fact be the ultimate goal because of its significant contribution to an individual's quality of life, the second key component of the model.

Quality of life is a subjective assessment of psychological and spiritual well-being and is characterized by feelings of satisfaction, contentment, joy, and self-determination (Iso-Ahola, 1980). Although certain external conditions may enhance these feelings, they are largely a product of one's psychological and spiritual state of mind that cannot be copied or reproduced. As we noted earlier, this outcome is important because it touches the heart

Activities that are meaningful and relaxing help clients achieve a high level of wellness.

of what life is about, what it means to be human. It is in this context that an individual can be treated as a whole person rather than one who has a dysfunctional part—like a machine that needs a certain part repaired. Placing the quality of life outcome between health status and functional capacity on the model indicates the need to consider the whole person regardless of the primary focus of the intervention. When selecting a treatment intervention to improve any of the five functions, a TRS must consider the needs, desires, and interests of the client. Finally, the centrality of quality of life in the model represents its primary focus for the therapeutic recreation profession.

A third outcome of health-care services involves an individual's ability to function mentally or cognitively, physically, psychologically or emotionally, spiritually, and socially. These domains can be defined as follows:

- Mental/cognitive function—the ability to learn and function intellectually
- Physical function—the ability of all body systems to function efficiently and effectively during work or play
- Psychological/emotional function—the ability to deal comfortably and appropriately with emotions
- Spiritual function—the ability to find meaning and purpose in life
- Social function—the ability to enjoy meaningful relationships with other people in one's environment

Since therapeutic recreation programs often focus on the strengths and abilities of the individual, identifying clients' **functional capacities** (potential ability to perform specific functions in each of the five domains of health status) is basic to further treatment or intervention. Assessment tools, both within and outside the TR field, have been developed to determine an individual's current level of functioning in each of the domains listed above (burlingame & Blaschko, 2010). In many cases TRSs evaluate and treat broader areas—such as lifestyle management skills and leisure attitudes and behaviors—that are affected by multiple domains; therefore, we have included leisure function as a separate component in our model. It is placed in parentheses to set it apart from the other domains and to reinforce its relationship to all five components (see figure 1.1). The profession has developed specific leisure assessment tools and intervention strategies designed to promote leisure function and leisure independence. The important consideration is to determine the needs of the client and develop a plan, usually in concert with other health-care professionals, that will enable the client to maintain or improve his or her total level of functioning. Chapter 4 will describe the assessment and planning process in greater detail, and later chapters outline the effects therapeutic recreation interventions might be expected to have on functional capacities of persons with specific impairments.

In summary, health-care outcomes are extremely important to consider in program planning. Therapeutic recreation has traditionally had a strong impact on the quality of life of individuals and a lesser impact on health status and functional capacities; however, the profession is actively involved in research that is helping to define its place among other health-care services that are competing for the same health-care dollars (Shank et al., 1996). Moreover, outcomes research is foundational to evidence-based practice, which is at the heart of the current focus to increase the quality of care while monitoring risk (Stumbo, 2003). Evidence-based practice applies the results of outcomes research to improve TR services. The TR profession is being held accountable for identifying through research which specific interventions result in health status, quality of life, and functional capacity improvements. At least for the time being, enhancing all three outcomes appears to be the unique role and function of TRSs as health-care providers. Future professionals must document the effects of therapeutic recreation interventions, use available scientific knowledge (outcomes literature), and reflect evidence of effectiveness in the interventions selected to achieve outcomes with the least cost to the client.

Service Delivery Model

We have stated that therapeutic recreation seeks to maintain or improve the health status, quality of life, and/or functional capacities of clients through the use of specially designed recreation or experiential activities and processes. The actual components of a therapeutic recreation program—how it is organized to accomplish its goals—are presented in figure 1.2. The scope of services involves (1) the diagnosis or assessment of need, (2) treatment or rehabilitation of a problem or need, (3) educational services, and (4) prevention and health promotion activities. Although most clients will receive a needs assessment regardless of setting or disability, all other services are provided on an as-needed basis. A needs assessment might determine that an indi-

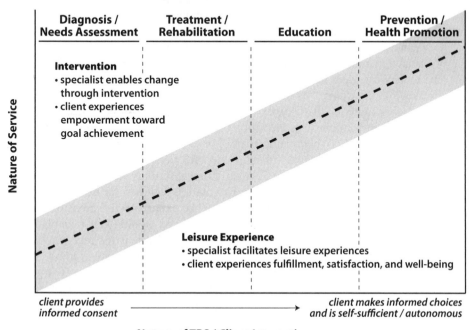

Figure 1.2   Van Andel's Service Delivery Model

vidual would benefit from rehabilitation services or education services. Another client may benefit from a prevention/health promotion program. Vertical dotted lines are used to indicate the flexible and interchangeable service components that are typically available in a comprehensive TR program. They also indicate the potential overlap among the services, since they are not mutually exclusive. A goal for a person with a closed head injury, for example, might be to increase cognitive functioning. Using computer memory games, a TRS might be able to help diagnose specific learning problems (needs assessment), provide exercises that would develop memory skills (treatment/rehabilitation), and teach specific educational skills that could be used in other vocational or leisure settings (education). Thus, although each classification of service is organized according to its primary goals, a given activity or program may achieve several different service goals.

Diagnosis/needs assessment includes a formal evaluation of the strengths, limitations, and abilities of the client. Assessment instruments will vary according to the client's disability and situation, but more tools are being developed and marketed to assist TRSs in this important process.

Treatment/rehabilitation involves interventions that have a direct or indirect objective of restoring or ameliorating the primary or secondary effects of a disease process or injury. For example, when individuals with mild depression are enrolled in an exercise program, they have been shown to produce natural antidepressants that directly reduce their symptoms. Similarly, a cognitive retraining program for individuals who have sustained brain injuries might be used to assist clients in recovering their memory or developing their attention span. **Education** is commonly used to teach specific knowledge or skills such as stress management techniques or self-care activities. **Prevention** or **health promotion** may also involve an educational component, but the primary goal of the intervention would be to promote and reinforce healthy lifestyle behaviors that will maintain or improve clients' well-being or functioning.

The scope of services has two dimensions, both of which may be present in therapeutic recreation programs. The model draws on Neulinger's (1976, 1981) concepts of leisure and work to define the nature of this relationship. The **intervention** side (non-leisure state of mind) emphasizes the action taken by the TRS and the effort of the client to accomplish specific therapeutic goals. The client's freedom and choice may be constrained by the professional judgment of the TRS as he or she determines the best approach for achieving the therapeutic goals. Clinical settings that use the traditional medical model (acute care hospitals and rehabilitation facilities, for example) operate almost exclusively from this service philosophy. The **experiential** dimension may be viewed as the play or leisure aspect of a TR program and would likely take place in a community or educational setting but also may be a direct or indirect outcome of many clinical programs. The leisure experience reflects a leisure state of mind characterized by the client's intrinsic motivation and sense of perceived freedom. The goal of the therapist is to facilitate a sense of freedom, satisfaction, and joy, because it is believed that these are key to experiencing quality of life (Coleman & Iso-Ahola, 1993; Iso-Ahola, 1980; Sylvester, 1987).

How can both intervention and experiential dimensions operate together as this model seems to suggest? Consider, for example, a group of clients that is advised to exercise as part of a treatment intervention. During the activity they may experience a sense of freedom and playfulness. As another example, clients with brain injuries are asked to play a game designed to develop memory or problem-solving skills; it is likely that some participants will enjoy what they are doing and have fun while also performing some difficult tasks. This dynamic interrelationship between intervention and leisure experience—work and play—is shown schematically by the dark gray area around the diagonal dotted line in figure 1.2. In many respects this is the ideal therapeutic situation, since psychobehavioral research shows that enjoyable experiences will be more effective in inducing long-term behavioral and attitudinal changes (Cousins, 1989).

The specific nature of the services provided, intervention or leisure experience, is dictated by the philosophy and goals of the TRS and the setting in which the interaction takes place. There may be some "purists," for example, who would advocate a leisure experience approach exclusively. The model represented by figure 1.2 is designed to accommodate these modifications by adjusting the diagonal dashed line up or down depending on the service philosophy advocated by a particular TRS or agency. Moving the line up, for example, would more accurately represent a service philosophy that de-emphasizes the intervention approach and endorses the experiential or play nature of the service. Thus, the model is intended to represent a continuum of service delivery—from the more intense, acute-care approach involving diagnosis and treatment found in hospitals or rehabilitation centers to the community-based focus of outpatient, day-treatment, or home health-care services that generally emphasizes education and health promotion. Clients may enter the system at any point on the continuum to receive the most appropriate mix of therapeutic recreation services. They would almost always require a needs assessment, for example, but this assessment may be done partly in the context of a treatment/rehabilitation or education service component of the program. Thus, the service delivery model does not necessarily indicate a "normal" sequencing of services from diagnosis to prevention, but rather an ordering that is more related to the degree of client autonomy in the context of a dynamic health-care service delivery system.

A final component of the service delivery model is the nature of the TRS-client interaction. As we will discuss in chapter 3, the relationship between the client and the TRS is complex and therefore difficult to describe in a service model. However, there are generalizations that can be made which are helpful in understanding how services are provided. First, the service philosophy will dictate to some degree the nature of the interaction. An acute-care center that uses the medical model approach will emphasize the patient's subordination to the therapist, while a community setting will tend to reinforce the client's need for autonomy and independence. Second, the nature of the client's impairment will also impact the relationship. Those who are severely impaired may be more dependent on others to make decisions regarding their health-care needs. Humane care dictates that clients be given as much autonomy as possible in determining what services they need and how they will participate. The ultimate goal of the TRS-client interaction is client independence. Finally, the nature of the service will affect the interaction. Needs assessment and treatment modalities generally require a more directive approach than education or prevention since the former tend to be closely related to the medical model and therefore reflect that philosophy of care. However, authority-dependency relationships should and can be avoided if the client is adequately informed about the nature of the service and the expected outcomes.

SUMMARY

Throughout the previous and present centuries many changes have influenced the field of therapeutic recreation. Some of the more significant factors include a broadening of the definition of recreation, a more holistic and global understanding of and concern for health, the return of people with disabilities to the community, and a more humanistic understanding of people with disabilities. Therapeutic recreation is defined as a holistic process that purposefully uses recreation and experiential interventions to bring about a change, either social, emotional, intellectual, physical, or spiritual, in an effort to maintain and improve health status, functional capabilities, and overall quality of life. Therapeutic recreation specialists provide a variety of services to a wide range of clients in many different settings throughout the health-care system and beyond.

Theorists have developed a variety of conceptual models to describe comprehensive therapeutic recreation practice. The two practice models primarily used in this text are the Therapeutic Recreation Outcome model and the Service Delivery model (Van Andel, 1998). The outcome model focuses on the goals related to maintaining or improving the client's health status, quality of life, and/or functional capacity. The service delivery model defines the four service goals as diagnosis/needs assessment, treatment/rehabilitation, education, and prevention/health promotion. Since play and leisure experiences are basic to our definition of what it means to be human, therapeutic recreation can make a significant contribution to the health and well-being of all individuals—even those who experience temporary or permanent disabling conditions.

Key Terms

community-based treatment Health-care services that are delivered in local facilities and agencies such as schools, senior centers, and clients' homes.

custodial A type of care that only meets the basic needs of the patient/client.

diagnosis/needs assessment The process of identifying client strengths and limitations, which can then be used to formulate treatment and program plans.

education Instruction designed to develop specific skills or knowledge.

experiential A personal interaction with an activity or one's environment.

functional capacity The potential ability to perform specific functions in each of the five domains of health status.

health A state of complete physical, mental, social, psychological, and spiritual well-being.

health status The relative level of physical, mental, emotional, social, and spiritual health as determined by various assessment tools.

holistic health An approach to health that integrates body, mind, and spirit.

humanistic Outlook that stresses the importance of human development, improved processes of human interaction, and the protection and restoration of the natural environment.

intervention Action taken by a professional person in cooperation with a given client to achieve a predetermined and mutually agreed upon treatment goal.

long-term care Health care that provides ongoing basic services to chronically ill individuals who are institutionalized for more than 30 days.

medical or clinical Health-care settings or agencies that provide acute treatment or rehabilitation services.

milieu An approach that recognizes the client's environment or surroundings as an integral aspect of therapy.

optimal wellness The highest level of well-being that is usually associated with the effective development and integration of the five dimensions of health—mental, physical, emotional, spiritual, and social.

outcomes The product or result of the treatment or intervention.

prevention or health promotion Services or activities that emphasize positive attitudes and behaviors toward personal health.

quality of life A subjective assessment of psychological well-being that is characterized by feelings of satisfaction, contentment, joy, and self-determination.

recreation A positive psychosocial response to a meaningful personal experience.

therapeutic recreation A holistic process that purposefully uses recreation and experiential interventions to bring about a change, either social, emotional, intellectual, physical, or spiritual, in an effort to maintain and improve health status, functional capabilities, and overall quality of life.

treatment or rehabilitation A process of restoring or stabilizing the health or functioning of an individual following impairment from disease or injury.

wellness A state of complete integration of the body, mind, and spirit.

Study Questions

1. What factors have contributed to a redefinition of therapeutic recreation?

2. What is the difference between recreation and therapeutic recreation services? What makes therapeutic recreation unique? Explain how each is related to health and wellness.

3. Identify and discuss the similarities and differences among the various therapeutic recreation practice models.

4. According to the various models, what are the primary treatment or intervention outcomes that therapeutic recreation programs seek to achieve? Give examples of how each is used in a given setting.

5. Interpret each of the three goals identified in the outcome model. What are examples of evidence for each outcome?

6. According to the Service Delivery model, what are the four service components used in comprehensive therapeutic recreation practice? What relationship do they have to outcome goals?

Practical Experiences to Enhance Student Objectives

1. Work with other members of the class to create a therapeutic recreation practice model or modify a model in the text that best expresses your present understanding of therapeutic recreation.

2. Write a short paper on why you are contemplating entering this profession. What are the most and least appealing aspects? What additional information do you need before you will be able to confirm your choice of a profession?

3. After further research on the nature of health-care service delivery systems described in this chapter, identify the strengths and weaknesses of each and develop a rationale for your own personal preference.

4. Identify several changes that are taking place in the health-care system today and suggest the implications each might have for the therapeutic recreation profession.

5. What therapeutic recreation service outcomes seem most important to you? Which ones would you be willing to pay for if you needed such a service? How much do you think they are worth?

6. Do you personally know anyone who could benefit, or has benefited, from therapeutic recreation services? Describe his or her situation and explain how his or her life could be, or has been, improved by such participation.

7. Discuss the intervention and experiential components of the Service Delivery model. Which dimension is most important, the intervention or experiential? Would you reposition the diagonal dashed line in figure 1.2? Justify your answer.

Discovering the Roots of a Profession

After reading this chapter, students will be able to:

✔ Outline the developmental stages of therapeutic recreation

✔ Describe the historical development of therapeutic recreation

✔ Demonstrate awareness of the roles of professional organizations

✔ Describe the status of therapeutic recreation as a profession

✔ Demonstrate an understanding of the philosophical perspectives surrounding therapeutic recreation

✔ Explain why the development of a philosophy is a dynamic process that continues beyond the completion of an introductory TR course

Why should a student considering a career in therapeutic recreation study the historical and philosophical evolution of the profession? Is there a link between the previous events and perspectives and the present-day knowledge and skills required of a therapeutic recreation specialist, or is this just another academic exercise?

Knowing the roots of a profession is critical to understanding its present and shaping its future. Understanding the evolution of therapeutic recreation comes "from understanding the 'story' of the development of the profession" (Austin, 2002a, p. 273). A survey of the history of therapeutic recreation provides insight into why, for instance, therapeutic recreation is considered an emerging profession, or why practitioners in various settings have differing views of therapeutic recreation. There are different definitions of therapeutic recreation. This seems to be inherent in the nature of the profession, as evidenced by a review of both its early and contemporary history.

To prepare you for the challenge of continuing the legacy of this profession we feel it is essential that you know its history. It is a story characterized by continuous change, varying philosophical perspectives, and eclectic influences from other disciplines.

INTRODUCTION

The beginning of civilization also commences the use of therapeutic experiences to treat people with illnesses and disabilities. Studies by archaeologists and historians reveal that earlier cultures used hot water springs, massage, and such medications as opium, hashish, sarsaparilla, acacia, and many other agents in the treatment of various diseases (Haworth & MacDonald, 1946).

These early principles of health care are seen in the Greek and Roman cultures between 700 BC and AD 400. Greek physicians reportedly treated the whole person— body, mind, and spirit—in health temples built to honor Aesculapius, the god of healing. Consideration was given to patients' feelings by building temples as curative centers in scenic areas and equipping them with mineral springs, bathing pools, gymnasiums, gardens, exercise grounds, and libraries (Bullock, Mahon, & Killingsworth, 2010; Frye & Peters, 1972; Sellew & Ebel, 1955; Sigerist, 1933).

Even in the age of rational medicine, which was ushered in by Hippocrates (460– 377 BC), the father of medicine, exercise was promoted for its value in treating obesity and other disabilities. Other contributions Hippocrates made to contemporary health care include the Hippocratic Oath (see exhibit 2.1) and the case study method of medical education whereby the physician learned, recorded, and taught the natural causes of illness through bedside observations. Rather than continuing to reuse earlier cures and treatment techniques, Hippocrates instituted the use of trial-and-error techniques, recording successful methods to be used with individuals exhibiting similar symptoms (Sigerist, 1933). These observations led Hippocrates to hypothesize that all diseases, including psychological disturbances, were somatogenic, or physiologically based, rather than—as the prevailing theory held—the result of conflicts with the gods (Ball, 1969).

The Romans contributed to the advancement of health care by establishing public health standards and creating a hospital system designed to provide soldiers access to medical care (Crawford, 2001; Frye & Peters, 1972; Sellew & Ebel, 1955). Galen, a noted teacher and physician in the second century AD, advocated an activity-based

---

Exhibit 2.1   The Hippocratic Oath

I swear . . . so far as power and discernment shall be mine, I will carry out regimen for the benefit of the sick and will keep them from harm and wrong. To none will I give a deadly drug even if solicited . . .

Into whatsoever house I shall enter I will go for the benefit of the sick.

—Hippocrates

The first code of ethics in medical practice is still used today throughout the health-care community.

treatment that emphasized the use of music, poetry, relaxation, and recreation in his work with Roman gladiators (Avedon, 1974).

During the later period of the Roman Empire, the rise of the Christian church brought a humanitarian concern to the care of all people, regardless of social class (Frye & Peters, 1972). Hospitals were built to care for those not able to purchase private health care. The church also advocated the value of human life and the desirability of preserving it through the application of scientific knowledge. These efforts represent the earliest form of social organization designed to provide health services. The continued commitment of health and human services, particularly to the poor, is still a hallmark of the Judeo-Christian community today.

The advances in health care brought about in ancient Greece and Rome are significant. The Greeks promoted the healthy development of the whole person and recognized the value of physical activity in combating atrophy and physical deterioration. The Romans addressed various social ills by implementing standards for clean water and public facilities, developing a hospital system, and constructing parks and large entertainment centers, such as the Coliseum and the Circus Maximus, for entertainment of the masses.

The Middle Ages spanned the period from the fall of the Roman Empire around AD 400 to the Renaissance, which dawned in Italy in the fourteenth century and spread to the rest of Europe by the sixteenth and seventeenth centuries. Life during the Middle Ages was difficult for the common citizen and often cruel for those in hospitals or institutions. Restrictions were placed on games and activities of any sort for fear it might lead to "insubordination" (Ball, 1969). Those hospitalized for emotional illnesses were often chained in cold, damp cells and used as a form of entertainment for the public, who would pay to see these "lunatics" (Crawford, 2001; Frye & Peters, 1972). Other individuals with emotional illness became identified as court jesters and village idiots by the nobility and townspeople. Throughout history, people who exhibited unusual or deviant behavior were often viewed by the public as a menace or nuisance, or a subhuman object of ridicule (Bedini, 1991; Bullock et al., 2010).

In medicine a distinction prevailed in the kinds of treatment given to the upper and lower classes. The physician, a noted scholar, served the upper classes, while a surgeon, a barber by trade, served the lower classes. The physician's position as an academic person was held in higher esteem than was the surgeon's, whose trade depended on the use of one's hands, which was characteristic of the lower class. In the seventeenth century, as a result of the work of Ambroise Pare, the status of surgeons began to come into parity with that of the professionals serving the upper classes (Sigerist, 1933). Pare believed the "whole man" needed to be treated both before and after surgery, so he introduced procedures that included the use of games, music, and reading to relieve boredom (O'Morrow & Reynolds, 1989). He is also credited with developing the artificial limb and glass eye.

Although much of the church's early philosophy of health care simply advocated custodial or caretaking services, it also began to advance a new concept: the provision of health education for the patient. However, by the late Middle Ages the influence of the church gave way to health care by public institutions as the influences of the Renaissance emerged.

In summary, health care is a product of centuries of work in a variety of cultures. The relationship between health and activity is long-standing and reflects an understanding that the best way to treat an illness is to treat the whole person—body, mind, and spirit. As we discuss the next era of the profession's history, you will begin to see how therapeutic recreation began to develop as a new modality in the care and rehabilitation of people with disabilities.

PRENATAL PERIOD OF PROFESSIONAL DEVELOPMENT (1800–1935)

One of the major questions developmental psychologists seek to answer is how much of one's development is influenced by genetic inheritance and how much is influenced by experience. As we consider the developmental history of therapeutic recreation, we need to examine what has contributed to its role and identity as a profession. No profession suddenly arrives on the scene without some previous developmental history. For therapeutic recreation, circumstances such as health-care reform, the development of public and private hospital systems, the recognition of play and recreation as effective tools for rehabilitation and social reform, and the growth of the playground movement in the nineteenth and early twentieth centuries served as the foundation for its development. Each event played a significant role in establishing the roots of the profession as we know it today.

Health-Care Reform

Although much of the health care for persons with mental illness in the eighteenth and nineteenth centuries may be characterized as dehumanizing, there were a

few positive developments that provided some hope for these individuals. Under the guidance of Philippe Pinel (1745–1826), a French physician, humane treatment of persons with mental illness and the economically disadvantaged was revived (O'Morrow & Reynolds, 1989). Pinel believed these people were capable human beings who deserved to be treated with compassion and dignity rather than being chained and locked behind bars. His remarkably successful approach became known as *moral treatment* and included the use of purposeful recreational activity like gardening and productive work experiences to restore mental and physical health so individuals could live and function successfully in society (Austin, 2002a; Davison & Neale, 1990). In some respects the moral

French physician Philippe Pinel's "moral treatment" approach utilized purposeful recreation activities to restore mental and physical health.

treatment approach established the context as well as the content of future recreation programs in institutions.

About this same time William Tuke (1732–1822), an English merchant and a Quaker, appalled at the conditions he found at York Asylum, worked with the Society of the Friends to establish the York Retreat in 1796. The retreat, a quiet country estate where individuals were encouraged to garden, talk with attendants, and take walks in the countryside, became a model for several institutions in the United States (Davison & Neale, 1990). For example, moral treatment programs could be found in small, private psychiatric hospitals such as the Asylum of New York Hospital, McLean Hospital in Massachusetts, and the Brattleboro Retreat in Vermont, where activities like chess, gardening, reading, walking, and needlework were used as therapeutic tools in the care of patients (Frye, 1962). Moral therapy grew to include social gatherings attended by hospital personnel as well as patients, thus creating a positive, caring environment for healing.

Unfortunately, *only* small, private institutions could afford to provide the individual attention required to meet the unique needs of each patient. Since the private hospitals in the United States simply could not care for all the people who experienced mental illness, hearing and visual impairments, developmental disabilities, and physical disabilities, larger hospitals and custodial care facilities were constructed in the mid-1800s. This growth parallels the changing social conditions brought on by the industrial revolution. Increasing immigration, urbanization, and deteriorating social conditions contributed to the rise in what the social community defined as bizarre or unusual behavior. Thus, broadly defined, mental illness again became a socially repugnant, "incurable disease" that required the individual to be removed from general society. It is not surprising that as the larger institutions housed greater numbers of people with mental illness, moral treatment declined. Characterized by little sensitivity to the dignity and value of these people, the eighteenth and nineteenth centuries were a dark time in the history of health care in the United States.

The mid-1800s also witnessed increasing experimentation in treatment practices. For example, Benjamin Rush (1745–1813), the father of American psychiatry and the first superintendent of the Pennsylvania Hospital in Philadelphia (the first general medical hospital in the United States), is credited with recognizing the therapeutic values of recreation activities as treatment for people with psychiatric illnesses (Austin, 2002a; Haworth & MacDonald, 1946). He also is noted for his hypothesis that mental disorders are caused by excess blood to the brain; therefore, his preferred treatment for individuals with mental disorders was to draw great quantities of blood from them. Rush also believed that many individuals who were mentally ill could be cured by frightening them half to death (Davison & Neale, 1990). Thus, the mid-1800s was characterized by a mixture of treatment approaches, some of which were more humane than others.

The humanitarian concern for institutional reform was championed, however, by the pioneer of modern nursing, Florence Nightingale (1820–1910). While caring for injured soldiers in hospitals in Scutari and Crimea, she organized classrooms, reading rooms, and recreation huts to combat such negative side effects of soldiering as drunkenness and inappropriate social behaviors. In 1873 she wrote a book, *Notes on Nursing: What It Is and What It Is Not*, about improving the rehabilitation environment. The text included guidelines for visitor conversation topics, promoted the psychological bene-

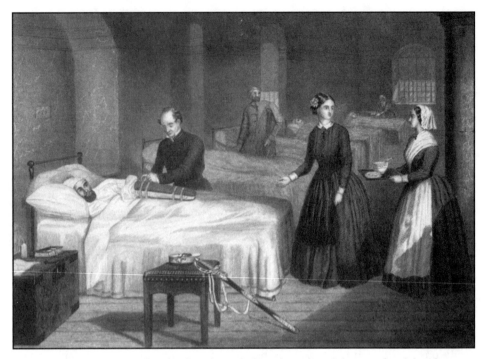

Florence Nightingale, the pioneer of modern nursing, championed the use of social and recreational activities to promote the rehabilitation of injured soldiers during the Crimean War (1853–1856).

fits of music and pets, and highlighted the need for variety in both the objects and the color of the hospital environment (Avedon, 1974; James, 1998). Under Nightingale's leadership, significant efforts were launched to improve the physical interiors of the previously constructed hospitals and custodial care facilities, thus creating more pleasant living environments.

The social reform movement of this period also influenced correctional facilities. Under the leadership of the Quakers in Pennsylvania and upon implementation of the Auburn system in New York, several progressive procedures were initiated. The goal of these procedures was to change the mentality of the prisoners by restricting communication between inmates and placing them in individual cells. Males and females were separated, as were older and younger offenders, and first-timer offenders and repeaters. Moreover, differential treatment methods were established for varying degrees of crime (O'Morrow & Reynolds, 1989). The concepts of probation and parole were introduced in the penal systems of Massachusetts and New York. Despite the improvements brought about by the reform movement, information on therapeutic recreation with legal offenders is scant. This is true of the past as well as of the present. With few exceptions—managing youth "at-risk" behaviors and programs targeting violence in urban areas—therapeutic recreation with legal offenders in our society has been and continues to be a low priority.

Development of Public and Private Hospital Systems

Prior to the industrial revolution, hospitals were primarily religious, charitable institutions that provided care for the poor, while the wealthy were often treated in their homes. During the mid- to late-1800s, hospitals became the center of medical education and practice for physicians, who were experiencing growing respect. Unqualified doctors and unproven treatments gave way to professionalization, specialized training, medical research, and more effective treatments. However, advances in medical practice did not necessarily guarantee improved care. As the medical profession gained stature, primarily through the success and popularity of clinical training programs, hospital administrators used their limited resources for hiring medical professionals who could participate in the latest psychological and medical research rather than employing support staff who had previously provided humane, moral care to patients (Brieger, 1976). Thus, health-care priorities were oriented around scientific research, while the moral treatment that had proven effective in the rehabilitation of people with mental illness often became secondary. As the number of individuals placed in public and private institutions increased in the late nineteenth century, great variations developed in the level of care. Specialty hospitals for those with visual impairments, physical disabilities, emotional disorders, or developmental disabilities frequently used diversional activities to improve patient morale, while in other institutions the recreation programs that were such a significant part of moral treatment in the previous century were simply not provided.

Reformers such as Dorothea Dix (1802–1887) brought attention to the inadequate custodial care of those in public institutions of all kinds, prompting the construction of a number of state-level institutions prior to the outbreak of World War I. This effort attempted to alleviate the overcrowding in jails and prisons and establish more humane care in institutions. However, to some extent, as more facilities were constructed to institutionalize a growing number of people with mental, physical, and social impairments, the social and moral attitude of "out of sight, out of mind" became more entrenched. It was not until well after World War II that significant institutional and social changes were fully realized. Nonetheless, the growing number of public and private agencies serving people with disabilities provided many opportunities for the development of new helping professions, including occupational therapy, physical therapy, and therapeutic recreation.

Rise of the Playground Movement

By the mid- to late-1800s the deleterious effects of the industrial revolution were obvious in America. Larger cities were characterized by growing slums surrounding industrialized complexes; children who had few opportunities for attending school were abandoned in the streets by parents who worked long hours in factories; horrible socioeconomic conditions were contributing to significant increases in juvenile delinquency; and the erosion of moral and social standards undermined the very structure of society. A variety of social, philosophical, religious, educational, and political changes were needed to combat these conditions. Social scientists and municipal leaders abandoned the popular philosophical Darwinian determinism and adopted the more pragmatic view that society could be reformed and revitalized (Knapp & Hartsoe, 1979). The Young Men's Christian Association (YMCA), under the leadership of Luther Gulick (1865–1900), established more than 1400 local branches by the turn of the century, all contributing to revitalizing the cities by providing leadership in social reforms, athletics, education, and youth work (Knapp & Hartsoe, 1979).

Another response to the erosion of cities was the establishment of playgrounds and parks where children could engage in more appropriate social activities. Play and recreation were espoused as forms of self-development and tools to combat delinquency and promote healthier social environments (Austin, 2002a; James, 1998). The playground movement, promoted by the social reformer and lawyer Joseph Lee (1862–1937) and by Luther Gulick (a physician by training), was formally organized in 1906 as the Playground Association of America. It was later (1930) renamed the National Recreation Association (NRA). As the primary advocate for expanding opportunities for play and recreation in urban areas, the NRA would serve as one of the professional roots for therapeutic recreation.

In 1918 the National Education Association established "the worthy use of leisure" as a necessary goal of school curricula and thus developed the first leisure education programs. It also opened school buildings and playgrounds for recreation and social gatherings. During this time, play and recreation became legitimized as tools for personal and social reform. Such legitimacy established the foundation for extending their use to other areas of community life such as health care.

Recreation as a Tool in Rehabilitation

In the early 1900s some special schools for children with developmental disabilities and other voluntary agencies, such as the Industrial Home for the Blind in New York, begin providing recreation and camping programs for children with disabilities living in the community (Avedon, 1974). The intent of many of these programs was to provide training and rehabilitation as well as create normal opportunities for fun and enjoyment. As quoted in Avedon, the director of the Vineland, New Jersey institution stated:

> It should be fully appreciated by teachers, parents, and superintendents that the playing of these games is not mere play, but definite training of the best kind. In many cases there is little else to be done. . . . It should not be forgotten that these games not only develop coordination and attention, manners, morals, self-control, altruism, patience, and many more desirable qualities. . . . [They] will help to make him a social rather than an antisocial being! (Avedon, 1974, p. 12–13)

In one of the earliest therapeutic recreation studies reported, the authors of a project at the Lincoln State School and Colony in Illinois noted that students with developmental disabilities made better emotional and social adjustments to their living situations when allowed to participate in play activities (Frye & Peters, 1972). Therapeutically designed recreation programs were thus becoming important educational and rehabilitation tools in these agencies.

The therapeutic use of recreation activities in health-care institutions took more time to evolve. The first step was the introduction of recreation as a diversion for people who were hospitalized. The stimulus for this movement was the American Red Cross, which used recreational activities to treat those who sustained various injuries in military combat during World War I (1914–1918) (James, 1998). Since the Red

Cross was the primary organization charged with providing humane care for injured soldiers, they recognized the negative effects of boredom and inactivity and began experimenting with the use of recreation leaders and volunteers to conduct bedside and group activities in military and Veterans Administration (VA) hospitals. Like the community recreation agencies of that time, the Red Cross wanted to create opportunities for entertainment, enjoyment, and fun, but for hospitalized people. As these programs gained recognition for their contribution to morale and to aiding the adjustment of military personnel to civilian life, they were established as a permanent part of the routine service provided in these institutions (Summers, 1962).

As a result of their success in military hospitals, recreation services began to be offered in state mental health hospitals during the 1920s and 1930s. In institutions such as St. Elizabeth's Hospital in Washington, DC, and hospitals in the Pennsylvania and Illinois state systems, recreation programs were provided primarily for diversion (while recognizing the therapeutic value)—to keep the patients occupied and reduce problem behaviors brought on, in large part, by the squalid conditions of institutionalization (O'Morrow & Reynolds, 1989). Since rehabilitation was not viewed as practical or appropriate for most individuals with mental and physical illness, many institutions functioned as caretaking or custodial agencies where these individuals would spend the rest of their lives. Thus, the institution took on the social dimensions of a community, where recreation programs were provided to meet the needs of both the patients and the staff. A survey of hospitals indicated that by 1959 nearly all larger, long-term care institutions such as state hospitals, veterans facilities, and specialty hospitals (for example, tuberculosis hospitals) offered organized recreation programs (Frye & Peters, 1972).

Throughout this period of professional development, play and recreation experiences began to emerge as important factors in defining quality of life, both within and outside institutions. Concern for humane care and recognition of the benefits of play and recreation, especially for those who were challenged by social, physical, psychological, or developmental disabilities, provided support for recreation programs.

Summary of Prenatal Period

The roots of the therapeutic recreation profession can be seen in several trends in the nineteenth and twentieth centuries. Health-care reform began to recognize the dignity of all people and the therapeutic value of humane treatment that included the social and environmental stimulation of recreation activities. The establishment of private and public hospital systems created the structure for health-care providers to experiment with programs and services that included recreation activities as a component of care. The playground movement reemphasized the role that play activities serve in social and environmental reform. Professional associations supporting therapeutic recreation were also spawned by this movement. And finally, recreation came to be viewed as a basic institutional service that improved morale and enhanced the treatment of those with disabilities, especially in long-term care facilities. With the development of a clear motive for service and the formation of a professional association (the National Recreation Association), the stage was set for the birth of the therapeutic recreation profession as we know it today.

BECOMING A PROFESSION

At first glance it may seem relatively easy to identify when a new profession is born. Many of us might simply look for the date the first professional association was formed and consider that the birthday. However, if we are to accurately understand the developmental viability of this profession, we need to consider the criteria that traditionally define a profession. Although many attributes have been suggested, there are five that are generally used to define a profession (Austin, 2002c; Carter, 1998; James, 1998; Mobily & Ostiguy, 2004). Social scientists suggest all professions must (1) provide an accepted and necessary public service, (2) consist of subgroups or professional organizations that have common goals and interests and control or self-regulate the profession, (3) establish standards of practice and a code of professional conduct that will protect the public good, (4) base practices on accepted scientific theories and evidence, and (5) establish a body of knowledge with formal preparation and continuing training and development. In light of these criteria, we begin to understand why it is so difficult to determine when professional status is achieved by the therapeutic recreation field. These commonly recognized standards will guide our review of the progress the field has made toward achieving professional status since the mid-1930s. By examining each criterion within a specified period we can begin to assess the developmental stage the profession has achieved.

BIRTH AND INFANCY (1935–1965)

Newborns were once viewed as "empty slates" waiting to be filled with information. We now know they are very complex individuals who are constantly responding and adapting to internal and external stimuli as the developmental process unfolds. Throughout infancy, children are dependent on others to provide nurture and basic care. So too, in its early stages of development, the field of therapeutic recreation presented a diverse background of experiences shaped by internal and external forces, while leaning heavily on the more established recreation and health-care professions for identity and support.

Service to Society

Throughout the decades prior to the 1940s, the primary purpose for recreation in hospitals was to satisfy the social and emotional needs of institutionalized children and adults. The most visible advocate of this philosophy of care, the Red Cross, trained and employed over 1800 recreation leaders during World War II (Frye & Peters, 1972; James, 1998). Before and after both world wars, Red Cross directives supported recreation as having a therapeutic value. Medical approval was required for participation and treatment teams included clients and family members in care planning and decisions. After World War II, medically approved recreation programs were introduced in VA hospitals. The rapid expansion of recreation programs in hospitals also necessitated recruitment of trained community recreation leaders who could step in quickly to organize the programs. After the war these workers carried the recreation philosophy with them as they assumed positions in other hospitals and institutions. It was this core of young professionals who identified with the larger rec-

Recreational activities were employed to rehabilitate soldiers who sustained combat injuries during World War I (1914–1918) and World War II (1939–1945).

reation movement and would later (1949) form a hospital recreation section within the American Recreation Society (Frye & Peters, 1972; James, 1998).

During the late 1930s a second approach to the use of recreation in treatment centers emerged. Recreation activities were used at such institutions as the Menninger Clinic in Topeka, Kansas, as a treatment tool or "therapy" for persons with psychological disabilities. Following the psychoanalytic model, psychiatrists at the Menninger Clinic used recreation activities to reduce tension and anxiety that was believed to be caused by unconscious conflict among inner motives or drives. Since it was assumed that pleasurable experiences were preferred over painful experiences, the focus of therapy was to help the patient work through the conflict. Traditional psychoanalytical treatment approaches used dream analysis or similar forms of free association to uncover the conflicting unconscious forces and to provide insights into alternative behavior patterns. At the Menninger Clinic, however, psychiatrists creatively adapted recreation activities to achieve specific treatment objectives such as the release of aggression. Typical recreational treatments for redirecting hostile emotions involved drawing a face on a punching bag and encouraging the patient to strike it. The face was intended to depict an overbearing parent, for example, and the bag then served as the substituted focus of the individual's hostility. More generalized tensions were treated through active games such as volleyball or tennis. Diversion of antagonisms, hatred, and frustration into healthy, aggressive outlets such as competitive sports was believed to be the most important contribution recreation could make to human welfare. Creative experiences were also encouraged for those who were not able to achieve satisfaction and fulfillment in personal relationships. It was frequently noted that symptoms of psychological disturbance would decrease as interest in woodworking, weaving, leatherwork, pottery, and so forth increased (Menninger, 1948).

Thus, recreation became an adjunctive or additional method of treatment in some institutions. Selected recreational activities were carefully matched with the particular needs of the individual and used to alleviate or reduce the primary symptoms of illnesses. Interventions that used recreation activities to achieve specific therapeutic goals were considered *a means to an end* and as such were perceived as *therapy*.

Despite the growth of recreation programs in hospitals and institutions, community programs for individuals with special needs, including socially and economically disadvantaged people, were limited at best. When services were provided, they were often segregated by program and at times by separate facilities as well. In an effort to address the lack of community services for people with disabilities, the NRA began providing a "consulting service on recreation for the ill and handicapped" in 1953. The service was headed by Beatrice Hill and included both hospital recreation and community recreation settings. A few years later, Hill left the NRA to form Comeback, Inc. (1960), a private consulting firm committed to promoting therapeutic recreation through research; training workshops for agency directors, recreation leaders, and volunteers; fund raising; publications; and by providing scholarships for undergraduate students (Avedon, 1974; Frye & Peters, 1972). She is reported to be one of the first to promote recreation services for individuals with disabilities living in the community, as well as services for hospitalized individuals and those in clinics, residential facilities for the elderly, and the homebound (Meyer, 1980b). It was largely due to her work that recreation was valued as a professional service for people with disabilities. Hill's contribution is significant to our historical understanding of therapeutic recreation because it represents an initial effort to connect hospital recreation with community recreation for people with disabilities. By combining the terms *therapy* and *recreation* to form *therapeutic recreation* and by providing services in both institutional and community settings, Hill was able to prepare the way for the unification of diverse professional special interest groups.

Early in the development of therapeutic recreation services two different philosophies emerged. The *recreation in hospitals* approach perceived the primary role and value of the profession as providing meaningful recreation opportunities and experiences for pleasure and enjoyment, while the *recreation therapy* approach emphasized the therapeutic use of recreation activities in the treatment and remediation of specific illnesses or disabilities. Some would suggest that these perspectives are quite different and therefore might be seen as twin births, while others believe they simply represent two different ways of looking at the same infant. Attempts to integrate these perspectives throughout the early years of the profession were unsuccessful. As the 1960s progressed, however, renewed efforts by leaders such as Hill began to bring these two philosophies closer together (Meyer, 1980b). The following section traces the impact of these ideological perspectives on the development of professional organizations.

National and state legislation also influenced the development of the profession's services. The Mental Retardation Facilities and Community Mental Health Centers Construction Act of 1963 (PL 88-164) reduced the size of and decentralized large state hospital systems and shifted the focus of care from custodial services to rehabilitation and education. The act also included monies for the employment of therapeutic recreators for both the outpatient and day-treatment programs in community mental health centers and a Bill of Rights section for people with developmental disabilities (Bullock et al., 2010).

Additionally, the social unrest of the early 1960s led to a reaffirmation of the need to provide social services, including recreation, to those living in poverty and those living in urban areas. In the Kerner Commission Report, the National Advisory Commission on Civil Disorders ranked poor recreation facilities and programs among the major grievances of urban residents. The political response was to declare "war on poverty" through the passage of numerous urban assistance programs, many of which provided recreation funds and services directly or indirectly to the community. In 1965 funds for recreation were also made available through the Older Americans Act, the Land and Water Conservation Fund, and the Housing and Urban Development Act. Public support for the field of therapeutic recreation and its use in improving the quality of life for people with social, economic, physical, and mental challenges continued to grow throughout the 1960s, and many of the programs initiated by the Economic Opportunity Act (1964), such as the Job Corps, Head Start, and the Community Action Program, continue in one form or another today.

Professional Organizations

As the ranks of hospital recreation workers grew, several professional organizations began to emerge. The first effort toward professional organization came from within the American Recreation Society (ARS) in 1948. An interim committee was organized to lay the groundwork for the Hospital Recreation Section (HRS), which became a reality during the 1949 New Orleans Congress. HRS members represented hospital recreation workers from military, veterans, and public institutions, many of whom had been recruited by the Red Cross from community recreation positions during World War II and had a service philosophy that emphasized providing leisure experiences to hospitalized individuals. The HRS quickly established a liaison with the American Medical Association (AMA) and the American Psychiatric Association (APA) and published *The Basic Concepts of Hospital Recreation* (1954) and five volumes of *Recreation in Treatment Centers*.

Not all recreation personnel who served those with disabilities, however, were comfortable with the HRS service philosophy. Many felt HRS was too closely aligned with the community recreation movement and did not adequately represent the recreational therapy perspective (Meyer, 1980b). Thus in 1952 a Recreation Therapy Section was formed within the Recreation Division of the American Association for Health, Physical Education, Recreation, and Dance (AAHPERD). The interests of the membership focused on developing recreation and physical education programs in schools serving students with disabilities and adapting physical education programs in inclusive school settings. A column was devoted to recreation therapy in the *Journal of Health, Physical Education, Recreation, and Dance*, and professional meetings were convened during national and district conventions (Frye & Peters, 1972). Since most members held college degrees in physical education, this organization served to link the interests of therapeutic recreation to college and university curricula, an element critical to the future development of accreditation standards.

The third organization to evolve was the National Association of Recreational Therapists (NART). In February 1953 Charles R. Cottle, director of recreation and education at Mississippi State Hospital, convened a meeting at Western State Hospital in Bolivia, Tennessee, for recreational therapists from state hospitals and schools serving people with mental illness or intellectual disabilities (ID) (Cox & Dobbins, 1970).

Most of the attendees were not affiliated with the American Recreation Society or the National Recreation Association and were looking for professional affiliations that would support the needs of those working in institutional programs and that endorsed the recreation therapy philosophy. NART's major contributions included developing standards for professional education, outlining professional qualifications for clinical practice, and defining the role of the profession (Hillman, 1970). Beginning in 1957 the organization also produced a quarterly journal, *Recreation for the Ill and Handicapped,* which stemmed from Cottle's publication, *The Inter State News.*

Even though the three organizations had different perspectives on service delivery, they recognized the need to work together to address common problems such as inequities in salary and practice benefits with other hospital employees (Cox & Dobbins, 1970). In 1953 representatives from each of the organizations met to form the Council for Advancement of Hospital Recreation (CAHR), which provided a cooperative structure for these organizations and served to strengthen the professional image of hospital recreation. Moreover, in 1959 each of the three organizations appointed representatives to a joint committee to identify existing philosophical differences and design a plan for uniform growth of the profession. Although the committee met for four years, it was unable to come to agreement on an appropriate direction for the profession and was disbanded.

Professional Standards

To assure the public that quality services are being provided, a viable profession establishes standards of practice, a code of ethics, and a process for credentialing or monitoring professional qualifications, including certification and licensure. Society's recognition of these standards of conduct is an indication of the profession's level of acceptance. One tangible product of the formation of the CAHR was the implementation of the Voluntary Registration Plan in 1956 (Frye, 1962). The plan, which included three levels of certification (hospital recreation director, hospital recreation leader, and hospital recreation aide), was used by the profession until 1969, when it was extensively revised (Carter, 1981).

Developing a Body of Knowledge

The body of knowledge for a profession is developed through research and disseminated through publications. Along with service to society, this research has been described as the most important quality of a profession (Goode, 1957). No matter how useful to society, a profession will not survive and mature without a substantive theoretical basis for its activity. Thus, any assessment of the status of a profession rests in large part on the quality and quantity of the research that forms its foundation. Several decades would pass before such a body of knowledge could be developed for the field of therapeutic recreation.

During the late 1950s and 1960s several studies examined the status of therapeutic recreation personnel in a variety of employment settings. Joseph Wolffe, a noted leader in the field of sports medicine, initiated a large research project that involved comparing outcome variables of more than 1,000 hospitalized persons who had received recreation intervention with those who had not. He reported that recreation interventions contributed to shorter hospitalizations, less need for medications, and fewer negative side effects of hospitalization (Wolffe, 1957). Another study was directed toward determining the status of programs, research, and practitioner needs in treatment centers in the United States (Weckworth, 1964). The results of these studies and other research from treatment programs such as the Menninger Clinic provided initial support for hospital recreation and recreation therapy during the early developmental years.

The development of journals and other publications was a primary contribution of the early professional associations. Specifically, the HRS published *Recreation in Treatment Centers* from 1954 until 1969, and NART published *Recreation for the Ill and Handicapped* from 1957 to 1967. However, it was not until Valerie Hunt wrote *Recreation for the Handicapped* (1955) and Josephine L. Rathbone and Carol Lucas authored *Recreation in Total Rehabilitation* (1959) that the profession could claim textbooks that were dedicated to promoting therapeutic recreation.

Training and Education

If a profession is to both use and extend its body of knowledge, it must develop a formal educational program that will be recognized and supported by the higher education community. Although the first known professional recreation course was taught in 1909, the National Recreation Association Leadership School began formal training of recreation personnel in 1926 (Ball, 1969). The most significant development of recreation curricula occurred in 1951 with the first master's degree programs offered by the University of West Virginia and the University of Minnesota (Frye & Peters, 1972). Formal training in hospital recreation became available in the early 1950s at the University of Minnesota and the University of North Carolina under the leadership of Fred Chapman and Harold Meyer, respectively. By 1953 the HRS Standards and Training Committee identified six colleges and universities with graduate or undergraduate degree programs in hospital recreation (Kraus, 1983).

As more degree programs in therapeutic recreation were established, leaders became concerned about their content. As a result of a study published in 1959 on the state of training in higher education, the NRA held a conference in 1961 to explore degree requirements and general competencies for therapeutic recreation personnel (Frye & Peters, 1972). A follow-up conference, known as the Recreation Education Accreditation Project, developed therapeutic recreation criteria for both undergraduate and graduate levels of study. The criteria guided the development of therapeutic recreation curricula throughout the next decade (Ball, 1968; MacLean, 1963).

In addition to formal curricula, annual therapeutic recreation conferences held alternately on the campuses of the Universities of North Carolina and Minnesota during the 1950s and 1960s contributed significantly to professional development. These conferences often featured noted physicians such as Alexander Reid Martin, former chairman of the American Psychiatric Association Committee on Leisure, and Joseph B. Wolffe (1957), who, along with Paul Haun (1965), wrote and spoke extensively on the value of recreation to the rehabilitation of individuals with disabilities. The credibility of these individuals and others, such as Beatrice Hill, was a significant factor in the promotion of hospital recreation as a viable profession.

Given this newfound status in community and political circles, recreation was included as a necessary service in several significant legislative acts in the early 1960s. The Vocational Rehabilitation Administration Act (1963) provided training and research funds for recreation programs for children and adults with mental illness and intellectual disabilities (O'Morrow & Reynolds, 1989). Nearly 300 graduate students from 11 different universities received training grants to complete studies in therapeutic recreation between 1963 and 1970. Since this law was the first to recognize the value of recreation in rehabilitation, it laid the groundwork for future legislation.

Summary of Birth and Infancy Period

In the early developmental stages of the profession, therapeutic recreation services emerged in two forms: as recreation for institutionalized people and as therapy for the treatment of specific disabilities. The professional organizations that formed during this period reflect these two distinct philosophies and, as a result, were unable to achieve consensus on an appropriate direction for the therapeutic recreation movement. Although the profession obtained the support of the AMA and the APA, little research was available to give it widespread recognition, and only a few universities offered therapeutic recreation courses at the undergraduate or graduate level. The profession had achieved some identity as a legitimate health-care service, but much work remained before it could satisfy the criteria designating professional status.

CHILDHOOD (1966–1980)

Childhood has been defined as the years from toddler to teenager. This period is characterized by a slow, steady growth process with social development being key to the maturation of the individual's self-concept. Self-concept is comprised of character traits that the child has come to value and gradually adopt as his or her own. The concept of self influences every aspect of our lives, including our attitudes toward others, our sense of independence, and our self-confidence. If we apply this analogy to therapeutic recreation, we recognize its "childhood" as a very critical time because the profession began to develop the traits that would form its sense of self—its identity. The following sections trace the distinct values the profession embraced during its maturation process.

Service to Society

A major factor in the delivery of therapeutic recreation services in the late 1960s was the downsizing of large institutions. President Nixon mandated that the number of people with mental illness and intellectual disabilities living in public institutions be reduced by one-third. This placed a greater demand on community-based health-care services, including therapeutic recreation. One organization, the San Francisco Recreation Center for the Handicapped (now called the Janet Pomeroy Center), served and continues to serve as a model for other community organizations. Founded by Janet Pomeroy in 1952, the center's primary purpose is to provide a variety of programs that contribute to the growth and development of children and adults with severe handicaps or intellectual disabilities through healthful and constructive activities. The organization's continued success is a tribute to the vision and support of the many community leaders and volunteers who have provided the required resources over the years (Pomeroy, 1969).

During the late 1950s and the 1960s other community-based programs for people with disabilities were established in several major cities, including Kansas City, Chicago, New York, and Cincinnati. However, the results of several surveys showed that only 25% of all public recreation agencies provided services for those with disabilities (Mitchell & Hillman, 1969). Another report published by New York University on the status of recreation services to children with disabilities noted a need to develop more inclusive programs, remove architectural barriers in community recreation facilities, and improve programs in hospitals and residential schools (Kraus, 1983). These results indicated that although some public recreation agencies responded to the need for community recreation programs for children and adults with disabilities, many appeared to relinquish the humanitarian vision of the early leaders of the recreation movement.

Fortunately, several private and nonprofit organizations attempted to fill the void. The American Foundation for the Blind (www.afb.org), the Association for Retarded Citizens (now known as The Arc of the United States, or simply The Arc, www.thearc.org), the United Cerebral Palsy Association (www.ucp.org), and the National Easter Seal Society (www.easter-seals.org), among others, provided such services as day and resident camping, homebound activities, professional training and publications, research, and adapted recreation aids. These associations continue to serve as resources for student materials, information, and employment possibilities.

The Special Olympics (www.specialolympics.org) program began in 1968 following a request by the Chicago Park District to the Joseph P. Kennedy Jr. Foundation for the funding of a national track meet for people with intellectual disabilities. Although the Special Olympics has been its most visible activity, the foundation has continued

Basketball was one of the earliest forms of wheelchair competition.

to support research, provide public information, and sponsor other activities such as the Unified Sports Model program designed to promote interaction between children with disabilities and able-bodied peers.

Recreation and therapeutic recreation services to people with disabilities were greatly expanded through several laws passed in this era. Advocacy efforts by voluntary and nonprofit organizations, including professional therapeutic recreation associations, assisted in the passage of several pieces of significant legislation. These include the Architectural Barriers Act of 1968 (PL [public law] 90-480); the Rehabilitation Act of 1973 (PL 93-112), specifically sections 502 and 504, which ensure equal access for persons with disabilities to all federally funded facilities and programs; the 1978 amendment to the Older Americans Act of 1965, which provides funding for research and recreation programs for senior citizens; and the Education for All Handicapped Children Act of 1975 (PL 94-142), which defined recreation as a "related service" that should be included as part of the individual educational plan (IEP) if it would enhance the special educational experience of the student (Bullock et al., 2010). As a related service, recreation included the assessment of leisure function, therapeutic recreation (specific, goal-oriented interventions), general recreation programs in schools and communities, and leisure education. Some TRSs used this law to justify consulting services or full-time positions in public and private schools serving students with disabilities. However, since recreation is a related—not a required—service, most school administrators did not push to add therapeutic recreation services unless strongly requested by parents during the IEP planning process.

This period witnessed changing attitudes toward people with disabilities. Individuals were no longer placed in institutions for life; but rather began to be accepted as a functional part of society. *Integration* and *normalization* were the buzzwords that promoted the inclusion of all people in the community.

Professional Organizations

By the mid-1960s several lay and professional organizations had been formed to promote various aspects of the community recreation field. Leaders of the profession believed consolidating forces would avoid competition, add to the political impact of the field, and improve its visibility with the public. Thus, in 1965, after much negotiation and debate, the National Recreation and Park Association (NRPA, www.nrpa.org) was organized as an umbrella organization to represent its affiliate branch organizations: the American Institute of Park Executives (1898), the National Recreation Association (1906), the National Conference on State Parks (1921), the American Association of Zoological Parks and Aquariums (1924), and the American Recreation Society (1938). Given the potential for participation in this 20,000-member recreation organization, the Hospital Recreation Section of the American Recreation Society, which was now a branch of NRPA, and the National Association of Recreation Therapists renewed efforts to merge. In October 1966 they agreed to become the **National Therapeutic Recreation Society (NTRS)**, the sixth branch of NRPA.

In addition to embracing the purposes of NRPA, NTRS proposed to (1) gather and disseminate facts and information with reference to therapeutic recreation, (2) further the rehabilitation of participants through recreation, (3) engender a spirit of cooperation between all professions and agencies related to their cause, and (4) develop standards for personnel, programs, and facilities that would result in improved services for participants. Through the board of directors, committees, and special task forces, members worked with NRPA to promote the profession and generate the documents needed to provide essential services to clients.

Throughout its early years NTRS benefited from inspired and energetic leaders who helped the organization achieve most of its goals. The last few years of the 1970s were particularly fruitful as the leaders focused their energies on such critical issues as legislation, a definition and philosophical statement of therapeutic recreation, personnel and program standards, credentialing, accreditation, and governance structure within NRPA. The governance issue was particularly problematic because many NTRS leaders desired greater organizational autonomy and felt constrained by the philosophical differences between the two organizations. In spite of many efforts to resolve the conflict, governance was an issue that seemed insoluble. A second controversial issue was the development of a definition and philosophical statement for the association. Both concerns would ultimately contribute to the formation of a new professional organization in the mid-1980s and the dissolution of NTRS as a branch of NRPA in 2010.

Professional Standards

A code of ethics, traditionally based on Judeo-Christian principles of moral behavior, guides the actions of professionals while providing the public with an expected standard of care. Ethical behavior is a distinguishing feature of professional practice. A code of ethics "provides the rules to eliminate the unqualified, reduces internal competition, and emphasizes the service ideal" (Meyer, 1980a, p. 10). As described by O'Keefe, an ethic of care "places social responsibility above professional status and financial reward" (2005, p. 73). NTRS in 1966 adopted a six-point statement of professional ethics that was later revised (1972) and accepted by the membership.

The national registration or credentialing plan, originally developed by CAHR in 1956, was substantially modified by NTRS in 1969 to reflect changes in education and training as well as current trends in therapeutic recreation practice (Carter, 1981). One aspect of the plan was the appointment of the Continuing Professional Development Review Board to review and endorse the ever-increasing number of therapeutic recreation training opportunities that would best serve the educational needs of the profession. Initial state-level credentialing efforts in the late 1960s and early 1970s resulted in Recreation Therapy Practice Acts licensing therapists in Georgia and Utah; while Georgia was unsuccessful in retaining its Practice Act, Utah has retained state licensure since 1975.

Closely related to the development of credentialing tools is the preparation and use of standards of practice. Therapeutic recreation standards for psychiatric facilities were developed by NTRS in 1971 and served as the basis for standards used by the **Joint Commission on Accreditation of Healthcare Organizations (JCAHO),** commonly known as The Joint Commission (www.jcaho.org). Significantly, these were the first therapeutic recreation standards adopted by a health-care accrediting agency. Doris Berryman (1971), working through a grant funded by the U.S. Department of Health, Education and Welfare, developed recreation standards for residential institutions that became the blueprint for two standards-of-practice documents: *Standards for the Practice of Therapeutic Recreation Service* and the *Guidelines for the Administration of Therapeutic Recreation Service in Clinical and Residential Facilities* published in 1980 by NTRS (Van Andel, 1981). A similar document addressing therapeutic recreation services in the community, *Guidelines for Community-Based Recreation Programs for Special Populations,* was published in 1979.

As curricula multiplied, professional leaders also expressed concern for maintaining quality academic programs that would serve the emerging profession. In 1975, after several years of planning, NRPA and the American Association for Leisure and Recreation (AALR), now American Association of Physical Activity and Recreation (APAR), developed an accreditation process for reviewing college and university recreation and park curricula. This Council on Accreditation (COA) of NRPA/AALR is now COAPRT—Council on Accreditation of Parks, Recreation, Tourism, and Related Professions. Although the primary focus was toward professional preparation in recreation, park resources, and leisure services, the 1977 version identified a specialization in therapeutic recreation at the undergraduate and graduate levels, the first specialization for which accreditation was granted.

With the development of standards of practice, credentialing, a code of ethics, and a growing organization, the therapeutic recreation profession was able to achieve some recognition among the other health and human service organizations. However, NRPA's financial reversals in the mid-1970s caused cutbacks in staff and services to all NRPA branches, including NTRS, and limited the organization's ability to adequately address critical professional issues.

Developing a Body of Knowledge

Since research and publications are so basic to the development and survival of a profession, they have been a primary concern of many therapeutic recreation leaders over the years. An identifiable body of knowledge about therapeutic recreation drew support from the proliferation of academic programs in the 1970s and an active professional organization. Two new NTRS publications, the *Therapeutic Recreation Journal* and the *Therapeutic Recreation Annual,* replaced *Recreation for the Ill and Handicapped* and *Recreation in Treatment Centers.* However, the *Therapeutic Recreation Annual* only survived for five volumes before it was discontinued in 1972 due to a financial crisis at NRPA. Other journals, such as the *Journal of Leisurability* (1974–2000) and the *Journal of Leisure Research,* also increased opportunities for publishing research and gave the young profession greater visibility.

In 1972 Virginia Frye and Martha Peters noted that one-third of all research in therapeutic recreation completed during the previous 50 years was undertaken between 1963 and 1972. However, despite the obvious growth in research efforts during this period, the quality of the studies became suspect. Some have suggested that the lack of research methods skills of these early researchers caused much of their work to be "localized, trivial, biased, fragmentary, and defective in design and methodology" (O'Morrow & Reynolds, 1989, p. 124). It would take more than a decade or two to develop the sophistication in research methods that were necessary to establish a solid theoretical base for the field.

Major textbooks began to appear in the early 1970s, the first of which was written by Frye and Peters (1972)—*Therapeutic Recreation: Its Theory, Philosophy, and Practice.* First editions of other academic texts, including *Therapeutic Recreation Service: Principles and Practices* (Kraus, 1973); *Recreation and Special Populations* (Stein & Sessoms, 1973); *Therapeutic Recreation Service: An Applied Behavioral Science Approach* (Avedon, 1974); *Therapeutic Recreation: A Helping Profession* (O'Morrow, 1976); and *Therapeutic Recreation Program Design* (Gunn & Peterson, 1978), rounded out a decade of significant publications that seemed to substantiate the growth of this young profession.

Training and Education

In the mid-1960s and 1970s, the focus of training and education shifted. The narrow emphasis on preparing recreation leaders for work with individuals with specific disabilities in custodial settings was broadened to involve the rehabilitation and education of a variety of people with disabilities in a decentralized, community service system. The opportunities for training also expanded, as evidenced by a growing number of university curricula offering courses in therapeutic recreation and a variety of excellent conferences, workshops, and institutes at the state, regional, and national levels. Notably, the first Midwest Symposium on Therapeutic Recreation was held in Chicago in 1971 with Karl Menninger, distinguished psychiatrist and longtime supporter of the therapeutic use of recreation in treatment and rehabilitation, serving as the keynote speaker. Other regions of the U.S. have used the successful Midwest Symposium as a model for providing a network of professional training and continuing education.

As previously noted, from the mid-1960s to the 1970s there was a substantial increase in the number of therapeutic recreation curricula. A 1969 study listed 35 programs offering a therapeutic recreation specialty at the undergraduate level and 26 at the graduate level (Stein, 1970). Only ten years later there were 116 undergraduate therapeutic recreation options within general recreation curricula and another 34 master's-degree programs (Anderson & Stewart, 1980). The authors of the study speculated the growth might have been the result of increased legislation supportive of people with disabilities and their need for recreation services. Health care also experienced tremendous growth during this time, which created many job opportunities for graduates and added to the popularity of therapeutic recreation programs within universities.

Summary of Childhood Era

This period of therapeutic recreation history reveals an emerging profession. A strong push toward professionalism occurred during the late 1960s and 1970s: a unified professional association was established, standards of practice were developed, the credentialing process was updated, and Practice Acts resulted in licensure at the state level. However, several areas of weakness remained: the profession lacked a clearly defined philosophy of service that was widely held by TRSs, the credentialing tools were voluntary and lacked uniformity, research studies and the accumulated body of knowledge were fragmented and had not achieved a recognized status in respected journals, the contributions of therapeutic recreation to client welfare were in very early stages of documentation and justification, and finally, the quality of academic training had yet to meet the test of job accountability. By 1980 the professional development of therapeutic recreation reached a critical stage, a period we will refer to as adolescence.

ADOLESCENCE (1981–1990)

Developmental psychologists describe adolescence as the period between the beginning of puberty and the achievement of independent adult status (Myer, 1986). As Myer notes, for some it is a time of storm and stress, of emotional turbulence caused by the tension between biological maturity and enforced dependence. While these descriptions are filled with scenes of disorder and turmoil, others might describe their adolescence as Tolstoy characterized it—a time of vitality without the cares of adulthood, a time of congenial family relationships punctuated by only occasional tensions, a time of rewarding friendships, a time of heightened idealism, and a growing sense of life's exciting possibilities (Coleman, 1980).

These conflicting views of adolescence may accurately describe the contrasting perspectives of various therapeutic recreation professionals during this decade. Some would say it was a time of growth and opportunity while others would report it as a time of chaos and constant battles. Both would agree, however, that it was a time of unprecedented change in health care and in the profession. For the field of therapeutic recreation, changes occurred in the service delivery system, employment practices, professional organizations, and educational requirements, to name a few. Strategic positioning and strategizing were constant themes of the profession as it prepared for "adulthood."

Service to Society

The 1980s saw changes in the delivery of health-care services and, consequently, therapeutic recreation services. Cost-containment efforts by governmental agencies and health insurance companies commenced in the 1970s (McCormick, 2002). Legislation was passed that denied approval of unnecessary services, prohibited unnecessary expansion of health-care systems, and dictated a reduction in the length of hospital inpatient stays. This dramatically reduced hospital income and resulted in numerous job losses, especially in mental health facilities. Increased competition between agencies, services, and disciplines challenged TRSs to demonstrate their effectiveness as treatment providers who could help accelerate the rehabilitation process and reduce the length of hospital stays. Cost-conscious administrators and external accrediting agencies, such as The Joint Commission and state health-care regulators, also pressured service providers to be more accountable for the quality, appropriateness, and outcome of their services.

Because the cost-containment efforts of the 1970s were not as effective as desired, new legislation in the early 1980s [Tax Equity and Fiscal Responsibility Act (TEFRA) of 1982 and the Social Security Amendment Act of 1983 (PL 98-21)] introduced reimbursement through a prospective payment system (PPS) (McCormick, 2002). Diagnoses were grouped with payment amounts pre-set. Thus, cost efficiency discouraged reimbursement for any additional services—further challenging TRSs to justify service reimbursement. More procedures and services were being performed on an outpatient basis, which traditionally had not been a strong employment area for therapeutic recreation. Outpatient services are usually provided on a fee-for-service basis, and since therapeutic recreation was not always recognized by insurance companies as a chargeable service, health-care agencies were not consistently able to provide therapeutic recreation services for their clients even when they were considered beneficial.

As an alternative to the traditional health insurance plan, which pays for treatment, a growing number of Health Maintenance Organizations (HMOs) promoted a philosophy of health promotion and disease prevention while restricting choices of service providers. Believing it was less costly to keep people healthy than to treat them after they became sick, HMOs began to spread across the country largely due to employer-supported efforts to control escalating costs associated with employee benefit packages. Although it would appear that therapeutic recreation had great potential to participate as an agent of health promotion, this role did not evolve until the early 1990s.

As the process of deinstitutionalization continued and more people with disabilities returned to community-based facilities, recreation and park agencies expanded therapeutic recreation services. With the passage of the **Americans with Disabilities Act (ADA)** (PL 101-336) in 1990, all public recreation programs were required to provide people with disabilities equal access to all programs and facilities. This law provided the impetus public recreation programs needed to hire TRSs and support the training of recreation professionals who could design and implement inclusionary therapeutic recreation programs.

Amendments to the Education for Handicapped Children Act in 1983, 1986, and 1990 recognized the need to initiate intervention services for infants and toddlers as early as possible and expanded funding in this area. The 1990 amendment (PL 101-476) also renamed the act the Individuals with Disabilities Education Act (IDEA), replacing *handicapped* with the more politically correct term *disability* (Cowden & Eason, 1991). TRSs who became familiar with the law and worked with local children's advocacy groups, such as The Arc, to market therapeutic recreation services were able to develop programs in selected school systems.

Trends in health care throughout the 1980s emphasized community-based services and required major adjustments for health-care providers. As we will discuss in the following section, these trends also had a significant impact on professional organizations as they sought to provide leadership to this dynamic field.

Professional Organizations

What is the primary purpose of therapeutic recreation? Is it a means to an end, often described as "recreation therapy," or is the value of therapeutic recreation the outcome of the recreation experience, an end in itself? The debate about the true nature of therapeutic recreation surfaced again in the 1980s. In an effort to bring some consensus to the profession, NTRS asked Lee Meyer of the University of North Carolina to identify the various historical perspectives and consider the implications of these views on the development of the therapeutic recreation profession. In his 1980 report, Meyer outlined the definitions of therapeutic recreation that had been articulated by various members of the profession over the previous decades: to provide opportunities for recreative experiences (recreation); to treat, change, or otherwise ameliorate effects of illness and disability (therapy); to enhance therapeutic effects of the recreative experience (therapeutic); and to eliminate leisure barriers, provide leisure skills and attitudes, and enable independent leisure functioning and the recreative experience (service continuum or leisure ability) (Meyer, 1980b).

After much debate, the membership of NTRS was surveyed to determine their ideological preference. The clear majority endorsed the leisure ability position, which was subsequently adopted by the NTRS board in 1982 (Reynolds & O'Morrow, 1985). However, adopting a philosophy of therapeutic recreation did not end the struggle for professional identity. Another concern was the inability of NTRS as a branch of the leisure-services-oriented NRPA to adequately respond to the professional needs of those in health-care settings such as hospitals and rehabilitation centers (Peterson, 1984). For more than a decade NTRS leaders unsuccessfully urged NRPA to recognize the importance of providing the staff and resources needed to address such issues as third-party reimbursement, credentialing, and working with external accrediting bodies such as The Joint Commission on health-care standards. Finally, Gary Robb, a past president of NTRS and the society's representative to the NRPA Board of Trustees, advised NTRS to "reconcile the fact that NRPA is a broad-based public advocacy organization for the parks and recreation field and that professional programs and concerns are only one of its many organizational functions" (O'Morrow, 1991, p. 23).

Not surprisingly, therapeutic recreation specialists in health-care settings argued that the newly adopted leisure-ability philosophy statement lacked the focus needed to support their work in the highly competitive health-care market. They preferred the therapy position because it seemed to be more consistent with the focus of other successful health-care professions such as occupational therapy and physical therapy and therefore more acceptable to administrators, insurance companies, and regulatory agencies. Thus, the stage was set for organizational change.

In 1984, under the leadership of many active professionals, the **American Therapeutic Recreation Association (ATRA)** was established (www.atra-online.com). Although the goals and programs of the organization were similar to those of NTRS, the process for achieving the goals was different. ATRA's organizational autonomy allowed its board to determine priorities and follow through with action plans without modification by a parent agency. ATRA developed a decentralized organizational structure that encouraged the formation of local affiliate chapters as active components of the system; promoted networking with other health-care agencies; supported the value of the therapeutic recreation process in health-care delivery systems; improved professional services; and initiated a proactive approach to organizational planning.

In 1987 ATRA adopted a philosophical statement that subscribed to a modified "therapy" position while also acknowledging the role of recreation services in therapeutic recreation (see exhibit 2.2). Such a philosophy represented the views of a large majority of the membership who worked in health-care settings where professional services were more likely to be judged by their effectiveness in improving the functional capacity, health status, and/or quality of life of the client.

One of ATRA's most significant contributions to health care is the role it has played in promoting therapeutic recreation as a legitimate health-care service. During the last half of the 1980s, ATRA was able to establish closer relationships with external regulatory agencies such as The Joint Commission, the Commission on Accreditation of Rehabilitation Facilities, now CARF International (www.carf.org), the

> **Exhibit 2.2   ATRA's 1987 Statement of Philosophy**
>
> Therapeutic recreation is the provision of treatment services and the provision of recreation services to persons with illnesses or disabling conditions. The primary purpose of treatment services, which is often referred to as recreation therapy, is to restore, remediate, or rehabilitate in order to improve functioning and independence as well as reduce or eliminate the effects of illness or disability. The primary purpose of recreation services is to provide recreation resources and opportunities in order to improve health and well-being. Therapeutic recreation is provided by professionals who are trained and certified, registered or licensed to provide therapeutic recreation.
>
> Statement taken from *ATRA Newsletter,* May–June 1990. Used with permission of the American Therapeutic Recreation Association.

Centers for Medicare and Medicaid Services or CMS (www.cms.hhs.gov) [formerly Health Care Financing Administration (HCFA), renamed in 2001], and other federal agencies; promote professional involvement through numerous affiliate chapters; develop and market a number of publications involving quality improvement, quality management, third-party reimbursement, treatment protocols, standards of practice, and research in therapeutic recreation; expand continuing education opportunities; promote the development of credentialing; and influence significant pieces of legislation affecting people with disabilities.

At the same time, NTRS spearheaded similar contributions by establishing National Therapeutic Recreation Week (1984, second week in July annually), attending the The Joint Commission Professional Technical Advisory Committee meetings (since 1987), and adopting a revised code of ethics. In 1990 NTRS revised its internship standards and guidelines for the administration of therapeutic recreation services to support professionals in a variety of settings, including those providing therapeutic recreation in the community. Although the reestablishment of two professional therapeutic recreation organizations was not without its difficulties, historical reflections will probably recognize the wisdom of this decision.

Professional Standards

The 1980s also saw the separation of the NTRS Registration Board from the NRPA. The National Commission for Health Certifying Agencies [which evolved into the National Organization for Competency Assurance in 1987, renamed the Institute for Credentialing Excellence (ICE) in 2009], required the board to be independent from NRPA if its certification plan was to be recognized. In October 1981, the **National Council for Therapeutic Recreation Certification (NCTRC)** assumed the management and administration of certification and recertification standards for therapeutic recreation personnel. NCTRC continued to establish national evaluative standards for certification and recertification, granted recognition to those who satisfactorily met the criteria, and monitored adherence to the standards.

In an effort to improve the credentialing program, NCTRC initiated the Job Analysis Project in 1987, which attempted to define the entry-level knowledge base through practitioner and curriculum studies. The findings concluded that professionals agreed on the important knowledge components required to practice therapeutic recreation and that the knowledge base should be stable and consistent—two factors necessary for developing a national certification exam (Oltman, Norback, & Rosenfeld, 1989). Following this study, NCTRC contracted with the Educational Testing Service (ETS), an agency that had a strong reputation for constructing occupational credentialing exams, to develop a 200-item national written exam. This exam was first offered in November of 1990.

While NCTRC was preparing to administer its exam for the CTRS, the National Certification Board of NRPA contracted with Applied Measurement Professionals to develop an exam for certifying leisure professionals, one section of which included questions on therapeutic recreation. This exam was also first administered in 1990. Given the move toward inclusion, basic knowledge in therapeutic recreation was viewed by the leisure profession as important to the provision of recreation services to persons with disabilities.

During the 1980s, members of NTRS and ATRA made contact with representatives from The Joint Commission and CARF International seeking incorporation of the Standards of Practice of Therapeutic Recreation Service into the review process of these groups. With the advent of ATRA's financial commitment to networking with health-care agencies, these relationships seemed to mature to the point where the profession was actively involved with key health-care organizations in defining criteria for quality client care. These initiatives required updating the professional standards of practice. By 1990 an ATRA Standards of Practice Committee had published a new set of outcome-oriented standards common to all contemporary health-care organizations, while NTRS had updated its Guidelines for the Administration of Therapeutic Recreation Services. The profession had begun to demonstrate that it was ready and able to take its place with other health-care professions and to make a contribution to the rehabilitation and social inclusion of persons with disabilities.

Developing a Body of Knowledge

In 1980, O'Morrow had aptly suggested that therapeutic recreation research should include studies that would assist in: (1) determining special activity needs, professional responsibilities and practices, appropriate use of therapeutic processes by practitioners with varying backgrounds, roles of individuals with disabilities in implementing therapeutic recreation plans, and rationales for using therapeutic recreation to resolve a problem; (2) guiding decisions inherent in the therapeutic recreation process; and (3) developing evaluative tools (O'Morrow, 1980). Many of these challenges were met throughout the next decade as TR research came of age. Articles submitted to the *Therapeutic Recreation Journal* were substantially improved in research methodology, instrumentation, design, and analysis, and reflected more conceptual and hypothesis testing and less survey research (Reynolds & O'Morrow, 1985). As the quality and quantity of research improved, new journals devoted to therapeutic recreation were established (first issue of the *Annual in Therapeutic Recreation* was published in 1990 by

ATRA), and other respected rehabilitation journals began to publish therapeutic recreation articles.

Academics within the field also published numerous new college texts and revised several others. It was clear that the profession had begun to define the unique knowledge and skills it needed to participate as a full member of the health and human service delivery system.

Training and Education

Following the unprecedented expansion in the 1970s, funding for colleges and universities declined in the 1980s, and several nationally recognized programs substantially restructured or closed. Nevertheless, in 1982 the NRPA/ AALR Accreditation Program was officially recognized by the Commission on Recognition of Postsecondary Accreditation, now known as the Council on Higher Education Accreditation (CHEA), a national agency that monitors academic accreditation programs. With this endorsement, recreation and park curricula and their therapeutic recreation options achieved a new level of acceptance as a discipline and a profession. The previous (1977) COA (currently COAPRT) recognition of the therapeutic recreation *specialization* was enhanced in 1981 when it was recognized as an *option,* with a list of competencies unique to therapeutic recreation curricula. These competencies were again upgraded in 1990 to better reflect job tasks in health and human service settings.

Opportunities for continuing education expanded with the addition of conferences sponsored by ATRA, state affiliate chapters, the International Symposium on Therapeutic Recreation, and various other regional symposiums. Other significant contributions to professional preparation were made by the Therapeutic Recreation Management School cosponsored by the University of Maryland and the Wheeling West Virginia Park Commission, and the Recreation Therapy Institute sponsored by the Department of Recreation Therapy at the University of North Carolina Hospitals and the Curriculum in Leisure Studies at the University of North Carolina.

Summary of Adolescent Period

The 1980s was a period of debate and transition toward autonomy for professional therapeutic recreation organizations. As the profession moved through adolescence, many practitioners perceived that its emancipation from a leisure-services-oriented parent organization (NRPA) was the only way to establish its identity as a legitimate health-care profession. Augmented by a developing body of research and a strong commitment to quality services, the profession was slowly emerging as a viable member of the health-care community. The changing nature of health care, however, suggested continuing challenges would emerge in the last decade of the twentieth century and early decades of the twenty-first century.

YOUNG ADULTHOOD (1991–PRESENT)

Daniel Levinson (1978) has suggested that following a separation from a preadult world, the young adult seeks to create a secure and stable environment in which he or she can launch a career and establish a family or become part of a social community.

Other researchers have identified early adulthood, a period roughly spanning the ages from 20 to 40, as a time of "affiliation and achievement, attachment and productivity, commitment and competence" (Myer, 1986, p. 102). These developmental characteristics appear to fit this period of therapeutic recreation's professional history. In some ways, like life, the profession is constantly in transition. TRSs will continue to discuss philosophical and theoretical issues that define who they are because the health-care environment is continually changing, challenging health-care practitioners to modify the roles and responsibilities they have traditionally adopted (Hunter, 1996). However, the field of therapeutic recreation is also entering a period that should offer more potential for productivity, competence, and achievement. With continued improvements in the quality and effectiveness of services provided to those with special needs, the growth and visibility of professional associations, the expanded body of research, the recognition and support from allied health associations, and the development of the professional credential and standards of practice, TRSs have established therapeutic recreation as a legitimate practice in the health and human service field.

Service to Society

Attitudes toward people with disabilities have continued to improve. Evidence of this change is the enactment of the Americans with Disabilities Act in 1990. Like its predecessors, this law prohibits discrimination on the basis of one's disability but is broader in scope and has stronger provisions for federal enforcement. Probably the most significant impact of the act for TRSs and those with disabilities is its implications for providing opportunities for all people to participate in community recreation programs. Public recreation and park agencies are now required to offer comprehensive services to people with disabilities; typically this means employing TRSs to design and implement specialized and/or inclusive recreation programs. The impetus to employ qualified professionals to develop inclusive programs was advanced when NRPA adopted in 1999 an NTRS-prepared statement on inclusion and when the first National Institute on Recreation Inclusion (NIRI) was held in September 2000. These efforts have led the way in making "public recreation facilities and programs accessible to persons with disabilities" (Austin, 2004, p. 42). In addition, amendments to the Individuals with Disabilities Education Act (PL 105-17, June 1997) and the Individuals with Disabilities Education Improvement Act of 2004 (IDEAIA, PL 108-446, December 2004) required transition planning to be in effect with the IEP (individual education plan) when a child is 14. Such transition could include community experiences that promote movement from school to post-school activities. Support for professionals to incorporate recreation as a related service was advanced through academic preparation and training like the Summit on Therapeutic Recreation as a Related Service (1995), sponsored by the University of North Carolina at Chapel Hill, and the annual NIRI conference.

The health-care field continues to rapidly change. Interventions in the twenty-first century bear little resemblance to twentieth-century practices. Bricks and mortar, as well as operational structures of hospitals and health services, are less relevant (Porter-O'Grady, 2003). "Advances in medical science and technology and the explosion in medical and health information accessible through the Internet" (Aiken, 2003, p. 165) have contributed to the globalization of health care and rising expectations with regard to personal care, health promotion, and disease prevention. "Predicted changes are occurring at the same time they are being experienced" (Porter-O'Grady, 2003, p. 60). Even clients and health-care providers in remote locations are adopting new knowledge, technology, pharmacology, and chemo- and biotherapeutics as they become available (Nosek, 2004). The aging population, a shift from acute to chronic conditions, and successes in medical care are contributing to an expanded role for health care beyond treatment and rehabilitation to issues like obesity, sexual predators, substance abuse, and the global encroachment of diseases. Advancements in health-care technology and health-care reform will dramatically affect therapeutic recreation services. TRSs will need to assume advocacy roles as they develop new services and programs to meet the changing needs of society. Moreover, TR professionals will need to network with a variety of health care, educational, social service, and community agencies to provide care that is efficient, evidence-based, and holistic (Aiken, 2003; Riley & Skalko, 1998). The 2009 congressional health-care reform bills are intended to improve quality, access, and cost containment, while focusing on prevention and wellness. TRSs, like other health-care professionals, will continually monitor their practices to assure accountable outcomes that promote health and positive lifestyle behaviors.

A 1979 Surgeon General's report, *Healthy People*, promoted a nationwide health and disease prevention agenda to focus on quality of life issues at the community level. Some 30 years later, the *Healthy People 2010* report is based on the premise that community-based health care systems are comprehensive, culturally competent, capable of achieving an increase in quality and years of life, and can eliminate health disparities among all individuals (Howard, Russoniello, & Rogers, 2004; U.S. Department of Health and Human Services, 2007). Included among the 10 leading health indicators that reflect national health concerns are physical activity, obesity, substance abuse, mental health, and violence. In other words, the health of the nation is to be measured with these indicators. TR initiatives are consistent with the *Healthy People 2010* outlook. Through active interventions like adventure challenge, aerobic exercise, and stress management, TRSs promote health and prevent secondary health conditions that accompany chronic illness. Health promotion through physical fitness and lifestyle awareness programs is widespread (Coyle, Boyd, Kinney, & Shank, 1998). Patient health education has experienced a resurgence with the increasing focus on a holistic view of health care that emphasizes health promotion and disease prevention (Austin, 2002b; Heintzman, 1997; Mobily & Ostiguy, 2004). The experience of war, terrorism, and natural disasters calls for TRSs to design and implement interventions that promote coping skills, physical rehabilitation, and lifestyle adjustments. These events require special intervention skills and an understanding of how therapeutic recreation programs can satisfy the unique needs of clients across cultures and delivery settings.

Professional Organizations

During the 1990s professional organizations developed joint agreements to address issues critical to the growth and promotion of the profession. Additionally, each organization advocated for inclusion of therapeutic recreation services through participation in CARF International, The Joint Commission, and CMS; through the development and distribution of reimbursement publications; and by supporting a paid lobbyist and legislative days on Capitol Hill. The memberships of the respective organizations were strengthened through grassroots training, updating of philosophical statements, and publication of protocol documents.

Throughout the early and mid-1990s the professional organizations addressed health-care reform issues. Publication of *Recreational Therapy: A Summary of Health Outcomes* by ATRA in 1994 predated the publication of a joint statement by ATRA and NTRS, *Therapeutic Recreation: Responding to the Challenges of Health-Care Reform.* To support the role of therapeutic interventions as viable contributors in health-care settings, ATRA and NTRS published reimbursement and protocol documents, became active in CARF International and The Joint Commission Coalition of Rehabilitation Organizations, and met with representatives of CMS to interpret the profession's position in federal health-care regulations.

In 1996, ATRA and NTRS established a Joint Task Force on Credentialing to support state efforts to become recognized health-care providers in state codes and regulations. The Alliance for Therapeutic Recreation was created in 1998 by ATRA and NTRS as a means to communicate, cooperate, and collaborate. A Joint Task Force on Long-Term Care was formed in 1999 by the Alliance to address the needs of professionals practicing in various types of long-term care settings. Early in 2000 the Alliance began to study issues in higher education surrounding professional preparation, and a task force was appointed in 2001 to develop a strategic plan to address higher education issues.

During the 1990s and into the first decade of the twenty-first century, each organization advanced its particular mission through political activities, grassroots training, and publication of updated position statements. ATRA increased the number of state affiliate chapters and treatment networks. The emphasis on recreation therapy was sustained through successful lobbying efforts in Washington, DC, leadership training and legislative summits, and "ATRA Day on the Hill." Moreover, publications like *Recreation Therapy: A Viable Option in Rehabilitation, Treatment through Prevention* (2003) advocated for application of the TR process in clinical settings. In March 2004 ATRA undertook one of the most far-reaching and impactful legislative efforts to include recreation therapy services as a covered benefit under Medicare in inpatient rehabilitation facilities (IRFs), inpatient psychiatric facilities (IPFs), and SNFs (skilled nursing facilities). The ATRA membership amassed financial resources to garner legislative action in 2007 to designate recreation therapy as a skilled rehabilitative modality included in the PPS (prospective payment system) rates' bundle of services in these three settings. Although H.R. 4248 (The Ensuring Medicare Access to Recreational Therapy Act of 2007) did not move beyond the U.S. House of Representatives, ATRA continues to work with CMS to list recreational therapy with other skilled modalities in Section 110.43 of the Medicare Benefits Policy Manual. Revised mission, vision, and definition statements (2009) reinforced the member-driven nature of the organization and the focus of recreation therapy as a treatment service (see exhibit 2.3). In 2006 the Board of Directors approved a diversity statement that recognized the value of diversity in recreation therapy practice and education (ATRA, 2006).

Exhibit 2.3

ATRA Mission Statement

The mission of the American Therapeutic Recreation Association is to serve as a member-driven association that collectively supports the recreational therapy profession.

ATRA Vision Statement

The vision of the American Therapeutic Recreation Association is to be the premiere professional membership association representing recreational therapists, consumers, and stakeholders.

ATRA Definition Statement

"Recreational Therapy" means a treatment service designed to restore, remediate, and rehabilitate a person's level of functioning and independence in life activities, to promote health and wellness as well as reduce or eliminate the activity limitations and restrictions to participation in life situations caused by an illness or disabling condition.

ATRA brochure, September 2009. Used with permission of the American Therapeutic Recreation Association.

The NTRS focus on therapeutic recreation across the human-service continuum and especially in the community was promoted through publication of a marketing guide and an advocacy manual; the updating of its philosophical position statement (1996) and its vision, mission, and definition (2000); the acceptance by NRPA (1999) of the NTRS Resolution on Inclusion; and the annual sponsorship of the NIRI conference. In a 2002 statement "Recreation Access," NRPA promoted legislative efforts to create access through continued support of ADA, IDEAIA, *Healthy People 2010,* and Rehabilitation Services Administration programs. These efforts reflect a national movement to promote inclusive recreation (Austin, 2004). Reduction in the size of NRPA's governing board in 2009 included a proposal to reduce its branches and sections to two branches, Citizen and Professional, with present branches (NTRS included) becoming "Networks." This proposal, accepted in July 2010 by the NRPA board of directors, challenges NTRS's capacity to advocate across the continuum and to serve TR professionals. Both ATRA and NTRS supported renewed efforts to articulate the benefits and efficacy of professional practice and the use of technology to enhance professional skills and service delivery.

Professional Standards

As the organizations articulated their roles in health-care reform and their contributions to client well-being, a number of tasks were undertaken that resulted in the revision and/or creation of personnel and practice standards. Research by NCTRC supported the viability of the certification examination and its revision as a result of a third job analysis. Likewise, the National Certification Board updated its certification exam and renamed the leisure credential. Interpretive guidelines for each organization's (ATRA and NTRS) code of ethics guided recreation therapists' actions as the TR process was carried out. Enhancement and revisions of each organization's standards of practice enabled professionals to better articulate their responsibilities to ensure accountability.

From 1981 to 1992, the NCTRC standards defined two levels of practice, professional and assistant. The Council determined that the number of people seeking certification at the assistant level did not support the development of an exam for the CTRA, and the level was officially discontinued on December 31, 1999. In 1993, NCTRC received federal trademark registration of the Certified Therapeutic Recreation Specialist (CTRS) and was accredited by the National Commission for Certifying Agencies (NCCA), the body whose standards guided the creation of NCTRC in 1981. Efforts to sustain state licensure were rekindled in the 2000s. Joining Utah's successful effort to support Practice Acts were North Carolina (2005), New Hampshire (2006), and Oklahoma (2009). NCTRC published a position statement on the legal regulation of recreation therapy practice in 2007 (NCTRC, 2007b).

Throughout the 1990s and early 2000s, NCTRC revised and updated certification criteria and the examination, conducted job analyses, and reported on the growth of the field (NCTRC, 1997, 2007a; Riley & Connolly, 1997, 2007). Requirements to become a CTRS include successful passage of a computer mastery test, completion of a bachelor's degree or higher with specified credit hours in coursework defined by the Professional Knowledge Domains, and an internship under a CTRS for a defined number of hours completing tasks spelled out by the Job Task Domains. Since many CTRSs tend to work in hospital settings providing direct care, test content areas focus on the APIE process (assess, plan, implement, evaluate) and documentation. Possession of the CTRS credential denotes that the individual practices according to the "most current therapeutic professional standards and ethical guidelines" (NCTRC, 2007b, p. 5) and intends to do no harm to clients. In May 2010, NCTRC introduced a Specialty Certification Program. Qualified CTRSs are eligible to apply for recognition in Physical Medicine/Rehabilitation, Geriatrics, Developmental Disabilities, Behavioral Health, and Community Inclusion Services. The purpose of the program is to acknowledge CTRSs who have reached advanced practice levels and possess competencies essential to ensuring quality care and risk management. In concert with professional organizations, NCTRC advocates for legislation to legally regulate practice with state licensure. Further, NCTRC, through promotional resources, supports the international recruitment of new students and retention of professionals. Students may become familiar with certification criteria and profiles of practicing professionals by review of Internet resources at http://www.nctrc.org and through information shared with educators during the academic year.

The National Certification Board also completed a second and third job analysis (1999, 2006). As a result of these analyses, the test specifications in therapeutic recreation were merged into one of the three remaining content areas: managing, programming, or operations. These analyses also supported the significance of inclusionary practices by all park and recreation professionals. Early in 2000 the credential name was changed from Certified Leisure Professional to Certified Park and Recreation Professional (CPRP). As with the CTRS credential, the first administration of a computerized CPRP exam occurred in 2001. Also like the CTRS credential, criteria were revised so only one certification level existed (CPRP). Strategic planning identified as goals the management of a national level plan (rather than a national plan administered by the states) and creation of a *mastery* level. In December 2010, NRPA in consultation with NCB began a job task analysis for the possible implementation of a *manager* or *executive* level certification. The certification is designed to identify professionals as they advance in their careers. State-level CPRPs' plans were transitioned to national-level management at NRPA (2008–2010) as NCB and NCTRC jointly agreed to initiate design of specialty inclusion certification (2009).

To maintain their credentials, professionals are required to complete recertification every five years for the CTRS and every two years for the CPRP. Each plan requires individuals to retain and update their competencies through (1) documented experience, (2) retesting, and/or (3) the accumulation of continuing education units (CEUs) and payment of a maintenance and renewal fee. CEUs are earned by attending professional conference sessions that have been approved for content areas outlined in the job analyses of each national exam.

During this time frame each professional organization updated its respective code of ethics and interpretive guidelines (ATRA in 1990, 1998, 2001 and 2009, NTRS in 1990, 1994, 1998, and 2001). This quest is imperative to becoming a legitimate learned-service profession (Sylvester, 2002). Because such codes are self-regulatory, they are perceived as evidence of a maturing profession. Consequently, with established criteria to govern practice, the profession is viewed as having moved closer to recognition as a true profession. Another indicator of professional maturity is the use of standards of practice to define a profession's scope of service and to measure quality of service delivery. Modifications and enhancements in the ATRA standards of practice (1993, 1998, 2000) included a self-assessment tool for program and administration practices implemented by professional and paraprofessional level practitioners (see exhibit 2.4). Revised NTRS standards of practice (1995, 1998, 2003) incorporated paraprofessional standards and criteria to assess the implementation of the TR process. Extensive field research at clinical agencies throughout the country substantiated the appropriateness of the ATRA document as a professional accountability tool.

Developing a Body of Knowledge

A common concern in the field has been the lack of research demonstrating the impact of therapeutic recreation on client outcomes (O'Morrow & Reynolds, 1989). In response, Temple University sponsored a state-of-the-art national consensus conference on the benefits of therapeutic recreation in rehabilitation. Researchers presented six papers outlining current research findings and recommended areas for future research (Coyle, Kinney, Riley, & Shank, 1991). The disciplines covered were physical medicine, psychiatry, pediatrics, chemical dependency, developmental disabilities, and gerontology. The most comprehensive project of its kind, the conference and its subsequent publication, *Benefits of Therapeutic Recreation: A Consensus View*, provided a significant resource for the profession as it defined its role in rehabilitation.

The impetus to support research on the efficacy of therapeutic recreation was sustained with ATRA's publication of *Research in Therapeutic Recreation: Concepts and Methods* (Malkin & Howe, 1993) and its identification of a research agenda "aimed at examining the effectiveness of recreation therapy interventions and promoting the quality of recreational therapy education" (ATRA, n.d.). Additionally, each year recip-

Exhibit 2.4   Table of Contents for ATRA Standards of Practice

Preface
Introduction
ATRA STANDARDS OF PRACTICE
   Direct Practice in Therapeutic Recreation
      STANDARD 1 **Assessment**
      STANDARD 2 **Treatment Planning**
      STANDARD 3 **Plan Implementation**
      STANDARD 4 **Re-Assessment and Evaluation**
      STANDARD 5 **Discharge and Transition Planning**
      STANDARD 6 **Recreation Services**
      STANDARD 7 **Ethical Conduct**
   Management of Therapeutic Recreation Practice
      STANDARD 8   **Written Plan of Operation**
      STANDARD 9   **Staff Qualifications and Competency Assessment**
      STANDARD 10 **Quality Management**
      STANDARD 11 **Resource Management**
      STANDARD 12 **Program Evaluation and Research**
SELF-ASSESSMENT GUIDE
   Scoring Summary Worksheet
   Documentation Audit
   Management Audit
   Outcome Assessment
   Competency Assessment
   Clinical Performance Appraisal
Bibliography
Glossary
ATRA Code of Ethics
ATRA Patient Bill of Rights

From ATRA *Standards for the Practice of Therapeutic Recreation Revised* (2000). Used with permission of the American Therapeutic Recreation Association.

ients of research monies awarded by ATRA present their findings during the annual meeting. Since 1993, NTRS also has awarded partial funding to projects that investigate the efficacy of therapeutic recreation services. A 2003 study (Wilhite, Keller, Collins, & Jacobson) ranking research agenda items reaffirmed the significance of an efficacy agenda. The highest priority rankings were TR's impact on global health-care outcomes like health status, rehabilitation outcomes, and overall quality of life as valued by all stakeholders. Research also is published in the respective publications, *Annual in Therapeutic Recreation* (ATRA) and *Therapeutic Recreation Journal* (NTRS). The first volume of the *American Journal of Recreation Therapy* appeared in 2002. Each issue presents results of research completed by professionals across practice settings.

    The field witnessed the publication of several new college texts on management, inclusion, and diversity, as well as revised editions of several fundamental texts (introduction, techniques, philosophy, program design, trends, and issues). The research, journal articles, textbooks, professional organization publications, and conference papers made available through electronic media continue to contribute to a knowledge base that distinguishes therapeutic recreation as a unique professional field.

Training and Education

Throughout the 1990s and early 2000s, the disconnect between TR preparation and accountability measures resulted in higher education curricular challenges (see figure 2.1). Although growth in both faculty and student numbers was anticipated, a decrease occurred in the number of undergraduate students and accredited programs.

Researchers reported that "very little agreement has been reached about how to package and structure therapeutic recreation curriculum" (Stumbo et al., 2004, p. 54). In 1995 ATRA conducted a curriculum conference to address the issues and factors affecting therapeutic recreation education. The resulting publication outlined core competencies for use in curriculum development as well as for continuing education for TR professionals (Kinney & Witman, 1997). The 2008 revision of this document, *Guidelines for Competency Assessment and Curriculum Planning for Recreational Therapy Practice* (West, Kinney & Witman), updated the curriculum guidelines and noted the critical importance of safe and effective practice in health-care settings (where a majority of the TRSs are employed). The ATRA Academy was created to facilitate regional training and develop audio programs (CDs) and Webinars for continuing education. To address inconsistencies in internship requirements and procedures,

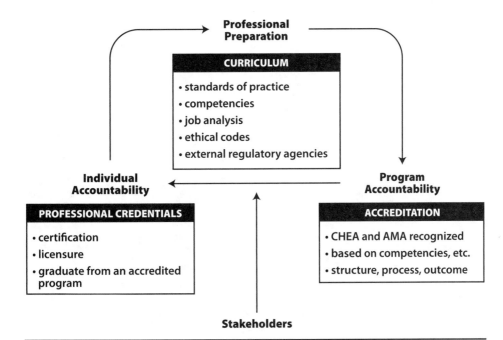

Figure 2.1   Quality and Accountability Cycle
Adapted from Stumbo (2009).

NTRS published a revised set of guidelines in 1997. ATRA followed suit in 1998. Both NTRS and ATRA realized recognition by peer professional groups was critical to acceptance of curricula across campuses. To this end, they advocated for and were included in the 1997–1998 AMA *Health Professions Career and Education Directory*, a biennial publication listing health-care careers and education programs (AMA, 2006).

The impetus and recommendations emanating from the 1995 ATRA curriculum conference contributed to the COAPRT appointing a task force in 1997 of representatives from ATRA, NTRS, and NCTRC (information only) to review and make recommendations on the professional preparation competencies and the standards for accrediting therapeutic recreation options. The revised standards published in 2000 required faculty to possess credentials in their respective expertise areas and required students to write outcome-oriented goals, to display competence in cultural diversity, and to comply with regulatory standards. New competencies identified in the revised standards included demonstrating an understanding of the roles of caregivers, inclusionary practices, holistic health, health-care delivery models, and human service systems trends. Also in 2000, the Alliance for Therapeutic Recreation formed a work group to identify issues and suggest strategies to resolve the continuing challenges faced by therapeutic recreation curricula in higher education. Subsequently, a Joint Task Force on Higher Education developed a strategic plan with goals aimed at increasing the consistency and strength of professional preparation programs. To further these goals, the Therapeutic Recreation Education Conference (TREC) was held in May 2005. Presentations covered topics affecting undergraduate and graduate education, credentialing, recruitment and retention, technology, health-care trends, and

The case study method of education is practiced during student internships.

faculty research and productivity, and were compiled in *Therapeutic Recreation Education: Challenges and Changes* (Carter & Folkerth, 2006), which summarized the state of affairs in higher education while providing information helpful to curriculum design.

Following TREC, the COAPRT undertook a strategic plan to bring the accreditation criteria into compliance with CHEA (Council for Higher Education Accreditation) recommendations to focus on outcome measures and management processes that are accountable and transparent. Revisions of standards and operating procedures (effective in 2013) ensued. A second TREC took place in June 2009. Undergraduate and graduate preparation and accreditation were again central discussion topics; also of concern was unification of the two professional organizations.

In 2009, prior to NTRS branch dissolution in 2010, an affiliate agreement was signed with COAPRT to develop learner outcomes to accredit TR as a specialty profession. With the impetus provided by publication of the ATRA 2008 document (*Guidelines for Competency Assessment and Curriculum Planning for Recreational Therapy Practice*), therapeutic recreation professionals explored accreditation alternatives—including alignment with health-care bodies to strengthen the viability of professional preparation programs. In 2009, the ATRA board voted to approach the CAAHP (Commission on Accreditation of Allied Health Programs). Subsequently in 2010, CAAHP accepted ATRA as a sponsoring member of educational programs in recreational therapy practice. CARTE (Committee on Accreditation of Recreational Therapy Education) was recognized as the accrediting body with standards drawn from the 2008 document.

A concern affirmed by research (Wilhite et al., 2003) remains the provision of effective services to culturally diverse individuals. While entry-level CTRSs tend to report having a satisfactory level of multicultural competence (Blair & Coyle, 2005; Stone, 2003), over one-third have not completed coursework on diversity. These authors also reported that those who attend multicultural workshops tend to report higher levels of multicultural awareness, knowledge, and skill. A profession's commitment to diversity is evidenced by the degree to which its training and professional preparation embrace the topic. There is a need to consistently present multicultural information commencing during entry-level preparation.

A second area of concern, and one central to recognition as a learned-service profession, is the expectation that entry-level professionals "are capable of meeting their ethical commitment to serve the public good" (Sylvester, 2002, p. 315). As with diversity, research reveals a paucity of ethics education in curricula (Nisbett, Brown-Welty, & O'Keefe, 2002). Without ethics education, how do professionals gain competence in applying professional codes of ethics to guide their practice? With ethics education, students are prepared to address a diverse constituency, to document service effectiveness, and to adapt to technological advancements. With infusion of multicultural and ethics information across the curriculum, moral leadership of the profession is advanced. Further, the profession is better positioned to provide the guidance the public desires from a learned-service profession (Sylvester, 2002).

Summary of Young Adult Era

The therapeutic recreation profession is in a period of transition that will likely continue for some time. To address the challenges created by health-care reform, the professional organizations developed publications on reimbursement and the benefits and efficacy of therapeutic recreation interventions. Additionally, these organizations advocated for inclusionary practices and promoted therapeutic recreation services through involvement in CARF International, The Joint Commission, and CMS. The changing nature of practice settings and services has compelled revisions in the standards of practice, codes of ethics, and professional certification and licensure standards. With the formation of the Alliance for Therapeutic Recreation, ATRA and NTRS established a mechanism to communicate, cooperate, and collaborate on issues critical to the advancement of the profession. Therapeutic recreation curricula remain diverse, without consensus on individual and program accountability measures. Yet, at the close of the first decade of the twenty-first century, history was repeated as professional unification and curriculum advancement were addressed, and one professional organization, ATRA, remained to serve the profession. The research base and body of knowledge have been disseminated through professional journals, published research, new and revised textbooks, and curriculum conference publications. Collectively, these accomplishments have better positioned the field for recognition by social scientists as a viable profession or "true" profession (Austin, 2004).

SUMMARY

This historical review of therapeutic recreation has identified the central forces, issues, and concerns giving direction to the formation of the profession. The therapeutic recreation field has evolved from two philosophical perspectives: one emphasized the use of recreation activities as a tool for therapy (recreation therapy) and the other acclaimed the product of the recreation experience (hospital recreation). These views were merged with the introduction of the term *therapeutic recreation* and the formation of a unified professional association, the National Therapeutic Recreation Society (1966–2010). For more than 40 years the therapeutic recreation field has worked to establish itself as a recognized health and human service profession, characterized by the service it provides to society, the formal organization of its members, recognized programs for training and education, professional standards of practice and ethics codes, and a reputable body of knowledge.

Although the profession has succeeded in achieving a level of maturity, the changes in society—and specifically in health care—will require its tenets to be subject to constant revision and adaptation. With the formation of the American Therapeutic Recreation Association in 1984, the profession's position in the health-care arena was strengthened. As the profession experienced practice shifts and newly emerging roles and responsibilities, accreditation, certification, and licensure standards evolved to reflect application of the therapeutic recreation process to diverse populations and settings. Although somewhat tenuous, creating the Alliance for Therapeutic Recreation in 1998 provided a mechanism to address issues resulting from transitions occurring across the care continuum. As we look to the future then, one concept seems constant—change. Having some understanding of the roots of the profession will enable the next generation of leaders to continue to develop the therapeutic recreation field into a viable and respected health and human service profession.

Key Terms

American Therapeutic Recreation Association (ATRA) An entity founded in 1984 as an independent professional therapeutic recreation organization that emphasizes the role of recreational therapy in health-care settings.

Americans with Disabilities Act (ADA) A law passed in 1990 that provided persons with disabilities equal access to programs, services, and facilities.

Centers for Medicare and Medicaid Services (CMS) The federal health care regulatory agency that monitors standards of care for Medicare and Medicaid programs. Formerly called the Health Care Financing Administration (HCFA).

Joint Commission on Accreditation of Healthcare Organizations (JCAHO, The Joint Commission) One of several voluntary health-care regulatory agencies that establishes and monitors standards of health care for hospitals and community agencies.

National Council for Therapeutic Recreation Certification (NCTRC) The national organization that coordinates and administers a voluntary credentialing program for therapeutic recreation professionals.

National Therapeutic Recreation Society (NTRS) A professional therapeutic recreation organization founded in 1966 as a branch of the National Recreation and Park Association (dissolved as a branch in 2010, now a Network within NRPA).

Study Questions

1. Briefly describe the events and factors that contributed to the emergence of the National Therapeutic Recreation Society in 1966.

2. Identify the five qualities of a profession and discuss the current status of therapeutic recreation in relation to each.

3. Identify the philosophical perspectives that have developed throughout the history of the profession. What were the historical factors that led to the emergence of each perspective?

4. Given your understanding of the history of therapeutic recreation, what factors will influence the evolution of these philosophical perspectives in the future?

5. What events led to the creation of the American Therapeutic Recreation Association in 1984?

6. What have been the similarities between ATRA and NTRS? What has each organization contributed to the advancement of the profession and what might each contribute to a new organization?

7. What is the role and purpose of the National Council for Therapeutic Recreation Certification? What is its history and significance in the therapeutic recreation profession?

Practical Experiences to Enhance Student Objectives

1. Talk with a person who is the same age as your parents and someone the age of your grandparents. Record their descriptions of (1) recreation as they were growing up, (2) medical treatment and care of the ill during their generations, and (3) their exposure to and experiences with people with disabilities.

2. Interview a professional (a doctor, nurse, psychologist, or related therapist) who has been involved with people with disabilities for some time. Ask this person to describe and document changes that have occurred in health care and medical practices as a result of technology and research. Ask this person to describe the role of health-care providers as they address the needs of a diverse population.

3. Develop a timeline that charts the growth of therapeutic recreation from the early 1930s to the present, including the significant influences on the development of the profession.

4. Explore the impacts of globalization on therapeutic recreation. What is the cultural impact on therapeutic recreation in various countries and do different countries differ in the practice of TR? How has the presence of war, natural and man-made disasters, and pandemics impacted health care worldwide?

5. Create a script for a play entitled *Whatever Happened to (insert your name)?* Project your professional growth. Identify where you would like to be in your career as a therapeutic recreation specialist five years after graduation. What will be the major influences on the development of your philosophy? How will your interpretation of therapeutic recreation change with time?

7. Conduct an Internet search or call the American Therapeutic Recreation Association (www.atra-online.com) or the National Council for Therapeutic Recreation Certification (www.NCTRC.org) to secure information that describes their services, resources, and philosophies.

Becoming a Helper

After reading this chapter, students will be able to:

✔ Describe the nature of helping

✔ Identify specific interpersonal and helping skills

✔ Demonstrate awareness of facilitation skills used in helping relationships

✔ Identify the unique needs of other people and develop empathy for them

✔ Describe interventions (modalities and facilitation techniques) used in therapeutic recreation

✔ Discuss ethical issues that may arise in the helping relationship

✔ Evaluate the influence of culture on the helping relationship

As we discussed in chapter 1, therapeutic recreation is a process that uses recreation activities and experiences to meet the specific needs of selected individuals. An essential ingredient in the process is the interaction between the helper and the client. As helpers, TRSs (therapeutic recreation specialists) need specific interpersonal skills that will enhance their ability to develop effective helping relationships with clients.

INTRODUCTION

Over the last several decades health care has become more sophisticated and scientific. Technology continues to change both the content and delivery process of most health and human services. Therapeutic recreation is no exception to this trend. In keeping with the movement toward increased accountability, the primary focus of care is the individual. Identifying the needs of the individual and determining which **interventions** (modalities and facilitation techniques) will best assist in meeting those needs have become the bottom line in all service delivery. As a consequence, therapeutic recreation programs have begun to provide individualized care that is based on evidence-based practices; this care includes standardized testing and individualized treatment or program plans based on which interventions best meet the client's needs and have proven effective in reducing the impact of the particular illness or disability.

The emphasis on individualized care has heightened awareness of the importance of the therapeutic or helping relationship between the **helper** and client. The basis of a helping relationship is **interpersonal communication** (the verbal and nonverbal interaction between two or more people), which provides the means by which a helper assists the client in mobilizing his or her resources to satisfy a need. Helping relationships are most effective when the helper communicates an attitude of empathy and acceptance. Empathy says, "I understand how you feel," and **acceptance** says, "I accept you as you are—no strings attached." These attitudes or emotional conditions are communicated to the client through facilitation skills. In this chapter we will identify and describe how these and related skills are used to develop helping relationships.

Becoming a helper involves a thorough understanding of the nature of the therapeutic relationship. Our intent is to provide a basic orientation to the knowledge and skills we judge to be important. Further study and practice will be needed to develop the level of competence required for effective helping.

WHAT CHARACTERIZES A HELPER?

Therapeutic recreation specialists enter into helping relationships because clients—either in their own eyes or the eyes of others—face choices, problems, or challenges that require resolution, or because they are not living as fully as they desire. The intent of the relationship is to help the client grow, develop opportunities, and more effectively manage options and resources as decisions are made—a positive psychology goal (Brammer & MacDonald, 2003; Egan, 2002). The self is an instrument to facilitate constructive change. Our personalities are the principle tools of the helping process (Brammer & MacDonald). Evidence suggests "if I want to become more effective I must begin with myself . . . our principle helping tool is ourselves acting spontaneously in response to the rapidly changing interpersonal demands of the helping relationship" (Brammer & MacDonald, p. 36). While course work tends to focus on *content;* that is, the therapeutic recreation experience, it is important during professional preparation to consider the *process,* the helping relationship, and how our own growth and interpersonal skills contribute to client impacts and outcomes. Internships and practical experience become avenues to explore "self as an instrument" and to integrate academic skills with awareness of personal qualities essential in the helping process.

Although no one cluster or list identifies uniform helper characteristics, research and opinions of experts tend to agree upon a composite set of behaviors that facilitate effective helping relationships (see exhibit 3.1). A partial listing includes self-awareness, cultural awareness, congruence, altruism, ethical integrity, honesty, responsibility, empathy, warmth and caring, positive regard and respect, openness, concreteness and specificity, communication competence, genuineness, and client empowerment (Brammer & MacDonald, 2003; Egan, 2002; Okun & Kantrowitz, 2008). The helping process is far more complex than simply relying on these qualities alone to facilitate favorable client outcomes. The process is dependent on many variables, including personality, emotional health, competence, and motivation of the helper and the client; type of intervention; attitudes; and congruence or harmony with the values and norms of diverse populations.

Students entering health and human service professions tend to know "they would like to be able to help people" (Purtilo & Haddad, 2002, p. 64). As described by Green-

---

Exhibit 3.1   Qualities of Effective Helpers

1. **Awareness of self and values.** Helpers need a broad awareness of their own value positions and their basic assumptions about people. To be an effective helper, the TRS suspends judgment of others. .

2. **Awareness of cultural experiences.** An effective helper has knowledge of populations other than his or her own and he/she is comfortable with cultural differences. Effective helpers examine their worldviews and respect the cultural context in which interventions occur.

3. **Ability to analyze one's own feelings.** An effective helper is aware of and controls his or her feelings. TRSs "detach" from their feelings to avoid projecting their feelings on clients.

4. **Ability to serve as a model and influence others.** Helpers are role models and social influences to their helpees and thus must have fulfilling lives to avoid using the helping relationship to satisfy unmet needs. TRSs are aware of how they are perceived by the clients with whom they interact. TRSs who are perceived as experts treat their clients as equals.

5. **Altruism and compassion.** An effective helper is keenly interested in people and in service. As described by Spears (1998), the TRS "assumes first and foremost a commitment to serving the needs of others" (p. 7). A compassionate philosophy comes from a worldview grounded in spiritual traditions that all of life is sacred and connected, while service is renewing and sustaining.

6. **Strong sense of ethics.** A TRS values the client's welfare and does nothing to harm him or her. The TRS who is aware of his or her own values understands issues involving ethics (Spears, 1998).

7. **Responsibility.** The effective helper assumes responsibility for providing structure, support, and energy to enable change, yet allows clients to use their judgment and assume responsibility for decisions made to improve their well-being. The TRS identifies the desires of clients and helps them clarify their goals while recognizing the uniqueness of each client (Spears, 1998). The effective helper is a skilled empathetic listener who realizes he or she has the opportunity to help make whole the client (Spears). Thus, the helping relationship for which the TRS is responsible is a process of transformation and integration that helps heal clients who, ultimately, are responsible for their behavior (Spears). The TRS has the foresight "to understand the lessons from the past, the realities of the present, and the likely consequences of a decision" (Spears, p. 7) the client makes about his or her well-being.

8. **Ability to empower others.** The ultimate goal of the helping relationship is self-help, or helping clients become effective change agents. The TRS facilitates the process by which clients add value to their life by learning new options and acting on their choices.

Adapted from Brammer, L. M., & MacDonald, G. (2003). *The helping relationship: Process and skills* (8th ed., pp. 36–44). Boston: Allyn & Bacon.

leaf (1977), the servant-leader's first order of business is "to make sure that other people's highest priority needs are being served" (p. 13). The test of an effective helper is to assess if, while being served, the client becomes "healthier, wiser, freer, more autonomous, more likely themselves to become servants" (Greenleaf, pp. 13–14). Becoming a health and human service professional, like becoming a leader who first experiences service to others, is a "transformational approach to life and work—in essence, a way of being—that has the potential for creating positive change throughout our society" (Spears, 1998, p. 5). It is a lifelong commitment that carries with it "expectations on the part of society, as well as privileges and responsibilities" (Purtilo & Haddad, p. 64).

The characteristics believed central to the development of servant-leaders include listening, empathy, healing, awareness, persuasion, conceptualization, foresight, stewardship, commitment to the growth of people, and building community (Spears, 1998). These qualities are inherent in the descriptions of effective helpers found in exhibit 3.1. DeGraaf, Tilley, and Neal (2001) believe these characteristics are founded on self-reflection, integrity, and passion. When these qualities are woven into our personal and professional lives we amplify our ability to be compassionate and effective servant-leaders. A unique aspect of health and human service work is that it requires delivery through the use of self as an instrument. Effectiveness of the self (instrument) is gauged by the degree to which clients experience change and growth. While servant-leader qualities and **interpersonal skills** are not necessarily inherent to most of us, they can be developed. Such development encompasses learning experiences, self-discipline, mastery of professional competencies, and cultivation of attitudes and behaviors appropriate to our roles as health and human service professionals.

One of the most important consequences of the effective use of interpersonal skills is the establishment of **trust** between the client and helper. Trust is an essential ingredient in the helping relationship since it decreases the psychological and physical stress associated with the client's need. For example, a hospitalized child's fears of the unfamiliar environment and impending medical procedures can be traumatic. A trusting relationship with a hospital staff member may reduce the anxiety and provide a source of security and hope. Trust is the tool that shapes respect for clients (Purtilo & Haddad, 2002). Trust helps us decide when to depend on the doctor or nurse, or when to be cautious about revealing personal details. If we believe the therapist is being honest, we are more likely to respect the guidance given. A trustworthy or respected helper creates an environment in which clients are more willing to "risk" sharing important parts of themselves and more likely to respond in a way that increases helper effectiveness.

Interpersonal skills also improve the quality of care provided to clients. Tension and stress are common emotional conditions that many of us find difficult to manage by ourselves. We may seek out a good listener, or someone with the ability to help us resolve the conflict. In these situations we usually identify a person with interpersonal skills. So too in therapeutic programs; helpers assist individuals in resolving conflicts that limit their ability to achieve the quality of life they desire. Helping may involve reducing the person's resistance to a therapeutic intervention or building confidence in the ability of the program to assist in meeting his or her needs.

In most health and human service settings, therapists interact with clients having backgrounds different than their own (Purtilo & Haddad, 2002). In some instances differences are apparent, for example, gender. In other cases, the difference is less obvious, as with educational background. Developing effective helping skills begins with "self-examination and consideration of what cultural differences mean" (Purtilo & Haddad, p. 37). "Human diversity is a significant factor in working with all people" (Brill & Levine, 2005, p. 71). Brill and Levine suggest students become sensitive to differences among people, understand their causes and effects, and be skillful in recognizing them. Because cultural differences affect every aspect of practice, a starting point is to become aware of our own cultural context and worldviews and how we project these views on others (Brammer & MacDonald, 2003). If we are sensitive to the influence of culture on our own values, attitudes, and behaviors, we are more apt to understand the effects on others of differences attributed to, for example, culture, occupation, illness or disability, and social status. When we understand clients and their situations contextually, we appreciate why, for example, a 20-year-old might respond quite differently than an 80-year-old to a life-threatening illness. A sensitive helper is comfortable with differences and respects each individual's unique attributes while recognizing it is impossible to know and respond effectively to all clients all the time.

Professionals who work with people who are terminally or chronically ill or with young children, for example, have found that acknowledging and accepting the feelings expressed by these individuals is basic to helping. Since many of us may be uncomfortable with issues related to death, anger, hostility, and overdependence, we might tend to avoid dealing with them unless we have the understanding and skills to do so. Therefore, before we explore the specific interpersonal skills required, we need to consider the general characteristics of clients.

WHAT CHARACTERIZES A CLIENT?

Most of us at one time or another have experienced some form of illness or debilitating injury either personally or through family members or friends. These experiences can help us begin to understand what a client may be feeling in a given situation. Perceptions will vary somewhat according to one's worldview or the context in which the illness or disability occurs. For example, people from certain cultures may be discouraged from seeking help from a stranger or entering into helping relationships involving self-disclosure (Okun & Kantrowitz, 2008). Ethnicity influences who is responsible for child care, individuals with disabilities, and aging parents. "Attitudes toward pain, methods of conveyance of bad news, management of chronic illness and disability, beliefs about the seriousness of illness, and death-related issues vary among different cultures" (Purtilo & Haddad, 2002, p. 36).

One of the first problems faced by a person who is ill or disabled is a series of losses that may include the dream of the "ideal" life, a sense of self-esteem, freedom, privacy, social acceptance and contacts, and quality of life (Purtilo & Haddad, 2002). Individuals will seek to cope with these losses by protecting themselves in various ways. The helper needs to consider these feelings of loss and despair and be prepared to provide needed support and encouragement to combat them. Therapeutic recreation professionals can do a great deal to help individuals regain a sense of dignity and wholeness by initiating meaningful treatment, rehabilitation, and education programs that reinforce their clients' strengths and interests while helping them adapt.

While most individuals will experience fear and frustration with their change of health status, some will enjoy the special privileges it might bring, at least temporarily. Those who work in psychiatric inpatient services, for example, are often told by the patient who is being encouraged to participate in an intervention, "I don't care to participate in pet therapy, I came here to rest." One implication of being "sick" is that you are exempt from social and personal responsibility, which obligates others to take care of you. Although it is still possible to escape responsibilities by being sick or having a disability, dramatic changes in the delivery of health care and the tightly controlled length of stays have limited this. Patients are transferred from acute care to outpatient rehabilitation within a few days after open heart surgery, for example; such rehab programs reinforce ability rather than disability.

In addition to the structure of the health-care delivery system, there are other incentives for getting well. These might include the desire for individual autonomy, self-respect, health, vigor, economic or social opportunities, or service to others. Depending on the level of commitment to these values, they can become powerful motivations for healing. However, these same values may exacerbate a sense of loss. A person who values the freedom, independence, and adventure of backpacking in the wilderness will face tremendous adjustments following a spinal cord injury that leaves him or her with paraplegia. Any significant permanent loss of function, health status, or quality of life will need to be mourned before the individual can move toward recovery and a sense of well-being.

The therapist helps identify significant values affected by the disease process or debilitating injury and creatively substitutes and adapts other experiences or activities that show how these values may still be achieved, or how they might need to be modified. This process often takes weeks or even months as the patient learns to accept the impairment and make the necessary lifestyle adjustments. It is important to remember that therapists should not impose their personal values and worldviews on clients but rather use their expertise to accurately discern and develop those values that seem contextually appropriate to achieve the goals and desires of clients. Since most individuals will likely be returning to the social setting from which they came, the therapist must also be aware of the various cultural factors that will influence the success of the rehabilitation process. These could include the values and attitudes of the family or support system if one exists, the resources available for continued participation and rehabilitation, and other attitudinal or communication barriers preventing acceptance of the disease or disability. The degree to which the new value system is compatible with these limitations and opportunities will impact the degree to which the client will be able to achieve his or her rehabilitation goals.

Every person also brings past experiences to a new relationship. Someone's feelings, either positive or negative, about a person in the past can be shifted or transferred to another person (Brammer & MacDonald, 2003). For example, if the helper sets limits on the behavior of a young client, the person may be reminded of similar experiences with an overbearing parent and begin to transfer the angry feelings he or she has toward the parent to the helper. **Transference** is particularly common in authority-dependence relationships and therefore should be recognized and understood for what it is—unresolved conflict with previous relationships. Although this complicates a therapeutic relationship, Brammer and MacDonald note that effective helpers are able to work through these barriers with the client by identifying and confronting the true source of the feelings and behavior and keeping the reality of the current situation in view.

Having some understanding of the worldview and cultural context in which people experience illness or disability can provide the specialist with a sense of how she or he might begin to develop a therapeutic relationship with them. However, helpers also must understand their own perceptions and motivations for helping, and they may need to modify and adapt their views of human development, functioning, and helping when interacting with clients from diverse cultures (Okun & Kantrowitz, 2008).

THE ETHICS AND PROBLEMS OF HELPING

In addition to becoming more sensitive to their own cultural context and worldviews, helpers should consider why they want to help. A primary reason may be a strong desire to help others effect changes that will improve their quality of life. Brammer and MacDonald (2003) note that "the love motive, in the Greek 'agape' sense of non-erotic personal caring, is strong in helpers. They believe they are helping out of a deep love of humanity focused on a particular person" (p. 41). Yet, we must recognize that we have basic needs such as self-worth, status, intimacy, and personal growth that are fulfilled by helping others.

Altruistic motivations for helping are extremely complex since they reflect many socially and theologically conditioned, as well as consciously chosen, values, behaviors, and attitudes. For example, if we view the client as an object that has come to us to receive our particular form of magical cure, our good intentions could lead to manipulation and control, which, in turn, dehumanize the individual and destroy any potential benefit. Therefore we should carefully assess client competency to determine under what circumstances and conditions our professional judgment would take precedence over that of a client (Purtilo, 1999). A common error is mistaking incapacity of function with incompetence to make personal decisions. People with physical disabilities frequently report waiters or store clerks asking an able-bodied friend what "she" or "he" wants rather than speaking directly to the person with a disability. Incapacity in one area of life cannot be generalized to other areas—especially when it involves autonomy and making choices. If it is necessary to substitute our judgment for the client's, we should make the decision based on what we believe he or she would want. Being able empathetically "to walk in clients' shoes" is a prerequisite to substituting judgment (Brammer & MacDonald, 2003).

A final principle suggests that we always balance the need for intervention against respect for client **autonomy**—the individual's ability to express his or her freedom to make choices (Austin, 2009). Although the traditional medical model of the therapist-patient relationship is characterized by an authority-dependence interaction, contemporary Western health-care models require that the helper give the client sufficient information to participate knowledgeably in the decisions required to initiate selected interventions. Known as **informed consent,** this process emphasizes the person's basic right to self-determination or autonomy by sharing in all decisions that directly affect him or her. Help, if it is to be helpful, must recognize and celebrate the values and autonomy of the person as a unique human being. While the tendency of the well-intentioned helper is to say, "I know what is best for you," respect for the individual and a desire to maintain his or her confidence and trust says, "These are the choices, which do you prefer?" Or, to simplify it even more, before you automatically begin pushing a wheelchair for a friend or client who seems to be struggling, ask if he or she wants or needs your help. Purtilo (1999) notes that, in practice, the concept of informed consent means that helpers constantly monitor their position of power so that in the process of helping they do not unknowingly compromise a person's desire to be independent.

The most difficult application of informed consent is with individuals who are incompetent or incapable of making decisions about their interventions; for example, those who are quite young, or who want to be cared for, or who, because of their disability, find it difficult to participate in decisions about their care (Purtilo, 1999). In these situations, family members or legal guardians are involved in the decision-making process. In other instances, notes Purtilo, advance directives give proxy consent for a once-competent person. Furthermore, there are some circumstances that may require an intervention against the apparent wishes of the individual; for example, family members may seek to protect the substance abuser from further harm, from jeopardizing his or her relationships with family and friends, or from slowly undermining financial and social stability. In this case, as well as others where intervention is warranted, we often find that the person really wants to regain control of his or her life but is unable to do so without the help of others.

Other areas of concern to aspiring helpers can best be illustrated by a case study. Mrs. Anderson, a 33-year-old mother of two young school-aged boys, was admitted to a rehabilitation unit following a diving accident in which she broke her neck and was left paralyzed from her neck down. As a physical education teacher, she had been demonstrating the use of the diving board for her class when the accident occurred. June, the recreation therapist, visited her often, playing selected CDs, decorating her room with cheerful posters, and talking with her about her family and home life. Because Mrs. Anderson was far from home, she had few visitors and her family could only come on weekends. She was extremely lonely and, as expected, became depressed by her circumstances. As a mother herself, June began to overidentify with her client's tremendous needs and soon oriented her day around Mrs. Anderson. She would be the first person June would see in the morning and the last person she visited before leaving. As Mrs. Anderson became more dependent on June and sought even more attention, other health-care professionals became concerned as they observed the detrimental effects of this relationship.

This true story illustrates several good lessons. Contrary to what you may think, helping is not always easy. It presents many challenges—some of which will creep up on us and overwhelm us before we realize what has happened. Since all helpers have needs and bring personal agendas to their relationships, all are vulnerable to these types of situations. Only by knowing and understanding your own needs and feelings, and being aware of situations that elicit these types of unhealthy responses, can you hope to avoid them.

But what are these situations? Could you identify them from the illustration? Circumstances in which it is most difficult for helpers to maintain professional distance include when a client is lonely, when the client's situation may elicit pity, or when there is some identification with the client (Purtilo & Haddad, 2002). The latter may occur when the client reminds the therapist of someone he or she has known or when the therapist's experiences are so similar that it is difficult to separate the client's feelings from his or her own. In June's case this occurred because the similar family situation engaged her emotions. June looked at the young mother and thought, "This could be me! How would I feel? How would I want others to care for me?" Having overidentified with the client, it was quite natural for June to feel the pain of Mrs. Anderson's disappointment and loneliness. June's initial emotions were reinforced by a sense of pity for Mrs. Anderson's catastrophic situation. How could June have avoided this slide into detrimental dependence? Was it possible for her to maintain professional distance and still show genuine concern for Mrs. Anderson?

To answer these questions we need to examine June's behavior more closely. June had a tendency to become "friends" with her clients and at times shared personal feelings and emotions with them. Although friendship is a goal for many social situations, it is generally not acceptable for most therapeutic settings. Professional distance and the nature of the relationship are often directly related to the level of communication between the parties involved. Powell (2002) has identified several levels of communication (see exhibit 3.2) that can serve as a guide to establishing therapeutic helping relationships. When professional distance is required, the level of

---

Exhibit 3.2   Levels of Communication

Level Five: Cliché conversation. Although we often communicate at this level, no genuine human sharing takes place. "How are you?" "It's good to see you," and "See you again" are said without thought and standard answers are expected. The person who responds to "How are you?" with a detailed description of a recent illness will likely be avoided in the future. This level allows you to acknowledge other people in social circumstances but does not encourage further involvement.

Level Four: Reporting facts. Almost nothing personal is revealed at this level. Although some sharing does take place, it only involves an exchange of general information about such subjects as baseball scores, fashions, or a good book.

Level Three: Personal ideas and judgments. People venture to give some information about themselves at this level. They may express an idea, judgment, or decision, which is usually guarded and is modified by the listener's response. If the listener looks disapproving, bored, or confused, the person probably will become anxious and hesitate to share more at this level.

Level Two: Feelings and emotions. Only people with mutual trust reveal themselves at this level. Love between friends cannot grow unless there is reciprocal sharing at this level, commonly known as gut-level communication. The individual wants the other person to understand that the emotion being expressed is deep-seated.

Level One: Peak communication. Mutual, complete openness and honesty are shared at this, the deepest, level. There is almost perfect mutual understanding. Obviously, not many human interactions take place at this level. It is an all-encompassing intimacy experienced rarely by most people and never by some.

Adapted with permission from Purtilo, R., & Haddad, A. (2002). *Health professional and patient interaction* (6th ed., pp. 231–233). Philadelphia: W.B. Saunders.

communication should not go deeper than level four, reporting facts (Purtilo & Haddad, 2002). If pity becomes the foundation of the interaction, it is usually because there has been extensive interaction at levels three and two. Rather than assuming full responsibility for Mrs. Anderson's care, June should have relied on coworkers to provide support. June's more frequent visits also contributed to the intensity and intimacy of this relationship. Although it was extremely difficult, June had to begin limiting the frequency and length of her visits, often making sure someone else was in the room to further modify the dependency that had developed between her and Mrs. Anderson. If June could not have made these changes it would have been necessary for her to withdraw from this situation and allow another therapist to assume responsibility for Mrs. Anderson.

As a helper June also had a tendency to want to solve everyone's problems, especially when the clients seemed particularly helpless themselves. She would often feel guilty if she was not successful in her efforts to resolve some of their pain and suffering. This attitude reflects the assumption of an extreme sense of responsibility and lack of respect for the client as an autonomous person. It takes courage to place the focus and the responsibility for the client's personal health and healing on the client, especially when that individual feels helpless and may initially be unable to assume that responsibility. Thus, a primary role of the helper is to **empower** clients to engage in the struggle for healing and, at times, for life itself (Brammer & MacDonald, 2003).

In spite of these potential problems, it is possible to develop and maintain a good professional relationship provided the therapist uses care and wisdom while working through difficult situations. One of the best strategies is to develop good working relationships with other staff members. The greater your isolation from other professionals, the greater the tendency to enter into unhealthy relationships with clients. However, in addition to a good professional support system, helpers need effective communication and interpersonal skills as a basis for building healthy therapeutic relationships. The following section outlines these important skills.

INTERPERSONAL FACILITATION SKILLS

Interpersonal skills that are used to develop trusting relationships with others are called **facilitation skills.** Human relations professionals have long debated the importance of certain skills over others and have failed to arrive at a consensus. For our purposes, since we are only introducing the topic, the primary focus will be on the practical skills that provide a basis for understanding the principles of **helping relationships**.

A number of skills have been identified as essential to the facilitation of trust relationships. Among these are requesting or leading, responding, informing, interpreting, warmth, attending, listening, summarizing, probing, empathy, challenging, and reflection (Brammer & MacDonald, 2003; Egan, 2002). **Inviting requests** or **leading** refers to the ability of the TRS to encourage the client to ask questions or initiate requests by anticipating where the client is headed. Many people are intimidated by professionals or by unusual circumstances or environments. One task of the helper is to create an open and relaxed environment that will be supportive of clients' needs—especially the need to inquire about and understand their surroundings, circumstances, and feelings.

Responding with information or **informing** is a skill that allows the helper to provide objective and factual information in a manner consistent with the client's level of understanding (Okun & Kantrowitz, 2008). Two important aspects of responding to questions are the proper **interpretation** of the request and the selection of appropriate information for the response. Most of us have experienced a situation in which our request for information was misunderstood, and as a result the response was irrelevant or unsatisfactory. Responses can also be more complex than the questioner was anticipating, as in the case of an adult responding to a child's simple question as if the child were an adult. Therefore, it is helpful to listen carefully and discern

An experienced helper creates an open and relaxed environment where clients feel free to ask questions and initiate requests.

what the questioner really wants to know. The TRS may attempt to restate or clarify the question before responding to avoid misinterpretation. When a hospitalized child asks, somewhat fearfully, "Why do they keep taking my blood?" the alert staff member will be able to hear the underlying question, which is, "Will I die if they take more of my blood?" The staff member may respond by saying, "It sounds like you might be worried about running out of blood if they keep taking it out of you." This response is a form of active listening, which we will discuss later in this section, and the example is descriptive of the process involved in clarifying the question in order to provide an appropriate response.

When a request has been made, the professional *responds with action*. People we trust are those who not only say they care and want to help, but who also follow through with concrete action to fulfill the request. You should be cautioned, however, to consider the implications of the request to determine the most appropriate response. Some clients, for example, may be quite manipulative and will ask the staff to give them something they are restricted from having or that has been denied them by another staff member. Others may have a tendency to become overly dependent on the staff and will make requests for services they should be performing for themselves. The therapeutic goals that are established in each individual's treatment plan are usually the best guides for responding to such requests, since the goals spell out selected therapeutic approaches. All professionals are "taken in" by inappropriate requests for

A therapeutic recreation specialist can convey warmth through physical touch and by focusing on the client's verbal and nonverbal communication.

action from time to time; a few of these experiences will teach the new professional to thoughtfully consider the appropriate response to each and every request for action.

Warmth refers to the ability of the specialist to communicate a sense of caring. Showing a personal interest in the person by acknowledging his or her uniqueness and expressing this concern in a friendly, genuine manner is a way of communicating this attitude. Warmth is often expressed through physical touch or nonverbal messages. Eye contact, leaning forward in your chair to listen more intently to the message, putting your hand on the person's shoulder, or simply smiling and nodding are all ways in which feelings of caring are shared with the other person. Warmth also can be communicated through tone of voice, softness of the eyes, respect for silence, openness to negative as well as positive feelings, and so forth. These responses are often called **attending** skills (Brammer & MacDonald, 2003), since the intent of the behavior is to focus on, or attend to, the verbal and nonverbal communication of the client. Specific behaviors that demonstrate attention and communicate warmth and acceptance are identified in exhibit 3.3. Despite the value of communicating warmth to others, we must always be mindful of the individual's cultural context as well as his or her needs. Inappropriate use of touch or a nonverbal message, for example, may interfere with, or in some cases destroy, trusting relationships. Each culture "places its own norms and meanings on eye contact and distance" (Brammer & MacDonald, p. 72). So, for example, sustained eye contact between the TRS and client may be offensive or inappropriate from the client's perspective. With some people touch may cause stress or discomfort. To illustrate, people who experience the psychological disorder called schizophrenia are extremely uncomfortable with being touched by others. With adolescents and others who are experiencing problems in areas of sexual adjustment, touch may be misinterpreted as a sexual advance. Physically abused people and hostile clients are also usually repulsed by physical contact. Clients read cues like touch, eye contact, or distance in the context of their worldviews, and thus their perceptions indicate the effectiveness of the helper's attending skills (Purtilo & Haddad, 2002). An attentive, sensitive presence invites a trusting relationship.

Exhibit 3.3   Guidelines for Attending

1. **Connect with the person when he or she is talking.** Maintain the most comfortable distance while recognizing the significance of visual contact. Direct prolonged eye contact or staring may be culturally inappropriate while frequent "looking away" may be perceived as uneasiness on behalf of the TRS.

2. **Maintain an open (natural), relaxed posture.** Avoid folding your arms or crossing your legs as this communicates a lack of interest or involvement in North American culture. Conversely, leaning toward the person can be interpreted as showing interest. A relaxed, natural presence communicates comfort and confidence and tends to place others at ease.

3. **Adopt a body orientation that conveys acceptance and equality.** If the client is sitting, the TRS might also sit in a chair so the interaction occurs at the same level, as often occurs when clients use wheelchairs.

4. **Consider the gestures you use while conversing with the other person.** Avoid blocking or interfering with the visual context or connection between yourself and the client or distracting the client with, for example, finger or foot tapping.

5. **Consider your verbal responses.** Take care not to interrupt or redirect the person toward a new topic. Verbal attending assures the client that the TRS is listening while helping him or her to continue addressing the issue.

Sources: Brammer, L. M., & MacDonald, G. (2003); Egan, G. (2002).

As with any technique, the skill of communicating warmth must be genuine and honest—a natural part of you. Genuineness and honesty are essential to **challenging** or pointing out what is occurring and what you infer from the client's feelings (Brammer & MacDonald, 2003; Egan, 2002). In other words, facilitation skills must become more than techniques. They must be integrated into the philosophy and lifestyle of the helper. Genuine caring comes from the heart, not the head. Effective helpers' feelings, words, and actions are congruent. Thus, the ultimate objective of the helper is to integrate the affective (feelings about others), cognitive (knowledge of building relationships), and the psychomotor (behavioral responses such as eye contact or gestures) into a personal system of relating—a way of interacting and living with others (see figure 3.1).

Another highly important facilitation skill is **listening.** "A considerable portion of a health professional's day is spent listening" (Purtilo & Haddad, 2002, p. 181). Listening may appear at first glance to be "a passive act of taking in the content of the helpee's communication, but actually it involves a very active process of responding to total messages" (Brammer & MacDonald, 2003, p. 71). It means listening with your ears to verbal messages while you observe and read the person's body language or nonverbal behavior and analyze and interpret the context of the message (Egan, 2002). Listening involves several skills that communicate to people that you hear and understand what they are saying, both verbally and nonverbally. *Passive listening* is simply the ability to remain silent and avoid interrupting the other person's message. Consideration of the other person's rights and recognition of his or her ability to be expressive demand our greatest effort to resist even well-intentioned interruptions. Passive listening skills also involve the ability to cope with pauses in the conversation or periods of

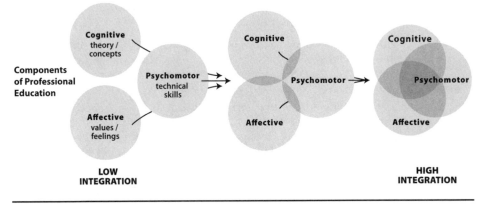

Figure 3.1   Movement toward Maturation as a Professional Person

silence. Learn to control the fear of silence by reviewing in your own mind the content and feeling of the conversation while allowing the other person time to reflect as well. Thus, silence can be useful for both the TRS and the client. At some point the professional might simply **summarize** or restate the central theme of the conversation to focus the conversation once again on the client's need. In short, effective helpers become comfortable with periods of silence and consistently focus their attention on the verbal and nonverbal messages being communicated (Brill & Levine, 2005).

Acknowledgment responses are verbal or nonverbal cues that indicate to the client you are listening. Head nods, hand signals, and responses such as, "Yes, I understand what you are saying" or "uh-huh" communicate a sense of understanding and acceptance to the client.

Encouraging words or phrases such as "Go on" or "Tell me more" (**probing**) are also useful communication tools that facilitate sharing. Since most of us use these types of phrases in our daily conversation, we simply wish to restate their importance to the listening process and suggest continued refinement of their use in helping relationships.

Active responsive listening, the most important listening skill, is a process that involves listening to and understanding both the nonverbal and verbal communication and the underlying thoughts and feelings of another person (Okun & Kantrowitz, 2008). In all communications between two parties there is a content message and a feeling about the content that is being shared by the sender. We often ignore or are simply insensitive to the feeling associated with the content, and therefore we need to be trained to listen to the whole message.

Active responsive listening implies the TRS is able to communicate a genuine understanding or empathy for the client (Okun & Kantrowitz, 2008). **Empathy** is described as the ability to put yourself in the shoes of the other person or to see the world through his or her eyes. The staff member in the previous example who listened to the feeling of the child's message about drawing so many blood samples was demonstrating empathy. Responding to both the content and the feeling assures clients of your interest and acceptance of them and thus facilitates the building of relationships.

In practice, active listening is a two-part skill that involves understanding the communication and then relating that understanding to the other person. The pediatric staff member used both of these skills in responding to the child's question. The active listening response usually involves a **reflection** on what (content) the client is saying and on how (feeling tone) it is being said (Brammer & MacDonald, 2003). Typical responses begin with, "You're saying" or "I hear you saying" or "It sounds like" phrases, which communicate the helper's attempt to empathize with the client. Initially these phrases seem a bit "canned," but with practice and adaptation to your personal communication style, they will begin to flow more naturally.

The next step in formulating a response is to reflect the feeling the client or patient is communicating. In the previous example, the staff member began by saying, "It sounds like you might be worried. . . ." This reflection should be closely followed by the reason for the feeling, ". . . about running out of blood." A simplified model that considers both aspects of the response is, "You feel . . . because. . . ." (Egan, 2002). There are numerous words and phrases that can be used to communicate clients' experiences, behaviors, and feelings. The words you select reflect that you understand the client and are trying to perceive the world as they do (Brammer & MacDonald, 2003).

At first glance, listening to and understanding clients in context may appear to be relatively easy to learn or, for some, may even be a description of what they already do. However, there are a number of situations that challenge the ability of both novices and advanced helpers to listen effectively as they attend to clients (Egan, 2002). Some common examples of ineffective listening are listed in exhibit 3.4.

Exhibit 3.4   Common Examples of Ineffective Listening

1. Helpers may listen inadequately because they are distracted by their own needs. We may be tired, approaching burnout, too eager to help, or unaware of cultural differences.

2. Helpers may evaluate or judge what the client is saying to be right or wrong. We may judge based on our perspective rather than the client's worldview and context. We may unknowingly be biased because of our cultural filters (Egan, 2002).

3. We may read the diagnostic label or respond to the classification listed on the client's chart rather than take into account the person's unique feelings, experiences, and context. A new TRS might rely on academic or book knowledge with initial listening responses until the ability to recognize the unique nature of each client is realized through experience.

4. A novice helper might also tend to respond to facts (content) rather than the "person" (feelings) or context. In some instances the client may be obsessed with facts (a person with emotional needs or the child with autistic-like behaviors); yet themes are embedded in the message. The TRS must help the client clarify and reflect on the total message.

5. A tendency to become sympathetic may result from hearing the "misery" in the person's story (Egan, 2002). When we sympathize rather than empathize, we lose sight of the whole picture—we are not only walking in the shoes of the person but also adopting his or her viewpoints rather than walking *with* the person in a reality that is probably much more complex. A TRS may become biased or one-sided and unable to accurately analyze all the alternatives and issues in their proper context.

Adapted from Egan, G. (2002). *The skilled helper* (7th ed., pp. 90–92). Pacific Grove, CA: Brooks/Cole.

Active listening is a skill that, when used appropriately, can be very helpful in building relationships and freeing others to grow and develop in new ways. "The stakes are high when a patient is trying to communicate with you" (Purtilo & Haddad, 2002, p. 183). All of the helper skills introduced in this chapter require effective listening. The ability to communicate warmth and to be an active responsive listener, along with the other facilitation skills introduced, enable the TRS to develop deeper, more meaningful relationships with others—a goal that is worthy of considerable time and effort. General guidelines to effectively communicate with clients are presented in exhibit 3.5.

Exhibit 3.5   Guidelines for Effective Communication

1. Concentrate on themes and be selective in what you listen to. Listen in paragraphs.

2. Use "I" statements to own your feelings and encourage the client to do the same.

3. Summarize in your own mind what you hear the person saying before giving feedback. When giving feedback, speak in the same vocabulary used by the client.

4. Talk directly to the client, clarifying any vague statements before proceeding. Time your response to facilitate rather than interrupt communication.

5. Listen from a contextual view rather than focusing on emotionally charged words or culturally sensitive topics.

Sources: Purtilo, R., & Haddad, A. (2002); Okun, B. F., & Kantrowitz, R. E. (2008).

INTERVENTION STRATEGIES—
MODALITIES AND FACILITATION TECHNIQUES

Building relationships allows the TRS to more successfully apply therapeutic techniques to assist clients in achieving specific therapeutic goals. TRSs use selected *modalities* (activities) together with *facilitation techniques,* which are "theoretically based methods in which the therapist structures the activity and his or her interactions with the client" (Kinney, Kinney, & Witman, 2004, p. 60). Selected techniques impact client function, health status, and/or quality of life. Professionals base "what they do in practice on what has been done in research" (Dattilo, 2000, p. 7). Evidence-based practices employ interventions that have documented evidence of treatment effectiveness with particular client populations. With such practices, the predictability and causality of intervention outcomes are improved and therapists, clients, regulatory agents, and health-care payers are assured of increased quality and accountability (Stumbo, 2003).

As costs of hospital treatment continue to escalate, insurance carriers are limiting the extent of care they are willing to provide in these acute care settings; thus, the length of inpatient hospital stays is decreasing. **Brief treatment** has become the buzzword for this orientation toward care. It focuses on assessing the precipitating problem for admission to the institution, determining a course of treatment, initiating treatment, and making plans for discharge back to the community as quickly as possible

(Witman & Batchelder, 1992). Consequently, therapists are reevaluating their role and function and are having to modify treatment goals and **intervention strategies** (selected modalities and facilitation techniques that helpers use to assist patients in effecting change) so they are compatible with the goals and treatment approach of the institution. Therefore, the interventions described in the following sections will be useful only to the degree they can be adapted to meet the needs of clients and the goals of the agency in which you will be employed (Kinney, Warren, Kinney, & Witman, 1999). Some strategies (adventure/challenge education, for example) may serve as a component in a comprehensive assessment program, while other interventions (aquatic therapy) may be more effective in community reintegration.

It is not our intent to thoroughly review and describe every modality or facilitation technique but rather to acquaint you with the basic concepts involved so you may develop an understanding of and appreciation for these techniques and how they might be used. Other chapters will describe how specific clients might benefit from these strategies and how they might be integrated into an actual program. Many techniques also require specialized training or certification, so we strongly suggest you receive adequate preparation prior to initiating these strategies.

Adventure/Challenge Education

The growing popularity of outdoor recreation has contributed to the use of adventure/challenge activities such as backpacking, biking, canoeing, caving, rappelling, ropes courses, rock climbing, and wilderness camping in the treatment and rehabilitation of people with disabilities. Adventure therapy, adventure-based counseling, wilderness therapy, and adventure/challenge education, described by the term *therapeutic outdoor programming*, involve (1) active engagement in sequenced activities in natural or indoor (climbing walls) environments, (2) the extensive use of experiential education, (3) real or perceived risks inherent in the experience, and (4) the use of problem-solving and group dynamics to stimulate physical, social, and psychological well-being (Austin, 2009; Ewert, Voight, & Harnishfeger, 2002; Shank & Coyle, 2002; Werhan & Groff, 2005). These activities provide rigorous, structured environments that create an "interplay between an individual's perception of risk and competence" (Groff & Dattilo, 2000, p. 17) so the individual is challenged beyond his or her comfort zone. Consequently, a well-supervised program contributes to im-

A well-supervised adventure/challenge program contributes to physical, social, interpersonal, and emotional health.

proved physical health, social skills, outdoor recreation skills, and interpersonal adjustment; coping with the stresses and pressures of dysfunctional environments; and appreciation for the natural environment. Moreover, it accomplishes these while also aiding the management of antisocial behaviors and group interactions among family and persons with and without disabilities, as occurs with inclusive outdoor programs (Ewert et al., 2002; Corson, 2002; McAvoy, Smith, & Rynders, 2006; Werhan & Groff). These outcomes are appropriate to persons with emotional and mental health issues, persons with cognitive disabilities, adjudicated youth, sexual abuse survivors, and children in pediatric rehabilitation (Bent, Johnson, Klaas, Rathsam, & Schottler, 2003; Corson; McAvoy et al.; Werhan & Groff).

Although these programs have been shown to benefit participants, there are physical and psychological risks that need to be controlled. The qualifications and preparation of the leader and the readiness of the participants to manage the risks are important considerations in implementing adventure/challenge programs. The Challenge Sequence Model (Roland & Havens, 1981) has been used effectively with children with behavior disorders as well as persons with physical and cognitive disabilities. The model includes seven steps, or participation levels: (1) goal setting, (2) awareness, (3) trust, (4) cooperative activities, (5) problem solving, (6) group challenge, and (7) adventure activities. Each step is closely monitored by the leader to assure the safety of each participant and maximize the effectiveness of the experience. Following the experience, participants are asked to share observations and feelings through debriefing or processing sessions that center around three questions: What happened? So what? and Now what? The *what happened* question focuses on the facts of the experience. *So what* reflects on how the experience affected each participant, and *now what* encourages them to suggest ways these lessons can be applied to the real world. This intervention strategy requires specialized training in adventure-based counseling, competence in technical and safety aspects, and processing skills (Shank & Coyle, 2002). Consequently, certification and training is required and available through various professional workshops and educational programs.

Animal-Assisted Activities/Therapy

The therapeutic use of animals has become an accepted intervention strategy to achieve specific outcomes in a variety of situations. The therapeutic use of animals elicits emotional, social, and behavioral responses that improve the health and well-being of people with disabilities (Dattilo, Born, & Cory, 2000). This intervention encompasses a variety of animals, from dogs and cats to horses, birds, and dolphins. It includes diverse forms of human interaction with animals in informal and structured engagements—from companion and helper animals to stroking and cuddling pets and viewing wildlife. When used informally like brushing or petting a dog to facilitate animal-human interactions that generally benefit the client's health (e.g., coordination and fine motor skills), the intervention is referred to as animal-assisted activities/therapy (Rathsam, 2002; Richeson & McCullough, 2002). Animal-assisted or pet therapy is not simply play—the APIE process is used and the outcomes of the structured intervention are documented in the treatment plan; for example, when hospitalized children or seniors improve their psychosocial adjustment and subjective well-being

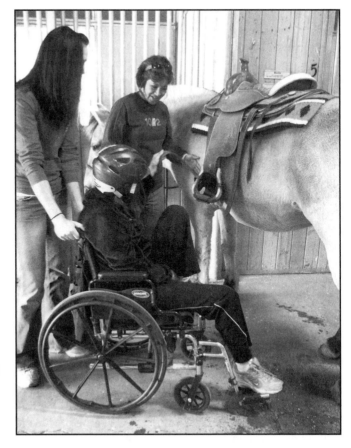

A number of organizations provide therapeutic horseback riding experiences to clients with physical and cognitive disabilities.

(Richeson & McCullough, 2003). Therapy may be offered in an individual format; for example, when small pets are brought into pediatric intensive care or the youth playroom, and through group interventions like hippotherapy, a passive form of riding that uses the movement of the horse as a treatment tool with individuals having physical or cognitive disabilities.

Outcomes attributed to various forms of human interaction with animals include reduction in anxiety and stress, enhanced social skills and interactions, decreased heart rate, improved ambulation, and improvements in self-esteem, sense of achievement, coping skills, and responsibility (Bole, Costa, & Frey, 2007; Dattilo et al., 2000; Sausser & Dattilo, 2000). Formal programs to certify trainers, accredit sites, and select and manage animals have been developed by organizations like the North American Riding for the Handicapped Association (NARHA, www.narha.org) and the Delta Society (www.deltasociety.org).

Aquatic Therapy

Aquatic therapy promotes psychological and physiological improvement while enhancing functional ability in all areas of life; moreover, it is a lifelong leisure activity

(Bintzler, 2006; Broach & Dattilo, 2000). Aquatic therapy uses swimming and various forms of active and passive water exercise to improve function and support inclusion. Interventions target outcomes like (1) improved bone density, strength, range of motion, endurance, balance, flexibility, and pulmonary function; (2) management of pain, mood disorders, and chronic fatigue; (3) reduction in spasticity, anxiety, and depressive symptoms; and (4) increased attention, freedom of movement, relaxation, energy, and social interactions (Berlin, Moul, LePage, Mogge, & Sellers, 2003; Broach & Dattilo, 2003; Broach, Dattilo, & McKenney, 2007; Shank & Coyle, 2002). The inherent qualities of the aquatic environment—buoyancy, hydrostatic pressure, resistance, and support—create a "freeing environment" and allow movements to be completed in the water that otherwise could not be accomplished on land (Broach & Dattilo, 2000). Also, the aquatic setting is conducive to group and long-term interventions. Individuals with varying abilities may participate in individualized or group exercise programs offered in community settings, allowing them to address their long-term rehabilitation and maintenance needs (Austin, 2009; Mobily, Mobily, Lessard, & Berkenpas, 2000). Thus, aquatic therapy is a viable option to consider as inpatient stays decrease in length and third-party reimbursers search for cost-effective alternatives.

Aquatic therapy is provided by therapeutic recreation specialists and other professionals, including physical and occupational therapists and physical education and recreation personnel. These helpers deliver services through warm and cold water programs to individuals with acute and chronic injuries, illnesses, and disabilities—including those with chronic pain and fatigue, arthritis, asthma, multiple sclerosis, depression, obesity, diabetes, heart disease, strokes, spinal cord injuries, cerebral palsy, muscular dystrophy, hip and knee replacements, and amputations (Austin, 2009; Bintzler, 2006). The aquatic environment demands respect, therefore thorough assessments and screening on land and in the water are precursors to intervention. Obvious contraindications include the presence of open wounds and tracheotomies. Less apparent yet equally significant precautions are taken with people who, for example, have high blood pressure or seizure activity. Organizations like the Arthritis Foundation and the National Multiple Sclerosis Society offer specialized training and award credentials. Students interested in aquatic therapy are encouraged to pursue these opportunities to enhance their competence and employability while becoming aware of aquatic safety and risk-management procedures.

Assertiveness Training

A popular action-oriented treatment for individuals who have difficulty expressing their true feelings is assertiveness training. This intervention involves role playing, modeling, and instruction on how to recognize and appropriately share feelings that may be difficult to express in social relationships, work settings, and other social situations. Assertive behavior emphasizes respect for oneself and others, with the ultimate goal being honest communication of feelings and ideas. Assertiveness training helps clients explore irrational beliefs that prevent them from being assertive. Through structured group experiences, clients practice techniques like "I statements" that enable them to be assertive rather than passive or aggressive (Austin, 2009; Shank & Coyle, 2002).

Assertiveness training helps people stand up for their rights and the rights of others, thus increasing their self-esteem (Austin, 2009). *Physical confidence therapy* (PCT) is a similar intervention that has been used effectively with adolescents and adults who exhibit low self-confidence and low self-esteem or who lack self-awareness, impulse control, and self-discipline (Beukema, 1977). In PCT a small group of four to six participants meets several times a week for 45 minutes to do a number of progressively structured routines involving group calisthenics, medicine ball passes, jousting, and attacking a tackling dummy. Each group member establishes personal goals and then performs the routine to the high standards established by the leaders before the group moves on to the next level. Significant time is spent discussing the experience, especially emphasizing the open expression of feelings by each group member. As with other action-oriented therapies, PCT requires adequate training and special expertise in **group treatment** techniques (care that is provided by one or more professionals to a group of clients, who also actively participate in helping fellow group members).

Assistive Technology

The therapeutic use of technology has steadily gained recognition as a therapeutic intervention. Efficacy studies support the use of special toys, augmentative and alternative communication (AAC), and video games as facilitation techniques (Broach, Dattilo, & Deavours, 2000). Limited research is available to support the general use of computers, technology, and virtual reality, yet each of these types of assistive technology is in use with individuals having various disabilities, and reported outcomes support increased independence, physical well-being, improved functioning in activities of daily living, and access to self-determined social and leisure opportunities (Austin, 2009; Broach et al., 2000; Broida & Germann, 1999). Efficacy studies investigating the effects of computerized leisure education (Dattilo, Williams, & Cory, 2003) and therapeutic recreation programs (McKenney, Dattilo, Cory, & Williams, 2004) on knowledge of social skills with youth with intellectual, emotional, and behavior disorders supports the use of computer-based interventions in the acquisition of social skills knowledge with these individuals. Assistive technology also includes items like adaptive toys, wheelchairs, and commercially developed devices that provide access to education, employment, transportation, and other activities of daily living (Bullock, Mahon, & Killingsworth, 2010).

Assistive devices such as microswitch-controlled toys have been used with individuals having severe developmental disabilities or communication deficits to promote choice-making and independent leisure functioning. Further, data from research with microswitch-based programs with persons with profound multiple disabilities shows that these interventions result in increased manipulation responses and elevated moods (Lancioni et al., 2006). Computer games are used in physical rehabilitation to promote cognitive reintegration, memory, attending, recall, and improved physical functioning, e.g., Wii fit (Austin, 2009; Drexler, 2009). Through virtual reality activities, clients develop community reintegration skills, enhanced feelings of competence and social acceptance by others, and experience a wide range of simulations that may, for example, desensitize them to a fear of heights (Reid & Campbell, 2006) or create pleasurable environments in which to relax (e.g., snoezelen rooms for individuals with developmental disabilities) (Patterson, 2004). Children and seniors use the Internet to communicate across geographic distances and to share their life stories through such networks as www.starbright.org and www.seniornet.org. With the aging baby boomer cohort, the number of computer/Internet users is likely to increase and "computer literacy may not only offset age-related declines" but also prolong independence and improve the quality of life and leisure (Lee, Godbey, & Sawyer, 2003, p. 27).

TRSs are encouraged to gain and maintain their competence in assistive technology as this form of intervention continues to become more sophisticated and offers an empirically sound intervention for a number of client populations. The future will see TRSs teaching clients to use the Internet for leisure (e.g., leisure education games) and also to locate services in their home communities like accessible golf courses and playgrounds (Johnson & Ashton-Shaeffer, 2003). Data will be collected from client assessments, efficacy research, and outcome studies through computerized applications. The delivery of community, home, and follow-up interventions to remote areas and underserved persons will become more common with computers and the Internet.

Behavior Modification and Management

Many of the interventions used in therapeutic recreation involve assisting clients with changing or modifying some aspect of their attitudes, **values** (principles, standards, qualities, or activities that are considered worthwhile to the individual), and/or behaviors. Frequently, these strategies involve techniques that are common to behavioral theory, which suggests that all learning occurs as a result of a conditioned response to a satisfying experience. The psychologist B. F. Skinner proposed that human behavior could be shaped by positively reinforcing desired behaviors and punishing undesirable behaviors. Although it has been criticized for being too simplistic and mechanistic, certain components of this approach (like token economies) have been shown to be effective in treating people with developmental disabilities as well as others who experience emotional and behavioral disorders (Wolfe, Dattilo, & Gast, 2003). A description of some of the most common techniques is found in exhibit 3.6. For additional information refer to chapter 6 in Shank and Coyle (2002) and behavior manipulation techniques in Porter and burlingame (2006).

Cognitive Retraining

The brain is a complex organism that controls much of our everyday functioning, including movement, emotions, mental processing, sensory perception, and memory. Consequently, people who have experienced strokes or head injuries often require significant retraining of cognitive and behavioral functions such as long- and/or short-term memory, social skills, visual-spatial skills, concentration, perception, planning, judgment, and communication. Memory and attention deficits contribute to an inability to regulate, inhibit, or monitor behavioral responses; referred to as *deficits in executive function,* they become apparent during social experiences. TRSs and other team members use a variety of techniques: repetition; simplify and redesign learning tasks to circumvent the injured area of the brain; sequence and structure learning from single to more complex tasks; and give consistent cues to assist patients in recovering functional capacities and leisure awareness. Memory activities and community out-

---

Exhibit 3.6   Overview of Specific Behavior Management Techniques

Aversion therapy: Developing an aversion to a stimulus by pairing that stimulus with vividly imagined noxious stimuli.

Backward chaining: Instruction starts with the last step in a sequence and when the client has acquired the last step, the next to the last step is taught and so on until the first task in the chain is accomplished.

Chaining: Leading the individual through a task sequence that progresses from the simplest to more complex skills.

Cognitive restructuring: Changing maladaptive behavior by demonstrating the irrationality of the assumptions on which the behavior is based and teaching the person more adaptive self-talk.

Contingency contracting: Increasing adaptive responses and decreasing maladaptive responses by drawing up a contract indicating the rewards and punishments contingent on the responses in question.

Extinction: Decreasing the frequency of behavior through lack of reinforcement.

Fading: Gradual decrease in physical guidance as client gains a skill.

Forward chaining: Instruction starts with the first step in a sequence and when the first step is acquired, the next step is taught in the task sequence.

Modeling: Establishment of an adaptive response by rewarding the client's imitation of that response as modeled by another person.

Negative reinforcement: Increase in frequency of behavior as a result of removing something unpleasant.

Positive reinforcement: Increase in frequency of behavior following a pleasurable stimulus or reward.

Premack principle: Form of reinforcement that pairs a preferred or liked item/activity with a less preferred so the less desired is reinforced.

Prompting: A physical, verbal, and/or visual cue to encourage a behavior.

Punishment: Anything that decreases a behavior, like time-out, a contract, or aversion therapy.

Shaping: Reinforcement of approximations of desired behavior until the desired behavior is reached.

Systematic desensitization: Extinction of anxiety by pairing anxiety-arousing stimulus with induced state of relaxation.

Time-out: Suppression of a maladaptive response by removing the client to a neutral environment, void of reinforcements, when he or she displays the response.

Sources: Alloy, L. B., Acocella, J., & Bootzin, R. R. (1996); Austin, D. R. (2009); Crawford, M. E., & Mendell, R. (1987).

---

ings (such as computer games, crafts, and group activities) that reinforce planning; increase attention, decision-making skills, and leisure awareness; and promote social functioning and community reintegration are typical of those used in cognitive-retraining programs (Austin, 2009).

Community Reintegration

Community reintegration is resuming roles and activities, including independent or interdependent decision-making and productive behaviors, with family and social supporters in natural community settings (Lewis, 2006). Interventions help clients who are returning to the community following medical and behavioral health issues (Shank & Coyle, 2002). These interventions are integral to the rehabilitation process and complete the therapy cycle (Armstrong & Lauzen, 1994). Consequently, community reintegration is found with outpatient, rehabilitation, skilled nursing, home-health, and community therapeutic recreation services (Ardovino, Todd, & Navar, 2002; Bocarro & Sable 2003; Lewis).

Clients whose care plans include community reintegration are those who have experienced strokes, spinal cord and head injuries, mental health issues, chemical dependency, and chronic pain. Interventions incorporate leisure education, assessments, resource guidance and counseling; problem-solving; time and stress management; fitness; functional and individual and family recreation skill development; and peer mentoring and socialization with peers without disabilities (Ardovino et al., 2002; Sable & Bocarro, 2004). Community reintegration experiences address the need created by reduced length of inpatient stays and recidivism attributed to managed care restrictions. Further, these interventions are in line with the "national public health agenda that focuses on health promotion and prevention of secondary conditions for people with disabilities" (Sable & Bocarro, 2004, p. 209).

Expressive or Creative Arts

Although limited, research does support the use of visual arts, music, dance or movement, and drama as facilitation techniques (Devine & Dattilo, 2000). Expressive or creative interventions encompass a number of specialists, including music and art therapists who rely on their respective media to diagnose and treat clients. TRSs use modalities like storytelling, journaling, writing, and a number of hands-on and visual arts to promote learning, expression of thoughts and feelings, improved functioning and social interaction, and exploration of the relevance of recreation experiences to the quality of one's leisure lifestyle (Martin & Wilhite, 2003; Trader & MacKinnon, 1998).

Bibliotherapy (reading materials that help clients become aware of their needs) has been used with hospitalized adults and children and the elderly with depression (Austin, 2009); oral histories and life review are created when journaling and story-telling with seniors (Shank & Coyle, 2002); and poetry therapy (reading, listening, writing, and discussing poems) is used with diverse groups of clients to evoke or express feelings (Moore & Coyle, 2007). These interventions lend themselves to individual and group therapies spanning the health-care continuum, from inpatient to outpatient settings.

The arts also provide tools to people with dementia that enable them to express themselves (Basting, 2006). Two programs with reported effectiveness are Memories in the Making (visual arts) and Time Slips (creative storytelling). During and following these experiences, clients demonstrate higher levels of normalcy and communication (Basting). One program found in many communities is Very Special Arts. This international organization strives to create a society where people with disabilities learn through, participate in, and enjoy the arts. It not only promotes increased access to the arts, but supports professionals and educators with resources and tools to facilitate arts programming in schools and communities (www.vsarts.org).

Group Processes

Use of the group process as an effective and cost-efficient model of treatment has been accelerated by managed care (Reeve, 2006). TRSs are likely to work with a number of informal and formal groups. Group treatment approaches are a preferred modality for psychosocial treatment among persons with mental illness (Revheim & Marcopulos, 2006). Interventions like cognitive behavior therapy, originally developed as an individual therapy, are now applied in the group context due to time constraints and cost effectiveness (Oei & Browne, 2006). Further, specific disciplines like social work, whose practices favor a mutual aid model, are employing group processes to meet therapeutic needs of persons with traumatic histories like post-traumatic stress disorder (Knight, 2006). In therapeutic recreation, structured groups are effective with social skills training, leisure education, physical activity, and adventure therapy (Austin, 2009; Caperchione & Mummery, 2006; Griffin, 2005).

The rationale for using group membership and processes to bring about individual and group change and healing is grounded in the social exchanges and multiple relationships that are created among group members and leaders (Knight, 2006; Oei & Browne, 2006). A sense of community is promoted as members help each other through the healing process. Group members become empowered as they realize they are "all-in-the-same-boat." Group cohesion is significant to promoting task and social interactions that result in behavior change. TRSs who support and (when necessary)

Structured group processes promote a sense of community and cohesion.

confront group members facilitate group cohesion which, in turn, has a positive effect on treatment outcomes (Oei & Browne). TRSs, therefore, maximize outcomes and optimize recovery when they are proficient in group development processes and leadership.

Horticulture Therapy

Horticulture interventions use a variety of plant materials to create therapeutic relationships and outcomes (Austin, 2009). Interventions range from creating indoor and outdoor gardens to watering potted plants and observing plant life. Horticulture is a catalyst for creativity and craft projects like building bird feeders and windowsill boxes (Shank & Coyle, 2002). The creation of a hospital garden benefits clients, caregivers, and staff (Johnson, Bland, & Rathsam, 2002). Moreover, beyond improving emotional health and social activity, gardening is a motivator of physical fitness and personal well-being among seniors (Ashton-Shaeffer & Constant, 2005; Austin, Johnston, & Morgan, 2006). Both individual experiences and group therapy sessions are found in rehabilitation hospitals, health-care facilities, and camps.

Leisure Education

Barriers to leisure experiences have been a concern since the early 1900s, when schools were encouraged to promote the worthy use of leisure, especially in urban settings where boredom and delinquency were primary social problems. Today, barriers may be economic, sociocultural, experiential, attitudinal, time related, or health related, among others. Leisure fulfillment contributes significantly to an individual's quality of life and since people with disabilities tend to face complex problems associated with the functions of daily living, removing barriers to meaningful leisure experiences has become a key component of many therapeutic recreation programs.

Leisure education helps clients develop the attitudes, knowledge, and decision-making skills required for optimal leisure functioning. A typical program includes components that develop the cognitive, affective, and psychomotor skills that are basic to participation in various recreation activities and social experiences; create awareness of leisure opportunities and provide the equipment, supplies, and other information needed to access these experiences; develop an understanding of and an appreciation for leisure and its role in enhancing quality of life; and provide opportunities to explore and experience a variety of leisure activities and social experiences that encourage appropriate leisure behaviors and promote health.

Evidence indicates that leisure education is widely and successfully used to facilitate independent and appropriate leisure expression across population groups (Dattilo & Williams, 2000; Kinney et al., 2004; Kinney et al., 1999). Leisure education components are used in a wide variety of settings and with a diverse array of individuals, including those who are incarcerated, survivors of trauma, physically disabled, aging, and youth with cognitive, emotional, behavioral, or developmental challenges (Caldwell, Baldwin, Walls, & Smith, 2004; Cory, Dattilo, & Williams, 2006; Griffin, 2005; Janssen, 2004; McKenney, 2002; Robertson, 2000). Specific outcomes reported in the literature include enhanced perceptions of freedom, locus of control, personal competence, decision-making and problem-solving skills, self-esteem, self-determination, and quality of life, as well as increased frequency and duration of leisure participation (Dattilo & Williams).

One significant component of leisure education that focuses on removing attitudinal barriers to participation and satisfaction is **values clarification,** the process of identifying and defining the personal beliefs that guide one's own behaviors. The intent is to help clients make autonomous decisions so their actions, feelings, and thoughts are consistent with their values. This facilitation technique encourages clients to consider what is important to them and then develop a value system to guide their behavior (Shank & Coyle, 2002). First used in schools as an avenue to character education and more recently recognized as a tool in the development of critical thinking, values clarification nevertheless remains undocumented as a facilitation technique (Easterbrooks & Scheetz, 2004; McKenney, 2002). Although viewed by some as a separate intervention technique, it is most often used in conjunction with other treatment programs. Various individual, group, and paper and pencil strategies, such as listing twenty things you love to do, are used to explore and clarify basic beliefs and values that may contribute to improved leisure satisfaction and quality of life (Austin, 2009).

At times, counseling techniques are used to facilitate the goals of leisure education. Some have referred to this as *leisure counseling* to legitimize or improve the status of this service. However, many professionals object to using this term in the context of an educational process and argue that employing a particular technique does not justify using it as a descriptor of a process. Leisure counseling is a tool that some practitioners use in treatment programs. Thus, it is important to distinguish leisure education—which focuses on the program content or curriculum that enables optimal leisure participation—from leisure counseling, which involves personal development beyond providing information to a client in the context of education. Counseling requires the use of specialized helping skills that have been shown to be effective in modifying attitudes, thoughts, and/or behaviors. Thus, to the extent a TRS uses these techniques to assist a client in removing barriers to leisure experiences, the process may be termed leisure counseling. A number of resources outline procedures a professional may use to implement both leisure education programs and treatment programs that address behavioral change; a review of these may help the entry-level professional distinguish the unique features of this broadly applied technique to change behavior and remove leisure barriers (Dattilo, 2008; Stumbo, 2002; Stumbo & Peterson, 2009).

Physical Activity

Physical activity is an umbrella term that encompasses aerobic and anaerobic exercise, sport, and any bodily movement produced by the skeletal muscles resulting in energy expenditure (Broach, Dattilo, & Loy, 2000; Austin, 2002; Shank & Coyle, 2002). The physiological value of physical activity has been widely recognized by physicians, physical therapists, exercise physiologists, and consumers. Forms of exercise like Tai Chi, resistance training or weight lifting, and yoga have been shown to improve functional capacity and quality of life. Documented outcomes include: (1) decreased pain, anxiety, and stress among persons with Acquired Immune Deficiency and spinal cord injuries; (2) reduced incidence of falls and symptoms of depression and improved physical functioning and independence among older adults; (3) reduction in symptoms found with depressive mood disorders; and (4) promotion of healthy lifestyles among youth with physical and cognitive disabilities (Allsop & Dattilo, 2000; Bonadies, 2004; Latimer, Martin-Ginis, & Hicks, 2005; Lynch, 2006; Mobily, Mobily, Raimondi, Walter, & Rubenstein, 2004; Passmore & Lane, 2006; Slawta, 2006; Stumbo, Pegg, & Lord, 2007; Tummers & Hendrick, 2004). Further, participation in physical activity acts as a nonpharmacological therapy since it reduces the effects of many health problems; moreover, interventions can be delivered in community-based recreation settings because minimal technical support or equipment is required (Mobily et al., 2004; Richeson, Croteau, Jones, & Farmer, 2006).

Even though most clients can participate in a carefully prescribed exercise program tailored to their physical abilities, strict protocols should be followed in implementing such a program, especially when clients have been sedentary. The intervention should always include adequate assessment procedures and approval of a physician prior to initiating the program, and the specialist should receive sufficient training to qualify him or her as an exercise leader.

Although limited, research tends to support the use of sports (adaptive) on the quality of life of individuals with disabilities and their families (Zabriskie, Lundberg, & Groff, 2005). Sports include a variety of individual and team competitions with adaptations made to accommodate specific functional limitations (Shank & Coyle, 2002). Results of studies on sports participation suggest that individuals realize positive overall health outcomes, including improvements in the quality of social and family life, physical health, and personal enjoyment (Zabriskie et al.; Barletta & Loy, 2006). A number of organizations support sports for persons with disabilities. Two of the more well known are Special Olympics International and the U.S. Paralympics, which hosts military veterans at USOC training sites.

Problem-Solving Skills

Problem-solving skills are fundamental to both effective professional practice and to clients' attainment of therapeutic recreation outcomes. A TRS uses problem-solving skills during the APIE process when he or she applies clinical reasoning to facilitate client outcomes (Hutchinson, LeBlanc, & Booth, 2002). Managers rely on their problem-solving skills to negotiate and facilitate progress toward achievement of unit goals (Carter & O'Morrow, 2006). Clients engage in problem-solving during social skills training, leisure education, and stress management interventions (Bray, Barrowclough, & Lobban, 2007; Hood & Carruthers, 2002; Stumbo & Peterson, 2009). Problem-solving experiences are commonly used in physical medicine and rehabilitation as well as in mental health services; for example, when clients consider how to negotiate physical barriers to gain access or when they examine the consequences of choices they make (Kinney et al., 2004).

Problem solving is an ongoing process that uses a series of steps to organize information in order to close a gap between existing and desired circumstances. Similar to APIE, the steps involve: (1) collecting information to assess and identify the problem, (2) generating alternatives and selecting solutions, (3) implementing a solution strategy, and (4) evaluating strategy effectiveness (Dixon, 2000). When clients are exposed to leisure experiences, they rely on decision-making and problem-solving skills to facilitate self-determination (Hood & Carruthers, 2002). These skills also are necessary when clients address stressful situations created by health problems (Kurylo, Elliott, & Shewchuk, 2001). Impulsive or careless problem-solving is correlated with increases in depressive symptoms while proactive problem-solving promotes perceptions of competence and self-control (Hood & Carruthers; Kurylo et al.). Problem-solving training is effective with those experiencing mental health issues, intellectual disabilities, and chronic physical health issues like pain, spinal cord injuries, and strokes; caregivers also benefit from such training (Bray et al., 2007; Hutchinson et al., 2002; Kurylo et al.; O'Reilly et al., 2004). Thus, TRSs continuously practice problem-solving during the APIE process, while clients employ problem-solving skills to promote self-direction and well-being as they accommodate alterations in their health status.

Reality Orientation

Reality orientation (RO) is used with clients who show signs of disorientation, confusion, and memory loss. Constant repetition of basic information such as the person's name, the place, time, and date is the key component of RO. Informal RO occurs 24 hours a day as everyone who comes into contact with the client repeats basic facts that orient clients to daily events, places, and things in the environment (Austin, 2009; Shank & Coyle, 2002). Formal RO occurs in didactic group therapy classes of four to six clients who meet at a routine time for 15 minutes to one hour per day, with the length of classes influenced by degree of confusion (Austin; Metitieri et al., 2001). In a typical class, participants review a reality orientation board listing such things as the name of the setting, the day, month, year, weather conditions, the TRS's name, and future events. Class discussions focus on helping the clients identify their own names, personal location, and personal events scheduled to occur during the day. Although numerous researchers have analyzed the efficacy of RO, the reviews are mixed (Austin; Metitieri et al.). Formal RO is one of the more frequently used techniques by TRSs and appears to be more effective than less-structured interventions (Kinney et al., 2004; Kinney et al., 1999). It is widely used in rehabilitation of individuals with dementia and persons who have experienced traumatic brain injuries (Metitieri et al.; Thomas et al., 2003).

Reinforcing desirable behaviors and eliminating undesirable behaviors requires a systematic intervention strategy that matches a specific approach or attitude to the client's behavior. **Attitude therapy** is a form of behavior modification often used in conjunction with reality orientation. It has been used effectively with a variety of clients by selectively applying the five attitudes of (1) kind firmness, (2) active friendliness, (3) passive friendliness, (4) no demand, and (5) matter-of-fact approach (McGuire, Boyd, & Tedrick, 1999). *Kind firmness* is used, for example, with depressed or insecure people. For instance, a TRS might respond to a client with, "I'm not going to listen to talk like 'I'm no good.'" In contrast, a *no demand* approach could be used with suspicious, frightened, or out-of-control clients who might respond more effectively to: "I'm not going to harm you or interfere while you are upset." Encouraging clients with repeated verbal support, referred to as *active friendliness*, is the most appropriate attitude for apathetic, withdrawn people who have had little success relating to others. Identifying these people, spending extra time with them, and praising them for any accomplishment, no matter how small, is a key to positive outcomes. *Passive friendli-*

ness is often used with clients who are suspicious, frightened, fearful of closeness, or distrustful of others. Staff make themselves available but do not, for example, insist that a client complete a task immediately. A *matter-of-fact* attitude is used with manipulative, irresponsible people or with those displaying expected behaviors. A therapist might respond to a late arrival with, "The program started at 10:00 a.m. Please listen as directions are given, and see me after the session if you have any questions." These types of measured responses—like the tenets of informal and formal RO—are most effective when used consistently across the patient care environment.

Reminiscence Therapy

Although research remains limited, therapeutic reminiscence and life review are popular interventions with older adults (Kinney et al., 2004; Kinney et al., 1999; Sheldon & Dattilo, 2000). Therapeutic reminiscence is a purposeful recall of past events. Life review—a specific type of reminiscence—involves evaluating the past in order to examine one's experiences and desires with the intent of achieving reconciliation or completing unfinished business. Legacy building uses audio and video recordings to capture life stories of terminally ill patients (Shank & Coyle, 2002). Reminiscence has been used with individuals experiencing depression and dementia. Reported benefits include enhanced self-esteem and coping, improved social interactions, decreased depression and confusion, resolution of issues among family and friends, mentoring of younger individuals, intergenerational understanding, cognitive stimulation, discovering meaning and purpose in one's life, and improved well-being (Austin, 2009; Sheldon & Dattilo; Waite & Tatchell, 2005; West, Quigley, & Kay, 2006). The TRS facilitates reminiscence therapy by prompting clients to recall memories of life events and experiences through reviewing historical events or through providing props and sensory cues such as movies, lectures, baking or cooking activities, music, and visual aids like digital scrapbooks. Depending on the type of client, intervention may be initiated one-on-one or in a small group, provided the audience is warm, accepting, and genuinely interested in having the person share with others. Disoriented persons may require more coaching and encouragement, including the stimulation of one or more of the five senses; for example, using taste and smell to remember significant experiences.

Although there is no established structure for reminiscing, therapists must recognize the importance of selecting the right time and a place where the individual feels safe and in control. Normally, group sessions occur weekly at the same time and place; involve 5 to 12 members, depending on their abilities; last less than an hour; and focus on a particular topic (Austin, 2009). For an aging person who once enjoyed baking, an invitation to help prepare the ingredients for baking bread may be all that is needed to stimulate latent memories. Reciting familiar prayers or singing hymns may bring special satisfaction to an individual who has strong religious roots. The key to effective reminiscence therapy is the therapist's ability to gather a comprehensive social history and to then use this data to access the long-term memories of the client.

Remotivation Therapy

In contrast with many intervention techniques that focus on client deficiencies, remotivation stimulates healthy personality development by focusing interaction around topics and interests that motivate the client to reestablish contact with the real world. Since people who are regressed, withdrawn, confused, or who have sustained a brain injury tend to focus on personal conditions, diverting attention from the illness to positive discussions of sports, hobbies, or current events increases self-respect, alleviates boredom, and stimulates social and cognitive functions. A typical remotivation group meets weekly, focuses on a theme or topic, and uses five sequential steps to reengage clients in everyday life:

1. *A climate of acceptance* is developed when the leader makes personal introductions and welcomes the group members.

2. *The bridge-to-reality phase* involves focusing the group's attention on a topic by reading a poem or quotation, playing a song, or showing a series of pictures designed to stimulate discussion.

3. *Sharing the world we live in* builds on the bridge-to-reality phase by inviting responses to carefully prepared objective questions on the selected topic.

4. *Appreciation of the work of the world* focuses the group's attention on jobs and tasks familiar to them.

5. *A climate of appreciation* is used by the leader to summarize the key points of the discussion and announce the time and date of the next meeting (Austin, 2009; Shank & Coyle, 2002).

Remotivation is often used in concert with other therapies, including reality orientation and resocialization.

Given the focus on stimulating personal growth through reestablishing relationships with real-world interests, remotivation techniques seem to reinforce the basic rationale for therapeutic recreation services: the strengths of an individual have value as a motivational force in treatment. Remotivation is more commonly used in geriatric settings than in mental health or in physical medicine and rehabilitation (Kinney et al., 2004; Kinney et al., 1999), however the data are mixed on its effectiveness (McGuire et al., 1999). Restoring wholeness must begin by recognizing the client as a whole person, which is the key to remotivation.

Resocialization

An important quality of a well-adjusted person is the ability to live in a community, or in relationship with others. People with chronic illnesses, such as those in geriatric settings, frequently experience isolation and decreased levels of social functioning. The goals of resocialization interventions are to improve interpersonal skills, renew interest in life events and activities, and stimulate contributions to the quality of life for others (Austin, 2009). Resocialization groups typically meet three times a week to share experiences in a nonjudgmental, warm, accepting atmosphere that is modeled and promoted by the leader. Refreshments contribute to the hospitality of the environment, and group members are encouraged to interact with one another, often discussing issues that are of mutual concern to those living in the social community.

Therapeutic recreation programs—whether structured around resocialization interventions or other social group activities—are uniquely suited to promoting social interaction skills; thus, it is not surprising that resocialization is one of the more frequently used intervention techniques (Kinney et al., 2004; Kinney et al., 1999). With careful planning and well-chosen activities, a program designed for those who may by circumstance or personality tend to avoid social interactions can contribute significantly to a client's quality of life.

Sensory Training and Stimulation

Training and stimulation programs designed to awaken one or more of the five human senses are used with children with developmental or neurological impairments, individuals with brain injuries, and with older adults. Pediatric recreation therapists may hang bright mobiles over a child's bed (visual stimuli). Therapists introduce sensory stimulation (through, for example, animal assisted therapy) to individuals in comas due to brain injuries in order to assess responsive levels and reality awareness and to reduce the depth and duration of a coma (Austin, 2009). Those working with aging adults may ask them to identify certain smells (olfactory stimuli) or describe the texture of an object (tactile stimuli). Sensory training programs attempt to maintain and improve an individual's perception and alertness in response to the environment while keeping clients in contact with reality (Austin, 2009; Wilhite, Keller, Gaudet, & Buettner, 1999). Although data are limited, benefits include cognitive improvements and enhanced progress in inpatient and outpatient rehabilitation (Wilhite, Keller, Gaudet et al., 1999).

Snoezelen, a form of sensory stimulation, is used with persons having multiple, severe, and/or profound developmental disabilities to promote learning through play and relaxation experiences (Patterson, 2004). Sensory-stimulating environments are created in empty rooms or through portable technology carts. Findings remain mixed, yet the intervention appears to be effective in decreasing stereotypic behaviors and increasing concentration levels, managing pain, and enabling relaxation (see also Assistive Technology on pages 87–88).

Social Skills Training

Social interaction skills are important to leisure behavior; they may be the primary reason for a leisure experience or its by-product. Although there are a number of approaches to social skills training, authors agree that many individuals with disabilities "(1) lack adequate social interaction skills, (2) are at risk later in life in terms of life functioning, and (3) need direct instruction concerning social interaction skills to overcome deficits" (Stumbo, 1995, p. 34). The goal of social skills training is to develop basic social and interpersonal skills that clients need to function in society. Clients are taught appropriate verbal and nonverbal responses for a variety of social situations, and they practice social skills such as maintaining eye contact, responding to instructions, carrying on a conversation, or having appropriate social interactions with a person of the opposite gender. Training sessions often involve modeling, role playing, giving feedback through videotaping, and assigning "homework" to practice skills in real-life situations (Austin, 2009).

Research conducted on the effects of social skills training indicates it is frequently used and benefits a variety of people with and without disabilities (Kinney et al., 2004; Kinney et al., 1999; Mueller & Roder, 2005; Mundy, 1997). Populations include children with learning disabilities; people with developmental and physical difficulties and persons with severe disabilities; those with mental health, chemical dependency, and behavior disorders; aging individuals; and those at-risk or already incarcerated. Social skills training breaks the downward spiral of rejection and social isolation by promoting expected social behaviors. With social competence comes improved self-esteem and self-control, awareness of the rights of others, and the potential for full social inclusion (Austin, 2009; Mundy; Stumbo, 1995).

Stress Management

Much has been written about the debilitating effect of prolonged stress on the body. Headaches, skin rashes, backaches, ulcers, asthma, and even cancer are a few of the illnesses that suggest a strong interrelationship between the body, mind, and spirit. Stress has also been linked to health indicators like obesity, hypertension, and elevated heart rate. It is estimated that "43% of the adult U.S. population experience adverse health conditions due to stress . . . [while] 75% of all visits to primary care physicians are stress-related" (Orsega-Smith, Mowen, Payne, & Godbey, 2004, p. 232). Our increasing use of and reliance on technology also adds stress while shifting our leisure preferences to sedentary, solitary, passive choices. On the other hand, evidence suggests "park environments play a unique role in promoting health and alleviating stress" (Orsega-Smith et al., 2004, p. 237). Leisure experiences are positively associated with perceived physical and mental health and physiological health indicators. The Centers for Disease Control and Prevention reports physical activity reduces the risk of dying early from heart disease and cancer while promoting mental health. These outcomes occur with aerobic or a mixture of aerobic and muscle-strengthening activities three to five times a week for 30 to 60 minutes each session (CDC, 2008). Although the literature examines a number of approaches to manage stress, individuals with disabilities may not possess the resources or have ready access to sources that address the effects of stress in their lives (Berg & Van Puymbroeck, 2005; Malley & Dattilo, 2000). Research supports the use of stress management techniques, especially in mental health (Kinney et al., 2004), where compliance with the CDC's physical activity recommendation was found to alleviate symptoms of depression—the most common mental health issue experienced today (Berg & Van Puymbroeck).

The emergence of a holistic model of health with a focus on disease prevention and health promotion has introduced treatment approaches like yoga and biofeedback, which are used by many therapists, including therapeutic recreation specialists, in many different settings (Austin, 2009). As we have already noted, physical activity has been shown to be an effective antidote to stress and as such is an important ingredient in therapeutic programs. Similarly, *relaxation techniques* are being used to treat the physiological and psychological symptoms of stress. For example, *aromatherapy* and *therapeutic massage* are gaining popularity as interventions to reduce anxiety, pain, and tension while enhancing well-being, particularly when used with relaxation techniques like *meditation* (Brownlee & Dattilo, 2002; Kunstler, Greenblatt, & Moreno, 2004).

Recent studies also have lent support to the role of **humor therapy** as an intervention strategy in reducing anxiety, moderating the adverse effects of daily stress, increasing pain thresholds, and creating a healthy immune system (Williams, 2002;

Williams & Dattilo, 2000). The biblical proverb that "a cheerful heart is good medicine" is gaining scientific support and should be considered in therapeutic recreation programs as well. Humorous movies, books, and CDs are used by many hospitals, including Duke Cancer Center, Good Samaritan Hospital of Los Angeles, and St. Joseph's Hospital in Houston, to help patients engage all of their innate resources to combat the negative effects of disease, treatment, and hospitalization.

Validation Therapy

Although data to support the efficacy of validation therapy are limited, it is becoming accepted as an effective technique to use with very old people with Alzheimer's-type dementia (Austin, 2009). Validation therapy employs empathetic communication to validate the feelings and needs underlying a client's unfinished life tasks (Austin). For example, TRSs interacting with a client acknowledge unresolved issues in past relationships or unfinished life responsibilities; therapists do not attempt to impose reality but rather accept the client's disorientation and validate their feelings and needs. Feil (2002) describes specific validation techniques and outlines the four phases of validation group meetings. Each group meets weekly, consists of seven or eight participants, and lasts 20 to 60 minutes. During phase one, "Birth of a Group: Creating Energy," the therapist greets clients and individuals are selected to open the meeting with a prayer, poem, or song. In phase two, "Life of the Group: Verbal Interactions," the therapist introduces a topic and encourages each member to respond. For the third phase, "Movement and Rhythms," group members actually complete movement activities like a dance step, exercise, crafts, or hitting/throwing balloon/beanbag. The last phase, "Closing of the Group with Anticipation for the Next Meeting," requires the person who opened the meeting to close with a song; refreshments are served and group members are reminded of the next meeting (Feil).

Overview

The modalities and facilitation techniques introduced in this section are used in a variety of settings and with many types of clients to accomplish the same goal: enhanced health, functioning, and quality of life. In some instances these techniques function as stand-alone programs, like adventure/challenge education or physical activity. In other situations, for example, community outings or computer classes, techniques like cognitive retraining and social skills training are used with other therapies to accomplish treatment goals. In the final section of this chapter we present leadership suggestions to enhance effective implementation of these techniques.

GENERAL LEADERSHIP INTERACTION AND INTERVENTION CONSIDERATIONS

As we review various aspects of helping, we recognize that there are numerous situations, settings, individuals, and philosophies that impact intervention techniques. Before we conclude this chapter, we want to briefly summarize a few of the more general skills and attitudes that you should consider when working with people with disabilities.

- Be yourself. Share your anxieties and fears with colleagues and seek their support in being genuine.

- Be professional. Integrity is a precious quality that must be nurtured and protected. Sharing confidential information with family or friends is a breach of trust, and trust is essential to effective helping relationships. Overinvolvement with clients also jeopardizes your ability to be objective.

- Collaborate or partner with clients. Active engagement in the change process by using the client's resources promotes growth while empowering clients to assume responsibility for their well-being.

- Exhibit culturally sensitive practices. Consider elements of multiculturalism associated with the APIE process. Consider and reflect in practice the impact culture has on both clients' and your beliefs about health, illness, and the role of the helping professional.

- Guard and maintain the dignity and humanity of the client. Consider the client in relation to his or her environment. The agency, family, and social network present assets as well as limitations to the client's autonomy and growth. Interactions may enhance or detract from the client's competence.

- Provide as much structure as is needed to promote a safe, secure environment that stimulates growth toward independence and personal fulfillment. A greater amount of structure is necessary for clients with psychological impairments such as psychoses or antisocial and other personality disorders.

- Use sequential activity experiences to promote increasingly socialized levels of group interaction. Clients who are severely disturbed may need to begin participation with a one-on-one or parallel level of interaction, move into a structured individualized or small-group activity, and then transition into group activities that include more direct social interaction.

- Use physical touch with discretion. A hug can be a beautiful way of communicating warmth and affection but may be interpreted differently by teenagers and young adults than by children. For some clients, physical touch may also be offensive or frightening. Although touch is extremely useful in promoting interpersonal relationships, be aware of the potential problems that may result.

- Plan a wide variety of activities that meet the cultural needs and interests of all clients. Consider the uniqueness of each client. New activity experiences provide new opportunities for growth for those who have limited interests.

- Encourage active participation rather than observation. Circumstances such as reactions to medications may limit a person's participation, but try to include all clients in some aspect of the activity (scorekeepers, judges, officials) and to increase their involvement.

- Motivate through example and through the strength of the helping relationship. Be enthusiastic but sensitive to "where the client is at." Communicate your sincere interest in the client's well-being with firm, consistent persistence.

Leadership is a complex assortment of attitudes and actions that motivate and guide others to achieve a goal. By following the suggestions listed here, you will be more effective in that critical role, and, more importantly, you will benefit the clients you serve.

SUMMARY

Therapeutic recreation is a human service profession that provides individualized care to clients who have specific social, psychological, or physical needs. Care is provided within the context of a helping or therapeutic relationship, which is established through the use of interpersonal communication skills. Helping relationships have been shown to improve the rehabilitation process; however, inappropriate relationships (such as codependent ones) can have a detrimental effect. Therefore, developing knowledge and communication skills for healthy interpersonal relationships is an important aspect of therapeutic recreation education. An integral aspect of helping relationships is sensitivity to the worldviews and cultural contexts of others. With experience, therapists realize that each individual is unique and learn to celebrate these differences.

Effective helpers possess many humanistic qualities, but the most important is their ability to communicate empathy and acceptance to the client. The expression of warmth through nonverbal behavior and active responsive listening is the most critical facilitation skill needed to demonstrate this acceptance. Other modalities and facilitation techniques frequently used by TRSs include adventure/challenge education, animal-assisted activities/therapy, aquatic therapy, assertiveness training, assistive technology, behavior modification and management, cognitive retraining, community reintegration, expressive or creative arts, group processes, horticulture therapy, leisure education, values clarification, physical activity, problem-solving, reality orientation, attitude therapy, reminiscence therapy, remotivation therapy, resocialization therapy, sensory training and stimulation, social skills training, stress management, relaxation techniques, aromatherapy, therapeutic massage, humor, meditation, and validation therapy.

Key Terms

acceptance Having positive regard for another person without a judgmental attitude.

active responsive listening The process of listening to and understanding both the verbal and nonverbal communication of another person and communicating such understanding to that person.

attending Verbal and/or nonverbal behavior that indicates the helper is responding to the client's needs.

attitude therapy Form of behavior modification used with RO involving measured responses to specific client behaviors.

autonomy The client's ability to express his or her own freedom to make choices.

brief treatment Time-limited treatment that typically emphasizes crisis intervention techniques with a goal of stabilizing and discharging a patient as quickly as possible.

challenging Communication skill in which genuineness and honesty are employed to point out what is occurring and what the helper infers from the client's feelings.

empathy The ability to put oneself in the place of another person and see the world through the other person's eyes.

empower Creating the proper psychosocial conditions that permit and encourage personal growth and autonomy in others.

facilitation skills Interpersonal skills that are used to develop meaningful relationships with others.

group treatment Care that is provided by one or more professionals to a group of clients, who also actively participate in helping fellow group members.

helper A person who interacts with another human being in such a way as to promote mutual growth.

helping relationships Positive, supportive relationships that facilitate growth in both the client and the helper.

humor therapy An intervention that stimulates laughter and promotes a positive state of mind.

informed consent The agreement of a client to participate in a given treatment after being told of all possible outcomes and risks.

informing Providing objective and factual information.

interpersonal communication The verbal and nonverbal interaction between two or more people.

interpersonal skills Attitudes and behaviors such as acceptance or active listening that enhance relationships between two or more people.

interpretation Explaining the meaning of events so clients are able to view their needs from a new frame of reference.

interventions Specific modalities and facilitation techniques that are used to alter problematic behaviors or situations.

intervention strategies Selected modalities and facilitation techniques that helpers use to assist the client in effecting change.

inviting requests The ability of the therapist to encourage clients to initiate questions.

listening A skill that communicates to another person that you hear and understand what they are saying, both verbally and nonverbally.

probing Verbal and nonverbal tactics to help clients explore issues more fully.

reflection An active listening response that rephrases the client's stated or implied feelings, observed or nonverbal behaviors, and/or what the client may have omitted or emphasized.

responding Communicating appropriate information to another person following the appropriate interpretation of his or her request.

summarize Tying together ideas and feelings to focus client awareness on the theme or explore the theme more fully.

transference Feelings about previous relationships are shifted or "transferred" to another person.

trust An essential condition in the helping relationship that is developed through genuine caring for others.

values Principles, standards, qualities, or activities that are considered worthwhile to the individual.

values clarification The process of identifying and defining the personal beliefs that guide one's own behaviors, which, for example, might be related to participation in leisure activities.

warmth A facilitation skill that enables the helper to communicate a sense of caring and understanding.

Study Questions

1. What is a helping relationship? What implications does it have for therapeutic recreation programming?
2. What are the characteristics of servant-leaders and how do they compare to qualities of effective helpers?
3. Explain the significance of trust in developing helping relationships.
4. What is meant by the ethics of helping? Discuss several ethical problems that helpers face.
5. What is the role of informed consent in a helping relationship? Identify several circumstances where a TRS might be challenged by the principle of informed consent and discuss the ethical implications of these situations.
6. Identify five interpersonal facilitation skills and discuss the importance of each in developing a helping relationship.
7. How does one's culture impact the helping relationship and the use of various interventions?
8. Identify and discuss the purpose of each modality and facilitation technique. Which strategies have proven effective for specific clients?

Practical Experiences to Enhance Student Objectives

1. Contact the following organizations to determine training options and resources available, and gather support for the effectiveness of various interventions:
   - American Dance Therapy Association, www.adta.org
   - Project Adventure, www.pa.org
   - Very Special Arts (VSA Arts), www.vsarts.org
   - American Art Therapy Association, www.arttherapy.org
   - Association for Applied and Therapeutic Humor, www.aath.org
   - American Music Therapy Association, Inc., www.musictherapy.org
2. Search Web sites for resources and information on various interventions:
   - ATRA, www.atra-online.com
   - World Health Organization, Disability and Rehabilitation Team, www.who.int/disabilities/en
   - Center for Applied Special Technology, www.cast.org
   - American Psychological Association, www.apa.org
   - North American Riding for Handicapped Association, www.narha.org

- The Delta Society, www.deltasociety.org
- Animal-Assisted Therapy & Activities, www.animaltherapy.net
- National Information Center for Children and Youth with Disabilities, www.nichcy.org
- Rehabilitation Engineering and Assistance Technology Society of North America, www.resna.org
- *Healthy People 2010*, www.healthypeople.gov
- Center for Universal Design, www.design.ncsu.edu/cud
- The Alliance for Technology Access, www.ataccess.org
- The National Institute on Disability and Rehabilitation Research—U.S. Department of Education, www.abledata.com

3. Contact the following commercial vendors and request a catalog:
   - Briggs Corporation, www.briggscorp.com
   - tfh, www.specialneedstoys.com
   - Danmar Products, www.danmarproducts.com
   - Access To Recreation, Inc., www.accesstr.com
   - FlagHouse, Inc., www.flaghouse.com

Program Design

After reading this chapter, students will be able to

✔ Identify professional standards of practice and competencies that influence program planning

✔ Identify the tasks involved in the assessment, planning, implementation, and evaluation (APIE) of individual intervention plans, critical pathways, department program plans, and protocols

✔ Identify the role of the assessment process and the use of assessment data in program planning

✔ Write measurable goals, objective statements, and strategic planning statements

✔ Describe the processes used to select intervention strategies appropriate to the client's and the department's goals and objectives

✔ Identify the tasks required of the TRS as programs and services are planned and scheduled

✔ Recognize roles of the team as programs and services are planned, delivered, and evaluated

✔ Explain a TRS's responsibilities as programs and services are implemented, including the monitoring and documentation of client outcome measures, program objectives, and quality indicators and making adjustments to programs and services following formative evaluation

✔ Discuss the importance of evaluation, quality improvement plans, and efficacy research, including the revision of individual and department programs and services, and the use of data in transition and long-range planning

✔ Explain the importance of theory and evidence-based practices in program design

The therapeutic recreation process of assessment, planning, implementation, and evaluation (APIE) is carried out by developing and delivering programs and services. These tasks require balancing targeted client needs with resources, balancing individual client objectives with program objectives, balancing quality client care with increasing fiscal responsibility, balancing responsive and appropriate services with reasonable length of stay, and balancing spontaneous decisions with long-range planning. All health-care providers are being held accountable for service effectiveness and quality. Increasingly, professionals are using theory and evidence-based practices to improve achievement of client outcomes and to provide a rationale for their programs. Current practice requires professionals to use research evidence (**evidence-based practices**) with clinical decision making to select interventions that are effective with clients having specific needs. This approach leads to the practice standardization and validation demanded by reimbursers, regulators, and professional standards.

INTRODUCTION

Programs and services are the means by which the helping process becomes a reality. A **program** is a preplanned intervention consisting of experiences with definitive outcomes. A **service** is an exchange between the TRS and client during the helping relationship that may be intangible yet promotes client growth and well-being. To illustrate, the intent of an inpatient leisure education program may be to increase the number of referrals to outpatient placements. As the TRS assesses client functioning, including awareness of leisure barriers, a service is provided when the TRS suggests how the client might access a number of outpatient leisure options.

A TRS is responsible for identifying, organizing, and managing resources to achieve measurable client and program outcomes in an accountable and cost-effective manner. To this end the TRS draws upon "the best research information possible in addressing client needs and getting to client outcomes" (Stumbo & Peterson, 2009, p. 83). Additionally, the TRS uses theories (**theory-based practices**) as the underpinnings or framework to guide practice and determine which programs and services best contribute to intended outcomes (Baldwin, Hutchinson, & Magnuson, 2004; Jordan, DeGraaf & DeGraaf, 2005). These processes involve integrating all the factors, information, and inherent interrelationships impacting practice. One conceptual model—the input, process, output (IPO) model—illustrates the relationship between planning and outcomes using the four phases of the therapeutic recreation process (assessment, planning, implementation, and evaluation) integrated with quality improvement standards (structure, process, and outcome) (see figure 4.1). The IPO model actually consists of four parts (input, process, output, and feedback), each of which represents one or more of the above-mentioned phases.

Input information describes all the influences affecting the client, the program, and the agency. Through assessments, TRSs gather this information and use it in the ongoing planning of programs and services. For example, the assessment of structure indicators includes factors like facilities, equipment, staff, finances, department policies and strategic statements, and organizational resources. The adequacy of these input factors influences the quality of programs and services as well as the degree of compliance with standards of practice and external regulatory standards.

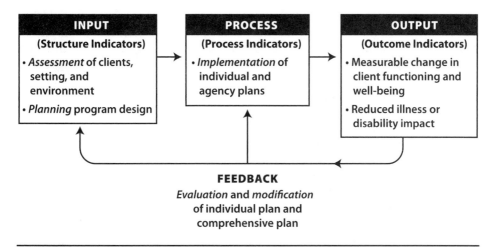

Figure 4.1   Input, Process, Output Model

In the process phase, programs and services are implemented. During implementation, the TRS monitors the client's progress and the effectiveness of the particular program or service. This monitoring is accomplished using process indicators that measure both interactions between the client and the TRS and the performance of therapeutic experiences. **Critical (clinical)** pathways (guidelines for intervention by team members according to specified time periods) and **protocols** (written procedures to implement specified programs and services by diagnostic category or activity type) are implemented and the TRS collects data that provides evidence of the quality of therapeutic interactions and modalities and facilitation techniques.

In the output phase, the TRS identifies the measurable changes in the client's functioning, health status, and/or quality of life that have occurred as a result of the program or service. Outcome indicators measure the degree to which the person has directly benefited from a program or service.

The fourth phase of the model, feedback, is the evaluation phase of the therapeutic recreation process. Client and program outcomes are compared to expectations written in individual and department plans and in **continuous quality improvement (CQI)** programs (written quality assurance plans mandated by professional standards of practice and external accrediting agencies to promote ongoing service quality) to determine the effectiveness of programs and services. The TRS assesses the differences or changes in the client between the time he or she entered and exited the program and ascribes these outcomes to specific interventions (Stumbo, 2003). This evidence may reinforce the program as originally planned, or prompt revisions to the program/services to (1) enable clients to better achieve desired outcomes or to (2) improve efficiency or effectiveness in the delivery of interventions.

The importance of pinpointing therapeutic recreation outcomes and using theory to guide practice and clinical judgment is captured in the Outcome Engineering model (Lee, McCormick, & Perkins, 2000). This model expands the APIE process to include an awareness of possible therapeutic recreation outcomes from the initial planning phase through documentation and evaluation of client performance. Evaluation results are used to improve performance and promote the benefits of programs/services to the client and various stakeholders (Lee et al.). The cyclical nature of the IPO model highlights the TRS's responsibility to implement quality improvement processes, which means he or she is continuously identifying and analyzing the factors impacting programs and services and, when necessary, modifying, redesigning, or discontinuing interventions to better address client needs. By using theories to explain what might have resulted and collecting evidence of the actual results, the TRS is justified in making these decisions.

A number of dramatic changes have affected and are continuing to influence the design and delivery of programs and services. Globalization, advancement in information technology, natural and human-generated disasters, terrorism, cultural and demographic shifts, and a health-care crisis triggered by chronic health diseases are among the challenges to be addressed by professional programs and services. To embrace change and impact individual client growth and quality of life, TRSs must move beyond the technical competencies defined in the IPO model and incorporate knowledge and skills grounded in conceptual and value orientations (Sylvester, Voelkl, & Ellis, 2001). In so doing, the TRS applies critical thinking and reflection to programming responsibilities (Lee & McCormick, 2002). The sensitive planner not only considers accountability demands, but also embraces, for example, collaborative opportunities, multicultural expression, and an ethic of caring with each client contact (O'Keefe, 2005).

The philosophy of health care has shifted from a focus on disease and illness to a wellness perspective. Moreover, there is growing recognition that the health of each individual is intertwined with that of the larger community. This holistic approach is embodied in the World Health Organization's International Classification of Functioning, Disability, and Health (ICF) and the U.S. Department of Health and Human Services's *Healthy People 2010—Understanding and Improving Health* (Howard, Russoniello, & Rogers, 2004; Porter & Van Puymbroeck, 2007). TRSs have adopted this outlook by using cross-disciplinary and cross-cultural communication to better design experiences that facilitate positive change and growth. Additionally, as fiscal realities dictate shorter length of stays, TRSs must apply the TR process (APIE) during brief intervention periods—integrating evidence-based outcomes with fiscal responsibility. Throughout practice, innovative delivery strategies not only ensure quality but also continuous improvement, safety and security of all involved, and documentation of program and service efficacy.

A planning model introduced by Stumbo (1996) conceptualizes the changing nature of TR practice. The Therapeutic Recreation Accountability model outlines the significance of quality indicators like assessment, protocols, and documentation to the delivery of outcome-based programs and services (Stumbo; Stumbo & Peterson, 2009). Additionally, this model depicts the relationship between program/client evaluation and quality improvement/efficacy research. Widmer and Ellis (1998) and Wilhite, Keller, and Caldwell (1999) presented therapeutic recreation service models that outline the role of the TRS in educating clients and facilitating experiences to promote health and happiness throughout the life course. Likewise, the Leisure and Well-Being Model (LWM) introduced by Carruthers and Hood (2007) identifies the importance of the leisure experience as an avenue to develop resources and enhance clients' well-being. The WHO's ICF model provides a framework for measuring health and disability at both the individual and societal level. This framework includes a list of body functions and structure, and a list of domains of activity and participation. The framework acknowledges the context within which functioning and disability occur by including environmental factors. This model allows the TRS to present experiences that facilitate recovery and health across delivery settings. These models, like the Outcome Engineering model, address the changing nature of day-to-day programming responsibilities. The development of accountable, cost-effective programs and services through team effort is a significant responsibility in agencies affected by external accrediting bodies like The Joint Commission and CARF International. Governmental and nonprofit agencies are also expected to offer safe, high-quality, culturally sensitive options.

This chapter first discusses the phases of the therapeutic recreation process (assessment, planning, implementation, and evaluation) as they would be applied to the preparation of *individual* plans, and then as they would be applied to the development of *comprehensive* therapeutic recreation programs. Descriptive models depict each phase and the respective technical subtasks necessary. Whether designing an individual plan or a program plan, the responsibilities of the TRS are similar. In the former, the tasks focus on one individual, while in the latter, the scope encompasses a group of clients. In either case, the product is a plan having measurable client and program outcomes for which the TRS is accountable. This systematic planning process enables the TRS to make spontaneous decisions that focus on immediate client needs, while networking with other professionals to develop and improve the quality of programs and services. This process lends itself to outcome studies and research to collect evidence to verify the impact of programs. Further, it is grounded on systems theory that presents a "process all practitioners can follow and achieve similar results" (Jordan et al., 2005, p. 48).

INDIVIDUAL PLANS

The design of an individualized plan is necessitated by a variety of federal and state regulatory agencies such as CMS; external accrediting agencies such as The Joint Commission and CARF International; third-party reimbursement companies and **managed care providers** (agencies like HMOs that monitor providers' health-care expenditures) such as Blue Cross-Blue Shield; and by professional organizations such as ATRA. The responsibility lies with the professional to prepare individual plans that satisfy the criteria of these entities (Stumbo & Peterson, 2009). The APIE process is driven by the needs of the client and is applied in a variety of settings to individualize benefits derived from participation (LeConey, Devine, Bunker, & Montgomery, 2000). In community settings the process may be used to develop support plans for inclusive recreation programs (LeConey et al.), while in rehabilitation settings the outcomes may focus on benefits important to case managers, like enhanced independent functioning and skills that carry over to everyday life (Sorensen & Luken, 1999). Thus, this process seeks to identify an agreed-upon set of tasks that all professionals practice regardless of position or setting (Mobily & Ostiguy, 2004). Professionals apply the modalities and facilitation skills (refer to chapter 3) within the APIE process to create helping relationships to effect client change. Throughout this text, the TR process refers to this combination of technical, theoretical, and professional behaviors used to effect growth and change among clients.

Assessment

The therapeutic recreation process begins with assessment, as shown in figure 4.2. During the assessment phase, a TRS identifies the assets, resources, and liabilities of a client relative to his or her worldview and the cultural context of the TR process.

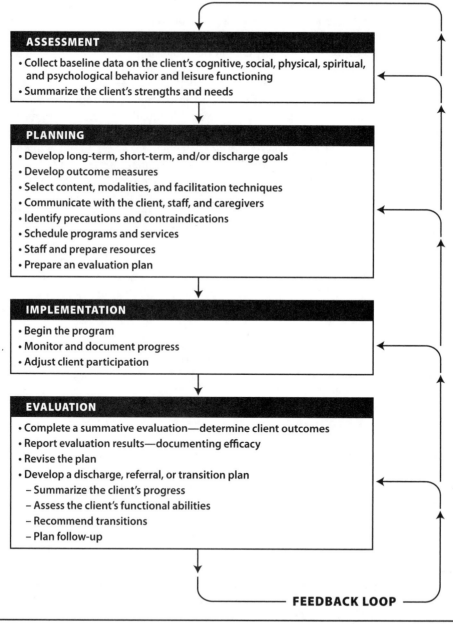

Figure 4.2   Individual Plan

This involves gathering baseline data on the individual's cognitive, social, physical, spiritual, psychological, and leisure functioning to determine his or her interests, expectations, strengths, limitations, program needs, and current status in each area (Austin, 2009). This information provides the foundation from which the TRS designs individualized plans in order to diagnose, treat/rehabilitate, educate, and/or promote improved functional capacity, health, and leisure well-being. The intent of interventions is to bring about a behavioral or functional change to improve the quality of life and leisure relative to the client's frame of reference. Assessment data on current functioning are gathered to establish a baseline from which changes resulting from program participation are measured (Stumbo, 2002; Stumbo & Peterson, 2009). Such an assessment helps the TRS determine which programs are most effective for a particular client or group of clients (Shank & Coyle, 2002; Stumbo).

Various tools and procedures are available to help the TRS determine program focus, client placement, intervention effectiveness, and the client's perspective on social, cultural, and environmental factors influencing growth and change potential (O'Keefe, 2005; Porter & Van Puymbroeck, 2007). Standardized instruments like the Leisure Competence Measure (LCM) and nonstandardized methods like narratives and video technology capture personal and environmental factors reflective of a client's perspective and culture relative to his or her life situation (Kloseck, Crilly, & Hutchinson-Troyer, 2001; O'Keefe). Exhibit 4.1 delineates the types of behaviors assessed in each functional area. A number of assessment instruments are listed in Exhibit 4.2 (see page 120). Descriptions of assessment areas may be found by review of these instruments.

Collecting Baseline Data on the Functioning Areas

Cognitive behaviors are displayed during thought processes as evidenced when, for example, the client chooses among alternative experiences or decides what cards to play or how many spaces to move while playing a table or board game. This area is important to assess since thought processes regulate body movement and behavioral aspects of participation (Stumbo & Peterson, 2009). Furthermore, this area affects the ability to learn and process information in life and leisure (Shank & Coyle, 2002). Cognitive functioning consists of a series of processes, beginning with concrete behaviors and advancing to abstract levels of thinking. Each process becomes more complicated and involves more behaviors. Thus, a recall of facts or listing of rules is less complicated than is creating a work of art. The most difficult cognitive task is to evaluate a situation in order to decide appropriate actions, such as occurs during inclusion experiences that require money management and selection of alternative travel options. Other cognitive areas assessed by TRSs include recognition; attention skills, including arousal, selective attention, concentration, and alternating attention; short- and long-term memory and retrieval memory; orientation to person, place, and time; judgment, problem-solving, and decision-making; abstraction; organization and planning; language; sequencing; and academic skills like counting and calculation (Porter & burlingame, 2006; Shank & Coyle; Stumbo & Peterson). Figure 4.3 (on page 115) lists the cognitive processes and gives an example of each.

Social behaviors are displayed as a person interacts with one or more persons and engages in major life activities and community life (Porter & burlingame, 2006; Shank & Coyle, 2002; Stumbo & Peterson, 2009). Social functioning includes the behaviors,

Exhibit 4.1   Assessment Categories in Therapeutic Recreation Instruments

Cognitive Behaviors are displayed in thought processes, intellectual functioning, learning, and knowing. Areas assessed may include:

- Attention and concentration
- Concrete and abstract processes
- Following directions
- Functional use of mental skills like reading, writing, counting, scoring
- Generalization and transfer skills
- Insight, judgment and decision-making
- Memory, organization and planning
- Orientation, problem solving
- Sequencing, strategy

Social Behaviors are displayed as individuals interact with others and engage in major life activities and community life. Areas assessed may include:

- Boundaries and personal space
- Communication skills
- Contact and physical proximity
- Cooperation and competition
- Engagement, etiquette, manners
- Participation, active, passive
- Social interaction skills, group behavior
- Support and relationships
- Teamwork and sportsmanship
- Trust, mistrust issues

Physical Behaviors are skills used in movement, sensation, and are fundamental to maintaining physical and emotional health. Areas assessed may include:

- Ambulation with and without assistive aids
- Balance, coordination, endurance
- Locomotor, nonlocomotor, and manipulative movements
- Fine motor control, flexibility
- Perceptual motor skills
- Sensory, strength
- Visual and auditory perception
- Wellness and overall physical health

Psychological Behaviors are the skills used in expression or communication of feelings or affect. Areas assessed may include:

- Anger management, frustration, tolerance
- Attention seeking, anxiety
- Autonomy, dependence, independence
- Coping, emotional control, expression
- Frustration and tolerance levels
- Locus of control, motivation
- Satisfaction, pleasure, enjoyment
- Self-concept, self-esteem, self awareness
- Self-regulation, stability
- Sensory integration issues
- Stress and tension relief
- Values

Spirituality is linked to subjective well-being and meaning in life and is observed with prayer, ritual, and expression of comfort. Assessment may address:

- Connectedness
- Meditation, rituals
- Meaning in life or purposiveness
- Perception of quality of life

Leisure and play behaviors are assessed to determine recreation competence and potential benefit from engagement. Leisure behavior areas assessed may include:

- Awareness, interests
- Barriers, participation
- Cultural and social influences
- Modifications and accommodations
- Patterns, resources, satisfaction
- Skills, time management

Sources: burlingame, j., & Blaschko, T. M. (2010); Porter, H. R., & burlingame, j. (2006); Genesis Medical Center, Davenport, Iowa, Therapeutic Recreation Services Department.

language, and attitudes displayed during interactions, within relationships, while engaging in volunteer and work experiences, and while participating in informal and formal recreation. Social interaction is a primary leisure experience as well as a by-product of leisure that serves to motivate participation in other leisure and life functions (Stumbo, 1995). Stumbo and other authors have suggested that social competence is multidimensional and that individuals who lack social skills are at risk later in life and, therefore, require direct instruction to overcome social skill inadequacies. Like cognitive skills, social interaction skills are assessed on a hierarchy (see figure 4.4), beginning with intra-individual interactions and advancing to group interactions. TRSs also assess social amenities, communication, sportsmanship, interactions with others of the same and opposite sex, cooperation, relating to peers and adults,

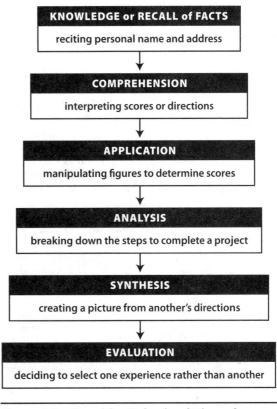

Figure 4.3   Cognitive Behavioral Hierarchy
Based on Benjamin S. Bloom et al. (1956), *Taxonomy of Educational Objectives, Handbook I: Cognitive Domain*. New York: Longman, as presented in Norman E. Gronlund (1970), *Stating Behavioral Objectives for Classroom Instruction*, pp. 20–21. New York: Macmillan.

waiting, taking turns, and sharing. Two aspects of these skills are considered. The first concerns instrumental interactions—the skills necessary to gain information or assure economic well-being—like acquiring and keeping a job. The second aspect focuses on affiliation needs like exchanging feelings during a recreation experience (Shank & Coyle). These skills are essential to full social inclusion. Since a person's self-concept mediates social behavior, the status of an individual's self-concept is also considered. For example, a person with a low self-concept may benefit from individual leisure experiences like card playing or video games prior to progressing into group activities, where the "self" is open to judgment by others. Social skills are influenced by and influence behaviors in each of the other domains. As a consequence, assessment in this area reveals functioning abilities and deficits in each of the other areas. The TRS's role in assessing social interaction is critical because social skills are an important component of holistic health, and because few other professions tend to consider this area (Stumbo & Peterson).

Physical behaviors involve gross and fine motor skills, use of the senses, mobility, flexibility, coordination, balance, sequencing and patterning of movements, perceptions, and fitness elements such as endurance, strength, and stamina. These skills are fundamental to maintaining physical and emotional health, preventing secondary conditions,

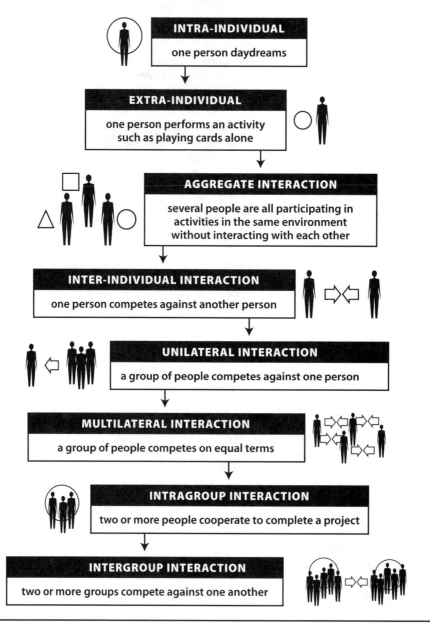

Figure 4.4   Social Behavioral Hierarchy
Adapted from Avedon (1974).

completing self-care functions, and engaging in an active leisure lifestyle (Porter & burlingame, 2006; Shank & Coyle, 2002). Assessments consider the frequency, duration, intensity, and number of body parts used to complete activities; increases in each of these result in a more difficult physical behavior. Although most leisure experiences appear to require physical skills, some, such as swimming, require more than others, such as the performing arts. TRSs assess clients' physical behaviors to ascertain the present functioning level as well as residual abilities (functioning unimpaired by the disability) used to complete specific skills such as grasping/releasing, ambulating, and responding to sensations. TRSs are likely to collaborate with physical and occupational therapists and speech, language, and audiology professionals in order to adapt assessments so performance is not compromised by the client's level of physical well-being and sensation.

Specific physical skills like grasping and releasing can be assessed during naturalistic observations.

Psychological behaviors involve the expression or communication of feelings. Like cognitive and social skills, this behavioral area can be presented in a hierarchy with lower-level skills, such as listening or responding, requiring less emotional involvement than those at higher levels, such as demonstrating appreciation or accepting responsibility for one's own behavior. Figure 4.5 lists psychological behaviors and gives an example for each. TRSs assess clients' emotional stability, anger management and control, attitudes toward self, locus of control, expression, and the value they place on the satisfaction they derive from different experiences and interactions (leisure and friendship, for example) as indicators of emotional status. Key outcomes of intervention are facilitating appropriate expression of feelings—especially enjoyment, satisfaction, and handling stress (Porter & burlingame, 2006; Shank & Coyle, 2002; Stumbo & Peterson, 2009). The value an individual places on leisure and interactions with the therapist during interventions is a measure of emotional well-being.

Spirituality is linked to subjective well-being as an integrative measure of health (Heintzman, 1999). Spirituality is a feeling of connectedness to oneself, nature, and a higher power and is an important factor in a person's perception of health and finding

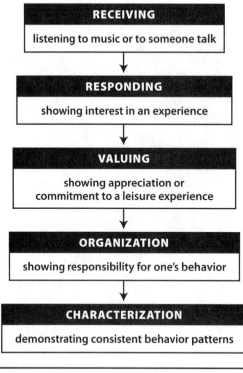

Figure 4.5   Psychological Behavioral Hierarchy

Based on David R. Krathwohl et al. (1964). *Taxonomy of Educational Objectives, Handbook II: Affective Domain*. New York: David McKay Co., as presented in Norman E. Gronlund (1970), *Stating Behavioral Objectives for Classroom Instruction*, pp. 22–23. New York: Macmillan.

meaning in life (Porter & burlingame, 2006; Shank & Coyle, 2002). The significance of faith and spiritual health to healing and well-being is supported by a number of scientific studies (Heintzman; Wallis, 1996). The nature of spirituality can be connected to a wilderness experience, art, music, nonverbal communication, friendships, and meditative relaxation responses that elicit peace in mind and body (Dailey, 2000). Other dimensions of spirituality a therapist subjectively assesses are "purposiveness or meaning in life, hope or optimism in anticipation of future events, and values" (Witmer & Sweeney, 1992, p. 141), which guide relationships and decision-making. Spiritual needs are commonly addressed in services with aging adults where the clients "need to feel connected, competent, useful, and successful" (Dailey, p. 3). The palliative care of hospice services exemplifies the importance of addressing the spiritual health of clients. Therapists observe motivational levels, ethical responses, and commitments to personal fulfillment. As suggested by Heintzman (1997), questions related to spiritual health are found in leisure wellness assessments and may be added to agency-generated tools. Spiritual assessments are used by the TRS to identify behaviors that cause spiritual distress, like anger and isolation, and to highlight strategies that promote comfort and meaning, like relationships, pets, nature, and humor (Dailey). The Spiritual Well-Being Scale (Ellison & Smith, 1991) offers a number of measures useful in assessing a person's perception of the quality of their lives; for example, "I feel that life is a positive experience"; "I feel unsettled about my future"; "I feel very fulfilled and satisfied with life"; "I don't enjoy much about life"; "I believe there is some real purpose for my life." While these statements reflect a person's values, other questions might identify the cultural context surrounding one's faith; for example, "What are the spiritual traditions in your home?" could reveal the importance spirituality plays in organizing the client's life (Hodge, 2005).

Leisure and play behaviors give TRSs an overview of clients' health and abilities relevant to a broad spectrum of life and leisure functioning. Leisure assessments are critical to gathering baseline data used in determining the effects of therapeutic recreation interventions (Stumbo & Peterson, 2009) and are required to ensure compliance with professional standards of practice (ATRA, 2000) and the standards of care established by accrediting bodies. Data from such an assessment reflect a person's leisure interests, assets, patterns, needs, barriers, and knowledge. Assessment information helps the therapist recognize the influence of the client's cultural values and way of life on the delivery of therapeutic programs. Accurate assessment increases the TRS's efficiency and effectiveness in designing programs and services and creates a better understanding of the role of leisure in individuals' lives and how it is impacted by their disabilities.

TRSs use a variety of techniques and instruments to collect assessment data. Generally, the selected methods include (1) self-report, (2) observation, (3) performance testing, and (4) secondary data sources (Shank & Coyle, 2002). Self-report methods include structured (directive) and unstructured (client-centered) interviews with clients and caregivers as well as self-administered questionnaires or surveys completed by the client (Shank & Coyle; Stumbo, 2002). TRSs may also directly or indirectly observe client behaviors in both natural and controlled settings. Through obtrusive (client is aware of observer) or unobtrusive (client is unaware of observer) observations TRSs systematically record behaviors in real-life situations (Stumbo & Peterson, 2009). Performance testing, the third method, requires clients to perform skills that assess, for example, balance and strength critical to preventing falls. Secondary data sources are sources other than the client; for example, family members, official records, and team documentation. Information gathered may confirm results of client interviews while avoiding unnecessary, repetitive staff assessments. By reviewing client and caregiver intake records as well as the results of standardized assessments, functional skills testing, and agency or program specific self-administered surveys, the TRS gains a holistic view of the individual in relation to his or her leisure attributes, culture, health, and the impact of the disability on the person's life.

When the TRS administers assessments and collects data directly from clients, these are considered primary data sources. Thus, the first three assessment methods (self-report, observation, performance testing) are primary data sources that yield client-generated data. The fourth method, secondary data sources, considers not only client medical and educational records, test results, and team meetings but also social histories, progress notes, home visits, and informal conversations with family members and related professionals (Austin, 2009). Secondary sources are used to enhance and elicit further explanation of primary data, particularly when collection from the client is limited, as in the case of older persons or those with limited ability to communicate. The TRS records data in individual plans as either objective assessment data or subjective assessment data. **Objective assessment data** are based on observable facts uninfluenced by emotion or personal prejudices, beliefs, or ideas. Such data are available from medical and psychiatric records, test results, diagnostic workups, laboratory reports, physical examinations, social histories, and recorded verbal communications that conform to agency protocol. **Subjective assessment data** are influenced by personal interpretation (and sometimes personal bias) and include discussions with colleagues and significant others as well as observations and impressions other professionals present either during staff meetings or by written documentation in a client's chart or program file. From a health-related focus, the assessment process must gather not only objective facts but also subjective information on the client's perception of his or her health and quality of life (O'Keefe, 2005).

A number of factors influence the selection of assessment tools, including the purpose for the assessment; instrument validity, reliability, and usability; client abilities; staff capabilities; availability of commercial and self-administered tools; access to computers and software programs for electronic health/medical records (EHR); content, level, and purpose of programs offered; agency characteristics and resources; practical considerations like constraints found with client length of stay, language preference or cultural norms; and anticipated use of assessment results (Mobily & Ostiguy, 2004; Shank & Coyle, 2002; Stumbo & Peterson, 2009; Sylvester et al., 2001).

Nowhere in the APIE process is the impact of culture more vivid than with assessment. Culture influences both content and data-collection methods. Factors like communication styles, time and spatial orientation, and eye contact; views on health, familial roles, autonomy, and independence; and the client's actual recreation and leisure experiences impact the choice of instruments and how information is gathered (Shank & Coyle, 2002; Stumbo & Peterson, 2009). Thus a TRS will purchase or design one or more tools and techniques to collect information to develop a comprehensive database. Tools available for purchase and/or use by permission are categorized according to their primary purpose and content, which allows the TRS to align the tool with the nature of the programs and services offered. Examples of instruments used (but not limited to) according to their purpose and content are included in exhibit 4.2.

Assessment data may be gathered during formal intake assessment periods or during routinely scheduled programs and services. The TRS should complete the process in a timely manner in accordance with the standards of regulatory agencies and agency protocols. With time-limited groups or in settings where intervention is short-term (five days or less), TRSs develop individual plans primarily during the intake or

---

Exhibit 4.2   Assessment Instruments

Leisure Attitudes and Barriers
Leisure Diagnostic Battery (LDB)
Leisure Satisfaction Scale (LSS)
Leisure Motivation Scale (LMS)
Leisure Attitude Scale (LAS)
Life Satisfaction Scale (LSS)

Functional Abilities
Comprehensive Evaluation in Recreation Therapy: Psychiatric/Behavioral (CERT:PB) and Physical Disabilities (CERT:PD)

Functional Abilities (cont'd.)
Functional Assessment of Characteristics for Therapeutic Recreation Revised (FACTR)
General Recreation Screening Tool (GRST)
Leisure Competence Measure (LCM)

Leisure Interests & Participation Patterns
Leisurescope Plus and Teen Leisurescope Plus
State Technical Institute Assessment Process (STIAP)
Leisure Interest Survey (LIS)

Sources: Stumbo, N. J. (2002); burlingame, j., and Blaschko, T. M. (2010).

admission period (the first 24 to 72 hours of intervention). With ongoing programs, the TRS may extend the process over a longer period of time (several days) as the client participates in programs.

Summarizing Clients' Strengths and Needs

Assessment findings guide the TRS in writing the individual plan. Initially, the TRS develops a statement summarizing the client's strengths, needs, and functional status. From this statement, the TRS writes clinical impressions and recommendations for intervention, referral, or for no service at all. This statement also guides the TRS during the planning phase when he or she is sharing assessment findings with the client and family to target and prioritize desired intervention goals. These statements may be documented in the client's record and presented to the **interdisciplinary team** (specialists from different professions who exchange information and resources to enable an integrated development of programs and services and client transition among agencies) during meetings (staffings) with team members, clients, and caregivers. Or, as with inclusion options, these statements may be shared with other staff, the client, and caregivers during program planning to aid in the selection of experiences offered by the agency. Such data become the baseline from which the client's progress and the plan's effectiveness are later evaluated.

A well-written individual plan (1) satisfies the criteria of accrediting agencies, (2) is tailored to the needs of the client, and (3) lays the foundation for interventions that will promote improved functional capacity, health, and well-being.

Planning

The second major step in the programming process involves two main tasks: (1) the development of an individualized plan consistent with professional and regulatory guidelines and the philosophy of the client and delivery setting and (2) the preparation of resources enabling this program to be delivered. When the tasks of this phase have been completed, priorities will have been set and services will be in place to meet individualized client goals and achieve measurable outcomes. The nature of this process is unique to each client and service setting. For example, in some settings, each plan is generated on a computer or recorded on a chart that is integrated into a treatment-team prepared care plan. In other settings, each client collaborates with the TRS during the intervention process to select goals, document participation, and outline discharge experiences. To comply with the ATRA (2000) standards of practice, the contents of a plan must include long-term, short-term, and/or discharge goals; objectives; intervention strategies; outcome evaluation procedures; discharge/transition plans; and referral, follow-up, and aftercare plans. Additionally, the plan must be compatible with the department's plan of operation and available resources; congruent with the overall treatment plan; reflect collaboration with the client, significant others, and team members; and be based on assessment data. Additionally, as outlined in the ATRA diversity statement (2006), plans should reflect culturally sensitive practices and acknowledge each client's perspective on health, functioning, and quality of life.

Stumbo's (1996) TRAM model identifies protocol development as a means of "increasing the standardization of intervention programs" (p. 253) by defining the input, process, and outcomes of programs and services. A **protocol** is a written plan that addresses a client's specific needs or diagnosis, such as impaired mobility or depression; or describes the procedures to implement an individual activity or program to help the client achieve desired outcomes (Grote, Hasel, Krider, & Mortensen, 1995). Protocols contain assessment, process, and outcome criteria; that is, recommended assessment areas and procedures, intervention techniques and programs, and expected outcomes that address specific client needs. Protocols are the bridge between program design and specific outcomes and, as a consequence, provide documentation for common professional practices essential to TRS accountability (Stumbo & Peterson, 2009). A TRS uses protocols to design individual plans. When a client presents more than one need or diagnosis, such as alcoholism and depression, the TRS draws from several protocols to prepare the individual plan. The following sections outline the steps involved in creating individual plans. Protocol design is considered later in the chapter within the discussion of comprehensive program plans.

Developing Long-Term, Short-Term, and/or Discharge Goals

The assessment summary may identify a number of client and caregiver interests and concerns. Consequently, the TRS and client prioritize specific areas to address. Consideration is given to client's expressed strengths and priorities as well as participation and environmental factors like family expectations, resources, and time available for intervention; premorbid lifestyle; agency mission; and the team's scope of care (Austin, 2009; Shank & Coyle, 2002). Goals are derived from the summary findings (needs and strengths) of the assessment process and are written to describe outcome behaviors needed to resolve the client's limitations or to support his or her abilities and interests. Thus goal statements are written after the direction of intervention is decided and incorporate the client's views toward health, helping relationships, and the cultural context in which the client is expected to function. Each plan has one primary discharge goal, and each long-term goal describes one skill needed to achieve the discharge goal. Thus, each plan may have several long-term goals. For each long-term goal, the TRS identifies several short-term goals—each identifying one skill needed to achieve that particular long-term goal. The nature of these statements varies with the setting. For instance, a person in a physical rehabilitation unit is expected to display behaviors specified in short-term goals during each phase or level of the rehabilitation process prior to attaining long-term goals and discharge from the agency. In a setting where TR services are received over an extended time period (five to seven days or longer), such as in a private residential facility or in an educational program, the behaviors targeted by the short-term goals are expected to be progressively displayed as the client achieves the overall long-term goals and as the team makes plans with the client to transition to another type of setting or program option. The sequencing of goal statements reflects client and staff priorities or the order in which client needs will be addressed. Goals, therefore, identify anticipated improvements in the client's status as a consequence of intervention. To illustrate, the goals of a client in physical rehabilitation might include:

Discharge goal: To live in a transitional program
Long-term goal: To participate in community re-entry experiences with significant others
Short-term goals: To identify accessible community leisure programs
                   To develop leisure skills compatible with those of significant others
                   To develop community travel and safety skills

Developing Outcome Measures

For each goal, written objectives specify measurable outcomes that target client change. In other words, each objective is a stepping-stone toward reaching a goal (Melcher, 1999) and identifies an outcome expected to result from involvement in a well-planned program (Stumbo, 1996). These outcome statements reflect a change in a person's functioning, health status, and/or quality of life. The TRS uses these measures to monitor progress and document client change (relative to his or her cultural perspective and views) during participation. At the conclusion of programs and services, these statements are used to evaluate outcomes. This evaluation ties participation in the chosen experience directly to client change and is the process by which the TRS establishes accountability, program quality, and evidence-based practices. Thus, several important characteristics are considered as outcome measures are developed (Stumbo & Peterson, 2009):

- Outcome measures are important to the client and attainable within the scope of intervention.

- Outcomes may be evident in clinical and functional status, quality of life, satisfaction with care, and cost or resource use, and result directly from intervention.

- Within the length of stay or intervention period, the outcome is achievable and able to be demonstrated and documented.

- The direct relationship between the outcome and intervention are meaningful and valued by client and caregiver.

Format for objective statements usually includes (1) minimal level of expected behavior change, (2) the condition under which the behavior is observed, and (3) the "criterion or standard of quality that the behavior should fulfill to demonstrate that the outcome measure has been achieved" (Sheehan, 1993, p. 131). Therefore, each statement has three features (Shank & Coyle, 2002; Stumbo & Peterson, 2009; Sylvester et al., 2001):

- Action verb denoting observable and measurable behavior outcome from either the cognitive, social, physical, psychological, or spiritual domain; or leisure behavior
- Conditions relevant to the performance of the outcome such as activities, timelines, or environment where the skill is to be performed
- Criteria describing how well the client must perform the behavior so the TRS is able to judge the client's progress and effectiveness of the experience

As stated earlier, outcome measures are determined by the therapeutic recreation goals and the team's goals. Each objective is written to reflect the same priority sequence as the goal statements: "This prioritization shows the importance and connection between the client's needs and outcomes" (Lee et al., 2000, p. 66). Also, objectives are sequenced to coincide with the hierarchies evident in each behavioral domain. Thus, in the cognitive area, clients are expected to acquire concrete skills such as counting before applying these skills to score keeping. Probable objectives describing one outcome in each behavioral domain for the discharge goal stated in the earlier example are presented:

Cognitive: After two weeks in recreation therapy, the client will identify at least two criteria of accessible community resources.

Social: After two weeks in recreation therapy, the client will talk 15 minutes with one caregiver about two or more mutual leisure interests.

Physical: During the community re-entry program, the client will ambulate using a wheelchair for at least 10 minutes with only two rest stops.

Psychological: Prior to discharge, the client will demonstrate adjustment to the acquired disability by verbally describing two adaptations made to complete a leisure activity during a community re-entry experience from the hospital.

Spiritual: Prior to discharge, the client will verbally describe the significance of the adapted activity as a positive experience to life satisfaction and well-being.

These statements measure the benefit of participation for each individual. When a client achieves each outcome measure in the individual plan, the objectives are considered relevant and important to the client and attainable through experiences offered (Stumbo & Peterson, 2009). The achieved outcome measurements become indicators of client benefits directly attributable to participation in a specific intervention.

Selecting Content, Modalities, and Facilitation Techniques

TRSs accomplish two tasks when selecting content, modalities, and facilitation techniques. First, specific experiences are selected to enable the client to achieve measurable outcomes, and second, leadership strategies and interaction strategies are identified to use with the client during the program. To accomplish the first task, the TRS analyzes each objective statement to identify all possible content that will help the client achieve his or her expected outcomes. Through the processes of activity and task analyses, the TRS selects, modifies, and sequences content to produce the desired client changes. **Activity analysis** involves identifying each cognitive, social, physical, psychological, and spiritual behavior performed during a specific leisure experience. Activity analysis, therefore, is the process used by the TRS to understand why an experience is likely to "help assure optimal therapeutic benefit for the client" (Austin, 2009, p. 219). **Task analysis** involves sequencing each skill, from the first to the last, to be performed in an activity. This task sequence is actually a listing of individual skills identified in the activity analysis process. Each task step becomes one measurable outcome for which objectives are prepared and progress is monitored. One experience rather than another is chosen or designed because it has inherent characteristics that better enable the client to achieve the outcome identified in the objective (Stumbo & Peterson, 2009). Skill sequencing enables the TRS to begin the intervention at a client's ability level and to determine when an individual has successfully mastered the skills to achieve an objective. The activity and task analyses listed below illustrate the skills necessary to complete the tasks in the objectives presented earlier.

Cognitive:	Recall accessible parking area criteria
	Comprehend accessible travel route to building entry
Social:	Identify leisure preferences of self and others
	Talk about leisure likes/dislikes
Physical:	Sitting balance, stamina, strength, endurance
	Grasp/release, elbow flexion/extension
Psychological:	Listening and responding to others
Spiritual:	Valuing benefits of leisure, accepting adaptations

Task Steps for wheelchair (w/c) ambulation:
- Transfer to w/c
- Maintain seated balance
- Grasp/release seat belt
- Grasp/release brakes
- Push w/c forward, backward, and make turns
- Stop w/c

After the TRS analyzes each objective to identify experiences that will enable the client to reach particular outcomes, he or she determines leadership strategies, modalities and facilitation techniques, and a program structure that will be supportive of the content, compatible with the agency resources and plan of operation, congruent with the client's culture and way of life, and will effectively and efficiently achieve the outcome measures in the individual plan. The frequency, duration, and organization of experiences, as well as the modalities and facilitation techniques used by a TRS during programs, are influenced by such factors as the available space and program time, program purpose, critical pathways and protocols, reimbursement guidelines, and the techniques used by other team members. A client's cultural background, caregiver support, and personal comfort with specific interventions (like aquatic therapy) also impact the selection and delivery of experiences (Porter & Van Puymbroeck, 2007; Sylvester et al., 2001). To illustrate using the previous example, during inpatient rehabilitation TRSs intervene one-on-one and in small groups with clients during sessions coordinated with other team members' schedules. To achieve the long-term goal of community re-entry, the TRS will need to schedule with the other therapists available transportation, the times of the outings, and the staff members who will assist. If other team members are using behavior management and sensory integration techniques when they interact with a client, these intervention processes will also be maintained during outings. Additional feasible experiences and interventions to support the discharge goal of living in a transitional setting might include:

- A leisure education session that includes social skills training and practice with caregivers and other clients conducted in a community setting
- Completing leisure awareness assessments during a one-on-one session
- A family dinner featuring ethnic foods in the lounge, allowing the TRS to use cognitive retraining techniques in a discussion on how to locate and use accessible restaurants

Communicating with the Client, Staff, and Caregivers

Communication facilitates cooperation and collaboration among staff, clients, and families as they become aware of each other's assets and needs. Sharing knowledge is critical to minimizing conflicting opinions, preventing misunderstandings, and maintaining consistency as programs and services are delivered. Further, when clients and caregivers are invested in the TR process, they tend to be more committed and motivated, and the client's assets are better used in achieving goals (Austin, 2009; Shank & Coyle, 2002). Communication and collaboration reflect an ethic of caring that values each client's perceptions (O'Keefe, 2005; Porter & Van Puymbroeck, 2007). Moreover, professional standards of practice require collaboration among professional disciplines and caregivers as the plan is developed and implemented.

This process is facilitated when each team member documents his or her respective entries on the appropriate planning forms or in the database. This information includes assessment data, goals, objectives, and recommended therapeutic experiences and intervention strategies. Agency protocol determines the actual documentation forms or computer programs used and methods for communicating with clients, colleagues, and significant others. A TRS usually records information in the client's file, chart, or individual program plan (IPP), which becomes a tool to educate and inform other professionals and caregivers of the TRS's intent. Formal (protocols and clinical or critical pathways) and informal written and verbal communication also serve to educate others about the nature and purposes of therapeutic recreation programs and services. After each health and human service professional has entered information, the plans are discussed during staff meetings, team meetings, caregiver conferences, and/or departmental meetings. To continue our earlier illustration, after a meeting with the client, team members discover that family members are not available for community outings, so friends must be recruited if the long-term goal of participating in outings with significant others is to be achieved. The client and team also conclude that stress management and relaxation training are additional, appropriate interventions. This information is then added to the IPP. Throughout the program, the TRS shares information with stakeholders about the client's progress and any adjustments necessary to ensure that programs and services align with outcome measures and the client and team's intentions. Realistically, a client's health may preclude involvement in the TR process from time to time. Yet, one theoretical belief is that the client's self-determination is instrumental in achieving his or her desired level of optimal wellness. Consequently, TRSs encourage client participation through sensitive responses and invitations at opportune times.

Identifying Precautions and Contraindications

As a result of each professional's input and input from the client and significant others, the TRS becomes aware of individual management precautions and contraindicated experiences and enters them in the IPP. For instance, a child may be a "runner" (darts away unexpectedly) or a person may experience medication side effects, display an aura before a seizure, or become resistant when faced with a challenging task or an "authority figure" like the TRS. Family members may use effective communication techniques, behavior management techniques, and "gimmicks" when motivating the individual to perform daily living skills or when administering medication, which may be helpful to professionals. Precautions are necessary when the concomitant effects of a disability or secondary limitations influence a patient's participation in experiences. For example, sudden noises and swimming in cold water increase spasticity; seizure activity may interfere with a client's ability to respond to a leader's verbal directions.

Since the desire is to facilitate change in functional capacity and relevant skills, TRSs also consider the environmental and personal context when planning programs, so necessary precautions will be applied. For example, the side effects of an anticonvulsant drug may not be noticed in a hospital setting yet they become apparent during community outings when the client increases his or her energy expenditure. Because therapeutic recreation programs and services often occur in settings familiar to the client, TRSs may observe and record behaviors not exhibited during inpatient stays or in the presence of other therapists. For example, a client's ability to maintain independent ambulation is more accurately assessed during community outings when natural accessibility barriers are mastered than when clients maneuver through TRS-designed hospital obstacle courses. The TRS would record this information in the IPP and discuss it during conferences to ensure that all who come into contact with the client respond consistently, supporting the client's goals and assets.

Scheduling Programs and Services

A TRS develops a client's schedule after completing initial assessments and conducting interdisciplinary or planning meetings. The client's objectives and preferences and the agency's resources and plan of operation influence schedule development. The schedule also reflects the directives of (clinical) critical pathways and agency protocols. The schedule identifies the frequency, duration, and nature of a client's experiences while in a particular setting or program.

Objectives identify desired participation outcomes and potential experiences and intervention strategies. After conducting activity and task analyses and reviewing assessment data, the TRS compares a client's skills to those required for successful participation in selected activities. From this, the TRS determines the approximate time or number of sessions needed for the client to achieve the expected outcomes. In

A client's intervention schedule reflects the preferences of the client and is coordinated with both agency and TR program schedules.

our example, for instance, the TRS reviews the client's assessment data on strength, endurance, and wheelchair tolerance, and identifies several alternative activities in which ambulation practice can occur. Then the TRS establishes the length and number of therapeutic recreation sessions so that the physical objective of ambulating for at least 10 minutes with only two stops is accomplished during the community outing.

Before finalizing each client's schedule, a TRS should assess the agency resources and plan of operation. The duration of a program and client-to-staff ratios may be identified during team meetings when operating standards and reimbursement options are considered. Where a seasonal calendar identifies a standard length of time per session or the number of calendar days per program, TRSs recommend appropriate participation options. Community settings represent this scheduling format. In hospitals, patient schedules are developed after considering activities of daily living (ADL) routines, mealtimes, medical rounds, number of patients and their functioning capacities or the case mix, transportation, available contact space or number of activity areas, skill level and number of staff or caseload, physical distance of programs from one another, number of other services in which patients are involved, recommended precautions and contraindications, costs to the patient, and length of stay and/or financial reimbursement permitted. As the participation environment is considered, the TRS adjusts the intensity and duration of intervention "to maximize the possibility of outcome achievement" (Lee et al., 2000, p. 66).

Regardless of the setting, the client's recommended schedule is a reflection of the client's preferences and is coordinated with the agency's comprehensive schedule and the therapeutic recreation program schedule. In hospitals, the team leader may use a (clinical) critical pathway to prescribe services. In community settings, the TRS recommends alternative programs that best enable the participant to achieve expected outcomes, and the participant decides his or her final schedule after, for example, considering available transportation, program location, and time of offerings. In either situation, the final schedule reflects compromises intended to utilize existing resources effectively and efficiently, to comply with governing standards and protocols, and to best address client preferences and environmental influences.

Staffing and Preparing Resources

Staff assignments are made following the design of client programs and services. Program orientation influences staffing patterns. In a diagnostic or treatment program with time-limited participation, staff are assigned to one-on-one bedside and/or small group interventions. When the purpose of the program is to teach skills or to prevent functional loss, staff may conduct group and one-on-one sessions over extended time periods. Policies on staffing hours, compensation, seniority, **privileging** (process used to grant staff the right to perform tasks essential to a particular job, providing that staff display and maintain competence), client-to-staff ratios, and the number, skills, and credentials of staff also influence staff schedules. Staff may possess culturally relevant skills like spoken language or religious preference, and as a consequence may elect to manage plans of clients having similar characteristics.

The total hours worked by each staff member is influenced by several additional factors: duration or length of direct client contact plus presession and postsession resource preparation and formative evaluation (the ongoing collection of information that allows a manager to make immediate, informed decisions as required); the extent of record keeping required; quality of computers and technical support; quality assurance and improvement, and safety and risk management duties; indirect leadership and supervision activities, such as informal client-staff or staff-staff discussions; and personal and professional training and development. A program manager weighs each staff member's responsibilities in each of these areas as he or she designs a master staff schedule.

Before a client enters a program, a TRS prepares the equipment, supplies, materials, areas, and facilities involved and ensures that documentation procedures are readied. Standards of practice and the nature of the setting influence these planning tasks. The types of records to be kept are identified by regulatory agencies and accrediting bodies (The Joint Commission and CARF International), and the documentation procedures for recording the required information are outlined by agency protocols. Likewise, the management of physical resources is influenced by quality improvement policies, safety and risk management policies, infection control policies, and other agency regulations.

Examples of tasks the TRS completes to ensure program readiness include:

- ordering and monitoring the condition of equipment
- securing releases
- confirming room reservations
- briefing part-time staff and volunteers

- writing daily session plans or reviewing (clinical) critical pathways
- preparing for entry or recording of participation data
- ensuring that assistive and adaptive devices are available at the program site

The nature of these preparations varies with each individual program; for example, the preparation for a one-on-one bedside session differs from the preparation required for a community outing with several participants.

Preparing the Evaluation Plan

The final step in planning is the preparation of an evaluation plan. This includes identifying, purchasing, and/or constructing data-collection instruments, establishing a schedule for collecting the data, and identifying when and how the client's involvement in the programs and services will be adjusted to reflect the findings revealed from the gathered evidence.

Formative, or process, **evaluation** occurs while a client is in the program and involves making immediate decisions regarding alternative intervention strategies and adjusting objectives to achieve expected outcomes. Through **summative**, or outcome, **evaluation**, a TRS gathers information after a client completes the experience and uses it to consider the effectiveness of the particular experience in enabling the client to achieve desired outcomes. A TRS designs or purchases instruments to collect both types of data. The techniques and tools to evaluate client progress and outcomes are similar to those used with assessment; staff may actually re-administer the same instrument as well as rely on written goals and outcome measures to guide data collection. Program managers employ standardized and agency-specific instruments to collect data not only on clients' functioning and health but also on the key elements that affect outcomes—content, leadership strategies and interventions, and resource management. Selecting evaluation instruments may lead a TRS to reconsider assessment processes, to collect new/different assessment information, and/or to redesign the individual plan.

A TRS establishes a data-collection schedule by reviewing each objective and considering the standards of regulatory and accrediting bodies and input from the client and team. In situations where individuals are in residence lasting approximately five to thirty days, formative evaluation occurs more frequently than when participants enroll in programs extending for longer time periods.

As noted earlier, objectives specify the amount of time in which an outcome is to be reached—"after two weeks," for example, or "before discharge." During team meetings, members set dates for monitoring the client's achievement of short-term, long-term, and discharge goals. These dates may correspond with insurance reimbursement protocols, such as those of managed care providers. Planning requires designating a certain number of periods for collecting data or arranging for staff time necessary to use naturalistic observation to evaluate progress.

While the evaluation plan identifies when and how changes are made if adjustments seem warranted, the data a TRS collects may or may not indicate adjustments to an individual plan. When data suggest outcomes are being achieved as planned, the TRS simply documents the effectiveness of prescribed programs and services in the plan. When deemed necessary by formative evaluation results, a client's schedule may be altered after meeting with the client and team, or a predischarge meeting (a form of summative evaluation) may result in changing outcome measures or rewriting the discharge goal to modify the length of time a client is engaged in a program.

"Accountability demands of external reviewers and payers are increasingly focused on the specific value and utility of particular services" (Witman, 1994, p. 85). Reimbursers are concerned with appropriateness, cost effectiveness, and quality of services as they benefit the client. TRSs document and monitor client progress to determine if targeted outcomes are achieved through individual plans. Data from evaluation of client outcomes have a direct relationship to comprehensive program evaluation (Stumbo & Peterson, 2009). As a central component, they become primary measurement thresholds and benchmarks in managing overall program improvements. Data collected also contribute to efficacy research to justify interventions. Data on client outcomes provide professionals with knowledge of what is positive and appropriate from the client's perspective; thus, client evaluation is not only essential to evidence-based practice but also to ethically based practice (Sylvester et al., 2001).

Implementation

The third major step in the programming process is the implementation of the individual plan. During this phase, the TRS uses technical leadership skills, specialized intervention techniques, and unique personal skills to establish a helping relationship so the "paper" plan becomes an action plan. TRSs integrate each individual's plan into the department or agency plan and monitor client and program progress so each individual participates in appropriate experiences. During implementation, formative evaluations identify adaptations and modifications that will enhance the client's experience. Similarly, ongoing interactions between TRSs and caregivers will enhance their involvement as the process unfolds. In those cases where a client's progress is not evident or newly displayed behaviors suggest untreated or unresolved problems, a TRS can network with other health and human service professionals to receive input helpful in revising the individual plan. The steps involved in program implementation are outlined below.

Beginning the Program

A client begins the process by being (1) integrated into ongoing activities, (2) placed in newly organized groups, or (3) scheduled for one-on-one sessions with the TRS. Some programs have definitive entry and exit intervals and a preset number of sessions; others are designed so the client chooses when to initiate or terminate involvement. In some settings, individualized client schedules are established by the team; while in other settings, the participant voluntarily follows a self-determined schedule.

An activity protocol helps staff organize each session and document the leadership and interaction techniques used during a program. Additionally, each plan includes objectives, needed activity resources, content sequence and timing, leadership techniques and intervention strategies, adaptations, safety and risk-management procedures, evaluation procedures, and space to comment on observed client outcomes. An activity protocol is also useful during interactions with caregivers and other professionals to communicate the course of a session. These protocols encourage consistency and enhance outcome achievement (Austin, 2009). Such a plan outlines formative evaluation criteria and provides a method to document client response to each experience. The actual protocol may be entered in a chart or computer file along with documentation of the client's response to the experience.

During program implementation, a TRS uses the "self" in a helping relationship with a client to achieve client goals. The TRS-client relationship, as well as the content of the program, becomes a tool to bring about therapeutic outcomes. The TRS observes the individual's entry into the program to detect reactions such as confusion or anxiety (which may be attributed to "newness") and to determine the compatibility of significant others' expectations with the client's potential and the objectives of the experience. The TRS continually gathers information by observing the verbal and nonverbal cues of the client, caregivers, and colleagues. Sensitive TRSs are aware of the impact of their cultural heritage on program implementation and adjust their interactions and appropriateness of the experience to facilitate relevant client outcomes.

TRSs employ specific leadership strategies to gain the client's attention, motivate his or her involvement, give directions, monitor the client's actions during an activity, bring the experience to closure, and debrief following the experience. TRSs also choose specialized modalities and facilitation techniques—such as behavior modification, stress management, assertion, reality orientation, values clarification, cognitive retraining, and sensory integration—to enhance the effectiveness of the helping relationship. They select those strategies which, in their judgment, are compatible with the content, congruent with the client's beliefs, and facilitate expected client outcomes.

Monitoring and Documenting Progress

Through formative (process) evaluation, a TRS collects subjective and objective data. The TRS might record data by session or throughout an ongoing program attended over a time period (usually a few days to several weeks). Data are organized according to each objective, outcome measure, or problem area. Data are recorded in the form of progress notes, program observation logs, and narrative comments with attendance report forms. If a clinical program keeps **problem-oriented medical records (POMR)** (a documentation form that organizes client data according to behaviors or problems; the chart is organized according to five categories: data base, problem list, plans, progress notes, and discharge summary), each problem is prioritized and all professionals complete chart entries by problem area rather than by their respective disciplines (Austin, 2009). The organization of documentation in the narrative portion of the treatment plans is referred to as **subjective, objective, assessment, plan (SOAP)** notes (a progress note format that organizes client data according to these four categories of information). Similar in format to SOAP notes is focus charting. The narrative portion of a focus note organizes information under the categories of **data, action, response, plan (DARP)** (Austin). Focus charting identifies client behaviors or concerns and the TRS's actions related to one particular service aspect, like an assessment or an implemented experience, using these four categories. Another documentation similar to SOAP charting is **PIE** charting (**P-problem, I-intervention, E-evaluation**). The subjective and objective information is combined to create a problem list with documentation of corresponding interventions and evaluation results (Shank & Coyle, 2002; Stumbo & Peterson, 2009).

Another format of clinical documentation uses a flow chart technique that is compatible with the structure of (clinical) critical pathways. Programs and services are presented according to the time sequence in which the client will receive the service. The TRS documents client response and outcomes corresponding to the planned intervention sequence. With **CBE (Charting by Exception)**, charting occurs only when findings are significant or when they deviate from the pathway or professional standard or protocol (Shank & Coyle, 2002; Stumbo & Peterson, 2009). A positive variance is a significant outcome or one achieved sooner than expected while a negative variance results when anticipated outcomes are delayed or unusual. If a hospital uses a **source-oriented** method of documenting, each professional discipline keeps narrative notes on patient achievements and progress toward stated outcome measures in one particular section of the chart (Austin, 2009). TRSs maintain observation logs and anecdotal records with activity protocols and attendance reports when programs are offered by recreation and human service agencies that emphasize education and health promotion rather than treatment. Regardless of setting, technology and the use of electronic health/medical records are impacting documentation of outcomes (Austin; Shank & Coyle; Stumbo & Peterson). Computer workstations may be located near intervention areas or in an office area, or employees may be issued laptops or electronic recording devices. The challenge is to carefully manage any individually identifiable health information as defined by HIPAA—Health Insurance Portability Accountability Act.

Monitoring a client's progress toward achieving his or her objectives is of primary concern and helps ensure that short-term, long-term, and discharge goals are reached. A TRS should document the appropriateness of the selected content, leadership strategies, modalities and facilitation techniques, and the management of resources in relation to a client's potential and objectives. TRSs should continually ask themselves if the client/caregiver is satisfied and whether alternative experiences, techniques, and resources could bring about the desired outcomes more effectively and efficiently.

Unanticipated outcomes and reactions are as critical to the therapeutic recreation process as are the intended consequences. Thus, as a program progresses, a TRS should document interpersonal and social interactions, expressed attitudes, and the reactions of clients, team members, caregivers, and any others affected by the programs. Observations and interviews in the recreation or leisure environment, along with review of completed projects, photos, and videotapes, help capture spontaneous responses crucial to understanding why clients do or do not achieve objectives. The use of these techniques facilitates client and caregiver understanding of therapeutic recreation and its contribution to client growth, change, and well-being.

Adjusting Participation

A TRS adjusts an individual's participation in a program when formative evaluation information suggests that the client will not achieve designated outcomes or when the client exhibits new behaviors or expresses concerns that are indicative of untreated or unresolved problems or new needs. When any of the preceding situations occur, the TRS chooses among several options, including reanalyzing and/or redoing assessments, rewriting goals and restating outcome measures, adapting or altering content, modifying leadership strategies or techniques, reconsidering input from caregivers and colleagues, changing the client schedule or staff assignments, using assistive devices or adaptive resources, altering the documentation process, and redesigning the evaluation plan. Each option is a reconsideration of one of the preceding planning steps.

If the TRS reconsiders the initial assessments and determines that the client's needs and assets were accurately identified, he or she then reconsiders the results of the activity and task analyses and redesigns the program content and intervention strategies. On the other hand, if after reconsidering the assessment findings the TRS discovers new client needs or untreated problems, he or she prepares another individual plan to adequately address these concerns.

As mentioned earlier, activity and task analyses are the primary tools used to ensure that selected content and strategies will enable the client to accomplish expected outcomes. Therefore, these two tools are also employed by the TRS to adapt content and modify leadership so a client's needs are met during interactions. When the TRS anticipates that the desired outcomes are not likely to be realized with the planned content and intervention strategies, the TRS reexamines the results of the initial activity and task analyses and adapts the program content so more or less complicated skills or different skills are used to successfully complete the experience. For example, a TRS might reexamine the skill sequence and select a different step in the sequence from which to commence the therapeutic experience. These processes also assist the TRS in making procedural or resource modifications, which result in decreasing or increasing the difficulty of an experience. Caregivers and team members who interact with and observe clients in other settings might also contribute ideas and resources helpful to program adaptation and modification.

Activity and task analyses are tools that enable a TRS to plan an experience from which the client will benefit fully. Additionally, they are the means by which staff can do more with fewer resources in less time and adapt to constantly changing work environments (DeGraaf, 1997). DeGraaf suggests using a creative approach to programming to enhance the quality of client experiences; for example, making the familiar unfamiliar by modifying the experience. Bullock, Mahon, and Killingsworth (2010) consider the nature of the client's participation in an activity prior to implementing any adaptations, which might consist of (1) finding, creating, or modifying equipment, (2) changing the method a client uses to perform the task, and (3) changing the rules or procedures to compensate for a skill required (p. 314). These authors believe the more extensive an adaptation, the greater the chance others are affected and the nature of the experience is compromised. Assistive devices are readily available through a number of commercial vendors as are a number of mechanical aids like lightweight wheelchairs or handgrips. With input from clients, caregivers, and team members, the TRS is capable of making creative adjustments to ensure the experience becomes more beneficial. If adjustments are made to the implementation of the client's IPP, they are documented in the activity protocols and the client's IPP and reported in appropriate meetings. This facilitates consistency. Examples of the types of resource adjustments a TRS might make are presented in exhibit 4.3.

Evaluation

The concluding phase of designing an individual plan involves collecting and reporting summative data and preparing a discharge or transition plan. This enables appropriate long-term planning, aftercare, and referral. During this phase the TRS focuses on determining the effectiveness of the IPP—has the client improved function-

Exhibit 4.3   Potential Resource Adaptations

Equipment	Methods	Rules/Procedures
• modify size/weight	• reduce number of items to manipulate	• alter number of positions
• adjust material colors		• allow more/less time
• decrease noise	• reduce number of facts	• adjust scoring
• modify surface texture	• alter number of steps in task	• alter distances
• control heat or light	• allow more/less choices	• adjust area size
• add/reduce equipment	• select from fewer alternatives	• add rest intervals
		• eliminate winning-losing
		• vary number of participants

ing, health, and quality of life? Outcome measures help the TRS determine the degree to which a client has benefited from therapeutic interventions. The specific steps involved in the evaluation phase are described below.

Completing a Summative Evaluation—Determining Client Outcomes

As already noted, summative evaluation occurs (1) when a client has completed a prescribed time period noted in the plan, (2) at the natural conclusion of a program having a certain number of sessions, (3) on a date specified in the plan, or (4) when the client/caregiver selects to terminate the experience. Data from the formative evaluation and input from the client, caregivers, and other team members supplement data collected by the TRS on the client's objectives. Data collected from several sources provide a better measure of congruence or consistency in client outcomes (Austin, 2009). These data may be collected with tools and techniques used in the assessment process, as well as with newly selected or newly prepared tools. Collectively, these data are used by staff to make recommendations for discharge, aftercare, and referral.

Summative evaluation is intended to (1) identify client progress toward achievement of plan goals; (2) determine if the content, leadership, and resources were effectively used to support the team's plan; and (3) establish if the client is satisfied with the process and outcomes. Thus, an evaluation plan includes instruments and procedures to help the TRS collect summative data on the content, leadership, and management of the plan of operation and also incorporates feedback from the client. Criteria for selecting these instruments are similar to those listed for assessment and formative evaluation tools.

When applying the evaluations used in the assessment process, TRSs report qualitative and quantitative comparisons between pre- and post-program participation results. For example, the CERT (PB & PD) scales are designed so the TRS records data by date of measurement over a period of time. Thus, progress is noted by functional change from initial intervention to the most recent date of data collection. The Leisure Competence Measure (LCM), conceptualized according to WHO-ICF philosophy and designed to be compatible with the Functional Independence Measure

(FIM), was developed "to document leisure functioning and to measure therapeutic recreation outcomes" (Kloseck et al., 2001, p. 32). Both pre- and post-administration of the LCM, for example, enables the TRS to record progress in a number of areas; for example, leisure awareness, leisure attitudes, leisure skills, social appropriateness to cultural/social behavior, group interaction skills, clinical participation, social contact, and community participation. Because the LCM is not an assessment tool per se but rather a tool to summarize results of therapeutic recreation assessments in a standardized way using the WHO-ICF, it enables the creation of an international database to provide evidence of intervention outcomes across populations and settings (Kloseck et al.). Summative information identifies behavioral changes, behavioral areas in need of further intervention, untreated or unresolved needs, and the effectiveness of therapeutic recreation in improving the person's health status and leisure functioning and in reducing the effects of a disability.

Reporting Evaluation Results—Documenting Efficacy

TRSs enter data on appropriate forms or in electronic files according to a prescribed format or agency protocol. They report the results during conferences, team meetings, or staff meetings with clients, caregivers, and team members. A TRS may be responsible for maintaining documentation on a given number of clients and for a certain number of programs. Therefore, in addition to documenting outcome measures, TRSs also report on program variables such as personnel, fiscal, and physical resource management. For instance, while maintaining client progress notes and session evaluations, a TRS might also complete monthly reports on part-time or volunteer hours, income and expenses for particular events, and supply inventories. Such data measure program effectiveness and the degree to which program management supports client outcomes.

The TRS uses client outcome data as benchmarks of quality and to study program effectiveness. Quality improvement emphasizes client satisfaction and continuous monitoring of resource use and staffing functions to satisfy client expectations. Quality assurance audits determine if the experiences a TRS provides are the most appropriate to ensure achievement of outcome measures. Outcome data from a number of participants are studied to determine program and service effectiveness. Such **efficacy research** (systematic data collection to determine service effectiveness and benefits to clients) documents the usefulness of particular interventions to address specific client needs. TRSs involved in quality improvement programs and efficacy research report outcomes through case studies and user satisfaction surveys.

When reporting evaluation results, the manner in which the TRS presents the information may be as important as the information itself. Caregivers eager to "see" progress may not "hear" all that is said. Value placed on outcomes like independent functioning or self-determined leisure may vary from culture to culture. Therefore, administrators should address sensitive areas—such as finances and family care-giving roles—with caution. Other factors that affect an evaluation report include the requirements of regulatory bodies, fiscal accountability measures, available computer technology and software support, quality improvement processes, and formal and informal interactions among health and human service professionals in the setting. Regardless of the particular factors influencing an evaluation document, all reports summarizing client outcomes should include:

- a brief account of goals and outcome measures
- a brief overview of content, leadership strategies, and modality and facilitation techniques
- a listing of assessment and evaluation tools
- a statement regarding any bias or concerns in the collection and interpretation of data
- recommendations to either continue, revise, or discontinue programs based on attainment or nonattainment of client outcomes.

Revising the Plan

The TRS, in cooperation with the client, caregivers, and colleagues, uses the findings of formative and summative evaluations to continue, revise, or discontinue programs. Programs are continued or revised when, with further or modified intervention, the client's outcomes are expected to be achieved. If, however, it is ascertained that the individual's needs cannot be adequately addressed, he or she has achieved the plan's discharge goal, or the individual is unwilling or lacks motivation to participate, the TRS terminates the experiences or the individual enters the next phase of programming identified in a discharge, referral, or transition plan. The team and client/caregiver collectively decide to continue, revise, or discontinue programs during meetings similar to those held as the client's progress in the program is monitored. They occur at intervals or dates identified during staff meetings and are based on length of stay permitted by third-party reimbursers, accreditation standards, available financial resources, and/or the setting's seasonal program schedule.

When a plan is revised, steps similar to those taken to adjust the plan following formative evaluation are repeated. Changes might include subtle revisions in the outcome criteria or substitution of one program site for another. Alternatively, the plan may be rewritten to focus on newly emerging client needs. For example, TRSs may rewrite goals and objectives to target different outcomes or alter programs and services to allow for increased or decreased length of stay or transition to another seasonal program.

A program or service may be discontinued when the resources of the setting or service level within the setting do not facilitate the diagnosis, treatment/rehabilitation, education, or promotion of client health and well-being. For example, someone may be transferred from a short-term to a long-term facility when his or her needs cannot be resolved in a few days. Programs also are discontinued when the plan's goals are realized, or when a recommendation based on the plan or the expressed desires of caregivers and the client is to discontinue a particular service level (inpatient to outpatient, for example) or a particular program (discontinue an evening lounge program, for instance, and recommend leisure awareness sessions with community TRSs). To illustrate using the previous example of the person in physical rehabilitation, inpatient services may be discontinued (1) because the individual has transitioned successfully to an outpatient program or (2) because the client indicates satisfaction with the level of community inclusion achieved and home health care provides training in community travel and safety skills. Regardless, as suggested by Shank and Coyle (2002) and implied by a caring ethos, closure is brought to the helping relationship. In the best-case scenario, the TRS and client reflect upon growth and change resulting from their collaboration while preparing for the future. Sometimes, however, discontinuation occurs abruptly, as with unexpected changes in health status or reimbursement decisions. In these instances, clients are discharged or transitioned to other units and staff plan interventions like reunions or legacy building, e.g., life review to acknowledge and document outcomes, or to celebrate life when illness or disability results in death.

Developing a Discharge, Referral, or Transition Plan

A discharge, referral, or transition plan is an extension of the original plan. It is developed during routine meetings with caregivers, colleagues, and clients and is intended to identify long-term options while ensuring continuity between phases of the health-care continuum or between alternative services. Transitions occur when clients move from inpatient to outpatient services or from outpatient services to inclusionary options. To continue with our earlier example, the treatment team may recommend that the client continue rehabilitation on an outpatient, rather than inpatient, basis because the person's ability to ambulate without assistance has improved to an acceptable level yet requires regular practice, or because the person has identified and participated in community outings to accessible recreation facilities; thus, the next logical step (appropriate to the plan's objectives) is to negotiate these outings in the company of significant others. Transitions also result within a particular setting or session when, for instance, clients attend additional hours of therapeutic recreation programs or when, within one session, increased leisure alternatives require clients to make more choices about participation. To ensure maximum success during these transition intervals, a written document describes the steps to continue services or to access alternative aftercare or referral services (Carter & Foret, 1994).

This planning takes place before a client actually leaves one program or transfers to another setting. Confidentiality of client information and the preparedness of a new environment are considered in these transitions. Information on a SOAP or focus note in a chart or in an individual educational program is considered confidential and therefore must be used with discretion and proper release. However, a community recreation leader, unaware of the side effects of certain medications or the signs of an impending seizure, for example, would require assistance from a TRS to prepare for an inclusive leisure education program. Therefore, TRSs should handle information in the discharge plan and disposition of the plan with the utmost care and according to the operational policies of the participating agencies.

A discharge, referral, or transition plan should include the following information.

- *Progress summary.* The TRS summarizes the client's progress toward the outcome measures and discharge goal(s) and shares the information with the client, team members, staff, and caregivers who are presently interfacing with one another or who will do so in the future. The TRS also notes the responses of the client to specific interventions and staff interactions.

- *Functional abilities assessment.* This item compares the client's exhibited functional capacities to the performance expectations of the environment to which transfer is anticipated. The TRS identifies what additional skills or assistance the client needs to function successfully in the new environment(s).

- *Transition recommendations.* By assessing anticipated options, the TRS prepares client outcomes and goals. The TRS also suggests specific experiences, such as leisure resource training, social and financial support, and support groups, that would be helpful to the client and provides the names of agencies offering various options.

- *Follow-up plan.* A follow-up plan is an outline of dates and procedures that will be used as the client transitions from one experience or program to another. The follow-up plan also lists referral contacts and the training and supportive assistance desired by colleagues, caregivers, and the client. The TRS should delineate the evaluation methods and strategies that will be used to report outcomes and client changes. Follow-up also includes making arrangements—through ongoing meetings, informal conversation, and sharing of written client and program reports—to ensure continued exchange of communication and resources among professionals.

COMPREHENSIVE PROGRAM PLANS

The design of a therapeutic recreation program in an agency or department encompasses tasks similar to those completed in the preparation of an individual plan. Instead of focusing on one person's needs, the TRS considers all of the individuals who utilize the programs or services offered by the agency. The TRS applies the APIE process as he or she integrates several individual plans into already existing programs or creates new programs to meet clients' needs. Since this planning sequence (see figure 4.6) is similar to the one employed with individual program planning, only those tasks not detailed in the previous section are presented here. By comparing the planning models, you will notice the similarity of the subtasks undertaken to develop individual and comprehensive TR program plans.

Assessment

The assessment data gathered from each client and documented in the person's individual plan determines whether he or she is integrated into already existing programs or whether new programs are created to meet clients' needs. In hospital settings, patients are assessed individually and assigned to a staff member's caseload, to new or predesigned group therapy sessions, and to ongoing activities like resource planning. In community settings, assessment data are collected on each participant either during individual assessment sessions or as groups participate in planned activities. Individuals then register or enroll in seasonal programs or enter into ongoing programs. Program experiences are organized to reflect assessed skill levels (introductory, intermediate, and so forth), inclusive services, or content areas suggested by medical/psychological diagnosis (aquatics for individuals with arthritis, for instance, or social clubs for individuals with intellectual disabilities). Thus, TRSs first consider the range of client characteristics, their health status, needs, preferences, and leisure behaviors prior to designing a program vision, mission, purpose, and goals.

As information is being gathered about clients, the TRS also considers the settings and the environments in which individuals attend programs and to which they

ASSESSMENT

Client
- individual client results, health status, preferences, needs, leisure behaviors
- assess client placement or assignment in relation to current program offerings

Setting (agency and/or department)
- service scope (programs and services offered; therapies available)
- personnel, physical and fiscal resources
- plan of operation
- political directives and agency/department culture

Environment (resources and external standards)
- professional literature, e.g. efficacy research, theories, evidence-based practices
- government, regulatory, professional standards and best practices
- discharge, referral, transitional setting, and caregiver expectations, e.g. cultural and social behaviors

PLANNING

- Develop program vision, mission, value, and goal statements
- Identify program components (diagnostic and treatment interventions, health promotion, and leisure education)
- Develop program protocols or specific activity plans (structure, process, and outcome criteria and client specifications)
- Disseminate program information to stakeholders in staffings and care meetings
- Prepare department or agency program schedule
- Secure and assign staff and resources to specific programs
- Prepare for quality improvement and monitoring program outcomes
- Prepare resources for data collection and evaluation plan documentation

IMPLEMENTATION

- Deliver program/service to individual clients or client groups
- Monitor and document progress of particular clients and outcomes of specific programs
- Modify programs and services to address formative evaluation results and client needs

EVALUATION

- Collect summative data on interventions, management, resources, and client outcomes
- Report evaluation results to stakeholders and clients
- Document effectiveness and outcomes through efficacy research and evidence-based practices
- Revise, discontinue, develop new programs/services

FEEDBACK LOOP

Figure 4.6   Comprehensive Therapeutic Recreation Plan

will later transition. The resources to develop programs and individual plans come from particular settings, such as a hospital or community leisure service department. Program effectiveness is judged by the client's ability to function successfully in the setting and surrounding environment. The TRS studies agency and department documents and applicable government, regulatory, and professional standards to ascertain program development criteria, expectations, and supportive theories and evidence (see figure 4.7). Information sought from these materials includes department and agency service scope; personnel, physical, and fiscal resources; plan of operation; and quality improvement, reimbursement, evaluation, and research criteria that substantiate best practices. By collecting and reviewing these materials, the TRS becomes aware of factors directly and indirectly influencing clients and caregivers during and after intervention and is better able to justify program decisions and offerings.

Figure 4.7   Influences on the Therapeutic Recreation Program

An agency or department service scope describes the types of programs and services that relate to the specialized needs of clients the agency or department serves and that influence the agency's interactions with other service providers. By reviewing the service scope, a TRS can identify the nature of clients and foci of an agency or department. For example, in hospitals, people who have experienced traumatic injuries require assessment/diagnosis and treatment/rehabilitation, while in community settings, people with behavioral and leisure functioning deficits require education and promotion of behaviors critical to health maintenance and inclusionary experiences.

Availability of personnel, physical resources, and fiscal resources can enhance or deter a person's access to therapeutic experiences. The number of staff and their qualifications; the availability of equipment, supplies, areas and facilities; and the monies appropriated to support therapeutic recreation also influence the quality of experiences clients receive.

The TRS studies the department's or agency's **written plan of operation.** This plan provides guidelines related to staff, clients, quality improvement, infection control, risk/safety management, security, utilization review, evaluation, and research. The plan includes vision, mission, value, and goal statements; programs and services offered; protocols and intervention plans; policies, procedures, and rules; staff credentials; quality improvement, and evaluation and research directives to assure accountability. The contents of this plan are derived from written documents such as administrative manuals, treatment and program protocols, professional standards of practice, and regulatory reports (refer to chapter 5 for discussion of a written plan of

The availability of personnel, their skills and qualifications, and the resources of the agency influence the quality of the client's experience.

operation). Further, the TRS reviews the professional literature to gather evidence of successful interventions and results of efficacy research. Theories are reconsidered to explore their relationship to programming and understanding human behavior. Unwritten or "political" directives can be gleaned through employment orientation and training sessions and through personal contacts at staff meetings, for example, or focus groups with caregivers and clients.

A summary of findings from comprehensive assessments guides the TRS's interactions with clients in a particular setting and enables the TRS to advocate for client needs. Such assessments will allow the TRS to develop specific therapeutic recreation plans, protocols, and policies and to effectively coordinate with agency colleagues.

Planning

From information gathered on the clients, setting, and environment, the TRS can formulate a written plan of operation for a particular program. This plan of operation is the counterpart to an individual program plan: the content is similar, as seen by comparing figure 4.2 to 4.6. However, the scope of the plan is broader, as it covers all the content and operational procedures of an agency or a program designed for a number of individuals. A TRS drafts vision, mission, value, and goal statements for the specific program that are compatible with the overall vision/mission of the agency and regularly updates these statements to reflect the agency's new initiatives. In addition to developing the program's values and goals, the TRS makes decisions on the components of the program and also prepares protocols outlining the intent of each of these components (explained below). The remaining tasks in comprehensive program planning and development are similar to those undertaken when individual programs are planned; however, they are broader in scope because they encompass the needs of all individuals serviced by the agency.

A comprehensive therapeutic recreation program philosophy (vision, mission, values, and goals; and/or separate philosophy and purpose statements) is prepared after review of the agency/department scope of care (programs and services available from the agency/department) and the assessment information. The philosophy outlines the nature of the program and guides the TRS as program components are designed. A **vision statement** is futuristic and focuses on programs/services that are better than the present (Taylor, 2006). Included in the statement are values and beliefs, the overall mission or purpose, and the goals that guide the TRS as actual programs are planned. A **mission statement** describes the primary reason for the existence of the program. Mission statements may be worded to reflect quality assurance indicators; that is, structure, process, and outcome measures. A mission statement describes in more detail the vision statement and reflects the practice model underlying the agency or department's offerings (Sylvester et al., 2001). From the mission or purpose statement, goal statements are developed. Program goals are similar to individual plan goals, but relate to all the clients and outcomes for a program. Like the mission statement, goal statements are brief and reflect the intents of the previous statements (vision and mission). Generic statements for a recreation therapy department in a hospital or a therapeutic recreation unit in a public parks and recreation agency might read as follows:

Vision Statement

The program vision is to provide comprehensive quality experiences through individualized goal-directed plans using valid and reliable professional techniques in a cost conscious manner. Of utmost importance is enhancement of client functioning, dignity, integrity, health, and well-being within the context of an ever-changing environment. Programs and services are accomplished through teamwork and dedication of qualified recreation therapy professionals who uphold professional standards of ethics, practice, and accountability.

Mission and/or Purpose Statement

(1) The program incorporates assessment, diagnostic, rehabilitative, educational, health promotion, and leisure experiences to promote improved client health and well-being while coordinating and supporting programs and resources with clients, colleagues, caregivers, and supportive professionals.

(2) To provide through a comprehensive therapeutic recreation program those experiences that (a) benefit client health and well-being by impacting cognitive, social, physical, psychological, spiritual, and leisure functioning; (b) support the individual plan; and (c) enable clients to attain functionally appropriate levels of health, leisure well-being, and satisfaction.

Goal Statements

To provide an opportunity for clients to improve their functioning potential through a variety of diagnostic, treatment/rehabilitative, educational, health promotion, and leisure programs.

To provide an opportunity for the enhancement of client goals through collaborative efforts with health and human service professionals and caregivers.

To provide an opportunity for clients to experience leisure that benefits their health and well-being while enabling satisfaction.

A component defines one aspect of an agency/department program. Components are selected because they enable clients to achieve their individual plan goals, because they are feasible based on resource availability, and because they may be effectively managed. Together, the selected components comprise the program. A TRS determines program components by reviewing the department-level or agency-wide mission and goals (which reflect the assessment information). For example, a TRS may determine generic components such as (1) diagnostic and treatment interventions, (2) leisure education, and (3) health promotional experiences. Each component is then further defined by a purpose statement and goal statements. Collectively, the purpose and goal statements of each component define the overall mission and goals of the program and the structure or manner in which services will be organized and delivered. While including elements of the *program's* purpose and goals, the *components'* mission and goals are more specific. Below is an example of a treatment component purpose and goals:

Component Purpose

To provide an opportunity for clients through diagnostic, active treatment/ rehabilitative interventions to improve cognitive, social, physical, spiritual, and psychological well-being and leisure functioning in order to alleviate the effects of the disability while enhancing life and leisure satisfaction.

Component Goals

To provide an opportunity to develop, modify, and enhance health and well-being behaviors.

To provide an opportunity to develop leisure skills, interests, and resources in order to reduce the impact of the disability as identified in the interdisciplinary plan.

To provide an opportunity for the client and caregivers to develop an awareness of and an ability to access future life and leisure needs, assets, resources, and alternatives.

For each program component, the TRS develops protocols or specific activity plans that include outcome measures in objective statements, content and modality and facilitation techniques, adaptations, safety and risk-management procedures, resources needed to conduct the activities, and formative evaluation measures. Collectively, information contained in protocols includes structure, process, and outcome criteria used in quality improvement and describes clients for whom the experiences are beneficial. Because they define the input, process, and projected outcomes of intervention, protocols are used to increase the standardization of therapeutic recreation programs and services (Stumbo, 1996; Stumbo & Peterson, 2009). Protocols are the cornerstone of evidence-based practices because they describe the "best practice" or standardization of specific interventions with specific clients and "result from recent research evidence, literature reviews, or professional consensus" (Stumbo & Peterson, p. 231). Protocols also enable managers to design research and evaluation projects to collect efficacy data (Carter & O'Morrow, 2006). Protocol development is an ongoing activity. The scope of programs/services determines the number of protocols written. As program component goals and purpose statements are updated to better align with agency or department goals and mission statements, new protocols are written to explain alternative experiences. TRSs may maintain protocols in clients' charts or databases with hospitalized patients or with the program planning documents or databases in community therapeutic recreation. An abbreviated example of an activity protocol that might be prepared for the treatment component with inpatients or individuals in community aquatics is presented in exhibit 4.4.

After protocols are developed, the TRS shares this information with clients, caregivers, and colleagues through staffings and planning sessions. The information is disseminated in order to enhance communication and understanding and to promote program benefits as viable contributions to client well-being. Program managers prepare the agency's program schedule using the activity protocols to identify experiences offered in each of the program components. Preparation of a program schedule finds the TRS matching client needs with the reality of the program's resources, including available intervention time, space, physical and human resources, demands of other health and human services, and client and caregiver resources and expectations. A computer-generated schedule allows the TRS to more easily make adjustments for changed client health status or changes in colleague or facility availability.

Following schedule preparation, the TRS manager secures and/or assigns staff to program offerings and readies resources necessary to deliver these offerings. The manager then develops and posts a staff and facility schedule to ensure adequate program coverage and equipment/supply access. Staff and facility schedules should be designed with enough flexibility to accommodate the changing nature of clients' health conditions or staff responsibilities.

Exhibit 4.4   Activity Protocol Example

Activity Protocol

Program Area: Aquatics; Activity: Warm Water ROM

Referral: Individuals with ROM limitations resulting from CVA, arthritis, CP, paralysis, chronic pain and fatigue, spinal cord and traumatic brain injuries, MD

Objective: increase ROM by 25%
increase stamina by 10%
enhance self-care or ADL skills, e.g., dressing, undressing

Program description: Uses a heated community pool, small group, ROM exercises to improve stamina, flexibility, ambulation, independence, joint range of motion, body awareness, and self-care. Meets twice per week for 30-60 minutes with CTRS providing active/passive ROM, water resistance, water aerobics, stretching, relaxation exercises.

Safety/risk management: Medical referral required. Assistance with water entry-exit provided. Non-slip footwear required. Ratio 1 to 2. Monitor heart rate and blood pressure. Staff certified lifeguards, CPR/first aid, and recreational therapy aquatic training. Shallow water programming. Controlled air and water temperatures.

Resources: Goggles, floats, adapted entry-exit, non-slip surfaces, earplugs, extra towels, thera-bands, music.

Content/leadership sequence:

Structure Criteria	*Process Criteria*	*Outcome Criteria*
warm-up/safety check self-monitoring ↓ review/new activity ↓ practice/taper off ↓ debrief/evaluate	stretching/relaxation exercises, lower/upper body in small group ↓ passive/active ROM water walking/floating aerobic exercises and individual ambulation ↓ sitercise/deep breathing shallow water, small group activity	recording pre-session vitals & ROM ↓ ROM all joints ambulate "X" distance sustain "X" minutes and move through full range ↓ post-session vitals and ROM measurements

Notes/observations: "x" number of pts. achieved "x" number of IPP goals

The concluding task in planning a comprehensive program is coordinating and integrating the formative and summative evaluations on each client into the agency's quality improvement and evaluation plans. The timing and monitoring of evaluations is influenced by the agency's fiscal year and annual report period and by external reimbursement expectations from managed care providers. Evaluation intervals usually occur monthly, quarterly, or as clients' insurance companies reimburse for services rendered (for example, after 72 hours or three to five treatment days). When an agency offers a continuum of services, reviews may coincide with the client's transition from one level or type of program to the next or with aftercare and referral plans. Staff, together with clients, caregivers, and other professionals, identify the time and resources needed to monitor and evaluate the quality and appropriateness of each program component in accordance with funding stipulations and the agency's vision/ mission, protocols, and calendar.

Implementation

Three primary subtasks similar to those identified during the implementation of individual plans occur when an agency offers a comprehensive therapeutic recreation program: (1) clients enter into one or more of the programs/services, (2) their progress, satisfaction, and program outcomes are monitored and documented, and (3) adjustments are made in the agency's programs to better enhance clients' well-being and to ensure program quality and effectiveness.

TRSs typically oversee the individual plans of several clients while also designing and implementing several different programs, which might range from leisure education programs to specialty interventions like stress management classes, aquatics, and adventure/challenge activities. Staff simultaneously write individual plans and session plans or protocols while preparing for and conducting one-on-one or group sessions lasting from a few minutes (bedside) to several hours (special events).

In accordance with agency protocol, a program planner may periodically be called upon to monitor and document the progress of particular clients and specific program outcomes. For example, a staff member may recommend that a particular client's schedule be modified and also that different resources be introduced during a leisure education program.

The TRS must consider how the adjustments resulting from program modifications will impact other program participants, the staff, program resources, and the agency schedule. Program implementation is cyclical in nature; as one program is being implemented, staff are preparing the next. For example, while staff lead activities, they complete formative evaluations so data are available to justify adjustments in future program delivery. These modifications may occur in current programs or in the next cycle of seasonal programs.

Evaluation

The concluding phase of comprehensive TR program planning is collecting and reporting data in order to make revisions in the program. This ensures that clients will experience quality programs and appropriate transitions and aftercare, and provides information for the TRS to improve program delivery and outcomes (Stumbo & Peterson, 2009). In other words, evaluation documents the benefits of applying the therapeutic recreation process. As an advocate, the TRS shares the benefits with case managers, for example, and appropriate supporters and caregivers to promote continuity between settings and services. This is particularly important when clients participate over extended time periods (months rather than days) and the desire is to maintain leisure functioning in inclusive experiences (LeConey et al., 2000). Program improvement and evaluation processes and tools are similar in format and content to those used with IPPs and when evaluating the implementation of one program session.

TRSs collect summative data on content, leadership, management, fiscal and physical resources, and on the degree to which program component objectives and goals were achieved. Staff members analyze this data and make recommendations to discontinue programs, develop new programs, or continue the current programs with appropriate modifications. These evaluations occur when clients have completed preplanned time periods and when programs come to natural endings following predetermined schedules. TRSs establish these time periods by considering the fiscal calendar, reimbursement protocols, accreditation standards, and operating calendars of other health and human service team members, such as special educators or hospital clinicians.

Evaluations focus on aspects of program quality including effectiveness, efficiency, and ethics (Sylvester et al., 2001). They answer the questions: Does analysis of data collected on clients' individual plans and program components suggest that content, leadership, and resources were (1) beneficial to the clients and (2) effectively and efficiently managed? Knowledge generated through evaluation guides TRSs' decision making and clinical judgments. That is, evaluation answers questions about the desirability of client outcomes and program experiences and provides evidence to suggest causal relationships between interventions and client outcomes (Sylvester et al.). TRSs collect data from participants, caregivers, staff, and administrators about staffing, programs and services, and resources. Data are analyzed and reported in program summaries, year-end reports, specialists' program reports, and annual reports. TRSs present and review these documents during staff meetings, administrative hearings with supervisors, and in sessions with professional and lay committees on quality improvement, safety audits, and budget preparation.

One method to evaluate comprehensive therapeutic recreation programs and services is through quality improvement (QI) programs (Stumbo, 1996; Stumbo & Peterson, 2009). QI indicators in mission statements and protocols comprise the targets or benchmarks that measure effectiveness and identify areas to be improved. When the TRS systematically collects data for a particular group or groups of individuals to document effectiveness, efficacy research determines the benefits of service delivery (Stumbo; Stumbo & Peterson). Efficacy research considers the interactions among content, leadership, management, fiscal and physical resources, and their relationship to achievement of client outcomes. Program effectiveness is recorded in case studies, quality improvement audits and reviews, and as critical pathways are monitored and revised. The reporting of program effectiveness and outcomes is crucial, since the "accountability demands of external reviewers and payers are increasingly focused on the . . . utility of particular services to effective and efficient" intervention (Witman, 1994, p. 86).

Agency or department programs are revised when decisions are made to reassign staff, reallocate monies, utilize different physical resources, or initiate new programs more compatible with clients' plans and aftercare and transition options. Major program modifications are instituted to coincide with seasonal calendars, fiscal year changeovers, and as major changes occur in program clientele.

SUMMARY

The programming process of assessment, planning, implementation, and evaluation (APIE) is applicable to individual plans and to comprehensive therapeutic recreation programs within departments or agencies. A client-centered, interdisciplinary approach benefits participants' health and well-being while reducing the effects of disability or illness. Likewise this approach aligns with perspectives of the WHO-ICF and *Healthy People 2010*, which realize that health and well-being are influenced by one's personal factors and community interactions. The APIE approach involves clients and significant others in the process and recognizes that programs are initiated and discontinued when clients do not realize desired outcomes or when they, for whatever reason, are no longer responsive to the offered programs.

During each of the four phases, specific tasks are undertaken that enable TRSs to design new programs or to redevelop previously existing ones. Assessment is a data-gathering or fact-finding phase. TRSs use information from assessments as they write goals and objectives during the planning phase. Goal and objective statements specify outcome measures and guide TRSs in selecting content, modalities, and facilitation techniques; securing the necessary resources, and preparing evaluation plans, which outline formative and summative evaluation processes and measures.

The implementation phase occurs when clients participate in therapeutic recreation programs. TRSs monitor and document clients' performances using various record-keeping techniques (POMR, SOAP notes, PIE, focus charting, flow charts, CBE). They evaluate program quality with standardized and staff-prepared tools and measure the results against internal and external regulatory standards. Formative evaluation guides program revision *during* program implementation.

In the concluding phase, evaluation, TRSs collect summative data. The TRS evaluates the evidence collected against the program's philosophy and approach to make deliberate decisions and judgments for future programming. They present reports on the effectiveness and quality of programs during staff meetings and program management meetings and prepare transition plans for clients. These reports also are used as quality improvement mechanisms and to develop databases for efficacy research. TRSs revise, update, or discontinue individual plans and comprehensive therapeutic recreation plans to ensure congruence between desired client outcomes and program quality. Decisions made in this final phase reflect financial and resource allocations and efforts to comply with internal and external standard-setting bodies, also recognizing the interrelationship between the client's health and culturally sensitive practices.

Key Terms

activity analysis Study of leisure experiences to identify the cognitive, social, physical, and psychological/spiritual behaviors present in each.

charting by exception (CBE) A documentation form that occurs only when there is a positive or negative variance from standards or protocols.

clinical, critical pathway Guidelines for intervention by team members pre-sented according to a time sequence similar to the flow-charting documentation technique.

continuous quality improvement (CQI) Written quality assurance plans mandated by professional standards of practice and external accrediting agencies to promote ongoing service quality.

data, action, response, plan (DARP) notes A documentation form in narrative focus charting that organizes client data according to these four categories of information.

efficacy research Systematic collection of data to determine service effectiveness and benefits of service delivery to the client.

evidence-based practices The use of research, literature, and consensus to select interventions effective with clients having specific needs.

formative evaluation Also known as process evaluation; the ongoing collection of information as programs are implemented that allows a manager to make immediate, informed decisions as required.

interdisciplinary team Specialists representative of different professions who exchange information and resources to enable the integrated development of client plans and transitions among health and human service agencies.

managed care provider An agency, like an HMO (health maintenance organization), that monitors providers' health care expenditures.

objective assessment data Information based on observable facts and uninfluenced by emotion or personal prejudices, beliefs, or ideas.

outcome measure Identifies the degree to which the client will benefit from program participation as stated in objective statements.

privileging Process used to grant staff the right to perform tasks essential to a particular job, providing that staff display and maintain competence.

problem, intervention, evaluation (PIE) Documentation form that organizes client data by problem with corresponding intervention(s) and evaluation listed by problem.

problem-oriented medical records (POMR) A documentation form that organizes client data according to behaviors or problems. The chart is organized according to five categories: database, problem list, plans, progress notes, and discharge summary.

program A preplanned intervention consisting of experiences with definitive outcomes.

protocol A written plan that describes the specific steps involved in the delivery of programs and services.

service An exchange between the TRS and client in a helping relationship that may be intangible yet promotes client growth and well-being, e.g., sharing information on resources or referral options.

source-oriented documentation System in which each professional discipline documents client achievements and progress toward satisfying the outcome measures in their section of the chart.

subjective, objective, assessment, plan (SOAP) notes A documentation form that organizes client data in the narrative portion of the treatment plan according to these four categories of information as the plan is written.

subjective assessment data Information based on feelings and personal experiences.

summative evaluation Also known as product or outcome evaluation; assessment that occurs after clients have concluded participation or programs have ended. Involves analyzing program and client outcomes to revise future plans.

task analysis Listing in sequence the skills required to perform a particular activity successfully.

theory-based practices Use of theories to guide practice and explain which programs and services contribute to intended outcomes.

written plan of operation A compilation of documents, such as policy and procedure outlines, job descriptions, and vision/mission statements, that serve as guidelines for the administration of a department or program.

Study Questions

1. What are the quality indicators (QI) described in the IPO model?
2. What cognitive, social, physical, psychological, spiritual, and leisure behaviors do TRSs consider during the assessment phase of designing individual plans?
3. What specific tools and techniques are employed by TRSs to gather assessment data? Provide examples of cultural sensitivity expressed during assessment.
4. According to the professional standards of practice, what must be included in individual plans?
5. What are the criteria for writing statements with measurable outcomes?
6. Why is the writing of client goals and objectives the first step in the planning phase of an IPP? What tasks follow?
7. What is the relationship between the individual plan and the comprehensive therapeutic recreation plan?
8. What is process, or formative, evaluation and when does it occur?
9. What is product, or summative, evaluation and when does it occur?
10. What types of information are included in discharge/referral/transition plans? Give examples of how this information is moderated by the client's culture.
11. What are the relationships among client and program evaluation and quality improvement and efficacy research?
12. Explain how evidence-based practices and theory are used in program design.

Practical Experiences to Enhance Student Objectives

1. Using the objectives for the discharge goal illustrated in the chapter and the three ways to adapt activities in exhibit 4.3, identify alternative experiences to satisfy the intent of each objective.
2. Interview a TRS about the planning process he or she employs in the agency/department where he or she works. Compare the steps taken by this person to develop either an individual or comprehensive program plan to the models presented in this chapter.
3. Conduct an Internet search of agency home pages to collect department and agency documents describing the comprehensive therapeutic recreation programs they offer. Using the CPP statements (vision, mission, and goals) presented as examples in the second half of this chapter, critique your collected resources and note how they might be improved.

4. Visit with a CTRS to gain permission to observe clients in programs. Then, for one person you observe, review available documentation to identify the following information:

   - subjective data
   - objective data
   - goals
   - outcome measures
   - content, and modalities and facilitation techniques
   - evaluation data
   - transition considerations

5. Discuss the spontaneous nature of client-TRS interactions with a person in the field. Identify unpredictable client experiences that could happen during planned programs. Are there particular events that cause unanticipated client reactions? How does the TRS accommodate these uncertainties and what are the responsibilities of a program planner in these situations?

6. Through Internet searches and personal contacts, collect and examine (clinical) critical pathways and protocols. Compare the QI indicators found in the collected documents. Discuss with a TRS their use with clients and their compatibility with regulatory standards.

7. Returning to the service delivery model presented in chapter 1, identify for each component the appropriate vision/mission/goal statements using the statements presented in this chapter as a model.

Therapeutic Recreation Management

After reading this chapter, students will be able to

✔ Demonstrate familiarity with the content of written plans of operation, including vision, mission, value, and goal statements; organization structure; scope of care and unit structure; programs and services offered; protocols and intervention plans; policies, procedures and rules; staff credentials; quality improvement; and participant/program evaluation and research

✔ Describe the basics of financial management practices, including methods of financing therapeutic recreation services, rate setting, cost allocation, and budgeting processes

✔ Discuss the significant roles of marketing, advocacy, and networking in therapeutic recreation

✔ Identify the elements of continuous quality improvement programs and productivity measurements

✔ Identify the elements of risk and safety management programs

✔ Describe a TR manager's responsibilities related to accessibility and inclusion

✔ Evaluate the impact of technology and information systems in therapeutic recreation management

✔ Discuss the role of ethics in managing therapeutic recreation practices

✔ Identify personnel functions essential to program operation

✔ Explain the importance of training, supervision, performance management, and diversity in the workplace

✔ Describe the role of the manager with teams, paraprofessionals, interns, and volunteers

Students about to enter the therapeutic recreation field will quickly learn that, in addition to client/program assessment, planning, implementation, and evaluation, the success of a program is highly dependent on many factors related to the management of services, such as fiscal and personnel management. Many fine programs fail not because they are inadequately planned, implemented, and evaluated, but because the underlying foundations or support systems are weak or inadequately managed. Since management has a direct bearing on the ultimate degree of success clients experience in therapeutic recreation programs, information is included in this introductory text to help you develop the ability to identify and appreciate issues that are critical to the operation of therapeutic recreation services in health and human service settings.

INTRODUCTION

Management is the process of accomplishing goals through others. In therapeutic recreation services, like other health and human services, good management is perceived as "a means of achieving increased efficiency among health-care personnel and better accountability" (Hunter, 1996, p. 799). Professionals find they must focus not only on their clients' needs but also on management issues surrounding service delivery that impact all constituents. TRSs are charged with providing safe, effective, innovative services that enhance client satisfaction and improve their functioning and quality of life, while keeping the lid on costs. In other words, they are expected to combine a caring ethos with operational savvy (Center for the Health Professions, 1998).

A number of factors underscore the need for TRSs to acquire an understanding of and degree of skill in management activities. The complexity and scope of health and human service organizations has grown considerably since the 1950s (Carter & O'Morrow, 2006). A more diverse, articulate, and well-informed clientele requires TRSs to relate to service users in complex ways (Hunter, 1996). A "customer" orientation compels TRSs to support their clients as they take on increased responsibility during interventions. Professionals are expected to link evidence-based practices to client outcomes in a results-driven environment impacted by global technology. Rising consumer demand and beneficiary roles, increasing fiscal challenges, terrorism, natural disasters, and the cost of catastrophic diseases worldwide also have impacted an already competitive and constrained health-care environment. Consequently, managers focus on **cost benefits** while TRSs document the impact of their services on client functional capacity, health status, and quality of life.

This chapter is organized into four sections: a written plan of operation, financial operations, technical operations, and personnel operations. Each section covers several topics. The location of therapeutic recreation services within the administrative structure of an agency or department influences the nature of the manager's functions. Also, the nature of the agency determines the extent to which certain management responsibilities are required. For example, the initial section of the chapter considers treatment protocols and program plans. Health-care settings are more likely to require that man-

Chapter 5 was revised with contributions from Dana Dempsey, MS, CTRS, and the staff of the Therapeutic Recreation Department, Scottish Rite Hospital for Children, Dallas, Texas; Sandra K. Negley, MS, MTRS/CTRS Expressive Therapies of the University of Utah Neuropsychiatric Institute, Salt Lake City; and Ray E. West, MS, LRT/CTRS, consultant, Chapel Hill, North Carolina.

agers design treatment protocols, while TRSs in special recreation associations are apt to prepare program plans. While the nature of accountability may vary from one setting to another, managers are responsible for implementing and monitoring protocols and programs to ensure safe, effective client outcomes *and* fiscal accountability. In other areas, as with staff credentials and program and/or client evaluation and research, managerial responsibilities vary little regardless of the type of agency or clientele.

Health care and human services are provided in a variety of settings and through diverse agencies and associations. While some organizations provide a full spectrum or continuum of care, others are single-focus agencies: A health-care facility that provides inpatient treatment, ambulatory care, home health care, and hospice care represents a wide range of services, while an agency like The Arc of the United States provides social and educational services (including recreation) to individuals with intellectual and developmental disabilities, representing a single-service focus. Thus, the functions to be managed vary with not only the complexity and scope of the agency but also with the nature of the clientele, the number of TRSs employed by the agency, the focus of the agency, and the internal and external standards governing agency operation. This chapter introduces a number of management functions that require varying amounts of a professional's daily work time. The extent to which TRSs divide their time between direct client service and functions like budgeting and marketing is unique to each position within each particular agency.

A WRITTEN PLAN OF OPERATION

According to professional standards of practice, a written plan of operation ensures that therapeutic recreation services achieve desired goals. A written plan of operation guides the TRS as services and resources are managed. Such a plan incorporates information found in policy and procedure manuals, governing codes and regulations, recorded minutes, and executive orders. It reflects the organization's goals and mission; when the agency's sole function is therapeutic recreation (as with special recreation associations), the plan of operation includes all written documents that define the services offered and describes procedures to manage resources and personnel (ATRA, 2000). Although variations exist among agencies, common elements of a written plan of operation include vision, mission, value, and goal statements; organization structure; scope of care, and programs and services offered; protocols and procedures; staff credentialing; quality improvement; and evaluation and research processes. Examples of these elements and documents unique to particular organizations are presented.

Vision, Mission, Value, and Goal Statements

A **vision** is a statement defining what an organization believes in and focuses on the future or end results; a **mission statement** defines the unique reason or purpose a therapeutic recreation service exists and the intent that it serves (Taylor, 2006). A vision statement "describes an image of the organization's preferred future" and provides "a description of what the organization will look like if it achieves its true potential" (Wegner & Jarvi, 2005, p. 111). The mission statement clarifies the vision and answers the question, "How will the world be different as a result of providing this therapeutic recreation service"? **Goals** provide direction, describing the outcomes and client benefits derived from the therapeutic recreation service or program. Goals connect the mission and vision by identifying how the agency intends to organize its work to achieve the preferred future. Writing clear vision, mission, and goal statements is a means to articulate organizational efforts and commit the therapeutic recreation service to continual improvement.

Therapeutic recreation providers may also have separate philosophy and value statements. A **philosophy statement** identifies the basic concepts, values, beliefs, and/or theories about a service or outcome so that services are connected to the mission and vision of the organization (Taylor, 2006). **Value** statements are reference points to describe a program to its stakeholders. Value statements are influenced by professional and regulatory practices, standards, and trends. Values guide the TRS during the helping relationship as interventions are implemented and are reflected in operational decisions of managers. Values appear with mission and vision statements: They are foundational to program direction, client health, performance expectations, and organizational change. Exhibit 5.1 provides vision, mission, and value statements for a special recreation association while Exhibit 5.2 contains a statement of purpose for a therapeutic recreation department in a children's hospital. Exhibit 5.3 contains the purpose, philosophy, and mission statements of a treatment team in a neuropsychiatric institute.

Organizational Structure

As mentioned in the introduction, a diverse array of agencies provides health-care and human services. The organization and autonomy of therapeutic recreation services is influenced by an agency's enabling legislation; in other words, the legal basis for the agency's existence; the agency's vision, mission, values, and goals; the nature of the agency's clientele; the types and number of other services provided by the agency; and the regulatory agencies that set the governing standards for the agency's programs and services. Organizational charts present schematics of how the parts of an organization are linked. Managers find these charts in agency policy and procedure manuals.

Therapeutic recreation services may be the sole function of an agency like a special recreation association (figure 5.1 on page 160). Another common structure finds TRSs organized into a separate department in a health-care setting (figure 5.2 on page 161) or a therapeutic recreation division of a public recreation agency (figure 5.3 on page 162). The organization of therapeutic recreation services must be compatible with the existing agency organizational structure. An agency's organizational chart will help the TRS identify "formal organizational relationships, areas of responsibility, persons accountable, and channels of communication" (Carter & O'Morrow, 2006, p. 27). Position descriptions complement organizational charts by defining the scope of responsibilities, specific duties required to be performed, scope of authority for decisions made, and reporting relationships, as well as necessary competencies and required qualifications and credentials. Collectively, the staff who assume the positions within each service unit enable an agency to achieve its mission. Although

Exhibit 5.1   Special Recreation Association: Vision, Mission, and Values

Our Vision

The Fox Valley Special Recreation Association (FVSRA) enriches the lives of people with disabilities within the communities it serves. Formed in 1976 as an extension of the Fox Valley, Geneva, St. Charles, Batavia, Sugar Grove, Oswegoland Park Districts and the Village of South Elgin Parks and Recreation Department, we provide a diverse range of year-round recreational opportunities to enable residents with disabilities to experience active, healthy, and playful lifestyles.

Through innovative partnerships and advocacy, FVSRA seeks to be regarded as THE community resource for individuals and families of people with disabilities within our service region. Recognizing the diversity of the member agencies and populations we serve, we pledge to be "customer focused" in our approach to governance and service delivery. We further recognize that our organization's long-term stability and consistency are vitally important to those we serve.

In the years ahead we will continue to focus on sustaining and improving high user satisfaction with the services we deliver as well as those we recommend to our customers. Through education, awareness, and advocacy we will strive to remove all barriers that may inhibit people with disabilities from achieving maximum enjoyment, satisfaction, and fulfillment in their lives.

Mission Statement

The Fox Valley Special Recreation Association exists to enrich the lives of people with disabilities. Working collaboratively with member agencies and community partners, we pledge to put PEOPLE FIRST.

Our Values

People First

We pledge that in all our actions the individual will be foremost and the disability secondary.

Fair & Equal Access

We pledge nondiscriminatory and equal access to all programs and services. We value the privacy and confidentiality of those we serve and are committed to honoring the trust and confidence placed in our staff.

Respect

We will always display the highest respect for the diversity of our participants, their families, member agencies, community partners, and one another.

Safety

Programs and services will always be operated in accordance with adopted risk management standards to ensure the utmost safety of participants, employees, and guests.

Commitment to the Cause

We strive to achieve the highest level of excellence in all we do. We will commit to the highest professional and ethical standards in all our work.

Partnering

We value strong partnerships with our member agencies and community organizations.

Communication & Outreach

Recognizing the many stakeholders that contribute to our success, we pledge to interact clearly and often, maintaining strong lines of communication.

Enriching Lives

We seek to continually identify and be responsive to community and participant needs and to provide high quality service, expanding opportunities for those we serve.

Used with permission of Carolyn J. Nagle, CTRS, Fox Valley Special Recreation Association, Aurora, Illinois.

Exhibit 5.2   Therapeutic Recreation Department: Statement of Purpose

We understand that recreation and leisure are basic needs and a necessary part of a well-balanced and healthy life. While a child is a patient of TSRHC (Texas Scottish Rite Hospital for Children), therapeutic recreation services will be provided upon referral supervised by a CTRS. Services are designed to contribute toward a child's growth, independent leisure functioning, and optimal health. This is achieved through the provision of a variety of leisure services including:

- leisure education focusing on personal interests, leisure support systems, and community leisure resources;
- leisure activities which promote a healthy sense of self and perspective of self in relation to society;
- a balanced selection of therapeutic recreation activities to develop and maintain essential recreation and leisure skills (e.g. activity, social interaction, communication, problem solving, conflict resolution);
- leisure experiences which provide therapeutic interactions and model appropriate behavioral expressions; and
- recreation and sports activities.

Used with permission of the Therapeutic Recreation Department, Texas Scottish Rite Hospital for Children, Dallas, Texas.

Exhibit 5.3   Expressive Therapies Department:
Purpose, Philosophy, and Team Mission

Purpose

The Expressive Therapies (ET) Services are an integral part of the client's treatment at the University of Utah Neuropsychiatric Institute (UNI). These services provide therapeutic intervention in order to meet the physical, social, emotional, cultural, recreation, health, and wellness needs of the clients. A specific treatment plan is designed to meet individual needs while also promoting various phases of group involvement to enhance functioning in family, social and leisure life. The Expressive Therapies Services also maintains a primary role in providing outreach and community services for the hospital through the challenge course program (R.O.P.E.S.) and other educational programs.

Philosophy

The Expressive Therapies Services assesses, plans, implements, and evaluates treatment through patient participation in a variety of group and one-on-one experiences. The prescribed interventions are used to improve patient's social functioning, leisure functioning, daily living, coping skills, self-esteem, personal awareness, expression of feelings, and overall knowledge of improved quality of life.

Team Mission

To provide safe, effective, and age-appropriate programming and clinical treatment for all levels of care, in a changing health-care environment; and to promote an atmosphere of staff/client support and respect.

Used with permission of the Expressive Therapies Department, University of Utah Neuropsychiatric Institute (UNI), Salt Lake City, Utah.

health-care and human service systems are being streamlined through the use of cross-functional teams and by mergers—with resulting structural changes from hierarchical to flat—organizational charts nevertheless help employees know to whom they are responsible and how the various jobs and services within the organization are linked.

Scope of Care and Unit Structure

The **scope of care** section of the written plan of operation describes the services provided as well as the goals and objectives for each service. Using the therapeutic recreation service model described in chapter 1, the scope of service section might include those services designed to facilitate diagnosis/assessment, treatment/rehabilitation, education, and/or health promotion. This section of the plan of operation defines the structure of programs and services offered by the specific unit.

A number of factors influence the scope of care and subsequently its structure. These include increased access to technology, health information, and global health care; focus on holistic and integrative health; sensitivity to personal, cultural, and community influences; demands of accountability, cost containment, safety, and quality; and the recognition of theory and evidence as integral to service justification and viability. These influences compel professionals to consider, for example, the WHO-ICF model and *Healthy People 2010* initiatives as they prepare a service scope.

Scope of care descriptions define the services provided and create complementary organizational structures to meet the needs of an ever-changing competitive environment. Although the past trend has been for TRSs to become more specialized, the future trend for health-care and human service providers is to develop multiskilled team members whose scope of care extends beyond a single client to all stakeholders, incorporates clients and caregivers as collaborators, and whose responsibilities encompass a full continuum of care from client education to experiences that contribute to health and quality of life (Carter, 1999; Howard, Russoniello, & Rogers, 2004; Hunter, 1996; Porter & VanPuymbroeck, 2007; Shank & Coyle, 2002). The scope of care and treatment modalities of the Expressive Therapies Department of the Utah Neuropsychiatric Institute (refer to exhibit 5.4 on page 163) illustrate the essential scope of care elements and the changing nature of TRS responsibilities.

Programs and Services Offered

The scope of care defines the types of programs and services offered by a service unit (refer to exhibit 5.4). For example, a continuum from inpatient to in-home services may be offered by departments in hospital settings. Programs and services with a more specific focus—like inclusion—are offered through, for example, nonprofit agencies (e.g., the Arc) whose missions are more specific. TRSs develop specific program plans for each program and service defined by the scope of care. Each specific plan identifies the particular unit goal supported by the program or service (Sylvester, Voelkl, & Ellis, 2001) as well as a purpose, goals, outcome statements, interventions, and leadership strategies (refer to chapter 4 for specific examples). Management responsibilities vary with the types of programs and services offered. Where a continuum of care is evident, a manager's tasks encompass all aspects of operation from personnel and financing through technical operations. If the scope of care is limited to,

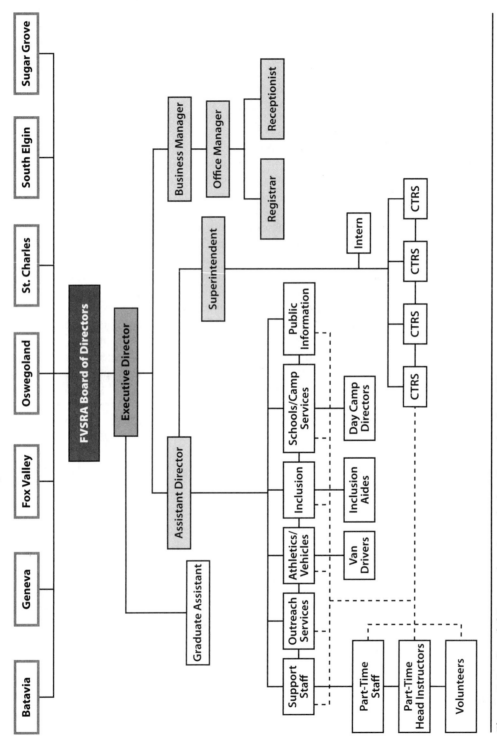

Figure 5.1   Special Recreation Association Organizational Chart

Used with permission of Carolyn J. Nagle, CTRS, Fox Valley Special Recreation Association, Aurora, Illinois.

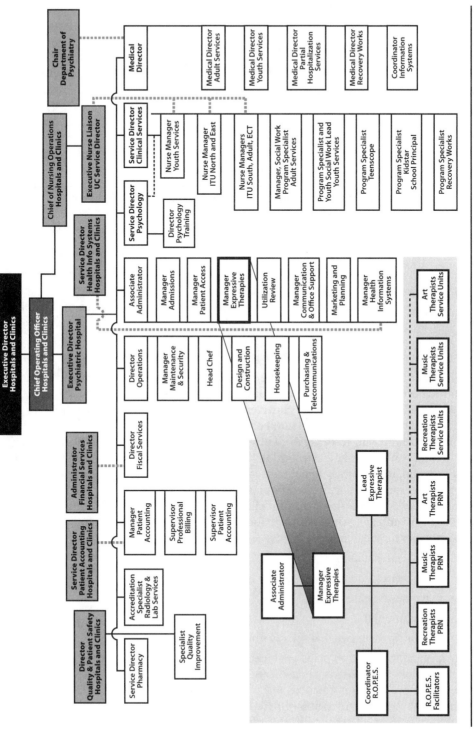

Figure 5.2   Hospital/Clinic Organizational Chart
Used with permission of the University of Utah Neuropsychiatric Institute (UNI), Salt Lake City, Utah.

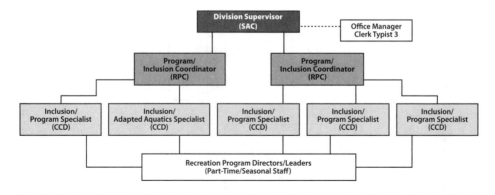

Figure 5.3   Recreation Commission, Division of Therapeutic Recreation Organizational Chart
Used with permission of the Cincinnati Recreation Commission, Therapeutic Division, Cincinnati, Ohio.

for example, programming inclusive options, a manager's tasks may focus on specific operational aspects like advocacy and networking. Regardless of setting, it is likely that to some degree managers will perform tasks considered in each area outlined in this chapter.

Protocols and Intervention Plans

Managers prepare protocols or intervention plans for each program and service area. Programs and services tend to be offered to clients with similar needs (Sylvester, Voelkl, & Ellis, 2001). Protocols and intervention plans outline best practices for a specific activity with a specific client(s) or client need(s) "that have been standardized and result from recent research evidence, literature reviews, or professional consensus" (Stumbo & Peterson, 2009, p. 231). Two types of protocols exist. One is written for a program, for example, aquatic therapy, while the other is prepared for a diagnosis or problem area, like depression (Stumbo & Peterson). Protocols tend to be used in hospitals, while intervention plans are more often found in settings other than acute and/or inpatient care. Although their formats are not necessarily uniform, the two protocol types have common elements:

- referral information
- assessment summaries of client assets and/or problems
- outcomes expected
- intervention(s)
- leadership strategies that specify safety and risk measures

Protocols and intervention plans are blueprints TRSs use as they interact with clients on a day-to-day basis. Managers use these to document benefits of therapeutic recreation, to assess staff performance, and to develop efficacy and effectiveness studies important to the standardization of practice, quality improvement plans, and validation of best practices. These documents may be found in manuals prepared for accred-

Exhibit 5.4   Scope of Care and Treatment Modalities

Scope of Care

- Patients with all psychiatric diagnoses as outlined under UNI's admission criteria
- Families of patients as it relates to client's treatment
- Serve patient ages ranging from four to very old, as outlined by UNI's admission criteria
- Programs receiving services:
  - Adult services
  - Youth services
  - Outpatient
  - Community

Treatment Modalities

Treatment modalities include: art therapy, music therapy, and recreational therapy.

- *Art therapy:* Art as a treatment modality is based on the knowledge that every individual has a latent capacity to project feelings, perceptions, and conflicts into visual forms. Art provides an expressive form for communication, socialization, and manipulation of the environment. It reflects an individual's ability to recall and convey the past, it documents aspects of the present condition, and it lends itself to communication and expression. The therapist will typically make use of verbal explorations and interventions as well.

- *Music therapy:* Music therapy is the scientific application of music in a therapeutic prescription to address non-musical treatment goals. A music therapist utilizes the medium of music to improve or maintain cognitive functioning, to facilitate social and emotional growth, to promote communication, and to facilitate reduction of stress. The music therapist designs sessions for groups and individuals based on client needs using interventions such as: music improvisation, receptive music listening, song writing, lyric analysis, imagery, movement, and toning.

- *Recreational therapy/therapeutic recreation:* Utilizes recreation and other activities as a form of "active treatment." Recreation interventions are designed for diagnostic observation, prevention, or treatment, to restore, rehabilitate or remediate in order to improve functioning and independence, as well as reduce or eliminate the effects if illness (ATRA, 2003). The primary goal is to preserve or improve the functional ability in order to enhance the client's coping skills, utilization of community integration, and overall quality of life.

Used with permission of the Expressive Therapies Department, University of Utah Neuropsychiatric Institute (UNI), Salt Lake City, Utah.

itation visits [Joint Commission (JC), CARF International] or state inspections (CMS), or in the programming sections of department operational manuals. A generic example is presented in chapter 4 (refer to exhibit 4.4).

Policies, Procedures, and Rules

The specific directions that establish how programs and services are to be operated are contained in an agency's policies, procedures, and rules. While the therapeutic recreation staff is obligated to follow the agency's policies and procedures, such as requiring documentation of a physician's order for therapeutic recreation in the medical record or documenting client preferences, additional rules may be necessary to maintain order and consistency in daily operations and staff performance. In other words, the agency's policy and procedure manual may include general instructions for conducting therapeutic outings, whereas the program's rules might identify staff-to-participant ratios or expected client behaviors.

The number of policies, procedures, and rules necessary for effective management of a TR program will depend upon the number and nature of the guidelines established by the agency. If an agency has elaborate and well-defined policies and procedures, then only those policies, procedures, and rules that relate specifically to therapeutic recreation service provision need to be developed. A guide to developing policies, procedures, and rules for therapeutic recreation is to determine what elements are minimally necessary to assure safe and effective service provision and achievement of client objectives and benefits.

Commonly, one or more manuals outlining policies specific to therapeutic recreation personnel, programs, participants, and administration are necessary. Policies may also appear in program brochures and agency reports. New or revised policies must be approved by appropriate governing boards and/or managers. When these documents are updated, managers provide training to inform staff, clients, caregivers, and agency administrators of the implications of new policies.

Staff Credentials

Managers are responsible for documenting in the plan of operation their staff members' credentials and the procedures that ensure staff maintain their competence in areas relevant to the programs and services offered. The importance of maintaining staff competence is set forth in a number of regulatory documents and by agents that guide the practice of health-care professionals (JCAHO, 2005). Standards require that staff competence be assessed annually and anytime there is a change in practice standards (Whelan, 2006). Further, the manager must define competencies for each position and ensure that employees maintain and improve their competence. **Competency assessment** is incorporated into the staffing process with written job descriptions, screening for position vacancies, initial skills assessments conducted during orientation, performance appraisals, and professional development plans.

The ATRA professional standards of practice identify the CTRS credential as the minimum level of competence necessary for staff members who deliver treatment services (ATRA, 2000). The CTRS credential encompasses job tasks critical to competent practice and knowledge and skills essential to competent entry-level performance (NCTRC, 2007). Yet, as noted by Dieser (2005/2006) and reported by Riley and Connolly (2007), the CTRS examination is rooted in a dominant culture and practiced predominately by Caucasian females. Consequently, relevance as an international measure of entry-level competence will be important to establish. Managers maintain copies of staff credentials like the CTRS certificate in their human resource files; when, if for example, an accreditation visitor from the Joint Commission requests documentation of staff competency, the manager can present appropriate certificates (e.g., registrations, certifications, licenses) and records of earned continuing education units.

In some health-care and human service agencies, particularly hospitals, established **privileging criteria** ensure staff are competent to practice and remain competent to deliver specific services like stress management, adventure-challenge, or aquatic programs. The manager outlines these criteria and identifies in the plan of operation how staff competence is assessed and maintained and privileging criteria are satisfied (Carter, Washington, Witman, & Beck, 1994).

Quality Improvement

Quality and patient safety are major concerns of health-care and human service organizations. What began with accreditation efforts to evaluate adequacy of client care in the 1950s has evolved in the twenty-first century to improving safety and providing patient-centered care using scientific information or evidence-based practices (Carter & O'Morrow, 2006; Lee & McCormick, 2002). The Patient Safety and Quality Improvement Act of 2005 brings to the forefront the importance of information technology for sharing ideas and increasing knowledge among clients and professionals in order to improve quality care and safety while reducing health-care costs and disparities (Kinnaman, 2007).

Professional standards of practice outline the components of quality improvement (QI) programs to be included in the plan of operation. These include monitoring and evaluation, peer review, risk/safety management, infection control, case review, and record documentation. In addition to legislation and professional standards of

One component of a quality improvement program is case review by the treatment team.

practice, external accreditation bodies like the Joint Commission and CARF International require written plans to monitor and improve patient safety and services while developing databases and sharing information with stakeholders so all make informed decisions about health care.

Utilization review describes a process used to assure medical necessity of services and care effectiveness. Retrospective (after service) and concurrent (during service) reviews examine the *frequency* (how often an intervention is scheduled, such as twice a day), *duration* (length of each intervention, such as 30 minutes), and *intensity* (need for specialized services such as aquatic therapy versus physical rehabilitation) of services provided to ensure they can reasonably be expected to improve the patient's functioning. As one element of the manager's QI program, procedures outline how patient charts or client case studies will be reviewed to document service necessity and effectiveness. Managers design quality improvement plans and incorporate them into operational manuals. A sample quality improvement plan is presented later in the chapter in exhibit 5.6. It is important to note that since the agency or program QI team may not necessarily have first-hand experience with TR standards of practice and efficacy research, the TR manager and staff must articulate salient theories and evidence to support TR practices and intervention outcomes.

Participant/Program Evaluation and Research

A written plan of operation describes both client and program evaluation types, and the research methods used by the TRS to measure outcomes, substantiate theories, and gather evidence of effectiveness, quality outcomes, and safety. An evaluation plan identifies formative and summative evaluation methods while outlining the relationships among evaluation and quality improvement factors. Professional standards of practice indicate that managers must identify procedures to protect human subjects and to use the results of evaluation and research to improve service function and demonstrate effectiveness (refer to chapter 4 for discussion on evaluation).

Research has become an important professional issue, partially as a response to pressures to demonstrate the efficacy of therapeutic recreation services (Carruthers, 1997/1998). Efficacy research is concerned with outcome measurement and documenting which services are most beneficial with respect to given client needs (Malkin, Coyle, & Carruthers, 1998). There also is a desire to document value to a clientele that is culturally diverse and that experiences TR interventions through a wide array of professional practice settings (Wilhite, Keller, Collins, & Jacobson, 2003). Further, the explosion of information, advancements in technology, and globalization of medicine require TRSs to use evidence-based practices to assure consistent and predictable outcomes and to manage the increasing amounts of specialized information on health and behavior (Buettner & Fitzsimmons, 2007). Measurement results are essential to assessment, which guides the TRS's decisions and judgments as the TR process is applied and to outcome documentation that relies on accurate data to affirm change (Zabriskie, 2003). Thus, evaluation and research are prerequisites to providing appropriate interventions, to demonstrating utility in emerging service areas, and gathering evidence to substantiate professional performance (Buettner & Fitzsimmons; Wilhite et al.; Zabriskie).

FINANCIAL OPERATIONS

"During the first half of the twentieth century, the practice of medicine was simple and straightforward" (Roth, 1997, p. 715). Fees were relatively small and payments could be made by the patient with exchange of goods and services. By the 1980s, economic constraints prompted the government to design a prospective payment system for diagnostically related groups (DRGs). A number of managed care options (MCOs) emerged to monitor service provision while controlling costs by ensuring payment based on usual and customary needs. For example, preferred provider organizations (PPOs) provide services on a fee-for-service basis with incentives of lowered rates when the PPO is used. In the late 1990s, the government reaffirmed a **prospective payment system (PPS)** for government providers—a method of reimbursement based upon paying a prearranged amount for specific services no matter what the actual cost of those services might be. Reimbursement for services according to reasonable cost was defined as those services essential to treatment of a specific patient or patient population based on a predetermined rate adjusted by case mix or RUG (resource utilization group)—used primarily in skilled nursing facilities (SNF). Another cost containment option involves "group" rate setting by private employers. A number of employers contract to cover their employee health-care needs by **capitation** (fixed payment defined for a range of health-care services for a specific group of individuals). As Roth (1997) notes, this change from fee-for-service or retrospective payment to gatekeeper or prospective payment has altered the face of traditional medical practice.

The twenty-first century finds managers challenged by increasing pressures to contain health-care costs while maintaining quality (Leeth, 2004). A number of converging factors have propelled health-care costs to rise almost three times faster than the Consumer Price Index (Scanlon, 2006). Complex reimbursement methodologies, rising consumer demand, more provider choices, swelling beneficiary rolls, technology, care for the uninsured, cost of malpractice insurance, care of chronic and catastrophic disease, and emergency preparedness for bioterrorism and national disasters have contributed to an economically constrained and competitive health-care environment (Carter & O'Morrow, 2006; Leeth; Scanlon). Consequently, TRSs practicing in all delivery settings need to document the benefits/outcomes and cost effectiveness of specific TR interventions for clients and **third-party payers** (insurance companies) to remain viable team members in integrated health-care systems. An emphasis on prevention, the promotion of quality-of-life behaviors, and recognition of the interrelationship among functioning in life activities and contextual (e.g., environmental and personal) factors present TRSs with the opportunity to carve out a unique niche in the health/human service delivery system (Porter & Van Puymbroeck, 2007; Shank & Coyle, 2002). To accomplish this, managers will need financial management savvy, the creativity to garner alternative resources, and the ability to document relationships between fees and client outcomes (Leeth). This section of the chapter outlines the manager's responsibility to prepare budgets, solicit revenues, set rates, and monitor and project fiscal year expenses and activities.

Financing Health and Human Services

Third-party reimbursement evolved after insurance carriers became involved in health-care financing. The *first party*, or client, receives services from the *second party* (health-care provider or organization) and the services are paid for by public and private insurance carriers, or *third party.* A variety of reimbursement methods are used by third-party payers including fee-for-service, cost-based reimbursement, and case group reimbursement (McCormick, 2002). In general, deductible payments (out-of-pocket amount to be paid by the person with insurance prior to reimbursement by the company), non-covered services, and co-payments (amount paid at the time of service) have increased as has the actual cost of health insurance.

The escalating cost of health care has prompted the development of a number of cost-containment programs, including coinsurance, second opinions for elective surgery, precertification (prior approval of a service), managed care plans, and prospective payment systems. While most "health-care systems lose between 3–5% of net revenues" (Leeth, 2004, p. 44), they must end their fiscal year with a **net revenue surplus** (profit) in order to survive in a competitive market. In addition to financing routine **expenses** (such as salaries, benefits, supplies, equipment, renovations, buildings, and other expenses), providers also finance charitable care and bad debts for an increasing number of uninsured or underinsured clients who cannot or do not pay their bills.

Human service agencies like public park and recreation departments or agencies like The Arc (voluntary nonprofit) rely on monies from the general fund (monies generated by taxation and paid to a government entity) and **fee-for-service** (charges assessed participants for the services they receive) as primary income. Limited funds come through third-party reimbursement when, for example, health-care partnerships result in aquatic therapy being documented as an intervention essential to rehabilitation. Additional sources of income include grants, sponsorships, fund-raising projects, donations, gifts, and cooperative ventures like partnerships with medical supply vendors and agencies that sign exchange-of-service contracts.

Therapeutic Recreation Financing

The federal government often defines practices that are eventually accepted by private insurers to determine their policies. In health-care settings, CMS (Centers for Medicare and Medicaid Services) defines **active treatment** as services provided under an individualized assessment and treatment plan, supervised by a physician, and considered a **reasonable** (shown to improve the client's functional capacity, health status, and/or quality of life) and **necessary** (required to meet specific diagnostic and treatment needs of a client) service (Passmore, 2007; Skalko, 1998). Private insurers have accepted these government criteria and tend to reimburse for services that constitute active treatment. Insurers review claims submitted by clients for services rendered and may deny payment or authorize whole or partial reimbursement. If a person's employer has entered into a plan operating under capitation practices, the person's expenses may be reimbursed at a set rate or not be covered by the plan. The difference between the insurer's payments and the actual expenses is either written off or paid directly by the client (Carter & O'Morrow, 2006).

When therapeutic recreation services are provided under the auspices of public agencies (local, state, federal government), revenue is based on taxation. Allocations from the general fund (city government) or legislature (state/federal agency) occur on an annual basis. These funds (referred to as appropriations) may be supplemented by matching government and nongovernmental grants. Allocations tend to be subject to changes in the tax base brought about by the economic and political climate (Carter & O'Morrow, 2006). As a consequence, therapeutic recreation providers may be subject to increments or unexpected decreases in their annual appropriations.

Fee-for-services are charged by public agencies to supplement allocations, and by private providers like profit and not-for-profit camps and service agencies like The Arc. Fees may be set to cover the full cost of operating a particular service, like a social skills class, or to cover a portion of the costs incurred with programs where costs far outweigh revenue, as would occur with a therapeutic equestrian program. Clients also may have to pay membership fees, distinguishing between those living within a certain taxing district versus those living outside the district. Or, membership fees may be set at an annual rate and include an identification card that permits entry to specific programs at no cost while minimal fees are attached to high-cost programs like aquatic therapy and adventure/challenge activities. Fees are sometimes based on a sliding scale determined by client financial status and the awarding of agency-generated scholarships to participants.

TRSs in health and human service agencies also rely on grants, contracts, gifts, donations, and foundation support. These sources typically fund innovative programs and specific options like participation in state-wide meets or unique services like cultural arts programs in inclusive settings. TRSs may work with advisory committees or foundations that have 501(c) (3) tax-exempt status to raise and disburse funds for particular events or participants. A primary funding source for social service agencies is the United Way (United Fund, Community Chest). Annual fund drives target certain financial goals. TRS managers submit requests to United Way, for example, and present their needs at budget hearings. Requests are evaluated based on both the amount of monies received by United Way from its annual fund drive and the funding priorities set by its board of directors. TRSs also acquire monies through foundations and grants. Foundations are often associated with prominent families in local communities or successful enterprises like the Mott Foundation. Grants are available through local, state, and federal government. Competition for foundation and grant monies may require the manager to submit specific application forms or a brief letter outlining the need for the monies and the relationship or role of the funder to the particular project; that is, how the funder will benefit from its contribution. In communities, service organizations like the Rotary or Lion's Club sponsor clients and raise monies or conduct fund-raisers to purchase, for example, handicapped accessible vans for the agency. TRSs may also contract for specific services like adventure-challenge therapies. Contracts cover liability associated with the experience, leadership during the experience, and any other specific services essential to safe delivery of the experience.

Rate Setting and Cost Analysis

As the budget is developed and services are planned, therapeutic recreation managers may determine and set service rates so clients and/or their insurance carriers are charged an appropriate fee. Managers take into consideration the portion of the intervention cost to be covered by the fee and the position of their agency on cost recovery or profit and loss. In some instances, the charges must cover all costs associated with the program, while in other situations the fee is expected to cover only a portion of the total cost. A number of techniques are used to determine charges. One approach determines the full cost of service provision by identifying direct and indirect costs. The managed care approach tends to use negotiated methods incorporating allowances, discounts, deductibles, and other risk-adjustment factors. *Parroting* means that rates are set to be compatible with other services provided by the agency (Thompson, 1996).

Rate setting requires the TRS to know the direct and indirect costs of service provision. This information allows the TRS to measure outcomes in terms of the actual cost of the service to produce a desired benefit. The price set for the service may be influenced by what the market will bear—taking into consideration **allowances and uncollectibles** (charges to those unable to pay that are passed on to other revenue or cost recovery centers, like other clients or programs). **Direct costs** include all those expenses directly tied to a particular service like salaries, fringe benefits, supplies, equipment, paperwork time, and preparation time pre- and post-intervention. **Indirect costs** like utility and maintenance expenses are necessary for service delivery and are usually shared with other services that use the facility. The sum of the direct and indirect costs is the actual service cost.

The TRS establishes rates per unit cost or charge per service unit. Therapeutic recreation services may be based on hourly rates, broken down into fractions of an hour, e.g., 15 minutes. These rates are influenced by market trends and, therefore, may fluctuate. Consequently, the American Medical Association (AMA) codes treatment and therapies annually; known as CPT codes (Current Procedural Terminology), each reimbursable intervention receives a five-digit number and descriptor. Some TRS interventions (like aquatic or group therapy) may be covered under these codes if found to directly contribute to the client's care plan, while others may not (Carter & O'Morrow, 2006). Length of interventions also varies with the nature of the setting and the patient's ability to tolerate the duration of treatment; for example, with inpatient physical rehabilitation or inpatient psychiatric treatment. As a consequence, physical rehabilitation sessions may average 30 minutes, while psychiatric treatments may be scheduled for 45 minutes—regardless, each 15-minute period has an associated unit charge (Passmore, 2007). Also, the salaries of TRSs vary by setting or geographic location, which influences the unit cost or service charge. Clients may actually be charged by time units, percent of total program fee, a per diem (daily) rate, or for specific services. The nature of the setting determines which type of billing is used. In some health-care settings, therapeutic recreation is considered a nonchargeable service by insurance companies, yet is a necessary support service to a chargeable service like physical therapy. Therefore, therapeutic recreation services would be considered part of the overhead or indirect cost of providing physical therapy and insurers may or may not elect to cover the costs.

Cost allocation is the process of determining the actual cost of a service and assigning this cost to the division where clients receive the service. Exhibit 5.5 is an example of a method used to allocate the costs of providing therapeutic recreation to a particular clientele in an agency. In this example, the allocation base is the direct personnel expense (therapists and assistants) plus the supplies and equipment (operational expense) plus the administrative/clerical support and overhead costs. Notice that the annual salaries and benefits used to provide therapeutic recreation services are $146,107. The operational costs and administrative and clerical support costs are included and, when added together with the overhead costs, determine the total cost ($292,149) of providing therapeutic recreation services for these clients. From this total we can determine the cost per hour or cost per day depending on which option, or **unit cost,** seems to be most appropriate to the setting and department. If 20,000 hours of client care were provided, it would cost $14.60 per hour. If 22,000 client days of therapeutic recreation services were provided, it would cost $13.27 per day. (Note: In this example, hours of patient care are the cumulative hours of care/treatment provided to clients by the agency. Patient days refers to the total number of days patients are involved in some type of therapeutic recreation service.)

Exhibit 5.5   Therapeutic Recreation Cost Allocation

Allocation Base: (Direct personnel costs, plus operational expenses, plus administrative and clerical costs, plus overhead = total costs)

Salaries and Benefits	$146,107
Operational Expense (supplies and equipment)	$14,400
Administrative/Clerical Support	$48,171
Subtotal	$208,678
Overhead @ 40%*	$83,471
Total Costs	**$292,149**

Cost per hour of patient care: (Divide total cost by number of hours of patient care) $292,149 cost per year divided by 20,000 hours of patient care per year = $14.60/hour

Cost per patient per day: (Divide total cost by number of patient days) $292,149 cost per year divided by 22,000 days of patient care per year = $13.27/day

* Overhead is calculated at 40 percent of direct costs. It includes various indirect expenses such as heating/cooling, electric, printing, maintenance, and housekeeping.

A few clients often account for a substantial proportion of health-care costs (Grimaldi, 1998). As a consequence, managed care providers have implemented risk-adjustment measures like **carve outs** (certain services are excluded from capitation rates and reimbursed on a fee-for-service basis, for example, mental health costs) to prevent unwarranted gains or losses from their enrollment mix. Setting rates and identifying all direct and indirect costs help the TRS accurately estimate resources necessary to provide services and determine the service benefits associated with particular costs. This type of documentation justifies service provision while contributing to cost-containment practices.

Budget Preparation and Monitoring

A budget is a plan used to allocate, monitor, and control the flow of resources (estimated revenues and expenditures) to ensure the program objectives are achieved in financial terms (Carter & O'Morrow, 2006). Therapeutic recreation services may stand alone as an identified budget or may be a portion of a larger departmental or division budget. Every budget starts as a proposal; it becomes the budget for a definitive time (year or more) when the appropriate individuals and boards have approved the proposal. A TRS plays a critical role in the budget preparation process and may also advise the financial department as the proposal is developed, presented, and approved. Likewise, once an approved budget is implemented, a TRS reconciles monthly/quarterly budget reports, may be consulted by the accountant/comptroller as the fiscal year progresses, and is responsible for remaining within approved budget parameters.

There are a number of budget formats used in health and human services. A common format is the **line-item** or object-of-expenditure; each item has an identified account line and very often is assigned a classification code or number (object class). These codes are similar regardless of setting. For example, personnel services is usually the 1000 code (Crompton, 1999). Another budget format is the **program budget**, which contains all the revenues and expenses for an entire program, like therapeutic recreation or a mental health/psychiatry unit. **Zero-based budgets** are formulated each fiscal year by ranking proposed services—with resources allocated based on the priority listing of services (Carter & O'Morrow, 2006). In health care, each service may periodically be required to justify budget continuation, yet the process is not referred to as a zero-based budget. Budget preparation commences at least three to six months prior to the actual **fiscal year (FY)** (the agency budget year, e.g., January 1–December 31, October 1–September 30, July 1–June 30, or April 1–March 31). Consequently, TRSs may be asked to estimate fiscal needs for the coming FY based on patterns of current revenues and expenses.

The operating budget consists of expenses and revenues. Expenses include salaries, supplies, equipment, and overhead. Revenues consist of fees and charges, grants, contracts, and insurance reimbursements. **Capital** expenses may be incorporated into the operating budget, but are more commonly broken-out in a separate budget. Capital expenses are larger sums of money associated with buildings or equipment; each agency sets the amount that defines a capital expense. For some, amounts over $50 may be capital expenses while for others equipment over $1,000 is a capital expense. Specific procedures and the timetable for budget development vary from agency to agency. In some, after an analysis of previous FY revenues and expenses, dollar figures are assigned to all departments; in others, the manager might request allocations by budget category. Usually the expenses are estimated first, and then the revenues are projected according to the agency's budget calendar. As the budget process unfolds, the TRS may be asked to provide additional justification or to reassess the submitted figures in order to revise the budget proposal. Also, throughout the FY, the TRS may be asked to complete specific financial forms related to, for example, committed or ongoing costs (salaries, rent, and insurance) and replacement costs to purchase new equipment. TRSs are expected to be aware of pending due dates and to submit appropriate forms or computer-generated data in a timely manner. Likewise, as the proposed budget is developed TRSs are expected to be aware of the expenses and revenues associated with the delivery of their services.

Once the proposed budget is approved by the governing authority, which may be the hospital or corporate board of directors, the finance committee, or the city council, it becomes the operating budget and is considered a legal document. The dollar amount assigned to each category or program may or may not reflect the requested amount, depending upon modifications made by the varying administrators and boards. Often actual allocations are organized such that monthly reports can be generated to detail activity in each budget category. TRSs may be required to reconcile specific accounts monthly or quarterly so year-end totals are balanced, or to ensure that at the conclusion of the FY the entire budget is balanced (e.g., not overspent) or each account is in-line with the FY allocations. The TRS also may be responsible for maintaining specific programmatic records like client contact time/units and full-time equivalents (FTEs; one FTE equals 40 hours of staff time/week or 2080 hours per year). A TRS who computes regular financial audits is better able to spot unexpected accounting errors and to project needed changes in account allocations. Also, managers will have the cost analysis information to document program effectiveness or justify resource reallocation.

TECHNICAL OPERATIONS

Technical operations encompass a number of day-to-day management tasks essential to the survival of quality therapeutic recreation programs and services. The health and human service industry faces increasing competition, necessitating that managers help control the costs of services to clients (**cost containment**). TRSs undertake a number of specific tasks to gain fiscal and political support for programs and services, achieve valued client and program outcomes on a consistent and predictable basis, identify and reduce safety risks to clients, create access to services, and to practice evidence-based care in an ethical manner. TRSs use technology daily as they document and schedule services. This section presents a number of topics in which the TRS needs to be well-versed in order to provide fiscally responsible and effective interventions in today's dynamic health and human service environment.

Marketing, Advocacy, and Networking

Marketing is both a tool managers use to benefit the department, client, employee, and profession and a concept that describes activities designed to identify client wants and needs and encourage clients to establish long-term relationships with service providers (Broida, 2006). TRSs use marketing techniques to survey client needs, identify service gaps, and develop products and services relevant to clients and caregivers (Kingma, 1998). *Value-added* services aim to give more than the client expects (Broida) and have generally been regarded as essential to the success of health and human service organizations (Fischer & Coddington, 1998). The value-added approach might focus on improving quality of care or accessibility through evidence-based practices, reducing unit costs through effectiveness studies, or achieving valued client outcomes on a consistent and predictable basis. The intent of marketing is to create exchange relationships in which TRSs provide value-added services so clients are satisfied and will return or remain within the service network.

Developing a marketing plan is similar to the TR process of assessment, planning, implementation, and evaluation (refer to chapter 4). One approach is to conduct a SWOT (strength, weakness, opportunity, threat) analysis. A SWOT analysis identifies the internal resources (strengths and weaknesses) of the agency and compares them to the external factors (opportunities and threats) in the environment. This enables managers to proactively respond to the trends and forces influencing the unit's stakeholders while identifying program design and evaluation factors that affect client health, functioning, and quality of life outcomes (Ipson, Mahoney, & Adams, 2005). In the assessment phase, this analysis identifies target markets and the preferences and needs of these individuals as well as the capabilities of the agency/department to address these preferences in relation to other agents providing services. Marketing goals are written and services are designed to achieve these goals during the planning phase. For example, as a result of the assessment, the TRS may determine that physicians, administrators, reimbursement agents, and caregivers are target markets for whom plans must be written so these people assume a more active role in supporting therapeutic recreation services. During the implementation phase, the TRS selects the most suitable avenues to gain support from the target markets, develops a timetable for advocating the client outcomes of therapeutic recreation services, and commences the activities to develop exchange relationships with each audience. The TRS might decide a series of presentations at "grand rounds" would best address physicians' and administrators' needs, while mailing brochures from professional organizations (e.g., ATRA, NCTRC) to insurers would be an effective way to promote valued client outcomes to third-party payers. In the evaluation phase, the TRS identifies whether the strategies used with each target market accomplished the respective marketing goals. A marketing audit establishes if the **market segment** (target audience with specific needs) has been reached with appropriate marketing tools. TRSs may actually count the number of responses or inquiries prompted by their brochures or interview caregivers to identify how, for example, their perceptions of therapeutic recreation have changed following National Therapeutic Recreation week.

TRSs are integral to achieving value-added outcomes as individuals and as collaborators and partners with clients and stakeholders (Ipson, Mahoney, & Adams, 2005). Managers facilitate this process by cultivating a work culture that enables TRSs to deliver high-quality, culturally sensitive programs. Managers link TRSs with sources to build networks that inform stakeholders about our profession and garner resources to benefit clients. When TRSs conduct effectiveness studies, contact their legislators, provide evidence of valued client outcomes (e.g., improved physical, cognitive, social, and emotional functioning in life activities), or facilitate client/caregiver participation in team meetings or on advisory boards, they are advocating the significance of our profession while creating client and community retention and loyalty.

Continuous Quality Improvement

Managers will continue to be pressed to refine the quality of health-care delivery while providing efficient, safe, and effective care at reasonable costs (Wojciechowski & Cichowski, 2007) with fewer available resources. Improved care and safety rely on evidence-based practices. Shorter lengths of stay mean less time for staff teaching and client interaction. Consumer's use of the Internet for health information continues to increase. Under these circumstances, professionals will be challenged to present best-practice alternatives so clients can make informed decisions.

During the 1980s, quality assurance (QA) was the preferred term for activities that improved health and human services. In the mid-1990s, the Joint Commission initiated efforts to focus on outcome-oriented measures. The intent was to identify client outcomes and to continuously improve service quality by focusing on performance and measuring the processes that improve results (McCormick & Darnsteadt, 1999). Continuous quality improvement (CQI) and performance improvement (PI) became the preferred Joint Commission terms. The early 2000s saw a significant shift to a focus on client safety, bolstered with quality-improvement related activities and evidence-based practices. With passage of the Patient Safety and Quality Improvement Act of 2005, stakeholders were encouraged to collaborate to increase knowledge among all constituents, decrease errors, and thus improve quality (Kinnaman, 2007).

Total quality management, or TQM, is viewed as an approach to increase the value of care while containing costs (Dansky & Brannon, 1996). TQM programs are characterized by CQI or PI, client orientation and satisfaction, employee empowerment, teamwork, and structured problem solving (Dansky & Brannon). TQM embraces change and recognizes that change is continuous. Moreover, the focus on safe, high-quality care resulting in continuous improvement relies on systematic measurement of outcomes and indicators to determine what values are important in service delivery (Carter & O'Morrow, 2006).

Indicators associated with CQI/PI are measurable components of care or service that reflect quality (Carter & O'Morrow, 2006; Garnick, Horgan & Chalk, 2006). Quality measures tend to include structure, process, outcomes, access, and patient experience (Garnick et al.). Access focuses on the client's service need and ability to receive it, while patient experience addresses actual participation. The three remaining measures tend to be incorporated into CQI/PI plans as criteria of program efficiency, safety, and effectiveness. **Structure indicators** relate to factors that must be present in order to provide a service, e.g., proper staffing, correct use of equipment, and adherence to policies. **Process indicators** describe the nature of the interaction between the client and the therapist and are represented by use of professional practice guidelines and evidence or consensus that particular interventions will achieve desired outcomes (Garnick et al.). **Outcome indicators** measure the effects of intervention on the state of the client's health in relation to contextual (environmental and personal) factors. External accreditation bodies like the JC review CQI/PI plans for data that reflect the safety and quality of care provided. The intent of the data collection is to manage undesirable trends, identify and manage sentinel events, and assure a proactive program that identifies and reduces unanticipated adverse events and safety risks to patients. Also, because professional standards of practice are organized according to these criteria, they assist the TRS in assessing CQI/PI. Exhibit 5.6 provides an example of a CQI/PI plan developed for assessments.

Efficiency is one of the areas targeted in quality improvement programs (Kinnaman, 2007). **Productivity measurements** compare the quantity of services provided with the amount of resources expended, like staff time used to produce a specific outcome or the ratio of inputs to outputs. For example, the number of units produced per day may define productivity (Passmore, 2007). Products "include patient outcomes, patient satisfaction, and production of unit charges" (Passmore, 2007, p. 45). Unit charges are charges per 15-minute intervals assigned to interventions lasting a certain period of time (30–45 minutes) on a daily basis. The personnel costs in service organizations are a significant pro-

Exhibit 5.6   Therapeutic Recreation Monitoring and Evaluation Procedures

Major Clinical Function/Aspect of Care:
Therapeutic recreation assessments

Indicators:
The therapeutic recreation assessment is individualized.
The therapeutic recreation assessment is completed according to standards.

Criteria:
Structure:
The assessment is completed, 91 percent of the time or more, according to the standards for structure, content, and timeliness developed by the department, the CMS (Centers for Medicare and Medicaid Services), and the Joint Commission.
Process:
The therapeutic recreation specialist, 91 percent of the time or more, informs the client of his/her responsibilities in the assessment and seeks collaboration in the process. If the client is unable to participate in the assessment, the therapeutic recreation specialist seeks involvement from the family or significant others.
Outcome:
The client/family or significant other is involved in the assessment to the extent possible, 91 percent of the time or more.

Sample:
Twenty-five percent of the caseload of each therapeutic recreation specialist will be assessed each quarter.

Methodology:
Assessments are compared against criteria and a percentage of compliance calculated for each therapist. Results are reviewed by the Therapeutic Recreation Supervisor and the Director. Compliance and noncompliance with the criteria are documented for the CQI/PI and for staff performance reviews. When noncompliance with the criteria is determined, a plan of corrective action is developed, implemented, and evaluated. Results are shared with appropriate administrative and medical staff and the Director of the CQI/PI.

Data Sources:
Client medical records.

portion of the budget, so productivity specialists may develop formulas to compare the amount of staff time used (for example, to complete assessments or conduct inclusion experiences) to the fees and charges for the services rendered.

If an agency requires productivity measurements, a TRS may establish productivity levels for specific activities and identify both barriers to productivity and avenues for improvement. To illustrate, a TRS may allocate 50% of his or her time for direct client services, 25% for paperwork, and 25% for meetings and caregiver contact. While the percentages may vary depending upon client population and setting, agencies concerned with productivity will monitor these and other activities to find ways to maximize the TRS's efforts. Because unit productivity becomes one element of annual evaluations, it is incumbent upon TRSs to participate in the development of program policies on productivity levels (Passmore, 2007).

Risk and Safety Management

Risk management involves developing processes and procedures for controlling the delivery of safe, quality services. The intent of risk and safety management, like quality improvement programs, is to develop, monitor, and evaluate procedures so both providers and participants avoid harm while operations are continuously improved. Concern for safety is personal and global. As a result of terrorist-related activities, catastrophic diseases, and natural and human-influenced disasters, safety and risk protocols have become part of our common experience. Moreover, as professionals we participate in those activities designed to diminish losses and risk to promote safety and security in the work setting.

The law requires TRSs "to act with reasonable care and prudence to prevent unreasonable risks of harm to participants" (Kaiser & Robinson, 2005, p. 593). *Negligence,* the term used to describe harm to person or property as a result of actions or failure to act as a reasonable and prudent person or professional, is established by four elements: duty, standard of care, proximate cause, and injury (Carter & O'Morrow, 2006). Duty is the TRS's obligation to the client as described in a job description, protocol, or supervisory plan. Standard of care refers to the TRS's responsibility to provide the same degree of care that another competent TRS in the same position would provide. Proximate cause means establishing that the TRS's action or inaction is the direct cause of injury. And, finally, an injury must exist for negligence to be present.

Several steps are involved in preparing and implementing risk and safety management programs. The manager (1) identifies potential areas of risk; (2) analyzes the frequency, causes, and severity of incidents; (3) educates staff, volunteers, and interns about the significance and consequences of risk and safety management practices; and (4) implements plans to monitor and evaluate services to prevent and correct behaviors. Potential risk and safety issues may relate to staff-to-participant ratios or staff skills like transferring or lifting a client; to programming issues like sequencing and adapting experiences so they are commensurate with client skills; or to participant management concerns like elopement, first aid needs, and compliance with requests. Because communication is identified as a primary factor in client safety violations (Scalise, 2006), managers and staff also monitor situations that might compromise clients' rights, privacy, confidentiality, and autonomy; for example, consent forms, medical charts, or transactions that reveal identifiable health information.

After risk and safety issues are identified and analyzed, the manager may develop training programs to reduce or minimize risks by educating all involved on how to better complete a task (like lifts); or the manager may develop protocols or impose policies to follow (like security procedures with elopement). In other situations where risk and safety issues are ongoing (like aquatic programs), managers may minimize risk through facility inspections and the use of forms (assumption of risk) that help determine the client's understanding of inherent activity risks.

Involving clients and professionals in routine safety and emergency experiences not only ensures preparedness but also demonstrates and engenders support of policies and safety and security practices. As communities become more culturally diverse with increasing numbers of aging and mobility-impaired residents, it will be important

Signage is intended to promote safety.

for TRSs to continue their training and advocate for inclusive risk, safety, and security preparations (Fox & Rowland, 2007).

Risk and safety practices are defined in practice standards and ethics codes of professional organizations and regulatory bodies like the JC and CARF International. TRSs will find operational manuals to be a good source of risk and safety management policies. Legal directives like the Americans with Disabilities Act also address risk and safety factors. Local health departments and national organizations like the Department of Homeland Security also impose safety standards. TRSs may find standard protocols require not only first-aid training but also credentials specific to a particular experience—like ropes-course training or lift training for accessible vans—as indicators of competency. Employees may be required to purchase professional liability insurance, or employers may provide such coverage.

Accessibility and Inclusion

Accessibility is important to most individuals at some point in their lives—when, for example, a temporary limitation results from a broken bone or an unshoveled sidewalk, or when a long-term adjustment like decreased visual acuity affects participation (Carter & LeConey, 2004). The term *accessibility* refers to the design and construction of areas and facilities so persons with disabilities can use the resource. In a broader context the word refers not only to physical but also to programmatic and attitudinal accessibility. The phrase *universal design* refers to providing options in an environment for all people. Thus, universal design of, say, a pathway, extends the concept of accessibility to include the needs of any person whether using a wheelchair, bicycle, motorized scooter, or baby stroller (Carter & LeConey).

The law that originally addressed physical accessibility, the Architectural Barriers Act of 1968 (PL 90-480), has been enhanced by the passage of new legislation. The Vocational Rehabilitation Act Amendments of 1973 (Section 504, PL 93-112) established the **Architectural and Transportation Barriers Compliance Board (ATBCB)** to ensure compliance with the Architectural Barriers Act and further extended accessibility to mean programmatic access (Bullock et al., 2010). With passage of the Americans with Disabilities Act (ADA) in 1990, each of the previous laws was strengthened. The ADA of 1990 is commonly referred to as the civil rights act for individuals with disabilities.

The American National Standards Institute (ANSI) guidelines, the **Uniform Federal Accessibility Standards (UFAS),** and now the Americans with Disabilities Act Accessibility Guidelines for Buildings and Facilities (ADAAG) define physical accessibility standards for all public facilities. These documents identify criteria for ramps, doors, outdoor areas, parking lots, building entrances, pools, restrooms, showers, stairs,

Legislative initiatives have increased access to recreational facilities for those with disabilities.

Supplements to the ADAAG outline accessibility criteria for recreation facilities like golf courses.

telephones, and water fountains, among others. Supplements to the ADAAG standards outline criteria for play areas, recreation facilities, and outdoor environments. Play areas are considered a collection of individual components; standards require that a minimum number of components be accessible within an area. Criteria are presented for ground level and elevated play components, ramps and transfer systems, and accessible routes and surfaces. Recreation facilities include "amusement rides, boating facilities, fishing piers and platforms, golf courses and miniature golf, exercise equipment and machines, bowling lanes, shooting facilities, and swimming pools, wading pools and spas" (Carter & LeConey, 2004, p. 18). Outdoor environments include trails, beaches, and picnic and camping areas. For ADA updates and resources, students may contact the compliance board at http://www.access-board.gov.

As noted earlier, ADA attempted to eliminate discrimination against people with disabilities while supporting inclusion in all aspects of life. Further, as noted by Klitzing and Wachter (2005), the provision of inclusive services in the community aligns the profession with initiatives like *Healthy People 2010* and the World Health Organization's (WHO) focus on health promotion and disease prevention. Inclusive experiences allow choices and recognize diversity. Managers and TRSs facilitate inclusion through in-service training with recreation staff, persons with/without disabilities, aides, and volunteers; use of individual inclusion plans, adaptive equipment, and task-analyzed skill-instruction; and by providing inclusion companions and assistants to recreation programmers (Klitzing & Wachter). Inclusion is a process that happens through collaboration and commitment. The process involves steps similar to APIE (refer to chapter 4) and commences with assessment questions like: Does everyone feel welcome? Can everyone be included? Is everyone prepared for inclusion? Inclusion resources like *Paths to Inclusion* are available online (www.IncludingAllKids.org) through funded initiatives. These sources present best practices synthesized from the collaborative efforts of numerous organizations and professionals.

A series of laws commencing with the Education for All Handicapped Children Act in 1975 (PL94-142) and continuing with amendments and revisions [Individuals with Disabilities Education Act of 1990, amended in 1997, 2004 (PL108-446) (Improvement Act of 2004)] mandate a free, appropriate public education for all children in the least restrictive environment. This legislation originally defined recreation as a related service consisting of four components: assessment of recreation and leisure functioning, leisure education, therapeutic recreation, and recreation in school and community agencies: PL108-446 identifies recreation, including therapeutic recreation, as a related service. An Individual Education Plan (IEP) is updated annually to address the student's participation in the general curriculum. TRSs participate in the IEP's design or advocate through professionals and parents to include therapeutic recreation. Such recreation enables students to attend, for example, after-school or summer programs where staff develop individual inclusion plans to support the IEP and document outcomes relevant to leisure and life.

Technology and Information Systems

Therapeutic recreation is driven by knowledge and evidence. Evidence-based practice relies on access to the most recent research on best practices. Computers and information systems help clients and TRSs access the rapidly changing knowledge base in health and human services and enable timely application of new information. Technology enhances not only access to health and resource information, but also networking, data analysis, and management tasks like personnel scheduling—all essential to improving client health literacy, safety, efficiency, quality of operations, and competence of TRSs (Conn, 2007; McKnight, McDaniel, & Ehmann, 2006; Wojciechowski & Cichowski, 2007).

Computer-based, integrated information systems are a cost-effective way to mix practice (e.g., assessment, documentation, and discharge planning) with management (e.g., resource utilization and budgeting). Computers are also an effective way to store information and to communicate globally. Communication over the Internet links clients worldwide and fosters friendships and support not otherwise possible. One such example is Starbright World (www.starbright.org), a private computer network that links youth with their peers and to information that may help them understand the challenges they face. A number of computerized database systems link various agencies while also comparing outcomes to performance measures across facilities. The MDS (Minimum Data Set) is a reporting system required by CMS that summarizes assessment data from all professionals for a particular client and electronically submits the information for reimbursement.

Other resources that help connect clients and practitioners with one another and with health information and resources include Listservs. For example, http://

www.onelist.com/group/rec-at is a Listserv on assisted technology and therapeutic recreation. Online programs like WebMD and the like (www.healthfinder.gov provides medical information while www.medscape.com has full text medical articles) contain a wealth of health information. Computers are used to develop new information and databases that advance our knowledge, research capabilities, and evidence-based practices. To illustrate, ongoing research using the Leisure Diagnostic Battery is generating a database that will add to our understanding of the assessment process. As the role of computers and information systems continues to evolve, clients will benefit from the development of health resource centers and Web sites, while professionals gain knowledge from evidence-based research and client-based practices.

Assistive technology has enabled individuals to become more involved in their communities. Assistive technology is any device used by a person to increase, maintain, or improve functional capacity (Bullock et al., 2010). Devices range from computers to voice amplifiers to powered wheelchairs. Access to the community also is enhanced by virtual reality environments that electronically simulate an environment for the client before he or she actually goes to the setting (Broida & Germann, 1999). Such experiences alleviate fears while increasing accessibility knowledge. Because people with disabilities are less likely to use the Internet for health information, and because research has found improved health literacy results from access to basic information, one important TRS role is to provide computer access and education during interventions (Wojciechowski & Cichowski, 2007).

Ethics and Practice

Ethics is concerned with what is good or bad, right or wrong. Ethical practices are defined by professional codes of ethics (ATRA, 2001; NTRS, 2001), employing organizations, laws like HIPAA, licensure acts at the state level, NCTRC, and each individual's value system. Consequently, each client and professional can be affected by the ethical behavior of many others. Managers often field questions from staff as to what is ethical and legal (Carter & O'Morrow, 2006). Managers also are responsible for staff growth and development, which may include changing old practices or acquiring new behaviors guided by a moral understanding of our role in society (Sylvester, 2002).

TRSs experience a number of situations during a routine workday that may result in ethical dilemmas, including client autonomy, confidentiality, social-sexual relations, professional competence, reimbursement, resource allocations, quality improvement methods, and efficacy research (Austin, 2009; Carter & O'Morrow, 2006; Mitty, 2007; Van Puymbroeck & Wahba, 2007). TRSs make decisions about, for example, releasing client information or charging for their services. Ethical decision-making models (Carter & O'Morrow) encourage TRSs to consider ethical obligations defined in codes of ethics (e.g., beneficence/nonmalfeasance, informed consent, fidelity) as well as theories (e.g., virtue ethics, ethics of caring) that influence moral development and reasoning prior to responding to a dilemma. This approach recognizes that ethics are shaped by human events in society (Sylvester, 2002). To illustrate, when a TRS makes a decision about the type of demographic data to collect during an efficacy study on a particular intervention, the moral needs of a multicultural society are considered along with the principles defined in ethics codes (Sylvester; Van Puymbroeck & Wahba).

With client health literacy improving, and science and technology continuing to intensify the rate of change, TRSs will experience challenges as they process increasing levels of information. Applying a moral decision-making process will help them respond in ways that promote client health; for example, determining which intervention is cost-effective, culturally sensitive, and improves quality of care. Legislation like the Health Insurance Portability Accountability Act (HIPAA) of 1996—which addresses a number of issues including fraudulent rate setting, the security and privacy of health information including electronic transactions, and denial of insurance because of previous medical conditions—is sometimes necessary to protect clients when professionals face dilemmas with unclear resolution. Because ethical practice is required by such legislation, licensure acts, and credentialing bodies, violations of ethics codes may be reported to employing agency ethics committees, credentialing organizations, and licensing boards. Actions of these entities may, for example, result in the loss of a credential.

PERSONNEL OPERATIONS

The nature of therapeutic recreation services has changed dramatically and will continue to evolve. As a consequence, personnel management functions will remain critical as professionals are called upon to deliver services to an increasingly diverse clientele living in a more complex and constantly changing environment. Recruiting, hiring, training, and supervising personnel are crucial management tasks since the programs and services offered are only as effective as the professionals employed by the agency.

Staffing needs in today's health and human service agencies are fluid and require multiskilled TRSs who are effective team members and communicators. Managers must oversee staff orientation, training, and supervision in order to maintain qualified and competent personnel. Since managers are responsible for the actions of their staff, they must ensure staff members adhere to professional and agency standards. Annual performance reviews, for example, are a managerial responsibility, as is implementing disciplinary action. Agencies strive to maintain a diverse workforce, which affects staffing functions from recruitment to the design of training programs. In addition, staff composition is affected by the changing nature of the workplace; for example, the number of available full-time positions or equivalents (FTEs) in an agency may necessitate employment of part-time staff, paraprofessional personnel, and the management of a volunteer program including student interns.

Position Design, Analysis, and Classification

Agencies have specific policies and procedures for the design and classification of positions. Further, these are influenced by legal regulations, court decisions, and professional standards of practice. The larger the agency or service system, the more comprehensive and complex these policies and procedures are likely to be. In large, complex systems, such as the federal or state systems, there often is a division of the personnel department devoted to analyzing and categorizing positions. Understanding the policies, procedures, and classification factors of an agency or institution will enable the therapeutic recreation specialist to write more complete job descriptions, which will therefore assure more accurate classification. This is important, since the designation of a position relative to other positions and the job market will determine an employee's salary. A clear understanding of these factors also will enable the TRS to be more effective in recruiting and training the right people for therapeutic recreation positions. Elements administrators often consider in classifying positions include the variety and difficulty of work; the authority and responsibility exercised; the degree of supervision versus independent functioning; the judgment/discretion exercised; the nature and extent of public contact; and the knowledge, skills, and abilities required to do the work. Generally, the more complex functions have higher classifications.

Recruitment, Screening, and Selection

Recruitment begins after an accurate job description has been developed and the position has been properly classified. Positions are usually advertised through college and university placement services, job fairs at conferences, advertisements in newsletters and newspapers, through Internet Listservs, and by position vacancy announcements sent to agencies known to provide therapeutic recreation services. Professional networking is an important recruitment vehicle. Prior to interviewing applicants, a department must determine the criteria to be used in screening the candidates. Preliminary screening occurs prior to on-site screening and traditionally is based on application forms, resumes, portfolios, and background checks. On-site screening and interviews usually involve only candidates who have met the predetermined screening criteria and may include an assessment activity or performance simulation to affirm desired agency-specific knowledge, skills, and abilities.

Typically agencies require the candidate to be a graduate of an accredited college or university with a degree or specialization in therapeutic recreation or recreation therapy (TR/RT) and to be certified by the National Council for Therapeutic Recreation Certification (NCTRC) and/or to be licensed, certified, or registered in states where state certification is also an option. Employers in the community may require the CPRP (Certified Park and Recreation Professional) credential from the National Certification Board. While agencies may require specific coursework or training beyond, for example, NCTRC criteria, managers may also review college transcripts to assure that certain courses such as anatomy, physiology, abnormal psychology, human growth and development, and specific TR/RT content courses have been successfully completed.

A candidate who is selected for the position satisfies the screening criteria, is available to fill the position when desired by the agency, and brings to the agency work-related skills and competencies suited to the character of the agency. Throughout the hiring process, the manager adheres to regulatory laws like ADA and EEOC and professional standards to ensure fairness in the selection of the candidate.

Staff Orientation and Training

Managers orient employees to their specific job responsibilities and to the expectations and protocols of the employing agency. This may occur during the probation-

During orientation sessions with new employees, managers explain performance expectations, supervisory processes, personnel policies, emergency protocols, and other agency practices.

ary period or may precede probation. Included in the orientation are explanations of the performance expectations, supervisory processes, competency and review procedures, personnel policies, and emergency protocols. Additionally, the staff orientation includes preparation of the new employee's professional development plan and an initial assessment of competencies necessary to complete daily tasks. This assessment also identifies training needs, like use of technology. During orientation, managers help employees write objectives that guide their supervisory interactions and form the basis of their professional development plans.

According to Carter and O'Morrow, "effective twenty-first century organizations are characterized as learning organizations" (2006, p. 235). With the accelerated pace of technological and social change in the world, TRSs must continue to acquire new knowledge and learn skills that translate into increased quality and safety during client care. Standards of practice present criteria that "encourage professionals to remain competent through continuing education and design of individual development plans" (Carter & O'Morrow, p. 236). To retain the CTRS credential, documentation of earned professional development points (e.g., CEUs) is required. TRSs can accomplish this by attending professional conferences, completing academic coursework, logging in to electronic seminars, and participating in professional exercises like research and publication.

Supervision

Managers conduct three types of supervision: (1) managerial supervision is intended to assure that staff members understand and comply with department and agency policies and initiatives; (2) clinical supervision is intended to improve staff interactions with clients and to enhance staff skills as therapeutic recreation professionals; and (3) supportive supervision is intended to improve morale and job satisfaction so team members remain harmonious and productive (Wenzel, 2006). The various forms of supervision occur when managers and staff participate in performance interviews, observations, case presentations, journaling, and quality audits. In many settings the manager performs all three forms of supervision. Initially, clinical supervision is experienced during internships when students and their supervisors set goals and evaluate progress toward competence as entry-level professionals (Hutchins, 2005/2006). Clinical supervision also is evident throughout one's career when supervisors instruct and consult in order to enhance intervention skills and the quality of the helping relationship. When the manager is responsible for all three forms of supervision, boundaries can become blurred among supervisory duties. Ideally, assigning the responsibility for clinical supervision to someone other than the manager who controls and assures productivity will help maintain the focus on staff growth and development.

Performance Management and Disciplinary Actions

While agencies have differing procedures for performance review and competency enhancement, the typical process involves a formal review at the end of a probationary period (three to six months) and on an annual basis. Thorough discussion of performance expectations during the recruitment process and clear explanations of competency assessment plans during the orientation period assure that the employee understands expectations and that no surprises will occur during performance reviews. Professional standards of practice and regulatory bodies like the JC and CARF International require that staff members have individual development plans to improve competency as one aspect of annual reviews; these plans are reevaluated at the end of each work cycle to assess improvements. Managers must ensure that staff maintain appropriate credentials, demonstrate current competence, periodically assess their educational needs, and have opportunities for professional development.

Agencies must have defined policies and procedures for resolving performance or conduct problems and for responding to employee grievances. Disciplinary procedures usually involve varying degrees of verbal or written warnings or suspension prior to termination, depending upon whether the infraction is a conduct or performance issue and the severity of the offense. Theft, for example, is usually considered a conduct issue which, if confirmed, results in immediate dismissal. However, since the cost of recruiting and developing employees is high and dismissals are often complicated by legal challenges, most agencies prefer to invest their resources in employee retention and development, which highlights the importance of effective recruitment and selection procedures and competent managers.

Staffing Patterns, Multiskilled Staff, and Teamwork

The organization of an agency's staff is influenced by the setting, the services provided, and the number of staff members and their classifications. In settings where a number of TRSs are employed, personnel may be assigned to particular units or program areas and held responsible for implementing the TR process with either specific clients (e.g., individuals with physical disabilities) or for specific services (e.g., aquatics). Where only one or a few TRSs are employed, they may deliver services throughout the agency to all types of clients. An example of the former type of setting might be a large hospital or special recreation district while the latter setting might be a social service agency (YMCA) or a public park and recreation department. Staff organization is reflected in agency and departmental charts (refer to figures 5.1, 5.2, 5.3), which you are encouraged to review as internships and future career options are contemplated.

By nature, TRSs have a broad service perspective and deliver services in a variety of settings. In a global economy, multiskilled staff members who can address the needs of diverse client groups are a valuable asset. Three broad skill categories include: (1) technical competencies associated with the APIE process; (2) social and emotional skills necessary to facilitate helping relationships; and (3) work skills that are reflected in the term "professionalism." Skills that complement the APIE process include cross-disciplinary knowledge, communication, teamwork, and analytical reasoning ("Preparing Students," 2007). In the second category, competencies include social and self-awareness, self-management, relationship skills, responsible decision-making, adaptability, creativity, and the vision to adjust to a diverse workforce and a fast-changing culture (Beland, 2007). Those associated with professionalism include a strong work ethic, sound philosophy, and maintenance of good working relationships with clients (Wozencroft, Voelkl, & McGuire, 2006). TRSs should also note on job descriptions certifications like first aid, aquatics, crisis intervention, and sign language. Staff members may be hired because of a specialized skill, yet be valued for their broad-based experiential background and willingness to maintain and gain credentials applicable to the agency's services.

Considerable focus has been placed on self-managed teams in the workplace as a key to improving performance (Carter & O'Morrow, 2006). The use of teams to devise solutions and improve care is critical when safety and quality improvement are management priorities (Insalaco, Ozkurt, & Santiago, 2007). Managers, as well as staff, may participate on quality improvement teams and various department or unit teams. Responsibilities of team members vary, yet as managers hire staff, they assess their potential as productive team members.

Diversity in the Workplace

Health and human services are becoming more diverse due to demographic shifts as well as opportunities created by technology to communicate across geographic boundaries. A diverse workforce is important to providing services with all populations (Blair & Coyle, 2005; Mitchell & Lassiter, 2006). Managers craft mission statements that address diversity and provide staff with resources that support diversity and embrace cultural sensitivity. Staff training, workshops, and infusion of cultural diversity into coursework have been found to be instrumental in preparing new employees and current staff to work well in diverse environments (Blair & Coyle). Specific competencies recommended for entry-level practitioners are "(1) an understanding of their own culture and its impact on other cultural groups and (2) an understanding of how clinical practice and communication are impacted by culture" (Getz & Austin, 2001, p. 26). Professionals who possess awareness and sensitivity to various cultural perspectives will increase their ability to deliver effective services; thus, not only is productivity influenced by one's cultural competence, but also workforce retention is enhanced through multicultural awareness and practices.

Paraprofessionals, Interns, and Volunteers

Changes in agencies and organizations, developments in technology, and the nature of health-care delivery today have implications for practitioner skills and practices. Identifying less costly ways to provide services has highlighted issues like specialization versus multi-skilling, and the relationship between professional and paraprofessional level personnel. Professional guidelines (ATRA, 2000) outline the working relationships between the TRS and the TRA (therapeutic recreation assistant). The latter assists and collaborates with the TRS in the assessment of clients and the delivery and evaluation of services, while the TRS provides appropriate levels of clinical supervision.

"The internship experience has become virtually universal in the training of all Certified Therapeutic Recreation Specialists who obtain their credential through the normal academic path" (Zabriskie & Ferguson, 2004, p. 28). Guidelines for the management of internships have been put forth by the professional organizations (Grote & Hasel, 1998; NTRS, 1997). The manager's role is to prepare staff to support student interns as they learn the professional practice of therapeutic recreation and transition into career tracks. Interns assume increasing degrees of responsibility yet must be clinically supervised as they learn how to establish—then relinquish—therapeutic relationships. The significance of the internship experience has increased as entry-level practitioners are expected to perform effectively soon after they acquire their first professional position.

Volunteers are another means to supplement a cost-constrained workforce. Managing volunteers includes activities similar to personnel operations associated with paid staff. TRSs may work through a human resources department to acquire volunteers or they may assume the entire volunteer management responsibility in their unit. Volunteers offer their talents, time, and financial resources to enhance services. Volunteer roles vary with the nature of the setting and clientele. Volunteers may assume supportive duties like fund-raising and resource acquisition or direct service duties as mentors or buddies during inclusion experiences. Managers develop and monitor volunteer protocols and facilitate volunteer recognition programs. The extent to which the agency uses volunteers influences both the manager's and staff duties in this area.

SUMMARY

Although not all TRSs become program managers, every TRS needs to know how to manage service delivery. All professionals will work for an agency that maintains accountability through the use of the four management components outlined in this chapter: a written plan of operation, financial operations, technical operations, and personnel operations. The written plan of operation is a comprehensive document or series of documents that provide the organizational structure for the department. The structural components of the plan include (1) statements of vision, mission, values, and goals; (2) organization structure; (3) a description of the scope of care and unit structure; (4) identification of the programs and services offered; (5) a compilation of the protocols and intervention plans; (6) a compilation of the policies, procedures, and rules governing service provision to clients; (7) guidelines for staff credentials; (8) procedures and criteria for quality improvement; and (9) a plan for evaluating programs and services and conducting research that documents benefits, outcomes, and effectiveness of evidence-based practices.

In this time of increasing pressure to control costs, professionals must be familiar with how health and human services are financed and the various alternatives for financing therapeutic recreation programs. In addition, specific techniques for determining the costs of individual interventions are necessary when participants are to be directly charged for the services they receive. Techniques for determining and allocating costs are also critical for administrators who wish to include the cost of a therapeutic recreation program as part of the agency's overhead or operating expenses. Specialists must be familiar with the budget process and be prepared to provide input as well as monitor expenses for programs and services.

Technical operations consider such functions as marketing, networking, and advocating to assure valued client outcomes on a consistent and predictable basis; using professional standards and evidence-based practices to advance safety, continuous improvement, and a high quality of care while maintaining productivity; developing risk and safety management programs; facilitating inclusion and access to programs and resources; using technology to communicate and to manage data; and performing tasks in an ethical manner. The quality and effectiveness of the department's programs and services is influenced by the attention and detail given to technical operations.

Proper management of personnel is essential to an effective therapeutic recreation program. Classifying positions; recruiting and selecting qualified employees; orienting, training, and supervising employees; assessing and maintaining staff competence; and evaluating staffing patterns and staff potential to function successfully on self-managed teams are all critical to the operation of efficient departments. Managers and staff daily experience diversity in the workplace. Through training and infusion of cultural diversity into coursework, the natural outcomes of diversity are addressed so new and existing employees bring awareness and sensitivity to their responsibilities. Entry-level professionals will encounter a mix of skills among staff and may work with paraprofessionals, interns, and volunteers. Understanding the manager's roles and responsibilities will help prepare you to face the challenges of providing quality services in a diverse, competitive, cost-conscious, and client-driven environment.

Key Terms

active treatment Services provided under individualized assessment and treatment plans that are supervised by a physician and considered as reasonable and necessary medical care.

allowances and uncollectibles Charges to those unable to pay that are passed on to other revenue or cost recovery centers like other clients or programs that are able to pay the service price.

Architectural and Transportation Barriers Compliance Board Established by the Rehabilitation Act of 1973 to ensure adherence to the Architectural Barriers Act of 1968. Aided in the preparation and publication of the Americans with Disabilities Act Accessibility Guidelines for Buildings and Facilities (ADAAG).

capital expenses Large sums of money associated with major purchases or construction of buildings that are either incorporated into the operating budget or for which the manager creates a separate budget.

capitation A fixed payment defined for a range of health-care services for a specific group of individuals. Employers contract with insurance companies to provide health-care coverage for employees for a specific rate.

carve outs Certain services that are excluded from capitation rates and reimbursed on a fee-for-service basis, like mental health costs.

competency assessment A process to ensure that staff competence is objectively assessed, maintained, and continually improved so quality performance in the provision of services is demonstrated.

cost allocation The process used to determine, identify, and assign the actual costs of a service to a particular department or program.

cost benefits Outcomes from intervention that are deemed worth the cost.

cost containment The process of designing programs to control the costs of services to clients.

direct costs Expenses—including personnel, supplies, and equipment—needed to provide a service.

expenses All costs incurred in the delivery of a service such as salaries, equipment, and supplies.

fee-for-service Charges assessed participants for the services they receive.

fiscal year (FY) The budget year of an agency; may or may not coincide with the calendar year.

indirect costs Expenses such as utilities, maintenance, and housekeeping that are also needed to provide a service. These costs are indirectly assigned (e.g. by a percentage) rather than being itemized by each service.

market segment Selecting and targeting a certain clientele (portion of the market) that is most appropriate for a specific service.

marketing The process of identifying the customer's needs and designing programs and services to ensure the customer establishes a long-term relationship with the service provider.

mission statement Briefly describes the reason and purpose a therapeutic recreation service exists.

necessary medical care A service that is required to meet specific diagnostic or treatment needs of a client.

net revenue surplus Profit.

outcome indicators Describe the effects of the service such as changes in functional capacity, health status, and/or quality of life.

philosophy statement Identifies the basic concepts, values, beliefs, or theories underlying services or outcomes.

policies, procedures, and rules Specific directions that establish how programs and services are to be operated.

privileging criteria Criteria that define the limits of professional practice based on the professional's competence and credentials.

process indicators Describe the nature of the interaction between the client and the service provider, such as assessments and documentation techniques.

productivity measurement The process of comparing the quantity of services provided with the amount of resources (such as staff and time) used to provide the service.

program budgets All the revenues and expenses for an entire program like aquatics, leisure education, or community outings; or for services like therapeutic recreation and senior programs.

prospective payment system (PPS) A method of reimbursement based upon paying a prearranged amount for specific services no matter what the actual cost of those services might be.

reasonable medical care A service which has been shown to be effective in improving a patient's functional capacity, health status, and/or quality of life.

risk management Identifying and developing processes for controlling the delivery of safe, quality services.

scope of care Identifies the programs and services available from the department.

structure indicators Resources that must be available for service delivery, like staff and equipment.

third-party payer A private insurance company or government agency that reimburses another institution or individual for services provided to a client.

Uniform Federal Accessibility Standards (UFAS) Criteria used to define accessibility prior to ADAAG.

unit cost The specific increment, such as an hour or a day, that is used to allocate a cost for a service.

utilization review The assessment of the necessity and effectiveness of a service in the care and treatment of clients.

vision Identifies an agency's basic values and beliefs and focuses on the future or end results, which define how it wants to be perceived by the public.

zero-based budget A form of budgeting that requires justification of each service in the next annual budget since in essence each account starts with a zero balance in the new fiscal year.

Study Questions

1. Explain why therapeutic recreation specialists should become familiar with basic management tools and techniques.

2. Identify the components of a written plan of operation and discuss their relevance to therapeutic recreation programming.

3. Identify the various forms of health-care financing and the alternative methods to fund therapeutic recreation services.

4. What information is needed to determine an appropriate fee-for-service?

5. What is active treatment?

6. Who is a third-party payer?

7. Identify and briefly discuss the tasks and skills used in the technical operations of a therapeutic recreation program.

8. Interpret the concepts of inclusion, accessibility, and universal design. What legislation has impacted these concepts?

9. Define and give an example of a structure indicator, a process indicator, and an outcome indicator.

10. Develop a rationale for conducting evaluation and research to document outcomes, benefits, and results of evidence-based practices.

Practical Experiences to Enhance Student Objectives

1. Visit the professional organization Web site (ATRA) to study the ethics code and standards of practice. Review the NCTRC Web site to identify criteria to become a CTRS.

2. Use the cost allocation form in exhibit 5.5 to determine the hourly cost of a therapeutic recreation service at an agency in your community.

3. Locate a copy of the accreditation standards published by the Joint Commission (www.jcaho.org) or Carf International (www.carf.org) and identify all the standards that apply to therapeutic recreation services.

4. Discuss the operating budget with an agency's therapeutic recreation administrators. Identify the sources of revenue, the primary expenditures, and the responsibilities of respective staff in preparing and monitoring the budget(s). Investigate the use of CPT codes and identify the codes that may be applicable in TR/RT settings.

5. Visit an agency that uses paraprofessionals, interns, and volunteers. Collect management documents and determine the processes used to recruit, train, place, evaluate, and reward paraprofessionals, interns, and volunteers.

6. Conduct an accessibility survey using the Americans with Disabilities Act Accessibility Guidelines (www.access-board.gov) as the standard for your survey. Then take measurements of areas and facilities and identify locations that are in compliance with the standards and those that require renovation to comply with the standards.

7. Discuss with practitioners the concepts of networking and advocacy. What activities occur during national TR/RT week?

II

AN OVERVIEW OF INDIVIDUALS WITH DISABILITIES

In Part Two we focus on the functioning abilities, programming implications, delivery settings, leadership considerations, and related health and human service concerns of individuals representative of the clients with whom you will someday establish a therapeutic relationship. The content in the first four chapters represents the diagnostic groupings listed under foundational knowledge of the professional knowledge domains of the National Council for Therapeutic Recreation Certification (http://www.nctrc.org/documents/5JobAnalysis.pdf).

In chapters 6 and 7 we consider individuals with physical, sensory, and communication impairments. The material is organized by the bodily system(s) impacted. Common characteristics of clients with the impairments studied in chapter 6 are limited physical abilities regardless of the impairment. In chapter 7, we discover that, for some individuals, the outcomes of illness, although not physically or visually apparent, may be life threatening (as is true with cardiovascular diseases and cancer) or lifelong (as with diabetes mellitus or chronic fatigue syndrome). Also, the degree of impairment attributed to the disability may not necessarily be reflective of the actual limitations (as is the case with sensory impairments).

Chapter 8 discusses individuals with cognition and related impairments (learning, motor skills, communication, feeding and eating disorders; intellectual disabilities; severe multiple impairments; and autism). The single common feature of these impairments is their origination during the growth and development process; otherwise, the range of abilities demonstrated by individuals with these impairments is diverse. You will become familiar with psychological and related impairments in chapter 9, where the *Diagnostic and Statistical Manual of Mental Disorders* is introduced as the primary tool of the medical model for interpretation of these impairments.

The remaining three chapters address individuals with impairments with whom therapeutic recreators are employed, although they are not specifically identified as impairment populations by the 2007 NCTRC National Job Analysis. Social impairments—HIV/AIDS, abuse and neglect, poverty and homelessness, and unlawful behaviors—are introduced in chapter 10. People who experience these circumstances are unable to mediate their personal lives and social relationships. Chapter 11 considers children and young adults who are hospitalized as a result of physical impairments, illnesses, elective surgeries, or chronic health-care conditions. We cover the psychosocial aspects of hospitalization on children and youth and their caregivers, the needs of pediatric clients, and the role of therapeutic recreation in family-centered care. In chapter 12 we discuss the process of aging and the illnesses and disabilities that affect well-aging individuals as well as aging individuals with impairments.

Each chapter has a similar format. The opening section presents clinical definitions, diagnoses, prognoses, and statistics. Symptomatology by behavioral domain is outlined in the Functioning Characteristics section. The next three sections—Purpose of Therapeutic Recreation, Delivery Settings, and Leadership Interaction and Intervention Considerations—outline the role of therapeutic recreation as it relates to individuals with specific disabilities. As you will recall, the therapeutic recreation process of assessment, planning, implementation, and evaluation occurs when the therapist enters into a helping relationship with a client. The section on Applying the Therapeutic Recreation Process uses a case-study approach to carry through this process with clients like those with whom you will someday work. A closing section, Related Considerations, presents information critical to our professional interactions and roles.

During their careers, therapeutic recreation specialists (TRSs) are likely to be exposed to individuals with impairments representative of each of the NCTRC groupings (cognitive, physical, sensory, and psychological) as well as the other populations we have discussed. The nature of health and human service systems is rapidly changing: hospitalized clients are in residence shorter time periods; clients residing in health-care facilities have greater health and human service needs (such as for skilled nursing); school-age children with disabilities are functioning in inclusive environments; clients at risk (e.g., children in poverty, individuals with AIDS) are becoming apparent in specific age groups; and some clients are living out their lives with chronic and life threatening (cancer) impairments. TRSs are impacted by these dynamics. To illustrate, many are now employed as inclusion specialists and as home health-care personnel. The intent of this text is to introduce you to both the traditional and evolving employment arenas, their practices, and their diverse clientele. The information presented is foundational to future coursework in this field; however, keep in mind that each reader's implementation of the concepts presented is influenced by his or her unique application of "self" through helping relationships, which mature with professional practice.

Musculoskeletal, Neurological, and Neuromuscular System Impairments

After reading this chapter, students will be able to

✔ Demonstrate an understanding of the functioning characteristics and leisure needs of people with physical impairments affecting the musculoskeletal and nervous systems

✔ Explain the nature of therapeutic recreation with those who have musculoskeletal, neurological, or neuromuscular impairments

✔ Identify therapeutic recreation delivery settings and interaction and intervention processes

✔ Describe application of the therapeutic recreation process with individuals having musculoskeletal, neurological, or neuromuscular impairments

✔ Identify considerations unique to therapeutic recreation programs for people with musculoskeletal, neurological, or neuromuscular impairments

In this chapter and the next, we will discuss physical impairments. These impairments affect the musculoskeletal, nervous, circulatory, and respiratory systems and include endocrine disorders and infectious diseases. These impairments are congenital or traumatic in origin and have temporary, chronic, degenerative, or terminal consequences. These impairments affect individuals of all ages and are diverse in nature. A common characteristic of the impairments in this chapter is that they limit physical expression. The complexity of physical impairments is exemplified by the many settings and services delivered: hospital rehabilitation units for traumatic brain injury, transitional living centers, pediatric hospitals, sub-acute programs, and sports programs for persons who are physically challenged, to name a few.

INTRODUCTION

The disorders discussed in this chapter limit the physical functioning of one or more of the body's systems. Since many of the body's systems work in concert, an injury or illness affecting one system may impact other systems. For example, when a person experiences a spinal cord injury (SCI) or trauma to the musculoskeletal system, the circulatory and respiratory systems may also experience dysfunction. The use of adapted equipment and assistive devices to compensate and substitute for physical limitations impacts a person's mobility and interactions with others and with his or her environment. Therefore, as TRSs design therapeutic recreation programs they must consider ways to make individuals' environments accessible to them.

The physical impairments presented in this chapter have been organized into three categories: musculoskeletal impairments affect the bones, joints, and muscles; neurological impairments affect the nervous system; and neuromuscular impairments affect both systems. Each of these three sections presents disabilities TRSs are likely to encounter, and although the primary label is "physical impairment," such dysfunction affects many of the body's systems and requires comprehensive therapeutic recreation services.

MUSCULOSKELETAL IMPAIRMENTS

Disabilities affecting the musculoskeletal system include: muscular dystrophy, arthritis, spina bifida, osteoporosis, myasthenia gravis, arthrogryposis, osteogenesis imperfecta, amputations, poliomyelitis and postpolio syndrome, orthopedic disorders, and thermal injuries. In this section, as in the following two sections, information is presented on etiology and symptoms, functioning characteristics, purpose of therapeutic recreation, delivery settings, leadership, and application of the therapeutic recreation process with specific case studies.

Muscular dystrophies (MDs) are a group of related muscle diseases that progressively weaken and cause atrophy of voluntary muscle groups. Muscular dystrophy (MD) itself is not fatal, yet its effects on the respiratory and cardiac systems cause death. The most prevalent form affects children, yet varieties of MD do occur in middle age or later.

Childhood muscular dystrophy (also known as *Duchenne*, or progressive muscular dystrophy) is the most common and severe form of muscular dystrophy and affects male children more frequently than female children (Mobily & MacNeil, 2002). It is genetically transmitted and congenital with no specific treatment to stop or reverse its

Physical disabilities tend to impact mobility and limit movement, yet the use of wheelchairs and other assistive devices can help individuals access recreational opportunities.

course. Although controversial, stem cell research with animals has been effective in restoring muscle function (Mackenzie, 2006). Symptoms begin to appear by age two or three but may appear as late as 10 or 11 and include a waddling gait, tendency to fall, *lordosis* (forward curvature of the spine), hypertrophy of calf muscles, and an inability to negotiate curbs or stairs, drink from a straw, or rise from a sitting position (Sherrill, 2004). Contractures develop in the ankle, knee, and hip joints, causing children to walk on their toes; this further increases the incidence of falling. As the degeneration process proceeds, muscles enlarge, resulting in a false appearance of physical well-being, which is why this form of muscular dystrophy is also referred to as *pseudohypertrophic* muscular dystrophy. By early teens, a person with childhood muscular dystrophy must rely upon a wheelchair for locomotion. Eventually, the person is confined to a bed and requires assistance with activities of daily living (ADL). This disorder results in death during adolescence or young adulthood, usually by age 30 (Mackenzie).

The most common form of adult muscular dystrophy among both males and females is facio-scapulo-humeral muscular dystrophy. Progression of this disorder is slow and persons may even experience periods of remission (Mobily & MacNeil, 2002). The first noticeable symptom is weakness in the facial muscles. Increasing weakness in shoulder and upper arm muscles precedes its progression to hip and thigh muscles. These symptoms may not begin to appear until a person reaches adolescence. Most often individuals are given a prognosis for a near-normal life span.

Another form of muscular dystrophy, limb-girdle, affects males and females equally and is similar to facio-scapulo-humeral except that the facial muscles are not as evidently impaired. Although weakness in thigh and hip muscles is more frequent than in the shoulder girdle, both lower and upper extremities are involved. The first symptoms may be difficulty raising the arms above the shoulder or difficulty climbing stairs. Degeneration progresses slowly, but severe motor limitations may result.

Arthritis is a term that describes more than 100 medical conditions that cause joint inflammation. Arthritis causes pain, stiffness, swelling, redness, heat, and decreased range of motion (ROM) at the joints. Osteoarthritis (OA) or degenerative joint disease (DJD) results from deterioration of articular cartilage that covers the ends of bones in the joints and is the most common form of arthritis (Porter & burlingame, 2006; Rooney, 2004). While degenerative but not necessarily progressive (moving from one joint to another), chances of developing osteoarthritis increase after age 60, but can develop at any age, with deterioration in the most commonly used joints and/or joints that have been injured (Mobily & MacNeil, 2002; King, Yang, & Malkin, 2006; Rooney). Rheumatoid arthritis, less common than OA, attacks the joint lining (synovium) and damages bone and cartilage. This results in inflammation and pain affecting joints on both sides of the body; symptoms may be present in the 20s and 30s, yet most people develop it in their 50s and 60s (Rooney). Because of its earlier age of onset (Mobily & MacNeil), it is known as the most debilitating and painful form of arthritis. Moreover, joint stiffness does not ease with activity, as with OA (Rooney). Further, rheumatoid arthritis may cause loss of appetite, lethargy, and anemia.

Juvenile rheumatoid arthritis affects children as young as six weeks; average age of onset is six years (Dunn & Leitschuh, 2006; Sherrill, 2004). In children the prognosis is positive, with only 10% of affected children experiencing functional impairments later in life (Dunn & Leitschuh). Systemic rheumatoid arthritis in children—sometimes called Still's disease—affects the entire body, while peripheral arthritis affects only the joints; the knee is most commonly involved. Onset may be sudden and painful, or progressive, with swelling that limits ROM.

Spina bifida, a nonprogressive congenital defect, results when, prior to birth, the vertebral arches fail to close completely around the spinal cord. Three types are generally identified. In spina bifida occulta, the vertebral column forms incompletely, yet there are no external manifestations of this impairment other than a clump of dark hair or a dimple on the back. Spina bifida with meningocele occurs when the coverings of the spinal cord (meninges) and cerebrospinal fluid protrude in a sac through the defect in the spinal cord. Motor and sensory deficiencies are not usually evident. Spina bifida with myelomeningocele (MM) occurs when the protruding sac also contains portions of the spinal cord. Motor dysfunction is usually evident.

Spina bifida is the second most common physical impairment in school-age children (cerebral palsy is most prevalent), and MM is the most prevalent form of spina bifida among adults and children (Sherrill, 2004). The degree of impairment caused by MM is determined by the location of the **lesion** (discontinuation of tissue or loss of function of a part of the body) on the spine. Sacral lesions cause weakness in the feet. Lumbar-thoracic (lower back) lesions result in paresis (partial paralysis) or *paraplegia* in the lower extremities and people with this form of spina bifida require leg braces or a wheelchair for ambulation. Secondary consequences of MM include incontinence, deformities of the spinal column (scoliosis) and feet, obesity, skin lesions and pressure sores, seizures, congenital heart disease, urinary tract and renal infections, and **hydrocephalus** if excessive amounts of cerebrospinal fluid accumulate within the cranial cavity.

Osteoporosis refers to loss in mineral content of bones, causing bone tissue deterioration and bone mass loss. The consequence is that bones become more porous and brittle and are less able to support the body's weight and withstand external forces on the skeleton—leading to an increased risk of fractures (Mobily & Ostiguy, 2004; Porter & burlingame, 2006). As the population ages, it is expected to reach epidemic proportions worldwide (Herson, 2007), especially among Caucasian and Asian women and those who are thin and small-boned (Crews, 2007). Osteoporosis is also a secondary outcome of, for example, cerebral palsy, spinal cord injuries, cancer, and situations in which excessive amounts of bed rest and physical inactivity are present. People with osteoporosis are more likely to experience fractures of the hip, spine, and wrist—including pathological fractures, which occur when a bone is broken as a person transfers from one position to another (Porter & burlingame).

Myasthenia gravis is a chronic disease characterized by progressive muscular weakness with remissions and exacerbations. Onset occurs at any age yet is most common in women in their 20s and 30s and in men in their 50s and 60s (Palmier, 2005). Symptoms vary, appear over extended time periods, and initially may go undetected. Facial and throat muscles are the first to be affected; especially ocular muscles (drooping eyelid) and muscles of mastication (difficulty chewing) (Mobily & MacNeil, 2002). As the disease progresses, back, abdomen, arm (more commonly than leg), and leg muscles are affected. Muscle weakness is most evident following exercise or at the end of the day, and, with rest, improves. If the respiratory muscles are affected this may result in fatal pulmonary complications.

Arthrogryposis multiplex congenital (AMC) is a nonprogressive congenital contracture syndrome characterized by stiff joints and weak muscles. Limited arm and shoulder movement result from "internal rotation at the shoulder joints, elbow extension, pronated forearms, [and] radial flexion of wrists" (Sherrill, 2004, p. 654). Further, flexion and outward rotation occurs at the hip joint and abnormal positions of the knees and feet are present. Some people use wheelchairs while others experience minimal affects. The primary disability is restricted ROM (Sherrill).

Osteogenesis imperfecta (OI) is inherited and present at birth or becomes evident in later childhood. Children are born with broken bones or they are prone to fractures through their early teens. OI is evidenced by a "short stature and small limbs that are bowed in various distortions from repetitive fractures" (Sherrill, 2004, p. 658). After age 15 the incidence of bone fractures decreases (Sherrill). Because child abuse is a frequent cause of fractures, undiagnosed or mild OI may be mistaken for child abuse. Until the condition arrests itself, youth may ambulate with wheelchairs and TRSs must be careful to avoid fractures during assists and transfers.

An **amputation** is the loss of all limb elements below a certain point (Porter & burlingame, 2006). Major causes of amputation are "trauma, including war-related injuries, diseases, and congenital limb deficiencies" (Esquenazi, 2004, p. 831). Congenital limb deficiencies (congenital amputation) are present at birth, while acquired amputation refers to a loss after birth. Limb deficiencies are more common than acquired amputations, with lower limb more common than upper limb amputations (Sherrill, 2004). Causes of amputation vary from country to country: Countries with recent history of warfare account for up to 80% of trauma amputations, while developed countries attribute amputations to vascular disease, diabetes mellitus, and tumors (Esquenazi). Functioning ability is influenced by the number of missing limbs, level of amputation, and portion of the limb remaining. To illustrate, when the remaining stump is long and the joint is intact, fitting a prosthetic device to the stump is easier and joint flexion and extension are possible. A number of secondary problems impact functioning with prosthetics and include pain, infection, skin breakdown, edema (swelling), contractures, phantom sensation (presence of amputated limb), deconditioning, and dermatologic problems associated with the liner, socks, sockets, or suspension mechanism (Porter & burlingame).

Poliomyelitis is an inflammation affecting spinal cord motor cells, causing varying degrees of temporary and permanent paralysis in the upper and lower extremities. **Postpolio syndrome (PPS)** (or sequelae) describes a number of returning symptoms affecting individuals who have had poliomyelitis. Polio means "gray" and myelitis indicates infection. The polio virus destroys only the motor nerve cells, leaving sensation intact. Polio can attack people of any age; the incidence is higher among females than males. A vaccination has virtually eliminated new cases in industrialized countries but not in developing countries. It is believed that up to 50% of polio survivors are affected by returning symptoms like new joint and muscle pain accompanied by joint disturbance and impaired mobility, muscle weakness at old and new sites, general fatigue, respiratory problems, progressive scoliosis, dysphagia, sleep apnea, and cold sensitivity (Acello, 2003; Gevirtz, 2006).

A number of **orthopedic impairments** (disorders affecting the bones, joints, muscles) manifest chronic conditions that require temporary or lifelong adjustments. Common congenital disorders include talipes (*clubfoot*) and *congenital dislocation of the hip*. Osteochondroses (growth plate disorders) such as *Perthes' disease, Osgood-Schlatter disease*, and *Scheuermann's disease* occur among school-age children and may require temporary casting or bracing. Postural deviations such as *scoliosis, kyphosis*, and *lordosis* require bracing or surgery to correct the spinal curvature and result in temporary activity restrictions. *Spondylitis* and *spondylolisthesis* are disorders of the spinal column requiring surgery to fuse affected vertebrae which, in turn, causes permanent stiffening of the back.

Thermal injuries are caused by flames, chemicals, electricity, sunburn, and prolonged contact with extreme degrees of heat and cold. People between the ages of 20 and 30 receive the highest number of thermal injuries, and persons under age 5 and over age 65 experience the highest mortality rates (Sherrill, 2004). Most thermal injuries occur in the home and may result in longer than usual hospitalizations, disfigurement, mobility impairments, chronic pain, and amputations.

The nature of tissue damage caused by a thermal injury is determined by the duration of time the tissue is exposed to the source of heat or cold and the intensity of the temperature. Burns are clinically identified by depth of tissue injury and percent of body surface involved:

- Superficial, or first degree, burns affect the epidermis and are characterized by pain, edema, and redness.

- Partial thickness, or second-degree, burns affect the epidermis and dermis to varying depths and are characterized by blisters and/or infection, loss of body fluids, and pain.

- Full thickness, or third degree, burns affect the epidermis, dermis, and all skin appendages, causing a charred, painless surface, or eschar, to develop.

To standardize estimates of percent of body surface involved, health-care professionals superficially divide the body into areas equal to multiples of 9% of its total surface, known as the **Rule of Nines**. The head and upper extremities are each 9%; the front and back of the trunk are each 18%; and, the lower extremities are each 18%. Since the skin is the largest organ of the body, the greater the extent of the burn, the greater is the damage to various support systems and the potential for complications (shock, fluid loss, infections) and death. For example, when a young or elderly person is burned over 18% of his or her body surface, the burn is considered to be critical. A young adult with the same surface area damage might not be considered to be in critical condition. Electrical burns are considered to be full thickness (or third degree) burns, even though the body surface damage appears minimal. Electricity flows through the body along the pathways of least resistance; that is, through the blood vessels. This causes blood clotting and tissue death, which can lead to heart stoppage, paralysis of respiration, or amputation.

Functioning Characteristics

Muscular Dystrophy

The Muscular Dystrophy Association of America defines eight functional ability stages of persons with muscular dystrophy (Sherrill, 2004):

Stage 1: Ambulates with mild waddling gait, lordosis, can climb stairs
Stage 2: Ambulates with moderate waddling gait, lordosis, uses assistance to climb stairs
Stage 3: Ambulates with moderate to severe waddling gait, lordosis, cannot climb stairs, can stand erect
Stage 4: Ambulates with severe waddling gait, lordosis, cannot stand from seated position
Stage 5: Performs daily activities independently using wheelchair
Stage 6: Pushes wheelchair but needs assistance with daily activities
Stage 7: Pushes wheelchair short distances, requires back support and ADL assistance
Stage 8: Functions from bed and needs assistance with daily activities

Initially, daily exercise slows the effects of muscular dystrophy. Functional ability deteriorates more rapidly once the person becomes a wheelchair user. Extended periods of bed rest contribute to muscle atrophy and respiratory complications. An individual with muscular dystrophy can sustain physical activity, yet fatigue should be avoided. His or her intellectual capacity is usually unaffected, yet social-emotional immaturity, withdrawal, depression, and lowered tolerance and motivation levels become evident as physical limitations increase.

Arthritis

Rheumatoid arthritis is a chronic disease that may affect different joints at different times. It is also progressive with periods of remission. Extended periods of bed rest due to acute attacks reduce cardiovascular endurance. Pain, stiffness, and deformities are unpredictable. Osteoarthritis attacks the weight-bearing joints and may worsen with weather changes, yet is predictable from day to day with joint changes extending over a period of time (Bullock, Mahon, & Killingsworth, 2010). Children with juvenile rheumatoid arthritis may experience periods of remission "interspersed with weeks of acute illness and maximum joint involvement" (Sherrill, 2004, p. 652). They require rest and daily ROM exercises. If steroids like cortisone are prescribed, normal growth patterns are inhibited. Arthritis does not affect cognitive functioning, though individuals may experience anxiety and fear of injury to inflamed joints. Social interactions are restricted by mobility impairments. Adjusting to pain, not feeling well, and deformity take an emotional toll on children and adults. Pain in weight-bearing joints may lead to joint replacement (Porter & burlingame, 2006). Also, pain and inactivity may lead to such secondary issues as obesity, depression, high blood pressure, and heart disease.

Spina Bifida

Spina bifida occulta may not cause disability, while MM results in paralysis and absence of sensation below the lesion level and urinary and bowel incontinence (e.g., the bladder must be emptied manually or by **catheterization**). When hydrocephalus is present [70–90% of the time in MM (National Dissemination Center for Children with Disabilities, 2004)], a shunt may be surgically implanted to drain fluids from the ventricles into the abdominal cavity. Children with hydrocephalus may also experience cognitive impairments. Problems result when the lack of sensation in the lower limbs causes skin breakdown that goes unnoticed (Mobily & MacNeil, 2002), or when an athlete sustains a hip dislocation and is unaware of the injury due to the lack of sensation (Naugle, Stopka, & Brennan, 2007).

Osteoporosis

Osteoporosis, or porous bones, causes bone fragility and increased risk of fracture. People may not realize they have osteoporosis until a fracture occurs (Porter & burlingame, 2006). Consequences of decreased bone mineral density (BMD) include not only vertebral compression and hip fractures but also abdominal protrusion, acute and chronic pain, kyphosis secondary to multiple fractures, decreased respiratory capacity and functional ability, depression, immobility, and increased morbidity and mortality rates (Limburg, 2007; Porter & burlingame). Fractures due to falls among older adults are more serious as they are likely to have latent osteoporosis with bones that heal more slowly than younger persons (Mobily & Ostiguy, 2004). Once detected, prescription medication may halt the loss of bone mass. Clients also are encouraged to increase calcium and vitamin D intake while engaging in weight-bearing exercise.

Myasthenia Gravis

Myasthenia gravis limits an individual from performing strenuous repetitive activities of long duration. Ambulation and movements against resistance may be labored (Mobily & MacNeil, 2002). Emotional stress, infection, and common colds intensify the effects of the disease.

Arthrogryposis

People with arthrogryposis experience limited arm and shoulder movement and may rely on a wheelchair to enhance mobility. Secondary conditions like congenital heart disease, urinary tract problems, overweight, low fitness levels, and respiratory problems impose limitations.

Osteogenesis Imperfecta (OI)

The ease with which bones become weak and break limits movement. Chest and spinal defects limit aerobic endurance and may be the result of osteoporosis attributed to lack of exercise (Sherrill, 2004). Psychosocial development is interrupted by repeated hospitalizations and rest periods necessary for healing.

Amputations

Functioning with an amputation is influenced by age of occurrence, number of limbs involved, and residual abilities. Acquired limb loss that results from diabetes with older adults, for example, is often more traumatic for individuals than congenital amputations. People with congenital amputations have no past experience with which to compare their loss, while those who experience limb loss during or after childhood must incorporate disability into their identities and, often, manage other health problems or concurrent injuries (Sherrill, 2004). Bilateral amputations have a greater impact on a person's ability to balance than do unilateral amputations. Joint loss affects residual abilities, especially range of motion. Functioning is also impacted by increases in energy expenditure to use a prosthesis, sweating in the remaining body parts, and loss of muscle mass and/or muscle atrophy around the stump.

Poliomyelitis & Postpolio Syndrome (Sequelae)

Acute poliomyelitis attacks cause high fevers, severe weakness, and muscle pain; and with the chronic form, progressive muscle weakening occurs. Some forms are remittent, yet between attacks weakened and contracted muscles do not regain their functional capacity. Individuals also experience skin discoloration, scaling, and atrophy. The most evident outcome of poliomyelitis is dysfunction of the lower limbs resulting in the use of crutches and/or wheelchairs for ambulation. In postpolio syndrome (PPS), symptoms range from mild to debilitating, and may wax and wane with muscle weakness progressing over a number of years. Functional challenges with ADL, mobility, and overuse syndrome (pain and muscle weakness after strenuous use) are in evidence (Sherrill, 2004). Psychological adjustment to altered lifestyles and the presence of muscle and joint pain impacts quality of life.

Orthopedic Impairments

Orthopedic impairments affect balance, ambulation, flexibility, and an individual's ability to complete self-care tasks. The emotional challenges an individual experiences due to orthopedic impairments are influenced by the person's age at the onset and the suddenness with which he or she must adjust to mobility limitations. Children and teens experience limitations in play, which may affect their social development. The time consumed by medical and surgical interventions reduces an individual's learning and work time.

Thermal Injuries

The skin has immune and metabolic functions and is important in regulating body temperature, fluids, and protein and electrolyte homeostasis (Kagan, 2000). Initial concern is excessive loss of fluids that may lead to shock (Mobily & Ostiguy, 2004). Also of concern within the first 48 hours is respiratory complications and edema (Porter & burlingame, 2006). Susceptibility to infection caused by the loss of functional skin barrier is an ongoing issue. Secondary impairments of thermal injuries are managed with extensive rehabilitation. When an individual receives a thermal injury, scar tissue grows from the periphery of the wound to its center. A thick covering (**eschar**) forms over the wounded area and causes contractures that limit range of motion. Jobsts (elastic supports) and isoprene splints or braces are used to apply pressure to healing areas and to manage scar tissue growth. Itching (pruritis) and skin sensitivity to sunlight and chlorine result with use of these devices. Extended periods of immobilization and social isolation will protect an individual against infection, yet result in contractures, decreased flexibility, and deconditioning. When eschar tissue is removed through debridement procedures, shaving, or washing, nerve endings are exposed and intense pain results. Frequent removal of jobsts or dressings to cleanse the surface area also is painful.

Purpose of Therapeutic Recreation

Muscular Dystrophy

Children with muscular dystrophy experience fewer opportunities to play and become even less active as they grow older. Adults experience change in work and social activities as degeneration progresses. Therapeutic recreation programs focus on outcomes that promote quality of life, such as enhancing social networks; improving self-control; promoting meaningful use of discretionary time; maintaining strength, flexibility, fitness, and range of motion; and sustaining independent functioning. Swimming, rhythmic breathing, and yoga are recommended to strengthen muscles used in wheelchair ambulation and respiration. Stretching, range of motion activities, and flexion-extension exercises prevent contractures. Exercises completed from a seated position aid posture and strengthen muscle groups used in transferring to and from a wheelchair and in ADL. Leisure education can aid an individual's adjustment to extended periods of wheelchair use and bed rest by developing his or her interests and skills in activities such as cognitive games, artistic expression, journaling, maintaining contacts with support groups via the Internet, and using light-touch equipment to activate a TV or remote control car, for example (Mobily & MacNeil, 2002).

Arthritis

Extent of joint involvement and damage, as well as chronic pain determine the participation of people with arthritis in therapeutic recreation programs. When in remission, an individual's participation may be unaffected. When pain is severe, however, treatment includes prescribed bed rest, heat applications, ROM exercises, and medication like steroids and nonsteroidal anti-inflammatory drugs (e.g., aspirin) to reduce inflammation and pain. TRSs use swimming, physical exercise and stretching, cycling, creative movement, relaxation, and throwing or target games like horseshoes to move the joints through their full range of motion and to prevent sitting or weight bearing for extended time periods. Leisure education experiences promote awareness of inclusive wellness options, adherence to routine physical activity and weight management practices, and adaptation to lifestyle changes and new leisure skills (Mobily & MacNeil, 2002; Porter & burlingame, 2006). Trauma to the joints such as that which can occur in contact sports or as a result of falls sustained during activity is contraindicated. Weight-bearing and gross motor activities may also cause pain and therefore should be avoided (Mobily & MacNeil).

Spina Bifida

TRSs select interventions to strengthen the upper torso, promote postural alignment, and prevent obesity, skin lesions and pressure sores, and secondary contrac-

Exercises performed in a swimming pool can help individuals with arthritis move the joints through their full range of motion.

tures. These exercises include chair aerobics, strength training, swimming, and archery to develop shoulder and arm strength; aerobic activities such as swimming to control body weight; and activities that require full range of motion (such as tossing a ball) to prevent secondary contractures. Clients need to maintain upper body strength when a wheelchair is the primary method of ambulation or used in sports competition. Through integrative play, sports, and recreation experiences, TRSs encourage behaviors necessary for meaningful participation, like friendship development and social relationships. TRSs assist youth as they adapt to the energy expenditure necessary to ambulate with mobility aids (Pollock et al., 1997).

Osteoporosis

Osteoporosis can affect people who are ambulatory as well as those with varying degrees of paralysis, such as individuals with spinal cord injuries. TRSs can help an individual retard the rate of calcium loss with paralysis by prescribing passive range of motion exercises and by placing individuals on tilt-tables. TRSs work with ambulatory individuals to design therapeutic recreation programs involving weight-bearing and resistance exercises such as walking and yoga, provided these activities can still be tolerated (Crews, 2007). TRSs may conduct fall prevention programs through outpatient clinics and community agencies like the YMCA.

Myasthenia Gravis

Individuals with myasthenia gravis have difficulty completing activities that do not permit rest periods or that require prolonged standing or walking. Therefore, TRSs design programs where breathing capacity is maintained. Swimming is one such activity, however prolonged exposure to ultraviolet light should be avoided. Social events and cognitive experiences (like journal writing) promote expression and self-control and discourage depression.

Arthrogryposis

Primary interventions are aimed at maintaining ROM. Aquatics and water exercise promote relaxation and fitness. TRSs working with adaptive physical educators encourage adjustment to assistive devices, participation in competitive sports and inclusive recreation to promote friendships, leisure education, and physical well-being.

Osteogenesis Imperfecta (OI)

As the incidence of fractures decreases, greater degrees of participation in physical activities like swimming and ROM exercises are possible as well as increased social experiences. As adults, participation using wheelchairs increases mobility and in some instances, individuals take part in competitive sporting events. TRSs help participants adapt to environmental barriers so unnecessary fractures are avoided.

Amputations

To participate in recreation and leisure activities, an individual may choose to use a **prosthesis** (an artificial or substitute limb or body part) like a Flex-Foot. Alternatively, some people may select to use a wheelchair to gain mobility and avoid damage

Athletes with amputations participate in a wide variety of recreational and competitive sports. Some choose to use a prosthetic limb, while others elect to use a wheelchair to gain mobility.

to the prosthesis or involved limb(s). In either case, the visual presence of a "loss" may affect others' perceptions of participants' capabilities. By promoting sports competition, TRSs can help individuals with amputations develop self-advocacy skills that break down physical and social barriers. As noted in the *Healthy People 2010* document, people with disabilities are less physically active than those without disabilities. Thus a primary focus of TRSs is to promote a physically active lifestyle (Porter & burlingame, 2006). Strengthening, endurance, ROM, energy conservation, activity adaptations, residual limb care, proper body alignments, and community recreation are client rehabilitation goals (Porter & burlingame; Sherrill, 2004).

Poliomyelitis & Postpolio Syndrome (Sequelae)

The use of braces, crutches, and wheelchairs affects movement and requires adaptations. The incomplete nature of paralysis makes judging the lesion level and degree of impairment difficult. Intellectual capacity is unaffected. TRSs are cautious with strenuous physical activity requirements and control temperature variations during intervention. Additionally, the promotion of a healthy diet, high in protein, occurs during formal wellness classes and through support group activities. Adults with postpolio syndrome can self-monitor their activity levels while using services offered at recreation centers, YMCAs, and private health clubs.

Orthopedic Impairments

Orthopedic disorders are usually treated with surgery, bracing, and casting. Activities that involve direct forceful contact to a specific joint or extended periods of weight-bearing are contraindicated for people with orthopedic disorders. Therefore, TRSs design treatment programs involving aquatic exercises and promote wheelchair sports. They also prescribe exercises that stretch and strengthen affected muscle groups. TRSs focus on helping individuals with chronic disorders adapt to their impairments and assistive devices. They also involve them in creative expression activities to release feelings and adjust to lifelong impairments.

Thermal Injuries

Thermal injuries and their rehabilitation limit a person's mobility and cause disfigurement, sometimes requiring reconstructive surgery. TRSs use range of motion and relaxation training to encourage individuals to develop the coping skills needed for extended periods of splinting and bracing. TRSs also design bedside activities to divert a patient's attention from the pain that occurs with skin grafting and debridement procedures. Individuals often wear pressure garments to prevent hypertrophic scarring (irregular scar tissue), which temporarily disguise deformities and limit mobility, yet when removed these garments may reveal a person whose features are quite different from his or her previous appearance. The TRS includes family and friends in the treatment procedures to foster emotional adjustments to the person's altered self-image. TRSs also prepare individuals for the client's return to the community through phased reintegration (Porter & burlingame, 2006). Therapy also includes encouraging participants to engage in physical activity so their appetite is enhanced and physical well-being is promoted. During physical activity, TRSs are mindful of the potential for dehydration and heat stroke because scar tissue has no sweat glands and other body areas compensate by sweating more (Sherrill, 2004).

Delivery Settings

People who experience musculoskeletal disabilities must cope with congenital or chronic impairments having lifelong manifestations. The progression associated with the muscular dystrophies and myasthenia gravis or arthritis result in intermittent hospitalizations as the degeneration causes increasing mobility limitations. Those with amputations and thermal injuries may require intensive inpatient care to address life-threatening complications following the trauma. People with disabilities like spina bifida, osteoporosis, arthrogryposis, osteogenesis imperfecta, postpolio syndrome, and orthopedic disorders experience ongoing visits with clinicians to adjust medication and adaptive and assistive devices.

TRSs working in hospitals function as integral members of treatment teams. As such they complete assessments, develop treatment goals, conduct leisure education sessions, and promote health practices that address impaired functioning—both directly attributable to the disability and to secondary complications (e.g., spasticity, contractures, and reduced ROM). TRSs in children's hospitals, camps, after-school programs, sports and fitness organizations, day programs, and residential settings (e.g., host homes) develop plans to use residual skills and mobility aids to enable optimal physical and social functioning so that clients can enjoy childhood activities. TRSs work with aquatic and equestrian specialists, for example, to support the outpatient goals of occupational and physical therapists. Also, TRSs co-lead family programs and support groups with social workers and home health-care staff. TRSs work hand-in-hand with community recreators to plan transitions, conduct and sponsor events (e.g., competitions like wheelchair sports), and coordinate compliance with ADA standards.

Leadership Interaction and Intervention Considerations

TRSs working with youth and adults with musculoskeletal disabilities address specific chronic needs through various therapeutic interventions and helping processes.

- Stretching exercises and deep-breathing exercises prevent muscle shortening and contractures and promote relaxation and pain management.

- Youth and adults experience pain and stiffness that may contribute to mood swings. Maintaining ROM is encouraged by avoiding stationary positions for extended time periods.

- Aquatics and activities conducted on padded exercise equipment protect the fragile musculoskeletal system and encourage the maintenance of cardiorespiratory fitness.

- Youth with spina bifida who have had a shunt inserted require precautions to prevent direct insult to the head, neck, chest, and abdomen (Sherrill, 2004). TRSs also monitor closely the participant's contact with surfaces since the lack of sensation may result in an unknown scrape or cut that could bleed excessively without client awareness.

- Participants may elect to remove prostheses and use a wheelchair to gain mobility and protect the artificial limb from damage that might occur during participation.

- Participants with thermal injuries may be sensitive to sunlight and pool chemicals; protective clothing or artificial shade is arranged (Sherrill, 2004). Activity is best conducted in areas where temperature and humidity are controlled.

- TRSs use leisure education to develop awareness of cognitive and expressive activities that promote psychological well-being and accommodate periods of wheelchair use and bed rest.

- Individuals with spina bifida and all people with spinal paralysis above S2 (except those with polio) have bladder dysfunction that requires different urination processes (Sherrill, 2004). TRSs are aware of bathroom schedules, meal regulations, catheterization routines, and the management of defecation with surgical procedures like ileostomies and colostomies (surgeries that create openings in the abdomen through which a tube is inserted to connect the intestine with a bag attached to the outside of the body for collection of fecal matter).

- Psychological development is delayed in children and adversely affected in adults due to motor limitations and access issues. TRSs use leisure awareness to promote self-efficacy, social skills training, and opportunities for community reintegration.

Applying the Therapeutic Recreation Process

The therapeutic recreation process is applied with a child who has recently undergone surgery to install an ileal loop. Plans are underway for Mary to return to her family's home in the community.

Assessment

Demographic information.   Mary is a 10-year-old with spina bifida with myelomeningocele (lesion located at T6) who has just had an *ileocystostomy* (surgical creation of an opening through the abdominal wall into the ileum in order to divert urine from the bladder). She lives with her family and attends public school. She is the middle child with an older brother and younger sister.

History.   Mary has experienced a number of hospitalizations to adjust braces, fit her wheelchair, and manage bowel and bladder. She relies on her wheelchair for ambulation, and physical therapists (PTs) have helped Mary adapt to changes in chair use and chair type. Her recent surgery was to install permanent appliances to manage urination.

Present behavior.   Mary will be an inpatient on the rehabilitation unit for three to five days. She experiences some scoliosis. She is one grade behind as a result of her hospitalizations. Her family is very active in a local YMCA.

Planning

Long-term goal.   The long-term goal of the TR process is to assist Mary in adjusting to her urinary appliance.

Short-term goals.   The two short-term goals are to help Mary learn to manage her appliance and to help Mary identify community participation opportunities.

Objective.   During a community outing Mary will participate in swimming and will complete all the tasks necessary to change her clothes prior to and following the swim. She will also properly empty/attach her urinary bag for the swim session.

Content. During a hospital tour that included a visit to the raised garden and horticultural area outside, Mary and the TRS practiced wheelchair (w/c) transfers and taking her coat on and off.

Process. Sessions with the TRS were scheduled for extended time periods, so Mary practiced draining her urinary bag and transferring from her w/c to comfortable furniture to play computer games and participate in pet therapy sessions.

Implementation

The TRS co-led sessions with the PT to provide Mary with supervised practice draining her appliance. Pet therapy volunteers arranged visits during which Mary had to transfer from her chair to hold and feed the animals. Mary and the TRS also practiced standing/stretching at frequent intervals to promote muscle strength to counter the scoliosis.

Evaluation

At discharge, Mary was able to drain her urinary device without assistance. The TRS documented daily contacts and noted her willingness to empty the bag. During the community outing, the TRS played leisure education games like Leisure Bingo, Leisure Charades, and Name That Leisure Activity. When Mary went home she and her family identified three activities per week for Mary to do after school and with her family.

NEUROLOGICAL IMPAIRMENTS

Several disabilities primarily affect the nervous system. Among the more common are cerebral palsy, convulsive disorders, strokes, and multiple sclerosis. **Cerebral palsy (CP)**, or Little's disease (named for the English surgeon who first identified its manifestations), can originate prior to birth, during birth, or in infancy (first two years of life) as a result of brain damage, injury, or malformation. Weakness, paralysis, poor muscle tone, and a lack of coordination are its primary characteristics. A person's normally controlled reflexes appear to be either uninhibited or exaggerated, resulting in the appearance of limited muscle control. Cerebral palsy is "the most common childhood physical disability and affects 2 to 2.5 children per 1000 born in the United States" (Krigger, 2006, p. 91). Individuals with cerebral palsy experience secondary impairments including impaired vision, hearing, and oral-motor functions; abnormal touch and pain perceptions; language, communication, and cognitive disabilities; gastrointestinal and growth problems; markedly reduced bone mass; and seizure disorders (Cooley, 2004; Krigger). Cerebral palsy is nonprogressive, yet compromises mobility and independence throughout the lifecourse.

Movement disorders are identified by the body area affected and by the exhibited symptoms. Identification by limb involvement is described below.

- quadriplegia (tetraplegia)—four limbs
- paraplegia—lower limbs
- diplegia—lower limbs with mild upper limb involvement
- hemiplegia—both limbs on one side
- triplegia—three limbs
- monoplegia—one limb

Quadriplegia cerebral palsy affects all of a person's limbs, as well as verbal expression.

When movement disorders are identified by exhibited symptoms, the classifications refer to the location of the lesion in the brain.

- Spasticity is caused by a lesion to the motor cortex (the upper central portion of the cerebrum, or brain, where motor neurons form tracts) and is characterized by hypertension, muscle contractions, and postural deviations as a result of an uninhibited stretch reflex. It is the most prevalent form of cerebral palsy; 70 to 80% of individuals with cerebral palsy display spastic clinical features (Krigger, 2006).

- Athetosis is caused by a lesion to the basal ganglia (the large mass of neurons within the center of the cerebrum) and is characterized by constant involuntary, uncontrollable, unpredictable, purposeless movements (appearing as overflow movements) that become less evident upon relaxation. It is the second most prevalent form of cerebral palsy [10 to 20% display athetoid features (Krigger, 2006)], and commonly affects the head and upper limbs.

- **Ataxia** (lack of muscle coordination, poor balance) is caused by a lesion in the cerebellum (the area of the brain below the cerebrum and posterior to the brain stem) and is characterized by balance and *proprioceptor* deficits, causing falls and uncoordinated movements. (Proprioceptor refers to sensations from certain muscles, such as those in the feet, that help a person define his or her relationship to space.) It is the third most prevalent form of cerebral palsy, affecting 5 to 10% of those with cerebral palsy (Krigger, 2006; Mobily & MacNeil, 2002).

- Rigidity is caused by a lesion affecting the motor cortex and the basal ganglia and is characterized by a diminished stretch reflex, stiffness, and hyperextension of body parts. This is the most severe form of cerebral palsy and is often accompanied by cognitive disabilities.

- Tremor is caused by a lesion affecting the cerebellum or basal ganglia and is characterized by involuntary, uncontrolled, rhythmic motions appearing either when a movement is initiated or at random.

- "Mixed" is the term used to describe the presence of more than one form of cerebral palsy. For example, spasticity and athetosis commonly coexist.

Seizure disorders, convulsive disorders, and **epilepsy** are neurological conditions resulting from abnormal brain functioning. A seizure is a sudden change in consciousness or behavior and is characterized by involuntary motor activity. Seizures may be a one-time occurrence, such as those that occur during alcohol or drug withdrawal, or they may accompany other disorders, such as cerebral palsy, brain injuries, severe intellectual disability, autism, stroke, and extreme old age (Sherrill, 2004). *Epilepsy* as a diagnostic category refers to a group of syndromes characterized by repeated seizures that occur on their own with no other cause (Mobily & MacNeil, 2002). Thus, not all people who have seizures are considered to have epilepsy.

According to the International League Against Epilepsy, seizures can be either partial (involve only one cerebral hemisphere) or generalized (involve both hemispheres) (Dubow & Kelly, 2003; Mobily & MacNeil, 2002). Partial seizures begin in one specific body site and travel up the limb, affecting all of the limb's muscles. When consciousness is not impaired the seizure is called a *simple partial seizure;* when consciousness is impaired the seizure is called a *complex partial seizure.* A *Jacksonian seizure,* characterized by jerky muscle **contractures** (shortening or reduction in muscle size caused by spasm, paralysis, disuse, or remaining in one position for a prolonged period of time), is the most common simple partial seizure (Sherrill, 2004). *Psychomotor seizures,* characterized by unexplainable short-term behavior changes that often are not remembered by the person, are complex partial seizures.

Generalized seizures involve all or several body parts. *Absence,* previously called petit mal, seizures are characterized by brief lapses in consciousness. A person who is talking and experiences an absence seizure may hesitate briefly and then continue speaking as if nothing has happened. *Tonic-clonic,* previously called grand mal, seizures are characterized by first rigid (or tonic) movements and then jerky (or clonic) movements, loss of consciousness, and sleep or a coma stage. An **aura** (warning, like an unusual smell or vision) is often reported just prior to a seizure. A *myoclonic* seizure is characterized by a sudden violent muscle contracture in one part of the body or in the entire body. *Atonic,* or drop, seizures resemble absence seizures except the individual experiences a momentary loss of postural tone.

Although more than 40 distinct forms of human epilepsy have been identified, the estimates of numbers of people affected by epilepsy are difficult to determine since only those whose epilepsy is uncontrolled come to the attention of physicians (Ackerman, 1999). Also, since medication effectively controls seizure activity, in some instances only family members are aware of the individual's needs and the medication side effects. It is estimated that 70% of children who experience more than one seizure are able to control their condition with the first medication they try (Ackerman); moreover, most persons who take daily medication for seizures experience 100% seizure prevention (Sherrill, 2004). TRSs need to be able to accurately document seizure behavior and behaviors resulting from medication side effects; thus, they must be familiar with the International League Against Epilepsy's classification system and the less commonly used clinical labels (Jacksonian, psychomotor, absence, tonic-clonic). The cause of most epilepsy (80%) is unknown and remains unexplained (Sherrill). The age of onset of the first seizure varies from prior to age 10 to after age 40, with 75% experiencing their first seizure before the third decade of life (Dubow & Kelly, 2003; Sherrill).

Interruption to the flow of blood through the brain results in a **cerebrovascular accident (CVA)**, or **stroke**. Although people of any age may experience a stroke, those 60 years of age and older, especially males, experience more strokes than other age cohorts (Sherrill, 2004). Hemiplegia and hemiparesis are the primary overt physical signs of a stroke. Damage to the right side of the brain causes left hemiplegia, or paresis, while damage to the left side of the brain causes right hemiplegia, or paresis. Cognitive deficits with right cerebral damage are evident in depth perception, intuition, and nonverbal perception. Individuals with these impairments experience difficulty in interpreting visual information, in orienting to their environments, and in estimating their abilities. Cognitive deficits with left cerebral damage are evident in speaking, understanding, reading, writing, and judgment. Individuals with these impairments respond to abstract information or new situations in a slow, disorganized, anxious, and emotionally sensitive manner.

A stroke is caused by a cerebral thrombosis, hemorrhage, or embolism. A thrombosis—a blood clot in a blood vessel of the brain—gradually slows or stops the blood supply to one particular area thereby causing a stroke. A cerebral hemorrhage is the rupturing of a blood vessel in the brain causing bleeding in and pressure on one particular area. A cerebral embolism results from a blood clot or fatty material in the arterial bloodstream that travels to the brain, lodges in a vessel, and interrupts the brain's blood supply.

Effects of a stroke are related to the age of the person at the time of the stroke, the severity and magnitude of the lesion, and the **premorbid** functioning (prior to the insult or injury; refers to one's previous abilities and lifestyle) of the person. In general, the younger the person, the less damaged the brain tissue, the shorter the coma, and the higher the quality of life prior to the trauma, the better the prognosis. An incomplete stroke or **transient ischemic attack (TIA)** occurs at any age and is characterized by total recovery, yet is a warning of severe cerebral pathology or impending stroke (Sherrill, 2004).

Multiple sclerosis (MS) is the most common demyelinating disease of the central nervous system for adults. Diagnosis usually occurs between the ages of 20 and 40, with women affected more often than men (Broach & Dattilo, 2003; Sherrill, 2004). With this disorder, the **myelin** surrounding and protecting the nerves in the brain and spinal cord is destroyed and replaced with scar tissue. These scars, or plaques, interrupt transmission of impulses to and from the brain, causing symptoms that vary widely from one person to the next. Each individual's unique symptoms are a result of where the plaques have formed in the brain or spinal cord. There is no known cause of MS and no known cure, though many of the symptoms can be treated.

Symptoms are diverse and unpredictable with no two individuals exhibiting the same features. Although there are several types of MS, it is generally characterized by attacks (exacerbation) followed by periods of improvement or remission [Center for Neurological Diseases/Rocky Mountain Multiple Sclerosis Center (CND/RMMSC), 1998; Sherrill, 2004]. Each type is descriptive of the disease's progression:

- Relapsing-remitting, attacks followed by some recovery of function
- Secondary-progressive, people with relapsing-remitting experience progression between attacks or after attacks have stopped
- Primary-progressive, commences as a progressive disease without attacks, usually diagnosed between ages 40 and 60
- Progressive-relapsing, progression evident from beginning with occasional attacks
- Benign MS, attacks are followed by nearly complete recovery with no functional losses for several years

Symptoms associated with an attack usually last 4 to 12 weeks then gradually disappear, leaving various degrees of disability (Sherrill, 2004). Most often the disease is progressive, each phase more severe than the previous with less improvement during subsequent remissions (Mobily & MacNeil, 2002). Yet when in remission, near-normal health may be experienced. "Over two-thirds remain ambulatory with or without aids 20 years after diagnosis; the remaining one-third require wheelchairs for mobility" (CND/RMMSC, 1998, p. 6).

Functioning Characteristics

Cerebral Palsy

Cerebral palsy is characterized by multiple involvements including visual impairments, seizures, tremors, emotional lability, distractibility, hyperactivity, abnormal reflex activity, poor motor coordination, scoliosis, joint instability, bowl and bladder dysfunction, altered growth and nutrition, and cognitive disabilities. Some individuals experience spasticity, which affects the flexor muscle groups used to maintain posture. When spasticity affects the lower limbs, it results in a scissors gait. If it affects the upper limbs, the forearms will be pronated (rotated so the palm faces back or down) with flexion at the elbows, wrists, and fingers. The muscles of a person with spasticity feel and look stiff; further, an exaggerated stretch reflex may result in a sudden, potentially dangerous, recoil of the upper/lower limbs when the person is startled or in harm's way. Surgery and bracing can correct contractures caused by spasticity, and the limbs may be strapped down to manage the stretch reflex.

Athetosis causes constant movement that is jerky and fast or slow and rhythmical. Excitement and tension exacerbate this movement. Individuals with athetosis experience uncontrollable head movements and facial contortions that impair speech, with involvement evident in all four limbs. A difference between persons with tremors and those with athetosis is that tremors—regular rhythmic movement patterns—tend to disappear during sleep and when the individual is completing tasks that require concentration. People with ataxia demonstrate a poor sense of balance, coordination, and kinesthetic awareness. They tend to walk unsteadily and misjudge the relationship between themselves and objects, and overstep or overreach as a result. Some individuals with cerebral palsy experience rigidity, which causes hyperextension, or an appearance of stiffness.

Individuals who experience distractibility and visual and speech impairments have difficulty acquiring and processing information. Cognitive disabilities appear with spasticity and rigidity. Movement and speech limitations may impede a person's social interactions and his or her development of social amenities. Emotional development is impaired by a distorted self-image and limited social opportunities.

Seizure Disorders

Seizure activity is precipitated by several conditions: stress, hyperventilation, excessive intake of alcohol and caffeine, hyperhydration, hyperthermia, high blood alkalinity, hypoglycemia, fatigue, infection, a blow to the head, and for women, menstrual periods (Ackerman, 1999; Sherrill, 2004). Therefore, when possible, TRSs avoid experiences that exacerbate these conditions. A seizure disorder can be a primary or a secondary impairment; consequently, functioning characteristics vary with diagnosis. A third factor TRSs consider is medication. Anticonvulsant drugs like Dilantin, Phenytoin, Carbamazepine, and Luminal (phenobarbital) are prescribed according to seizure type and frequency. Adverse effects like reduced coordination and concentration, drowsiness, fatigue, slurred speech, and emotional irritability impact functioning and therapists' intervention plans. For people with seizure disorders, the foci of intervention are psychological, lifestyle, and social functioning more so than physical and health-care needs.

Strokes

The symptoms of stroke vary depending upon whether the person experiences left hemiplegia or right hemiplegia. Individuals with left hemiplegia experience more **visual neglect** (a lack of visual awareness on the side of the body opposite the brain lesion) than do individuals with right hemiplegia. They tend to have difficulty with spatial and perceptual tasks, to be impulsive and careless, and to be unaware of their deficits. Individuals with right hemiplegia experience speech and language deficits, yet understand what is said to them. They have a tendency to approach newness with caution and to be sensitive to having had a stroke.

People who have experienced a stroke may be depressed and emotionally labile, exhibiting unpredictable and inappropriate behavior, possibly crying. Quality control problems (inability to guide and check one's own behavior) result in the person displaying unexpected behaviors, like being humorous when a subdued response is more appropriate. A person's capacity to acquire, retain, and generalize information is reduced. Individuals who have had a stroke may experience contractures, seizures, spasticity, and shoulder **subluxation** (shoulder joint nearly dislocates; shoulder appears dropped and is usually held in a sling), which are painful and reduce his or her range of motion. Aphasia and/or dysphagia are also present. **Aphasia** (difficulty understanding or using language meaningfully) may be expressive (understands but can't articulate or write); receptive (articulates/writes but lacks comprehension); and/or mixed (both expressive and receptive) (Mobily & MacNeil, 2002). With secondary impairments there is an increased risk of complications (Pang et al., 2005).

Multiple Sclerosis

Symptoms of multiple sclerosis vary with the portion of the nervous system affected by plaques. Double vision or reduction in the visual field, unusual weakness, fatigue, and numbness are initial signs of multiple sclerosis. With its progression, an individual's speech becomes slurred or monotonous, his or her gait becomes stiff or staggered, and tremors, spasticity and paralysis may occur. These characteristics disappear during early stages of remission, but become more prominent in later periods when remission occurs less frequently. People with MS also experience bowel and bladder problems, depression, dizziness and vertigo, pain, sexual dysfunction, swallowing discomfort or loss of the ability to swallow **(dysphagia)**, sensory disturbances, loss of balance and coordination, and decreased strength. Cognitive and emotional deterioration become evident as the disease progresses. Fatigability and thermal sensitivity or heat intolerance are common throughout the course of the disease. Both primary (related directly to the disease process) and secondary (caused by other disease-related factors like weakness and deconditioning) fatigue impact a majority of people with multiple sclerosis (McFarlane, 2007). Overheating as a result of physical exertion may result in worsening of existing symptoms and development of new symptoms (Wenzel, 1999).

Purpose of Therapeutic Recreation

Cerebral Palsy

Because cerebral palsy primarily affects the nervous system, movements over prolonged periods of time result in overstimulation, tension, and fatigue. A TRS can help clients develop tolerance through fitness and cardiovascular activities like water aerobics, weight lifting, and individually prescribed programs that incorporate relaxation and stress management techniques. TRSs can promote motor functioning with experiences that incorporate bilateral movements, balance, extension, spatial relationships, and free gross motor actions. Examples of these activities include cycling, therapeutic horseback riding, swimming, and target activities. The National Disability Sports Alliance (NDSA) (originally incorporated as the USCPAA) uses functional levels rather than neurological capability to equalize competition among athletes with cerebral palsy, stroke, traumatic brain injury, or any condition that requires the use of motorized chairs. Athletes compete according to the classes listed in exhibit 6.1 (Sherrill, 2004) in individual sports including track and field, swimming, cycling, and cross-country.

Cerebral palsy is a lifelong impairment. Most people with cerebral palsy live in community settings—primarily with family. After the developmental period, challenges to their health status include not only secondary issues like contractures, dental hygiene, and nutrition but also the ability of family to provide care as they age (Cooley, 2004). TRSs support education and transition plans through leisure education and inclusion, while providing transportation assistance to supplement family availability throughout the school years and into adulthood. TRSs can help individuals develop a sense of self and positive self-image, become aware of community resources, maintain adequate fitness levels, engage in fall-prevention exercises and those helpful to maintaining proper posture, and participate in expressive outlets like creative arts. Research has shown that engagement in virtual reality experiences, an intervention requiring further assessment, results in feelings of competence and social acceptance (Reid & Campbell, 2006). Therapists also assist in the acquisition and adaptation of equipment and adjustment to and use of braces [orthoses or **ankle-foot-orthoses (AFO)**] and assistive devices like bowling ramps.

Exhibit 6.1   NDSA Classes of Competition

Class	Functional Level
1	Motorized chair—severe involvement in four limbs; motorized wheelchair is used for mobility
2	Athetosis, 2L (lower) or 2U (upper)—moderate to severe involvement in four limbs; 2L propels chair with feet; 2U relies on arms
3	Moderate triplegia or quadriplegia—moderate involvement in three or four limbs; propels wheelchair with short choppy arm pushes
4	Diplegia—moderate to severe involvement in lower limbs; propels chair with continuous pushes; good strength in trunk and upper extremities
5	Assistive devices—walks and participates with assistive devices or wheelchair; moderate to severe spasticity; involvement is either hemiplegia or diplegia
6	Athetosis, ambulatory—moderate to severe involvement in three or four limbs with severe balance and coordination problems; ambulates without assistance
7	Hemiplegia—mild to moderate spasticity with spastic arm bent in pronated position and spastic leg noticeably smaller than normal leg; ambulates without assistance
8	Minimal involvement—minimal involvement in one or two limbs with noticeable loss of coordination

Seizure Disorders

The interventions TRSs use with clients experiencing seizures vary from individual to individual. Reluctance to allow people with epilepsy to participate in sports stems from both physicians and overprotective parents (Dubow & Kelly, 2003). Evidence suggests that most benefit from exercise, with little evidence to support an increase in seizure frequency or risk of injury due to physical activity. During activities in which a fall could injure the head or cause unconsciousness (such as cycling or adventure/challenge courses), clients are required to have supervision and to wear protective headgear. TRSs can aid clients by controlling excessive environmental stimuli and designing therapeutic recreation programs to foster progressive physical well-being. By educating individuals about their disorder, TRSs can reduce the stigma and fear that contribute to the social isolation, diminished self-concept, and stress associated with a seizure disorder. Therapeutic recreation programs (like camping and skiing) combined with education and psychotherapy have been found to improve the self-esteem of children (Regan, Banks, & Beran, 1993). Role playing, creative expression, and relaxation training also help clients to develop coping abilities and promote lifestyle adjustments.

Strokes

The therapeutic response to a stroke depends on whether the individual has left or right hemiplegia. Because a person with left hemiplegia tends to overestimate functioning ability, the TRS asks clients to demonstrate their skill in particular areas. To compensate for visual neglect, the TRS presents verbal feedback and arranges tasks where objects are transferred from the right to the left hand. TRSs also minimize visual distractions and nonverbal actions to aid clients in their recovery. A TRS communicates with a person with right hemiplegia using concise, specific words and verifies comprehension of information. They offer frequent feedback and reinforcement to ease the anxiety associated with new tasks.

The initial interventions TRSs prescribe focus on improving strength, endurance, and ROM; adjusting to visual neglect; and preventing contractures and spasticity. Usually clients regain function sooner and more completely in the lower extremities than in the upper extremities. Treatment/rehabilitation incorporates spatial and perceptual tasks and bilateral movements. Therapeutic experiences include swimming, stretching exercises, relaxation, striking activities such as tennis and golf, and riding a three-wheel bicycle. Long-term intervention focuses on helping clients reintegrate into the community, enhance their self-image, manage depression, use discretionary time purposefully, and develop cardiorespiratory well-being. An increasing number of aging persons survive strokes and live in the community. Consequently, education on the importance of physical activity, fall prevention, relaxation, motivation and self-control, and maintenance of recreational exercise is integral to client health, reduction in further incidences and complications, and long-term recovery (Mobily & MacNeil, 2002; Pang et al., 2005). TRSs design programs that include leisure education, community awareness outings, avocational skill training, and social networking to facilitate a sense of community. Support groups aid clients and their caregivers in adapting to lifestyle changes, accessing resources, and maintaining social networks.

Multiple Sclerosis

Intervention goals vary whether the client is experiencing an attack or remission (Mobily & MacNeil, 2002). Interventions address secondary conditions like depression, chronic pain and fatigue, heart disease, and deconditioning resulting from physical inactivity. Yet the effects of multiple sclerosis are exacerbated when individuals become overactive or when the temperature of their environment becomes too warm. Consequently, TRSs must closely consider the intensity and duration of physical exertion and the ambient temperature when designing programs. Clients are primarily concerned with developing endurance, balance, flexibility, strength, and stamina; preventing fatigue and contractures; maintaining ADL skills; managing pain and depression; and adapting to lifestyle changes. These needs can be ameliorated with activities such as aquatic therapy, walking, and stationary bicycling, as well as ROM, breathing, and mild physical activity programs that incorporate stretching, strength, balance, flexibility, and endurance exercises. TRSs encourage individuals with MS to continue their social routines in community settings. By drawing on the psychosocial support of their environment, individuals can enhance their adjustment to their disorder while maintaining their sense of well-being (Gulick, 1997). Leisure education encourages lifetime leisure skills, aquatics participation, and supports inclusion. TRSs also emphasize the importance of relaxation exercises in preventing the stress attributed to the chronic nature of MS (Levine, 2001). In later stages, TRSs encourage chair exercises to relieve pressure that ultimately contributes to **decubitus ulcers** (pressure sores or ulceration in the skin and soft tissue as a result of extended periods of pressure to the area).

Delivery Settings

Neurological impairments are managed through hospitalizations (strokes); medications (convulsive disorders); rehabilitation (multiple sclerosis); and residential and community day programs (cerebral palsy). TRSs are employed in physical rehabilitation programs or settings; skilled nursing facilities (SNF); sub-acute, outpatient, and home health care; day-treatment programs; and with organizations like Easter Seals and United Cerebral Palsy.

TRSs design individual treatment plans in conjunction with members of cardiac rehabilitation teams, provide community accessibility awareness, coordinate sports clinics and events with wheelchair athletes, and assist clients and caregivers in the acquisition and adaptation of supportive devices like sports wheelchairs, card holders, computers, and hand grips. Therapists encounter people with seizure disorders in chemical dependency units, long-term residential treatment centers, and community mental health programs. With clients in these settings, TRSs consider secondary diagnoses like cognitive disabilities as well as lifestyle adaptations (James & Crawford, 2001). Likewise, when TRSs address the needs of youth or aging adults who have experienced strokes and are residing in children's hospitals or long-term care facilities, respectively, assessments and rehab plans account for concomitant issues and adjustments to the chronic nature of the disability.

Leadership Interaction and Intervention Considerations

TRSs address the needs of children and adults resulting from both the primary neurological disability and the secondary manifestation of these disabilities:

- Heat intolerance (thermal sensitivity) caused by MS requires that the TRS plan activities [cool water (80–83° F) vs. warm water (84–88° F) therapy] so heat and humidity are avoided (Veenstra, Brasile, & Stewart, 2003).

- TRSs promote experiences like aquatic therapy that are "somewhat beneficial and potentially enjoyable treatment that can be utilized to help manage the symptoms of MS" (Broach & Dattilo, 2003, p. 238).

- Regular stretching exercises promote relaxation and prevent contractures; exercise level is monitored to avoid fatigue.

- TRSs are familiar with the side effects of medications (Betaseron, Avonex, Copaxone) used to treat MS. The flulike symptoms, depression, and shortness of breath, for example, although transient, cause discomfort and interfere with performance.

- If clients experience seizures, activities like swimming, horseback riding, and repelling are closely supervised and completed with partners.

- TRSs document the nature and duration of seizure activity to assist medical staff as they study the relationship between activity level, seizure behavior, and drug therapy. TRSs also monitor medication side effects that interfere with physical and social behaviors.

- TRSs facilitate psychological well-being by helping clients and friends consider the impact of their perceptions about seizures on social interactions.

- Abnormal reflexes interfere with movement during activities in which a TRS helps an individual with cerebral palsy transfer from, for example, a wheelchair to a pool deck; therefore, TRSs are cognizant of these reflexes and compensate handling techniques accordingly.

- Continuous movements are easier for individuals with spasticity, while individuals with athetosis do better if rest and relaxation occur between movements (Dunn & Leitschuh, 2006).

- For those with cerebral palsy, concomitant deficits in perception, vision, and communication are remediated by outlets like music, breathing exercises, and sports participation.

- A TRS distinguishes between a right and a left hemiplegic to compensate for the deficits attributed to left (right hemiplegic) or right (left hemiplegic) brain damage. For the right-hemi, a TRS uses brief, concrete statements, demonstration, and modeling; with the left-hemi, the TRS is alert to impulsive behaviors and carefully monitors "overestimation" of abilities.

Applying the Therapeutic Recreation Process

The therapeutic recreation process is applied to an adult with cerebral palsy living independently in the community.

Assessment

Demographic information.   John is a 40-year-old adult with spastic quadriplegia cerebral palsy. He resides in an apartment building designed to accommodate individuals with physical disabilities on the first floor and ambulatory adults with developmental disabilities on the second and third floors. A married sister lives with her family in the same community.

History.   John graduated from high school and completed an independent living program conducted by United Cerebral Palsy. He is employed by a small retail food company. He has been living in the apartment building under daily supervision for 10 years. He has participated in the programs and services of the therapeutic recreation division of the city park and recreation department since early childhood. He relies on public transportation.

Present behavior.   John uses a wheelchair for ambulation. He transfers with assistance. His IHP—Individual Habilitation Plan—requires physical therapy to maintain range of motion and transfer skills. The TRS from the therapeutic recreation division annually re-administers the LDB and Leisurescope Plus to review John's leisure attitudes and patterns. The social worker employed by the apartment complex routinely monitors self-care and ADL.

Planning

Long-term goal.   The long-term goal of the TR process is to maintain a social network.

Short-term goals.   The two short-term goals are to maintain wheelchair ambulation and to participate in community social events.

Objective.   While attending two weekly social recreation activities, one in the apartment complex and one in the community, John will transfer in and out of his chair at least once per event with a one-person assist. He also will push his chair to and from the activity site or to the public transportation pick-up and delivery point without assistance.

Content. Friday night activities in the building's recreation room include billiards, table hockey, ping-pong, card games, shuffleboard, and board games. Weekend activities include warm-water aerobics, bowling, movies, and sporting events. The apartment complex contracts with the therapeutic recreation division to provide staff who plan, supervise, and evaluate the activities.

Process. A TRS from the department coordinates with United Cerebral Palsy to identify participants whose IHPs recommend therapeutic and social interventions. Semi-annual meetings with physical therapists, social workers, and vocational staff coordinate IHP activities. In John's situation, the TRS and PT co-treat during the weekly warm-water aerobics. During the Friday night game room activities, the team has recommended that contracted staff ensure that John participate in activities like shuffleboard and table hockey that require arm extension and transfers from his wheelchair.

Implementation

TRSs co-lead with physical therapists during aquatic therapy and provide contracted recreation staff and house parents with in-service training on leadership and management of game room activities. Monthly in-services include lifts and transfers, adapting game room experiences, assistive aids and devices, and therapeutic benefits of recreational games. TRSs attend programs at least once a month to provide social skills training, monitor client IHPs, and evaluate implementation of activities by contracted recreation staff.

Evaluation

Annual meetings coordinated by United Cerebral Palsy are attended by the TRS and other contracted therapists for the purpose of updating and revising client IHPs. The TRS makes participation recommendations based on the results of the annual review/re-take of the short form of the LDB and the Leisurescope Plus. John and his sister also attend. Semi-annual meetings are also held to ensure communication and to adjust programs with seasonal schedule changes.

NEUROMUSCULAR IMPAIRMENTS

Disabilities affecting the musculoskeletal and nervous systems include spinal cord and traumatic head injuries; progressive muscular weaknesses of adulthood including Huntington's and Parkinson's diseases and amyotrophic lateral sclerosis (ALS); Guillain-Barré syndrome; and Friedreich's ataxia.

The spinal cord, housed in the vertebral column, has 31 pairs of nerves branching out and transmitting information to the working muscles: 8 cervical nerves (C1–C8), 12 thoracic nerves (T1–T12), 5 lumbar nerves (L1–L5), 5 sacral nerves (S1–S5), and 1 coccygeal nerve (see figure 6.1). When the spinal cord is injured, transmission of impulses through these nerves is impaired. As a consequence, motor and sensory function are permanently impaired below the lesion level. **Spinal cord injuries (SCI)** are usually acquired through some kind of trauma. Motor vehicle accidents, falls, violence (including combat), and participation in high risk sports like diving and snow skiing are the primary causes of the trauma. The majority of the individuals who sustain injuries are young males between 16 and 30 years of age, and the most common injury is tetraplegia or quadriplegia (Sherrill, 2004).

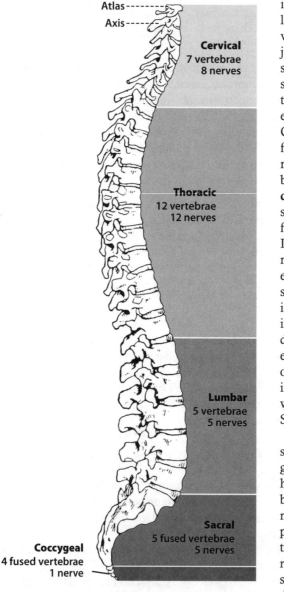

Description of the injury is identified by level and degree of lesion and amount of residual voluntary function. Level of injury is identified by a letter representing the specific area of the spinal cord that was injured and the numbers of the vertebrae closest to the injury. Thus, a C3 and C4 injury involves the third and fourth vertebrae in the cervical or neck area. Lesions also are labeled complete or incomplete. A **complete lesion** results in absence of sensation and motor function below the injury level. In an **incomplete lesion**, the spinal cord is not completely severed so varying amounts of sensation and motor function exist below the injury. The level of injury is used in rehabilitation to describe two classifications: Severance of the cord above the second thoracic vertebra (T2) results in tetraplegia or quadriplegia while severance at or below T2 to S5 results in paraplegia.

A third SCI classification is a spinal fracture (Porter & burlingame, 2006). A person who breaks his or her back or neck injures the bones around the spinal cord but not the cord itself. Fractures, compression, or hyperextension may traumatize the vertebrae but not result in paralysis. A number of secondary complications are evident with SCI. **Autonomic dysreflexia (AD)** or **hyperreflexia** is a life-threatening complication seen with individuals with T6 or higher lesions. Any stimulus below the

Figure 6.1   Vertebral Column Viewed from the Right Side

Source: Carter, M. J., and S. P. Le Coney. 2004. *Therapeutic Recreation in the Community: An Inclusive Approach.* 2nd ed. Champaign, IL: Sagamore.

level of injury may cause pain, discomfort, and high blood pressure resulting in a stroke (Porter & burlingame): Examples include full bladder, bowel impaction, pressure sores, tight clothing, fractures, hyperthermia, medical tests, or any painful stimulus (Vogel, Hickey, Klaas, & Anderson, 2004). The skin is prone to developing decubitus ulcers that can become infected. The bladder could become infected, so a catheter and collecting device are used to regulate urine flow. Contractures, spasticity, osteoporosis, and edema further limit movement. Heterotopic ossification (HO) is a complication that also limits movement and results from overgrowth of bone in the primary joints (Porter & burlingame). If respiratory or cardiovascular complications occur, the body's breathing capacity and ability to regulate body temperature and blood pressure will be upset. Weight control problems result from inactivity and contribute to fitness problems. Depression, denial, anger, sexual dysfunction, and pain may affect the person's adjustment to the trauma.

Traumatic brain injury (TBI) refers to an injury to the brain caused by sudden direct trauma including penetrating (i.e. gunshot wound) and nonpenetrating (i.e., closed head injury resulting from a car accident) injuries. If an individual sustains an injury to the head from a laceration, for example, the injury is referred to as a head injury; consequently, there may or may not be a TBI with a head injury (Porter & burlingame, 2006). TBI is a global health issue with at least 10 million TBIs annually resulting in death or hospitalization (Langlois, Rutland-Brown, & Wald, 2006). "More than half of those with TBI are men between the ages of 15 and 24" (Jennings, 2006, p. 29). During war the incidence of TBI increases, with falls, motor vehicle crashes, assaults, and blasts as leading causes (Langlois et al.; Warden, 2006). Further, TBI may lead to increased risk of other health conditions like alcoholism, epilepsy, depression, and PTSD. While mortality rates due to TBI have decreased, many experience lifelong physical, cognitive, behavioral, and emotional consequences. The sequelae vary widely depending on the site and extent of the brain damage (Sherrill, 2004). Recovery and change are lifelong processes, vary with age, and may result in permanent behavioral deficits (Jennings; Sherrill).

The Glasgow Coma Scale (GCS) is used to predict degree of recovery and severity of a TBI. Scores range from 3 to 15, with 13–15 considered mild, 9–12 considered moderate, and 8 and below severe with the client in a coma (Porter & burlingame, 2006; Sherrill, 2004). In general, the longer one remains in a coma and experiences amnesia the more severe the injury, while the closer the score is to 15 the better the prognosis.

Like a stroke, the particular brain area damaged affects the nature of the impairments. Brain trauma can produce bilateral effects (impairments affecting both the right and left sides of the body) and mixed behavioral patterns. The behavioral (emotional and personality) changes caused by a TBI are more long lasting and impacting than either the physical or the cognitive impairments. Physical impairments include aphasia (inability to understand or use language meaningfully), **apraxia** (inability to carry out purposeful movement), ataxia, bowel and bladder dysfunction, sensory and perceptual deficits, poor balance, respiratory limitations, seizures, spasticity, tactile defensiveness, and skull defects (sometimes a portion of the skull bone must be removed to compensate for brain swelling). Cognitive impairments include attention and memory deficits, disorientation, distractibility, mental fatigue, **perseveration** (the persistent repetition of a verbal or motor action), confusion, and deficits in information processing, perception, concentration, judgment, planning, sequencing, and problem solving. Emotional impairments include agitation, anxiety, irritability, apathy, egocentricity, impulsivity, lack of inhibition, depression, denial, withdrawal, emotional lability, and a lowered level of emotional tolerance. Social deficits include disinhibition, poor social judgment, socially inappropriate behaviors, and inability to respond to social cues (Lloyd, Malkin, & Poppen, 1997; Porter & burlingame, 2006).

Two progressive diseases of middle and late adulthood, **Huntington's chorea** (also known as **chronic progressive chorea**) and **Parkinson's disease**, affect the neuromuscular system, resulting in cerebral tissue degeneration, severe disability, and death. The onset of Huntington's disease usually occurs between the ages of 30 and 50, while Parkinson's disease commonly begins between the ages of 50 and 79—Parkinson's being the more prevalent impairment (Porter & burlingame, 2006). Initial clinical signs of Huntington's disease are sudden jerky muscle movements in the trunk, limbs, and head. Progressive impairments are noticed in memory, impulse control, mental functioning, and personality. Parkinson's disease is characterized by muscle rigidity, **bradykinesia** (slowness of movements), a unique resting tremor (a to-and-fro movement affecting one extremity then spreading to the other extremities or the opposite side), stiff facial expression, and a shuffling gait with stooped posture (Porter & burlingame). The trembling that begins in the hands eventually becomes apparent in other movements and is a key feature of the disease (Sherrill, 2004).

Amyotrophic lateral sclerosis (ALS), or Lou Gehrig's disease, progresses rapidly from its onset, which begins between the ages of 30 and 60, to death within one to ten years. Random physical impairments include weakness, atrophy, spasticity, exaggeration of tendon reflexes, and a tendency to fatigue easily. Cognition, awareness, and personality remain unaffected.

Guillain-Barré syndrome (GBS) is a transient neuromuscular disease affecting youths and adults. Ascending GBS, the most common form, is characterized by muscle weakness ascending from the lower limbs to the trunk, upper limbs, and eventually to the facial muscles, causing bilateral and symmetrical deficits and destroying the myelin sheaths covering the peripheral nerve axons. As these sheaths regenerate, muscle strength returns; recovery may begin two to four weeks after progression ceases (Porter & burlingame, 2006). If muscle strength is not recovered, respiratory weakness and permanent paralysis are predominant features.

Friedreich's ataxia, an inherited disease, affects children and teens and is caused by degeneration of the sensory nerves of the limbs and trunk (Dunn & Leitschuh, 2006). Clinical signs include clumsiness, poor balance, easy fatigability, lack of agility, atrophy of limb muscles, and thick, slurred speech. Secondary complications are progressive heart failure, spinal deformities, and diabetes mellitus.

Functioning Characteristics

Spinal Cord Injuries

People with spinal cord injuries have varying functioning abilities depending on their level of injury. Some degree of function may return within 6 to 18 months after injury, yet only a few recover all functioning (Porter & burlingame, 2006). Life expectancy is somewhat less than the general population but is longer for those with less severe (level and category) injuries. Mortality rates are higher during the first year after injury among those with severe injuries (Porter & burlingame; Vogel et al., 2004). The higher the lesion (C1–C3), the more restricted an individual's movement and the greater the loss of sensation, as the spinal cord no longer innervates muscle groups below the injury site. Injury above C3 paralyzes the diaphragm muscles, causing respiratory difficulty. Individuals with ultra high lesions (C1–C3) rely on artificial respirators and motorized wheelchairs with mouth sticks, headpieces, and microswitches to move about and to manipulate objects.

Lesions above T2 paralyze all four limbs (tetraplegia/quadriplegia). Lesions at or below T2 paralyze both legs and the lower trunk (paraplegia). The list below gives the functioning levels of individuals who have experienced spinal cord injuries at the areas indicated (Dunn & Leitschuh, 2006; Levine, 2001; Sherrill, 2004).

- C4—neck and diaphragm control, no upper extremity function; can manipulate wheelchair with mouth stick
- C5—functioning in neck, diaphragm, and some shoulder muscles—none in wrist or hand; elbow flexion; can propel wheelchair with rim projections and perform activities with the arms
- C6—elbow and shoulder flexion, abduction, wrist extension; can grasp large-handled, lightweight objects; can transfer oneself into and out of wheelchair and can propel wheelchair; may drive a car with hand controls
- C7–8—elbow extension and flexion, finger extension, weak grasp and release of small objects; can transfer into and out of wheelchair independently and can propel wheelchair independently
- T1–5—can grasp and release small objects, some arm movement, limited trunk stability; must wear seat belt or brace for posture and body alignment
- T6–9—trunk stability, upper extremity strength enables sustained grasping; can stand with braces; can transfer into and out of wheelchair independently and can propel wheelchair independently
- T10–12—complete abdominal and upper back control, weak lower back; wheelchair used as alternate ambulation form
- L1–5—flexion (L4) and extension (L5) of the hip and lower leg (L5) movement; independent ambulation with assistive devices
- S1–5—bladder, bowel, and sexual (may return after cessation of spinal shock) function affected at this level or any level above

Traumatic Brain Injuries

Individuals with traumatic brain injury progress through several cognitive and emotional recovery stages. Each stage lasts varying lengths of time—from a few hours to several months. Treatment and intervention are designed to manage behaviors presented at each level (Stumbo & Bloom, 1990).

Level I	no response, comatose
Level II	generalized response—nonpurposeful, inconsistent
Level III	localized response—inconsistent reaction to specific stimuli
Level IV	confused, agitated, nonpurposeful behavior; inability to process information

Level V   confused, inappropriate, nonagitated behavior; alert, highly distract-
            ible; responds to simple commands
Level VI   confused but appropriate behavior; goal-directed; uses external input
            for direction
Level VII   automatic, appropriate behavior; robotlike compliance with routine;
            shallow recall; increased awareness of others
Level VIII purposeful, appropriate behavior; alert, oriented, independent func-
            tioning

Aggressive treatment stabilizes comatose individuals. As with SCIs, the first six
months of intervention are most critical and indicative of the long-term recovery prognosis. Cognitive impairments result in disorientation to time, place, and persons and
may require others to assume responsibility for planning and follow-up. Physical
impairments affect the client's ability to complete self-care tasks, maintain employment, and travel in the community. Personality changes make others feel like they no
longer "know" the individual. Social networks are lost. The client's unawareness of
inappropriate social behaviors may require others to provide cues and monitor acceptable interactions. Communication impairments may require augmentative devices to
enable expression. A person who has experienced a TBI may not exhibit readily
apparent signs. As a consequence, an observer may be unaware of the individual's deficits. Clients experience impaired self-awareness and depression, both of which impact
functional recovery (Evans, Sherer, Nick, Nakase-Richardson, & Yablon, 2005). Clients lack awareness of the severity of their deficits and their impact on functioning;
along with low motivation, these contribute to decreased efforts during rehabilitation.

Huntington's and Parkinson's Diseases

People with Huntington's chorea exhibit involuntary head and limb movements.
Their speech becomes thick and difficult to understand. People with Parkinson's disease stand and walk in a stooped position. Impaired balance and poor coordination
lead to increased risk of falls. Muscle stiffness causes fatigue after minor exertion.
Their speech is slow and low in volume. Depression may become manifest as independent functioning decreases; Alzheimer's disease may later develop (Mobily &
MacNeil, 2002).

Amyotrophic Lateral Sclerosis

Muscle involvement patterns in ALS are scattered. In lower extremity involvement, weakness, fatigability, and need for ambulation aids result. In upper extremity
involvement, arms and hands experience muscle weakness yet the hands maintain
fine motor coordination. Breathing becomes labored; speech becomes thick, low in
volume, impaired, or nonexistent; and swallowing is compromised or absent.

Guillain-Barré Syndrome

Guillain-Barré syndrome causes muscle paralysis and affects the entire body
within one to three weeks of onset. Individuals with this syndrome require mechanical respiratory support during acute phases. Flaccid paralysis and denervation atrophy affect the hands and feet. Return of functionality varies from several weeks to
several years, with 80 to 90% of clients experiencing little or no remaining disabilities
(Palmier, 2005).

Friedreich's Ataxia

Friedreich's ataxia is characterized by an unsteady gait, foot deformity, curvature of the spine, and involuntary rapid eye movements. The pace of degeneration varies; an individual may use a wheelchair by his or her teens, while another may remain minimally affected throughout life (Sherrill, 2004).

Purpose of Therapeutic Recreation

Spinal Cord Injuries

Although the most visible evidence of a spinal cord injury is loss of movement and physical functioning, the traumatic onset of these injuries often leaves individuals with emotional scars. After stabilization, the rehab focus is to enhance functioning through skill development and adaptive equipment, reduce medical complications, and facilitate adjustment to an altered lifestyle (Porter & burlingame, 2006). Reintegration in work, leisure, and physical activity is an important rehab goal. Nevertheless, though individuals return to their home communities after rehab, the hours they spend doing meaningful work tend to decrease and the forms of participation tend to be less physically active (Schönherr, Groothoff, Mulder, & Eisma, 2005; Tasiemski, Kennedy, & Gardner, 2006). Consequently, TRSs promote exercise and participation in recreation as a means to buffer stress and improve subjective well-being (Latimer, Martin Ginis, & Hicks, 2005; Lee & McCormick, 2004). TRSs work not only with physical functioning and adaptive skills but also with social and emotional skills that impact health.

TRSs work with individuals to strengthen and stretch upper extremity muscle groups, which prevents contractures and enhances respiration. Individuals may experience muscle spasms below the lesion level, where some control (though incomplete) exists. Passive stretching, relaxation, medication, and immobilization of the limb(s) can prevent these spasms from occurring. As individuals with spinal cord injuries do not perspire below the lesion level, TRSs must take precautions to ensure that participants do not dehydrate and that their temperature does not rise too high.

TRSs encourage individuals to participate in athletic competitions and physical activity (swimming and chair aerobics, for example) to improve their physical well-being and reduce the incidence of secondary impairments like cardiovascular disorders (Beaudouin & Keller, 1994). Competition and the associated social events add to the person's quality of life and help promote attitudinal changes. A number of sport organizations make competition available to elite athletes worldwide. Wheelchair Sports/USA (WS/USA) and Disabled Sports/USA (DS/USA) sponsor competition in activities like athletics or track and field, aquatics, power lifting, shooting, wheelchair basketball, quad rugby, archery, and winter sports. TRSs encourage physical fitness interventions to enhance resiliency and explore new active recreation options to sustain inclusion and social engagement (Rogers, Lee, & Yang, 2007).

TRSs help clients develop social networks, use adaptive and assistive devices, access community resources, adapt to increased amounts of free time, and develop satisfying leisure behaviors. Researchers have found that therapeutic recreation provides clients with hope and a sense of future possibilities, adaptive resources, motivation, confidence, skill development, assistance with coping and adapting to the

Assistive devices like a Hoyer lift facilitate aquatic experiences that improve physical well-being.

disability, and community integration opportunities (Caldwell, Dattilo, Kleiber, & Lee, 1994/95). The spiritual/psychological value of therapeutic recreation interventions is noted in the research reported with individuals with SCIs and secondary health complications (Coyle, Shank, Kinney, & Hutchins, 1993). Life satisfaction is negatively impacted by depression and the loss of social support systems. TRSs can facilitate adjustment to the disability by promoting the development of assertiveness skills; leisure education; pain and stress management; community re-entry; and personal, family, and social leisure involvement.

Traumatic Brain Injuries

Treatment with clients who have experienced a traumatic brain injury corresponds to the level of cognitive and emotional recovery. Intervention commences with the client's present functional capacities and progresses with increasing information loads and cognitive processing demands (Mobily & MacNeil, 2002). The Rancho Los Amigos Scale of Cognitive Functioning identifies eight levels of cognitive functioning organized into four intervention stages (Porter & burlingame, 2006):

Functioning Level	Recommended Interventions
Level I	coma stage: sensory stimulation, passive ROM, music
Levels II and III	low arousal stage: sensory stimulation, orientation, cognitive retraining

A number of disabled sports organizations sponsor competitions for elite athletes.

Levels IV, V, and VI   post traumatic amnesia stage: leisure education, aquatic therapy, table and board games, orientation, community integration

Levels VII and VIII   post-confusional stage: memory books, community integration, social skills training, computer games, virtual reality, leisure resource awareness, relaxation, and stress and anger management

TRSs design programs that focus on helping clients reintegrate into the community, become aware of community resources, develop physical well-being, develop and maintain support systems, and restructure cognitive patterns. To ameliorate depression and feelings of loss of independence, therapeutic recreation programs incorporate expressive arts and social events. These activities help individuals develop their communication abilities and regain social contacts.

It is important for TRSs to manage the environment in which therapy occurs. They should eliminate distractions and overstimulation; structure interactions with repetition, routine, and consistent and quiet feedback; and monitor session length so clients do not become bored or fatigued (Mobily & MacNeil, 2002). TRSs must also be prepared to confront clients who use unacceptable language or display irresponsible and inappropriate behaviors.

Huntington's and Parkinson's Diseases

Therapeutic recreation programs for persons with Huntington's chorea or Parkinson's disease focus on helping individuals manage the side effects of the medications used in treatment as well as the physical effects of the disorders. Aquatic therapy is useful for managing involuntary muscle movements and muscle rigidity. Walking with supervision enhances balance and cardiorespiratory endurance. Relaxation training with breathing exercises help manage stress and strengthen respiratory muscles (Sherrill, 2004). Community reintegration experiences provide emotional support and counter depression, but must be structured such that clients do not become fatigued (Porter & burlingame, 2006).

Amyotrophic Lateral Sclerosis

Therapeutic recreation programs for people with ALS include a variety of experiences and activities. TRSs work with individuals on range of motion exercises to prevent muscle contractures; exercises to strengthen arms and legs to help clients use ambulation aids; and walking, stationary bicycling, and aquatics to strengthen respiratory muscles. Programs also include cognitive activities and humor to enhance clients' decision-making abilities, to help clients recapture pleasurable moments, and to retain human relationships (Young & McNicoll, 1998).

Guillain-Barré Syndrome

The degree of residual muscle weakness determines services needed by individuals with Guillain-Barré syndrome. Activities such as aqua-aerobics enhance the functioning of muscle groups affected by paralysis. Bicycle riding promotes strength and cardiorespiratory endurance. Animal-assisted therapy and sensory stimulation are used when clients experience lengthy periods of paralysis. Stress management is used to address the pain and anxiety that may accompany the sudden unexpected onset of the disease.

Friedreich's Ataxia

Initially, therapeutic recreation programs for individuals with Friedreich's ataxia promote activities that enable mobility and hand motion; however, with time, clients' muscle strength and exercise tolerance diminish. When this occurs, the TRS promotes exercises that involve gross motor skills, rather than fine motor skills, to support clients' residual abilities. Aquatic activities are useful because they permit freedom of movement not experienced in other settings. As individuals' verbal skills diminish, TRSs train them to use movement and music as alternative forms of expression.

Delivery Settings

Individuals who experience SCI or TBI require immediate stabilization at acute-care facilities. Once primary health-care needs are addressed, individuals transition to sub-acute and physical rehabilitation units with the ultimate goal to return home or to alternative living arrangements like transitional living centers and host homes. People with progressive adulthood muscular weaknesses may transition from their own homes to long-term care facilities. Individuals with Guillain-Barré are hospitalized and may require intensive care during the period of paralysis, followed by long-term rehabilitation to regain muscle strength and functional living skills as the paralysis subsides. Children with Friedreich's ataxia attend school where physical education specialists coordinate IEP objectives; as adults, such people typically transition into inclusive settings.

TRSs are employed in settings that encompass physical rehabilitation, transitional care, long-term care, and day programs. They manage comprehensive programs in inpatient settings and oversee educational, health maintenance, and recreational services at aquatic facilities, day-treatment programs, and public therapeutic recreation programs. In hospitals and rehabilitation centers the entire treatment team is involved in planning, while in community settings the TRS designs activity protocols to include in individual habilitation or rehabilitation plans.

Leadership Interaction and Intervention Considerations

TRSs address both primary and secondary manifestations of neuromuscular impairments:

- The sequelae (conditions following, for example, an SCI or TBI) are individualized and depend upon the individual's age, site, and extent of damage. TRSs consider the behavioral manifestations (depression and mood swings) and pain tolerance levels as programs and services are planned. It is also important to establish a communication system at the beginning of a program to ensure that the client's needs are met and emergencies properly handled.

- Swallowing difficulties (dysphagia) in later stages of Parkinson's are considered as the TRS plans meal functions.

- Activity restrictions with SCI cause obesity and reduce fitness. TRSs use passive and active ROM, and extension (rather than flexion actions) to promote maximal oxygen intake and caloric activity.

- For individuals with physical impairments, TRSs plan shorter exercise periods and select lighter equipment. Also, appliances and mobility aids require activities to progress at a slower pace and within a larger area to allow clients to maneuver; they also may cause clients to tire more easily.

- Like a person who has experienced a stroke, someone with a TBI experiences right or left hemiplegia, so responses may be slow and disorganized (right hemi) or the individual may appear to be self-centered and less sensitive to needs of others (left hemi). The TRS focuses on the individual's abilities, offering assistance only when necessary. Rehabilitation periods are lengthy, so the TRS's patience is likely to be tested (Mobily & MacNeil, 2002).

- Leisure education with caregiver support groups increases their awareness of resources in the community. Leisure education also can be used to foster a client's social connections (Carter, Nezey, Wenzel, & Foret, 1999).

- Accessibility of support areas like restrooms, parking lots, water fountains, and telephones are a prerequisite for program planning.

- When TRSs employ the buddy system, clients are able to compensate for one another's functioning abilities.

Applying the Therapeutic Recreation Process

The therapeutic recreation process is applied with a client who has recently experienced a closed head injury as the result of an auto accident.

Assessment

Demographic information.   Rich is a 24-year-old male recently transferred from a sub-acute unit to a regional hospital's inpatient physical rehabilitation unit. He sustained a closed head injury in a multi-fatality auto accident and was comatose for seven days.

History.   When placed in the rehab unit, Rich was assessed on the Rancho Los Amigo Hospital Cognitive Functioning Scale at level III. Premorbid leisure behaviors included hunting and fishing. He was employed as a farmer on the family farm.

Present behavior.   Rich responds to specific stimuli like turning his head toward a light or a sound. He responds inconsistently to one-step commands like "pet" the dog or "hold" the object. Awareness of name, placement, and family members is inconsistent. He is easily agitated by noises and moving stimuli.

Planning

Long-term goal.   The long-term goal is for Rich to transfer to a transitional living center (TLC).

Short-term goals.   The four short-term goals are for Rich to be able to (1) orient to time and place, (2) perform self-care with assistance, (3) verbalize needs with cues and prompting, and (4) respond to two-step commands.

Objective.   After four weeks in the rehab unit, Rich will respond to two-step commands during the sensory stimulation and animal-assisted therapy sessions at least 50% of the time.

Content.   The TRS conducts daily 15- to 20-minute sensory stimulation sessions at bedside. Twice weekly pets are brought to the room. With each contact, 24-hour RO (reality orientation) procedures are used.

Process.   The TRS uses behavior management strategies like repetition, reinforcement, and task analysis, and attitude therapy like no demand and kind firmness during the sessions. In each session the TRS requires response to each of the five senses; the same sequence is followed each session and sessions are conducted by the same therapist at the same time daily. The TRS uses animal-assisted therapy with family members since a number of pets live on the farm.

Implementation

The TRS begins at bedside, then progresses to one-on-one in the treatment room. Initially, one or two family members participate during animal-assisted therapy. Ultimately the TRS has the family take the lead in these sessions. The TRS records affective responses and social deficits while documenting the team's rehab goals. The TRS conducts caregiver support groups at which prognosis of TBI and placement alternatives are considered.

Evaluation

The Rancho cognitive functioning scale is the primary evaluative tool. TRSs periodically administer or re-administer the LCM (Leisure Competence Measure) and report on its compatibility with the team's FIM (Functional Independence Measure) scores. Weekly staff meetings assist the team and family in developing transition goals.

RELATED CONSIDERATIONS

Adaptations, Modifications, and Resources

Adaptation is an umbrella term that describes assessing, prioritizing, and managing variables to facilitate changes necessary to move toward desired outcomes (Sherrill, 2004). The effects of each impairment are unique from the perspective of the client and various stakeholders. To illustrate, while spinal cord injury results in various levels of limb paralysis, a person with a C3 requires different personal assistance than a person whose injury is at T12. Likewise, while the team addresses the physical impact of a TBI, participation barriers could arise if short-term rehab goals do not account for the length of recovery to address altered personality and social behaviors. Another variable considered with physical impairments is the secondary and "hidden" outcomes like chronic pain and depression. These psychosocial variables are considered along with assistance needs and participation factors as the therapist makes appropriate adaptations so clients achieve desired degrees of health and quality of life.

The WHO ICF model (International Classification of Functioning, Disability and Health) describes contextual factors (environmental and personal) that either facilitate or become barriers to one's health (Howard, Browning, & Lee, 2007). Using the coding system introduced by the ICF, the therapist can determine the influence, for example, of technology, natural environment, attitudes, and policies on client performance. With this assessment information the TRS prioritizes client goals and adaptations, and makes decisions regarding appropriate supportive resources. As clinical decisions are made, the TRS takes into account the following:

- Will adaptations completely alter the original intent of the experience or equipment? (Also, how important is the original intent to the client's goals and objectives?)
- How will the client react to the adaptation?
- How will other clients react to the adaptation?
- How will the adaptation affect the quality of life of everyone involved?

Adaptations are individualized, temporary in nature, and based on each client's strengths; they enable clients to demonstrate their skills without interfering with their impairments. Examples of potential adaptations are found on page 135 in exhibit 4.3 and range from obvious adjustments like using a wheelchair to ambulate during sporting events to the less noticeable—like longer rest periods during competition. Adaptations are continued as long as they empower the client and enable enhanced performance. CTRSs consult supportive resources as they plan interventions and transitions with clients and caregivers. A number of magazines, catalogs, and organizations provide resources appropriate to persons with physical impairments; a number of sites are presented below (although this list is not all-inclusive):

Resource	Internet Site
Government	
Disability Info.gov	www.disabilityinfo.gov
AbleData	abledata.com
United States Access Board	access-board.gov
Organizations	
National Center on Accessibility	ncaonline.org
The Center for Universal Design	design.ncsu.edu/research/cud
National Center on Physical Activity and Disability (NCPAD)	ncpad.org
Agencies	
Easter Seals	easterseals.com
United Cerebral Palsy	ucp.org
National Sports Center for Disabled	nscd.org
Adaptive Sports Center	adaptivesports.org
Breckenridge Outdoor Education Center	boec.org
Magazines and Catalogs	
Sports 'n Spokes, Paraplegia News	pvamagazines.com
Palaestra	palaestra.com
Access to Recreation, Inc.	accessstr.com
Program Development Associates	disabilitytraining.com
Special Populations, Flaghouse	flaghouse.com
TFH USA	specialneedstoys.com

SUMMARY

The physical impairments studied in this chapter are those that affect the bones, joints, and muscles (musculoskeletal impairments); the nervous system (neurological impairments); and both the musculoskeletal and nervous systems (neuromuscular impairments). The muscular dystrophies, arthritis, spina bifida, osteoporosis, thermal injuries, and amputations are among the prevalent disabilities affecting the musculoskeletal system. Among the more prevalent impairments affecting the nervous system are cerebral palsy, seizure disorders, strokes, and multiple sclerosis. Spinal cord and traumatic brain injuries are the more prevalent disabilities affecting both systems.

The focus of therapeutic recreation interventions varies with the nature of the delivery setting and the client's functional capacity and degree of adjustment to the impairment. Therapeutic recreation specialists promote improved health and quality of life through interventions that build on clients' residual capacities and rehabilitate disabilities. Because several of the impairments discussed in this chapter have lifelong impacts, TRSs provide experiences for clients and caregivers to educate them about these effects. The existence of an impairment may also affect an individual emotionally; clients may experience anger, depression, personality changes, and loss of inhibitions. Therapeutic recreation specialists can provide experiences that promote fitness, strength, social interaction, self-efficacy, redefinition of self-image, diversion from chronic pain, environmental and attitudinal accessibility, decision-making skills, and inclusion, all of which help clients build or rebuild their self-esteem. TRSs also adapt equipment and use techniques like cognitive restructuring, passive range of motion exercises, and behavior management programs to enhance clients' health and well-being. TRSs make referrals to supporting agencies and use the Internet to link clients and access information.

Key Terms

amputation The absence of a portion of or a complete limb.

amyotrophic lateral sclerosis (ALS) Also known as Lou Gehrig's disease, ALS is a progressive disease acquired in adulthood that affects the neuromuscular and nervous systems and results in premature death.

ankle-foot-orthoses (AFO) Braces that control spasticity and provide stability for the ankle and foot (identified by their initials).

aphasia Inability to understand or use language meaningfully.

apraxia Inability to carry out purposeful movement.

arthritis Inflammation of the joint.

arthrogryposis multiplex congenital (AMC) Nonprogressive congenital contracture syndrome characterized by stiff joints and weak muscles.

ataxia Lack of muscle coordination, poor balance.

aura A warning like an unusual smell or vision that is reported prior to a seizure.

autonomic dysreflexia or hyperreflexia Life threatening pathology common in quadriplegia, caused by release of hormone into the body that is stimulated by a full bladder. Characterized by sudden high blood pressure, slowed heartbeat, sweating, and headaches.

bradykinesia A slowness and paucity in movement that characterizes Parkinson's disease.

catheterization A means of withdrawing urine from the bladder via a tube and collection bag.

cerebral palsy (CP) A nonprogressive disorder of movement or posture due to malfunction of or injury to the brain. Several types of cerebral palsy (spasticity, athetosis, rigidity, ataxia, and tremors) are a result of the specific location of the brain injury.

cerebrovascular accident (CVA) Also known as stroke, CVA occurs as a result of interruption to the flow of the blood through the brain. Affects primarily the physical and cognitive functioning of a person yet may be evident in other areas.

complete lesion The spinal cord is completely severed, resulting in the absence of sensation and motor function below the injury level.

contractures Shortening or reduction in muscle size caused by spasm, paralysis, disuse, or remaining in one position for a prolonged period of time.

decubitus ulcer A pressure or bed sore.

dysphagia Discomfort or loss of ability to swallow.

epilepsy A central nervous system disorder marked by transient periods of unconsciousness or psychic disturbance, twitching, delirium, or convulsive movements.

eschar Charred surface tissue that develops when burns are experienced; causes contractures as the tissue heals.

Friedreich's ataxia Inherited disease affecting children and teens in which sensory nerves of the limbs and trunk are degenerated.

Guillain-Barré syndrome (GBS) Transient neuromuscular disease of youth and adults characterized by muscle weakness.

Huntington's chorea (chronic progressive chorea) Progressive disease of the neuromuscular system that results in cerebral tissue degeneration, severe disability, and death.

hydrocephalus Abnormal accumulation of fluid in the cranial vault; may result in an enlarged head, muscle weakness, and convulsions.

ileocystostomy Surgical creation of an opening through the abdominal wall into the ileum in order to divert urine from the bladder.

incomplete lesion The spinal cord is not completely severed at the point of injury, resulting in varying amounts of sensation and motor function below the injury.

lesion Discontinuation of tissue or loss of function of a part of the body.

multiple sclerosis (MS) A neurological disease characterized by periods of exacerbation and remission with progressive degeneration caused by plaques, which interrupt transmission of impulses to and from the brain.

muscular dystrophies (MDs) A group of progressive disorders evidenced by diffuse weakness of muscle groups. Muscle cells degenerate and are replaced by nonfunctional fat and fibrous tissue.

myasthenia gravis Chronic disease characterized by progressive muscular weakness with remissions and exacerbations.

myelin Protective covering around nerve fibers.

orthopedic impairments Disorders that affect the bones, joints, and muscles.

osteogenesis imperfecta (OI) Also called brittle bone disease, this is a congenital condition in which children are born with broken bones and deformed limbs or are prone to fractures.

osteoporosis Loss of calcium causes bones to soften and weaken, becoming susceptible to fractures.

Parkinson's disease Progressive neuromuscular disease of middle and late adulthood, characterized by muscle rigidity, bradykinesia, tremors, and postural instability.

perseveration The persistent repetition of a verbal or motor action.

poliomyelitis Inflammation affecting spinal cord motor cells causing temporary or permanent paralysis while leaving sensation intact.

postpolio syndrome (PPS) (sequelae) A number of returning symptoms or conditions that follow and affect people who have had poliomyelitis.

premorbid The conditions prior to or before the onset of an illness or disability, such as behavior patterns or leisure interests.

prosthesis An artificial or substitute limb or body part.

Rule of Nines Method used to standardize estimates of the percent of body surface burned. The body areas are divided into portions equal to multiples of 9% of the body surface.

seizure disorders Neurological conditions resulting from abnormal brain functioning, characterized by involuntary motor activity.

spina bifida A series of spinal cord defects caused by abnormal fetal development. The major types include myelomeningocele—an outpouching of the spinal cord through the back of the bony vertebral column that has formed incompletely; meningocele—an outpouching consisting of only the coverings of the spinal cord and not the cord itself; and spina bifida occulta—the failure of the back arch to form (no outpouching exists and the bony defect is covered with skin).

spinal cord injury (SCI) Damage to the vertebrae of the spine accompanied by paralysis resulting from the interruption of the nerves and pathways going from the brain to the involved limbs. The location and extent of damage are the major determining factors in degree of paralysis.

subluxation The near dislocation or visibly dropped shoulder on the affected side of a person who has suffered a stroke.

thermal injuries Injuries caused by flames, chemicals, electricity, sunburn, and prolonged contact with extreme heat or cold.

transient ischemic attack (TIA) Incomplete stroke causing dysfunction in speech, memory, perception, and muscle weakness, lasting for a few hours and serving as a warning of an impending severe stroke.

traumatic brain injury (TBI) An injury to the brain caused by an external force that produces either a diminished or altered state of consciousness (coma) and either temporary and/or permanent impairment in cognitive, physical, social, and behavioral functioning.

visual neglect Also known as visual field neglect, visual neglect is associated with strokes. Characterized by a lack of visual awareness on the side of the body opposite the brain lesion.

Study Questions

1. What are the primary and secondary functioning characteristics of clients with physical impairments?

2. What are appropriate therapeutic recreation objectives for people with physical impairments?

3. What specific interventions are used in diagnosis, treatment/rehabilitation, education, and promotion of well-being with clients with physical impairments?

4. Explain potential psychosocial and cognitive impacts of physical impairments on clients' leisure experiences and well-being. How do they affect clients' participation in activities of daily living?

Practical Experiences to Enhance Student Objectives

1. Contact the following agencies in your community, state, or at the national level and request their latest publications, videos, or Internet resources on disabilities and program services that they sponsor or provide:

   • Muscular Dystrophy Association: http://www.mda.org

   • Arthritis Foundation, Disease Center: http://www.arthritis.org/conditions/diseasecenter

   • Spina Bifida Association: http://www.sbaa.org

   • United Cerebral Palsy: http://www.ucp.org

- Epilepsy Foundation of America: http://www.efa.org
- American Heart Association: http://www.heart.org
- International Myotonic Dystrophy Organization: http://www.myotonicdystrophy.org
- International Osteoporosis Foundation: http://www.iofbonehealth.org
- National Multiple Sclerosis Society: http://www.nmss.org
- Multiple Sclerosis Association of America: http://www.msaa.com
- Brain Injury Association of America: http://www.biausa.org
- National Spinal Cord Injury Association: http://www.spinalcord.org
- National Easter Seals: http://www.easterseals.com
- U.S. Access Board: http://www.access-board.gov
- U.S. Department of Justice ADA: http://www.usdoj.gov/crt/ada/adahom1.htm

2. Try "simulating" the following impairments, as described.

   - Spend a day (or part of a day) in a wheelchair. Attempt to go about your routine daily activities.

   - Participate in at least two recreational activities that you enjoy (1) on crutches, (2) without using your arms, or (3) in a wheelchair.

3. Spend a day at a rehabilitation center or sub-acute program that provides treatment services. What adaptations did you notice that facilitated client ambulation? What types of assistive devices were used during therapy sessions? Describe the roles of other therapists, like PTs and OTs.

4. Visit a setting that includes people with physical impairments but is not treatment oriented (for example, a wheelchair sports program). Compare this experience with number 3 above; in particular, note the differences in client functioning, mobility, and staffing.

5. Make contact with Paralyzed Veterans of America (http://www.pva.org); Wheelchair Sports, USA (http://www.wsusa.org); National Disability Sports Alliance (http://www.ndsa.org); Disabled Sports/USA (http://www.dsusa.org); BlazeSports Clubs of America (http://www.blazesports.com); and the Paralympic Committee (http://www.paralympic.org) and request information on sport participation, rules, competition, and resources.

Sensory and Other Hidden Impairments

After reading this chapter, students will be able to

✔ Demonstrate an understanding of the functioning characteristics and leisure needs of people with physical impairments affecting the circulatory, respiratory, endocrine, and sensory systems

✔ Demonstrate an understanding of the functioning characteristics and leisure needs of people with cancer, chronic pain, and chronic fatigue syndrome

✔ Describe the role of therapeutic recreation with clients having circulatory, respiratory, endocrine, visual, hearing, and communication impairments

✔ Describe the role of therapeutic recreation with people with cancer, chronic pain, and chronic fatigue syndrome

✔ Identify the therapeutic recreation delivery settings and interaction and intervention processes appropriate for people with the impairments discussed in this chapter

✔ Identify considerations unique to therapeutic recreation programs and services for people with the impairments studied in this chapter

In this chapter we will study physical impairments affecting several body systems and introduce the subjects of sensory and communication impairments. While the previous chapter considered impairments that usually result in visually apparent disabilities, the impairments introduced in this chapter have effects that may or may not be visually apparent. Some of these impairments are life threatening (cancer), while others cause mild to severe long-lasting limitations (hemophilia, chronic fatigue syndrome). Consequently, as TRSs plan and deliver programs and services they are challenged to consider not only the physical needs of clients but also their psychosocial needs.

INTRODUCTION

The heart, which is the core of the circulatory system, controls the flow of blood throughout the body, which in turn provides nourishment to the body. Thus, when a dysfunction in this system occurs, the body's functioning is impaired. Coronary heart disease, hypertension, congestive heart failure, and strokes (cerebrovascular accidents) are among the most common circulatory system impairments.

Dysfunction in the organs of the respiratory system—nose, lungs, pharynx, larynx, trachea, and bronchi—results in breathing difficulties. Chronic bronchitis, emphysema, asthma, cystic fibrosis, hay fever, and tuberculosis are conditions that affect youths and adults and cause functional limitations. Diabetes mellitus, an endocrine disorder, affects youths and adults and is a major world health issue, as is obesity—a significant risk factor with the chronic illnesses introduced in this chapter.

Cancer can affect any of the body's systems and results in temporary or permanent impairments or death. Pain interferes with every aspect of a person's daily life. Chronic pain exacerbates already present diagnoses like arthritis, substance-related disorders, and cancer. A syndrome reported worldwide, chronic fatigue syndrome, affects all of the body's systems. Like pain, chronic fatigue syndrome impacts individuals for extended time periods and has associated effects like depression. A number of characteristics typify the disease; however, fatigue is the most common.

Sensory and communication impairments, such as vision and hearing loss, may occur as primary physical impairments or may be associated with other physical impairments, such as cerebral palsy and traumatic brain injuries. Communication limitations result when a person's capacity to learn speech and language are impaired—as with learning disabilities or with receptive or expressive language disabilities, which are commonly experienced by people who have sustained a head injury or stroke.

CIRCULATORY IMPAIRMENTS

For most of the populations worldwide, the last 100 years has seen improvements in health status compared to previous times. During this span, the causes of death and disability have shifted from nutritional deficiencies and infectious diseases to chronic diseases like cardiovascular disease (CVD), diabetes, and cancers (Lonn & Grewal, 2006). Although the rates of CVD peaked between the 1950s and 1970s, it is the leading cause of disability worldwide, exacerbated by rising rates of obesity and diabetes. These chronic diseases have created an ongoing global health and economic burden (Lonn & Grewal; McConnell, Jacka, Williams, Dodd, & Berk, 2005).

In the United States, "heart-disease-related deaths outnumber the next seven causes of death . . ." (Cheek, Jensen, & Smith, 2004, p. 4). Chronic diseases, including obesity, are not only the most prevalent and costly, they are among the most preventable since they are a function of people's daily choices (Rosenberger, Sneh, Phipps, & Gurvitch, 2005). The causes of many chronic diseases are grouped into two categories: (1) static risk factors like age, sex, race, and heredity that can not be altered and (2) lifestyle factors that can be altered like diet, exercise, tobacco use, stress, high blood pressure, and elevated low-density-lipoprotein cholesterol (LDL-C) (Mobily & Ostiguy, 2004; Sherrill, 2004). Consequently, TRSs commonly work as members of cardiac rehabilitation teams that assess and plan lifestyle changes, pharmacological and surgical interventions, education and health promotion, and reintegration experiences.

Cardiovascular disease affects the heart and blood vessels. It may develop as a primary impairment or result from other diseases such as rheumatic fever, HIV/AIDS conditions, obesity, and diabetes. CVD may be acquired or **congenital**: acquired CVD develops after birth and affects primarily the arteries that supply oxygen to the heart and brain, while congenital conditions develop prior to birth and are likely to be defects in the structure of the heart walls and valves (Sherrill, 2004).

Children are more likely to experience congenital rather than acquired conditions (Sherrill, 2004). Although present at birth, some cardiovascular diseases have no apparent symptoms and are not detectable until childhood or adulthood—for example, **Marfan syndrome** (an inherited connective tissue disorder that causes cardiovascular abnormalities) and **hypertrophic cardiomyopathy** (an inherited disease that causes sudden death in adolescents or young adults). Four common conditions account for most of the congenital heart defects (Sherrill). Ventricular septal defect (VSD) is a hole in the heart between the left and right ventricles. Patent ductus arteriosus (PDA) is caused when the opening between the aorta and pulmonary artery fails to close when the newborn begins to breathe on its own. Pulmonic stenosis valvular (PSV) occurs when there is obstruction in the outflow from the right ventricle into the pulmonary artery. Lastly, Tetralogy of Fallot (TOF) results in "blue babies" or **cyanosis** (bluish skin tone caused by a lack of oxygen or abnormal hemoglobin in the blood) and is caused by VSD, PSV, an enlarged right ventricle, or abnormal position of the aorta causing it to receive blood from both the right and the left ventricles (Sherrill).

In most cases, surgery is undertaken in the first few weeks of life to correct the structural defect. Prior to surgery, children with congenital defects experience respiratory infections, fatigue, vertigo, breathlessness, loss of consciousness, chest pain, edema, slow physical growth, pneumonia, lung infections, variance in blood pressure and pulse rates, murmurs, arrhythmias, and cyanosis. Periodic medical examinations will help detect symptoms that begin to develop as the child grows older and becomes more active. Also, during adolescence, defects like aortic or pulmonary stenosis worsen and result in congestive heart failure.

The most prevalent acquired heart disease is **coronary heart disease (CHD)**, which includes myocardial infarction, acute ischemic (**coronary**) **artery disease (CAD)**, atherosclerosis, and angina pectoris. CAD results from a narrowing of the coronary arteries, which causes a decreased blood supply to the heart. It is the number one cause of death to persons age 25 and over and is attributed to static and lifestyle risk factors (Mobily & MacNeil, 2002; Sherrill, 2004). With chronic exposure to risk factors, lipid and fibrous materials accumulate—forming blood clots that obstruct the arteries (thrombosis) or break off and travel to and obstruct blood flow in other arteries (embolism); in the latter instance a stroke results when obstruction occurs in the brain, while in the former situation a heart attack results from obstruction of the coronary arteries (Mobily & MacNeil; Porter & burlingame, 2006).

High blood pressure, or **hypertension** (habitual reading of 140/90 mm Hg or higher), is an acquired heart disease that may be considered a disease itself or a risk factor that contributes to other heart diseases (Mobily & MacNeil, 2002). The blood exerts a greater than normal force against the inner walls of the blood vessels and causes the heart to work harder (Mobily & MacNeil). A person may not experience pain or discomfort and be unaware the condition exists unless a checkup identifies blood pressure issues (Sherrill, 2004). **Arteriosclerosis**, a group of diseases characterized by thickening and loss of elasticity of the artery walls (hardening of the artery walls), may accompany hypertension. **Atherosclerosis** (a form of arteriosclerosis) is a degenerative process in which deposits of cholesterol and other fatty substances (called atheromas or atherosclerotic plaques) accumulate. When these deposits build up, artery walls are narrowed, contributing to high blood pressure, aneurysms (deformities in blood vessels), heart attacks, and strokes. Thus atherosclerosis is the primary cause of CAD and is mostly attributed to lifestyle issues like obesity and high blood pressure. PAD, or peripheral arterial disease, is a chronic arterial occlusion in the lower extremities attributed to atherosclerosis. Prevalence increases with age. Pain or weakness experienced when walking is relieved with rest (Aronow, 2007). Like other forms of acquired heart disease, predisposition to PAD results from modifiable risk factors like cigarette smoking.

Rheumatic fever/rheumatic heart disease is an acquired CVD that begins in children, most often between the ages of 5 and 15, as a result of rheumatic fever (Mobily & MacNeil, 2002). The valves of the heart become inflamed and scar as a result. This scarring prevents proper opening and closing of the valves. Subsequent back flow of blood (regurgitation) and reduced ease of blood flow (**stenosis**) caused by narrowing passageways affect the blood supply throughout the entire body. Medication, primarily penicillin, is used to treat the symptoms of rheumatic fever and to prevent attacks from recurring.

A heart attack or **myocardial infarction (MI)** occurs when the oxygen demand of the heart muscle is greater than the coronary arteries supply (Sherrill, 2004). Without an adequate supply of oxygenated blood, the part of the heart muscle served by the artery dies. This lack of oxygen is signaled by **angina pectoris**, severe chest pain behind the breast bone, and may be evidence of or a precursor to the more severe pain associated with a heart attack. Pain radiates to the jaw, neck, shoulders, or arms and is evidenced by sweating, shortness of breath, nausea and vomiting, and generalized weakness (Sherrill). Although heart attacks may occur at any age, the majority occur among individuals over 65, with men at greater risk until "age 70 when both sexes have the same incidence" (Porter & burlingame, 2006, p. 39). The most common cause of an MI is a blood clot.

Congestive heart failure (CHF) results from progressive weakness of the heart muscle, which impairs the pumping action of the heart and causes accumulation of fluid in the body's tissues (Mobily & MacNeil, 2002; Porter & burlingame, 2006; Sherrill, 2004). CHF may be caused by a number of issues including but not limited to CAD, MI, high blood pressure, and heart valve imperfections. CHF affects both sides of the heart yet may be more pronounced on one side (Porter & burlingame). Left heart congestion is the most common and causes fluid buildup in the lungs, shortness of breath, and wheezing, while right heart congestion causes fluid retention in the legs and feet and enlargement of organs (Sherrill). When heart muscles are unable to pump received blood, known as systolic dysfunction, organs and tissues do not receive oxygenated blood and the ventricles may enlarge. Conversely, with diastolic dysfunction, the heart's ability to stretch is reduced, which limits its holding capacity and causes blood to back up in the circulatory system, forcing fluids into bodily tissues (Porter & burlingame). CHF may progress slowly without any signs; and for people who remain in bed or do not sit upright each day, this may be the primary cause of death because the heart does not get its needed exercise (Sherrill).

Congenital and acquired cardiovascular conditions result in conduction abnormalities, heart rate irregularities, valve defects, and heart murmurs. Electrical impulses cause the heart to beat. Disruption in these impulses affects heart function. ECGs or EKGs (electrocardiograms) identify conduction disorders. The heart may beat fast, slow, irregularly (dysrhythmias), or experience blocks or delays when disorder in electrical impulses is manifest. Fibrillations (rapid quivers), tachycardia (excessive fast heart rate), and bradycardia (slow heart beat) display ECG patterns different than that characteristic of a normal heart. Imperfection in the heart valves that open and close to force the blood within the heart to flow in the right direction typically cause heart murmurs, heard as gurgling or hissing in the physician's stethoscope. Regurgitation, stenosis, and prolapsed valves are the three types of defects. A prolapsed valve has slipped or fallen out of place. An MVP, or mitral valve prolapse, is evident in Marfan syndrome (Sherrill, 2004).

Hemophilia is a blood disorder resulting from an inability to coagulate or clot properly. A hereditary deficiency of coagulation factor VIII (hemophilia A) or of coagulation factor IX (hemophilia B) are the most common types and result in prolonged internal or external bleeding after an injury (Dunn & Leitschuh, 2006). People with hemophilia experience swollen joints, movement limitations, and black and blue spots (Sherrill, 2004). When internal bleeding is extensive, as evident by discoloration and swelling, blood transfusions are necessary. Repeated hemorrhages into the joints result in hemophilic arthritis. Affected body parts are splinted to minimize bleeding.

Anemia, reduced oxygen-carrying capacity of the blood, is attributed to a deficiency in red blood cells or hemoglobin—the oxygen-carrying pigment within the red blood cells (Sherrill, 2004). Anemia occurs independently from or as a characteristic of other impairments like cancer, kidney disease, or lead poisoning. People who have difficulty chewing and swallowing, such as those with cerebral palsy or severe intellectual disability, are at higher risk of acquiring iron deficiency anemia (Sherrill). People with anemia experience chronic fatigue, lowered activity levels, pallor, increased heart and breathing rates, irritability, and lethargy.

Sickle cell anemia is an inherited blood disorder that develops at the time of conception. Symptoms such as pallor, poor appetite, fatigue, and pain in the back, abdomen, and extremities appear after a child is six months old (Sherrill, 2004). Normal hemoglobin is replaced by a hemoglobin variant. The shape of red blood cells changes to a sickle or crescent shape that makes it more difficult for the cells to travel through the veins, resulting in partial or complete blockage causing cell death and pain (Porter & burlingame, 2006). Those with sickle cell anemia appear to have a jaundice condition (yellow) in the whites of the eyes, are prone to infection, and experience pain in muscles and joints, especially in the rib cage. Sickle cell anemia goes through cycles of painful flare-ups followed by remissions. Flare-ups can be caused by, for example, increased body temperature, strenuous physical exercise, and dehydration, factors that could be present during recreational experiences (Porter & burlingame). With age, children become aware of their limitations and are able to manage the periodic physiological crises, yet growth is slower than usual and the life span may be abbreviated.

Functioning Characteristics

Several symptoms indicate the presence of heart disease: angina pectoris (chest discomfort); shortness of breath (**dyspnea**); edema (swelling) in the feet, ankles, or abdomen; dizziness; fatigue; indigestion; double vision; lethargy; weakness; apathy; poor memory; and depression. Since these same symptoms confirm the presence of other disabilities, a medical examination is required to rule out all other possibilities. People with heart disease experience several "hidden" disabilities, including the possibility of impending heart failure and death, chronic pain, prolonged physiological stress, mood and anxiety disorders, and major depression (McConnell et al., 2005; Porter & burlingame, 2006).

The American Heart Association (www.americanheart.org) describes the degree of heart damage by a person's functional activity levels (Dunn & Leitschuh, 2006; Mobily & MacNeil, 2002):

Level	Functional Activity
No restrictions	Heart disease present yet no limitation and no symptoms present with activity.
II	Slight limitation. Comfortable at rest, yet with more than ordinary physical activity symptoms like fatigue, palpitation, dyspnea, or anginal pain result.
III	Marked limitation. Comfortable at rest, yet with less than ordinary physical activity symptoms like fatigue, palpitation, dyspnea, and angina appear.
IV	Discomfort is experienced with any physical activity and symptoms of heart impairment appear.

This description helps a TRS identify the energy levels that a person with heart disease can comfortably expend during activity. A **MET**, or basic metabolic unit, is an estimate of oxygen consumption or energy cost required to complete an activity. One MET is equivalent to the amount of oxygen used while sitting quietly; four or more METs are used in daily activities. Thus, a person at level III or IV is advised to participate in activities that require no more than one to four METs—painting or playing cards, for example. A person at level I or II may expend 5 or more METs and participate in activities like golf and bicycling (Sherrill, 2004). Thus, METs provide a way to evaluate energy expenditure while measuring client function and progress. Inactivity and increased amounts of free time following cardiac trauma during acute care may exacerbate the risk factors (smoking, cholesterol intake, sedentary lifestyle, stress, and coping with boredom) that precipitated the heart disease (Van Puymbroeck & Ashton-Shaeffer, 2007).

Purpose of Therapeutic Recreation

The diversity of cardiac damage and functioning necessitate a comprehensive approach to recovery, secondary prevention, and general health promotion. Treatment focuses on the assessment and rehabilitation of functional capacity. A baseline assessment of functioning is determined and goals are set that stay within the cardiac parameters set by the physician (Porter & burlingame, 2006). During interventions therapists monitor heart rate, oxygen saturation levels, blood pressure, and respiration; perceived levels of pain and exertion; and also note conditions like dizziness, nausea, or feeling faint (Porter & burlingame). Therapists also consider environmental features like humidity, temperature, wind chill, and elevation as they may have an effect on client vital signs. Pharmacological interventions are introduced to reduce adverse cardiovascular issues, which requires therapists to be familiar with their effect on exercise response. Surgeries like catheterization, coronary artery bypass, transplants, percutaneous transluminal coronary angioplasty (PTCA), and ambulatory (outpatient) procedures alleviate symptoms and repair/replace defects. Education and health promotion focus on lifestyle adjustments that reduce risk factors such as hypertension and excess weight and cholesterol (Mobily & MacNeil, 2002).

As team members, TRSs address recovery, prevention, and health promotion by incorporating interventions that address hidden disabilities and promote self-regulation, like stress and time management, relaxation, humor, and leisure education. Therapists present passive interventions during hospitalization and employ techniques to adapt activities to avoid unsafe cardiac loads (Porter & burlingame, 2006; Van Puymbroeck & Ashton-Shaeffer, 2007). Additionally, TRSs raise awareness of the relationship between lifestyle issues and leisure—like snacking while playing computer games, or by watching rather than participating. They also promote family and caregiver support through, for example, self-monitoring of heart rates, blood pressure, and dietary habits. As a client's exercise tolerance improves, therapists support community reintegration and transitions from inpatient to outpatient programs. They also promote adherence to lifestyle and pharmacological therapies necessary for lifelong risk-factor modification.

Delivery Settings

Although not all individuals with heart conditions (e.g., uncontrolled arrhythmias or poorly controlled hypertension) benefit from cardiac rehabilitation/secondary prevention programs, one goal of cardiac rehab is to reintegrate clients into successful functional status in their home communities (Porter & burlingame, 2006). Generally, cardiac rehab is presented in four phases, each with particular delivery settings. Inpatient rehabilitation, Phase I, begins immediately at bedside while the patient is in the coronary intensive care unit in an acute-care hospital. Ambulation and low-intensity physical activity progressing up to 5–7 METs are intended to develop self-care skills and help the patient positively manage lifestyle adaptations (Bartels, Whiteson, Alba, & Kim, 2006). Phase II occurs at a rehabilitation facility and/or in the home for a period of 12 weeks and consists of exercise and ambulation within the 5–7 MET limit, avoiding any resistive activities (e.g., isometric exercises). This phase includes education on risk factors and support systems necessary to maintain rehabilitation protocols

(Bartels et al.; Porter & burlingame). Phase III, consisting of cardiac programs in settings like the YMCA or independent rehab clinics, focuses on developing healthy lifestyles while continuing supervised activity. This phase lasts 12 weeks, with exercise three times per week. Strength training is introduced to lower blood pressure and heart rate in order to decrease the heart's workload (Bartels et al.; Porter & burlingame). In Phase IV, lifelong maintenance phase, an exercise prescription is designed to promote the maintenance of exercise habits (Bartels et al.; Porter & burlingame). Periodic stress testing occurs to re-assess each exercise prescription.

While the focus of cardiac rehab/secondary prevention programs appears to be on exercise, comprehensive rehab programs incorporate periodic assessments, nutritional counseling, risk-factor management, psychosocial interventions like horticultural therapy, and programs like therapeutic recreation that foster healthy behaviors and compliance with these behaviors to reduce disability and promote an active lifestyle (Balady et al., 2007; Wichrowski, Whiteson, Haas, Mola, & Rey, 2005). Consequently, as members of cardiac rehab/secondary prevention teams, TRSs interact with clients in settings across a continuum from intensive care to home health care, where lifestyle management is the focus of intervention.

Leadership Interaction and Intervention Considerations

TRSs involved in cardiac rehabilitation address prescriptive exercise goals and promote lifestyle changes through specific interventions:

- TRSs provide education and training on selecting leisure experiences according to prescribed MET levels/activity.
- Therapists conduct assessments that examine educational needs, health status, risk factors, leisure resource awareness, psychosocial support, and fitness.

Cardiac rehabilitation usually includes an exercise prescription that is designed to maintain lifelong exercise habits.

- Therapists monitor the client's self-regulation of heart rate, blood pressure, caloric intake, and exercise regimens.

- TRSs teach clients to monitor wind chill and temperature-humidity indexes to assure appropriate environmental conditions; for example, if it is colder than 30 °F or hotter than 80 °F, outdoor exercise is discouraged.

- TRSs are aware that a variety of medications are used in cardiac programs and that these drugs may result in activity contraindications and side effects like reduced heart rates or clotting ability that require precautionary measures (refer to related considerations on page 286).

Applying the Therapeutic Recreation Process

The therapeutic recreation process is applied to an adult with coronary heart disease who has recently undergone cardiac catheterization with the insertion of a **stent** (stainless steel tube either latticed or resembling a spring, implanted in the area of the heart artery narrowed by plaque).

Assessment

Demographic information.   Bob is a 45-year-old male who teaches and coaches in a large metropolitan school. He is married with two teenage children and his wife also teaches in the same school system.

History.   Bob's father died at chronological age 50 as a result of an MI and his brother has a history of hypertension and arteriosclerosis. During Bob's annual physical, results of a stress test prompted the primary care physician to hospitalize Bob immediately; Bob also reported chest pain and frequent periods of tiredness and fatigue. Tests revealed coronary blockage; catheterization and insertion of the stent occurred within 12 hours of admission. Bob was released after four days in the cardiac intensive care unit, where he received inpatient services.

Present behavior.   Bob's rehab required 30 days of Phase II level exercises and meetings with a nutritionist. Bob now carries out a prescribed exercise program (Phases III and IV) through the YMCA.

Planning

Long-term goal.   The long-term goal is to maintain the prescriptive fitness program.

Short-term goals.   The two short-term goals are for Bob to self-monitor graduated exercise practices and to comply with recommended nutritional practices.

Objectives.   While participating three times per week in self-directed exercise, Bob will take and record pulse rate, blood pressure, and MET levels and remain within 60–70% of his functional capacity. Bob will maintain a weekly log, recording caloric intake and social-emotional conditions surrounding daily leisure and relaxation periods.

Content.   A TRS in physical rehab has consulted with an exercise physiologist and incorporated into Bob's prescription a walking-cycling program. The physical therapist and exercise physiologist consulted with the TRS to locate and arrange to use the YMCA to implement the program. A special diet was designed by the hospital dietician in consultation with Bob's wife.

Process. Through the state chapter of the American Heart Association, the TRS acquired contact information for the YMCA and a family support group. The TRS also administered a leisure inventory and shared literature with family members on stress and relaxation.

Implementation

The TRS consults with Bob and his family during inpatient visits and continues to share literature on exercise, diet, risk-factor management, and stress management. Periodically, the TRS and rehab team assess whether Bob is properly monitoring and recording activity frequency, intensity, and time. The TRS makes a monthly visit to the YMCA to assess Bob's activity levels and documentation. During inpatient stays the TRS walked with Bob to help him learn to regulate his intensity levels.

Evaluation

Stress testing occurred initially at six months, then at yearly intervals. Social histories and inventories monitored psychosocial stressors and risk factors like eating habits. The TRS administered the Leisure Satisfaction Scale and Life Satisfaction Scale during inpatient stay and one year post-surgery. The Leisure Motivation Scale was used during family support groups to help Bob and his family become aware of significant motivational characteristics/needs.

RESPIRATORY IMPAIRMENTS

Respiratory impairments prevent the body from adequately ventilating the lungs, which in turn leads to the body receiving an insufficient supply of oxygen and retaining carbon dioxide. People who have **chronic obstructive pulmonary disease (COPD)** may have one or a combination of chronic bronchitis, emphysema, and asthma (Porter & burlingame, 2006). COPD is a preventable and treatable chronic disease "characterized by airflow limitation that is not fully reversible and is usually progressive" (Anzueto, 2006, p. S46). Hay fever and cystic fibrosis are also chronic respiratory diseases. Tuberculosis (TB) is a well-known impairment yet is no longer considered a common cause of death. People with asthma may also have hay fever, or hay fever may be a precursor to asthma. Worldwide, the diseases that comprise COPD are the most common chronic lung diseases and the burden of COPD is projected to increase as tobacco use rises in developing countries (Ries et al., 2007).

Chronic bronchitis is an inflammation of the lining of the bronchial tubes with an increase in mucus and mucus-secreting cells (Porter & burlingame, 2006). The bronchi connect the windpipe to the lungs. When the bronchi are inflamed or infected, less air is able to flow to and from the lungs. A brief attack of acute bronchitis may accompany a cold. In chronic bronchitis there is a chronic mucus-producing cough (to clear the mucus or phlegm) that persists over extended time periods without other underlying explanations for the cough. Shortness of breath (dyspnea) is also experienced. Since smoking is the most common cause of chronic bronchitis, the cough is referred to as a "smokers' cough" (Dunn & Leitschuh, 2006).

Emphysema is a condition in which there is overinflation and subsequent destruction of the walls of the alveoli or air sacs in the lungs. This results in a smaller total number of effective air sacs (e.g., there is less surface area to exchange oxygen with carbon dioxide). The lungs lose their elasticity and, as a consequence, there is poor air exchange and shortness of breath (Porter & burlingame, 2006). Persons with emphysema may breathe 20 to 30 times a minute while the normal pattern is 14 times a minute (Sherrill, 2004). The heart pumps harder to compensate for the bloodstream's lack of oxygen, so heart failure becomes a possible complication (Sherrill). A barrel-shaped chest develops from repeated lung overexpansion as the nonfunctional alveoli attempt to receive an adequate oxygen supply and rid the body of carbon dioxide (Mobily & MacNeil, 2002).

Asthma, or reactive airway disease, is a chronic (always present) lung disease characterized by inflammation and increased sensitivity of the airways, obstructed airflow caused by narrowed airways and, in some instances, production of excessive thick mucus that further obstructs the airways (National Jewish Medical and Research Center, 1995). The obstructed airways produce the asthma symptoms: coughing, dyspnea, wheezing, and tightness in the chest. Asthma symptoms can vary from very mild to severe. Some people have seasonal symptoms while others experience symptoms daily; and for some, the symptoms develop suddenly, becoming asthma attacks. Attacks occur only occasionally and progress through three stages: (1) coughing that warns of an impending attack, (2) followed by dyspnea upon exhalation, (3) then severe bronchial obstruction with airways clogged from mucus that causes wheezing (Sherrill, 2004). Asthma episodes may be brief or last several days. Prolonged episodes and severe bronchial obstruction may result in *status asthmaticus,* which is life-threatening and requires hospitalized treatment.

Asthma affects all age groups and is a serious chronic illness worldwide. The "prevalence of asthma has increased in recent decades, especially in

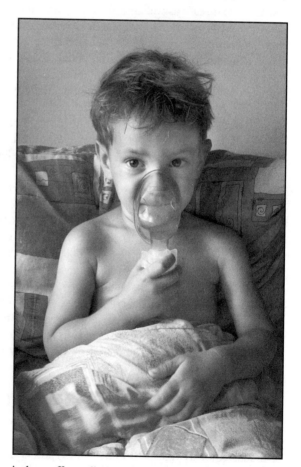

Asthma affects all age groups, but is seen primarily in children and youth.

urban areas with a Western lifestyle" (Huovinen, Kaprio, & Koskenvuo, 2003, p. 273). The number of emergency room visits and high drug costs make the economic burden of asthma a growing concern. Childhood asthma has genetic predispositions and many children with asthma have allergies to pollens, mites, mold, and animal dander. Episodes of asthma are usually triggered by a condition or stimulus. Children are more likely to have EIA (exercise induced asthma) than adults. Additional asthma triggers other than allergies and exercise include viral infections, emotional stress and excitement, cold air, occupational dusts, air pollution, irritants like cigarette smoke, sensitivity to drugs like ibuprofen, nocturnal asthma, household paints and cleaners, chronic sinusitis, and hormonal changes. Asthma is seen primarily in children and youth (Mobily & MacNeil, 2002). Sufferers have good and bad days influenced by weather changes, high pollen counts, environmental pollutants, or infection (Sherrill, 2004).

Hay fever or pollen allergy, also referred to as seasonal allergic rhinitis or pollenosis, is an allergy to a common substance that can accompany or be a precursor to asthma. Complications from repeated hay fever attacks can include chronic sinusitis and lowered resistance to disease as well as loss of sleep and appetite during hay fever season.

Cystic fibrosis (CF) is a genetic disorder caused by an abnormal or inadequate supply of a hormone or enzyme that affects the excretion of mucus, saliva, and perspiration (Hubbard, Broome, & Antia, 2005). Cystic fibrosis causes the membranes lining the internal organs to secrete an abnormally thick and sticky mucus that clogs the bronchial tubes and lodges in the windpipe, thereby obstructing breathing. This mucus also obstructs the pancreatic ducts, preventing digestive enzymes from reaching the small intestine and resulting in malnutrition (Sherrill, 2004). A high level of salt in sweat indicates a person has CF. Other symptoms include persistent coughing, wheezing, or pneumonia; excessive appetite but poor weight gain; and bulky, foul-smelling stools. Although the median age of survival has risen, a shortened lifespan results from complications created by lung infections and inability to properly digest food.

Tuberculosis (TB) is one of the leading causes of mortality and morbidity around the world: some 9 million people become ill with active TB each year, and nearly 2 million die (WHO, 2010a). Case rates in the United States have declined each year since 1992, with slightly less than 13,000 cases reported in 2008; yet despite available therapy, there continues to be a high prevalence in foreign-born and HIV positive individuals (CDC, 2009). TB is acquired by inhaling the germ from someone who has coughed or sneezed. Normal body defenses prevent the infection from causing the disease. If the disease becomes active, however, inflammation can cause extensive lung damage. Anyone at any age may be infected. The tuberculin skin test (PPD) reveals whether a person has been infected. A chest x-ray identifies whether the disease has become active.

Functioning Characteristics

Symptoms of other medical problems sometimes mimic respiratory impairments. Coughing, fever, shortness of breath, bronchial obstruction, wheezing, fatigue, change of mucus color to yellow or green, unexplained increase or decrease in weight, obesity, anxiety, depression, pain, difficulty sleeping or sleepiness, and general feelings of ill health are symptoms of respiratory disorders as well as many other chronic illnesses. Fear of wheezing or dyspnea causes some people with respiratory disorders to limit activity levels. This reduction in activity sets up a cycle of deconditioning that allows for disease progression. People with respiratory impairments commonly have permanent chest deformities (kyphosis, barrel-shaped chest, pigeon chest, or Harrington's groove—a depression along the lower edge of the thorax), distended abdomens, allergies, sinus trouble, and upper respiratory infections (Sherrill, 2004). A child with CF chills quickly due to a lack of adipose tissue. Cold dry air and high humidity predispose people to attacks, as does outdoor activity during pollen season, in dusty areas, and in smoke-filled environments. Dramatic weather changes and alterations in body temperature, specifically overheating, trigger exacerbations. Side effects of medications for COPD and asthma include increased heart rate, high blood pressure, dizziness, seizures, insomnia, diarrhea, and nervousness. With some medications, like steroids, long-term effects include osteoporosis, hypertension, diabetes, and interference with a child's growth (National Jewish Medical and Research Center, 1995).

Purpose of Therapeutic Recreation

The primary goal of pulmonary rehabilitation is to control and alleviate symptoms and optimize functional capacity, restoring the client to the highest level of independent function (Ries et al., 2007). Clients are encouraged to become more physically active and to learn how to cope and reduce disability from a chronic illness—the ultimate goal of comprehensive rehab is to improve quality of life through self-management and adherence to health-enhancing behaviors.

TRSs assess and report functional levels in treatment and education plans, conduct rehab programs to maintain physical capacity and emotional adjustment to chronic illness, implement leisure education programs, promote healthy lifestyle behaviors, and facilitate community reintegration. Periodic re-administration of the *spirometry* test helps the team adjust the rehab program. This breathing test helps determine severity of breathing difficulty while identifying improvement in pulmonary efficiency (Porter & burlingame, 2006; Sherrill, 2004). The client inhales deeply then exhales rapidly into a tube to determine lung capacity and forced expiratory volume for one second (FEV_1). With a drop of 10% or more from a normal reading, therapists re-evaluate rehab goals and interventions.

Therapists encourage clients to moderate their physical activities. By performing appropriate warm-up exercises and, in some cases, taking medications before exercising, an individual can avoid breathing difficulties. TRSs take into consideration environmental conditions such as pollutants and weather variations: Warm humid rather than cold dry climatic conditions are recommended when engaging in exercise and recreational experiences (Sherrill, 2004). Programs also include diaphragmatic and pursed-lip breathing exercises and relaxation techniques to improve expiration capacity.

The extent of lung damage or the lung capacity determines the type and amount of activity an individual with a respiratory impairment can tolerate without excessive fatigue. Prescriptive programs focus on improving the functioning capacity of the individual's respiratory muscles. Aerobic exercise, swimming, cycling, walking, and jogging strengthen chest muscles, enhance cardiorespiratory fitness, and promote the cough reflex that aids in mucus drainage. Golf, tennis, bowling, and weight training strengthen abdominal and shoulder muscles. Blowing activities, laughing, and playing wind instruments facilitate the elimination of residual air from the lungs.

A TRS who works with an individual with a respiratory disability is challenged to address the person's perceived and real barriers to activity. A fear of attacks may cause inactivity. This contributes to obesity and stress, which in turn trigger attacks. Leisure education promotes risk reduction and lifestyle changes (Mobily & MacNeil, 2002). Through resource awareness, TRSs promote the use of adaptive equipment to minimize exertion in ADL and leisure (Porter & burlingame, 2006). Where fear of stigmatization and pain are barriers, as with CF and TB, TRSs use social engagement, humor, and spirituality experiences as distraction and coping mechanisms (Hansel et al., 2004; Hubbard et al., 2005).

Delivery Settings

People with COPD, asthma, and CF generally spend some time each year convalescing at home or in the hospital from attacks complicated by colds, flu, and respiratory illness (Sherrill, 2004). Treatments for respiratory impairments include postural drainage, nebulizer breathing therapy, oxygen therapy, medications (bronchodilators, anti-inflammatories, and antibiotics), immunotherapy, gastrointestinal therapy, and counseling. Graded exercise programs or reconditioning exercises—which occur under medical supervision in outpatient clinics, the community, and the home—are prescribed. A TRS, in concert with the respiratory therapist and other team members, prescribes activities to promote physical well-being and psychosocial adjustment.

Leadership Interaction and Intervention Considerations

TRSs working with people with respiratory impairments are sensitive to the client's need to maintain body alignment and posture and encourage the use of warm-up and cool-down exercise. They are careful to avoid prescribing experiences in which participants might become fatigued, dehydrated, or inadvertently pushed to exertion; therefore, TR programs for people with respiratory disorders include intermittent activity and rest periods. They also incorporate diaphragmatic breathing through activities like parachute play and progressive relaxation exercises. Breathing patterns are also improved through activities like yoga (Sherrill, 2004).

Therapists educate clients and family members about elements that trigger attacks, like chlorine in indoor pools (Ratner & Griffiths, 1995). TRSs advise clients to: (1) consume a sufficient amount of warm fluids to facilitate coughing up excess mucus, (2) breathe through the nose rather than mouth to warm and moisten the air before it gets to the lungs, (3) breathe deeply and slowly during vigorous exercise, (4) maintain fluid intake before, during, and after exercise, (5) practice pursed-lip breathing (purse the lips like blowing out a candle or whistling) when the client feels short of breath from activity, and in some cases (6) take salt tablets when the client is likely to perspire excessively (Porter & burlingame, 2006; Sherrill, 2004).

Through leisure education, TRSs acquaint clients with activities such as board games and personal management strategies like instituting a buddy system to monitor participation levels. The use of self-efficacy concepts, problem-solving, and cognitive behavior therapy bolster performance and increase the likelihood of exercise compliance and management of stress, anxiety, and depression that lead to exacerbations and attacks (Burgess, Kunik, & Stanley, 2005; Porter & burlingame, 2006; Scherer & Shimmel, 1996). Social skills interventions reduce isolation and improve the integration of disability management into everyday life (Christian & D'Auria, 2006).

Applying the Therapeutic Recreation Process

Assessment

A one-week resident camp cosponsored by a children's hospital and respiratory clinic is held every summer. Additionally, through a family support group, fall and spring weekends are held at the camp. Self-esteem inventories (before and after) and modified fitness tests are administered as part of the camp program. Campers are primarily youth with asthma and CF.

Planning

Objectives of the program include educating youth to the signs, symptoms, and triggers of respiratory distress; managing treatment routines; promoting family adjustment to chronic illness; and cultivating self-care skills and healthy routines. During the resident camp a medical team from the hospital remains on the grounds, while the weekend camps are staffed by physicians, nurses, and respiratory therapists from the clinic. Parents are included in opening and closing day activities of the resident camp because the program is also intended to provide caregiver education. The weekend camps include clients and caregivers and are intended to provide updates on medical care, managing chronic illnesses, and promoting family well-being. TRSs at the hospital work with camp staff to plan resident and weekend camps.

Implementation

Campers plan their own daily activities. Each camper experiences an individualized medical session with one of the medical staff on a daily basis. Medical staff participate in camper programs, helping participants learn to monitor their breathing and exercise routines. Campers keep journals, and staff members document each person's progress daily. Evening debriefings address choices and decisions made during programs, leisure preferences, and personal management of medical needs.

Evaluation

Campers, staff, and caregivers complete post-camp assessments. Parents participate in closing day activities, when projects and accomplishments are displayed; they attend small group seminars with medical staff; and they participate in one favorite program (i.e., aquatics, outdoor skills, environmental education) with their child.

ENDOCRINE IMPAIRMENTS

The pituitary, thyroid, and adrenal glands are major *endocrine glands* that secrete hormones which regulate growth and maintain homeostasis. Malfunctioning of the endocrine glands causes growth deviations like *cretinism*, associated primarily with intellectual disabilities (ID), and obesity deviations. Metabolic impairments also are evident in rare syndromes like Hurler's and Tay-Sachs, forms of severe ID, and cholesterol and diabetic disorders. Obesity is one of the leading worldwide health issues.

Further, obesity increases the risk of cardiovascular disease and Type II diabetes and is a known issue in various cancers and respiratory impairments, other chronic illnesses presented in this chapter. This section first considers diabetes and then discusses obesity.

Diabetes mellitus (DM), called diabetes, which literally means "passing through" was named for its most common symptom, frequent urination (Sherrill, 2004). It is one of the most common, complex, chronic inherited diseases with an unknown cause. The prevalence of the disease is increasing worldwide and threatens to overwhelm health systems and undermine economies (Manning, 2007). Diabetes is attributed to a combination of genetics, environment, and behavior—it is exacerbated by eating habits. The prevalence of diabetes is going up because obesity is on the rise. Diabetes is manifest by abnormally large amounts of sugar in the blood and urine. A person with diabetes has an insufficient supply of insulin available to act on carbohydrates; therefore, sugar accumulates in the body and is eliminated in the urine. The body is denied heat and energy ordinarily produced by this sugar, resulting in weight loss, lack of energy, and continual hunger.

Type I diabetes, insulin-dependent diabetes mellitus (IDDM), affects primarily children and youths and results when the pancreatic beta cells do not manufacture enough insulin. Type I diabetes develops abruptly and is usually detected after an individual experiences sudden weight loss, frequent urination, drowsiness and fatigue accompanied by higher than normal sugar levels in the blood and urine (Sherrill, 2004). These individuals are lean and are susceptible to blood glucose swings and insulin reactions. They use insulin pump therapy, insulin pens, or inject insulin into their bloodstream; monitor glucose levels; and balance food intake and exercise to maintain normal insulin levels (Sherrill). Type I diabetes, also known as brittle diabetes, is the most difficult form of diabetes to control and is a lifelong condition.

Type II diabetes, non-insulin dependent diabetes mellitus (NIDDM), mainly affects adults and is the most common form of diabetes. Symptoms are the same as Type I except weight loss is not rapid (Sherrill, 2004). The pancreas produces insulin, but either not enough or the cells do not use it properly so glucose builds up in the bloodstream (Porter & burlingame, 2006). Type II diabetes tends to develop slowly and may be present several years prior to detection. It is associated with older adults, obesity, a family history of diabetes, ethnicity, and physical inactivity (Porter & burlingame). Diet, exercise, and oral medication may control glucose levels, with insulin used if necessary.

Obesity is excess body fat. An individual is *overweight* when his or her weight is 10–20% above the ideal for the person's age, sex, height, body build, and cultural expectations; obesity is defined as 20% or more above ideal weight (Porter & burlingame, 2006; Sherrill, 2004). Child and adult obesity has risen alarmingly over the past two decades in developed countries (see figure 7.1). Obesity associated with inactivity is considered to be at epidemic proportions and is a global health-care concern (Kaur, Hyder, & Poston, 2003; Murphy & Carbone, 2008; Yang, Telama, Viikari, & Raitakari, 2006).

Obesity, like diabetes, is a chronic illness and "each is a risk factor for future morbidity and mortality" (Mobily & MacNeil, 2002, p. 302), making prevention an important goal. Each also imposes substantial direct and indirect costs on health-care systems, including, but not limited to, diagnostic and treatment services and lost wages and productivity; in addition, obesity can entail costs associated with incidences of coronary heart disease, Type II diabetes, and hypertension (Rosenberger, Sneh, Phipps & Gurvitch, 2005). Another similarity is causation; environment, behavior, and genetics are factors in both obesity and diabetes. Endocrine disorders

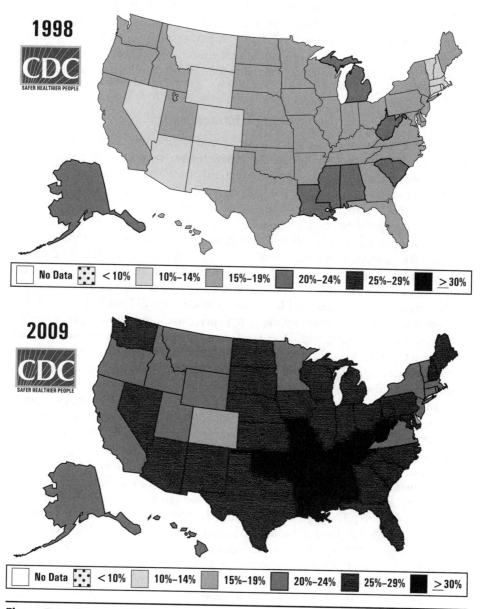

Figure 7.1   Percent of Obese U.S. Adults, by state, 1998 and 2009
Centers for Disease Control and Prevention, 2010.

contribute to 10% of those with obesity (Sherrill, 2004). Interaction between hereditary and environmental factors "result in an imbalance between caloric intake and output" (Sherrill, p. 507). This imbalance may be related to cultural practices or familial patterns such as sedentary leisure behavior or learned eating to cope with stress (Porter & burlingame, 2006). Certain medications used to manage chronic conditions like diabetes, cancers, and psychosis (e.g., sulfonylureas, corticosteroids, and antipsychotics) also cause weight gain (Porter & burlingame; Sherrill). Another similarity is the long-term, daily management required to monitor glucose levels (diabetes) and weight (obesity) (Mobily & MacNeil; Porter & burlingame). TRSs typically interact with obese and diabetic clients through leisure education and health promotion programs rather than in treatment and rehabilitation, as with cardiovascular and pulmonary interventions.

Functioning Characteristics

People with diabetes must monitor their blood sugar levels several times daily—especially before, during, and following activity to ascertain the need to administer sugar or insulin to prevent insulin shock (reaction) or a diabetic coma from occurring. A glucometer is used to measure the level of glucose in the bloodstream. A drop of blood from the fingertip is placed on a paper strip inserted into the meter; an electronic reading reports the level. Desired levels vary according to when the blood sample is taken; after meals the range is higher than before meals or during routine daily activities. The suggested normal range is 80–120 mg/dl (milligrams per deciliter) (Sherrill, 2004). High or low blood sugar is evidenced by a lack of energy, confusion, delayed reaction, loss of manual dexterity, and a tendency to tire easily.

If a person's blood sugar level is too low, below 80 mg/dl (that is, the blood contains too much insulin), insulin shock, or **hypoglycemia**, results and sugar is needed. The onset of insulin shock is rapid and is caused by an insufficient amount of carbohydrates in the diet, delayed meals, and prolonged strenuous physical activity. Insulin reaction is characterized by intense hunger, sweating, nervousness, nausea, headache, fatigue, raised pulse rate, pale skin color, sudden moodiness or behavior changes, seizure, and diplopia (double vision). Confusion, irritability, muscle weakness, loss of consciousness, and death result if glucose is not administered. People with Type I diabetes take insulin daily and continuously monitor blood glucose and balance food intake with exercise to avoid hypoglycemic attacks.

If a person's blood sugar level is too high, **hyperglycemia** results. It can be caused by injection of too little insulin or the body's inefficient use of insulin (Porter & burlingame, 2006). Hyperglycemia may progress from lethargy to drowsiness to diabetic coma (Sherrill, 2004). During a diabetic coma the body begins to break down fats to use as fuel because insulin is not available to metabolize glucose. High blood glucose levels (more than 120 mg/dl other than before, during, or immediately following meals) cause increased urination, dehydration, and loss of electrolytes. Signs of hyperglycemia include nausea, fatigue, and increased thirst. In ketoacidosis, which usually occurs with Type I, excess ketones (waste products from fat metabolism) develop, impair muscle glucose use, and increase blood glucose levels (Jimenez et al., 2007). "Any condition that raises ketone levels increases the risk of hyperglycemia" (Sherrill,

p. 511); examples include vomiting, overeating, alcohol intake, and failure to take enough insulin to offset activity levels. Symptoms of ketoacidosis usually develop slowly, appear several days prior to loss of consciousness, and include extreme thirst, fatigue, nausea, abdominal pain, leg cramps, high blood sugar levels, and high levels of ketones in the urine. Hyperglycemia with ketoacidosis may include the above signs as well as difficulty breathing, fruity odor to the breath, inattentiveness, confusion, and loss of appetite (Jimenez et al.). Signs of a diabetic coma include a flushed face, sweet breath odor, and a rapid pulse. Death may result if insulin is not administered.

Although diabetes itself does not kill, uncontrolled blood glucose levels—whether Type I or II—cause illness, disability, and death from heart disease, kidney failure, nerve damage, and increased susceptibility to infection (Manning, 2007). Diabetes increases the risk of blindness, amputations, complications from pregnancy, heart disease and strokes, and nervous system damage (Mobily & MacNeil, 2002; Porter & burlingame, 2006; Sherrill, 2004).

Long-term management of obesity is like managing addictions; the problem can be solved temporarily but never cured (Sherrill, 2004). Of those who diet, only an estimated 10% achieve lifetime weight control. Childhood obesity is a strong predictor of obesity in adulthood (Porter & burlingame, 2006; Sherrill). When underlying conditions are ruled out, lifestyle management is concerned with inactivity or sedentary behaviors, eating habits, cardiovascular endurance, social engagement, and self-responsibility for monitoring behaviors and seeking support. Children with disabilities are more likely than other children to be sedentary (Kaur et al., 2003; Murphy & Carbone, 2008), and physical inactivity during childhood tracks into adolescence and adulthood.

Weight increase results from poor dietary habits, selecting foods higher in fat and calories, and eating larger portions. Overweight and obese people tend to engage in sedentary leisure time activities like watching TV, playing video games, and using computers—activities that also limit social interaction. Further, motor impairment, peer pressure, and/or personal discomfort contribute to avoidance of social situations. With increasing weight, greater amounts of energy are necessary to engage in appropriate levels of physical activity; but poor cardiovascular endurance itself promotes inactivity, creating an unhealthy cycle. Self-responsibility for monitoring behavior is essential to adopting an active lifestyle. Without a change in attitude, it is difficult to maintain and appreciate the benefits of a daily exercise program—particularly given the additional time and energy necessary to manage weight. Modern lifestyles that promote fast food and sedentary leisure behaviors challenge long-term obesity management.

Purpose of Therapeutic Recreation

TRSs are most likely to implement education and health promotion programs with individuals whose primary or secondary impairment is diabetes. With obesity, TRSs design education and health promotion experiences to manage weight, promote proper nutrition and physical activity, and facilitate psychosocial well-being and support (Edwards & Poff, 2008; Porter & burlingame, 2006). Treatment of both Type I and Type II diabetes involves assessing and monitoring diet, exercise, blood sugar levels, medication, and secondary complications. People with Type I diabetes tend to be lean, while those with Type II tend to be overweight. To regulate weight control and maintain consistent blood sugar levels, TRSs help individuals adopt and maintain a high-carbohydrate, low-fat diet consumed in several smaller meals. In addition, when obesity is the primary issue, TRSs emphasize the value of and need to adopt (1) regular exercise habits, (2) proper nutrition, and (3) time management skills. With diabetes and obesity, relaxation and stress management help clients cope and gain self-control of risk behaviors that create barriers to positive lifestyles (Porter & burlingame, 2006).

Education programs for diabetics focus on lifestyle changes and managing blood sugar levels before, during, and after meals and exercise to prevent complications. Additionally, TRSs facilitate the practice of medication self-administration during social experiences. TRSs incorporate heart and blood pressure monitoring to help participants prevent and detect heart disease. Health promotion efforts with diabetic and obese clients help them identify and minimize stressors that trigger poor eating habits (Porter & burlingame, 2006). Leisure resource awareness promotes options and choices that remove physical activity barriers and identify pleasurable activities. With social experiences, clients gain self-confidence while participating with others having common interests—this promotes continued involvement. Through values clarification, assertion, and problem-solving experiences, TRSs enable a sense of client self-responsibility. Family education and support are key factors when working with younger clients (Edwards & Poff, 2008; McAuliffe-Fogarty, Ramsing, & Hill, 2007).

Delivery Settings

Individuals with diabetes and obesity have a chronic illness and, like those with respiratory impairments, may experience inpatient hospital treatment; but unlike someone with COPD, for example, hospitalization may not be exclusively for diabetes or obesity but rather for complications like stroke, kidney disease, amputations, and even depression. TRSs interact with clients during inpatient, outpatient, and home health-care services (e.g., aging adults with diabetes). In community settings, TRSs are involved with medical specialty camps, family interventions, and education and training of recreation personnel who facilitate physical activity with youth and adults in gyms, parks, and playgrounds (Braswell, 2006; Burlingame, 2007; McAuliffe-Fogarty et al., 2007).

Leadership Interaction and Intervention Considerations

Interventions with diabetes and obesity are multifaceted, taking into consideration how the individual and environment interact to influence behavior. A team approach targets behaviors across the health-care and human-service continuum. Regardless of setting, the intended outcome is client self-monitoring that promotes a healthy lifestyle. To accomplish this, team members use a number of techniques and strategies to foster compliance, self-care, and safety:

- Behavior modification is used to promote environmental change associated with caloric intake and activity levels.
- Goal setting promotes healthy behaviors while phasing-out unhealthy behaviors.
- Cognitive restructuring focuses on dietary change and increasing physical activity.
- Stress management techniques facilitate relaxation and time management.

- Journaling helps monitor physical activity intensity and duration, energy intake, and insulin regimen.

- Accessible, attractive play spaces and arrangement of exercise equipment encourage social interaction of clients and encourages family members to support and monitor physical activity levels.

- Humor, satisfaction, and enjoyment are valued and noted; clients are encouraged to engage in forms of physical activity that are pleasurable.

- Aquatic therapy introduces a non-weight-bearing option less stressful than land-based physical activity.

- Group problem-solving experiences provide crucial support that helps clients make permanent lifestyle behavior changes.

TRSs are aware of recommended safety precautions specific to diabetes. Increased exercise activity reduces the body's need for insulin, as does a diet of complex carbohydrates. Too much insulin and physical activity and too little food result in the rapid onset of an insulin reaction. By consuming sports drinks, fresh and dried fruit, or other foods with rapidly absorbed carbohydrates, participants can restore the proper insulin level in their bodies (Colberg, 2000). Too little insulin and physical activity and too much food result in the gradual onset of a diabetic coma, which requires treatment by insulin and immediate medical attention. Therapists are sensitive to mood swings and are comfortable approaching clients when signs of hypo- or hyperglycemia are manifest. Individuals with diabetes must practice precautions with cleanliness and foot care and must monitor skin breakdown at injection sites; spread of infections and poor wound healing are leading causes of amputations (Mobily & MacNeil, 2002).

Applying the Therapeutic Recreation Process

The therapeutic recreation process is applied with an adult whose primary diagnosis is hypertension with secondary complications from Type I diabetes.

Assessment

Demographic information. Tom is a 60-year-old male participating in an employee wellness program prescribed by his physician to help manage high blood pressure and diabetes.

History. Tom is anticipating retirement. He has successfully managed his diabetes since childhood. Since chronological age (CA) 56 he has taken prescription medications (antianginal agents) to reduce blood pressure and heart rate; most recently this has reduced his exercise tolerance and caused adjustments in his walking program.

Present behavior. Tom has recently enrolled in his company's wellness program so his physician can monitor exercise routine, diet, and medication levels.

Planning

Long-term goal. The long-term goal of the TR process is to sustain Tom's walking program.

Short-term goals. The two short-term goals are for Tom to self-regulate insulin levels/administration and to manage stressors.

Objectives. While participating three times a week in the company wellness program, Tom will record pulse rate, blood pressure, and sugar levels and adjust exercise intensity, duration, and caloric intake to maintain appropriate levels of each. Once a week Tom will record in an exercise log the psychosocial climate surrounding his participation in the wellness program.

Content. A TRS on staff with the hospital that contracts to provide the company wellness program routinely walks with participants. The therapist discusses leisure activities and relaxation techniques with participants and reviews weekly journal entries.

Process. The TRS encourages participants to maintain a leisure log and report variables that trigger stress. During monthly wellness luncheons the TRS and a dietician review Tom's and his wife's menu planning and activity routines.

Implementation

The TRS and rehab team prepare monthly charts. The TRS reports exercise level and behaviors affecting management of diet and exercise. An incentive program is maintained to encourage Tom to self-monitor the intensity, frequency, and duration of activities as well as an insulin regimen specific to each activity.

Evaluation

The pre-retirement program encouraged completion of life and leisure satisfaction measures and routine fitness tests. The TRS met with wellness participants to review implications of these measures on lifestyle behaviors.

CANCER

Cancer is a group of diseases characterized by uncontrolled growth and spread of abnormal cells that can affect any body system. "One in eight deaths worldwide is due to cancer . . . it is the second leading cause of death in economically developed countries (following heart disease) and the third leading cause of death in developing countries (following heart disease and diarrheal diseases)" (Garcia et al., 2007, p. 1). Worldwide, the three most common cancer sites are also the three leading causes of cancer deaths (breast, lung and bronchus, and prostate). While more than half of all new cancers and cancer deaths worldwide are potentially preventable, anyone can develop cancer, with the risk of diagnosis increasing with age (Garcia et al.; Porter & burlingame, 2006).

Cancer is caused by multiple mutations in the genes that control cell division. Normal body cells grow and divide in a coordinated manner, while cancer cells multiply out-of-control, overpowering the growth-control mechanism. These cancer cells destroy adjacent normal tissue and spread to other body parts. Secondary cancerous cells (**metastases**) develop and destroy cellular structure of the organ at the new site. A tumor is a growth of new cells (neoplasm) having no useful function. A benign tumor will remain at the site of its origin, while a malignant tumor has the potential to spread to other tissues.

Throughout one's lifetime, a number of risk factors affect the probability that an individual will develop or die from cancer. These factors are organized into four categories (Porter & burlingame, 2006): Behavioral factors are controlled by the client (e.g., smoking, diet, sunlight exposure, amount of physical activity); biological factors are physical attributes (e.g., gender, age) that may increase cancer risk but with behavior and environmental modifications these may be reduced; environmental factors (e.g., pesticides, water and air pollutants) may also increase cancer risk; and genetic factors (hereditary) may increase risk of particular cancers (breast). Researchers believe many cancers result from a combination of hereditary and environmental factors.

A physician may detect cancer as a result of conducting a screening test, which could include imaging or x-ray, laboratory tests and pathology reports from a **biopsy** (fine needle aspiration, punch, or endoscopic), or surgical removal of a tumor. Staging at the time of diagnosis describes the extent and spread of the disease and helps determine the prognosis and the appropriate treatment plan. The extent of the cancer or stage is determined by three variables, each identified by a letter, which comprise the **TNM system** (worldwide nomenclature) (Garcia et al., 2007; Porter & burlingame, 2006):

- *T* denotes the size and extent of the primary tumor
- *N* denotes the absence or presence of regional spread in the lymph nodes
- *M* indicates absence or presence of distant metastatic spread

Numbers are added to the letters to note the extent of the malignant disease, with 1 being early and 4 being advanced:

- Primary tumor size: T0 T1 T2 T3 T4
- Regional lymph node spread: N0 N1 N2 N3
- Distant metastasis: M0 M1

Summary staging describes how far a cancer has spread from its point of origin: *in situ* is present in the layer of cells where it began; *localized* is limited to the organ where it began; *regional* has spread to lymph nodes near the organ; and *distant* has spread from the primary site to distant organs and lymph nodes (Garcia et al., 2007; Porter & burlingame, 2006).

A clinical classification (cTNM) is based on evidence prior to treatment and physical examination supplemented by diagnostic studies [computed tomography (CT) scan] or blood chemistry tests. A pathological classification (pTNM) is based on information from surgical removal of the tumor or tissues (biopsies). Completeness and accuracy of cancer staging is essential to planning appropriate care.

Cancers are identified by the primary organ they involve and by the site of origin: skin cancer is referred to as **epithelioma**; glandular cancer is called **carcinoma**; muscle, fibrous tissue, tendon, or bone cancer is called **sarcoma**; lymph tissue cancer is **lymphoma**; and cancer in the white blood cells is known as **leukemia**. Leukemia constitutes the highest incidence of cancer in childhood (Sherrill, 2004).

Functioning Characteristics

Being diagnosed with cancer may be a life-changing event (Porter & burlingame, 2006). People exhibit characteristic normal responses: disbelief, denial, despair, "why me," followed by anxiety, depression, anorexia, insomnia, or irritability (Roth &

Massie, 2001). Psychological reactions of patients are influenced by the nature of their cancer: For example, the emotional well-being of a person who is undergoing successful treatments and is likely to have a lifespan free of recurrence is very different from a person whose cancer is incurable and who requires palliative and supportive therapy to address the complications from the disease. Both live with fear, yet in the latter situation such fear is intensified by pain, nausea, anorexia, insomnia, and problems of infection and bleeding. Other factors affecting psychological reactions are the client's ability to cope with stressful events, emotional maturity, emotional and social support of others, and societal and cultural attitudes (stigma) toward cancer and its treatment (e.g., cancer treatment is time consuming, routine is interrupted, overall health and energy are lacking) (Porter & burlingame; Roth & Massie). Simultaneously, clients must satisfy obligations while maintaining a sense of confidence about the outcome and managing the financial burden.

The seven warning signs of cancer may be symptoms of advanced stages of cancer and require aggressive treatment: unusual bleeding or discharge, a lump or thickening in or under skin tissue, change in size or color of a wart or mole, sores that do not heal, change in bowel or bladder habits, chronic hoarseness or nagging cough, and chronic indigestion or difficulty swallowing. The primary cancer treatments consist of one or a combination of surgery, radiation therapy, and **chemotherapy** (the administration of drugs to treat various cancers) (Garcia et al., 2007; Sherrill, 2004). With each, a person's functioning is temporarily or permanently affected. During surgery, the tumor and surrounding tissue are removed, thus affecting the particular organ where the cancer originated and the complete system of which it is a part. Some cancers (cancer of the larynx and the colon, for example) necessitate removing an entire body structure. Radiation therapy used alone or in conjunction with surgery and/or chemotherapy controls, weakens, or destroys cancer cells, or controls symptoms of recurrent cancers and relieves pain. The side effects of radiation include nausea, vomiting, weakness, profuse sweating, loss of appetite, weight loss, fatigability, and pain. Radiation depresses the bone marrow and results in the lowering of red and white cell production. This leaves an individual susceptible to infection. The complications from chemotherapy are similar to those of radiation. Lowered white cell counts permit infection to be a life-threatening issue. Chemotherapy so markedly reduces platelet cells that bleeding episodes become cause for concern. Hair loss (**alopecia**) is the most evident side effect of chemotherapy. While some treatments reduce or minimize a cancer, they may not change expected survival time, consequently both survival and anticipated clinical response to therapy are important factors considered as the team designs a treatment strategy (Lenhard & Osteen, 2001).

Purpose of Therapeutic Recreation

Cancer treatment results in impairments similar to those associated with other physical impairments. For example, surgery that causes facial disfigurement requires rehabilitation similar to the cosmetic restoration needed following thermal injury. An amputation due to cancer is treated like one due to a traumatic accident. Cancer of the nervous system has effects similar to those of neurological impairments (convulsive disorders, MS).

Therapeutic recreation specialists also address the psychosocial impacts of cancer. Clients' fear of death and recurrence of the disease, their anticipation of unbearable chronic pain, and the side effects of treatment create anxiety, frustration, and feelings of insecurity. Frequent hospitalizations and treatments disrupt social relationships and cause dependency. TRSs attempt to design programs that provide diversionary relief; promote health and well-being; manage grief, depression, and end-of-life issues; and facilitate social involvement and continued peer and family support. Leisure education programs encourage self-determination and life evaluation. Relaxation and stress management promote pain control. Wellness experiences release tension, promote physical activity, and build self-esteem. Cognitive stimulation and expressive experiences help clients manage depression, develop coping strategies, and create a positive self-image. Reminiscence enables end-of-life-review with caregivers (Porter & burlingame, 2006).

Delivery Settings

People with cancer experience periodic hospitalizations for surgery and various treatments. TRSs work with youths and adults with cancer in **oncology** (study of the growth of tumors) units and with children in specialized treatment centers or freestanding children's hospitals. TRSs also participate in the delivery of self-help and support programs such as Little Red Door residential camps and Recovery Clubs. Therapeutic recreation specialists are part of a team that includes surgical and medical oncologists, social workers, radiation therapists, psychologists, physiatrists, clergy, physicians' assistants, and speech, physical, and occupational therapists, all of whom are highly skilled in the psychological and medical aspects of cancer. Team members are involved in hospice services, home care, and ongoing bereavement support.

Leadership Interaction and Intervention Considerations

TRSs help clients and their families cope with physical impairment and psychosocial needs, as well as manage the grieving, depression, and isolation that result from a life-threatening disease. Clients, caregivers, and friends address the fear of recurrence and the anticipation of unbearable pain and death. Intervention strategies vary with the setting, cancer stage, treatment side effects, prognosis, and client preferences (Porter & burlingame, 2006). Specific strategies used with clients and caregivers include the following:

- Journaling and expressive therapies assist in the management of anger and frustration and help redefine a person's self-concept after losses that cause self-image changes.
- Guided imagery and muscle relaxation help reduce stress and anxiety.
- Nature and outdoor experiences create avenues to spiritual health.
- Leisure education and group processes foster problem-solving, alternative coping strategies, lifestyle adaptations, and participation in realistic choices (Porter & burlingame).
- Medical play helps children and families manage fear of cancer treatment (see chapter 11).

Outdoor activities can enhance self-esteem and provide a welcome diversion for a child facing the prospect of ongoing cancer treatments.

- Adventure-challenge experiences with youth facilitate improvement in physical and psychological outcomes, enhance self-esteem, and improve health-related quality of life (Stevens et al., 2004).
- Humor activities counter episodes of sadness.
- Animal-assisted therapy diverts attention and promotes care of others.
- Behavioral interventions and social experiences support lifestyle practices like diet and exercise that are risk factors for comorbid conditions (heart disease and diabetes).
- Wellness and physical activity programs promote a focus on quality of life for the whole family unit while supporting the client's physical wellness (Mobily & MacNeil, 2002).

Applying the Therapeutic Recreation Process

The process is applied in a research hospital with an adult with terminal cancer.

Assessment

Demographic information.   Becky, chronological age 44, is a home health-care nurse, married with a 16-year-old daughter.

History.   Becky scheduled a physical because she was feeling fatigued and had experienced an unusual number of colds, both of which she attributed to stress.

Present behavior.   Blood tests came back with an elevated white cell count. The diagnosis was myelodysplastic anemia, which if untreated develops into acute myelogenous leukemia (an adult form of leukemia) within six months to a year. Initial diagnosis occurred in April.

Planning

Long-term goal.   The long-term goal of therapeutic recreation is to facilitate quality of life during treatment to arrest leukemia.

Short-term goal.   The two short-term goals are to participate in diversionary bedside activities and to include family members in the treatment and education process.

Objectives.   Patient will participate with family members in bedside activities daily. Patient will complete daily cardiovascular exercise, i.e., walking, riding stationary bike, or exercises from seated position with family members assisting.

Content.   The family education program included an inventory of family activities enjoyed by Becky's siblings and her husband and daughter. Scrabble, backgammon, and cards were activities found to interest all family members. Family members were asked to assist Becky in walking or riding the stationary bike to prevent pneumonia and blood clots.

Process.   In September, family members moved to an apartment across from the hospital. A younger sister and older brother were found to have compatible blood types. Family members and Becky attended daily education sessions with the oncologist, nurse educator, and representatives from the team, i.e., physical therapist, chaplain, recreation therapist, and psychologist. On the day of admission, blood tests revealed Becky was in a blast crisis, diagnosis of leukemia. A stem cell donation, rather than bone marrow transplant, was determined to be the appropriate protocol.

Implementation

During the five days prior to the stem cell donation, family members and Becky daily played board games or cards and attempted to take short walks in the hallway. Becky experienced fatigue, diarrhea, and was beginning to lose her hair due to total body radiation. Sores developed in her mouth, throat, nose, and other soft tissue areas; her skin was burnt, and she bruised easily. The recreation therapist visited Becky and family members and provided the needed equipment daily. The therapist also advised family members where to access local restaurants, churches, and leisure resources.

Evaluation

The stem cell donation was successful; Becky was released to her home on October 1 with an IV pump (to administer morphine). Becky's family returned to their homes. On October 30, Becky experienced a second blast crisis. She died in her sleep. The therapist was successful in achieving the treatment objectives.

CHRONIC PAIN

The International Association for the Study of Pain (www.iasp-pain.org) defines pain as "an unpleasant sensory and emotional experience associated with actual or potential tissue damage or described in terms of such damage" (Merskey & Bogduk, 1994). Chronic pain syndrome (CPS) presents a major challenge to health-care providers worldwide due to its complex history, unclear etiology, and resistance to most medical treatment (Singh & Patel, 2005). *Acute* pain results from disease, inflammation, or injury to tissues; usually comes on suddenly; can be diagnosed and treated; tends to be confined to a period of time; and serves as a protective mechanism to signal a problem or the resolution of a problem (National Institute of Neurological Disorders and Stroke [NINDS], 2001). Chronic pain, on the other hand, implies a persistent pattern of pain that serves no useful function and is compounded by environmental and psychological factors. In some instances, acute pain may progress to chronic pain. "Pain is the most common complaint that leads patients to seek medical care" (Singh & Patel, 2005, Frequency, para. 1).

Chronic pain can affect any age group although the prevalence of pain among the elderly is reported to be higher than other age cohorts (Stumbo, 2006b). "Low back pain is a major health and socioeconomic problem in Western countries" (Woolf & Pfleger, 2003, p. 652). An aging population, the increasing prevalence of back pain with age, and the increasing weight of individuals combined with lack of exercise will increase the burden of musculoskeletal pain dramatically in the foreseeable future (Brooks, 2006). Chronic pain conditions are present with musculoskeletal diseases like arthritis (Jakobsson & Hallberg, 2002); terminal illnesses like cancer (Hill, Cleeland, & Gutstein, 2001); respiratory impairments like cystic fibrosis (Hubbard et al., 2005); and with life-altering experiences like thermal injuries, cardiovascular diseases, poliomyelitis, and traumatic incidents like spinal cord injuries (NINDS, 2001; Singh & Patel, 2005). Additionally, the American Psychiatric Association (2000) classifies pain disorder as a form of somatoform disorder. Such disorders have as a common feature the presence of physical symptoms in one or more anatomical sites that warrant clinical attention and are severe enough to impair social and occupational functioning. Chronic pain lasts six or more months while acute pain lasts less than six months (APA). While pain disorder may be associated with either psychological issues or general medical conditions, several associated psychiatric disorders are observed among people with CPS, including depression and anxiety disorders.

Fibromyalgia (achy pain and stiffness in soft tissues throughout the body or in specific locations like the shoulders) is a CPS that manifests as generalized muscle aches with generalized tender points (Mobily & Verburg, 2001). The diagnosis is based on the presence of widespread (all four quadrants of the body) pain for a period of at least three months. Pain is felt in response to slight pressure at at least 11 tender points on the neck, shoulders, back, hips and upper and lower extremities. Usually considered a disorder of women 20 to 50 years of age, it is also observed with youth, males, and older adults as well as in relatives of clients with fibromyalgia. Thus, genetics and the environment may be contributing factors (Chakrabarty & Zoorob, 2007).

Pain is a psychophysiological experience mediated by a number of personal and cultural factors: intensity and anatomical site of the intrusion, the person's physical and psychological condition, the meaning and the context of the pain experience, the way the person has learned to label and communicate pain, and the person's and significant others' perceptions about pain.

Functioning Characteristics

Chronic pain syndrome is characterized by a cycle of pain. CPS leads to decreased movement, inactivity, weight gain, poor sleep, and fatigue. These, in turn, decrease concentration, foster social isolation, and present challenges to performing daily activities (Kunstler, Greenblatt, & Moreno, 2004). Individuals with fibromyalgia may complain of headaches, morning stiffness, and low back pain, with cold humid weather aggravating their symptoms (Chakrabarty & Zoorob, 2007). Chronic fatigue syndrome is common to fibromyalgia and CPS. A loss of stamina, strength, endurance, and flexibility causes muscle pain when efforts are made to become active. Mobility is reduced. The pain cycle continues as the pain is perceived, anxiety builds, and muscle spasms cause more pain (Simon, 1996).

CPS interferes with relationships. Social, recreational, occupational, and family activities are disrupted, which contributes to stress and tension that, in turn, result in depression. Loss of or diminished employment can result in financial problems. Mood swings, stress, and anxiety are common. Quality of life is diminished.

Purpose of Therapeutic Recreation

Treatment of CPS is unique to each person. A team approach attempts to interrupt pain behavior, improve functional abilities, reduce medication use, prevent relapse, decrease depression and anxiety, provide pain relief, and improve sleep patterns—facilitating a better overall quality of life. A number of pharmacological and nonpharmacological interventions are employed in pain management. Combinations of medication, exercise, psychoeducational strategies, complementary therapies, cognitive behavior therapy, and surgical interventions help clients cope more effectively and set realistic self-management goals (Chakrabarty & Zoorob, 2007; Singh & Patel, 2005).

Pain management tends to be addressed initially by medical interventions, including medication, surgery, nerve blocks, and radiation. The intent is to reduce or possibly eliminate the pain (Stumbo, 2006a). A multidisciplinary approach with nonpharmacologic interventions tends to empower clients toward self-management; approaches pain management from a holistic perspective; and complements medications (possibly reducing dosages) while having fewer undesirable side effects (Chakrabarty & Zoorob, 2007; Stumbo, 2006a). TRSs help clients cope more effectively, acquire wellness behaviors, improve self-efficacy, find satisfaction and socialization in previously lost or newly acquired leisure behaviors, and achieve relaxation and enhanced levels of physical activity while reducing tension and pain (Kunstler et al., 2004; Singh & Patel, 2005; Stumbo, 2006b). TRSs promote stress management and time management skills and encourage physical activity (walking, bicycling, and swimming) to address deconditioning during inpatient rehab. Educational strategies include problem-solving, decision making, guided imagery, restructuring, relaxation, activity balance and pacing, assertiveness training, leisure skill development, and communication techniques. Relapse-prevention efforts and the promotion of social support and family caregiving help clients address their isolation while confronting self-defeating behaviors (e.g., avoiding exercise due to heightened perceptions of pain) and setting new "rules" about living within the limitations of their injury or illness (Barkin et al., 1996).

Psychological interventions in conjunction with medical interventions tend to increase the effectiveness of treatment programs (Singh & Patel, 2005). Alternative therapies used by TRSs include aromatherapy, massage, meditation, aquatic therapy, breathing exercises, yoga, tai chi, and physical activity (Kunstler et al., 2004; Mobily & Verburg, 2001). Biofeedback, chiropractic therapy, acupuncture, herbs and dietary supplements, and electrical stimulation are complementary interventions TRSs may encounter with a multidisciplinary approach (Chakrabarty & Zoorob, 2007; NINDS, 2001).

Delivery Settings

Treatment for chronic pain generally occurs on an outpatient basis; however, hospitalization may result when the treatment of choice is invasive or as a consequence of comorbidity, like illnesses associated with aging. People on medication reduction programs or those who are being treated for psychiatric issues are likely to be in inpatient units, while those whose pain is associated with chronic disabilities like arthritis or musculoskeletal injuries are likely to be under the care of a primary physician. Hospice care (cancer) occurs in the home. Clients also receive treatment at freestanding pain management centers and from private psychotherapists. TRSs work as members of multidisciplinary teams treating clients in psychiatric and physical rehabilitation units and are consultants and therapists with outpatient clinics and caregiver support groups.

Leadership Interaction and Intervention Considerations

TRSs use a variety of cognitive-behavior strategies to help clients change the way they perceive and respond to pain (Stumbo, 2006a). Clients are encouraged to assume

A multidisciplinary approach to treating chronic pain syndrome might include therapies like yoga, breathing exercises, tai chi, massage, and meditation.

an active role in choosing interventions and treatment planning. Client preference is an important determinant of continued participation in physical activity programs. With aging clients in health-care settings, exercising control is critical to their satisfaction—an important healthcare outcome (Kunstler et al., 2004). Group interventions lend themselves to psychotherapy and social support—techniques that moderate depression and anxiety. Through visual imagery, drama, and movement experiences, clients learn to redefine their self-image. Leisure education helps clients learn to solve problems and make decisions. TRSs also assign projects for clients to complete between sessions so they develop self-monitoring practices. Other strategies TRSs employ with individuals with chronic pain include assertiveness training and systematic desensitization (to help clients change their thought processes associated with pain). Therapists use behavior management strategies like goal setting and contracts to promote the maintenance of positive routines (physical activity and diet) and to prevent relapse. Flexibility, stretching, and cardiovascular conditioning increase physical functioning and are a part of wellness programs. Relaxation techniques, including meditation, also are employed to relieve tension and manage pain.

Applying the Therapeutic Recreation Process

The therapeutic recreation process is applied to an adult with fibromyalgia.

Assessment

Demographic information.   Betty is a 26-year-old female who is a caregiver for her mother and has made a recent career move to enable her to provide in-home care for her parents.

History.   Betty's fibromyalgia is controlled by daily exercise, a strengthening regimen, and with tricyclic antidepressants. The diagnosis was made within the last two years.

Present behavior.   The fear associated with increasing pain and profound fatigue has resulted in Betty taking NSAIDs (nonsteroidal anti-inflammatory drugs), increased dosages of a tricyclic antidepressant, and treatments with a physical therapist. A TRS at the hospital wellness center conducts aquatic therapy, relaxation, and caregiver support sessions. The TRS uses the LDB Form C to assess self-perception, leisure needs, and Betty's personality to select the most beneficial leisure activities.

Planning

Long-term goal.   The long-term goal of Betty's treatment is to relieve the intensity and duration of severe pain episodes.

Short-term goals.   The two short-term goals of her treatment plan are to improve Betty's ability to relax and to maintain her daily exercise routine.

Objectives.   Betty will participate daily in 30-minute exercise sessions, monitoring her heart rate and pulse and recording vitals in her wellness log. Betty will attend a weekly group session and practice relaxation techniques (deep breathing, meditation, muscle relaxation), documenting both stressors and destressors in her wellness log.

Content.   The TRS from physical rehab coordinates outpatient wellness and caregiver support groups. Exercises include land and water aerobics as well as activities that alternate strengthening with endurance. Group sessions educate clients on how to implement relaxation techniques like visual imagery, deep breathing, muscle relaxation, and humor. Support group topics include sleep habits, pain cycle, body mechanics, respite resources, leisure needs, and medication side effects.

Process. The TRS conducts early morning, noon, and evening wellness programs and meets with each client initially to review the team's plan. Thereafter, the TRS and the client meet monthly to assess the client's self-monitoring of vitals and quality of life measures.

Implementation

The TRS participates with clients during wellness sessions and on the rehab team staffings. He or she reviews the client's self-monitoring via chart audits. Life and leisure satisfaction measures are administered before and after wellness sessions. LDB Form C and FIM scores are kept in the client's chart. Leisure education exercises during support group meetings focus on leisure needs, resource awareness, decision making, and problem solving.

Evaluation

The TRS attends staff meetings and reports Betty's progress toward her goals. LDB Form C and FIM scores are reviewed monthly, with life and leisure satisfaction measures taken pre- and post program.

CHRONIC FATIGUE SYNDROME

Chronic fatigue and immune dysfunction syndrome (CFIDS), commonly called chronic fatigue syndrome (CFS), mimics the symptoms of other diseases like lupus, multiple sclerosis, fibromyalgia, depression, cancer, and tuberculosis. The syndrome has been reported worldwide. Prevalence rates are higher in well-developed countries than in underdeveloped countries. Most studies report a rate three to four times higher in women than in men; youth younger than 10 rarely experience CFS while adolescents (10–17 years) are more vulnerable; and people in their 40s and 50s tend to be most commonly impacted (Centers for Disease Control and Prevention [CDC], 2008; Wyller, 2007). Because the etiology of the syndrome is unknown, treatment protocols remain unclear and there is no known way to prevent the disease.

Like cancer and pain, the disease can affect all of the body's systems. A definition developed under the leadership of the CDC includes fatigue and symptom criteria as well as exclusionary criteria that prevent people from receiving a diagnosis of CFS if specific conditions are present (2008). Each fatigue criterion is clinically evaluated and must be in evidence: unexplained, persistent, or relapsing chronic fatigue that is new, has not been lifelong; does not result from exertion; is not alleviated by rest; and causes a substantial reduction in daily activities (CDC, 2009). Patients must also report four or more concurrent symptoms present for six or more consecutive months that do not predate the fatigue: short-term memory or concentration impairment; sore throat; tender cervical or axillary lymph nodes; headaches of a new type, pattern, or severity; unrefreshing sleep; muscle pain; multijoint pain without joint swelling or redness; and postexertional malaise lasting more than 24 hours (CDC). If the following conditions are present, CFS is not applicable: "hypothyroidism, sleep apnea and narcolepsy, major depressive disorders, chronic mononucleosis, bipolar affective disorders, schizophrenia, eating disorders, cancer, autoimmune disease, hormonal disorders, subacute infections, obesity, alcohol or substance abuse, and reactions to prescribed medications" (CDC, 2008, para. 1). This interpretation is the most encompassing; other reported definitions deviate very little. One definition requires the presence of mental fatigue and accepts symptoms that might indicate a psychiatric disorder; another descriptor requires a new or definite onset of fatigue; and yet another excludes symptoms of mental illness (Wyller, 2007).

The hallmark of CFS is persistent severe fatigue. CFS is characterized by gradual or acute onset of a flu-like or viral illness followed by unremitting severe fatigue, systemic complaints, and nervous system involvement like tremors that usually subside in a few weeks. Symptoms wax and wane over a long period of time, with individuals experiencing periods of exacerbation and remission. Symptoms vary from person to person and may vary over time with each individual. The course of the disease varies from months to years; some recover completely, others grow worse; full recovery without treatment is rare.

Functioning Characteristics

Chronic, persistent, disabling fatigue is the primary clinical manifestation of CFS. Patients report feeling feverish (even though their body temperatures fall within the normal range) and experiencing chills, joint and muscle pain, and recurring dull headaches. They also report difficulty concentrating and remembering recent events, feeling depressed, experiencing panic attacks, and exacerbation of the symptoms after exercise.

CFS affects each person differently. Some remain homebound while others resume work even though they continue to experience fatigue. A functional classification defines degree of impairment by ability to perform daily activities:

1. mild—person is mobile and carries out routine activities
2. moderate—person has reduced mobility and limited ability to perform daily activities
3. severe—person uses wheelchair and performs limited self-care
4. severe—person is bedridden and unable to care for self (Wyller, 2007)

The initial complaint with youth may not be fatigue but rather headaches and abdominal or limb pain; functional impairment and inactivity may be marked (Garralda & Chalder, 2005). CFS is characterized by activity peaks followed by extremely long rest periods; yet individuals often are able to perform light to moderate exercise without exacerbating their symptoms or cognitive performance (Nijs, Paul, & Wallman, 2008).

Individuals share one common reaction: a sense of giving up what has been previously earned. Recovery comes slowly. Symptoms are erratic and unpredictable. As the illness goes into remission, individuals express fear of its unannounced return. With each headache or cold-like symptom, fear is rekindled. Depression and loss of self-esteem often result from the loss of the individual's previous lifestyle and the uncertainty of the future.

Purpose of Therapeutic Recreation

Because the cause of CFS remains a mystery, the clinical course varies, and there is no cure, treatment is aimed at relieving symptoms and improving functional capacity and well-being (Schwalm-Lopez & MacNeil, 2005). A multidisciplinary approach with drug and nondrug therapies includes symptom management, cognitive behavioral strategies, graduated exercise programs, alternative therapies, and support (CDC, 2008; Schwalm-Lopez & MacNeil; Wyller, 2007). Prescriptive medications like nonsteroidal anti-inflammatories (NSAIDs) and antidepressants are used to improve sleep and relieve pain. Cognitive behavioral therapy in concert with graduated exercise programs increase activity level while attempting to replace negative thoughts and behaviors with positive ones that promote control over symptoms. Alternative therapies (e.g., tai chi, acupuncture, aquatic therapy, stretching, and massage) and support groups help clients relax, improve coping skills, reduce anxiety, and promote a sense of well-being.

Support, education, and health promotion are significant TRS roles. Interaction with clients through support groups and individualized leisure education sessions tends to reduce anxiety, promote acceptance, and enable the development of coping strategies. Clients are introduced to the benefits of exercise and balancing physical activity during daily routines. Social engagement is fostered, as is the acquisition of new passive leisure pursuits like journaling (Schwalm-Lopez & MacNeil, 2005). Through skill assessments and skill-development programs, therapists teach clients to select alternative experiences, set priorities, and monitor daily routines. Health promotional strategies help clients practice preventive strategies (relaxation, yoga, moderating daily activity levels, and balanced diet) that reduce the risk of later life problems. Therapists promote self-worth by helping clients focus on the present, realigning their short- and long-term goals, and selecting experiences that are meaningful, satisfying, and enhance clients' quality of life perceptions. Self-efficacy and personal control ease the adjustment to the unpredictable course of recovery.

Delivery Settings

Assessment and diagnosis occur in inpatient settings, while treatment and education occur in outpatient and home settings. A multidisciplinary approach is maintained. TRSs in psychiatry, rehabilitation, and home health-care settings support team efforts to develop individualized programs and promote family education. Services are similar to those provided to people with chronic pain.

Leadership Interaction and Intervention Considerations

Generally, TRSs focus on the symptoms that affect the person's functional ability and activities of daily living. TRSs confront clients when their behaviors adversely affect recovery. To illustrate, a TRS may mediate an individual's physical activity level to prevent an emotional relapse and the frustration the client associates with poor performance. Throughout their interactions, TRSs encourage humor and goal-setting that help clients adjust to the present. By assisting clients in redirecting thought processes and by employing behavioral strategies like visualization, a TRS helps clients abandon the sick role and adopt a more positive perspective. Through therapeutic activities like tai chi, journaling, and imagery, individuals learn to manage the interactions among rest, exercise, nutrition, stress, and social experiences. The TRS encourages clients to develop self-management strategies so they "pace" or balance activity with rest to avoid overexertion and relapse (Nijs et al., 2008).

Applying the Therapeutic Recreation Process

The therapeutic recreation process is applied to a 34-year-old female whose primary diagnosis is CFS.

Assessment

Demographic information. Kate is a 34-year-old female currently working part-time as a result of CFS symptoms. She is the mother of two children and, with her husband, lives and works in a major metropolitan area.

History. Kate was previously employed as a full-time supervisor in retail. She was active in her children's school functions and exercised with her husband regularly. Fatigue and memory/concentration problems interfered with work, causing Kate to take a brief medical leave; muscle and joint pain increased as did flu-like symptoms.

Present behavior. Exacerbation of Kate's symptoms necessitated reduced work hours; after exercise or housework her symptoms became more apparent. Kate is being treated by her primary physician following diagnosis of CFS at a research hospital.

Planning

Long-term goal. The long-term goal of Kate's treatment is to maintain social relationships.

Short-term goals. The two short-term goals are to sustain family activities and to maintain social contacts outside the family.

Objectives. Kate will participate in one activity per day with family members. Kate will visit at least twice weekly with members from her church.

Content. A monthly support group attended by all family members discusses implications of CFS, including social and recreational impacts. A social worker and TRS co-lead the group. Homework activities require family members to keep activity logs and participate in leisure and self-awareness exercises.

Process. The TRS teaches family members to use debriefing techniques with a leisure education workbook. The social worker documents self-reported ADL activities, while the TRS records social contacts and recreational events reported by family members.

Implementation

Family members attend individual psychotherapy sessions and the support group each month. Kate completes daily relaxation routines and plans balanced meals with family members. Family members walk together, ride bikes, and complete leisure education exercises on self-esteem and leisure resource awareness. A family log is used to record individual members' daily school, work, and leisure.

Evaluation

A battery of tests to assess deconditioning was repeated semi-annually. Cognitive reassessment also was repeated semi-annually. The social worker and TRS used self-reports to measure objective achievement. Scores on life and leisure satisfaction scales were also compared and reported in the staffings conducted by the research hospital team.

SENSORY LOSSES AND
COMMUNICATION IMPAIRMENTS

People with sensory losses and communication impairments experience a diminished ability to effectively respond to stimuli. Sensory losses and communication impairments often accompany physical impairments, like cerebral palsy and multiple sclerosis, and cognitive impairments, like autism. When more than one primary sensory loss is experienced, as with a person who is deaf-blind, a dual-sensory impairment exists.

Prevalence of sensory impairments varies with age groups and between developed and undeveloped countries. It is believed that two-thirds of the children under age 15 with permanent hearing losses reside in developed countries (Olusanya & Roberts, 2006), while 1–2% of those with visual impairments worldwide live in developed countries (Langelaan et al., 2007). Prevalence increases with age; by 75, 50% of the U.S. population has significant hearing losses at higher frequencies and at least two-thirds over age 65 have serious visual problems (Sherrill, 2004). These statistics are expected to increase worldwide with the aging of the general population. Hearing loss is the most common disabling condition in the U.S. and Canada (Smith, Austin, Kennedy, Lee, & Hutchison, 2005).

Visual acuity, the ability to distinguish forms or details, is expressed in a numerical ratio. This ratio compares the number of lines read from the Snellen chart at a particular distance to the number of lines normally read at that distance. Several terms are used to describe visual impairments (Sherrill, 2004):

- Legal blindness, 20/200—the ability to see at 20 feet what the normal eye sees at 200 feet

- Travel vision, 5/200 to 10/200—the ability to see at 5 to 10 feet what the normal eye sees at 200 feet

- Motion perception, 3/200 to 5/200—the ability to see at 3 to 5 feet what the normal eye sees at 200 feet (usually movement rather than a still object)

- Light perception, less than 3/200—the ability to distinguish a strong light at a distance of 3 feet from the eye, but unable to detect movement

- Total blindness, or cecutiency—the inability to detect a strong light shone into the eye

- Tunnel vision—a field of vision that is 20 degrees or less

Legal blindness refers to visual acuity that is 20/200 or less in the better eye after correction, or to a field of vision that is limited to an angle of 20 degrees or less out of the normal 180-degree field of vision (Smith et al., 2005). **Low vision** means that a person possesses a visual acuity of at least 20/200 but no greater than 20/70 in the better eye after correction, or 30 degrees or less visual field (Dattilo, 2002). Most people with visual impairments perceive light or motion. They can read large print, yet are unable to see an object or a portion of an object or the surrounding environment (Smith et al.).

People born without sight are considered to be congenitally blind, while those who lose sight after birth are referred to as being *adventitiously* blind. Causes of visual impairments include refractive errors (blurred visual image due to improper focus of light rays), muscle imbalance (when the muscles surrounding the eyes are not synchronized), genetic disorders, diseases, and accidents.

Refractive errors include (Mobily & MacNeil, 2002):

- Myopia, nearsightedness—the ability to see objects close-up but not at a distance
- Hyperopia, farsightedness—the ability to see distant objects but not close-up objects
- Astigmatism—blurred vision for both far and near objects

Muscle imbalance results in several visual distortions:

- Nystagmus—rapid side-to-side and up-and-down eye movements
- Strabismus—eyes cross or turn out
- Amblyopia—dominance by one eye due to inability of the two eyes to focus clearly on an object

Genetic disorders, or hereditary conditions that cause impairments, include:

- Achromatic vision—color blindness
- Albinism—lack of pigment in choroid and irises resulting in lack of sensitivity and refractive errors
- Retinitis pigmentosa—rods and cones don't rejuvenate, causing night blindness, tunnel vision, loss of central vision

Infectious diseases that cause birth defects contribute to several visual impairments, as do some adulthood diseases (especially diabetes):

- Cataracts—fogging, clouded, opaque spots on the lens
- Conjunctivitis—inflammatory disease of the conjunctivas
- Diabetic retinopathy—vascular changes cause hemorrhaging in the retina, blindness results
- Glaucoma—increasing pressure within the eye causes visual loss, commencing with peripheral vision

Visual impairments caused by accidents and injuries include punctures, retinal detachment, lens dislocation, and retinopathy of prematurity (ROP—a disease of the retina caused by poorly regulated oxygen in incubators).

The sense of hearing, like visual acuity, is characterized by several units representative of the attributes of sound. Sound *intensity*, or loudness and softness, is measured in decibels (db). A sound of 0 db is barely audible while sounds over 100 db are painful. *Frequency*, high or low pitch, is measured in units of Hertz (Hz) (20–20,000 Hz is the normal frequency range). Frequency measures determine whether the hearing loss is constant at different pitch levels. Finally, *spectrum*, or timbre, is the attribute of sound that makes one tone or series of tones distinguishable from another (spectrum ranges from pure tone, or single frequency, to complex tones, which occur during normal speech). Hearing losses are measured by the degree of speech heard per decibel level—the higher the number value, the more significant the loss (Sherrill, 2004):

- 25–40 db—slight hearing loss, cannot understand whispered speech
- 41–54 db—mild hearing loss, understands conversation at a 3- to 5-foot distance
- 55–69 db—moderate hearing loss, understands loud conversation at close range
- 70–89 db—severe hearing loss, may hear loud voices about 1 foot from ear
- 90 db or more—profound hearing loss, aware of vibrations rather than tonal patterns

A person who is **deaf** is unable, with or without a hearing aid, to process linguistic information. A person who is **hard of hearing** has experienced hearing loss, but is able to process linguistic information either with or without a hearing aid. A hearing loss of 70 db in the better ear separates those who are deaf from those who are hard of hearing (Sherrill, 2004). A congenital hearing loss refers to a hearing loss that is present at birth; an acquired, or **adventitious**, loss refers to hearing loss that occurs later in life. A prelingual loss refers to hearing loss that occurs prior to language development; a postlingual loss refers to a hearing loss that follows language development. Children with prelingual hearing losses have difficulty developing language skills.

When a hearing loss is attributed to physical obstruction in the conduction of the sound waves to the inner ear, such as that caused by impacted wax, a conductive hearing loss exists. Infection in the middle ear (*otitis media*) accounts for a majority of conductive hearing losses (Sherrill, 2004). Damage to the cells or nerve fibers that receive and transmit sound stimuli causes a sensorineural hearing loss. High-tone nerve deafness that accompanies the aging process is a sensorineural hearing loss. This form of hearing loss also results from nerve injury at birth, brain infections, illness of the mother during pregnancy, contagious diseases, and prolonged exposure to intense sounds (over 130 db). Mixed hearing losses, both conductive and sensorineural losses, are experienced particularly by the elderly.

The sources of some visual and hearing losses are unknown. Other sources include congenital defects, drug and alcohol abuse, maternal infections, injury, sexually transmitted diseases, heredity, and association with multiple disabilities (Sherrill, 2004). Usher's syndrome is another leading cause of dual-sensory impairments (deafness and blindness). This syndrome affects infants in the womb. These infants are born with hearing loss, accompanied by progressive blindness (retinitis pigmentosa). A person with a visual ratio of 20/200 or a field of vision of 20 degrees or less who also has a hearing loss of 25 db or more is considered to have a dual-sensory impairment (Dunn & Leitschuh, 2006).

Communication impairments result from perceptual and emotional factors associated with specific learning disabilities like aphasia. They also are evident with cognitive and physical impairments such as intellectual impairments, strokes, head injuries, or cerebral palsy. Diseases associated with aging like Parkinson's disease and Huntington's chorea affect the neuromuscular system and also result in communication impairments.

Perceptual-motor deficits, such as laterality, directionality, and space and time discrimination, which are evident with learning disabilities, result in communication impairments. When a person's receptive language abilities are impaired, as occurs with individuals who have experienced a stroke or head injury, he or she neither comprehends spoken words nor remembers their sequences. Expressive language deficits refer to impairments in speaking and writing abilities, as observed with children with autism. Impaired communication occurs with the aging process and a number of disabilities. Communication disorders are covered in chapter 8 and where appropriate throughout the text.

Functioning Characteristics

Visual Impairments

The attendant effects of a visual impairment are determined by the individual's age at the onset of the loss and the degree of vision that remains. When vision is lost prior to or at birth, a person's opportunity to acquire information from observation of others is absent. On the other hand, when vision is lost after age 7, language and motor development have reached a level that permits an individual's adjustment to new social environments. Similarly, when a person is totally or legally blind, he or she has less opportunity to acquire information from the environment than a person who still has the ability to perceive travel, motion, or light.

People with visual impairments may exhibit stereotyped behaviors like rocking back and forth or putting their fist or fingers into their eyes. These same behaviors are evident with severe multiple disabilities and autism and result from the need for physical activity thwarted by their respective impairments. To avoid objects and help maintain balance, these individuals may walk leaning forward with their arms extended. Lowered fitness levels result from sedentary lifestyles, overprotection, and lack of access to instruction (Sherrill, 2004). Comprehension of abstractions is difficult; this affects cognitive and social functioning. Also, when nonverbal gestures, expressions, and social amenities are missed, such individuals may appear expressionless and insensitive to the cues and verbal comments of others. With increasing age, deficits in social competence become more obvious (Sherrill). Work-related aspects like using computers and driving are affected; ultimately, visual impairments contribute to less than average employment rates among working-age adults and loss of independence in the older adult population (DiStefano, Huebner, Garber, & Smith, 2006; Langelaan et al., 2007). Moreover, visual impairments, when compared with hearing impairments or chronic disabilities like Type II diabetes, affect health-related quality of life more profoundly (Langelaan et al.). People with visual impairments have learned to use other senses to gain information and to interact. Consequently, others might perceive "exceptional memory" when, actually, the person relies on highly developed alternative sensory channels to process environmental input (Bullock, Mahon, & Killingsworth, 2010).

Hearing Losses

People who are born deaf or who lose hearing before speech and language are acquired experience greater disabilities—especially in the areas of language development and conceptual thinking—than those who acquire losses later in life (Smith et al., 2005). In addition to the loss of usual conversational methods, people with hearing losses exhibit such characteristics as a shuffling gait, restlessness, unusual head tilts and

Children with hearing losses miss the incidental learning that occurs during play.

rotations, and balance disorders. These individuals also experience an inability to access audible environmental information such as sirens, auto horns, and background sounds. Young children may miss the incidental learning of behaviors, rules, and strategies that occur during spontaneous play (Sherrill, 2004). Children with profound deafness may appear hyperactive as a result of their inability to communicate with the hearing world (Smith et al.). The social-emotional consequences of missed interactions and the anxiety created by an inability to express feelings may exacerbate the physical and cognitive losses. Frustration also results from environmental barriers like poor lighting or background noise that affects people wearing hearing aids or those who read lips (Sherrill).

Dual-Sensory Impairments

People with dual-sensory impairments need to develop a method to communicate, like finger spelling or using a telecommunication device for the deaf (**TDD**). Isolation attributed to visual and hearing losses results in limited social opportunities important to fulfilling well-being needs. Also, reduced opportunities for physical activity limit avenues to develop awareness of one's self-image that in turn affects self-concept development. One's self-concept mediates socio-emotional health. With lowered levels of physical activity, ADL become more physically challenging. Among adults, higher levels of unemployment and underemployment further reduce social and intellectual opportunities that impact health-related quality of life (Lieberman & MacVicar, 2003).

Communication Impairments

Communication impairments are experienced by a variety of individuals. People with multiple impairments often lack reading, writing, and attendant skills used to receive information. Aging adults may experience a diminished capacity to hear low and high tones like whispers or shrill voices. People with learning disabilities exhibit characteristic forms of communication impairments. For example, individuals with dyslexia reverse letters as they read and write.

Purpose of Therapeutic Recreation

Visual Impairments

Therapeutic recreation specialists help create accessible environments for individuals with visual impairments (Bullock et al., 2010). TRSs also encourage participation in physical activity and sports in order to promote self-confidence, provide sensory stimulation, manage obesity, and create avenues to social experiences and community resources. Therapeutic recreation facilitates leisure skill development and resource awareness. Therapists support training in fundamental skills like spatial awareness and balance and provide educational and health promotion experiences that create safe environments, foster self-directed participation, and promote physical activity in community and home-based activities (e.g. with older adults).

Therapists create accessible environments and opportunities in a number of ways. During the provision of direct services, therapists orient participants, adapt equipment, modify activities, act as sighted guides, and use a variety of tactile, kinesthetic, and auditory sensations to create accessibility. TRSs provide **orientation and mobility (O and M)** training to help clients gain access to leisure experiences. TRSs also assist caregivers and service providers in marketing and delivering services; for example, planning alternative communication avenues to use in the event of an emergency. Early intervention is important to remediate delays in the development of play and social

A community inclusion activity for a client with a visual impairment features a game of bocce.

skills as children cannot progress without help in aggregate or parallel play because they are unaware of others present (Sherrill, 2004). Through play groups, TRSs promote movement exploration, sensory stimulation, adaptation to environmental barriers, and social interactions—all of which foster increased access and participation.

Therapists also help clients develop sports skills and access participation in competitive events. The United States Association for Blind Athletes (USABA), and the International Blind Sports Association (IBSA) sponsor regional, national, and international events in which athletes with visual impairments compete. Individuals compete according to visual abilities, as shown in exhibit 7.1 (Sherrill, 2004). Popular sports include power lifting, swimming, track and field, goal ball, gymnastics, and winter sports like downhill and cross-country skiing (Sherrill). The growing rehabilitation needs of military veterans are being addressed through the collaboration of the USABA, the Blind Rehabilitation Service of the Department of Veteran Affairs, and the Blinded Veterans Association. Through clinics, participants are instructed on how to adapt various sports and to integrate into community-based sports programs ("Blinded Military Members," 2008).

Exhibit 7.1   USABA and IBSA Competition Classes

Class	Visual Abilities
B1	Visual abilities range from no light perception in either eye to light perception and inability to recognize shape of hand
B2	Field of vision up to and including 20/60 and/or limitation in field of vision of five degrees and ability to recognize shape of hand
B3	Field of vision greater than 20/60 up to 20/200 and/or field of vision between five and twenty degrees

---

Through aquatics, movement exploration, and fitness activities, clients are taught to monitor their movements and expressions and develop an awareness of proper posture, relaxation, and self in relation to others and objects in the environment. Leisure education programs encourage self-directed experiences by acquainting clients with reading devices such as opticons and books published by the American Printing House for the Blind, which prints books with enlarged print. With the increasing number of aging persons, visual impairments are also more prevalent. Consequently, leisure education helps older clients develop home-based activities and encourages them to remain socially engaged (Stevens-Ratchford & Krause, 2004).

Hearing Losses

People with hearing impairments vary in their ability to hear and to benefit from the amplification of hearing aids. They are dependent to varying degrees upon their visual and haptic (touch) senses to interact with others and their environments. When the hearing loss is attributed to destruction in the semicircular canals, the individual also experiences a loss of balance. Individuals' hearing abilities may be enhanced by hearing aids worn behind the ear, in the ear, on the chest, or in eyeglasses. These devices selectively amplify sounds, so users must learn to distinguish those that are essential. Digital hearing aids allow clients to tune out certain frequencies and thus eliminate prevailing sounds that interfere with understanding words (Sherrill, 2004). Individuals with conductive hearing losses experience more success with hearing aids than do individuals with sensorineural losses.

In addition to considering an individual's residual hearing ability and use of hearing aids, a TRS also considers the type of communication method preferred by the participant, as research has reported this affects leisure patterns (Wachter, 1994). Finger spelling (particular hand position is used for each letter of the alphabet), speech reading (observing the speaker's lips, mouth, facial expressions, and gestures), cued speech (spoken words supplemented by hand signs near the face), **American Sign Language** (ASL, the dominant language of the deaf community), signed English (signing English in the order it is spoken), and **Pidgin sign** (signing in English and ASL) represent manual and oral communication methods (Sherrill, 2004). Therapists control environmental distractions and lighting conditions since the effectiveness of these communication modes are influenced by such factors, e.g., wearing solid, dark-colored clothing improves effectiveness of finger spelling and sign language (Smith et al., 2005).

Therapists assist clients as they develop skills and access sports sponsored by associations like the USA Deaf Sports Federation (USADSF—www.usadsf.org) or the Deaflympics (International Committee of Sports for the Deaf—www.ciss.org). Leisure experiences offer social avenues, expressive and creative outlets, tension release, relaxation, sensory development, physical activity, and contribute to self-determination, well-being, problem-solving ability, decision making, spontaneity, and functional independence.

Persons in the deaf community seem to be less constrained in sports than in other leisure areas since sports rely less on verbal communication (Sherrill, 2004; Tsai & Fung, 2005). Inclusive recreation can present challenges due to the use of different modes of communication, deaf identity, attitudes, and social competence (Coco-Ripp, 2005; Lieberman & MacVicar, 2003; Sherrill). Thus, TRSs play a crucial role in creating opportunities with family and friends. Through leisure education and participation in ongoing communication training, TRSs reduce barriers and promote positive attitudes and social outcomes (Tsai & Fung).

Dual-Sensory Impairments

For people with dual-sensory impairments, activities that feature movement and arts and crafts provide opportunities to communicate and interact with others and to release emotions. TRSs working with individuals with dual-sensory impairments provide feedback through tactile and kinesthetic cues. Physical activity like walking and stationary bicycling enhances clients' personal comfort, health-related fitness, and ability to complete ADL tasks. Cognitive and cultural experiences such as card games and theater performances foster one-on-one and small-group social interaction. Individualized leisure experiences with companions encourage an individual's social integration and independence. Through leisure education, TRSs address barriers like lack of knowledge about community resources, leisure options, and adaptations.

Communication Impairments

TRSs working with individuals with communication disorders train their clients to use a variety of speech and language systems and communication aids to facilitate social interaction and promote independent behaviors. The intent of intervention is affected by the nature of the primary impairment, i.e., learning disability, stroke, or head injury. TRSs help create avenues for expression while working in tandem with treatment, rehab, education, and health promotion goals of, for example, physical rehabilitation or special education programs.

Delivery Settings

People who experience sensory and communication impairments may reside in their own homes, in congregate living centers in the community, or in residential settings such as state-operated schools for individuals with visual or hearing impairments. People with other physical impairments and those who are aging also may experience sensory and communication impairments. Therefore, TRSs are found in residential settings and throughout the community. TRSs work with adapted physical educators, vocational rehabilitation personnel, and orientation and mobility instructors to help individuals improve their daily functioning and physical and psychosocial well-being.

Leadership Interaction and Intervention Considerations

Visual Impairments

By following a number of guidelines, a TRS facilitates the client's participation in therapeutic recreation experiences.

Teaching strategies. TRSs design activities that include whole-part-whole instruction; physical guidance and guided discovery; sound-source devices and audible targets; marked boundaries; demonstration and tactile modeling; large print, Braille, or audible cassette systems; and the pairing of haptic (touch) with auditory senses. Boundaries, foot and hand placements, and starting, stopping, and turning points are identified with texture variations, voice commands, and audible goals.

Clear, concise directions using task-analyzed sequences paired with touch (after asking) may be necessary to teach a skill. The pace of an activity may be slowed to accommodate mobility aids and objects that may unexpectedly intrude into the environment. Visual awareness is enhanced by controlling the glare and shadows in the room or facility; wearing a hat or sunglasses may help, though the amount of lighting to provide optimal visual conditions varies from person to person (Smith et al., 2005). Physical boundaries are explored through all of the senses: to illustrate, echo and sound detection help discern distance between objects while light variations (natural daylight versus artificial illumination) and odors (chlorine smell) help clients distinguish and remember locations. Guide ropes or rails mark paths and trails. Yellow or orange painted balls aid partially sighted participants (Sherrill, 2004). Unnecessary noises and objects are eliminated from the environment.

Orientation and mobility. An essential initial task is to establish "communication" between the therapist and the participant. When approaching or walking away, the TRS states his or her name and tells the client he or she is departing (Smith et al., 2005). It is important to identify the client's residual vision capabilities and the best position for the therapist to assume during a conversation. A next step is to orient the client to the environment. Therapists may use a clock or a compass face to describe location of objects; for example, the door is at nine o'clock and the ladder into the pool is at noon. Using a letter of the alphabet to describe the entry-exit route helps clients remain on course. By providing reference points, the therapist encourages clients to use all senses as they orient to the area.

A number of techniques are available to guide participants during activities. Laser canes offer a degree of independence, yet may be perceived as a stigma. Guide dogs are trained with their owner and are considered "on duty" when they are in their harness. Sighted guides or partners enhance social interactions. The client grasps the guide's arm at the biceps just above the elbow, the guide's arm remains close to the side of the body, and he or she walks a half step in front of the participant. The guide reports the direction in which doors open and close, stairs ascend or descend, and the presence of curbs and ramps. As a skill is demonstrated, the participant may wish to place his or her hands on the therapists' to follow movements. With each experience, emergency procedures are practiced, hazards identified, and warning signals committed to memory.

Hearing Losses

Specific leadership strategies appropriate to people with hearing losses are outlined below. TRSs use various sensory and environmental cues to engage participants in activities; however, their initial task is to establish communication with participants and ensure their safety. They also take precautions to ensure that participants' hearing aids and earmolds are properly managed. These include securing and protecting hearing aids and earmolds from direct trauma such as a flying ball, wiping perspiration away from participants' hearing aids and earmolds during the course of an activity, and replacing ineffective batteries or molds. Specific intervention strategies include the following:

- Stand within the participants' view and permit participants to move so the leader is in view. Keep the lips fully visible and the mouth empty. Shadows, glare, shade, and sunshine interfere with speech reading and signing.

- Present directions only when participants are facing you. Clients may swim with their face out of the water in order to communicate. Keep background noise to a minimum and speak to the participant, not the interpreter.

- Repeat short sentences or be prepared to write down words. Speak in a normal tone using facial expressions and gestures to accentuate feeling and meaning. Speak distinctly but naturally.

- Model proper skills as an avenue to skill development.

- Use guided discovery and physical guidance to introduce movement patterns. Place participants so they are able to observe others performing the skill.

- Use visual cues to start and stop participants. Train participants to use their vision to spot dangerous situations.

- Demonstrate instructions like "fast" or "slow" so participants can discriminate movement variations. Terms having more than one meaning like "out" may require demonstration to explain multiple interpretations.

- Assist participants in compensating for unsteady balance by requiring them to lower their center of gravity and widen their base of support.

- Position mirrors in the room to allow participants to view and develop their movements and skills.

- Incorporate relaxation experiences to encourage self-awareness.

- Incorporate rhythm activities to facilitate participants' development of the motor skills essential for maintaining poise in social situations.

- Train participants to focus on leader cues and instructions so they learn to discriminate between immediate sounds and background intrusions.

- Request verbal feedback or demonstration by participants to ascertain their level of comprehension and ability to comply. Use questions to determine comprehension.

- Have several alternatives to accommodate a child who is easily distracted or requires increased levels of guidance to maintain attention (Smith et al., 2005).

Dual-Sensory Impairments

The TRS establishes a communication avenue with dual-sensory-impaired clients that might involve certain touch signs on the body, spelling the manual alphabet on the client's hands, or allowing the client to feel the TRS's face and mouth as he or she speaks. TRSs follow a routine so clients learn what to expect with each interaction. Clients acquire skills using kinesthetic cues, and TRSs employ the techniques listed earlier in the sections pertaining to visual and hearing impairments.

Communication Impairments

When working with clients with communication impairments, TRSs use the strategies employed with people with learning disabilities, autism, strokes, and head injuries, as communication impairments are often secondary outcomes of these other disabilities. Interventions used with people with hearing losses are also applicable. Art, dance, and movement are nonverbal experiences, yet they foster therapeutic expression and enhance an individual's self-concept. TRSs who are aware of contributing factors, such as environmental or psychological issues, will also employ interventions appropriate to social and emotional impairments. The nature of the communication impairment (receptive or expressive) may guide the TRS in selecting how best to communicate with the client.

Applying the Therapeutic Recreation Process

The therapeutic recreation process is applied to a young girl with a dual-sensory impairment.

Assessment

Demographic information.   Susie is a female of chronological age (CA) 14 with congenital visual and hearing losses (dual-sensory impairment). She resides with her family and two siblings in a suburban community.

History.   The cause of these losses is unknown, although antibiotics administered to the mother during the first trimester of fetal development may be a contributing factor. Diagnosis of the dual-sensory impairment was made at 24 months of age. Susie has less than 20/70 acuity in her better corrected eye with less than a 20-degree field of vision. Results of an audiogram reveal a threshold of 90 db in the right ear and 95 db in the left ear. Physical and speech therapists have provided interventions since age 3, with academic placement in classes for children with sensory impairments since age 6. TRSs have intervened as related service providers during the school year and over the summer. Susie communicates using ASL and walks using a laser cane.

Present behavior. Susie is functioning at third/fourth grade levels. She attempts little social interaction, displays frequent signs of tension and frustration, and has a "flat" affect. Her mobility is limited to the home and classroom. Her posture is rigid with a forward tilt and continuous rocking motions. Background information was collected from existing assessments in the IEP and by interviews and observations. Deficits exist in language development, visual memory, mobility, and psychosocial development. Assets include limited family support, access to an orientation and mobility (O and M) specialist, and a prescription for year-round intervention.

Planning

Long-term goals. The three long-term goals of Susie's TR intervention are to improve expression, initiate peer interaction, and to increase mobility.

Short-term goals. The three short-term goals are to increase use of sign language, increase group participation, and to improve mobility in outdoor environments.

Objectives. The objectives of Susie's TR intervention are as follows:

- By the conclusion of the academic year, Susie will use at least three new signs to identify requested leisure experiences.
- Following her participation in the leisure education program, Susie will attend at least three school-related social events with two other classmates.
- Before and after each day of the summer day program, Susie will ambulate (using her cane) between the pool/park area and the transportation area.

Content. Susie will be enrolled in a sensory stimulation program, fitness activities, aquatics, computer class, and leisure education during the school day. In the summer, Susie will attend a day program cooperatively managed by the school and the therapeutic recreation division of the park district. The entire program will focus on activities of daily living (ADL), speech, and hearing in the morning and recreation in the afternoon.

Process. The TRS will employ orientation techniques to acquaint Susie with respective activity areas. Therapy will employ Susie's haptic sense, sense of smell, and kinesthesia to orient her to the outdoors. Susie will also practice spatial awareness (relationship of body to the environment). The TRS will use the face of a clock to establish reference points in the classroom, pool, and park. Texture variations will denote each program area. The TRS will also employ behavior management to reinforce Susie's responsiveness and skill demonstration. An O and M specialist will participate with family members in IEP workshops and visitation days.

Implementation

The TRS co-led Susie's aquatics and leisure education classes during the school year. In the summer, therapeutic recreation staff assisted in the morning program and directed the afternoon portion of the program. Routine and structure typified each day. Each experience was presented in 20–30-minute intervals, and each day included sensory/tactile awareness, movement exploration, fitness or aquatics, leisure education and community integration, ADL, language, mobility training, and computer classes. The special education teacher, low-vision specialist, and speech therapist worked together to maintain the IEP. The TRS reported the extent to which sign language, peer interaction, and ambulation occurred during Susie's involvement in the program.

Evaluation

The IEP objectives served as the primary evaluative criteria along with input from family members and speech and hearing consultants. Although the goals are annually updated, the objectives are reviewed and revised quarterly, when appropriate. Susie interacted with the computer through residual visual and hearing skills and was able to express her activity interests. Activities from the Therapeutic Recreation Activity Assessment (TRAA) were adapted to assess the effectiveness of the program in improving Susie's functional abilities.

RELATED CONSIDERATIONS

Circulatory Impairments

A person in cardiac rehabilitation is exposed to a variety of medications that may affect his or her physical performance or capacity for physical exertion (Sherrill, 2004):

- Antianginal agents [angiotension-converting enzyme (ACE) inhibitors, alpha- and beta blockers, calcium channel blockers, nitrates] reduce blood pressure and heart rate (nitrates increase heart rate and improve blood supply and oxygen to the heart), thus reducing physical work capacity and exercise tolerance.

- Antihypertensive agents (diuretics) decrease peripheral resistance by relaxing small muscle cells. With exertion, the body excretes increased amounts of sodium and water, which results in muscle cramps and hypotension during physical activity (heart rate is not affected).

- Antiarrhythmic agents (digitalis is one example) lower the heart rate but do not affect blood pressure, thus masking the true heart rate during rest and exercise. As a result, prolonged and intense exercise may bring on cardiac arrest.

- Anticoagulants [heparin and warfarin (blood thinners), aspirin, for example], which are often prescribed with other cardiac medications, inhibit the blood from clotting. Individuals who take this medication must be aware that excessive bleeding may occur if they sustain bruises and cuts during physical activity.

Respiratory Impairments

Respiratory impairments are treated with medications, postural drainage, oxygen, and exercise. As a preventive measure, individuals with respiratory impairments should also monitor the humidity and the allergens in their environment. A TRS who is familiar with the operation of aspirators, metered-dose inhalers (MDIs), and oxygen tanks will reassure clients with these disabilities. Likewise, a TRS who is familiar with the medications (anti-inflammatory and bronchodilators) and their side effects, postural drainage procedures, and diaphragmatic and pursed-lip breathing techniques can do much to assure clients of their safety. By involving clients in stress management, problem solving, and relaxation activities, TRSs can help to allay emotions that otherwise might precipitate respiratory distress.

Endocrine Impairments

People with diabetes mellitus and obesity have needs similar to those of clients in cardiac rehabilitation. It is critical for them to monitor their activity and exercise levels, food selection and intake, and insulin in order to control blood sugar levels. The TRS is aware that injection therapy (insulin shots) involves different types and amounts of insulin that are affected by eating and activity schedules, while pump therapy allows more freedom in carrying out daily routines. Skin care is also important to monitor as breakdown may be a sign of circulatory issues. With obesity, TRSs help clients with time and stress management, encouraging the self-control necessary to manage risk factors that create barriers to healthy lifestyle adjustments and behaviors. Even with the use of behavior strategies, TRSs realize that changing clients' attitudes toward activity is a daunting task.

Cancer

If you are considering employment in situations (oncology units, hospice) where individuals are being treated for cancer, you may wish to assess your own feelings about managing grief and death. Cancer treatments result in discomfort and disfigurement, and the course of cancer may lead to death. A TRS who decides to work with individuals with cancer must be knowledgeable about bedside activities, medical play, life review techniques, activities appropriate to isolation areas, and experiences that divert attention from pain and loss of self-identifying features. TRSs also facilitate caregiver support groups and promote health and leisure wellness for all family members.

Chronic Pain

Each individual's experience of pain is highly variable. Consequently, a medical team employs several treatment approaches when working with individuals with chronic pain. These include biofeedback, hypnosis, electrical stimulation to the brain or localized pain area, pharmacologic therapy, and surgery (as a last resort). Pharmacologic therapy is used with caution as certain populations, like the elderly, have elevated risks of side effects, and all individuals sustain the possibility of becoming drug dependent. The International Association for the Study of Pain (www.iasp-pain.org), the American Pain Society (www.ampainsoc.org), and the American Chronic Pain Association (www.theacpa.org) support pain research and education and conduct client support meetings to complement professional services.

Chronic Fatigue Syndrome

The causes and duration of CFS are unique to each individual. TRSs working with such individuals assess clients' functional needs to recommend graduated adjustments in, for example, physical activity and leisure interests. During a client's recovery, TRSs use leisure education to promote access to information on support groups and ways of coping in the home and work environments. Health professionals can access information about CFS from the Chronic Fatigue and Immune Dysfunction Syndrome Association of America (www.cfids.org). The Centers for Disease Control and Prevention (www.cdc.gov) posts information on its Web site on CFS. As with chronic pain, CFS may be treated with drug therapy. Thus, a TRS should be aware of the uses and side effects of various drugs and support clients when they experience reactions to medications that may impact their participation in therapeutic recreation experiences.

Sensory and Communication Impairments

TRSs use touch as an interaction technique with people who have sensory and communication impairments. Gestures and movements are a form of communication, and a TRS is acutely aware of when to use the haptic sense and the kinesthetic approach to intervene with such individuals and of how body language serves as a communication medium. Orientation and mobility training and speech certification are available to TRSs interested in working with these individuals.

TRSs interacting with people with visual impairments rely on a variety of tools, including modified equipment, teaching techniques, and assistive resources. Catalogs available from the American Foundation for the Blind (www.afb.org) offer equipment and supplies, as do commercial vendors. **Brailling** (tactile inspection of an object) helps clients develop an awareness of objects and their relationships to activities. Instructional techniques incorporate touch as skills are demonstrated so clients develop an awareness of movement patterns. When guide dogs are used, they enhance a client's independence, though TRSs should exercise judgment before moving in to assist or pet the dog.

The term "deaf community" is used to describe the cultural and language differences that distinguish those with hearing losses from the hearing, speaking world (Sherrill, 2004). Some within the deaf community do not advocate people-first terminology (i.e., "person" with hearing loss rather than "the deaf"), and as a consequence, there is uncertainty as to appropriate terms to be used with people having hearing losses (Bullock et al., 2010). Some deaf persons prefer to be seen as a distinct culture with ASL as their communication system, while others see themselves as a part of the speaking community; as suggested in the research, these preferences affect recreation participation patterns.

A number of assistive devices create greater access to the hearing world. Cochlear implants (electrode devices surgically implanted in the mastoid bone) enhance hearing, but may prevent wearers from sitting in front of computers (similar to a pacemaker and microwave ovens). Over 200 assistive listening devices and systems (ALDS) are available (Sherrill, 2004). Closed-caption television, TDDs, and electronic metronomes are examples of devices that convert sound to meaning via light or vibrations. TRSs might find the Laurent Clerc National Deaf Education Center to be helpful in locating devices (www.clercenter.gallaudet.edu).

SUMMARY

The physical and sensory disabilities studied in this chapter may not be as visually apparent as those reviewed in the previous chapter, but they may be more life threatening (cardiovascular disorders, cancer). Heart disease and cancer remain leading causes of death and disability. Respiratory ailments, endocrine impairments, chronic pain, and chronic fatigue syndrome, though not life threatening (per se), have lifelong impacts. Therapeutic recreation specialists who work with individuals with the impairments discussed in this chapter deliver services in inpatient, outpatient, and home health-care settings. They address the notion of "hidden" impairments and the individual's responsibility for self-care through lifestyle adjustments. TRSs use leisure education and health promotion to help individuals achieve well-being and healthy lifestyles.

People with sensory and communication impairments experience varying degrees of ability to respond to environmental stimuli. The age of an individual at the onset of an impairment and the degree of residual ability are the primary factors that influence his or her functional ability. Congenital impairments leave people without the knowledge of how others experience environmental stimuli, and as a consequence, have a greater impact on individuals than adventitious, or acquired, impairments. When working with individuals with sensory or communication impairments, a TRS first establishes a communication avenue with each participant and then orients participants to the activity setting.

Since many of the disabilities covered in this chapter are lifelong or have terminal consequences, TRSs working with such individuals also interact with a number of different specialists. A TRS's role is influenced by input from these specialists, the client's adaptations to the disability, and the aging process (with age, the impact of these disabilities becomes more evident).

Key Terms

adventitious Acquired after birth.

alopecia Hair loss, a side effect of chemotherapy.

American Sign Language (ASL) The use of hand gestures and body positions to represent words and concepts.

anemia Reduced oxygen carrying capacity of the blood.

angina pectoris Temporary pain and discomfort that occurs whenever part of the heart muscle cannot get enough oxygen-rich blood through the coronary arteries to meet the heart's needs.

arteriosclerosis A group of diseases, including atherosclerosis, in which the artery walls harden, thicken, and lose elasticity.

atherosclerosis A progressive degenerative disease in which deposits of fatty substances, or plaques, thicken the inside linings of the coronary arteries, thus narrowing the passageway for blood circulation to the heart.

asthma Chronic lung disease characterized by inflammation and increased sensitivity of the airways, which results in obstructed air flow.

biopsy Method used to identify cancer cells by fine needle aspiration, punch, or endoscope.

blindness Visual acuity of 20/200 or less in the better eye after correction, or a field of vision that is limited to a 20-degree angle or less (out of the normal 180-degree field of vision).

brailling Tactile inspection of an object.

carcinoma Glandular cancer.

chemotherapy The administration of drugs to treat various cancers.

chronic bronchitis Inflammation of the lining of the bronchial tubes.

chronic obstructive pulmonary disease (COPD) A medical term generally applied to people with one or a combination of respiratory disorders including chronic bronchitis, emphysema, and asthma.

congenital Present at birth.

congestive heart failure (CHF) Progressive weakness of the heart that causes accumulation of fluids in the body's parts.

coronary artery disease (CAD) Condition characterized by narrowing of coronary arteries, causing reduced blood supply to the heart.

coronary heart disease (CHD) Range of cardiac conditions that result in narrowing of the coronary arteries, causing a decreased blood supply to the heart.

cyanosis A bluish skin color, which is caused by a lowered oxygen supply in the blood.

cystic fibrosis (CF) A genetic disease involving defective production of enzymes in the pancreas, causing secretion of a thick mucus that clogs the bronchial tubes and obstructs breathing.

deaf The inability (with or without a hearing aid) to process linguistic information.

diabetes mellitus (DM) A chronic metabolic disorder in which abnormally large amounts of sugar are manifest in the blood. Type I diabetes (insulin-dependent diabetes mellitus [IDDM], or brittle diabetes) affects youths and results when the pancreas does not pro-

duce enough insulin. Type II diabetes (non-insulin dependent diabetes mellitus [NIDDM]) commonly affects adults and results when the body is unable to use insulin, causing abnormally high blood sugar levels.

dyspnea Difficulty breathing or shortness of breath.

emphysema Condition in which lungs lose their elasticity, resulting in poor air exchange and shortness of breath.

epithelioma Skin cancer.

fibromyalgia Achy pain and stiffness in soft tissues throughout the body or in specific locations like the shoulders.

hard of hearing Describes a person who has experienced hearing loss, but is able to process linguistic information.

hemophilia An inherited blood disorder affecting males and resulting in chronic recurrent bleeding into the joints when they have been traumatized.

hyperglycemia High blood glucose levels resulting in a diabetic coma or keto-acidosis.

hypertension High blood pressure.

hypertrophic cardiomyopathy An inherited disease that may cause sudden death in adolescents or young adults; usually detected after the individual receives an abnormal electrocardiogram and is accompanied by a murmur or hyperdynamic cardiac pulse rate.

hypoglycemia Low blood sugar levels that can result in insulin shock.

leukemia A disease of the blood-producing organs that is characterized by an uncontrollable production and growth of white blood cells.

low vision A visual acuity of at least 20/200 but no greater than 20/70 in the better eye after correction, or 30 degrees or less visual field.

lymphoma Lymph tissue cancer.

Marfan syndrome An inherited connective tissue disorder that causes cardiovascular abnormalities. Clinical manifestations include long, thin extremities, hyper-extended joints, chest deformity, and dislocated optic lenses.

MET A basic metabolic unit used to measure energy cost to complete an activity.

metastases Secondary cancerous cells that develop and spread to other body areas.

myocardial infarction (MI) A heart attack.

oncology Study of the growth of tumors.

orientation and mobility (O and M) Specific techniques used to train people with visual impairments to ambulate.

Pidgin sign Signing in English and ASL.

sarcoma Muscle, fibrous tissue, tendon, or bone cancer.

sickle cell anemia Inherited blood disorder characterized by sickle-shaped red blood cells and a deficiency in the number of red blood cells.

stenosis A narrowing of a heart valve or the area near it resulting in decreased blood flow.

stent Stainless steel tube either latticed or resembling a spring, implanted in the area of the heart artery narrowed by plaque.

TDD Telecommunication device for the deaf.

TNM system Worldwide nomenclature used to describe the stage of cancer: T denotes the size and extent of the primary tumor; N denotes the spread of cancer; and M denotes the evidence of distant metastatic spread.

Study Questions

1. What are the primary and secondary functioning characteristics of people who have physical impairments affecting the circulatory, respiratory, endocrine, and sensory systems?

2. What are the clinical signs of cancer, chronic pain, and chronic fatigue syndrome?

3. Identify appropriate therapeutic recreation interventions and safety precautions for people with cardiac and respiratory impairments, obesity, diabetes, and sensory and communication disorders.

4. What therapeutic recreation strategies are used with pain and fatigue?

5. What are specific leadership strategies employed with people in cardiac rehabilitation and oncology?

6. Describe how a TRS creates accessible experiences for people with sensory impairments.

7. What precautions does a TRS take when intervening with people with respiratory impairments, diabetes, and those who are on cardiac medications?

Practical Experiences to Enhance Student Objectives

1. Contact the following agencies and request information on the health issue each addresses, and the services they sponsor or provide for individuals with such impairments:

- Cystic Fibrosis Foundation, http://www.cff.org
- American Lung Association, http://www.lungusa.org/
- American Cancer Society, http://www.cancer.org
- World Health Organization, http://www.who.int
- American Heart Association, http://www.heart.org
- American Diabetes Association, http://www.diabetes.org

2. Try simulating some of the impairments discussed in this chapter as described below.

- Eat a meal blindfolded.
- Participate in at least two recreation activities that you enjoy (1) without the use of sight, (2) using ear plugs, (3) taking your pulse rate and blood pressure before and after participation.

3. Spend a day in either a cardiac rehabilitation unit or an oncology unit. Take notes on what you observe. Describe the purpose of therapeutic recreation and roles of the TRS.

4. Visit a TR program that includes people with hidden impairments (asthma, chronic pain) but that is not treatment oriented. Compare this experience with the one described in number 3 above.

Cognitive
Impairments

After reading this chapter, students will be able to

✔ Identify the functioning characteristics and leisure needs of people with learning, motor skills, communication, feeding and eating disorders, and those with intellectual disabilities, severe multiple impairments, and autism spectrum disorders

✔ Describe the intent and outcomes of therapeutic recreation with each population

✔ Describe the interaction and intervention processes appropriate to each population

✔ Explain how the therapeutic recreation process is applied with participants representative of each population

✔ Identify unique considerations affecting therapeutic recreation with each population

In this chapter we will discuss cognitive impairments that originate during an individual's growth and development and which may result in physical, sensory, communication, emotional, and social impairments. Classification systems and terminology regarding cognitive impairments vary worldwide; moreover, there is wide diversity among individuals with learning and intellectual impairments. Individuals with severe impairments rely on assistance to complete self-care, while others complete their daily routines with no help or with minimum support. Finally, these impairments may be associated with others—like cerebral palsy and visual losses—presented in other chapters.

INTRODUCTION

The people studied in this chapter are identified in the *Diagnostic and Statistical Manual of Mental Disorders,* Fourth Edition Text Revision **(DSM-IV-TR)**, a publication of the American Psychiatric Association (APA), as having disorders that originate during childhood or adolescence or are diagnosed in adulthood (APA, 2000). These people experience disorders that persist without remission or exacerbation throughout their lives. The impairments discussed in this chapter occur in cognitive, social, psychological, and motor skill development. They may impact the acquisition of a specific academic skill, as with learning disabilities (LDs), or the acquisition of general skills, as demonstrated by intellectual disabilities (IDs), severe multiple impairments, and autism spectrum disorders.

In this chapter, persons with LD are discussed separately from those with ID; with international classification systems, however, there may be overlap (Dunn & Leitschuh, 2006; Sherrill, 2004). Today, there are more schoolchildren with LDs than with any other disability (Smith, Polloway, Patton, & Dowdy, 2008), and adults with LDs can be found in all professions. LD is a cognitive disability—a disorder of thinking and reasoning—yet individuals may also experience challenges in social interactions, emotional maturity, attention span, and motor skills. An intellectual disability perhaps best represents the wide diversity of effects a cognitive impairment can have. People identified as having a mild degree of intellectual impairment function adequately in most activities of daily living and in most social encounters, while people with severe degrees of impairment experience both physical and social challenges. The wide diversity of people with intellectual disabilities requires the TRS to assume the roles and responsibilities of leisure educators as well as trainers and advocates of social inclusion.

A person with an intellectual disability who also is emotionally or physically impaired appears "different" from other individuals, yet among clients with severe multiple impairments there are more individual differences than there are similarities. TRSs rely on structured, individualized, goal-directed interventions employing behavioral strategies and caregiver/team collaboration to accomplish meaningful quality of life outcomes.

Individuals described by the terms *pervasive developmental disorders* (PDD) and *autistic spectrum disorders* (ASD) exhibit a range of impairments (severe to mild) in social interaction, verbal and nonverbal communication skills, and in imaginative activity. They also demonstrate a limited repertoire of activities and interests, which frequently are stereotyped and repetitive. Throughout your career, you will encounter not only children who are autistic but also children and adults who display "autistic-like" behaviors. The functional characteristics and behavioral expressions are extremely complex and individually unique.

DISORDERS USUALLY DIAGNOSED IN INFANCY, CHILDHOOD, OR ADOLESCENCE

Learning disorders are identified when an individual's achievement on standardized tests in reading, math, or written expression is below that expected for his or her age, schooling, and level of intelligence (APA, 2000). It is a generic term that describes a heterogeneous group of disorders usually identified as a result of difficulties in the acquisition and use of academic skills (Peniston, 1995). A number of interpretations have been applied to learning disorders. As a consequence, specific learning disabilities were defined in the Individuals with Disabilities Education Act (IDEA, PL 101-476) as "one or more of the basic psychological processes involved in understanding or in using language, spoken or written, which may manifest itself in an imperfect ability to listen, think, speak, read, write, spell, or to do mathematical calculations" (Dunn & Leitschuh, 2006, p. 529). To satisfy the criteria of the federal definition, an IQ of 70 or higher and a severe discrepancy between intellectual ability and academic achievement in one or more areas (e.g., oral, written expression; listening, reading comprehension; basic reading skills; mathematics calculation and reasoning) must be present (Dunn & Leitschuh; Sherrill, 2004). Interpretation of the federal law by various states allows documentation of a "severe" discrepancy between IQ and achievement to be optional, which further confuses the issue of prevalence figures and determination of those eligible for academic support.

The American Psychiatric Association identifies a number of disorders, including learning disorders, that are commonly manifest during the developmental years and may result in significant difficulties in employment or social adjustment during adulthood. The learning, motor skills, communication, and feeding and eating disorders defined in the *DSM-IV-TR* are listed in exhibit 8.1, and an example of each is included in parentheses (APA, 2000). Attention-deficit and disruptive behavior disorders also found in this APA category are considered with psychological impairments in chapter 9.

Causes of learning problems are complex and not well understood (Dunn & Leitschuh, 2006). Evidence suggests neurological dysfunction; hereditary factors; trauma experienced before, during, and after birth; medical problems; and environmental causes (Dunn & Leitschuh; Smith et al., 2008). Learning disorders coexist with impairments like cerebral palsy and intellectual disability, which are evident at birth, or can occur later in life, as with the communication disorders that may accompany traumatic brain injuries and strokes.

Functioning Characteristics

Inadequate or inappropriate functioning of individuals with specific learning, motor, communication, and feeding and eating disorders is most evident in social situations, when performing activities of daily living, and with activities that require motor skills. A characteristic common to each behavioral area is the discrepancy among exhibited skills. For example, a child may speak fluently yet not be able to write his or her name or address, while an adult may be an avid bridge or rummy player yet tend to sit too close to other players and frequently interrupt their conversations.

Motor deficits are observed in a number of areas. One of the more visually apparent is clumsiness; this characteristic is most evident when complex activities require motor sequencing, planning, and information processing (Sherrill, 2004). Perceptual-motor weaknesses are evident in poor spatial relationships, figure-ground and depth-perception problems, and an immature body image (Sherrill). Inability to perceive the "whole" may result in a sound being heard yet not associating it with the cause, or seeing a word yet not associating it as part of the sentence (dissociation). Visual and auditory memory def-

Exhibit 8.1   Disorders that Commonly Manifest in Developmental Years

Learning Disorders

Reading disorder—impaired ability in word recognition and reading comprehension (dyslexia)

Mathematics disorder—impaired ability in understanding, recognizing, copying, and following numbers and sequences (dyscalculia)

Disorder of written expression—impaired ability to compose written text (dysgraphia)

Motor Skills Disorders

Developmental coordination disorder—impairment in development of motor coordination (dyspraxia)

Communication Disorders

Expressive language disorder—acquired or developmental impairment in expressive language development (expressive aphasia)

Mixed receptive-expressive language disorder—acquired or developmental impairment in both receptive and expressive language development (receptive aphasia)

Phonological disorder—inability to make articulations of speech sounds appropriate for the individual's age and dialect (**echolalia**—the senseless repetition of a word or sentence spoken by another person)

Stuttering—disturbance in the normal (appropriate for the person's age) fluency and time patterning of speech (circumlocution)

Feeding and Eating Disorders of Infancy and Early Childhood

Pica—persistent pattern of eating nonnutritive substances that result in conditions such as lead poisoning (paint) or toxoplasmosis (infection caused by ingesting dirt or feces; associated with intellectual disability)

Rumination—repeated regurgitation and rechewing of food occurring after feeding that results in malnutrition causing developmental delays in behavioral areas and potentially resulting in death (associated with intellectual disability)

icits affect individuals' short- and long-term retention; for example, their ability to recall safety rules from one session to the next. Task completion in general is affected by the inability to block out stimuli and concentrate on a task (distractibility); the inability to switch from one task to another (**perseveration**); and the inability to stay with a specific task, or random shifting and daydreaming (disinhibition) (Dunn & Leitschuh, 2006).

Several deficits create social-emotional difficulties. Inability to resolve conflicts, manage frustrations, initiate conversations, demonstrate empathy, or work in groups interferes with positive adjustment as an adult (Smith et al., 2008). Likewise, the inability to evaluate one's own behavior and identify inappropriate behavior or mistakes may create adult challenges; in other words, an overly optimistic view regarding their disabilities may mask deficits. Language deficits contribute significantly to social difficulties (Smith et al.).

Pica and rumination, viewed as secondary impairments in children and adolescents with cognitive and physical impairments, result in growth and developmental delays and the discomfort and irritability associated with hunger. Thus, in addition to considering the therapeutic recreation strategies associated with the primary impairments, TRSs must also closely observe clients during activities. Children with pica either ingest what is in their reach at the time the compulsive behavior strikes, or they ingest specific items (such as those made of wood) within their reach. Children with rumination run the risk of choking and malnutrition from the repeated regurgitation of food. Both types of behavior may continue into adulthood. If so, substances ingested may vary with age. For example, younger children may grab anything in their immediate range, while older children may select specific items such as stones. Regurgitation that occurs with older persons may not cause malnutrition as it does with youngsters who immediately regurgitate following feedings.

Purpose of Therapeutic Recreation

Therapeutic recreation specialists intervene (1) to prevent and remediate inappropriate interactions; (2) to assess and facilitate the acquisition of skills supportive of academic, motor, and social-emotional functioning; inclusion; and community involvement (Litner & Ostiguy, 2000; Sitlington, 1996); and (3) to promote health and well-being (Sherrill, 2004). Cognitive experiences (for example, board games) that include counting numbers, keeping score, and reading directions reinforce academic interventions. Adventure/challenge experiences enhance sensory integration, which supports improved cognitive functioning. Children and adults learn to establish friendships and develop appropriate social skills and group behavior through inclusion and camp experiences (Peniston, 1999). Self-concept, health, and physical well-

Outdoor recreation activities enhance sensory integration, while group participation helps clients establish friendships and develop appropriate social skills.

being are enhanced through aquatics, relaxation, leisure education, cooperative games and sports, and expressive therapies. With adults, empowerment and self-determination are promoted by assertiveness and social skills training (Johnson, 1995).

TRSs working with youths with pica and rumination use observation and behavioral assessments to identify clients' interests. They then use this information to plan experiences that focus clients' attention on preferred experiences and the immediate benefits gained through participation. Intervention periods address the three broad goals listed earlier and are structured so clients' time away from directed or supervised experiences is kept to a minimum.

Delivery Settings

Individuals with learning, motor skills, communication, and feeding and eating disorders reside with caregivers, spouses, family members, and in congregate living centers sponsored by mental health services. Children interact with resource teachers, behavior management specialists, and classroom teachers while adults may seek support from rehabilitation personnel and psychotherapists. Additionally, TRSs may work with individuals with pica and rumination in early-intervention programs for high-risk infants, in outpatient clinics supported by physical and occupational therapists, and in programs for children and adults with intellectual and physical impairments. As treatment team members, TRSs address academic, emotional, and social needs while monitoring clients' interactional behaviors, resource awareness, and leisure skills acquisition.

Leadership Interaction and Intervention Considerations

The heterogeneous nature of people with learning, motor skills, communication, and feeding and eating disorders results in a multidisciplinary service network. TRSs intervene to support and supplement special physical educators, community recreators, and treatment team members. Complementary leadership interactions are listed below.

- To control and structure the intervention environment, TRSs ensure that sensory stimulation, like extraneous visual stimuli, is kept to a minimum and structure activities that involve a limited number of people in defined spaces (Peniston, 1999).

- Activity and task analyses determine the nature and sequence of social interactions inherent in experiences (Dunn & Leitschuh, 2006; Peniston, 1999). Clients experience success and are apt to display appropriate interactions with a social sequence that commences with individual and cooperative experiences and progresses to intergroup interactions (from walking to competitive team games).

- Behavioral approaches incorporate various reinforcement measures, lead-up activities, and learning cues to enhance independent, internally motivated behaviors. Routine, structure, consistency, and documentation of baseline behaviors are essential features of such programs (Litner & Ostiguy, 2000; Smith et al., 2008).

- Leisure education experiences that involve goal setting, identifying priorities, and practicing time management facilitate transition to the adult world and responsibility as an employee (Smith et al., 2008).

- Cooperative games, initiatives, and adventure challenge education foster opportunities to develop social skills, friendships, enhanced self-concept, and motivation to continue physical activity involvement and group experiences (Sherrill, 2004).

- When providing directions and safety precautions, a leader may need to employ visual, auditory, and haptic cues to ensure comprehension. For example, an individual who is dysgraphic would be helped by having oral rather than written directions.

- The incorporation of equipment with contrasting colors and sounds, brightly marked boundaries, and tactile variance to distinguish foreground objects from background surfaces compensates for sensory deficits (Peniston, 1999; Sherrill, 2004).

- Experiences that require balance and movement exploration enhance spatial awareness, directionality, laterality, and coordination.

- Overlearning a skill through repetition, and completion or observation of the whole task before doing part of the task compensates for the tendency to dissociate parts from the whole (Peniston, 1999).

- Leaders bring safety and security to the intervention and design positive environments by stating expectations, boundaries, consequences, and rewards prior to client involvement (Peniston, 1999). Leaders supervise by providing firm, immediate (i.e., "here and now") intervention and follow-through, which encourages compliance and appropriate behavior (Litner & Ostiguy, 2000).

- Programs emphasize self-initiated behaviors, self-esteem, self-regulation, problem solving, and forming social relations. Social skills training includes negoti-

Spatial awareness, balance, and fine motor control are enhanced through this form of animal-assisted therapy.

ating, conflict resolution, and accepting and giving praise and criticism (Johnson, 1995).

- Modeling, role-playing, and positive self-talk are strategies helpful to learning motor sequences and socially appropriate behaviors. Such also help moderate impulsivity and resolve conflicts (Sherrill, 2004; Smith et al., 2008).

- TRSs use cues, prompts, and reinforcement to focus the attention of children with pica and rumination on the immediate experience.

- With pica, TRSs remove from the environment any nonedible items that could be grabbed and stuffed into participants' mouths.

- With rumination, TRSs do not acknowledge sucking noises and participants are positioned so ejection of food is inhibited.

Applying the Therapeutic Recreation Process

Tommy is an elementary-school-age child who experiences deficits in coordination, reading, expression, and attention. A TRS employed with a special recreation association coordinates with administrators in the elementary school to plan year-round services and transitions from school to community that are to begin by age 14 (as required by the 1997 amendments to the Individuals with Disabilities Education Act).

Assessment

Demographic information.   Tommy is an 8-year-old with learning, motor skills, and attention-deficit disorders. He is in the second grade in a neighborhood elementary school. He lives at home with his parents and two older brothers, 12 and 14 years of age.

History.   Tommy's mother was 35 when she gave birth to him. Medical records reveal no medical problems at birth. His father is dyslexic. Tommy was diagnosed with reading and writing disabilities at age 5 (pre-school). He has been on Ritalin twice daily (8 AM and 2 PM) for hyperactivity, also since age 5.

Present behavior.   Tommy is hyperactive and highly distractible. Perceptual problems, especially in the visual and motor areas, persist. His measured (Stanford-Binet) IQ is 100. He exhibits poor eye-hand coordination and motor planning and is clumsy. Tommy has a low frustration level and is socially immature.

The TRS obtained the above information through the early intervention specialist. Recommendations in the individual educational plan (IEP) suggested that the parents enroll Tommy in a summer therapeutic recreation program. The results of parent interviews indicate that Tommy has strengths in individual activities like swimming and some team activities, including soccer.

Planning

Long-term goal.   The long-term goal of Tommy's therapeutic recreation plan is to improve social skills.

Short-term goal.   The short-term goal is to increase Tommy's ability to function in inclusive experiences.

Objective. After two months, Tommy will demonstrate behaviors appropriate to small-group activities 80% of his participation time by not becoming verbally or physically abusive to other participants or withdrawing from the experience, and by complying with participation directions and safety rules.

Content. The program will focus on motor and social skills development by incorporating cooperative games, creative expression, computer games, small group initiatives, motor skills training, aquatics, and physical activity.

Process. The objective and goals will be accomplished through modeling, a structured environment, consistent routine, socially sequenced activities, and natural consequences and rewards. Additional interventions include the buddy system, family participation, relaxation experiences, and adventure/challenge experiences.

Implementation

Tommy attended the summer program and made plans to enroll in the after-school and weekend programs year-round. The TRS used the General Recreation Screening Tool (GRST) to assist in planning activities. Inclusion through the buddy system in recreation experiences occurred on weekends during the summer. Family members were involved in outings and in the collection of formative and summative data. An activity checklist was maintained at the recreation center, in the home, and at the school.

Evaluation

The objectives in the IEP and the recreation plan served as the evaluative criteria. The TRS and the special physical educator kept notes recording behavioral observations and the success of the activity checklist, which provided formative data. A quarterly meeting with the family and school personnel provided summative data per criteria of the objectives in the IEP and the recreation plan. The outcomes of the meetings were reported by the school **social worker** and special physical educator for incorporation in the revised IEP. The TRS revised the recreation plan to complement the education program and assist the recreation staff in their future inclusion of the participant.

Related Considerations

Individuals with learning, motor skills, communication, and feeding and eating disorders experience difficulty during social interactions. The social immaturity that results—in part from their inability to perceive subtle social cues (that is, to read body language) and regulate their own behaviors—causes peer denial and rejection. Inclusion and appropriate involvement in the community are primary outcomes of therapeutic intervention (Sitlington, 1996). Techniques like videotaping, adventure/challenge courses, relaxation, assertion, and animal-assisted therapy are employed to develop self-awareness, awareness of others, role expectations, and coping skills.

Children with physical impairments, social impairments, and certain cognitive impairments may experience some of the deficits ascribed to children and youths with learning, motor skills, communication, and feeding and eating disorders. For example, a child with cerebral palsy may also have perceptual and sensory deficits. Likewise, children with autism and children who have been abused may display behaviors observed in children who are dyslexic. With treatment, learning disabilities may be remediated by adolescence, yet social-emotional deficits may remain through adulthood. Helpful information can be found by contacting the following organizations: National Center for Learning Disabilities (http://www.ncld.org) and Learning Disabilities Association of America (http://www.ldanatl.org).

TRSs working with children with pica keep their clients' hands constantly busy so nonnutritive substances remain out of reach. TRSs also are trained in how to activate the gagging reflex to prevent ingested items from being swallowed. TRSs working with children with rumination position their clients so they cannot arch their backs or hold their heads back in order to regurgitate their meals. They also instruct caregivers to ignore the apparent satisfaction the child gains from sucking sounds.

INTELLECTUAL DISABILITY

Definitions of intellectual disability vary throughout the world. One reason for this is different professions interpret the classification schemes and definitions from their respective viewpoints. A second reason is eligibility for services is determined by definitions; so definitions may be broadened or restricted to impact eligibility. Two of the existing contemporary interpretations of intellectual disability are elaborated in the following paragraphs. The *DSM-IV-TR* identifies mental retardation as one of the categories of disorders diagnosed in infancy, childhood, or adolescence; the American Association on Intellectual and Developmental Disabilities (AAIDD) [formerly the American Association on Mental Retardation (AAMR)], defines intellectual disability broadly as deficits in various cognitive and adaptive ability areas.

The *DSM-IV-TR* identifies the person who is mentally retarded as one who experiences (1) significant subaverage general intellectual functioning, accompanied by (2) significant impairments in adaptive functioning, with (3) onset prior to age 18 (APA, 2000). The phrase *significant subaverage general intellectual functioning* refers to an IQ of less than 70 on the Wechsler Intelligence Scale for Children—Revised, and less than 68 on the Stanford-Binet Intellectual Scale or two standard deviations below the mean for general intellectual functioning (Sherrill, 2004). The phrase *significant impairments in* **adaptive functioning** refers to how effectively people cope with life demands and meet standards of independence expected for their age, sociocultural background, and community setting (APA, 2000). Scales like the Vineland Adaptive Behavior Scales are used in conjunction with a reliable independent source, like a developmental or medical history, to determine whether the second criterion is characteristic of an individual. As mentioned above, to be identified as having an intellectual disability, a person must display these characteristics prior to a chronological age of 18.

According to the *DSM-IV-TR*, four degrees of severity reflect actual intellectual impairment (APA, 2000). Each of the four levels is distinguished by an IQ range as outlined below.

Degree of severity	IQ Range
Mild	50–55 to approximately 70
Moderate	35–40 to 50–55
Severe	20–25 to 35–40
Profound	Below 20 or 25

Most of the people with an intellectual disability fall into the mild level of severity and are first diagnosed during early elementary school when minimal motor impairment and academic difficulties appear (APA, 2000).

People who experience moderate degrees of cognitive impairment represent 10% of those with intellectual disabilities (APA, 2000). Since they exhibit clinical or physical signs such as delayed walking or talking, a diagnosis is usually made early in life.

Individuals with severe degrees of cognitive impairment are a small proportion of those with intellectual disabilities and represent individuals who may display multiple impairments. These people are capable of acquiring **functional skills** such as personal care, walking, recognition of survival words, and the ability to use manual communication.

Individuals with profound levels of cognitive impairment often exhibit secondary impairments such as seizure disorders or cerebral palsy and represent the smallest proportion of persons with intellectual disabilities.

AAIDD defines intellectual disabilities (ID) as significant limitations in intellectual functioning and adaptive behavior skills in three categories—conceptual, social, and practical—with origin before the age of 18 (AAIDD, 2008; Sherrill, 2004). With both the APA and AAIDD definitions, criteria are similar. AAIDD describes adaptive behavior in more detail by presenting three categories. Conceptual skills include language, reading, writing, money concepts, and self-direction. Social skills are interpersonal relations, responsibility, self-esteem, gullibility, naiveté, following rules, obeying laws, and avoiding victimization. Practical skills include personal and instrumental activities of daily living, maintaining a safe environment, and occupational skills that could include leisure skills (Dunn & Leitschuh, 2006; Sherrill).

AAIDD further describes adaptive skills through an elaborate system of supports/resources and strategies that promote development, education, interests and personal well-being; are determined through individualized assessment; and intend to optimize functioning (AAIDD, 2008; Sherrill, 2004). Need for support is assessed in nine areas, with leisure and recreation introduced in several of the activity categories including human development, teaching and education, home and community living, health and safety, behavioral, social, and protection and advocacy. Thus, comprehensive assessments move beyond IQ-based decisions to determine resources necessary to enhance health and social inclusion (Mobily & MacNeil, 2002; Sherrill).

An intellectual disability, like severe multiple impairments and autism, is considered a developmental disability. Developmental disabilities (DD) have been defined by federal legislation in effect since 1963, originally the Mental Retardation Facilities and Community Mental Health Centers Construction Act of 1963 (PL 88-164) (Bullock, Mahon, & Killingsworth, 2010). According to the 1994 Developmental Disabilities Assistance and Bill of Rights Act Amendments (PL 103-230), "the term developmental disability means a severe, chronic disability of an individual 5 years of age or older that (1) is attributable to a mental or physical impairment or combination of mental and physical impairments; (2) is manifested before the individual attains age 22; (3) is likely to continue indefinitely; (4) results in substantial functional limitations in three or more of the following areas of major life activity: (a) self-care, (b) receptive and expressive language, (c) learning, (d) mobility, (e) self-direction, (f) capacity for independent living, and (g) economic self-sufficiency; and (5) reflects the individual's need for a combination and sequence of special, interdisciplinary, or generic services, supports, or other assistance that is of lifelong or extended duration and is individually planned and coordinated" (p. 7). This definition encompasses the levels and characteristics presented by the APA and AAIDD for mental retardation/intellectual disability as well as for a number of other disabilities like cystic fibrosis, cerebral palsy, spina bifida, deafness, and blindness. The subtle differences between an intellectual disability and a developmental disability are twofold: (1) An intellectual disability is usually present at birth while a DD may occur up to the age of 22; and (2) low IQ scores are necessary with intellectual impairments but not DD (Porter & burlingame, 2006). Consequently, DD services may encompass people with a broader range of abilities.

In developed countries, intellectual disability affects 1–3% of the population (Porter & burlingame, 2006) with those identified as severe (IQ under 50) having an incidence of 3 to 5 per 1,000 individuals (Sherrill, 2004). With the exception of individuals with severe ID, the life expectancy of people with mild retardation is the same as that of the rest of the population (Dunn & Leitschuh, 2006). Caregivers and professionals face a number of challenges as the number of older citizens, including those with ID, continues to increase throughout the world.

There is rarely one cause for an ID, since it may occur at any time during the first 18 years and is defined by the interaction between the person, the environment, and the support services provided. Causes are grouped according to the time when they may have originated. **Prenatal** (occurring or existing before birth) causes include chromosomal disorders, metabolic errors, brain formation disorders, and environmental influences like alcohol and drug abuse during pregnancy or maternal diseases (Sherrill, 2004). **Perinatal** (occurring from the 28th week of pregnancy through 28 days following birth) causes include head trauma at birth, abnormal delivery, and infections. **Postnatal** (any time before age 18) causes include head injuries, infections, degenerative disorders, seizure disorders, toxic-metabolic disorders, malnutrition, and familial/environmental causes like child abuse and neglect (Bullock et al., 2010; Sherrill).

Chromosomal abnormalities, one of the prenatal conditions, may cause cognitive impairments having clinically defined syndromes. Fragile X syndrome and Down syndrome (DS) are chromosomal disorders. Fragile X syndrome may result in mental functioning that varies from severe to average. Characteristic behaviors may include hyperactivity and autistic-like functioning (Sherrill, 2004). Intellectual functioning varies widely among those with Down syndrome (Sherrill). A number of features distinguish Down syndrome from other forms of ID.

Even though family resemblance is present, a person with Down syndrome has unique clinical features that include: short stature and limbs, with square, broad hands and feet; almond-shaped slanting eyes; flattened facial features and back of skull, with a short neck; and a small oral cavity, causing mouth breathing and tongue protrusion (Sherrill, 2004). Children with DS demonstrate delays in motor milestones. They are predisposed to respiratory infections, heart and lung problems, and poor muscle tone, which impacts participation in endurance activities (Dunn & Leitschuh, 2006).

Alzheimer-type neuropathology is present in about 15 to 40% of older adults (age 40 and older) with DS, and may cause decline in self-care and cognition (Sherrill, 2004). Moreover, there is evidence that people with DS age earlier than people who are not disabled (Bullock et al., 2010; Porter & burlingame, 2006). The occasional display of stubbornness appears to be a central nervous system difficulty. Obesity and high blood cholesterol also are associated with DS. **Atlantoaxial instability** affects recreation participation in a small percentage of individuals (Dunn & Leitschuh, 2006). Atlantoaxial refers to the joint between the atlas and axis (C1–C2, cervical vertebrae). Instability refers to abnormal mobility in the joint caused by lax ligaments and muscles surrounding the joint. Activities that could result in hyperflexion or hyperextension of the cervical spine, such as gymnastics or swimming, require close observation and possible restrictions. Useful information may be accessed through the National Down Syndrome Congress (http://www.ndsccenter.org) and National Down Syndrome Society (http://www.ndss.org).

Unknown prenatal conditions cause some infants to have distinct facial features or anomalies of the head. A person with *microcephalus* is identified by a small head. The severity of intellectual disability is increased as the size of the head decreases. Microcephalus is an indicator of conditions like fetal alcohol syndrome, which is caused by heavy alcohol consumption during pregnancy (Sherrill, 2004). *Hydrocephalus*, a large head caused by an excessive amount of cerebrospinal fluid accumulating in the ventricles of the brain, is associated with spina bifida and can lead to the development of an intellectual disability as the fluid pressure damages the brain. Individuals with Apert, Cornelia de Lange, and Prader-Willi syndromes exhibit craniofacial abnormalities, noticeable stature differences, and varying degrees of ID (Sherrill).

Functioning Characteristics

With the exception of people with unique syndromes, individuals vary greatly in the extent to which they demonstrate characteristic behaviors (Dunn & Leitschuh, 2006). Impaired intelligence and impaired adaptive functioning affect each of the other behavioral areas. The acquisition of social skills depends on an ability to reason in social situations and to allow reasoning to govern actions. As modern-day social changes quicken and intensify, decision-making skills become more critical during social experiences. The lower the level of measured intelligence, the greater the impact of a cognitive impairment on communication skills critical to managing ADLs and social relationships.

Verbal and nonverbal communication are the primary means of initiating and maintaining social contacts. Intellectual deficits limit the ability to discriminate meanings and sounds, to discern gestural patterns, and to generalize from one social situation to another. "Social maturity and satisfactory adjustment is acquired in play situations throughout the formative years" (Dunn & Leitschuh, 2006, p. 500). People with disabilities have fewer relationships than their peers (Schleien, Green, & Stone, 2003). A lack of social competence contributes to limited opportunities for inclusion (Cory, Dattilo, & Williams, 2006; Lord, 1997).

The demands of the situation also determine the effects of cognitive impairments on social functioning. Visibility, extent of deviation, and value placed on group membership influence the reactions of others toward individuals with cognitive impairments. You are probably aware of the stares experienced by persons with Down syndrome, whose appearance is different from the expected. Conversely, most people will not initially recognize those individuals with cognitive impairments who neither possess outward signs nor appear uncomfortable in social situations.

Emotional adjustments are part of the maturation process for all people, yet for those with intellectual disabilities, stress and conflict are created by an inability to identify, understand, control, and express their emotions. A person's self-concept lies at the heart of emotional adjustments; and though rejection and physical avoidance by others are expressions that may not be fully understood by an individual with an ID, they still bear on the development of a positive self-concept.

An inability to set realistic goals may characterize individual efforts. Without this skill, clients experience difficulty assessing self-knowledge, skills, and relationships with others. Clients must be able to link the cause to the effect in order to set realistic goals and accept responsibility for their behaviors. For example, clients who speak too loudly in a social group may not realize this is the reason why others in the group shy away, so they may not modify this behavior without prompting from the TRS.

People with an ID exhibit developmental delays and variability in motor performance, depending on the severity of the cognitive deficit. A general lack of coordination is evident with a shuffling gait, poor posture, slower than usual development of eye-hand coordination, and difficulty tracking objects. A lack of body rhythm is evidenced by an uneven running pattern or in a broken walking gait. People with an ID tend to be overweight or obese and this impacts motor performance and predisposition to physical activity; fitness is lower than that of peers without an intellectual disability (Sherrill, 2004).

Poor motor planning is attributed to decreased body awareness and kinesthetic perception. For example, observe a person with an ID climbing stairs; often he or she will take one step at a time, always placing the same foot on the next step. This demonstrates poor motor planning. The inability to transfer and generalize from one experience to another brings about the appearance of routine, mechanical motor patterns that have a perseverative quality. For some, once the motor pattern begins, internal control of the behavior seems to disappear. This overflow results in rapid involuntary stereotyped motor movements (tics) and the inability to stop a behavior, such as running beyond first base.

The degree of ID determines the extent to which cognitive behaviors are impaired. The development of functions such as auditory and visual memory, the ability to speak, and the capacity to understand abstract concepts may be delayed. Impinging stimuli easily distract clients, and generalization and transfer of learned behaviors from one experience to another is less spontaneous. Articulation and expressive language problems also interfere with the learning process. The ability to follow a logical thought pattern, to evaluate an activity, and to use a problem-solving approach to acquire new skills is limited. You may have observed the confusion or resistance that results when a person with ID is required to make a decision following the presentation of several choices.

Purpose of Therapeutic Recreation

Therapeutic recreation interventions with people with ID emphasize a balanced leisure lifestyle; decision making; leisure-skill and resource development, selection, and use; participation in age-appropriate experiences; inclusion within the community; physical well-being; ADL and self-care; environmental awareness and personal and community safety skills; communication; and development of functional skills fun-

Activities like playing cards help develop functional skills like counting.

damental to leisure experiences (Dattilo & Guerin, 2001; Porter & burlingame, 2006). Protocols focus on remediation of cognitive behaviors and leisure-skill deficits. Leisure education interventions remediate communication, social, and behavioral deficits, while self-initiated leisure functioning is promoted through participation opportunities that facilitate feedback and recognition of involvement.

Therapeutic recreation often includes social interactions that foster practice of verbal and nonverbal communication and acquisition of expected social behaviors. People with ID have difficulty understanding the meanings of words with more than one interpretation. Also, they do not recognize subtle nonverbal social cues. Appropriateness of voice tone and level and knowing when to laugh or talk are acquired social skills. Experience in social amenities such as exchanging greetings, using the appropriate restrooms, selecting and wearing proper clothing, making change, and identifying directional signs and signals can be gained through sensory awareness activities, leisure education, dining out, and participation in competitions like Unified Sports promoted through Special Olympics International (SOI), or international events for elite athletes sponsored by The International Federation of Sports for Persons with Intellectual Disability (INAS-FID—part of the Paralympic movement) (Sherrill, 2004).

Therapeutic recreation experiences become the medium through which individuals identify and express feelings and enhance the self-concept. Interventions that encourage self-improvement goals, the expression of likes and dislikes, and receipt of praise and recognition commensurate with performance lead to an improved self-concept. This results in expression of feelings reflective of the client's true emotions. Expression of emotions and awareness of other people's values can be facilitated during spectator events, inclusive experiences with buddies, adventure/challenge initiatives, and through physical activity and assertiveness training.

Therapeutic recreation provides an opportunity to enhance motor performance, fitness, perceptual-motor and motor planning skills, body rhythm, coordination, cause-and-effect relationships among movement patterns, and skill generalization and transition in community recreation (Dattilo, 2002; Dunn & Leitschuh, 2006; Sherrill, 2004). TRSs provide the support, assistance, and accommodations that facilitate inclu-

The praise and recognition that result from participation in spectator events can improve the self-concept of youth with Down syndrome.

sion. Improved physical skills lead to social inclusion and enhanced self-care (Schleien et al., 2003). Aquatics, sports, and fitness activities encourage physical activity that occurs in inclusive settings. Individuals leaving school systems and entering adult life or moving into community living arrangements may have excess time available with few meaningful interactional and employment opportunities (Dunn & Leitschuh; Smith et al., 2008). Thus, there is a need to develop age-appropriate behaviors, friendships, self-initiated involvement, and active rather than sedentary participation. Health-related fitness skills and lifelong leisure skills prepare individuals to use their time in rewarding and self-fulfilling ways. Leisure education, community integration and volunteer experiences, creative arts, and social-skills training are effective techniques and appropriate adult experiences in which cognitive skills are practiced and inclusion is fostered (Dattilo, 2002; Miller, Schleien, Brooke, Frisoli, & Brooks, 2005).

Delivery Settings

Individuals with ID reside with primary caregivers, in congregate community housing, in long-term facilities, and independently in housing supervised by nonprofit social service agencies. Services are provided through therapeutic recreation divisions of public park and recreation organizations, by special recreation associations, and by social agents like Special Olympics (www.specialolympics.org). The Arc provides social services and promotes self-advocacy in many communities (www.thearc.org). In residential settings, therapists may work in rehabilitation, activity, or therapeutic recreation departments to develop and monitor client progress through, for example, individual habilitation plans (IHPs). The Individuals with Disabilities Education Act (IDEA) of 1997 recognized that transitional services (beginning at age 14)—a coordinated set of activities written into the IEP—are essential to independent living and community participation. TRSs involved with school systems promote acquisition of lifetime skill training based on personal preferences.

The heterogeneous nature of ID is underscored by the diversity of delivery settings and services offered. Clients with mild impairments participate in inclusionary experiences like Unified Sports, while those with severe impairments may attend camps and aquatic programs alongside individuals with multiple impairments and developmental disabilities.

Leadership Interaction and Intervention Considerations

Individuals with ID "can easily participate in community recreation programs" (Bullock et al., 2010, p. 221). The degree of cognitive impairment influences the level of support provided by a TRS during functional skill development and leisure experiences. The acquisition of the skills necessary to take control over leisure participation is critical. A variety of professional practices have been found to support inclusive participation and to address the individual needs of people with varying degrees of cognitive impairment (Klitzing & Wachter, 2005). A comprehensive approach to TR service delivery incorporates administrators, family members, supportive living staff, rehabilitation and social-service personnel, and the TRS and client.

A number of management and leadership practices applicable to a variety of settings and clients are presented here; however, keep in mind that degree of impairment, setting, and program objectives determine the appropriateness of recommended practices.

- The initial step in establishing program focus (rehabilitation, education, health prevention/promotion) is assessment. Assessing a person's preferences in a variety of settings is the foundation for developing decision-making skills, which in turn help the individual assume responsibility for self-initiated leisure and to make successful transitions (Dattilo & Guerin, 2001; Schleien & Ray, 1997). Environmental analysis establishes the context in which participation is likely to occur. TRSs can better plan for skill transfer and generalization when the environmental supports are known (Dattilo & Guerin; Schleien, Germ, & McAvoy, 1996).

- A number of behavioral techniques have been found to promote performance on practical, concrete tasks. These include positive reinforcement, task analysis, skill sequencing, chaining, shaping, visual and verbal prompting, fading, modeling, and/or skill demonstration (Bullock et al., 2010; Schleien et al., 1996). Social recognition and token economies are positive reinforcers. The TRS uses task analysis to divide an activity or event into the sequence required to complete the skill. The skill sequence for catching a ball would include grasping, releasing, visual tracking, receiving a rolled ball, and receiving a thrown ball.

We refer to this step-by-step skill sequence as a *chain*. *Shaping* occurs when the TRS reinforces each displayed approximation in the skill sequence. TRSs use *prompting* to guide clients physically through an experience. The command, "Susan, watch me," is a verbal prompt. Gradual withdrawal of this assistance is called *fading*. With skill acquisition, the TRS relies less on modeling and more on repeated demonstrations with peer partners, family members, and leaders.

- Deficits in communication are evident when participants hesitate to initiate conversation, take time to plan what to say, and respond to how something sounds rather than what is said. TRSs encourage reciprocal communication by waiting before talking to allow client-initiated communication and asking "what" or "how" questions rather than framing sentences so "yes" or "no" responses are appropriate (Dattilo & Guerin, 2001). A TRS realizes a client's ability to understand speech may be more developed than his or her actual speaking vocabulary, and for this reason avoids speaking "down" to participants (Bullock et al., 2010).

- A structured environment encourages participants to focus on the topic at hand (Bullock et al., 2010). Structured cooperative games are used to reinforce appropriate social skills (Dunn & Leitschuh, 2006). Participants learn by doing. Practice and repetition through activity variation leads to comprehension. Performance is best the first few times a skill is attempted (Dunn & Leitschuh). New skills introduced early in a session are more apt to be acquired.

- Program-specific goals guide intervention (Germ & Schleien, 1997). TRSs focus on client abilities, recognizing that participants may have yet to achieve their potential because of a lack of expectations (Bullock et al., 2010). TRSs also are aware that participants are encouraged to transfer skills from one situation to another if circumstances and expectations are similar from one environment to another. TRSs are aware that a top down perspective—basing program goals and outcomes on the demands of the next environment where the client will recreate—facilitates skill acquisition and transfer (Smith et al., 2008).

- Explicit directions and descriptions are broken down into one or two steps and are precise (Bullock et al., 2010; Dunn & Leitschuh, 2006). For example, "Watch me, and repeat what I do" is more specific than "Stand over there." Hands-on learning and visual aids, along with repetition, are helpful. Circle formations facilitate modeling, imitation, demonstration, and peer interaction.

- Increased decision making is facilitated by requiring participants to select among the alternatives and to weigh the consequences of each choice. With repeated trial and error opportunities, clients acquire knowledge of alternatives that match their competence. A client's perception of control over the experience is enhanced as preferences are made known.

- Adaptations of program materials, equipment, and/or activities are among the more common inclusionary practices (Klitzing & Wachter, 2005; Schleien et al., 1996). Allowing time to adjust to change in routine or a new situation also promotes participation (Bullock et al., 2010).

- Rules and safety precautions are stated before experiences begin because clients may lack the judgment to understand dangerous situations or the difficulty of a task (Bullock et al., 2010). Expected conduct is also outlined prior to participation and consistently monitored during participation; this approach nurtures client safety awareness.

- Preparation for participation is just as important as the activity itself. Functional skills are acquired as clients change shoes, remove coats, and take care of equipment. Skill acquisition in areas like counting, identification of colors, sharing, and taking turns enhances functional capacity and is an intervention outcome.

- Because clients need to understand cause-and-effect relationships, leaders identify consequences of actions such as "kicking the ball too hard" or "not listening as directions are given." The leader's feedback is immediate, identifies the ABC (antecedent, behavior, consequence), and constructively relates client performance to outcome.

Applying the Therapeutic Recreation Process

Diane is a young adult with a mild ID. She will receive academic and related services, including therapeutic recreation, until the age of 21.

Assessment

Demographic information.   Diane is a young woman of chronological age 16 with a speech impairment and arthritis. She is presently living with her parents in a major metropolitan area.

History.   Diane's mother gave birth at age 36. Medical records reveal birth trauma. Diane was diagnosed with an ID during a preschool program. She has been in a resource classroom since first grade, with speech and physical therapies scheduled weekly.

Present behavior.   Diane enjoys bowling, dancing, family camping, and swimming. She frequently sits for long periods of time watching TV and DVDs; consequently, her weight is becoming an issue. Deficits exist in fine motor skills and endurance. She easily becomes upset, sulks, and appears shy and withdrawn with newcomers. Diane has joint stiffness and talks with a lisp.

The TRS obtained the above information through review of the social worker's reports, the data provided by a **psychometrist** (a specialist who uses tests to measure mental and psychological ability and functioning) from the administration of the Stanford-Binet, and an IEP with transitional services developed by interviews and observations with family members and Diane. Diane's list of needs includes: improved use of leisure, improvement of fine motor skills, enhanced physical activity, and increased social adjustment. Diane's assets include exposure to some forms of recreation, mastery of fundamental academic skills, and ability to respond verbally.

Planning

Long-term goal.   The long-term goal of Diane's TR intervention is to participate in inclusive leisure activities.

Short-term goals.   The short-term goals are to expand her social contacts through school activities and increase her level of physical activity.

Objectives. By the end of the semester, Diane will have participated with three other peers once per week in a community resource activities period.

During the semester, Diane will participate in at least two physical activities for at least 30-60 minutes, twice weekly.

Content. Activities will include drama, leisure education, wellness, horticulture, and social facilitation groups to encourage verbal expression.

Process. A variety of behavioral strategies like reinforcement, repetition, and modeling will be used in classroom and home-based leisure education programs. Weekly leisure education sessions include resources, communication and social skills, decision-making, leisure awareness, and self-determination skills (assertiveness, making choices). Family members will be encouraged to engage in physical activity with Diane.

Implementation

Diane participated in the school-based program as her parents simultaneously attended monthly in-service sessions designed to help them adjust to Diane's future placement outside of the home and to allow them to interact with the parent support group. Leisure education programs that involve families, choice making, and social interaction have been found to be successful in promoting independent functioning with clients like Diane (Ashton-Shaeffer, Shelton, & Johnson, 1995; Dattilo, 2002; Schleien et al., 2003; Schleien & Ray, 1997; Williams & Dattilo, 1997).

Evaluation

The objectives served as the primary evaluation tool. The TRS also used measures presented in the leisure education activities and inclusion models to assess progress on individual participation experiences. At the end of each semester, TRSs will review Diane's plan. They will recommend revisions in the program or her parents' involvement in the program and identify dates to make the adjustments and to determine the status of long-term goals.

Related Considerations

The assessment portion of programs with clients with cognitive impairments not only identifies exhibited abilities but also identifies clients' likes and dislikes. TRSs use observation techniques to determine the preferred activities of clients who have limited skill repertoires or a limited ability to communicate preferences. This assessment also includes analyzing environmental factors such as activities valued by peers and identifying natural reinforcers. With this information, TRSs develop programs that include age-appropriate skills and generalization of acquired skills to inclusive settings (Mobily & MacNeil, 2002). TRSs create an atmosphere that promotes social inclusion by articulating the tenets of inclusion and the practices that foster support (Schleien et al., 2003). Refer to exhibit 8.2 for an articulation of the NRPA's position on inclusion.

The TRS gives careful consideration to the structure of each intervention session, including timing of activities, skill requirements, sequence of activities, organized use of equipment, and movement and organization of clients. Each session follows a routine schedule that permits clients time to readjust or "debrief" before leaving the activ-

Exhibit 8.2   National Recreation and Park Association Position Statement on Inclusion

Diversity is a cornerstone of our society and culture and thus should be celebrated. Including people with disabilities in the fabric of society strengthens the community and its individual members. The value of inclusive leisure experiences in enhancing the quality of life for all people, with and without disabilities, cannot be overstated. As we broaden our understanding and acceptance of differences among people through shared leisure experiences, we empower future generations to build a better place for all to live and thrive.

Inclusive leisure experiences encourage and enhance opportunities for people of varying abilities to participate and interact in life's activities together with dignity. It also provides an environment that promotes and fosters physical, social, and psychological inclusion of people with diverse experiences and skill levels. Inclusion enhances individuals' potential for full and active participation in leisure activities and experiences. Additionally, the benefits of this participation may include:

- providing positive recreational experiences which contribute to the physical, mental, social, emotional, and spiritual growth and development of every individual;
- fostering peer and intergenerational relationships that allow one to share affection, support, companionship, and assistance; and
- developing community support and encouraging attitudinal changes to reflect dignity, self-respect, and involvement within the community.

Purpose

The purpose of the National Recreation and Park Association (NRPA) Position Statement on Inclusion is to encourage all providers of park, recreation, and leisure services to provide opportunities in settings where people of all abilities can recreate and interact together.

This document articulates a commitment to the leisure process and the desired outcomes. Accordingly, the NRPA Position Statement on Inclusion encompasses these broad concepts and beliefs:

Right to Leisure

- The pursuit of leisure is a condition necessary for human dignity and well-being.
- Leisure is a part of a healthy lifestyle and a productive life.
- Every individual is entitled to the opportunity to express unique interests and pursue, develop, and improve talents and abilities.
- People are entitled to opportunities and services in the most inclusive setting.
- The right to choose from the full array of recreation opportunities offered in diverse settings and environments and requiring different levels of competency should be provided.

Quality of Life

- People grow and develop throughout the life span.
- Through leisure an individual gains an enhanced sense of competence and self-direction.
- A healthy leisure lifestyle can prevent illness and promote wellness.
- The social connection with one's peers plays a major role in his/her life satisfaction.
- The opportunity to choose is an important component in one's quality of life; individual choices will be respected.

(continued)

Support, Assistance, and Accommodations

- Inclusion is most effective when support, assistance, and accommodations are provided.
- Support, assistance, and accommodations can and should be responsive to people's needs and preferences.
- Support, assistance, and accommodations should create a safe and fun environment, remove real and artificial barriers to participation, and maximize not only the independence but also the interdependence of the individual. People want to be self-sufficient.
- Support, assistance, and accommodations may often vary and are typically individualized. Types of support, assistance, and accommodations include, but are not limited to: qualified staff, adaptive equipment, alternative formats for printed or audio materials, trained volunteers, or flexibility in policies and program rules.

Barrier Removal

- Environments should be designed to encourage social interaction, "risk-taking," fun, choices and acceptance that allow for personal accomplishment in a cooperative context.
- Physical barriers should be eliminated to facilitate full participation by individuals with disabilities.
- Attitudinal barriers in all existing and future recreation services should be removed or minimized through education and training of personnel (staff, volunteers, students, and/or community at-large).

    The National Recreation and Park Association is dedicated to the four inclusion concepts of:

- *Right to Leisure* (for all individuals)
- *Quality of Life* (enhancements through leisure experiences)
- *Support, Assistance, and Accommodations*
- *Barrier Removal*

in all park, recreation, and leisure services. Properly fostered, inclusion will happen naturally. Over time, inclusion will occur with little effort and with the priceless reward of an enlightened community. Encouraged in the right way, inclusion is the right thing to plan for, implement, and celebrate.

Adopted by the NRPA Board of Trustees as an NRPA Policy, October 24, 1999. Used with permission of the National Recreation and Park Association.

ity and entering another program. Clients' entry-level skills vary, and within any given session clients with different skill levels may be present. A challenging task for the TR professional is to individualize a group experience. The use of activity and task analyses helps a TRS determine skill requirements and the progression to be mastered from entry-level to successful skill demonstration. Clients respond better to activities when they progress through them according to individual ability levels, taking on increasingly more difficult tasks as each step in the skill sequence is mastered (Mobily & MacNeil, 2002).

The TRS focuses on voice tone, eye contact, amount of physical assistance offered to clients, and the appropriateness of participants' interactions among each other and between themselves and the TRS. Participants can become distracted by subtle behaviors. They also may have difficulty interpreting the meaning of actions used to help them understand how to complete a task. For example, a prompt using physical guidance may instead be interpreted as a caring touch.

Therapeutic recreation activities provide a rich environment for learning. Specific activities offer TRSs and community recreation personnel the opportunity to observe, analyze, and evaluate behaviors. Therapeutic recreation also is a medium for training colleagues and caregivers in how to intervene and how to advocate to include others in leisure (Klitzing & Wachter, 2005; Wall & Gast, 1997). Through program observations/in-services with colleagues, TRSs provide inclusion training on topics like necessary and reasonable accommodations, ecological assessments, and the benefits to agency staff of client volunteers (Miller et al., 2005; Scholl, Dieser, & Davison, 2005). The TRS assumes the role of a leisure educator with caregivers. This might involve answering questions about adapted equipment and community resources, facilitating the organization of family advocacy groups, and sharing ways to adjust family leisure experiences to include family and community members (Schleien et al., 2003).

SEVERE MULTIPLE IMPAIRMENTS

An individual with a severe multiple impairment has either a profound disability or a combination of disabilities that require extensive ongoing support services in more than one major life activity (e.g., toileting, feeding, ambulation) to enable meaningful social participation, self-fulfillment, and enhanced quality of life (Dunn & Leitschuh, 2006; Schleien, Fahnestock, & Miller, 2001). People with severe multiple impairments include those who have serious mental illnesses; severe and profound ID; autism; developmental disabilities; are medically fragile, or **dually diagnosed** (a label used to describe the co-occurrence of two primary dysfunctions, like ID and psychiatric disorders, cerebral palsy and deafness, and dual sensory impairments) (Dunn & Leitschuh; Schleien et al., 2001).

Clients are heterogeneous; that is, there are more differences among them than similarities. The same impairment may appear to have different effects on different individuals. Individuals with pervasive developmental disorders like autism experience delays in speech, communication, and learning and have inappropriate social behaviors and sensory disabilities that contribute to the variability among clients. Likewise, individuals with cerebral palsy or clients with an ID and emotional issues exhibit individually unique characteristics.

For clients with severe multiple impairments, there is no explicit relationship among the degrees of involvement in each behavioral area. An individual with a severe emotional impairment may be intelligent yet unable to express these abilities because the emotional disturbance predominates. Each additional impairment appears to have a multiplicative, rather than an additive, effect. Thus, a severe impairment in one area may well have a significant impact on skill development in other behavioral areas.

Because there is not an explicit definition of severe multiple impairments, accurate estimates of the number of individuals is uncertain. Prevalence estimates for severe and profound ID range from 4–6% of those with ID; it is estimated that 7–8% of the school-age population require special education services because of serious emotional disorders (APA, 2000; Sherrill, 2004). Severe multiple impairments result from chromosomal abnormalities, genetic deficiencies, metabolic disorders, prematurity, **Rh incompatibility** (a condition in which the mother's blood is Rh negative and that of the fetus is Rh positive, causing the mother to form antibodies that affect the fetus), infectious diseases, malnutrition, maternal alcoholism, brain damage, and oxygen deprivation. Traumatic injuries, poisoning, abuse, and neglect may also result in severe multiple impairments.

Functioning Characteristics

The characteristic differences among individuals with severe disabilities are greater than their similarities. Individuals may

- display abnormal retention of reflexes
- require assistance with self-help skills
- exhibit challenging behaviors like self-injury, aggression, property destruction, and stereotyped movements
- lack the ability for clear, understandable communication
- display either emotional lability or a flat affect
- have difficulty walking or sitting without support, and experience deficits in strength, flexibility, agility, and coordination
- have difficulty applying skills learned in one environment to another
- have difficulty responding to commands and familiar surroundings (Dunn & Leitschuh, 2006; Sigafoos, Tucker, Bushell, & Webber, 1997).

Language patterns are described as telegraphic, perseverative, and echolalic. Individuals may appear to be unresponsive to objects and people and display few self-initiated interactions. They may appear awkward or clumsy, lack control over their motor behavior, and be nonambulatory or nonindependently mobile. They may become tense, rigid, or easily overstimulated when introduced to new experiences.

Individuals may be dependent on their relationship with others to make clear choices like selecting leisure options and objects (Zijlstra & Vlaskamp, 2005). A lack of spontaneity or responsiveness to play objects and people limits the interactional relationships fundamental to social inclusion and leisure experiences (Schleien et al., 2001). Intellectual limitations may preclude participation in leisure experiences that require reasoning and language development. With the variety of characteristics evidenced, TRSs are challenged to first assess client behaviors to ascertain each client's behavioral assets and then identify the interplay among developmental skills, as severe deficits in one area, physical for example, may mask cognitive abilities and vice versa.

Purpose of Therapeutic Recreation

Therapeutic recreation is designed to improve functional, communication, social, and leisure skills; choice-making; and independent functioning. The goal is for clients to have satisfying and meaningful leisure experiences that enhance their health-related quality of life (Patterson, 2004; Schleien et al., 2001; Zijlstra & Vlaskamp, 2005). TRSs assist team members by providing opportunities for social inclusion, physical activity, experiences in community-based or natural settings, and by training volunteers to support clients (Dunn & Leitschuh, 2006; Sherrill, 2004; Smith et al., 2008). The TRS facilitates development of fundamental motor skills necessary to maintain a comfortable posture, ambulate, and manipulate recreation objects. Interventions such as structured stimulation, passive range of motion, and snoezelen promote self-help, relaxation, increased levels of engagement, enjoyment, and meaningful interactive leisure experiences (Lancioni, Singh, O'Reilly, Oliva, & Basili, 2005; Patterson). Independence is increased as clients become better able to point to symbols on a **Bliss board** (a non-oral means of communication requiring the individual to point to abstract symbols that are associated with actual experiences or written words; the individual combines and modifies the symbols to replicate the English language), for example, or nod their heads or squeeze the TRS's hand to express a need or preference; or use low-tech (picture notebook) or high-tech (computer or microswitch) devices to encourage reciprocal communication.

Leisure education is intended to increase clients' skill repertoires, choice making, social interaction skills, and use of unoccupied time. Introduction to leisure toys such as those used in expressive arts has been found to reduce challenging behaviors while

Trained inclusion buddies facilitate client expression and contribute to meaningful leisure experiences.

encouraging self-initiated activities, like using the tape recorder or listening to music (Sigafoos et al., 1997). Individualized experiences with positive outcomes enhance the person's self-concept and social competence. Participants gain opportunities to explore leisure preferences, experience positive outcomes like happiness, and improve independent manipulative responses (self-direction) by using computers, electronic games, and microswitch technology (Facon & Darge, 1996; Lancioni et al., 2006; Raschke, Dedrick, Heston, & Farris, 1996).

Delivery Settings

People with severe multiple impairments may reside in congregate living situations, in long-term residential facilities, or with caregivers. TRSs employed by public and human service agencies provide services under the auspices of rehabilitation, activity therapies, or therapeutic recreation departments. Interdisciplinary teams develop individual treatment or program plans and provide training so consistency in intervention strategies is maintained throughout the client's lifetime. Services range from early intervention and skill development classes through schools to practicing social skills in natural settings like restaurants and private homes.

Leadership Interaction and Intervention Considerations

Early and continuous intervention with clients is critical to developing and enhancing lifelong skills. Intervention relies on naturalistic or ecological assessment with definitive objectives presented in a structured consistent format. Sessions include variable practice and opportunities for choice-making and social engagement. The interdisciplinary approach incorporates parents and other caregivers, with the TRS providing instruction and support in how to lead and adapt experiences and use behavioral interventions throughout the client's lifetime (Schleien et al., 2001; Wall & Gast, 1997).

A list of general interaction techniques to facilitate individualization of the helping process is presented below.

- Using a **kinesthetic approach** to teach a task, the TRS manipulates the client's limbs so he or she feels the sensation of movement in the muscles or joints. This approach helps to redirect challenging behaviors while recognizing that some clients lack the comprehension or strength to perform the complete task independently.

- The TRS helps the client focus on the task at hand by directing the person's eye contact. Additionally, the existence of basic reflexes interferes with intended movements. For example, a TRS attempting to position a client may inadvertently trigger a response such as the tonic neck reflex, the outcome of which could interfere with the desired action.

- The most innocuous word, item, or behavior can trigger an undesirable client reaction. Give precise, concrete, verbal directions such as, "Julie, throw the blue ball to me." Sudden movements, new voices, multicolored clothing, or jewelry can become the objects of attention. Soft colors and background sounds filter out disruptions and create a calming atmosphere.

A TRS uses a kinesthetic approach to help a client feel the muscle movement required to aim an arrow at a target.

- A behavioral intervention process using reinforcement, task analysis, cues, prompts, and sequencing individualizes instruction (Schleien et al., 2001). Backward chaining is effective because clients work into self-reinforcing tasks. Natural reinforcers provided by reactive recreation equipment, such as remote-control vehicles that use switches, result in sensory feedback and increased engagement, which enhance client interaction (Facon & Darge, 1996; Lancioni et al., 2006).

- Cues are the signals or requests that encourage clients to respond. Cues and prompts are presented in a sequence from least to most intrusive (from verbal cue to physical guidance) (Schleien et al., 2001). When the reinforcing value of equipment encourages interactions, the TRS is able to fade or reduce the use of cues and prompts, thereby fostering self-initiated behaviors.

- The TRS may find the use of relaxation techniques such as massage and rubbing or tapping the opposing muscle groups of contracted body parts effective in reducing muscle tension.

- The TRS is able to respond more effectively to the diverse needs of each person through structured small-group or one-on-one helping relationships preceded by preference and environmental assessments (Dunn & Leitschuh, 2006).

- The TRS assesses and evaluates progress through individual observations. The cumulative effect of severe multiple impairments is interactive. Gains in one area may not be readily apparent because of delays or deficits in another.
- Training in leisure experiences that will be used with a person's future peers facilitates age-appropriate skill development, skill generalization, and social inclusion. Training in functional skills such as travel skills, money management, and social greetings also enhances skill transfer and the maintenance of leisure skills in new settings.
- Skill remediation and generalization are enhanced when intervention focuses on functional skill development using lead-up and follow-up strategies as well as practice and repetition in the environments where the skill is to be applied (Dunn & Leitschuh, 2006; Schleien et al., 2001; Sherrill, 2004).
- The TRS makes a conscious effort to present alternatives that reflect clients' preferences in order to encourage them to choose and practice self-reinforcing experiences.

Applying the Therapeutic Recreation Process

Jimmy is a teenager who is multiply disabled. The TRS working with Jimmy interacts with caregivers and other team members to ensure that his individual intervention plan is properly implemented.

Assessment

Demographic information.   Jimmy is 18 years old. He resides with his parents and two siblings in a private home.

History.   Jimmy was born prematurely after a difficult labor. He was diagnosed with an ID, cerebral palsy, and communication impairments during his first year. He has had speech therapy and physical therapy since the age of 3.

Present behavior.   Jimmy recognizes his name. He communicates by nodding his head or pointing a finger but lacks meaningful verbalization. He displays challenging behaviors, spasticity, and is unable to ambulate using a wheelchair. The TRS gathered the assessment information using the General Recreation Screening Tool (GRST), by observing Jimmy during his daily activities, and through interviews with caregivers. Data obtained from his social worker, physician, speech therapist, and physical therapist supplemented the information the TRS gathered. Jimmy experiences deficits in emotional control, verbalization, coordination, and self-care. His assets include family support, his awareness of and willingness to interact with familiar people, and exposure to fundamental motor skills and activities.

Planning

Long-term goal.   The long-term goal of Jimmy's TR intervention is to improve communication.

Short-term goal.   The short-term goal is to increase Jimmy's ability to make interests known.

Objective. After six months, Jimmy will communicate the desire to move to a different area or to use a different piece of recreational equipment by employing a manual sign.

Content. The program will consist of activities of a sensory motor nature that do not require use of a wheelchair. The activities will involve the use of makeshift tactile objects, such as beanbags, balls, and Styrofoam objects, and will occur in a small, stimulus-controlled area. The TRS will require Jimmy to choose different objects and locations in the room.

Process. The TRS will employ physical guidance, shaping, modeling, verbal reinforcement, and directed questions to help Jimmy demonstrate his preferred interests. During this phase of program development, the team will develop the schedule for physical therapy, speech and hearing exercises, education, occupational therapy, and therapeutic recreation. They will plan conferences with his parents to report progress, to aid the family in learning communication and behavioral management techniques, and to plan family leisure experiences.

Implementation

Each therapeutic recreation session followed a structured routine: passive exercise; motor skill development; ambulation; small-group circle activity with balls, parachutes, and target throws; and mat exercises. During evening hours, staff encouraged his parents to participate in expressive arts and drama, modified lead-up games, aquatics, and walks in the local park.

Evaluation

During monthly staff meetings, TRSs reported Jimmy's progress on a behavioral checklist developed by the team. The social worker and parents will meet for quarterly conferences to review Jimmy's progress and to review his parents' success with various communication and behavioral management techniques. A yearly case review of Jimmy's individual habilitation plan (IHP) is mandated by state law.

Related Considerations

A comprehensive service network facilitates inclusion while addressing each client's unique needs. The knowledge and skills required of each team member include behavior management, skill sequencing, adaptation and modification procedures, functional skill training, orthopedic equipment use, management and care of seizures, referral procedures, computer applications, environmental assessment and observation skills, and alternative communication methods. The TRS should also be knowledgeable regarding the uses and side effects of tranquilizers, muscle relaxants, and anticonvulsant drugs. Commercial recreation equipment may lack durability and age-appropriateness; therefore, TRSs incorporate into activities objects that are pliable, large, and that possess reactive and sensory qualities.

Since clients with severe multiple impairments use a variety of orthopedic and prosthetic devices, program planning should consider interior and exterior facility accessibility. Also, such specialized equipment as mirrors, standing tables, pushballs, and mats, if available, enhance client responsiveness. Before beginning a session, a leader should designate areas for temporarily unused wheelchairs and "individual" areas to manage clients' behavioral needs.

Communication is a lifelong need. Many people with severe multiple impairments are either nonverbal or have a limited understanding of what they hear. A client's responsiveness is enhanced by verbal feedback. Sentences should be kept short, lack pronouns, and consist of functional language, rather than professional vocabulary. TRSs learn the necessity of repeating verbal directions using the same words and the importance of positioning the client in close proximity to the speaker. Even when a TRS does not understand a vocalization, an acknowledgment is given so the client recognizes that his or her attempts at vocalization do communicate. Nonverbal clients learn to associate gestures, facial expressions, and other forms of body language with the meanings they convey. Through trial and error, the TRS develops communication avenues. Possible techniques include pantomime communication and manual communications, including the American one-hand manual alphabet, finger-spelling into the palm of the client's hand, and adapted ASL (American Sign Language). Helpful resources may be acquired by contacting the Association for Persons with Severe Handicaps (www.tash.org).

Light-touch communication devices allow a client to "talk" to the TRS.

AUTISM

For this developmental disability, definitions and classification systems vary within and among countries and have changed over time. One system used in the United States, the APA's *DSM-IV-TR*, presents criteria for pervasive developmental disorders (PDD) that include autistic disorders (AD) and Asperger's disorders (AS). The term *autism* will be used, unless otherwise specified, to refer to individuals across the autism spectrum disorder. These disorders range along a continuum from severe, called classic autism or autistic disorder, to a lesser degree of impairment, referred to as Asperger's syndrome. Features characteristic of individuals are impairments in the development of reciprocal social interactions, verbal and nonverbal communication skills, and in their repertoire of activity and interests (APA, 2000). Every individual with autism has a unique combination of characteristics and behaviors which change with age and environment (Sherrill, 2004). The word *autism* is derived from the Greek word *autos*, which is translated as "self" and means withdrawn and self-absorbed. Children with autism display aloofness and social withdrawal very early in life. People with autism have a lifelong impairment; with intensive, structured early intervention about one-third of these individuals live and work independently as adults (Sherrill).

Before the age of three a child with autism may appear to be developing as expected, although parents may later recall that the child did not display the anticipated awareness of parental love. Parents have reported the following behaviors: becoming either limp or rigid when picked up, staring at lights, scratching or rubbing the covers, and failing to point to or reach for objects, including food. Deviations in speech patterns and eye contact are usually first noticed. Developmental deviations include walking without crawling, reciting a string of numbers without first being able to count or speak understandable sentences, and manipulation of objects while lacking a rhythmical walking pattern.

Autism is associated with ID, fragile X syndrome, tuberous sclerosis, and seizures (Sherrill, 2004; Strock, 2007). Although it is difficult to use standardized intelligence tests, and few diagnostic tools are available to accurately identify functional deficits, a large proportion of those with autism have intellectual disabilities (APA, 2000). Seizure activity may be present in children or may develop by adolescence; estimates range from one-fourth to one-third of all children with autism (APA, 2000; Hawkins, 2001; Sherrill).

Prevalence rates for autism around the globe range from 2 to 6 per 1,000 children, with boys four times more likely than girls to experience the disorder (CDC, 2008; Strock, 2007). Studies suggest an increase in the prevalence of autism. It is uncertain whether this represents a true increase since changes in diagnostic criteria, improved identification, and public and professional awareness may be contributing factors (Dunn & Leitschuh, 2006; Karande, 2006; Strock). Although not definitive, studies suggest that causes of autism are neurobiological and genetic (Karande; Sherrill, 2004). Early in fetal development, defects in genes that control brain growth and regulate how neurons communicate may disrupt normal brain development (NINDS, 2006). Also, there is an increased risk of autism among siblings (Sherrill).

Functioning Characteristics

Criteria for a diagnosis of autism vary among professionals and caregivers; consequently, characteristics associated with the spectrum are described from various perspectives. Psychologists and medical professionals tend to use the APA criteria, while educators reference the IDEA (Individuals with Disabilities Education Act) definition, and caregivers advocate for definitions presented through groups like the Autism Society (www.autism-society.org). Regardless, presenting characteristics are the foundation for further diagnostic assessments and range from mild to severe. We will first present the APA descriptors for classic autism or autistic disorders (AD) followed by a brief discussion and comparison with Asperger's disorders (AS).

A distinguishing feature of autism is a lack of play and social interaction skills. The APA (2000) criteria identify four social impairments:

- marked impairment in use of gestures to regulate social interaction
- lack of spontaneous seeking to share interests
- lack of social or emotional reciprocity
- failure to develop peer friendships

Children with autism fail to develop appropriate responsivity to people and to assign appropriate symbolic meaning to objects. They tend to treat people indifferently and interchangeably. A child may accept the extended hand of a parent or a stranger with the same lack of enthusiasm, while simultaneously perseverating on an object held in the other hand. Inappropriate play with objects may involve fixation on a particular feature, like a buzzer, or inappropriate use of the toy such as spinning a record continuously at eye level. They demonstrate a pathological need for sameness and to create order, for example, rearranging the chairs in the room before the activity can begin (Sherrill, 2004).

A second distinguishing feature of autism is impaired verbal and nonverbal communication skills. As identified by the APA diagnostic criteria (2000), this impairment may be manifest in several ways:

- delay or lack of spoken language
- repetitive use of language
- lack of make-believe play or social-imitative play
- inability to initiate or sustain a conversation

A child with autism might communicate by screaming, biting, kicking, or grabbing people or objects. Echolalia, pronoun reversal, and perseveration on words or topics are common. A person might use single words to communicate meanings, and speech is often labored phrases in flat, hollow tones. Speech is used to talk to oneself rather than others (Sherrill, 2004). Sentences spoken by individuals with autism sound like run-on statements **(idioglossia)** because these individuals leave off ends of words or replace a complete word with fragments of the word.

A third distinguishing feature of autism is a restricted repertoire of activities and interests. This is manifest in several ways (APA, 2000):

- stereotyped and repetitive motor mannerisms
- preoccupation with stereotyped and restricted interest patterns
- inflexible adherence to routines or rituals
- preoccupation with parts of objects

Children with autism appear to lack coordination and have odd or inappropriate movements and gestures such as hand clapping, whirling about, hoarding or collecting objects, walking on their toes, making objects spin, or a lack of eye contact with others yet prolonged staring at lights or running water. Interpersonal contact is closed off either by their physical positioning away from others or their idiosyncratic activity with an inanimate object. A response to another person's entry into their "world" may be self-abuse, such as hair pulling, or stimulatory behaviors like darting about aimlessly.

Children with autism display deficits in cognitive skills. For example, an individual might have difficulty comprehending abstract thought processes and logic, yet memorizes pages of material without knowing the meaning of the content. Over- and underresponsiveness to sensory stimuli is displayed when, for example, the child appears to enjoy a siren yet darts about aimlessly when bells ring. Emotional impairments also are exhibited, as when a child walks on a fence with no apparent fear of falling. Social interactions are affected by lack of appropriate nonverbal social behaviors (e.g., eye contact, gestures), and **functional deafness**, in which the child appears not to hear noises and speech (Sherrill, 2004). In the cognitive and physical areas, behavioral assets include the ability to concentrate on routine tasks, good long-term memory, and well-developed motor skills (Hawkins, 2001). Additionally, "the tendency for ritualistic and repetitive behaviors results in an enhanced ability to memorize instructions and follow through with the utmost of accuracy" (Schneider, 2000, p. 13).

As mentioned earlier, individuals with Asperger's syndrome represent expression of autistic characteristics to a lesser degree. Unlike AD there are no significant delays in cognitive and language development, self-help skills, and adaptive behaviors except social interactions and curiosity about the environment (Sherrill, 2004; Smith et al., 2008). One distinguishing feature is an obsessive interest with a single object or topic to the detriment of everything else (NINDS, 2005). Unlike individuals with AD who are withdrawn from the rest of the world, a person with AS is isolated because of his or her poor social skills and narrowed focus. Children experience motor development delays, are awkward, poorly coordinated, emotionally vulnerable, and highly active. As adults, depression and anxiety disorders may become apparent; yet, they manage employment and, with emotional support, maintain an independent lifestyle (NINDS; Smith et al.). Also, some adults with AS were diagnosed with classic autism (AD) as youth (Sherrill).

Purpose of Therapeutic Recreation

Intervention is a lifelong process (Hawkins, 2001). Leisure skills are important because they are building blocks for social interaction and because they enable safe, appropriate use of free time (VanBourgondien & Schopler, 1996). Recreation experiences prepare individuals "to pursue their free time and to achieve an enhanced quality of life" (Coyne & Fullerton, 2004, p. 4). Researchers have determined that play interventions increase language and social skills in children with autism (Thorp, Stahmer, & Schreibman, 1995). An interdisciplinary effort focuses on the development of interactive social and communication skills, appropriate social behaviors, community living skills (Hawkins, 2001), skill generalization, appropriate interactions with the environment, functional cognitive skills, effective motor behaviors, physical well-being, and daily living skills (Coyne & Fullerton). Through leisure education, TRSs aid clients in the development and practice of collateral skills like counting, reading directional signs, and locating community recreation options that support social inclusion. Relationships, social acceptance, and friendships are built around mutual interests and talents like music, art, or computer games (Coyne & Fullerton). TRSs also provide support to families during in-home training (Sherrill, 2004).

Interventions function to reduce perseverations and self-stimulatory behaviors, improve health and wellness, gain control over sensory input, improve relaxation, understand cause-and-effect relationships, develop recreation skills, and acquire the ability to appropriately interact with people and objects. TRSs design therapeutic recreation experiences that require eye contact, attention, imitation, cooperation, expression, and sensory motor awareness. Through structured interventions, displayed energy is redirected into functional physical activity; that is, movement patterns and interactions with leisure objects and peers. The therapeutic experience is planned so clients increase choice-making and self-control while realizing a sense of accomplishment. Verbal and visual feedback help clients associate the consequences of their actions with their behaviors. Clients' nonfunctional behaviors, such as aimless wandering and **atavisms** (reappearance of behaviors or characteristics after a period of absence), are redirected toward strength areas, such as looking at books or listening to music. Clients' strengths in nonlanguage areas like dance, music, and mechanical skills (computer use) become ideal avenues through which to create forms of verbal and nonverbal communication that enhance well-being.

Delivery Settings

Due to the heterogeneous nature of AD and AS, TRSs encounter clients in clinics, schools, private homes, and communities. An innovative option has been the creation of residential farming communities (Schneider, 2000). As Schneider reports, these communities accommodate the needs of people with autism by, for example, reducing excessive noise found in supportive work environments, while building on their assets, like a tendency to take more time to process information, resulting in a slower work pace. Team members include physicians; **psychologists** (specialists holding a master's or doctorate degree in psychology, who have received training in the mental processes and human behavior, and who hold a license to evaluate and treat mental and emotional impairments); speech, physical, and occupational therapists; social workers; and special educators and physical educators. These professionals work with family members to design individual care plans that are implemented through the application of behavioral, functional, and developmental techniques (Hawkins, 2001; Stone, 2007).

Leadership Interaction and Intervention Considerations

To meet individual needs through recreation requires eye contact, attending skills, tolerance for others, and interactive language. The unusual behaviors of people with autism are starting points from which to develop functional and leisure skills. An attraction for assembly-line-like behaviors (repetition) and matching items requires that all objects be durable and retain their appearance after extended use. Even if an object breaks while in use, a client may continue to manipulate it.

TRSs train leisure companions and parents in strategies that enable communication and emotional support, facilitate acceptance of the stereotypic behaviors, and encourage the use of behavior intervention processes. Staff regard companions and parents as team members and encourage them to interact with clients using similar intervention processes to facilitate skill development and generalization. The general leadership techniques outlined below are applicable in a variety of intervention settings.

- The therapeutic recreation environment should be structured and predictable. Expectations are conveyed by performing certain activities at a definite time with the same equipment and in the same location. Consistent routines are maintained (Schneider, 2000). The TRS identifies the sequence of events so clients are better prepared for a change in routine.

- Physical features of the leader and the setting are considered. A colorful cell phone or the sun's shadow is a distraction. The TRS needs to consider such important questions as, Can the objects become harmful? Are there places where clients could hide that might be unsafe?

- During each session, time is planned for learning new skills one-on-one and then practicing in group situations, and for working with "collected" or personal items. The TRS also plans a time and place for relaxation (away from social and sensory overload) and "meltdown" (following outbursts) during intervention.

- Peculiar behaviors like hand flapping that do not negatively affect either the client or others are ignored and/or replaced by, for instance, holding a meaningful object. A calm, predictable, firm, consistent leadership style is reassuring to clients.

- Clients' tolerance levels for touch vary, and they may display **tactile defensiveness** (discomfort caused by touch, one's own or others') (Sherrill, 2004). Physical guidance is used with discretion as clients are helped to acquire skills. As the client completes the skill, the TRS uses verbal and visual input to label the client's actions and feelings. This helps the client comprehend and transfer skills and meanings.

- The TRS first gains eye contact with the client, then presents directions with appropriate choices or options so clients acquire the ability to express likes and dislikes and make satisfying choices. Incorporating models like pictures or photos helps choice-making.

- A variety of leisure skills focusing on the same goal are taught in several settings, including the environment in which they will be used. This fosters skill acquisition, transfer, and generalization. For example, social interaction may begin in the home with family board games. An individual with Asperger's syndrome, for example, who becomes interested in a particular board game or computer game may develop this into a leisure pursuit that involves social interaction and enables lifetime satisfaction (Coyne & Fullerton, 2004).

- Existing and **splinter skills** (skills that are part of a sequence yet can be performed out of sequence), such as organizing or counting, are used by the TRS as points from which subsequent task-analyzed sequences are developed. Continuous naturalistic assessment of the client, environment, and task guide each TRS intervention.

- Incorporating client strengths like fundamental motor skills (running or climbing) or visual awareness (like photos) into interventions leads to a decrease in challenging behaviors and more positive interactions (Coyne & Fullerton, 2004).

- Tactile activities (sensory awareness) such as play with water, sand, textures, and leisure materials (reactive toys) that provide sensory feedback (sound) are reinforcing and sustain enjoyment. Aerobic experiences on motorized exercise equipment minimize stereotypic behaviors (Sherrill, 2004).

- Inclusion provides natural role models, cooperative rather than competitive experiences, preferred experiences, and built-in feedback with achievement recognition. Experiences like walking on the sidewalk along a busy street expose clients to real dangers and, therefore, train clients to respond appropriately. Likewise, physical activity like bicycling or jogging on a trail may replace "darting about" while improving physical health.

- Behavior intervention processes are effective in managing self-injurious and self-stimulatory actions. This approach is most effective when learning is individualized and monitored by each team member as client interactions occur. Contingencies are established—for example, putting on a coat precedes going outdoors; listening with the group to a CD or DVD precedes individual time. Cues such as a finger to the lips help the person maintain appropriate behavior for the duration of skill completion. Inappropriate behaviors are interrupted with abrupt commands like, "Michael, follow me." Token economies and behavior support plans encourage clients to recognize accomplishments. Imitation, modeling, prompting, and fading are also useful in teaching new skills and increasing the amount of positive reinforcement received by the client (Goodman & Williams, 2007; Kurt & Tekin-Iftar, 2008; Sherrill, 2004).

Applying the Therapeutic Recreation Process

Joe is a child with autism who lives with his family. A team of clinical therapists works with Joe to help him develop functional skills, especially ADL, social, and communication skills.

Assessment

Demographic information.   Joe is 7 years old and lives with his parents and one younger sibling at home.

History.   Joe's mother reported that the first nonroutine visit to a pediatrician occurred at 18 months because Joe displayed unusual feeding behaviors. Between 18 and 36 months, both a neurologist and a **psychiatrist** (a licensed physician who specializes in the diagnosis, treatment, and prevention of mental and emotional impairments) examined the child. Joe appeared to be hard of hearing and had no meaningful communication. Autism was diagnosed by 3 years of age.

Present behavior.   Joe is nonverbal, perseverates on handheld objects, darts about aimlessly, claps his hands repetitively, establishes no eye contact, displays limited self-help skills, resists touch, and displays self-abuse when routine is interrupted.

Pediatric, neurological, and social worker assessments contained the above information. The TRS used the Functional Assessment of Characteristics for Therapeutic Recreation (FACTR) to assess the social, communication, and physical deficits resulting from developmental delays (Stone, 2007). Through family therapy sessions, the TRS completed client observations and family interviews. Joe's needs, as listed by the team, include improved sensory awareness, verbal communication, eye contact, self-care, social interaction, and reduction in self-abusive behaviors and perseveration on manipulated objects. Joe's assets are listed as intervention at an early chronological age; interaction with and responsiveness to family members; and gross motor coordination.

Planning

Long-term goal. The long-term goal of Joe's TR intervention is to improve responsiveness to sensory stimuli.

Short-term goal. The short-term goal is to increase awareness of auditory and visual stimuli.

Objective. After one semester in the program, Joe will respond 50% of the time when a visual cue is used to prompt participation in a leisure activity.

Content. Joe will participate in activities that require him to attend to visual and auditory stimuli. Examples include listening to CDs/DVDs and stories, singing, playing musical instruments, and stopping and starting activities with prompts.

Process. The behavior processes that the TRS will use include a contingency reinforcement schedule, ignoring unharmful behaviors, prompting, cuing, and backward chaining. Sensory awareness experiences will use each sense modality.

The TRS will share this information with Joe's family, education personnel, the social worker, and the speech therapist during monthly conferences. Family members will participate in monthly training sessions.

Implementation

Each therapeutic recreation session followed a routine: All children sat in a circle in their assigned positions, and fundamental motor skills were followed by rhythm activities, exploratory (sensory) play, and individual play. All staff recorded the frequency and duration of both appropriate and inappropriate responses to sound and light stimuli.

Evaluation

Team members reported Joe's monthly progress toward each objective of the IEP. Formal revision will occur each school year.

Related Considerations

Impairments associated with autism affect life functions. A team approach facilitates comprehensive intervention. As a team member, the TRS should be familiar with psychopharmacology; behavior interventions; psychological, neurological, developmental, and motor assessments; functional skill training; alternative communication methods; computer applications; seizure management; and family interventions. Deficits in oral and written receptivity, expression, and attending skills limit or preclude the use of standardized instruments. Consequently, observation is a primary assessment/evaluation technique. Also, measurement focuses on specific behavioral ranges, since the desire is often to eliminate one behavior or acquire one new response.

TRSs are alert to clients' safety, especially considering their unawareness of real dangers and of routine interactions with potentially harmful objects. Each interaction and response to a client's behavior is planned and consistent. Progress tends to be slow and challenging. The pervasive nature of autism impacts the client and caregiver during most endeavors. Yet, TRSs have the opportunity to develop social-expressive skills that support treatment objectives and foster quality of life. The Autism Society (www.autism-society.org) offers helpful resources.

SUMMARY

People with learning, motor skills, and communication disorders may or may not exhibit clinical signs of their impairments. These disorders are often discovered as the child is exposed to academic settings and skills. TRSs intervene to remediate social and motor skills and promote improved self-care and self-concepts. Therapeutic experiences also serve as assessment and diagnostic tools when observations occur in the natural environment. Two feeding and eating disorders of infancy and early childhood, pica and rumination, were also discussed. These disorders are viewed as secondary impairments associated with cognitive and physical impairments. Children with pica ingest nonnutritive substances, while those with rumination repeatedly regurgitate food. TRSs use behavior strategies to refocus attention to constructive experiences while also addressing primary intervention goals.

Clients with an ID experience limitations in personal capabilities, adaptive skills, and cognitive functioning that become evident prior to age 18. Individuals with mild degrees of dysfunction may experience difficulty during the academic years yet experience inclusion as adults. People with more severe dysfunctions often experience secondary physical and motor impairments. TRSs intervene to promote physical activity and health; the development of friendships, cognitive, motor, self-care, and leisure skills; and the acquisition of functional skills useful to the management of free time and self-initiated engagement.

People with severe multiple impairments and pervasive developmental disorders like autism are each unique, yet have similar functioning characteristics and needs. We introduce the APA criteria to describe features of classic autism while also presenting Asperger's syndrome, a less severe autism spectrum disorder (ASD). Their impairments affect more than one behavioral area, develop before the age of 18, and usually continue indefinitely. Clients may require some degree of support throughout their lifetime. A team approach works best to deliver individualized, comprehensive programs. Therapeutic recreation goals center on developing functional skills (e.g., communication, motor, and interactive social skills) and leisure skills while eliminating unacceptable or self-abusive behaviors so clients experience meaningful leisure and enhanced quality of life. TRSs incorporate a client's talents, like an interest in music and reactive equipment, to increase self-control and provide a sense of accomplishment. Families need guidance to develop a support network and to learn how to pursue recreation as a unit with or without the impaired sibling. TRSs provide training and support to leisure companions and colleagues to facilitate social inclusion.

Therapeutic interventions are delivered in a structured environment with flexibility, persistence, consistency, firmness, and routine. Progress and successes may come slowly. The TRS should be skilled in the use of behavioral intervention processes, understand the use and side effects of various medications, and know how to use alternative verbal and nonverbal communication methods and assessment and evaluation techniques.

Key Terms

adaptive functioning A criterion of intellectual disabilities that refers to how effectively people cope with life demands and meet standards of independence expected for their age, sociocultural background, and community setting (APA, 2000).

atavism A reappearance of a behavior or characteristic after a period of absence.

atlantoaxial instability Atlantoaxial refers to the joint between the atlas and axis or C1–C2 of the spinal column; instability refers to abnormal mobility caused by lax ligaments and muscles surrounding the joint.

Bliss board A non-oral means of communication requiring the client to point to abstract symbols that are associated with actual experiences or written words; the client combines and modifies the symbols to replicate the English language.

DSM-IV-TR The fourth edition text revision of *The Diagnostic and Statistical Manual of Mental Disorders,* published by the American Psychiatric Association for the purpose of categorizing and classifying behaviors.

dually diagnosed A label used to describe the co-occurrence of two primary dysfunctions.

echolalia The senseless repetition of a word or sentence spoken by another person.

functional deafness The appearance of not hearing noises or speech.

functional skills Skills used in daily routine tasks in an individual's natural environment.

idioglossia Pronunciation of words so that it appears the person is speaking a "personal" language.

kinesthetic approach Instructional method in which the client's limbs are manipulated through an action by the TRS, so the client feels the sensation of movement from the muscles and joints.

perinatal Occurring from the 28th week of pregnancy through 28 days following birth.

perseveration Uncontrollable repetition of a word, phrase, or gesture.

postnatal Occurring after birth, prior to age 18.

prenatal Occurring or existing before birth.

psychiatrist A licensed physician who specializes in the diagnosis, treatment, and prevention of mental and emotional impairments.

psychologist A specialist holding a master's or doctorate degree in psychology who has received training in the mental processes and human behavior and who holds a license to evaluate and treat mental and emotional impairments.

psychometrist A specialist who uses tests to measure mental and psychological ability and functioning.

Rh incompatibility A condition in which the mother's blood is Rh negative and that of the fetus is Rh positive, causing the mother to form antibodies that affect the fetus. This condition results in ID in the absence of immediate blood transfusions.

social worker A professional who collects data on a client's background and relationships, education, work experience, and social contacts. These specialists assist clients and their families with personal concerns such as finances, living arrangements, childcare, and marriage.

splinter skills Skills that are part of a sequence yet can be performed out of sequence.

tactile defensiveness Discomfort caused by one's own touch or the touch of others.

Study Questions

1. For each population discussed in this chapter, identify cognitive, physical, sensory, emotional, social, and communication impairments that affect their participation in therapeutic recreation.

2. Identify the primary objectives of the therapeutic recreation process with each population discussed in this chapter.

3. List at least three specific interaction and intervention processes recommended for use with each population.

4. What assessment and evaluation approaches are used with the case studies presented in this chapter?

5. What personal qualities are recommended for TRSs selecting to work with these populations?

Practical Experiences to Enhance Student Objectives

1. Review human growth and development charts and compare them to an instrument such as the GRST (General Recreation Screening Tool). Document the time intervals and expected behaviors.

2. Develop from the instrument a behavioral assessment tool that would account for necessary functional and recreative behaviors.

3. Interview a psychometrist to determine how baseline data are gathered on clients with more than one major impairment.

4. Visit with a team of professionals who work with individuals with intellectual disabilities (a social worker, psychologist, nurse, and mental health worker, for example) to discuss their perceptions of the needs of their clients and their respective team duties.

5. Observe people with intellectual disabilities in therapeutic recreation programs (attend Special Olympics or a unified sports event or an early intervention program). Develop progress notes on your observations. Describe specific leadership interaction patterns and intervention processes used by the TRS.

6. Visit with a person with an intellectual disability and his or her family members. Participate in their home activities. Observe the manner in which the family members interact as a unit and the adjustments they make in their leisure when the family member with an impairment is present. How is leisure affected? What are the family's assets and needs?

Psychological Impairments

After reading this chapter, students will be able to:

✔ Identify the functional characteristics of the major classifications of psychological disorders according to *The Diagnostic and Statistical Manual of Mental Disorders*, Fourth Edition Text Revision

✔ Discuss the theoretical perspectives and treatment approaches with psychological disorders

✔ Describe the purpose of therapeutic recreation in agencies serving individuals with psychological disorders

✔ Identify the role of the therapeutic recreation specialist in the delivery of services to individuals with psychological disorders

Society defines **abnormal behavior** as any behavior that deviates significantly from the perceived norm. There is a growing tolerance for greater variations in acceptable behavior, which makes it more difficult to label certain patterns of behavior as "abnormal." Despite this problem, social and medical scientists have established a complex classification system for psychological disorders, *The Diagnostic and Statistical Manual of Mental Disorders*, Fourth Edition Text Revision (*DSM-IV-TR*), a publication of the American Psychiatric Association (APA, 2000). Physicians in treatment settings commonly use this system to describe behaviors and define treatment methodologies. Therefore, the purpose of this chapter will be to review the abnormal

Chapter 9 was revised with contributions from Glenda P. Taylor, PhD, CTRS, Longwood University, Farmville, Virginia.

behaviors outlined in the *DSM-IV-TR* together with various treatment approaches and interventions that might be used to assist clients in resolving their personal conflicts. The final sections of the chapter cover the actual application of these concepts to therapeutic recreation.

INTRODUCTION

Mental health services have become increasingly varied, not only in numbers of people experiencing mental illness, but in the education required to understand the complexity of multi-diagnoses, and the demand for innovative treatment interventions to meet the unique needs of each client. Globally, 450 million individuals are receiving mental health services, with 57 million of those in North America [WHO, 2006; National Institute of Mental Health (NIMH), 2006]. Mental disorders are the leading cause of disability among those 15–44 years old, with nearly half of those diagnosed (45%) meeting the criteria for two or more disorders (NIMH). Mental health and mental illness are understood within the context of a constantly changing world. A brief overview of mental health and mental illness precedes a review of the major theories that have attempted to explain the causes and, subsequently, approaches for treating psychological disorders.

The term "mental health" encompasses more than the absence of mental illness. The World Health Organization defines health as the state of complete physical, mental, and social well-being. Positive mental health includes (Jahoda, 1958):

- A positive attitude toward self, which enables a knowledge and acceptance of strengths and limitations and sense of self-identity.
- Growth and the ability to achieve self-actualization.
- Integration or the ability to adaptively respond to the environment, develop a unifying philosophy of life, and manage responses to stressful situations.
- Autonomy, or the ability to function independently, accept responsibility for choices made, and act in a self-directed manner.
- An accurate perception of reality with the capacity for empathy and respect and concern for the wants and needs of others.
- Environmental mastery, which facilitates the ability to achieve a satisfactory role within society in love, work, and play and the ability to adapt, adjust, change, and problem solve when faced with life situations.

Mental health is viewed in the context of our social, cultural, economic, and political environments (Disley, 1997). Behavior that is considered "normal" and "abnormal" is culturally relative; that is, expected behavior is considered to be within the norm of a particular culture (Mobily & McNeil, 2002). Thus, a competent TRS understands the cultural concepts that uniquely define each client (Disley; Townsend, 2006). For example, each culture is unique with respect to communication, space, social organization, time, environmental control, and biological variations (Townsend). A culturally competent professional is sensitive to the client's culture, its rules and beliefs, and is able to translate this into helper behaviors exhibited during the TR process (Dieser & Peregoy, 1999; Lee & Skalko, 1996).

As the severity of mental illness increases and the person's behavior moves away from the perceived cultural norms, the more likely that person is viewed by society as being different. Society tends to ascribe a view toward mental disorders that stigmatizes clients and becomes part of the lived illness experience (Castillo, 1997). A stigma is identified by the WHO (2001) as a hidden burden. Stigma describes a mark of shame, disgrace, or disapproval that results in an individual being shunned or rejected by others. Thus, being stigmatized has a detrimental effect on recovery, ability to access services, the type of treatment and level of support received, and acceptance in the community (WHO).

Our society lives by a set of explicit and implicit norms or rules that identify acceptable and unacceptable behavior. For those living in relatively homogeneous sociocultural environments, there is general agreement as to what norms govern their lives. Others find themselves in more complex, highly pluralistic, or diversified environments where there are great variances among established norms. As our society becomes more diverse, fewer behaviors are classified as abnormal. Recognizing this fact helps us to understand the ever changing, dynamic nature of psychological behavior disorders.

MAJOR THEORETICAL PERSPECTIVES ON PSYCHOLOGICAL DISORDERS

Although there has been great progress in the treatment of people with psychological disorders, the concept of abnormal behavior continues to be unclear. Throughout the age of civilized humanity, the nature and cause of abnormal behavior have been debated. We usually analyze and understand behavior through the use of a system of beliefs called *theories*. There are numerous psychological theories today, all of which claim to describe the nature of human behavior.

One of the earliest explanations of human behavior came from the *physiological or biological* viewpoint and suggested that, like physical impairments, mental impairments had a biological cause with symptoms that were behavioral rather than physiological. This approach suggests that abnormal behavior results from biochemical imbalances in the brain. Under this theoretical model, therapeutic recreation specialists would develop an understanding of the physiological functions of the body and explore the implications of increased physical activity, for example, on these physiological processes. Additionally, this view supports the use of psychotropic drugs and electroconvulsive therapy.

The most purely psychological paradigm is the *psychodynamic or psychoanalytic* theory, which was originated by Sigmund Freud (1856–1939). He and his followers assume that all behavior is the result of unconscious motives. According to psychodynamic theory, anxiety arises from conflict among three ego states labeled the id, ego, and superego. Each person attempts to control unacceptable motives, such as anxiety, by building defenses, such as repression, denial, rationalization, intellectualization, and projection; however, if a person is unable to control anxiety, it will result in some form of neurotic behavior. Therapists seek to resolve the unconscious conflicts through freeing the ego, or rational state of mind, to function more effectively. From a therapeutic recreation perspective, working within the framework of the psychody-namic model involves becoming familiar with the psychodynamic theories and termi-nology. The function of therapeutic interventions would be to assist the client in gaining new insights (associations) into psychic conflicts as well as to provide ego sup-port, or to build up the inner self.

In response to their disenchantment with the introspective approach of psycho-analysis, John B. Watson (1913), Edward Lee Thorndike (1935), and B. F. Skinner (1953) proposed that behavior was the direct result of learned responses that had been reinforced over time. *Learning* or *behavioral* theorists use techniques such as modeling, contingency management, and systematic desensitization to modify maladaptive behavior (see exhibit 3.6 on page 89). Since many of the behavioral techniques are easily learned and adaptable to many situations, therapeutic recreation personnel fre-quently use these techniques to assist clients who seek to modify abnormal or mal-adaptive behavior. For example, identifying and reinforcing more appropriate leisure behaviors is a key aspect of the rehabilitation programs for clients who abuse alcohol or drugs.

Recently, *cognitive behaviorists* have proposed that even more important than the external stimuli are the individuals' perceptions and thoughts about those stimuli. Normal and abnormal behaviors are part of the same continuum. According to this theory, unconventional thoughts or irrational beliefs (Ellis, 1984) and external stimuli move the individual toward abnormal behavior. Behavior is not automatically deter-mined by certain circumstances, but each individual must take full responsibility for how he or she responds to each event or situation. Cognitive therapy has taken several different forms, including reality therapy, assertion training, and biofeedback. TRSs who work in behavioral health settings will likely participate in one or more of these treatment modalities. In addition to advocating and developing a genuine helping relationship, cognitive therapies require practitioners to have specific skills in inter-viewing, monitoring thoughts, reality testing, and teaching of coping skills and relax-ation techniques.

Several recent psychological approaches to mental disorders emphasize the dig-nity of all human beings, their ability to grow and change, their freedom to make choices about their lives, and their personal responsibility for their behaviors. This *humanistic perspective* emphasizes growth and self-actualization rather than a cure or identification of the cause of behavioral disorders (Mobily & MacNeil, 2002). When individuals make poor choices that limit or block their natural movement toward self-actualization, abnormal behavior is the likely outcome (Rogers, 1951; Maslow, 1968). Thus, advocates of the humanistic approach seldom focus on how problems develop but concentrate on interventions that will free the person to make responsible choices.

Although retaining many of the common assumptions of the humanistic theorists including free will and responsibility, *existential theorists* such as Victor Frankl (1963) perceive behavior problems to be related to people's failure to find meaning in life. The therapist's role is to help the client make sense of life's circumstances by placing them in a larger context, a philosophy of life (Davison & Neale, 2001). Finding meaning and purpose in life is often associated with spirituality and religious beliefs. Another popular variation of both the humanistic and existential models is Gestalt therapy, which uses a variety of techniques such as metaphors, attention to nonverbal cues, projecting feelings toward an imaginary person in an empty chair, and "I" messages to help clients understand their needs and facilitate achievement of personal goals.

For therapeutic recreation personnel working within the humanistic or existential frame of reference, the major focus is toward developing authentic relationships with clients. It is through discovering who they are in relation to others that clients will be able to remove impediments to self-fulfillment and personal autonomy. Values clarification exercises, as well as assertion skills exercises or psychodrama techniques, might be specific therapeutic recreation strategies used with these psychological treatment perspectives.

CLASSIFICATIONS OF PSYCHOLOGICAL DISORDERS

One of the central constructs of mental health is the detailed classification system outlined by the American Psychiatric Association (2000) in the *DSM-IV-TR*. This system serves several purposes: distinguishing one psychiatric diagnosis from another; helping clinicians prescribe the most effective treatment; providing a common language among health-care professionals; and exploring the still unknown causes of many mental disorders (Sadock & Sadock, 2003). The classification system has facilitated evidence-based research, and in the case of therapeutic recreation, provides substantiation of the effectiveness of specific interventions to produce certain outcomes.

With the publication of the *DSM-IV-TR,* the American Psychiatric Association incorporated the *International Classification of Diseases* (ICD) developed by the World Health Organization. This ensured compatibility of coding and uniform reporting of national and international health statistics regarding psychological impairments worldwide. These codes are significant identifiers as they are used in insurance billing for reimbursement (Sadock & Sadock, 2003).

Multiaxial Evaluation

The *DSM-IV-TR* has five dimensions, or axes, each of which is used to rate the behavior of an individual (see exhibit 9.1). This multiaxial classification system requires that each individual be rated on each of the five axes to reflect more accurately the nature of the impairment. Axis I consists of clinical disorders and other conditions that may be the focus of clinical attention. Axis II is used to identify personality disorders and mental retardation/ID, and what may be a long-term, underlying problem such as a maladaptive personality type or use of defense mechanisms. The remaining axes are used to identify specific factors that are contributing to or being affected by the disorder. Axis III lists any physical disorder or general medical condition that is present in addition to the mental disorder. Axis IV is used to code the psychosocial and environmental problems that contribute significantly to the development or exacerbation of the current disorder. The clinician assesses the stressors in the person's life against those experienced by the average person from a similar sociocultural background. Information about stressors may be important in formulating a treatment plan that includes either managing the stress or developing coping strategies to deal with the stress. Axis V is used to classify the individual's current level of adaptive functioning in social relationships, occupational functioning, and psychological functioning. This scale provides a baseline of functioning. Therapeutic recre-

Exhibit 9.1   *DSM-IV-TR* Axes of Behaviors

Axis I: Clinical disorders and other disorders that may be a focus of clinical attention
1. Disorders usually first evident in infancy, childhood, or adolescence
2. Substance-related disorders
3. Schizophrenia and other psychotic disorders
4. Delirium, dementia, amnesic, and other cognitive disorders
5. Mood disorders
6. Anxiety disorders
7. Factitious disorders
8. Somatoform disorders
9. Dissociative disorders
10. Sexual and gender identity disorders
11. Eating disorders
12. Sleep disorders
13. Impulse control disorders
14. Adjustment disorders

Axis II: Personality Disorders and Mental Retardation
1. Personality disorders: paranoid, schizoid, schizotypal, histrionic, narcissistic, antisocial, borderline, avoidant, dependent, obsessive-compulsive
2. Mental retardation

Axis III: General Medical Conditions

Axis IV: Psychosocial and Environmental Problems

Axis V: Global Assessment of Functioning (GAF) Scale
The GAF scale, based on a continuum of mental health and mental illness, rates the current level of functioning on a 1–100 scale with 1 = death and 100 = no symptoms.

Excerpted from *The diagnostic and statistical manual of mental disorders* (2000). (4th ed., text revision). Washington, DC: American Psychiatric Association.

ation plans reflect the initial score and record the degree of change during the course of treatment and at discharge.

Although the classifications identified by Axes I and II are important to the TRS, the information gained from Axes III, IV, and V are particularly relevant to consider in a treatment plan. Physical problems or limitations (Axis III) will indicate a certain tolerance for activity or a need to develop physical fitness, for example; stress levels (Axis IV) as well as functional capacities (Axis V) can often be addressed through therapeutic recreation interventions. Thus, an understanding of the *DSM-IV-TR* classifications is an important consideration in planning programs for individuals with psychological disorders.

Because of the comprehensive nature of the *DSM-IV-TR* classification system, it is neither possible nor appropriate to review each classification in detail here. Rather, we will describe the functioning characteristics and treatment approaches that are most commonly experienced by therapeutic recreation personnel. The chapter contents will be organized according to Axis I and Axis II categories. Axis I disorders considered include: those diagnosed in infancy, childhood, and adolescence (excluding Axis II mental retardation/ID, which is discussed in chapter 8); substance-related; schizophrenia; mood; anxiety; dissociative; eating; and, impulse-control disorders. The somatoform, factitious, sexual and gender identity, and adjustment disorders will not be addressed in this text. Axis II personality disorders considered include: paranoid, antisocial, borderline, and passive-aggressive disorders.

In addition to identifying and defining the major symptoms in each category, we will describe those functioning characteristics that are most critical for diagnosis/ needs assessment, treatment/rehabilitation, education, and health promotion/prevention through therapeutic recreation programs. This brief introduction will not be sufficient, however, to develop a thorough understanding of these disorders. It should be noted that the National Council for Therapeutic Recreation Certification (NCTRC) requires all therapeutic recreation students who wish to become certified to complete a course in abnormal behavior.

FUNCTIONING CHARACTERISTICS AND TREATMENT APPROACHES

Considered in this section are the behavioral characteristics and interventions of individuals experiencing diagnoses on Axis I and II. As TRSs develop treatment plans, characteristics most pertinent to each client's situation are assessed to assure realistic goals. TRSs realize a number of variables like medication or family support influence client functioning and response to selected treatment approaches.

Disorders Usually Diagnosed in Infancy, Childhood, and Adolescence

Stages of growth and development are unique to each individual and continue over the life span. The period from birth to adolescence is a time of extremely rapid growth and change. It requires the successful incorporation of an incredible number of developmental skills and activities. Knowledge of the appropriateness of behaviors at each developmental level is vital to planning and implementing therapeutic recreation programs (Townsend, 2006).

Three especially stressful periods in a child's life are between the ages of 6 and 7, 9 and 10, and 14 and 15. It is during these critical times that developmental disorders occur in areas such as motor behavior, eating, sleeping, elimination, speech, emotional development, and social conduct. We quickly recognize the common nature of these developmental problems. As is the case with adult disorders, it is frequently difficult to determine whether the behavior is normal or maladaptive. Further, diagnosing psychological disorders in childhood is not easy because behavior that is appropriate to one developmental stage may not be appropriate to another (Schwartz, 2000). Usually parents, teachers, or physicians make the judgment, basing it on their own norms concerning normal developmental behavior. Davison and Neale (2001) address the psychological disorders of children and adolescents by considering behaviors that are classified as *overcontrolled* and those that are classified as *undercontrolled*.

Overcontrolled Behavior

The most frequent overcontrolled behaviors that tend to become disorders are childhood fears, social withdrawal, depression, and feeding and eating disorders. Phobias may manifest in fear of the dark, ghosts, or animals for example (Townsend, 2006). Sleep disorders (sleepwalking, insomnia, anxiety dreams, night terrors, and the like) are not uncommon experiences for many children, as are elimination problems such as enuresis and encopresis; however, prolonged or recurring problems may indicate that a child has more serious fears and anxieties.

Separation anxiety disorder is excessive anxiety concerning separation from the home or from those to whom the person is attached (APA, 2000). The prevalence of this disorder is estimated at about 4% in children and young adolescents; it is more common in young children (Sadock & Sadock, 2003). Temperament (e.g., extreme shyness) and stressful life events may be related to the development of anxiety disorders. Phobic anxiety may be communicated by parents to the child by direct modeling (Sadock & Sadock). In particular, parents can teach the child to be overanxious about perceived danger. Anticipation of separation may result in tantrums, crying, screaming, complaints of physical problems, and clinging behavior (Townsend, 2006). One study (Lofthouse, Fristad, & Splaingard, 2007) on sleep problems associated with early onset bipolar spectrum disorders, found that over half of the children (N = 133) age 8 to 11 had sleep problems associated with separation anxiety.

Treatment for anxiety in children may include cognitive behavioral therapy (Velting, Setzer, & Albano, 2004), family therapy, education, and pharmacological interventions. The TRS, in concert with other professionals, utilizes group therapy to provide feedback for appropriate social behavior. Same-age peers provide safe environments for the child to learn to give and receive support. Treatment teams use interventions like music and art therapy, creative crafts, and low-organized games to create expressive outlets and develop coping strategies.

Selective *mutism* is a childhood condition in which a child remains completely silent or near silent in social situations, most typically in school. These children usually can speak competently when they are not in a socially stressful situation, or when they are in familiar settings such as their home (Sadock & Sadock, 2003). The disorder appears more common in girls and younger children. These children may be extraordinarily shy and are often teased at school, which may induce them to refuse to go to school. Treatment includes individual therapy, cognitive-behavioral therapy, family therapy, and education sessions that all incorporate behavior management strategies.

Although once a controversial diagnosis, there is consensus that depression exists in childhood and can be differentiated from anxiety syndromes. The criteria to identify a major depressive disorder in children and adolescents are similar to those used with adults (APA, 2000); yet the symptoms may manifest differently in childhood. Characteristics of childhood depression emerge more as the child's age increases, with a higher rate expected in adolescence due to the stressors associated with this age range (Kamphaus & Frick, 1996). Symptoms vary with the age of the child and for young children may include: feeding problems, tantrums, and lack of playfulness and expressiveness; for children ages 3 to 5, self-reproach, phobias, and accident proneness may manifest; from ages 6 to 8, vague somatic complaints, aggressive behavior, clinging to parents, and risk-taking might be exhibited; and for those children ages 9 through 12, excessive worrying, morbid thoughts, and a belief that they somehow have disappointed their parents may be in evidence (Townsend, 2006). Townsend suggests the common denominator of depression in children is loss.

Depression in adolescents may be harder to recognize due to alcohol and substance abuse, which are both likely to be sought first before treatment (Sadock & Sadock, 2003). Victimization and bullying are potential risk factors for adolescent depression and suicide (Klomek, Marrocco, Kleinman, Schonfeld, & Gould 2007). Bipolar disorder emerges during adolescence and significantly impairs functioning in school, with peers, and at home with family (NIMH, 2000). When manic, symptoms include irritability and a tendency to destructive outbursts; and when depressed, symptoms include more physical complaints, frequent absence from school, poor performance at school, running away, complaining, unexplained crying, social isolation, poor communication, and extreme sensitivity to rejection and failure.

Treatment for severe depression or when there is imminent danger of suicide is hospitalization; pharmacological interventions are used for moderate to severe depressive disorders with follow-up provided through outpatient services. McArdle (2007) recommends cognitive-behavioral and interpersonal psychotherapy as the treatment of choice. Dieser and Ruddell (2002) support the use of attribution retraining with hospitalized youth. Therapeutic interventions are designed to alleviate the child's symptoms and strengthen the child's coping and adaptive skills. Social skills training, problem-solving strategies, and cognitive retraining seem to help children identify and express feelings and also incorporate experiences that contribute to a sense of mastery, competence, and self-esteem (Kaslow & Thompson, 1998).

Feeding and eating disorders that arise during childhood and adolescence often reflect emotional problems. Obesity (excess body fat due to overeating) may be the result of a response to stress or simply a normal activity associated with a child's family situation (refer to chapter 7 for an in-depth discussion on obesity). Disorders of anorexia nervosa and bulimia nervosa are first observed in adolescence or early adulthood. The individual who experiences anorexia nervosa does not eat for fear of gaining weight. The individual with bulimia nervosa, on the other hand, engages in episodes of overeating followed by induced vomiting or use of laxatives to purge the body of the excess food. These disorders are often linked with depression. Many theories have been proposed to explain anorexia and bulimia, including biological, psychodynamic, and family influences, like the mother's role in responding to the child's physical and emotional needs with food; spousal conflict; and power and control issues. Further discussion on eating disorders is addressed later in this chapter. Two childhood feeding and eating disorders, pica and rumination associated with ID, are presented in chapter 8.

Behavioral, cognitive, and humanistic therapies have all been used to address these complex problems, but much remains unknown. Action-oriented therapies, such as assertiveness training, physical confidence therapies (Beukema, 1977), and adventure therapy (Kaptian, 2003) may be used to promote appropriate self-expression and feelings of control. For the younger child, individual counseling with play therapy techniques are valuable. For the older child, social activities such as games and group discussions with other clients offer opportunities for social success and growth (Miller & Jake, 2001).

Undercontrolled Behavior

Attention-deficit and conduct disorders are the most common undercontrolled behavior disorders. Attention-deficit disorders (ADD) may include hyperactivity

(ADHD), impulse control problems, and attention problems. ADHD is a neurobehavioral syndrome characterized by persistent inattention, distractibility, over-arousal, and impulsivity and is associated with low self-esteem and impaired academic achievement (Nickel & Desch, 2000). ADHD usually becomes evident in preschool or early elementary years and is more prevalent in boys than in girls, with the ratio ranging from 2 to 1 to as much as 9 to 1 (Nickel & Desch; Sadock & Sadock, 2003). Children with ADHD manifest a variety of impairments in executive functions and a poor working memory (Nickel & Desch). Most research points to a physiological basis for ADD and ADHD, and therefore the most effective treatment has been the use of central nervous system (stimulant) drugs such as Ritalin. The outcomes of this treatment include an increased attention span, control of hyperactive behavior, and improvement in learning ability. Psychosocial interventions such as social skills groups, training for parents, and behavioral interventions at school and home are often efficacious in the overall management of children with ADHD (Abikoff & Hechtman, 1996; Sadock & Sadock; Welsh, Burcham, DeMoss, Martin, & Milich, 1997).

Disruptive behavior disorders include oppositional defiant disorder (ODD) and conduct disorder. These disorders result in impaired social and academic function in a child. ODD is more prevalent in children who have had a succession of different caregivers and in families that use harsh, inconsistent, and neglectful parenting practices (Nickel & Desch, 2000). ODD is characterized by a pattern of negative, defiant, disobedient, and hostile behavior toward authority figures (APA, 2000). Conduct disor-

A TRS can help a defiant youth learn to deal more appropriately with authority figures.

der is a set of behaviors that evolves over time; is usually characterized by aggression and violation of the rights of others; and tends to be more common in boys (Sadock & Sadock, 2003). Conduct disorder is not easy to treat as an isolated problem; and the co-morbid presence of ADHD makes its management more complicated (Glanzman & Blum, 2007). Chaotic family situations and poor role models contribute to these disorders, which exacerbate treatment issues. Children who exhibit these behaviors usually have not developed a strong moral sense of right and wrong or achieved a sense of responsibility for their actions (Ryall, 1974). The most promising treatment involves interventions that include comprehensive therapy services in the community targeting the child, the family, the school, and in some cases the peer group (Glanzman & Blum; Borduin et al., 1995; Sadock & Sadock). Effective strategies include behavioral, cognitive, family systems, and case management techniques that emphasize individual and family strengths, and action-oriented interventions that require daily or weekly efforts by family members (Henggeler, Schoenwald, Borduin, Rowland, & Cunningham, 1998). Individual psychotherapy and pharmacological interventions for symptoms that contribute to conduct disorders are also used.

Substance-Related Disorders

Substance-related disorders contribute to more deaths, disabilities, and illnesses than any other preventable health condition (Kunstler, 2001; Mobily & MacNeil, 2002; Sadock & Sadock, 2003). Alcoholism is the third leading cause of preventable death in the United States (Townsend, 2006). Alcohol remains the most commonly consumed substance in combination with other substances by users age 12 and over. Illicit drug use and heavy alcohol use are associated with depression and anxiety disorders. People who are homeless, legal offenders, those infected with the HIV virus, children of abusers, and individuals with antisocial personality disorders exhibit higher incidences of substance-related disorders. A high prevalence of additional psychiatric disorders is found among persons seeking treatment for alcohol, cocaine, and opioid dependence (Sadock & Sadock). People who rely on the use of substances for nonmedical purposes and who experience diminished psychological and physical functioning are identified in the *DSM-IV-TR* as persons with substance-related disorders (APA, 2000).

Drug and alcohol abuse impact the individual, the family, and society. Research has identified a hereditary factor involved in developing substance-use disorders, in particular with alcoholism, but less so with other substances (Townsend, 2006). Children of alcoholics are three times more likely than other children to become alcoholics (Harvard Medical School, 2001). Individuals who are raised in families with chemical-dependent persons learn patterns of dysfunctional behavior that carry over to adult life: These dysfunctional behavior patterns are termed co-dependence (Townsend).

Drug and alcohol use occur during leisure and are commonly considered to enable "having a good time." Dieser and Voight (1998) note "the greatest potential for substance abuse among young people and adults is during their leisure time" (p. 79). Preliminary results of one investigation suggest "that individuals expect that drinking will enhance their leisure experiences" (Carruthers, 1993, p. 242). The American Medical Association recognized chemical dependence as a disease in 1956 (Blakely &

Drug and alcohol abuse negatively impacts individuals,
families, and society.

Dattilo, 1993). People in treatment for substance abuse require comprehensive interventions that address "social, psychological, familial, and physical dysfunction issues
which vary according to the type and severity of drug consumption" (Malkin, Voss,
Teaff, & Benshoff, 1993/94, p. 40).

The *DSM-IV-TR* presents 11 classes of substances from which dependence or
abuse results: alcohol, amphetamines, caffeine, cannabis, cocaine, hallucinogens,
inhalants, nicotine, opioids, phencyclidine (PCP), and sedatives. Two additional classifications identify disorders resulting from (1) multiple substance use or **polysubstance dependence** (use of three or more drugs with none being dominant), and (2)
disorders attributed to, for example, steroid use, classified as "other" or "unknown"
substance-related disorders. Several terms are used to describe the features of substance-related disorders (APA, 2000).

Substance dependence is a cluster of cognitive, behavioral, and physiological
symptoms that indicate continual use of the substance, resulting in tolerance, withdrawal, and compulsive drug-taking behavior. Use of the substance continues despite
knowledge of its effects on daily functions and decline in significant functions like
work and recreation.

Tolerance varies across substance type and with initial use and is defined as the
need for increasingly larger or more frequent doses of a substance in order to obtain the
desired effects originally produced by a lower or less frequent dose (Townsend, 2006).

Withdrawal also varies with substance type and is a maladaptive behavior change
resulting when blood or tissue concentrations of a substance decline, often resulting in
the consumption of the substance to relieve or avoid unpleasant physiological and
cognitive effects.

Substance abuse results from repeated use of substances and causes failure in role
obligations; multiple legal, social, and interpersonal problems; and the potential for

physically harmful situations. An individual who abuses a substance is more likely to have recently begun to consume the substance yet less likely to exhibit signs of tolerance or withdrawal symptoms upon its disuse.

Addiction is a behavioral pattern characterized by continued involvement associated with acquiring, using, and recovering from the substance's effects; and there is a tendency to revert to drug use after attempts to quit or withdraw. Addiction is the final step in the progression from drug use through tolerance to abuse then dependency and eventually addiction.

Although individuals who consume substances do so primarily for the same reason—to change their mood and feelings—the body's response to a particular drug(s) is influenced by several individual factors. Quantity or dosage and the time it takes for the drug to travel and be absorbed into an individual's body affect the response he or she experiences. A person with a small frame and a low body weight experiences a more intense response to substances than does a person who is larger or heavier. Likewise, younger children and older adults experience more severe reactions than do other individuals. Use of substances may or may not progress to addiction. Factors like familial patterns, availability of the substances, and enabling systems like peers and the attitudes of significant others are powerful determinants.

Chronic drug users who enter treatment have a variety of medical and psychological needs. Initially, the withdrawal of drugs from their bodies is accompanied by physical and emotional behaviors like convulsions, tremors, disorientation, and anorexia that require medical monitoring. Since drug use results from a variety of influences, including anxiety, dysfunction in the family, depression, desire for sensation and control, and personality and attention deficits, these factors must also be addressed. The functioning characteristics most evident with each substance class are summarized in the following paragraphs.

Alcohol

People who depend on or abuse alcohol tend to be dependent on or abuse other substances like cannabis, cocaine, heroin, amphetamines, sedatives, or nicotine (APA, 2000). Symptoms of use include: relaxation, loss of inhibitions, lack of concentration, drowsiness, slurred speech, and sleep (Townsend, 2006). Literature suggests there are common characteristics associated with optimal leisure experiences and alcohol consumption. "Individuals do most of their drinking in their leisure and . . . they anticipate that drinking will create positive effects" (Carruthers & Hood, 1994, p. 9). As a consequence, the TRS must consider the person's reliance on alcohol to create feelings of enjoyment, control, and spontaneity as interventions are planned. Initial mood and behavioral changes occur with a **blood alcohol level (BAL)** of .05% (the equivalent of a 150-pound person consuming two drinks in succession). At a BAL of .2% noticeable loss of motor skills and emotional control are present, and unconsciousness occurs at .3 to .4% BAL. Chronic heavy drinking results in cirrhosis of the liver, heart disease, cancer, gastrointestinal irritations, sexual dysfunction, and irreversible brain and nervous system damage. Moreover, in a pregnant woman, the developing infant may be born with a group of symptoms known as Fetal Alcohol Syndrome (FAS). The diagnosis of FAS is defined by four criteria: maternal drinking during pregnancy, a characteristic facial appearance, growth retardation, and brain damage.

Amphetamines

Like cocaine, amphetamines are synthetic drugs that stimulate the central nervous system (CNS) and have outcomes similar to those that naturally occur with an adrenaline rush. With use symptoms include: hyperactivity, agitation, euphoria, insomnia, and loss of appetite (Townsend, 2006). Doctors frequently prescribe amphetamines (such as Ritalin) to treat narcolepsy, epilepsy, obesity, and ADHD. Persistent use of amphetamines results in a diminution of its pleasurable effects, yet an individual who abuses amphetamines will continue their use even in the presence of adverse effects (aggressive behavior, for instance). Small doses of amphetamines cause a heightened sense of well-being, restlessness, hostility, and aggressiveness; chronic use results in mood changes, malnutrition, hallucinations, suicidal ideation, heart problems, compulsive and meaningless behavior, and social isolation. Chronic users of amphetamines take alcohol and opiates to reduce the unpleasant "jittery" feelings; thus, multiple dependencies are common among people who use amphetamines. Symptoms of an overdose include cardiac arrhythmia, headache, convulsions, hypertension, rapid heart rate, coma, and possible death (Townsend).

Caffeine

The average caffeine intake per person in America is 200 milligrams per day (APA, 2000). Some individuals who drink large amounts of coffee experience dependence-like characteristics and exhibit tolerance, yet the symptoms do not clinically impair functioning. People who drink two to three cups of brewed coffee per day display restlessness, nervousness, diuresis, and gastrointestinal complaints. Increased amounts are associated with cardiac arrhythmia and the exacerbation of anxiety and somatic symptoms.

Cannabis

Marijuana and hashish are probably the most widely used illicit substances in the world (APA, 2000) and often are used in combination with other substances like nicotine, alcohol, and cocaine. Cannabis users tend to be younger than those who consume other substances. Symptoms of use include relaxation, talkativeness, lowered inhibitions, euphoria, and mood swings. Use begins with a "high" feeling followed by lethargy; impaired memory, judgment, and motor performance; and distorted sensory perceptions. Chronic heavy use may result in weight gain, emphysema, and the risk of developing malignant disease.

Cocaine

Like amphetamines, cocaine is a central nervous system stimulant that increases the body's motor activity, respiratory rate, blood pressure, and body temperature. *Crack* is a popular form of highly concentrated cocaine that is 10 times more powerful than cocaine. With both cocaine and crack, the high wears off relatively quickly and users then crash, feeling depressed and requiring rest to recuperate. This "rush-crash" cycle creates a need for frequent dosing to maintain the "high," which quickly leads to addiction. Chronic use may cause depression, seizures, and respiratory and/or cardiac failure. Cocaine and crack use during pregnancy may cause harm to the fetus. A cocaine-addicted baby experiences problems during infancy and childhood like heart failure or malformations, short-term memory loss, hyperactivity, speech delays, and poor motor development and play skills.

Hallucinogens

Such drugs alter mood, thought, and the senses (usually vision); they comprise a diverse group of substances, including lysergic acid diethylamide (LSD)—an odorless, colorless chemical—and substances such as mescaline. More than any other substance, the effects of hallucinogens vary with each experience and from use to use. Hallucinogens impair an individual's thinking processes and memory as well as the ability to distinguish past and present. Perceptual changes develop during or shortly after use and abate after several months but can last longer; users' reality testing remains intact (that is, they are aware that hallucinogens cause abnormal perceptions). Symptoms presented with an overdose include agitation, extreme hyperactivity, violence, hallucinations, psychosis, convulsions, and possible death (Townsend, 2006).

Inhalants

Most inhalants depress the central nervous system, which causes an individual to experience intoxication. Symptoms last 60–90 minutes. Large doses may result in death from CNS depression or cardiac arrhythmia (Townsend, 2006). Gasoline, glue, paint, paint thinners, and spray paints are examples of inhalants that produce psychoactive and physical effects. Inhalants reach the lungs and bloodstream very rapidly, causing euphoria, nausea, and coughing. Extended use of inhalants leads to memory loss, fatigue, depression, brain damage, coma, and weight loss. Inhalants are legal, inexpensive, and easy to access. They are most commonly used by adolescents in group settings. Tolerance for inhalants may develop, yet withdrawal symptoms are usually fairly mild (Sadock & Sadock, 2003). Intoxication usually requires no medical attention and resolves spontaneously (Sadock & Sadock).

Nicotine

The World Health Organization (WHO) estimates there are one billion smokers worldwide, with tobacco use killing more than five million people a year. Up to half of current smokers will eventually die of a tobacco-related disease (WHO, 2010b). All forms of tobacco use can result in nicotine dependence and withdrawal. Moreover, smokers are more likely than nonsmokers to be heavy drinkers and illicit drug users. Coronary heart disease, cancer, and chronic obstructive pulmonary disease (COPD) are leading causes of long-term complications and death related to tobacco use. And, individuals who have never smoked but are chronically exposed to secondhand smoke are at increased risk of lung cancer and heart disease. Withdrawal symptoms begin within 24 hours of last use and decrease in intensity over days, weeks, or sometimes longer; they include craving for nicotine, irritability, anger, frustration, anxiety, difficulty concentrating, restlessness, decreased heart rate, increased appetite, weight gain, tremor, headaches, and insomnia (Townsend, 2006). A smoker may forego social and recreational activities because the activities occur in smoke-free settings.

Opioids

Persons with opioid dependence use heroin most widely. Opioids (or narcotics) like heroin and morphine are medically prescribed as analgesics (pain relief), anesthetics, and cough suppressants. They relieve pain, diarrhea, and dysentery, yet they may also cause mild anxiety, insomnia, and/or fear. People using physician-prescribed opioids may become dependent upon or abuse the drug. Users consume larger and larger doses to achieve the same effects; eventually, regardless of dosage, the pleasurable effects are not realized and the drug is consumed to avoid withdrawal symptoms. Users are unaware of or ignore potentially harmful situations in their environment and may place themselves in dangerous situations. Opioid users typically develop tremors, seizures, and impaired memory. Prolonged use may result in a coma, respiratory depression, unconsciousness, and death.

Phencyclidine (PCP)

Also known as angel dust, PCP is a stimulant, depressant, and hallucinogen often found mixed in other street drugs. PCP is associated with 3% of substance abuse deaths and 32% of substance-related emergency room visits nationally (Sadock & Sadock, 2003). A person who first attempts to use PCP will either find the substance too unpredictable and abandon it or will quickly become a heavy user. Heavy users also tend to use alcohol, cocaine, and amphetamines. Those who become dependent on PCP attribute their continued use to its euphoric effect rather than to an avoidance of withdrawal symptoms. Repeated use of PCP leads an individual to lose coordination, dissociate with his or her environment, experience memory loss and feelings of apathy, demonstrate aggressive behavior, and, at higher doses, experience hallucinations, seizures, and respiratory depression.

Sedatives

Also known as hypnotics or anxiolytics, these substances are sleeping pills and benzodiazepines commonly prescribed for anxiety. Those who abuse sedatives may begin by gradually extending a prescription against medical advice or by increasing the dosage and frequency of a prescription. Sedatives are sometimes used to alleviate unwanted effects of other substances like cocaine or amphetamines. Hypnotics impair one's motor function, memory, concentration, and judgment and may also result in persistent delusions, tremors, and severe depression leading to suicide attempts.

Polysubstance dependence

People who use three or more substances—excluding caffeine and nicotine—but do not rely on one as the dominant drug may develop dependence. Users of alcohol, marijuana, cocaine, and sedatives are likely candidates for polysubstance dependence.

Other (unknown) substance-related disorders

This APA category is reserved for substances not listed in any of the other areas. Anabolic steroids, **over-the-counter (OTC)** drugs, and prescription medications have psychoactive effects. Although the use of steroids causes immediate increase in muscle size and strength, effects are temporary and with repeated use may result in lack of energy, aggressive behavior, depression, coronary heart disease, and cancer. Over-the-counter drugs relieve minor symptoms of illness, yet when used longer than needed can lead to respiratory difficulties, hepatitis, and gastrointestinal disorders.

Schizophrenic Disorders

The most severe and one of the least understood of the psychological disorders is schizophrenia (Sadock & Sadock, 2003). "An estimated 1% of the world's population experiences this disorder" (Mobily & McNeil, 2002, p. 87). Experts believe that schizophrenia seems to be the result of several related psychological and biological factors. Some individuals have a strong genetic link to the illness, whereas others may have only a weak genetic basis which gives further credence to the notion of multiple causations (Townsend, 2006).

The distinguishing feature of this disorder is the person's inability to perceive, process, and then respond to reality or environmental situations. With schizophrenia the various psychic functions seem to become dissociated from each other, causing severe disorganization of thinking, feeling, perceiving, and interacting with the environment. Although the primary symptom of schizophrenia is the inability to think coherently, there are several other symptoms that demonstrate the severe nature of this disorder (see exhibit 9.2). Recent assessment techniques emphasize using excessive "positive" symptoms, such as hallucinations, delusions, and bizarre behaviors, and "negative" symptoms, such as flattened emotions, poverty of speech, apathy, and an inability to experience pleasure in leisure activities or social relationships, to more accurately distinguish between various schizophrenic disorders (APA, 2000).

Antipsychotic medications and drugs called "atypical antipsychotics" have been used to modify or control the symptoms associated with schizophrenia. However, 10–20% of individuals who take antipsychotic medications have significant long-term side effects, which cause secondary problems like **tardive dyskinesia** (a condition that is characterized by various involuntary movements like tongue thrusting or muscle twitching) ("Long-term risks," 1993; Sweet et al., 1995). Other side effects, such as extreme sensitivity to solar rays, can result in critical conditions, such as severe burns. Therefore, TRSs need to be extremely cautious when working with individuals who are on these medications. In spite of some of the negative side effects, taking medication may be the difference between maintaining a moderate level of functioning and becoming totally disoriented.

Psychosocial therapies include a variety of methods to increase social abilities, self-sufficiency, practical skills, and interpersonal communication (Sadock & Sadock, 2003). A combination of drug treatment and group therapy has shown to be effective with outpatients. The social interaction, sense of cohesiveness, identification, and

---

Exhibit 9.2   Common Symptoms of Schizophrenia

Disorders of Thought and Language
  Delusions
  Incoherence
  Loose associations
  Lack of insight

Disorders of Perception and Attention
  Distractibility
  Hallucinations (especially auditory)

Disorders of Affect
  Blunted or flat affect
  Inappropriate affect

Disorders of Motor Behavior
  Bizarre, repetitive behaviors
  Marked hyperactivity or inactivity

Impairments in Life Functioning
  Social withdrawal
  Lack of social skills
  Avoidance of eye contact
  Difficulty in holding job

Adapted from Davison, G. C., & Neale, J. M. (2001).

reality testing achieved within the group setting have proven to be effective therapeutic processes (Sadock & Sadock).

Behaviorists have used social and vocational skills training, role modeling, and reinforcement programs to support and strengthen the appropriate behaviors of clients with schizophrenia while ignoring the psychotic or inappropriate behaviors (Mueser & Liberman, 1995; Paul & Menditto, 1992). When compared with insight-oriented treatment or milieu treatment, social reinforcement seems to provide better results, especially for individuals who have less severe symptoms or those controlled with medication.

Family-oriented therapists have focused on communication patterns and interactions among family members. Family education that reduces the level of expressed emotions, and thus decreases stress in the home, has been shown to be an effective treatment technique, especially in reducing relapse (Davison & Neale, 2001; Ho, Black, & Andreasen, 2003; Sadock & Sadock, 2003). TRSs can contribute to improved family interaction by initiating leisure education programs that involve family members in common leisure interests that will facilitate positive social and emotional outcomes.

Mood Disorders

Mood disorders (formerly *affective disorders*) encompass a large group of disorders in which pathological mood and related disturbances dominate functioning (Sadock & Sadock, 2003). Extremes in the emotions of sadness and elation become a source of distress if they are protracted over a period of time. Mood disorders are best considered syndromes consisting of a cluster of symptoms sustained over weeks to months, which represent a marked departure from a person's habitual functioning and tend to recur, often in periodic or cyclical fashion (Sadock & Sadock).

Mood disorders appear as mania or depression according to the respective positive or negative dimension of the moods. Their symptoms affect a person's thinking, feeling, motivation, and physiological functioning. Manic behavior generally consists of hyperactivity and endless energy; depression involves a mood of despair, hopelessness, and heaviness. Depression may appear in different forms depending on the age of the individual, but it usually involves reduced motivation and energy; disturbances of appetite, sleep, and sex drives; difficulties in thinking; recurrent thoughts of death or suicide; psychomotor retardation or agitation; melancholy; and feelings of worthlessness and guilt (Davison & Neale, 2001; Sadock & Sadock, 2003).

Bipolar disorder involves mood swings from mania to depression and affects approximately 5.7 million American adults, or about 2.6% of the U.S. population age 18 and older in a given year (NIMH, 2006 revised). The manic phase of the illness frequently occurs first, followed by a depressive phase, possibly after a more normal interlude. This cycle may recur several times over short or long periods of time. Unlike major depression, bipolar disorder is much less common, occurs equally in both sexes with age of onset in late adolescence or the early twenties, and has a strong link with heredity (that is, individuals who experience this disorder are more likely to have had parents or relatives who had a similar illness) (Mobily & McNeil, 2002).

Research suggests that a cognitive-behavioral intervention that reduces stress by adjusting irrational thoughts and improving interpersonal behaviors can be effective in modifying mood swings (Basco & Rush, 1996). However, physiological processes are a well-known component of mood disorders and most treatment regimens include some form of pharmacological intervention. Common medical treatment for bipolar disorder consists of one of several "mood-stabilizing" drugs including lithium and volproate. The effect of the drug is to balance the highs and lows of mood swings. Clients frequently discontinue this medication—against medical advice—because they "feel fine" and no longer sense the need to take it. In general, noncompliance is a major issue among individuals with bipolar disorder due to the uncomfortable medication side effects, denial of illness, and co-morbidity ("Treatment Challenges in Bipolar Disorder," 2006). The inevitable result is a recurrence of the bipolar cycle, until once again the client's moods can be maintained by medications. Individual, group, and family therapies and family psycho-education are recommended as interventions to reduce relapse (Fristad, Goldberg-Arnold, & Gavazzi, 2002); while cognitive therapy is recommended as secondary to pharmacological treatment, particularly with a mania diagnosis (Lehmann, 2003; Townsend, 2006).

Anxiety Disorders

A common description of anxiety is a subjective state of fear and apprehension that stimulates changes in the physiological and cognitive functioning. Low levels of anxiety are adaptive and can provide the motivation required for survival. Anxiety becomes problematic when the individual is unable to prevent the anxiety from escalating to a level that interferes with the ability to meet basic needs (Townsend, 2006). The *DSM-IV-TR* describes 13 different anxiety disorders experienced by 40 million American adults ages 18 and older in a given year. Each type of anxiety disorder presents different maladaptive behavior patterns, for instance: phobic disorders reflect persistent, abnormally intense fears; panic disorders involve sudden, periodic attacks of intense anxiety; generalized anxiety disorders exhibit a "free-floating" anxiety that tends to pervade and interfere in all areas of life; obsessive-compulsive disorders manifest behaviors such as repeated ritualistic hand washing; and post-traumatic stress disorders result from a jarring external event to the individual, such as rape, natural disasters (floods, tornadoes, fire), or combat. "Psychic numbing," or shock, is often the initial response to a catastrophe; this is followed by a passive, suggestible stage and subsequently, for most people, by recovery. Individuals who experience these disorders are in touch with reality and are usually able to cope with normal life functions depending on the degree of their emotional dysfunction. However, physiological distresses, such as headaches, backaches, insomnia, accelerated pulse rate, and memory loss may accompany generalized anxiety disorders and may severely limit an individual's participation in daily activities. Anxiety disorders are frequently present with depressive disorders or substance abuse (NIMH, 2006 revised). For instance, there is a danger of persons with panic disorders self-medicating (i.e., using alcohol and illegal substances), often as a result of not understanding that a panic disorder is a serious disorder (Goodwin & Pine, 2002). Two anxiety disorders with which TRSs intervene in mental health settings are considered more in depth.

Obsessive-Compulsive Disorder (OCD)

This disorder usually has an onset during puberty or earlier, depending on gender and environment (Stein, 2002). Associated with OCD are major depressive disorders and social phobias (Sadock & Sadock, 2003). The essential feature of OCD is recurrent obsessions or compulsions sufficiently severe to cause marked distress to the person. The most common compulsions involve washing and cleaning, counting, checking, requesting or demanding assurances, repeating actions, and ordering (APA, 2000). The individual recognizes that the behavior is excessive or unreasonable . . . yet the relief from discomfort that it provides compels the person to continue the act (Townsend, 2006).

OCD is associated with moderate to severe interference with socializing, family relations, and ability to study/work; also decreases in self-esteem and suicidal thoughts (Lochner et al., 2003). OCD is managed with pharmacotherapy and responds reasonably quickly with changes in thought and behavior patterns (Gold-Steinberg & Logan, 1999). Successful interventions include cognitive behavioral therapy, and group, family, occupational, recreational, and play therapies. Family psychotherapy is particularly beneficial in the treatment of children and adolescents, because it shows parents how to stop participating in children's rituals while providing education and support for the family (Gold-Steinberg & Logan). A psychodynamic approach aids individuals with OCD to become aware of the disorder's impact on self-image and others' perceptions of them. Shame and secrecy associated with OCD in children interfere with appropriate peer relationships and social development (Gold-Steinberg & Logan). By trying to hide obsessions or compulsions, children may hesitate to engage in social interaction. Therapeutic recreation and play provide children the opportunity to relax and feel free to "let go" of control and compulsions.

Posttraumatic Stress Disorder

According to the *DSM-IV-TR*, posttraumatic stress disorder (PTSD) is the development of "symptoms following exposure to an extreme traumatic stressor involving direct personal experience . . . or witnessing . . . or learning about unexpected or violent death, serious harm, or threat of death or injury experienced by a family member or other close associate" (p. 463). Examples of traumatic stressors include military combat, experiencing violent personal assault, being kidnapped or taken hostage, being tortured, being incarcerated as a prisoner of war, experiencing natural or manmade disasters, surviving severe automobile accidents, being diagnosed with a life-threatening illness, rape, and experiencing a burning building (Sadock & Sadock, 2003; Townsend, 2006). While this disorder can occur at any age, approximately 7.7 million American adults age 18 and older have PTSD (NIMH, 2006 revised).

Persons with PTSD re-experience the traumatic event in their dreams and in their daily thoughts; they are determined to evade anything that would bring the event to mind; they may undergo a numbing of responsiveness along with a state of hyper-arousal, depression, anxiety, and cognitive difficulties such as poor concentration (Davidson & Foa, 1993; Sadock & Sadock, 2003). Memories, often triggered by a traumatic reminder, arise when the person is least expecting them: These are referred to as "flashbacks" (a reliving of the event) and they may cause intense feelings of fear, helplessness, and horror. Some clients experience "survivor's guilt" or dysfunctional grieving (Townsend, 2006).

PTSD can occur in children and adolescents; prevalence rates are likely underestimated (Sadock & Sadock, 2003). The stressors in children may be a sudden, single incident or chronic trauma such as physical or sexual abuse. Children witnessing family or other types of violence may exhibit nightmares, physical symptoms such as stomachaches and headaches, and regressive behaviors such as enuresis. Some children may withdraw from play experiences, others are hyper-vigilant during play, and some act out (Taylor, 1985). Behaviors evident in children and adolescent victims of trauma include sexual acting out, substance abuse, and delinquency (Sadock & Sadock). Because children do not have coping mechanisms (as do adults) to deal with trauma, they may show symptoms of PTSD for one or more years. Play therapy, in particular "traumatic play" (a specific form of re-experiencing), consists of repetitive acting out of the trauma or trauma-related themes in order to develop coping strategies (Sadock & Sadock).

With adults, treatment intends to provide support, encouragement to discuss the event, and education about a variety of ways to cope (Nicholson, 2004; Sadock & Sadock, 2003). Additional interventions include cognitive-behavioral therapy, individual psychotherapy, and pharmacotherapy (Hitt, Kitchner, & Bisson, 2004); trauma-based counseling (Hodges, 2003); and debriefing after the event (Miller, 2004). When combined with pharmacotherapy, relaxation therapy reduces numbing and is an effective intervention, particularly when it includes breathing retraining and muscle relaxation (Ruzek et al., 2007). Technology in the form of *virtual reality exposure therapy and training* and driving simulators are being used to re-create different experiences (accidents) so clients can gain coping skills ("Post-traumatic stress disorder," 2007; Rowe, 2007).

Dissociative Disorders

One somewhat rare disorder that recreation therapists may encounter is that of dissociative identity disorder (DID)—formerly multiple personality disorder. Persons with dissociative disorders have lost the sense of having a single consciousness. They feel they have no identity, are confused about who they are, or experience multiple personalities (Sadock & Sadock, 2003). Within this category, APA (2000) identifies five disorders: dissociative amnesia, dissociative fugue, dissociative identity disorder, depersonalization disorder, and dissociative disorder, not otherwise specified. *DSM-IV-TR* characterizes DID as "the presence of two or more distinct identities or personality states that recurrently take control of behavior [accompanied by] an inability to recall important personal information that is too extensive to be explained by ordinary forgetfulness" (p. 526). Women tend to receive this diagnosis more than males (Sadock & Sadock). Abreaction and switching occur with DID. An *abreaction* is an emotional release or discharge after recalling (reliving) a painful experience (Sadock & Sadock). *Switching* (in a matter of seconds) from one personality to another is often triggered by psychosocial stress. The dominant personality at any given time determines the person's behavior. Suicide attempts are present with DID and the alternate identities engage in deviant behaviors of which there is no memory (Fink, 2005). Persons with DID are often mistakenly misclassified with other disorders such as depression, borderline and antisocial personality disorders, schizophrenia, epilepsy, and bipolar disorders (Townsend, 2006). Children may learn to dissociate when abuse is inflicted by the parent or primary caregiver from whom the child cannot physically escape (Whitman & Munkel, 1991).

Treatment for DID incorporates an interdisciplinary team as this disorder presents challenging symptomology to clinicians (Turkus & Kahler, 2006). The most effective therapies involve insight-oriented psychotherapy, cognitive-behavioral therapy, family therapy, creative and expressive therapies, clinical hypnosis, and interventions that strengthen the ego (Cleveland Clinic, 2007; Turkus & Kahler). The primary goal of therapeutic interventions is to integrate the personalities into one, which requires acknowledgement of the existence of multiple personalities and the reason for their existence (Townsend, 2006).

Eating Disorders

From a nutritional perspective, it is difficult to understand how people within affluent cultures all over the world are starving from lack of food (Townsend, 2006). Eating disorders were commonly thought of as a Western culture-bound phenomenon. Although more rare among non-Western cultures, they do occur; however the characteristic features are not the same (Bushnell, 1997). Society and culture influence people, and individuals with anorexia nervosa find support for their practices in society's emphasis on thinness and exercise (Sadock & Sadock, 2003).

The most well-known disorder is anorexia nervosa. Individuals engage in willful periods of dieting that lead to starvation and/or engage in periods of binging and purging. Of the reported number of individuals with anorexia, 90% are females, yet research indicates that males are currently being recognized as having eating disorders (APA, 2000; Crisp, 2006; Miller & Jake, 2001). Common age of onset for anorexia nervosa is mid-teens, with 5% experiencing onset in their early 20s (Sadock & Sadock, 2003). People with anorexia nervosa refuse to maintain appropriate body weight, have a distorted body image, and have a fear of obesity. Weight loss occurs with reduction of food intake, compulsive exercise, self-induced vomiting, and abuse of diuretics and laxatives. The prognosis varies from spontaneous recovery without treatment, recovery with varied treatment, a fluctuating course of weight gains followed by relapses, to a gradually deteriorating course resulting in death caused by complications of starvation (Sadock & Sadock). According to the NIMH (2006 revised), the mortality rate among people with anorexia is about 12 times higher than the annual death rate due to all causes of death among females ages 15 to 24 in the general population.

Individuals with bulimia nervosa engage in frequent periods of overeating (consuming 3,500–5,000 calories in one sitting) or of constant eating, either of which is followed by self-induced vomiting, use of laxatives or diuretics, fasting, and/or compulsive exercise. Hence, bulimia nervosa is often referred to as the **binge-purge syndrome.** These individuals have an overriding concern for body shape and weight. Bulimia is more common among females than among males: About 15 to 20% of college-age women practice forced vomiting or use laxatives while isolated episodes of binge eating and purging have been reported in up to 40% of college women (Dunn & Leitschuh, 2006; Sadock & Sadock, 2003). This disease is difficult to detect because the person usually conceals the binges or binges only when he or she is alone, and because the person may not appear emaciated: People are usually able to maintain their normal weight even though they exhibit frequent fluctuations (Sadock & Sadock; Sherrill, 2004). Bulimia seldom is totally incapacitating.

Two other diseases identified by the APA (2000) as eating disorders, pica and rumination, are more prevalent in young children than in adults and are associated with such predisposing factors as intellectual disabilities (see chapter 8). A new challenge for recreation therapists is to formulate innovative interventions for working with obese individuals. Obesity is not classified as a psychiatric disorder by the APA in the *DSM-IV-TR* but rather is coded as a nutritional disease under the *International Classification of Disease (ICD Selected General Medical Conditions and Medication-Induced Disorders)* because, to date, it has not been consistently associated with a psychological or a behavioral syndrome (see chapter 7 for a discussion of obesity).

The physical outcomes of anorexia and bulimia are most evident. The individual is usually under- or overweight and experiences frequent weight fluctuations. Other physical characteristics include thin, brittle, or lost hair; raised fine white hair on the cheeks, neck, and forearms; anemia; muscle atrophy; seizure activity; difficulty staying warm; dehydration; fatigue; muscle spasms; uncontrollable diabetes; and degenerative arthritis. These individuals experience low self-esteem, depression, anxiety, mood swings, feelings of loss of control, inability to relax or experience pleasure, and fear of success and failure. They tend to be self-critical, judgmental, perfectionist, set unrealistic expectations, display obsessive-compulsive behaviors, and to transfer their frustration with themselves to family and friends. As anorexia and bulimia progress, individuals develop eroded tooth enamel, varicose veins, and high blood pressure and cholesterol levels. If left untreated, these disorders may cause death due to starvation. Other complications include liver and kidney impairments, strokes, and heart problems induced by electrolyte imbalance.

People with anorexia and bulimia may not seek assistance for their disorder until their condition necessitates immediate medical attention. When this occurs, intervention takes place in the hospital or on an outpatient basis, where the individual attends a day-treatment program in a psychiatric unit or hospital-based eating disorder clinic (Mobily & MacNeil, 2002). Some people are treated in adolescent psychiatric units or in free-standing eating disorder clinics. Once the physical condition is no longer life threatening, other treatment modalities may be initiated. Noncooperation on the part of the individual typically makes treatment for anorexia nervosa difficult. Treatment includes aggressive medical management, nutritional counseling, behavior modification, cognitive behavioral therapy, and individual and family psychotherapy. With bulimia, treatment is similar to anorexia nervosa, but concentrates on interrupting the binge-purge cycle and helping the client regain control over eating behavior.

Impulse-Control Disorders

Individuals who experience impulse-control disorders follow their impulses to behave in a certain manner without regard to the consequences of their behavior. Before the act there is a sense of increasing tension or arousal; during the act there is relief or gratification; afterwards there is a sense of pleasure and satisfaction (Sadock & Sadock, 2003). Following the act there may or may not be guilt or regret (APA, 2000). Individuals function reasonably well in other aspects of their lives. Co-morbidity factors are common; for example, pathological gambling is found with substance abuse. Six categories of impulse-control disorders are presented in the *DSM-IV-TR*.

We will address pathological gambling, as it is a disorder that TRSs might experience and it is found with other psychiatric disorders presented in this chapter (Carruthers, 1999; Coyle & Kinney, 1990).

Pathological gambling is characterized by persistent and recurrent maladaptive gambling that causes economic problems and significant disturbances in personal, social, or occupational functioning (Sadock & Sadock, 2003). Gambling and poverty go hand-in-hand. Gambling victimizes the poor . . . those who can least afford it usually gamble the most. Inner-city residents are hurt the most by expanded gambling (Gambling with the Good Life, 2006). With increased availability of legalized gambling, there is an increase in prevalence rates. Lifetime prevalence rates of pathological gambling range from 0.4 to 3.4% in adults and 2.8 to 8% among adolescents and college students (APA, 2000). The urge to gamble tends to increase with stress or depression. The course for most is insidious, commencing with social gambling that becomes chronic with regular or episodic patterns.

Treatment is complicated as the gambler usually does not come forward voluntarily. It is often legal problems, family pressure, or other psychiatric complaints that bring the person to treatment. Gamblers Anonymous (GA) is an effective treatment for some; however it is believed that the drop-out rate is high. Behavioral therapy, cognitive therapy, and psychoanalysis have been used with pathological gambling with varying degrees of success (Townsend, 2006). A cognitive approach provides the opportunity to gain insight that may result in subsequent behavioral change. Insight psychotherapy may be effective after clients have been away from gambling for several months (Sadock & Sadock, 2003).

Personality Disorders

Individuals who exhibit distorted patterns of relating to, perceiving, and thinking about themselves and their environment are described as having personality disorders. These maladaptive habits of thought and behavior become evident by adolescence or even earlier. The qualifying characteristic of a personality disorder is its chronic, or long-standing nature, and its pervasive involvement of the total personality. The individual with a personality disorder is not in pain or distressed; the tendency is to view the behavior as healthy, not deviant. As a consequence, a person with a personality disorder may not take responsibility for, but assign the "problem" to others (Kinney & Kinney, 2001). Persons with these disorders are unlikely to seek psychiatric help, and are often coerced by family members to begin treatment (Kinney & Kinney). The *DSM-IV-TR* identifies 11 categories of personality disorders. We selected to present four of the most common seen by TRSs: (1) paranoid personality—people are often perceived as odd and eccentric, (2) antisocial personality—people are often seen as dramatic, emotional and erratic, (3) borderline personality—the individual appears in a constant state of crisis, and (4) passive-aggressive personality—people tend to resist expectations of others while exerting subtle control.

Paranoid Personality Disorder

People who are paranoid are suspicious of almost all situations. They are extremely distrustful and jealous of others, which limits their friendships and seriously affects their emotional and social adjustments, as well as their cognitive processes.

Persons appear hypervigilant and "on guard," ready for any real or perceived threat. Any perceived deviation from loyalty supports their underlying assumptions, with an honest mistake viewed as deliberate. As a consequence, it is difficult to get along with a person having this disorder. The treatment of choice is psychotherapy with pharmacological intervention for the anxiety and agitation often exhibited.

Antisocial Personality Disorder

A person with this impairment expresses a predatory attitude toward others. As the most severe and most prevalent of the personality disorders, it affects 1% of females and 3% of males in the United States (APA, 2000). In classifying this behavior, the two criteria that must be met are (1) evidence that the behavior has existed since early adolescence and (2) that the deviant attitude affects or permeates the total personality or behavior of the person. This personality type includes the following characteristics: aggressiveness, impulsiveness, recklessness, deceptiveness, criminal activity, inability to hold a job, inability to sustain meaningful sexual relationships, inability to act responsibly, a lack of remorse, and no sense of shame or guilt. Although several of the above must be present to confirm an antisocial personality disorder, the two defining characteristics appear to be absence of a sense of responsibility and absence of a sense of shame or guilt (Hare et al., 1990).

Antisocial personality disorders are considered among the most difficult of all personality disorders to treat. Co-morbidity factors such as anxiety, depression, mood disorders, and substance abuse require medication; however, a person with an antisocial personality is not likely to remain compliant with medication protocols. Individual psychotherapy focuses on development of appropriate interpersonal skills and instilling a moral code. When individual therapy is not successful, the physician may prescribe group and/or family therapy (Mayo Foundation, 2007).

Borderline Personality Disorder

Individuals with borderline personality disorders are characterized by extraordinarily unstable affect, mood, behavior, object relations, and self-image; and, almost always appear to be in a state of crisis (Sadock & Sadock, 2003; Townsend, 2006). Because of a chronic fear of abandonment, clients with borderline personality disorder have little tolerance for being alone. They prefer a frantic search for companionship, no matter how unsatisfactory, to dealing with feelings of loneliness, emptiness, and boredom.

Treatment may occur in a structured protective environment, for example hospital or day program, where clients who are excessively impulsive, self-destructive, or self-mutilating are given limits, and their actions observed (Sadock & Sadock, 2003). Treatments of choice include pharmacotherapy and psychotherapeutic interventions that focus on distress tolerance, affective regulation, changing distorted beliefs, and introducing new social and relationship problem-solving skills (Hunt, 2007). With adolescents, family treatments are used, especially with co-morbid factors like substance abuse.

Passive-Aggressive Personality Disorder

An individual with this personality disorder will indirectly resist the demands of others. Such a person would not openly refuse a request to perform a certain task but would procrastinate or make errors in the process of complying with the request, which is a hostile way of controlling others. Passive-aggressive individuals believe that life has been unkind to them, and they express envy and resentment over the "easy life" that they perceive others have (Townsend, 2006). They tend to manipulate themselves into a position of dependence. Townsend explains the overall clinical nature of this disorder:

> They demonstrate passive resistance and general obstructiveness in response to the expectations of others. As a tactic of interpersonal behavior, passive-aggressive individuals commonly switch among the roles of the martyr, the affronted, the aggrieved, the misunderstood, the contrite, the guilt-ridden, the sickly, and the overworked. In this way, they are able to vent their anger and resentment subtly, while gaining the attention, reassurance, and dependency they crave. (p. 725)

Psychotherapy is considered to have good outcomes. Although challenging for the therapist, the therapist must confront the passive-aggressive behaviors as they occur. If depression or suicidal ideation is present, antidepressants are administered.

PURPOSE OF THERAPEUTIC RECREATION

Therapeutic recreation contributes to the assessment, treatment, education, and health promotion of individuals with psychological needs and disabilities. Naturalistic assessments occur as TRSs observe and engage clients in team-planned interventions to enhance emotional health and educate clients about alternative coping strategies and lifestyle management. Outcomes promote relapse prevention and physical well-being. Treatment teams and families partner to address environmental influences and facilitate positive social interactions. Reducing anxiety while improving "self" are central to client recovery.

Disorders Usually Diagnosed in Infancy, Childhood, and Adolescence

Since play is so basic to child development, many children who experience behavior disorders also lack appropriate play skills. The role of therapeutic recreation in the treatment of childhood disorders becomes that of assessing fine motor and gross motor play skills, determining the level of play behavior, and planning interventions that will meet individualized needs. The scope of programs ranges from teaching play skills (kicking, throwing, balancing, running) to reinforcing efforts to increase social skills (communicating or playing with others). The goal is to enhance self-esteem and coping skills while decreasing inappropriate behavior.

Therapeutic recreation interventions that include family members can also be effective treatment measures, since recreation experiences can become the basis for developing healthier ways of relating as a family (DeSalvatore, 1989; DeSalvatore & Roseman, 1986; Hart, 1984; Malkin, Phillips, & Chumbler, 1991). Providing families with the skills necessary to plan, organize, and implement appropriate leisure activities should be an essential program focus.

Adventure/challenge activities are used for the treatment of conduct disorders. According to Cockerham (2002), wilderness programs have earned a well-respected niche in the continuum of care for troubled youth and families. The modality is incor-

Outdoor adventure activities can be a very effective component of treatment for youth with conduct disorders.

porated in programs for at-risk and adjudicated youth (Jones, Lowe, & Risler, 2004; Walsh, 2002). Residential psychiatric treatment programs view adventure therapy as an adjunct to therapy (Williams, 2000). These experiences demand total personal involvement by stretching individuals to their physical and psychological limits, which, in turn, affects the self-concept and its related components (Ewert, 1983, 1988). A major component of adventure therapy is the debriefing process: The TRS facilitates discussion that enables clients to apply lessons learned to the real world. Adventure-based Counseling (ABC) and low-element challenge courses are group-oriented programs that help participants learn to share responsibility, develop cooperative problem-solving skills, and increase self-confidence and well-being (Glass & Myers, 2001).

Satisfying social needs such as trust, belonging, acceptance, and loving and being loved is critical to a healthy adjustment to society. Adolescents, for example, are frequently struggling with identity questions such as, "Who am I?" and "What value or good am I to others?" They may rebel against their parents or other authority figures by acting out and in the process lose a great deal of self-respect. An effective treatment program must recognize the need to correct these distorted perceptions by incorporating experiences that address clients' social needs.

For youths, many social contacts center around leisure experiences, which become key training laboratories for learning and practicing important developmental or functional skills. For the adolescent who has had difficulty controlling aggressive impulses when interacting in stressful social situations, a competitive game allows the client to practice new coping behaviors within a controlled, supportive environment. Successful experiences in these situations build confidence for facing real-world situations in the future. Social skills training may also involve instruction in basic interviewing, asking a friend on a date, or dealing with authority figures. An interdisciplinary approach to programming for social skills training reinforces recreation therapy sessions during outpatient treatment (Rothwell, Piatt, & Mattingly, 2006).

Therapeutic recreation activities are an important part of therapeutic interventions with children and adolescents for several reasons. Observing play behaviors is a useful method of assessing a child's disorder. Therapeutic recreation interventions allow children and adolescents to explore and develop new behaviors that will help them cope more effectively with their world. Play skills are necessary for mastery of future developmental stages. Play is also an excellent tool for helping clients understand themselves and the world in which they live—especially as it relates to traumatic events in their lives. The goal of a therapeutic recreation program with youth is to facilitate appropriate experiences that will improve functional life skills so clients can enjoy an enhanced quality of life.

Substance-Related Disorders

Therapeutic recreation contributes to the treatment and rehabilitation (recovery and relapse prevention) of individuals with substance disorders. A primary role of the TRS in treatment is to help the person access healthy alternatives that cause sensations similar to those experienced with substance use. Quality sobriety is dependent upon improved quality of life and adapting to a lifestyle that allows for gratification and rewards from leisure, significant others, and relationships found at work, home, and in social experiences (Kunstler, 2001). Other treatment goals include the mastery of stressors and development of coping skills like proactive decision making and problem solving. In recovery, clients need to develop feelings of control, competence, and mastery (Kunstler). TRSs help individuals develop the ability to manage and structure their free time and select leisure experiences in which they gain feelings of self-esteem, self-efficacy, and the opportunity to build trusting relationships. Therapists remain role models throughout intervention, promoting "playfulness" and relaxation while encouraging clients to adopt a lifestyle that increases their health and manages their use of problem substances.

TRSs assess social and personality needs; treat self-defeating behaviors like dependency and low tolerance thresholds; help clients develop communication skills, self-control, cooperation, and trusting relationships; and enhance independent functioning, support networks, and physical well-being. Outcomes promote quality sobriety and prevention of relapse. Prevention of relapse is dependent upon developing, practicing, and incorporating into the person's value system leisure options perceived as challenging, rewarding, and self-governing. TRSs continually confront attention seeking, denial, and impulsive and manipulative behaviors as they collaborate with clients in the implementation of structured, success-oriented experiences. Interdisciplinary practice provides opportunities to co-treat in family therapy and structured family programming.

Schizophrenic Disorders

In addition to the role leisure education may play in family education, therapeutic recreation interventions may focus on clients' social withdrawal and motor behavior symptoms, as well as the underlying stressors that may be contributing to these inappropriate responses. Withdrawal appears to be a generalized response of individuals who experience the delusional world of schizophrenia. To counteract this retreat from reality, therapists encourage and motivate clients to participate in well-structured exercise groups, social interactions, and recreation experiences. Overly intense, emotionally charged group interactions, however, tend to be too threatening and should be avoided (Drake & Sederer, 1986).

Therapeutic recreation offers useful mechanisms for increasing attention spans by providing opportunities for decision making, developing language skills, and learning and following rules (Beck, 1982; Conroy, Fincham, & Agard-Evans, 1988). Whether therapists are interested in assessing or developing cognitive skills, recreation interventions provide an excellent tool to achieve these goals.

Although more research is needed to support the stress reduction theory, increased physical activity appears to help clients manage and vent emotional pressures (Berger & Owen, 1988; de Vries, 1987; Li, 1981). Evidence suggests a work-related stress management program also has positive effects on clients' perceived work-related stress (Lee, Tan, Ma, Tsai, & Liu, 2006). Recreation experiences thus become a coping mechanism for combating stressful situations that might otherwise force the client to withdraw into a solitary, delusional world.

Mood Disorders

Although the nature of intervention varies with the client's emotional state, a number of interventions have immediate and long-term benefits. Evidence indicates that a physically active body is more capable of coping with stressors than one that is less physically fit (Russoniello, 1991). Physical activity stimulates production of neurotransmitters (hormones) that have been linked to the stabilization of mood disorders (Griest, 1987; Sime, 1987; Townsend, 2006). In general, studies have found that physically active individuals have reduced probability for developing depression (Martinsen, 2005). Armed with these insights and the support of other team members, the TRS slowly moves the inactive client toward a more active lifestyle. As a general rule, clients will benefit from therapeutic recreation programs that not only increase their aerobic fitness but also encourage and motivate them to develop individualized fitness plans.

People with emotional disorders frequently experience decreased self-esteem and a distorted self-concept. Their perceptions of themselves reflect their struggles with anxiety and failure. Society's general attitude toward psychological disturbances and psychiatric care is itself a factor that undermines one's self-worth. Viewing such individuals as sick or helpless, a response known as **learned helplessness,** only reinforces clients' diminished self-perceptions and further complicates the rehabilitation process. Thus, a major focus of therapeutic recreation with individuals with mood disorders is that of building self-esteem and improving clients' attitudes and perspectives toward themselves. TRSs also help clients explore the causes of decreased self-esteem and encourage them to participate in programs established to increase their self-esteem.

Cooperative activities can enhance self-esteem and improve clients' attitudes and perspectives toward themselves.

Leaders in an activity-based program can do this effectively by selecting and sequencing activities that provide positive reinforcement to participants.

With pharmacological interventions, a period of two to three weeks is required for drugs to stabilize a client's mood swings. During this time the TRS assists the client through structured activities that are appropriate to the particular phase (manic or depressive) of the client's illness. Typically, individuals in the manic phase will need assistance in channeling their boundless energy into meaningful, esteem-building activities. In contrast, depressed individuals will require short-term, success-oriented activities, since their level of motivation is extremely limited.

Anxiety Disorders

The physiological approach emphasizes the use of medications to reduce anxiety. However, a growing body of evidence suggests that therapeutic recreation programs may be able to reduce anxiety by encouraging more active lifestyles. Exercise is beneficial for mental health as it reduces anxiety, depression, and negative mood while improving self-esteem and cognitive function (Callaghan, 2004).

The psychodynamic treatment paradigm attempts to expose unconscious material that is being repressed by the ego state of mind and is causing the anxiety. Therapeutic recreation programs that assume this perspective may incorporate activities that use expressive art forms such as dance, drama, painting, and poetry to assist the individual in freeing and expressing unconscious thoughts and fears. Psychodrama (guided dramatic action) facilitates insight, personal growth, and integration on cognitive, affective, and behavioral levels (American Society of Group Psychotherapy and Psychodrama [ASGPP], 2006).

Behavioral therapies, in contrast, focus on removing the symptoms of anxiety with classical conditioning techniques. Cognitive therapies will focus on the control and mastery of anxiety-producing situations by teaching coping skills through, for example, stress management, biofeedback, and other forms of desensitization. Therapeutic recreation may involve teaching relaxation techniques, assertion therapy, or similar stress reduction activities. A group of South Korean researchers found that a meditation-based stress management program can be an effective adjunct to pharmacotherapy in relieving anxiety symptoms (Lee et al., 2007). Therapeutic recreation programs serve as a useful laboratory for applying and testing new adaptive behaviors.

Since the focus of humanistic therapy is developing a better understanding of self, therapeutic recreation may use a values clarification approach to help the client determine which leisure experiences would be most satisfying. The professional would then seek to provide the client with the skills and understanding needed to participate in these selected activities. Other meaningful approaches might include programs designed to increase self-esteem and self-confidence.

Dissociative Disorders

As with other emotional disorders, an important goal of interventions is learning to manage stressful situations. Thus the recreation therapist considers the primary nature as well as the secondary features of DID like depression. Physical activity provides relief from anxiety while improving health. Social skills training promotes self-confidence and also reduces psychosocial stress (Mobily & MacNeil, 2002). Feelings of mastery, control, and a sense of success act to relieve symptoms of depression and result from self-selected experiences. Self-paced, repetitive, process-oriented activities like creative arts and horticulture therapy promote relaxation and opportunities to "be in control." Play therapy is used with younger children in order to provide a catharsis for events like repeated abuse that might have led to dissociative disorders. Witman and Preskenis (1996) reported the successful use of adventure programming with a 37-year-old male diagnosed with a multiple personality disorder (DID), major depression, PTSD, and narcissistic personality traits. The authors' noted that each client's unique needs must be considered and, as a consequence, group therapy can be challenging.

Eating Disorders

TRSs working with individuals with anorexia and bulimia must first assess and treat their physical health needs. After clients begin to abstain from the compulsive use of food and to address weight management issues, interventions begin to focus on feelings that have been repressed by addictive eating behaviors (Mobily & MacNeil, 2002). The intent of the interventions is to help clients identify what is really important to their self-esteem, rather than to allow them to believe their value is dependent upon body shape and size. The body of a person with an eating disorder is a battleground for interpersonal conflict, with food as the ammunition, and treatment is an inward journey to change the belief that only weight and shape define well-being.

Overall, TRSs diagnose and assess clients' functioning, work with clients to treat/ rehabilitate their social and emotional deficits, and promote recovery and the prevention of relapse of the disorder. Because eating is a leisure experience, TRSs have the opportunity to demonstrate how food consumption is affected by the client's feelings, yet is an experience like any other leisure activity (such as reading or walking) that clients control by making choices and acting on them.

Therapeutic recreation helps improve the emotional well-being of individuals with anorexia and bulimia by using structured interventions to relate feelings to experiences. Strategies like group and family therapies help clients dissolve barriers like isolation, guilt, shame, and loneliness (Mobily & MacNeil, 2002). When clients share such feelings within a group, the environment of shared concerns helps them develop an awareness of self-responsibility for recovery.

Leisure education experiences promote physical and social-emotional well-being and help prevent relapsing into old habits. Wellness experiences focus on balance, pacing, and the relationships between exercise and food intake without focusing on weight and appearance. Interventions to reduce compulsive exercise include teaching and practicing stress management techniques, increasing awareness of compulsive exercise as a problem, and developing a healthier attitude towards exercise (Miller & Jake, 2001). Through values clarification and self-awareness experiences, clients become aware of the relationship between their beliefs and their past and present

Therapeutic recreation interventions can promote physical well-being by helping clients develop a healthier attitude toward the benefits of physical activity.

behaviors. By learning to set physical and emotional boundaries, clients regain control and self-efficacy in their lives. When clients learn to make decisions for themselves and to follow behavior management plans, they gain coping skills and assume responsibility for their well-being. Additionally, decision making positively channels their need for control. From the most acute phase throughout recovery, a recreational therapist intervenes as an interdisciplinary team member to treat and promote healthy behaviors (Miller & Jake, 2001).

Impulse-Control Disorders

Carruthers (1999) identified the problems associated with pathological gambling that TR specialists might address in collaboration with the interdisciplinary team:

- tendencies toward under- or over-arousal
- maladaptive thought processes
- anxiety
- poor coping skills
- poor impulse control
- low self-esteem
- lack of social support
- difficulty maintaining friendships and interpersonal intimacy
- boredom proneness
- lack of constructive leisure

A study by Wood and Griffiths (2007) identified "escape" as the prime characteristic of the gambling experience that fuels continued problem gambling. Goals of intervention include developing coping and stress management skills, relationship and communication skills, and establishing a non-gambling lifestyle (Carruthers). Coyle and Kinney (1990) recommended that TRSs working with compulsive gamblers recognize that gambling is a form of recreational involvement, and as a consequence, there may be similarities in the reason for engaging in gambling and other recreational experiences. Thus, rather than substituting recreational experiences to inhibit the gambling urge, the TRS provides interventions that will encourage the gambler to explore the positive and negative consequences of their recreational behaviors. TRSs use leisure education strategies to promote awareness and adaptation of lifestyle changes resulting in healthy behaviors and social interactions.

Personality Disorders

Personality disorders represent a mixture of many different disorders, which makes it difficult to generalize across treatment approaches for all individuals who may be diagnosed with a personality disorder. For example, a person with antisocial personality disorder is likely to have substance abuse problems, and a person with avoidant personality disorder may also exhibit social phobia (Davison & Neale, 2001). The following paragraphs present some general TR approaches with people with personality disorders; however, it is important to understand the specific needs of each client and adapt the program accordingly. One further note: as might be expected, antisocial personality disorders are common among criminal offenders, and therefore many correctional programs (see chapter 10) must consider the implications of this disorder for therapeutic interventions.

It is generally agreed that individuals who are classified with personality disorders are some of the most difficult to treat because of the long-standing nature of the problem and because they often lack the motivation to change their behavior; that is, they do not see their behavior as inappropriate. Since most of these disorders appear to have little physiological basis, therapeutic interventions have focused on social-psychological treatment.

The psychodynamic approach suggests that the superego, which would normally control behaviors like antisocial impulses, is not sufficient to keep irrational conduct in check. Psychoanalysis and counseling might help to develop the superego, but these techniques usually require a highly motivated client who desires to relieve tensions and anxieties caused by internal conflicts. People with antisocial personalities, however, do not tend to sense conflict and therefore do not respond well to insight-oriented therapy unless it is accompanied by behavior modification techniques.

Behaviorists reject the notion of personality disorders, claiming that these unacceptable behaviors are maladaptive responses that occur as a result of specific reinforcing stimuli. They develop elaborate reinforcement programs to counteract negative behaviors and enhance positive behaviors. Highly structured programs that minimize the client's use of manipulative behaviors are most effective. As the client demonstrates greater ability to make responsible decisions, therapists progressively modify the structure until the client needs little or no external structure or control. Other behavioral-cognitive techniques, such as modeling, contingency contracting, or social skills training are more appropriate and are extremely useful for TRSs who work with individuals with personality disorders.

The humanistic view of personality disorders recognizes the need for increasing individual responsibility but tends to value personal choice above social conformity. Improving the client's self-concept and helping the client make constructive choices is the primary goal of therapy. Therapeutic recreation programs emphasize experiences that build self-confidence, self-esteem, and self-worth. For some individuals physical conditioning may achieve this goal, while for others it may require participation in an art form. The key is knowing and satisfying the underlying need of the individual.

DELIVERY SETTINGS

As we consider the need for therapeutic recreation in mental health, we might ask: What specific needs does therapeutic recreation meet that are not met by other disciplines and services? Furthermore, what tools or intervention techniques do TRSs possess that will aid in the habilitation or rehabilitation process? One of the problems with answering these questions quickly and easily is the situation we have confronted repeatedly in this chapter, namely, the lack of agreement on the cause and treatment of these disorders. The situation becomes even more complex since most settings use a combination of therapeutic modalities, depending on the needs of the client and the training and orientation of the staff. The complex and unique nature of each person and the wide range of personality disturbances rule out a simple, consistent approach to all disorders. The point is, the purpose and value of therapeutic recreation will vary according to the type of disorder, the psychological treatment approach used, the needs of the individual, and resources available in the setting.

Since passage of the Community Mental Health Centers Act in 1963, the focus of treatment has moved from large residential hospitals to local community-based service centers that provide inpatient services, often through local general hospitals; emergency or crisis intervention services (on a 24-hour basis); consultation to schools, police departments, and other community agencies; short-term care (including partial hospitalization programs, halfway houses, aftercare services, and a broad range of outpatient services); and research and education (Sadock & Sadock, 2003). Acute inpatient units, both locked and unlocked, are found in general medical hospitals with separate units designated for youth and adults. Assessment and intervention may occur within a 48-hour time period or for as many as two or three days: A five to seven day placement is considered "long."

Therapeutic recreation personnel employed in acute and community mental health settings are generally responsible for interventions on several units, with interventions offered seven days a week and during the evenings. Treatment may consist of individual and group therapy. The TRS may provide individual leisure education sessions, facilitate stress management, anger management, social skills groups, and provide opportunities that increase coping skills for better lifestyle management. The therapist may also design exercise and wellness programs; programs to assist clients in accessing community agen-

Therapeutic recreation personnel in community mental health settings address a wide range of youth needs.

cies that provide recreational and leisure opportunities; and co-treat with psychologists, social workers, and occupational therapists to increase the client's functional skills.

LEADERSHIP INTERACTION
AND INTERVENTION CONSIDERATIONS

A comprehensive therapeutic recreation program will focus on diagnosis/needs assessment, treatment/rehabilitation, education, and prevention/health promotion goals. Many different experiences can contribute to accomplishing the goals identified in an individual treatment plan (see exhibit 9.3).

A thorough physiological and psychological evaluation is a prerequisite to treatment for psychological impairments. Comprehensive assessments help team members classify and define the overall level of function and the client's strengths and areas of limitation. With the exception of those who embrace the behavioral perspective, mental health professionals depend heavily on verbal communication such as interviews and written communication (e.g., standardized paper and pencil tests) to assess and treat people with psychological disorders.

Therapeutic recreation programming, in contrast, is experiential based and, as such, provides a forum for assessing and treating clients in a more natural setting.

Exhibit 9.3   Examples of Program Goals and Activities

Goals	Suggested Activities
Diagnosis/Needs Assessment • Determine strengths/limitations	• Assessment tools, behavioral observation
Treatment/Rehabilitation • Improve physical fitness • Increase cognitive development and functioning • Improve social interaction skills • Increase self-concept and self-esteem • Increase leisure functioning	• Physical activity, exercise prescriptions • Mental games, rules and directions, problem-solving strategies, cognitive retraining • Group games, social skills training • Adventure/challenge and initiative games, group processes • Leisure education, self-esteem programs, behavior modification, values clarification
Education • Develop problem-solving skills • Develop self-help skills • Develop community living skills	• Problem-solving exercises, initiatives • ADLs, assertiveness training, animal-assisted therapy, aquatic therapy • Role playing, money management activities, resource awareness
Prevention/Health Promotion • Facilitate personally satisfying and healthful experiences	• Expressive and creative arts, horticulture, social activities, health and wellness, stress management, relaxation

Naturalistic observation (also known as field or behavioral observation) is one of the most basic assessment tools used by behavioral and social scientists, since it allows the professional to view the person within a normal or natural environment. Generally, the more natural or "homelike" the setting, the more clients' behaviors will represent what is considered natural or normal behavior for them. Since one of the professionals' objectives is to assess client behaviors accurately before, during, or following treatment, TRSs must be concerned about the representative nature of behaviors—that is, are the behaviors a good picture of the person's normal performance? From these observations, judgments can be made regarding the nature of the problem or need, the type of intervention that should be provided, the client's response to specific treatment interventions, and ultimately, the effect of the program in meeting the needs of the client. It should be noted that in the current brief-treatment practices, clients are often engaged in treatment/rehabilitation or educational activities that then become one component of the diagnostic assessment.

TRSs also use other assessment tools to evaluate clients' functional capacities, dimensions of health and well-being, and their quality of life. A few are listed in exhibit 9.4. You should become familiar with several valid and reliable measures that

---

Exhibit 9.4   Therapeutic Recreation Mental Health Assessment Tools

Psychosocial function

Social Fear Scale*
Interaction and Audience Anxiety Scales*
Stressful Situations Scale*
Assertion Inventory*
Profile of Mood States-BI Scale*
Loneliness Rating Scale*

Multidimensional Locus of Control Scale*
Index of Peer Relations*
Life Satisfaction Index*
Comprehensive Evaluation in Recreation Therapy—Psych/Behavioral (Parker et al., 1975, revised by burlingame, 1998)

Physical Function

I CAN: Health and Fitness (Wessel, 1976)
Bruininks-Oseretsky Test of Motor Proficiency (Bruininks, 1978)
Physical Best (American Alliance for Health, Physical Education, Recreation and Dance, 1988)
Therapeutic Recreation Activity Assessment (Keogh Hoss, 2002)

Cognitive Function

Problem-Solving Inventory*
Functional Assessment of Characteristics for Therapeutic Recreation, Revised (Idyll Arbor, 1996)

Leisure Function

I CAN: Sport, Leisure, and Recreational Skills (Wessel, 1979)
Leisure Diagnostic Battery (Witt & Ellis, 1987)
Leisure Competence Measure (Kloseck & Crilly, 1997)
Leisurescope Plus (Schenk, 2002)
Life Satisfaction Scale (Lohmann, 1976)
Leisure Step Up (Dehn, 1995)

*See Corcoran, K., Fischer, J., & Barlow, D. H. (1994). See also burlingame & Blaschko (2002) for functional and leisure-related assessments; Jansma & French (1994) for physical-function-related assessments; and Stumbo (1994/95) for psychosocial skills assessments.

aid in diagnosing and treating people with psychological disorders. Selecting the appropriate assessment tools depends on many factors—the nature of the disorder, the philosophy or treatment approach (i.e., biological, behavioral, humanistic, existential, cognitive, or psychoanalytic), client's length of stay, purpose and scope of the therapeutic recreation service, the level of staff training, and staff-to-client ratio.

The trend toward shorter hospitalizations and brief treatment has focused diagnostic and treatment activities on the specific needs of the client. Generally, assessments must be completed within 48–72 hours of admission and staff have less than two weeks to achieve their goals. Implications for all service providers are to identify what they can contribute to the rehabilitation process and use the most effective treatment modalities to accomplish those goals.

Specific leadership strategies used during intervention are intended to create a structured, predictable environment with clearly identified outcomes. Specifically, TRSs implement programs using the following strategies:

- Calm, consistent, patient explanations and directives are stated in a matter-of-fact manner.

- Prior to interaction, expectations, acceptable and unacceptable behaviors, and desired outcomes are stated and clarified. The rationale and consequences for desired behaviors are explained.

- Immediate reinforcement and acknowledgement of success occurs when desired goals are achieved.

- Interventions emphasize cooperation rather than competition (and labels like "winners and losers").

- Written instructions and information promote reality and client assumption of responsibility.

- Information is stated positively rather than negatively, i.e., avoid "do not do" statements.

- While providing positive reinforcement, the TRS confronts the use of defense mechanisms like excuses or denial.

- Encourage clients to verbalize anger, for example, while providing options and choices to express frustration; purposefully ignore behaviors that are not harmful.

- Trust builds over time; TRSs model desired behaviors and plan interventions that allow for increasing degrees of social competence and expression of self in group settings.

- TRSs remain aware of environmental factors that may cause stress or create unsafe experiences; unusual behaviors or statements are documented.

APPLYING THE THERAPEUTIC RECREATION PROCESS

Charlene, 16 years old, is in the hospital because of recurring mood swings and agitation that could not be controlled on an outpatient basis. She has a history of illegal drug use, including mescaline, marijuana, and alcohol. This is her third admission. Her physician referred her to therapeutic recreation for evaluation and treatment.

Assessment

The *DSM-IV-TR* assessment indicated the following: Axis I, mood disorder; Axis II, antisocial personality disorder; Axis III, some loss of cognitive processing skills; Axis IV, family conflict and recent loss of boyfriend; Axis V, highest level of functioning this last year was 69; current functioning is 52. The therapeutic recreation assessment of Charlene must include (1) an outline of her involvement in therapeutic recreation activities during past admissions and (2) her current level of functioning in the major assessment categories (cognitive, social, physical, psychological, spiritual, and leisure/play domains; see exhibit 4.1 on page 114). Two general types of assessment tools are used: behavioral observation and formalized testing.

Behavioral or naturalistic observation involves observing clients in real-life situations, such as during their participation in an activity. The TRS records these observations in an objective manner as soon as possible after the behavior occurs. Objective reporting describes what took place and does not make a subjective interpretation of those events. Reporting that "Charlene refused to participate in any activity" (objective), as opposed to recording "Charlene doesn't like to play with her peers" (subjective), is an example of this principle. Alternatively, you may report that Charlene said, "I don't like to play with those guys because they're too rough." This is a factual statement, not an interpretation.

The TRS looks for patterns in verbal and nonverbal cues to determine how the client is responding to a given situation. Observations include not only the actual behaviors but also the antecedent event and consequent events. The antecedent event is that stimulus or precipitating factor that occurred immediately before the behavior. The consequent events are any events that follow the behavior. Both types of events have effects on the behavior itself and therefore may provide further insight into the cause for certain types of behaviors.

The use of formal assessment tools, such as those listed in exhibit 9.4, can also generate diagnostic information. When applying these evaluation tools to gather information on certain behavioral functions, it is important to note that no test can provide an adequate picture of the total person. Even if a battery of tests such as a self-concept scale, physical fitness test, perceptual-motor test, leisure interest test, and a social adaptive test were used, you would still end up with a checkerboard perspective of the person. Developing a holistic perspective of the client is one of the major contributions of therapeutic recreation.

Planning

From a review of the *DSM-IV-TR* and assessment data, the TRS determines Charlene's goals:

- develop and improve interpersonal skills
- increase self-awareness, especially in social situations
- identify problems correctly and define alternative behaviors
- develop a mutually satisfying interpersonal relationship
- improve leisure skills in socially oriented activities

Charlene's objectives are to identify two appropriate and two inappropriate social behaviors during the brief intervention period and participate in at least one social experience two or three times per week without acting out or displaying negative behaviors during the intervention.

To accomplish the goals and objectives during the brief-treatment period, the TRS identifies the content and processes. Charlene is asked to participate in two group activities and in one activity that involves a one-on-one interaction with the TRS. The one-on-one activity involves daily care of horses and riding three days per week for one hour each day. The group activities involve swimming and a community living class. The physician also places Charlene on medication that is intended to control her mood swings. Charlene agrees to this plan and indicates special interest for the one-on-one activity.

Implementation

Since the treatment setting uses the learning and cognitive therapy approach, the TRS begins by developing a contract with Charlene to clarify mutual expectations and responsibilities. Charlene and the treatment team also agree on the consequences of completing or breaking the contract. The contract is a useful tool for those situations that demand more structure, since the standard of behavior is clearly defined and understood by all parties.

Implementation also involves the application of other selected intervention techniques that are designed to facilitate the therapeutic relationship and achievement of treatment goals. For Charlene, the rehabilitation team decides to use reinforcement techniques for demonstrating use of interpersonal and problem-solving skills. For each skill she uses in her daily activities she receives one token, and when she has earned a total of five tokens she may select and attend one social skills class. Each staff member who works with Charlene also has to model the interpersonal and problem-solving skills.

Evaluation

Following each activity, the staff documents Charlene's responses to the interventions using behavioral observation techniques. The rehabilitation team meets regularly to review the progress in each area of treatment. The TRS shares observations and suggestions for further refinement of the program and begins to develop a discharge plan that will help Charlene transition back into the community. After two weeks Charlene shows sufficient progress to return home and continue treatment on an outpatient basis.

RELATED CONSIDERATIONS

Therapeutic recreation specialists must be aware of the side effects of the drugs most commonly used at their agencies, since all such medications have obvious implications for programming. Drugs that affect balance or coordination or that cause other extrapyramidal symptoms, for example, will require a modified and restricted program to ensure the safety of the client. As a result of the complex psychiatric and general health of the client, pharmacological treatment also is complex. Each drug type will have contraindications or precautions and drug interactions. By documenting the observed neurological side effects of a particular medication, the TRS assists medical professionals in monitoring the client's treatment and contributes to the well-being of the client.

The major classifications of behaviors involving drug treatments are identifiable by the drugs' functional descriptions: antidepressants, antipsychotics, and antianxiety agents. All medications have certain side effects, which may at times be more incapacitating than the primary problem. For example, psychotropic drugs (haloperidol [Haldol], trifluoperazine [Stelazine], and chlorpromazine [Thorazine]), which are used to treat psychotic disorders, cause neurological changes in the extrapyramidal system of the brain resulting in the side effect of pseudo-parkinsonism. The client often appears physically rigid, may experience tremors, such as the hands shaking, has a very dry mouth or over salivates, walks with an abnormal gait, and may be extremely restless and agitated. Symptoms may appear one to five days following initiation of antipsychotic medications, especially in women, the elderly, and dehydrated clients (Townsend, 2006).

Electroconvulsive therapy (ECT) is part of the treatment for behavioral disorders, particularly severe mood disorders, that do not respond to more conventional therapy. ECT involves the mechanical inducement of a convulsion via an electric shock to the nondominant side of the brain. Although the specific physiological effect of ECT is not yet clear, research suggests that this is the treatment of choice for severe, unremitting depression (Klerman, 1988; Sadock & Sadock, 2003). The common side effects are a temporary memory loss and confusion. ECT is contraindicated for individuals with increased intracranial pressure, cardiovascular problems, severe osteoporosis, acute and chronic pulmonary disorders, and a high-risk or complicated pregnancy (Townsend, 2006). Special care must be taken when including these clients in interventions, since they may temporarily lose all knowledge of how to complete the experience that may have been quite familiar to them before treatment.

Family therapy focuses on the dynamics or interactions among family members to identify and resolve interpersonal conflicts that contribute to psychological disorders. As we have indicated, family therapy is often part of the treatment of childhood disorders and has also proven useful for the treatment of addictive disorders, such as alcoholism. TRSs work closely with family counselors, as well as with other treatment team members, to provide expertise to family members in areas such as play behaviors, family leisure experiences, development of interpersonal behaviors through leisure activities, and personal use of leisure.

Although we have focused on psychologically impaired clients, you should recognize that much of what has been discussed in this chapter could also apply to people in correctional facilities (see chapter 10). More than half of all prison and jail inmates have a mental health problem (James & Glaze, 2006) of an acute or chronic nature, and thus, their behaviors may be understood from this perspective. Some correctional facilities with mental health units offer programs for inmates having psychological diagnoses, as well as provide special education services to those who are ADD or ADHD or have conduct disorders.

With the trend toward shortened inpatient hospitalization, and the use of the rehabilitation/recovery model once pharmacological interventions outcomes are met, it is anticipated that TR professionals may find their interventions more applicable to outpatient rather than inpatient service (Keogh-Hoss, Powell, & Sable, 2006). This trend is consistent with the need for cost-effectiveness in the provision of medical care (Townsend, 2006). Health-care service delivery requires outcome measurement in all areas of treatment. TRSs must be able to connect intervention outcomes to those outcomes valued by health-care stakeholders (McCormick & Funderburk, 2000). Our profession will continue to increase its role in community mental health services across all levels of care as we continue to provide quality, cost-effective, evidence-based services.

SUMMARY

In this chapter we briefly discussed mental health and mental illness and its cultural context. We have defined "abnormal" behavior as a culturally relative term that describes substantial deviation from perceived norms of society that continues for an extended period of time.

The numerous disorders are classified in *The Diagnostic and Statistical Manual of Mental Disorders* (*DSM-IV-TR*). The major categories of psychological disturbances were reviewed according to their Axis I or Axis II classification. Since each major treatment perspective (i.e., biological, behavioral, humanistic, existential, cognitive, or psychoanalytic) views and treats these disturbances differently, the TRS must become familiar with the disorder and the preferred treatment perspective in the respective setting in order to integrate the therapeutic recreation process with other treatment methods.

The nature of psychiatric care has changed significantly since the nineteenth century. The primary advancements have been a clearer understanding of the etiology and nature of various psychological impairments, and the development and sophistication of psychological assessment tools, therapeutic treatment strategies and interventions, and pharmacological interventions. Increased efforts to prevent psychological disturbances and the emphasis on local treatment have also changed the manner in which clients receive health-care services.

Therapeutic recreation specialists have emerged as effective members of behavioral health care teams. They contribute to the physical, psychosocial, cognitive, and leisure functions as well as to the quality of life and wellness aspects of the client's rehabilitation. Comprehensive services include providing diagnostic/needs assessment, treatment/rehabilitation, education, and prevention/health promotion experiences that are based on client needs. By using formalized tests and behavioral observations, TRSs assess clients' needs. This assessment guides the development of treatment plans. The application of certain interventions and leadership strategies facilitate implementation of the plan. Evaluation helps TRSs determine clients' progress by comparing current performance with the goals for treatment and guides TRSs in planning future treatment goals.

Key Terms

abnormal behavior Behavior that deviates substantially from perceived norms of society.

addiction Final step in the progression from tolerance to abuse to dependence on a substance that results in impaired functioning.

binge-purge syndrome A reference to bulimia nervosa that describes the behaviors characteristic of the disorder.

blood alcohol level (BAL) A rating describing the percent of alcohol in someone's blood.

learned helplessness A behavioral response of an individual toward life that is characterized by passivity and dependence on others.

naturalistic observation The systematic process of observing behaviors in an ordinary (as opposed to clinical) environment and recording and analyzing the observations (also referred to as field or behavioral observation).

over-the-counter drugs (OTC) Drugs like antihistamines that have psychoactive effects.

polysubstance dependence A person who uses three or more drugs but does not depend on one for dominant use.

substance abuse The repeated use of substances that causes failure in role obligations; multiple legal, social, and interpersonal problems; and potentially physically harmful situations.

substance dependence Cluster of cognitive, behavioral, and physiological symptoms indicating continual use of a substance resulting in tolerance, withdrawal, and compulsive drug-taking behavior.

tardive dyskinesia A condition that is characterized by various involuntary movements like tongue thrusting or muscle twitching.

tolerance The need for increased amounts of a substance to achieve intoxication.

withdrawal Maladaptive behavior change resulting when blood or tissue concentrations of a substance decline, often resulting in the consumption of the substance to relieve or avoid unpleasant physiological and cognitive effects.

Study Questions

1. What factors influence our definition of abnormal behavior and what are the problems associated with such a definition?

2. Identify five purposes for the use of therapeutic recreation services with individuals with psychological or behavioral disorders.

3. Identify and discuss various interventions that might be used to achieve diagnostic/needs assessment, treatment/rehabilitation, educational, and prevention/health promotion goals.

4. Describe the elements that might be included in a comprehensive therapeutic recreation assessment for a person with a psychological disorder and suggest some appropriate assessment tools that you might use.

Practical Experiences to Enhance Student Objectives

1. Visit or volunteer at a community mental health center or hospital. Become familiar with the services they provide and the psychological interventions and approaches they use.

2. Assess the behavior of a child, a peer, or a parent using an assessment tool such as those described in exhibit 9.4.

3. Form small groups and discuss the concept of abnormal behavior. Attempt to arrive at some consensus of opinion on specific behaviors that the group members would define as abnormal. What criteria did you use? Why is this such a difficult task? Is it becoming easier or more difficult to define abnormality? Why?

4. Complete an Internet search of Web sites that present information on mental health issues like the American Psychiatric Association, National Institute of Mental Health, Alcoholics Anonymous, or Narcotics Anonymous. Identify best practices and research supportive of evidence-based practices.

Social Impairments

After reading this chapter, students will be able to

✔ Describe the functioning characteristics and needs of people with HIV/AIDS; those who have been or are abused, neglected, homeless; and those who are legal offenders

✔ Identify the intent and outcomes of therapeutic recreation with these individuals

✔ Outline the interaction and intervention processes used with these individuals

✔ Describe the application of the therapeutic recreation process with representative clients

✔ Identify considerations affecting the therapeutic recreation process with clients

In this chapter we will discuss a broad spectrum of social impairments: HIV/AIDS; child maltreatment; poverty and homelessness; and criminal behaviors. We have chosen to refer to the individuals considered in this chapter as people with "social disabilities" because an array of nonspecific characteristics affects the management of their personal lives and social relationships. These individuals are socially disadvantaged and may have health issues as a result of poor lifestyle decisions, extraordinary life stressors, long-standing behavioral issues that have not been addressed, and in general being misunderstood and disempowered.

Chapter 10 was revised with contributions from Glenda P. Taylor, PhD, CTRS, Longwood University, Farmville, Virginia.

INTRODUCTION

One of the foremost world health concerns is the spread of HIV (human immuno-deficiency virus) and AIDS (acquired immune deficiency syndrome). HIV/AIDS conditions are transmitted sexually or through contact with the body fluids of a carrier. If acquired, HIV/AIDS progresses through three stages, the last of which results in death. With congenital HIV/AIDS, two patterns of the disease are evident in infants and children. Although these patterns may not result in death, youth can experience lifelong disabilities. TRSs who work with children, youth, and adults promote socially responsible behaviors, educate about healthy alternatives, and implement rehabilitation programs designed to minimize the impact of the disease on physical, mental/spiritual, and social well-being.

Child maltreatment encompasses acts of **commission** or abuse (inflicting injury or allowing injury to result) and acts of **omission** or neglect (failure to act on behalf of a child). Symptoms and characteristics are nonspecific (could be indicative of other situations) and result from multiple and interactive factors like spousal abuse, social isolation and poverty, and at-risk home life (single-parent homes). Trauma from maltreatment is manifest in many aspects of a person's life. TRSs provide supportive environments for youth at-risk and intervene in the cycle of violence that results in adult criminal behavior.

Homelessness is an extreme manifestation of poverty. People who move in with friends or family are among the "hidden" homeless. The visible homeless are found in shelters, in parks, and along city streets. A central theme apparent in personal histories of children and adults who are homeless is flawed interpersonal and family lives. TRSs address these individuals' needs to enhance self-esteem, develop employment skills, process losses and unresolved grief, access essential resources, overcome isolation, manage stress, and improve developmental and functional skills.

Unlawful behavior affects individuals worldwide. Because of the gravity of these behaviors, the World Health Organization supports a program entitled Global Campaign for Violence Prevention that develops model prevention programs and provides technical support to reduce maltreatment and death attributed to violence. Of those individuals under some form of correctional supervision, the majority are on probation or parole. The percentage of youth who are "at-risk" of criminal behavior is increasing; thus, the scope of therapeutic recreation services includes prevention programs conducted through public park and recreation departments, as well as intervention programs in prisons and correctional facilities. These services include assessment, treatment/rehabilitation, education, and promotion of rational decision-making and socially healthy behaviors. Services with at-risk youth can play a valuable preventive role in modifying behaviors like substance abuse that contribute to criminal acts.

Collectively, these sometimes invisible populations represent a growing segment of the worldwide population. There is commonality in their lack of political power, feelings of fear, low self-esteem, limited decision-making and resource acquisition skills, and unclear goals and aspirations. Therapeutic recreation programs for these individuals address learned helplessness, dependency, devalued personalities, depression, abusive behaviors, social incompetence, and feelings of entitlement. The sections that follow review each of these populations.

HIV AND AIDS

HIV (human immunodeficiency virus) and AIDS (acquired immune deficiency syndrome) are conditions found worldwide. They have attracted the attention of both the popular press and the medical community because, since the first reported cases of AIDS in 1981, there is still no cure or immunization, the incidence of HIV infection continues to rise, and if AIDS develops the outcome is fatal. The prevalence of the disease is now of pandemic proportions (Gostin, 2004). The estimated number of people living with HIV/AIDS ranges from 30–36 million and nearly 2.5 million are children (Avert, 2008). Persons of color and the poor bear a vastly disproportionate burden, and the rates of infection among women are rising, especially among African Americans and Latinas of child-bearing age (Gostin). The fifty and older group is also a cohort identified with increasing rates of HIV/AIDS. Levy-Dweck (2005) suggests this group is a hidden and growing population, with 10–15% of new HIV/AIDS cases occurring in this cohort. According to Levy-Dweck, "52% of older Americans living with HIV/AIDS are African American or Hispanic/Latino" (p. 40).

HIV/AIDS is a viral infection that is either acquired or congenital. Acquired HIV/AIDS occurs "through contact with the blood, semen, vaginal secretions, breast milk, and amniotic fluid of carriers" (Sherrill, 2004, p. 541). If acquired, HIV/AIDS progresses through three stages, each with unique signs. In Stage 1, HIV infection, most people do not know they are infected since the condition is **asymptomatic** (symptom-free): This stage may last for many years. When the AIDS virus enters the bloodstream, it begins to attack white blood cells. This results in the production of antibodies that are detected by an oral swab, blood draw, or urine test, with results available within a few minutes or days after infection. In Stage 2, HIV disease, individuals experience weight loss, chronic diarrhea, fevers of unknown origin, chronic fatigue, night sweats, coughing, and increased susceptibility to infections (Sherrill). Each client's response to HIV is unique. If the virus progresses to the symptomatic state, the immune system is impaired. The client may exhibit shortness of breath, oral or vaginal candidiasis ulcers, dry skin, skin lesions, peripheral neuropathy, shingles, seizures, or dementia (Smith, 2003). In Stage 3, AIDS, the disintegration of the protective immune system results in the presence of opportunistic infections and diseases leading ultimately to death: pneumocystis pneumonia (PCP) and Kaposi's sarcoma (KS), a cancer, are the most common diseases (Dunn & Leitschuh, 2006). The length of time living with AIDS has increased dramatically with advances in treatment.

Congenital HIV/AIDS occurs when infected antibodies are passed on perinatally by HIV-infected mothers (Sherrill, 2004). In the progression of the disease, two general patterns of illness are observed. About 20% of children develop serious disease in the first year of life; most of these children die by age four. The remaining 80% of infected children experience a slower rate of disease progression (National Institute of Allergy and Infectious Diseases [NIAID], 2003). Many children do not present with serious symptoms of AIDS until they enter school or reach adolescence. However, the growth and development of children with HIV infection are compromised. They are often slow to reach milestones in motor skills and development such as crawling, walking, and talking. As the disease progresses, many children develop neurologic problems such as difficulty walking; poor school performance; seizures; ID; cerebral palsy; and symptoms of

HIV encephalopathy (NIAID; Sherrill). As with adults, children with HIV develop life-threatening opportunistic infections. Pneumocystis pneumonia is the leading cause of death in children with AIDS; another cause of death is cytomegalovirus (CMV) disease. A lung disease called lymphocytic interstitial pneumonitis (LIP) (rarely seen in adults) presents frequently in HIV-infected children, making breathing progressively more difficult and often resulting in hospitalization (Dunn & Leitschuh, 2006; NIAID; Sherrill).

HIV/AIDS is a chronic, life-span illness affecting people of all ages worldwide. The number of people living today with AIDS (prevalence) is at its highest level, due to a treatment introduced in 1996—highly active antiretroviral therapy (HAART). This is an early, aggressive multiple-drug treatment referred to as "cocktails." HAART helps reduce drug resistance, a common cause of treatment failure (Smith, 2003). TRSs are likely to find HIV/AIDS among those with substance disorders, psychological impairments, neurological disorders, and youth-at-risk.

Functioning Characteristics

People with HIV/AIDS live with complex, chronic medical conditions. They experience a number of physically and psychologically debilitating symptoms and, if medications are an elected form of treatment, a number of side effects that interfere with daily functioning. Initial symptoms include a persistent cough and fever accompanied by shortness of breath or difficulty breathing, skin rashes, white coating or patches on the tongue, diarrhea, night sweats, rapid weight loss, swollen lymph glands, and extreme tiredness. As the immune system deteriorates, opportunistic diseases like PCP, KS, and cytomegalovirus (as part of disease progression, CMV retinitis may develop and result in blindness) result in death. Adverse effects from medications like zidovudine (AZT or Retrovir) include abdominal pain, diarrhea, cramps, anemia, nausea, chronic fatigue, confusion, seizures, and decreased interest levels. Infants and children experience similar dysfunction; they also fatigue easily, are malnourished, experience respiratory problems, and are more susceptible to infections. As a consequence, they miss school and opportunities to socialize.

The disease process of HIV/AIDS manifests serious psychosocial problems. The social isolation experienced by many persons with HIV/AIDS is a result of discrimination, rejection, and stigma. Education about the transmission of the disease helps allay fears and decrease isolation (Smith, 2003). Clients also may experience guilt from previous lifestyle activities and self-blame for becoming infected. Common psychological issues that present as co-morbidity factors include neuropsychiatric, mood, and substance-use disorders, and cognitive impairments (Remien & Rabkin, 2001).

Purpose of Therapeutic Recreation

Therapeutic recreation for people with HIV/AIDS involves assessment, treatment/rehabilitation, preventive education, and health promotion. Through leisure education, clients are given information that enables them to make lifestyle decisions that deter or prevent further transmission to others (Grossman, 1997). Health promotion activities encourage clients to adopt and maintain habits like good nutrition and adequate exercise that minimize a disease's further impact on physical well-being (Mobily & Ostiguy, 2004).

TRSs who work with people with HIV/AIDS focus on "prevention education or enhance coping with a progressive disease which has no curative treatment" (Grossman, 1997, p. 127). They also focus on facilitating day-to-day expression and the maintenance of functional independence (Grossman & Caroleo, 2001). TRSs help clients adjust to and cope with the stressors associated with living with a chronic and possibly fatal disease (AIDS is fatal; HIV may not be). Another goal is to alleviate the self-worth gap created by the loss of roles that would normally contribute to self-identity, like employment or parenting. Participation in a therapeutic recreation program may actually change participants' attitudes, resulting in the belief that the length of their lives has been increased (Caroleo, 1999). Finally, TRSs help clients reduce feelings of isolation, guilt, social stigma, and learned helplessness (Grossman & Caroleo).

Delivery Settings

People with HIV/AIDS receive treatment in a variety of settings. They will usually receive initial diagnoses, treatments, and service referrals in a primary care environment. They may receive episodic health care in inpatient acute-care centers. Drop-in clinics and residential and home health-care settings address individuals' emotional and social concerns. Psychotherapy and counseling address family planning, substance abuse, and legal and financial matters. Hospice and voluntary, community-based organizations provide ancillary and outreach services and resources.

TRSs are involved with clients with HIV/AIDS in inpatient, outpatient, and day-treatment agencies. TRSs employed in hospitals, free-standing clinics, and long-term settings focus on diagnosis, treatment, and remediation of physical health needs and social and psychological adaptations. Advocacy groups such as the Gay Men's Health Crisis (GMHC) have used TRSs to facilitate social interaction and support. This agency serves not only males but women and their families (GMHC, 2007).

TRSs facilitate client and caregiver support groups during in-home interventions and they provide school-based leisure experiences. They also work in foster care and transitional homes, shelters, public recreation departments, camps, hospice facilities, prisons, substance abuse centers, and at pediatric sites. DeRosa (2003) outlines policies and procedures that minimize risk of disease transmission during public play and recreation, including competitive sports at all levels. The decision to participate and to disclose one's HIV status is usually made on a personal basis, yet is affected by legislation like HIPAA that protects personal health information. Consequently, training and education are important to minimize risk while respecting each participant's confidentiality.

Leadership Interaction and Intervention Considerations

People with HIV/AIDS vary in chronological age, background, and exposure to leisure and therapeutic interventions. In addition, the functions of the TRS vary with clients' needs and the service setting. As a result, TRSs use a broad array of strategies, including stress management training, education about sexual practices and relationships, biofeedback, visual imagery, physical activity, nutrition education, leisure education, empowerment, self-efficacy and assertion exercises, expressive arts, volunteer activities, and experiences that help clients cope with death. Specific considerations are outlined below.

- Autonomous experiences allow clients to drop in and out as health permits while enabling immediate self-appraisal (e.g., exercise classes, free weights, aquatics).
- Volunteer opportunities and participation in the planning and delivery of experiences facilitate a client's expression of choices, self-control, and empowerment.
- Clients should develop new social networks to replace those that diminish after diagnosis. TRSs can help individuals replace unoccupied time with experiences that remediate stress caused by decreased health and well-being.
- Values clarification and self-awareness assessment tools identify behavioral motives. TRSs determine why, for example, youths abuse substances, display risky behaviors, and select various leisure alternatives.
- Children and teens with HIV/AIDS need to continue reaching their developmental milestones, thus programming includes the use of age-appropriate experiences to achieve functional skill development goals and promote family recreation.
- Financial consideration is a necessary part of planning. Youths may be without parents, adults may no longer be employed, and both may have limited caregiver support. Support groups alleviate stressors, including financial concerns, on the caregivers and may provide opportunities for observation of the client-caregiver dynamics helpful to the intervention process.
- To help clients experience satisfaction and happiness, TRSs create environments of unconditional positive regard and incorporate social and creative experiences that encourage humor (laughing) and loss of inhibitions.
- Physical tolerance is monitored because fatigue exacerbates HIV/AIDS. Also, clients may come to programs with already limited physical energy. Yet exercise, particularly aerobic exercise and progressive resistance training, has been noted to significantly improve cardiopulmonary and psychological status (O'Brien, Nixon, Tynan, & Glazier, 2006).
- Through adventure/challenge and camping experiences, youths receive emotional support and social approval while experiencing risk—factors necessary to building self-concepts and peer relationships while alleviating loneliness and depression.
- Horticulture and animal-facilitated therapies bring to interventions a sense of love, growth, and life.
- Leisure education is an avenue to supportive relationships and alternative experiences. By allowing clients to express their feelings, make decisions, and solve problems, leisure education enhances their optimal mental and spiritual health.

Applying the Therapeutic Recreation Process

Tom has recently been diagnosed with AIDS. He receives outpatient services through a mental health clinic. The Activity Therapy Department employs a TRS who functions as a member of the interdisciplinary team.

Assessment

Demographic information.   Tom is 26 years old and was recently diagnosed with AIDS. He lives with his parents, maintains his job part-time, and attends outpatient mental health clinic programs.

History.   Tom was a teen drug user and was diagnosed with HIV infection six years ago. Premorbid leisure included fishing and auto racing.

Present behavior.   Tom has experienced 20% weight loss, PCP, and episodes of flu-like symptoms. Nonwork time is spent watching TV and alone. During assessments, Tom appeared anxious, unable to concentrate, and unresponsive.

Planning

Long-term goal.   The long-term goal of Tom's intervention is to promote self-worth.

Short-term goals.   The two short-term goals are to improve motivation and to express interest in personal well-being.

Objective.   After three months of participation in a leisure facilitation class, Tom will (1) show improved outcomes on leisure satisfaction and motivation scales; (2) participate in at least one more leisure experience each week with family or support group members; and (3) self-report to the TRS at least one experience during the week that resulted in feelings of improved physical or mental and spiritual well-being.

Content.   Classes will include self-awareness exercises, an introduction to alternative outdoor experiences, attendance at auto races/events, role-playing scenarios with other group members representing family and loved ones, and time management, relaxation, and physical activity.

Process.   The TRS will administer assessment tools intended to ascertain Tom's present functioning and motivate him to become aware of how his needs are met through leisure. A time budget study will require Tom to document his behavior. In the support group, legal and financial issues will be discussed, as will be ways to promote physical well-being.

Implementation

The TRS used drop-in activities to establish rapport with participants. Clients attended meetings of the social services team as interventions were planned. Family members participated in private psychotherapy. Clients were required to adhere to the Centers for Disease Control and Prevention precautions to prevent HIV transmission during programs.

Evaluation

Assessment tools served as both formative and summative measures. A consumer advisory group monitored the program's confidentiality and budget options. Team meetings were conducted to monitor quality of life issues and intervention outcomes.

Related Considerations

Each agency or department should have written policies and procedures that address safety, risk, and infection control. Physicians normally recommend against collision sports like football to protect others from blood spills, and "wounds that might seep blood should be kept covered during a sport activity" (Sherrill, 2004, p. 544). Although the risk of contracting HIV/AIDS during first-aid procedures is minimal, the risk can be further minimized by following certain guidelines when giving first aid to a person with a bleeding injury (Sherrill):

- Wear disposable plastic or latex gloves.
- Clean any blood spills using a household bleach solution of one part bleach to 10 parts water.
- "Towels and clothing with blood contamination are safe after hot-water/detergent washing but should be stored in tied plastic bags until laundered or trashed" (p. 544).
- When finished caring for first-aid emergencies involving blood, wash the hands with soap and water.
- All toys and equipment should be properly cleaned between users to prevent the spread of infectious agents (Wachtel, 2003). Most institutions will have biohazard bins to place these toys for cleaning.

Although TRSs are aware that disclosure of HIV/AIDS status could be a violation of client confidentiality, exceptions to preferred ethical practice arise when harm to the client or others becomes possible. The TRS is obligated to inform the client of circumstances under which confidentiality of client information is not maintained. TRSs receive training in the management of blood-borne pathogens and may be encouraged to obtain a Hepatitis B vaccine because of the similarity of transmission with HIV/AIDS conditions and Hepatitis B. A number of resources and networks provide personal and professional support and up-to-date information. The national AIDS hotline number is 1-800-342-AIDS. The Centers for Disease Control and Prevention (CDC) Internet address is http:// www.cdc.gov. The Gay Men's Health Crisis internet address is www.gmhc.org.

PROBLEMS RELATED TO ABUSE AND NEGLECT

Violence affects people from all walks of life throughout the world. The WHO's Global Campaign for Violence and Prevention highlighted child-abuse prevention in its 2002 publication *World Report on Violence and Health* (Krug, Dahlberg, & Mercy). While risk of fatal abuse varies among low-, middle-, and high-income countries, worldwide over 50,000 children each year are murdered at the hands of someone in a relationship of responsibility. As stressors impact people's lives, the breadth of violence increases. Violence ranges from intimate partner violence to youth and sexual violence. Violence in the home forms the context of many children's lives. Witnessing violence in childhood can have long-term ramifications, including psychiatric disorders and suicide and has a lifelong sequelae including depression and violence towards others.

The needs of children who witness domestic violence are described by the broader category of *child maltreatment*. Most often the outcomes, interventions, and legal implications of services for these children are placed within the realms of abuse and neglect. **Abuse** is an act of commission or inflicting injury or allowing injury to result to a child while **neglect** refers to an act of omission or failure to act on behalf of a child. The WHO definition and typology is similar to that found in the federal Child Abuse Prevention and Treatment Act (CAPTA), as amended by the Keeping Children and Families Safe Act of 2003 (Child Welfare Information Gateway [CWIG], 2008): "An act or failure to act on the part of a parent or caretaker which results in death, serious physical or emotional harm, sexual abuse or exploitation; or an act or failure

The most common form of child maltreatment is neglect. Such neglect may or may not result in outwardly visible signs.

to act which presents an imminent risk of serious harm." The WHO's global definition of abuse includes all forms of physical and emotional ill-treatment, sexual abuse, neglect, and exploitation that results in actual or potential harm to a child's health, survival, development, or dignity at the hands of a person in a relationship of responsibility (Krug et al., 2002).

Abuse is usually divided into three categories (Durall, 1997). The first category, physical abuse, was the first form to attract professional and public attention (Pearce & Pezzot-Pearce, 1997). Physical abuse is nonaccidental injury that may result when the caretaker is angry or frustrated. Forms of commission include shaking, burning, and beating, usually to the back of the body from the neck to the knees (Durall). Physical abuse may be suspected when the parent or other adult caregiver offers conflicting, unconvincing, or no explanation for the child's injury; describes the child as "evil" or in some other very negative way; uses harsh physical discipline with the child, and has a history of abuse as a child.

Sexual abuse, the second category, includes any act of sexual assault like rape, incest, sodomy, as well as exploitation upon or with a minor for the gratification of the perpetrator or a third party. Incest is defined as "the occurrence of sexual relations between close blood relatives" (Sadock & Sadock, 2003, p. 886). Exploitation refers to any act like promoting prostitution or selling pornography that depicts minors engaging in or simulating sexual contact (Durall). Cases of sexual abuse and exploitation are not reported to authorities as frequently as cases of physical abuse; consequently, the true rate may be underestimated. Of the reported cases, rates tend to be higher among females than males and in extrafamilial cases than in intrafamilial cases.

Psychological maltreatment or emotional abuse, the third category, commonly refers to chronic acts, usually verbal, that interfere with the psychological and social development of a child. Examples include belittling or rejecting the child, ignoring the child, blaming the child for things over which he or she has no control, isolating the child from normal social experiences, and using harsh and inconsistent discipline (CWIG, 2008). This category may include spousal abuse that occurs in the presence of the child (Durall). Most believe this form of maltreatment to be inherent in other forms of abuse and neglect.

The most common form of maltreatment is neglect: It is estimated there are "five to six times as many neglectful families as overtly abusive ones" (Jewell, 1999, p. 12). Child-rearing practices that are inadequate or dangerous do not necessarily result in visible signs, usually occur over time, and are often categorized as either physical or emotional neglect. Physical neglect includes failure to provide adequate shelter, supervision, safety, support, food, and clothing. Failure to provide praise, security, affection, and social support exemplify emotional neglect.

Because problems related to abuse and neglect are a focus of clinical attention, a section of the *DSM-IV-TR* outlines categories of physical and sexual abuse and neglect of children. The codes are used when "the focus of clinical attention is severe mistreatment of one individual by another through physical abuse" (APA, 2000, p. 738). Inclusion of these codes occurs because maltreatment may be related to the other mental disorders described in the manual.

Most child maltreatment is at the hands of parents, relatives, or unrelated caretakers (Sadock & Sadock, 2003). A higher incidence of girls than boys are sexually assaulted. Infants from birth to one year of age have the highest rate of maltreatment victimization. The actual occurrence rates are likely to be higher than reported because maltreatment may go unrecognized, and because those in a position to report the abuse are often reluctant to do so.

Certain types of families are more at-risk of encountering maltreatment. A person who abuses is more likely to have been abused as a child. He or she may experience undue amounts of stress or lack parenting skills. In a situation where an adult's social and emotional needs are not met, a child may assume the role of "adult companion" and become the target of the adult's frustrations. A child is also vulnerable to an adult who abuses substances, is experiencing financial difficulties or divorce, and has limited access to recreation and other social services. Single, remarried, and dual-career parents are more at-risk of maltreating their children than are other parents.

Children who have already been abused are at higher risk of being reabused because of learned attention-seeking behaviors. Youths who act-out or violate parental expectations and school policies are also at-risk. Likewise, children with disabilities are at a significantly higher risk of being maltreated (Sadock & Sadock, 2003). Identified risk factors for children with disabilities include an increased dependency on parents and adult caregivers and increased family stress and isolation. As the above discussion illustrates, multiple and interacting factors contribute to child abuse and neglect. There is rarely one cause that adequately explains behavior resulting in harm to a child.

Functioning Characteristics

Unless an injury is traumatic, the symptoms and characteristics of maltreatment are nonspecific; that is, each could be indicative of other situations. The appearance of specific symptoms and behaviors that cluster repeatedly over time is indicative of mal-treatment; or a sudden dramatic change in behavior might suggest maltreatment. Mal-treated children are at risk of developing a number of problems as diverse as inadequate emotional development and lowered cognitive functioning to poor peer relationships, depression, anorexia, delinquent behaviors, suicide, and substance abuse. There is overlap in characteristics of children exposed to different subtypes of maltreatment; some children exhibit only transient symptoms while others display none (Pearce & Pezzot-Pearce, 1997).

Characteristics and behaviors of maltreated children might include regression or delay in achievement of developmental milestones, "failure to thrive" syndrome, sud-den personality changes, poor self-image, behavioral extremes (aggression to with-drawal), excessive passive or aggressive behaviors, self-destructive or risk-taking behaviors, a tendency to cling to or avoid adults, repeated attempts to postpone going home, wearing clothing to cover up injuries, and sexual promiscuity (Jewell, 1999; Sadock & Sadock, 2003). Many of these behaviors are likely to be exhibited during play, recreation, and social experiences rather than in formal academic or clinical set-tings. Long-term effects of maltreatment include lowered self-esteem, marriage diffi-culties, ingrained lack of empathy, depersonalization, conduct disorders, phobias, psychosomatic complaints, major depressive disorder, suicidal behavior, posttrau-matic stress disorder, substance abuse, reluctance to seek therapy, repetition of the same sexual abuse rituals to others, and feeling strange, scared, or anxious and not knowing why (Durall, 1997; Jewell; Sadock & Sadock). "Children who are abused for long periods . . . are more likely to be profoundly damaged than those who have expe-rienced only brief episodes of abuse" (Sadock & Sadock, p. 889). Likewise, children with disabilities are likely to also have a poorer prognosis. Even though persistent abuse or neglect may result in death, children remain silent for fear of losing their families as a result of divulging family secrets.

A child who adopts protective social strategies like defensiveness or withdrawal brings to adulthood a distorted role perception and distrust of others that contributes to isolation and an inability to form close, lasting relationships (Meister & Pedlar, 1992). Additionally, the cycle of violence that begins with child maltreatment can lead to delinquency and adult criminal behavior (Earle, 1997).

Purpose of Therapeutic Recreation

The scope of services for children who have experienced maltreatment is compre-hensive. Through observation in natural play environments, TRSs assess the develop-mental needs of youth. Leisure education and therapeutic interventions are used to enhance motor and self-concept development and to foster social and communication skills in relationship building, expression, coping, and resource awareness. TRSs help youth develop appropriate age behaviors, family expectations, and skills to express their needs and frustrations (Jewell, 1999). TRSs provide education and training to assist in the identification and management of stressful situations that might support child maltreatment; for example, by teaching stress-reduction and time-management techniques to single parents or dual-career parents. TRSs also prevent the occurrence of abuse and neglect and promote well-being by facilitating access to safe and supportive environments like after-school programs for youth in high-risk situations (Witt & Baker, 1997). Essential to the therapeutic process is developing a trusting relationship with adults in a safe, culturally sensitive environment. As positive role models, TRSs help youth reestablish trust in adults (Jewell).

An essential component of the therapeutic process with children who have experienced maltreatment is the opportunity to develop trusting relationships with adults in a safe environment.

Delivery Settings

Youths and adults who have experienced abuse may enter the health care and human service system on their own volition, as a result of a traumatic injury, or as a consequence of a predominant clinical or legal incident like depression, suicide attempt, becoming a runaway, or substance abuse. Delivery settings are broad in nature and scope. Intervention may be initiated with removal from the abusive or neglectful situation. Consequently, youths are treated in hospitals, foster care settings, shelters, private residential clinics, and through referral and outreach programs of schools, camps, and the juvenile justice system. Adults participate in neighborhood support networks, day treatment, outpatient clinics, private psychotherapy, and short-term inpatient psychiatric programs.

TRSs intervene as team members in treatment settings, as counselors in summer and year-round camps and residential programs, and as therapists and support staff in after-school programs and support groups. TRSs are employed in private residential settings that treat emotionally disturbed youths and adults with psychological needs. TRSs co-treat with team members like mental health staff, social workers, and correctional officers. TRSs who work within public park and recreation departments monitor youth offenders assigned to community service and provide therapeutic programming for children and youth with behavior disorders; these services are likely to include maltreated children and youth. Day programs for offenders and individuals who are homeless or unemployed also serve those who are currently experiencing or have previously experienced maltreatment.

Leadership Interaction and Intervention Considerations

Below is a list of some of the skills and interventions that TRSs use when working with individuals who have experienced maltreatment.

- Outdoor adventure activities that are followed by a formalized debriefing process can create a climate that promotes problem-solving, cooperation, and shared feelings, and also enhances self-concept (Jewell, 1999). With younger children, debriefing is facilitated by using expressive arts to interpret emotions and thoughts.

- Educational programs for families and youth at-risk that incorporate strategies like time and stress management, assertiveness, physical activity, values clarification, relaxation, and journaling are effective treatment interventions for "at-risk" behaviors and for coping with ongoing stress (Jewell, 1999). Residential treatment centers use adventure experiences with youth and their families to promote healthy family interactions.

- Youth perceive outdoor experiences as offering a sense of safety and security not found "inside" where family members are, or have been, the aggressors.

- Devaluation of self contributes to participants' overcompensation and desire to achieve and perform exceptionally well. During play, recreation, sports or at leisure, this characteristic is evident with attention-getting behaviors, lack of impulse control, inability to lose graciously, and a desire to be "number one." A TRS, recognizing the underlying motive of such actions, helps individuals

Outdoor activities that are followed by a formalized debriefing process can create a climate that promotes problem-solving, cooperation, and shared feelings.

channel energy toward recognizing self-improvements and attaining realistic goals. Thus, esteem-building experiences like setting goals and making "I" statements are critical intervention protocols.

- Participants tend to prefer individual experiences—youth who have witnessed family violence tend to be hyper-vigilant—or indicate they lack recreation and play companions. Play therapy is an alternative form of expression with young children who tend to avoid contacts and engagements. To enhance social functioning, a TRS first schedules cooperative projects with a few others—like planning an outing (adults) or canoeing (youths)—and then gradually introduces experiences with larger groups.

- Leisure education strategies incorporate choices, goal setting, social skills training, and values clarification, thus enabling participants to affirm values, develop social involvements, and select experiences commensurate with their abilities.

- TRSs are cognizant of environmental features such as the time of day an activity is performed (night or day) or activity locations that may heighten clients' feelings of insecurity or powerlessness. When individuals reside in shelters, an alternative safe location is used with interventions to introduce "normalcy" and routine in family engagements.

- TRSs are alert to unusual visible signs of abuse (bruises, burns) and report such evidence to proper authorities while maintaining client confidentiality, since this reporting may place the abused at further risk of abuse from the aggressor.

- Physical activity relieves tension and offers the TRS opportunities to assess developmental delays attributable to maltreatment. Psychosomatic symptoms may result from abusive situations and can negatively affect an individual's performance. TRSs articulate the relationship between emotional and physical well-being and help clients manage conditions such as hyper- and hypo-activity.

- Structure, consistent expectations and routines, active listening, and reinforcement promote psychological wellness (Durall, 1997).

- Experiential activities like expressive and creative arts, and animal-assisted therapy encourage expression, playfulness, and altruistic behaviors (Durall, 1997).

- The provision of respite care through after-school programs or day camp may prevent the child from being in the wrong place at the wrong time (Jewell, 1999). Such experiences also allow youth to pursue age-appropriate options rather than, for example, taking responsibility for parental relationships and the raising of siblings.

Applying the Therapeutic Recreation Process

As young children, Joe and his brother were abused by their natural mother. Joe's adoptive family is supportive and has accessed leisure resources through the park and recreation department. Joe does not appear to be physically impaired, although abuse at an early age with subsequent placements in a number of foster homes has exacerbated his cognitive, behavioral, and social deficits.

Assessment

Demographic information.   Joe is 18 years of age and living with his adoptive parents. He attends school in an inclusive setting where he is identified as having a behavior disorder.

History.   Joe and a younger brother became wards of the state at ages 3 and 1, respectively, when abandoned by their mother. Medical examination revealed physical abuse. The brothers were placed in separate foster care homes. Joe was adopted at age 10 after living in three other homes.

Present behavior.   Joe comprehends and complies with verbal requests yet neither verbalizes nor initiates conversations. When presented with alternatives, he makes known his preferences. Joe functions in groups yet does not verbally interact with other group members. In his early home environment, withdrawal and isolation were effective coping mechanisms and are difficult patterns to reverse. Functional living and job training are included in his school curriculum. He has attended aquatic therapy programs through the therapeutic recreation division of the recreation commission.

Planning

Long-term goal.   The long-term goal of Joe's TR intervention is to improve social functioning.

Short-term goals.   The two short-term goals are to increase verbal and nonverbal expression and to increase personal interactions as a group member.

Objective. After six months of intervention Joe will (1) respond to at least two yes-no questions from the TRS each session, and (2) verbalize to at least one other person in a group each time the young adult social club meets.

Content. Joe will attend speech therapy and individual psychotherapy sessions during the school day and will participate in the teen social club, which is cosponsored by the mental health clinic and the therapeutic recreation division. The intent of the club is to help students apply functional living and community orientation skills acquired through the academic program. Experiences incorporate social training, time and money management, activities that help participants to access transportation, and independent living tasks.

Process. To determine Joe's functioning relative to the academic community, home, and leisure settings, the TRS administered the FACTR-R (Functional Assessment of Characteristics for Therapeutic Recreation-Revised). The assessment was completed by observing Joe during initial aquatic therapy and social club sessions. From the assessment the therapist identified the skills that needed improvement and could be remediated through therapeutic recreation. A behavior management program will be implemented by a therapy team consisting of a vocational rehabilitation specialist, psychologist, social worker, special educator, and TRS. Year-round training is recommended in Joe's individual transition plan (ITP).

Implementation

Consistency in daily routine was emphasized. The family documented Joe's verbal and group interactions. Joe was rewarded for his progress through verbal praise and additional swimming opportunities. During social club meetings, members were paired with community buddies to facilitate inclusionary experiences. Team meetings were held twice a year, and Joe's ITP was updated annually. A behavior specialist routinely monitored Joe's social/emotional behaviors.

Evaluation

TRSs kept critical incident records to record verbal responses during activity sessions. The buddy system was monitored to determine the number of new social contacts Joe made, as well as his verbal and nonverbal interactions. Observations were made twice yearly prior to the team meetings to reevaluate functional outcomes reported on the FACTR-R.

Related Considerations

"Increasingly, violence against children . . . may lead to crime perpetrated later in life by the victims themselves" (Earle, 1997, p. 67). Of those who abuse, the majority have been abused by their own parents and, with chronic maltreatment, aggressive and violent behavior are likely outcomes (Sadock & Sadock, 2003). Yet, many cases of abuse and neglect go unreported. Because of the acknowledged link between child maltreatment and crime, criminal justice, health care, and social service personnel are partnering to intercede in the "cycle of violence." Staff training provides TRSs with their employer's policies on maltreatment—especially information on how to recognize and report suspected acts of commission and omission. Training also provides

TRSs with awareness of culturally sanctioned leisure behaviors and child-rearing practices. TRSs sensitive to precipitating factors intervene to protect both the aggressor and the child.

TRSs are aware that they may be on the receiving end of misdirected anger, fear, hostility, and rejection that has accumulated from living in an abusive or neglectful environment. A TRS blends firmness, structure, discipline, and consistency with objective listening and positive feedback, yet realizes behavioral change comes slowly. TRSs are cognizant that their gestures and verbal interactions may be interpreted differently by clients. As a consequence, they seek out appropriate assistance when, for example, youth shy away from physical contact, display excessive dependency needs, or accuse a TRS of inappropriate interactions with themselves or other participants. Further, the TRS is aware that children and youth can be perpetrators (e.g., initiate abusive behaviors) and as a consequence adhere to intervention practices that sanction inappropriate physical contact and document incidents to assure safety of staff and participants.

POVERTY AND HOMELESSNESS

Poverty continues to be a pervasive problem in the twenty-first century. A worldwide economic downturn disproportionately impacts the poorest people, women, and children. The poverty level is increasing in female-headed households and among those employed yet earning less than the poverty threshold. Poverty impacts children and youth throughout their early lives and results in deficits in physical, socio-emotional, and cognitive development. Children of poverty may experience mental illnesses, ADHD, conduct disorders, antisocial behavior, drug use, and depression. Thus, there is a direct relationship between poverty and disability and developmental delays.

Homelessness is an extreme manifestation of poverty (Ward, 1995). The conditions into which a person is born are major predictors of poverty and homelessness. People who lack a fixed, regular, and adequate nighttime residence and who have a temporary nighttime residence supervised publicly or privately are considered to be homeless. People living doubled-up with friends or family or in makeshift housing arrangements are among those who constitute the hidden homeless. The visible homeless—those who sleep in shelters, welfare hotels, and outdoors in public places—are not necessarily the poorest. Those found in jails, foster homes, detox centers, and doubled-up with friends or relatives are among those considered to be living in poverty (Jencks, 1994).

Estimates of the number of people who experience homelessness at some point in their lives vary because there is no uniformity in the meaning of the term or in reporting methods. Most estimates rely on counting people who are in shelters or on the streets. This approach identifies the number of people who use services like shelters and soup kitchens, or who are easy to locate on the street or in a park, but results in underestimates of homelessness (National Coalition for the Homeless, 2008). Each year, more than 3 million people experience homelessness, including 1.3 million children (National Law Center on Homelessness & Poverty [NLCHP], 2008).

Families and children are among the fastest-growing groups of people who are homeless and experience extreme poverty. One third of all homeless are families with children under 6 years (NLCHP, 2008), accounting for the majority of the youth living with homeless parents (National Center on Family Homelessness, 2008). Older children who are homeless often are runaways and are likely to have experienced maltreatment; additionally, one of every three homeless youth has a diagnosable psychiatric disorder like posttraumatic stress (Koch, 2007). Authorities often place children of families found living in public places in foster care, congregate living centers, with families of friends, or in other transitional placements (Jencks, 1994).

The majority of those who are homeless are adult unmarried or unaccompanied males, single parent families, and families with children living in urban areas (U.S. Conference of Mayors, 2008). Such individuals commonly experience mental illness, physical disabilities, and are victims of domestic violence (U.S. Conference of Mayors). People with severe drug or alcohol problems who have served time in jails and prisons on felony convictions also number among the homeless, as do an increasing number of veterans who rely on veteran's hospital domiciliaries for temporary shelter.

Homelessness is caused by a lack of available and affordable housing, elimination of government entitlement programs, family breakup, domestic violence, underemployment and unemployment, mental health system reforms, an increase of minimum-wage service economy jobs and the elimination of unskilled and semiskilled occupations, and tightened eligibility standards for supplemental government services.

Functioning Characteristics

People without homes are a heterogeneous population. Presented characteristics are nonspecific, as they are indicative of a variety of needs. One medical or social need may be masked by another, as illustrated by a battered woman fleeing abuse who is homeless, or a runaway child whose health status is described as endangered and who has a reported history of physical and sexual abuse. Hidden characteristics like

Although the homeless are a heterogeneous population, adult, unmarried males comprise a large segment.

illiteracy, fear of crime, disempowerment, and inaccessible facilities and services tend to exacerbate the conditions of people experiencing poverty and homelessness.

"The problems of poverty, homelessness, poor physical and mental health, and social isolation combine to create a set of critical unmet needs" (Kunstler, 1993, p. 19). General characteristics of people who are homeless include learned helplessness, dependency, alienation, low self-esteem, unresolved loss and grief, depression, anxiety, flawed interpersonal competence, lack of information, self-defeating behaviors, lowered fitness levels, chronic stress, and large amounts of discretionary time and a lack of standards as to how to constructively use this time (Klitzing, 2004; Sessoms & Orthner, 1992). Children who are homeless tend to be sick, hungry, hospitalized, and have many more mental health problems than other children (National Center on Family Homelessness, 2008).

Purpose of Therapeutic Recreation

People who are living in poverty and are homeless are as diverse as their respective demographic features. Therapeutic recreation services, therefore, encompass an array of goals from assessment of social and emotional well-being to behavioral changes, leisure skill development, and lifestyle management. Because the effects of poverty and homelessness are cumulative and chronic, intervention is both intermittent and long-term.

Therapeutic recreation interventions contribute to quality of life concerns such as regaining a sense of identity, increasing self-esteem, experiencing positive social interaction, coping with stress, and becoming engaged in the community (Klitzing, 1993, 2004). Homeless mothers and their children learn "how to play together, develop social and leisure skills, and participate in physical health and fitness activities" (Kunstler, 1993, p. 21). Therapeutic recreation helps develop a sense of connectedness. "The chronic homeless person can experience a sense of ownership . . . and feelings of empowerment" as they increase their sense of influence and control (Harrington & Dawson, 1997, p. 24). Through leisure education, participants cultivate their decision-making and planning abilities, awareness of available programs and services, and alternatives to substance abuse during nonwork hours (Kunstler). TRSs also help clients develop life skills and educational and vocational interests, and facilitate access to medical and social service networks through case management and support groups.

Harrington and Dawson reported that recreation in shelters serves to "ameliorate the condition of homelessness . . . and perhaps empower them to make positive changes in their lives" (1997, p. 26). These authors noted that the intent of programs offered in shelters was to "improve the self-esteem of homeless individuals, allow them the opportunity to relax and release stress, and to enable them to socialize with others and build relationships with the community" (p. 26). Klitzing (2004) found for women living in shelters, leisure provided opportunities for getting away, social support, and diversionary experiences.

Delivery Settings

Case management, placement, and referral are directed by the physical and psychological functioning of the person. People whose clinical symptoms require medical intervention are serviced in inpatient and day-treatment hospitals and health-care centers. Adolescents and adults who have violated laws or statutes and require protective services reside in prisons, community restitution centers, halfway houses, and foster care homes. Other existing services and programs include day-treatment programs, AIDS houses, individual and group counseling, services for children in after-school programs, shelters, clubs, soup kitchens, youth centers, and church affiliated programs.

The role of the TRS varies with each setting. Hospital and clinical services focus on physical health care, and clients' goals address coping with environmental contingencies, enhancing physical and psychological skills, and stabilizing interpersonal functioning. TRSs working with individuals in outpatient settings incorporate experiences that enhance self-direction, empowerment, stress and time management, social interaction and engagement, goal prioritization, community and self-awareness, and life and leisure well-being.

Leadership Interaction and Intervention Considerations

In this section we present some general principles and interventions that should be considered by students who are planning to work with individuals who experience poverty and homelessness.

- Intervention is holistic, collaborative, and comprehensive and occurs in the client's neighborhood. TRSs' tasks include training, referral, family and parent education, consultation with psychiatrists and criminal justice personnel, and creating avenues to access transportation, funding, and leisure experiences.

- The term *accessibility* implies more than physical accessibility. Also considered are financial and participation requirements, facility location, staff attitudes, the presence of nonhomeless users, cultural sensitivity, and program promotion (Ward, 1995). Some of the barriers addressed include user fees, the presence of gangs or drug dealers, and program publicity through media—neither available to nor understood by clients.

- Intervention is nonjudgmental and empathetic; however, expectations are set and rules are enforced. Supportive listening without patronizing or giving advice on unsolvable issues encourages clients to set realistic goals and make decisions while examining the consequences of their actions.

- Clients are involved in program delivery to experience self-determination, control, resource acquisition, social support, and interdependent functioning (Dail, 1992; Klitzing, 2004). They address disenfranchisement by taking on communal responsibilities. TRSs help individuals feel similar to their peers rather than different (Klitzing, 1993).

- TRSs incorporate such interventions as stress and time management and assertiveness training so clients can learn to better meet daily survival needs. Expressive and creative outlets like music, comedy shows, and dancing help clients release tension and allow anger and frustration to dissipate (Polzer, 1995).

- In residential placements like Veterans Affairs Medical Centers, prisons, and mental health centers, treatment protocols include daily living skills and incentive activities like gardening and operating coffee houses.

- Intervention with children is both structured and unstructured so they develop playfulness and academic support skills. Programs include physical activity, gardening, small animal projects, libraries, and environmental education to promote healthy development (Kunstler, 1993).

- Therapeutic recreation helps people cope with social decompensation (Harrington & Dawson, 1997). TRSs who work in shelters design programs to develop clients' social skills, provide positive role models, and involve clients in experiences to facilitate connections and networks in their home communities and environments.

- Through leisure education, TRSs strive to empower clients to exercise initiative and act independently (Harrington & Dawson, 1997). Experiences include money and travel planning, developing alternative leisure skills, grieving seminars, self-care classes, and designing and following through on life and leisure plans.

Applying the Therapeutic Recreation Process

Assessment

A free-standing medical care facility in a metropolitan area services individuals from the surrounding rural areas, including those who are homeless. The number of

Interventions with children whose families have experienced poverty or homelessness may include structured and unstructured play.

residents in state facilities has been reduced by one-half during the last few years. All available subsidized housing units are full and the Salvation Army provides the only shelter. Weekly lunch and evening meals are provided through two community churches. The school system provides after-school programs during the year and daily lunches at day-camp sites in the summer. Downtown areas are serviced by metro buses. A YMCA supports a youth center year-round. TRSs within the medical facility service the psychiatric, chemical dependency, physical rehabilitation, and children's units. They provide day treatment and outreach for nonresidents.

Mothers with young children are the fastest growing group of persons who are homeless in the community; males in their late teens and early twenties are another significant group. As in other areas where farming and skilled labor are declining, this metropolitan area is not equipped to provide for increasing numbers of unemployed and underemployed individuals.

Planning

The director of recreation therapy from the hospital is a member of the mayor's committee on the homeless, along with other social service providers. The city budget director and superintendent of schools also serve on the committee. The committee's mission is to develop a referral network.

The recreation therapy director and the United Way director will update a community directory. Human service department social workers will plan visits to the youth center, churches, and the Salvation Army to assess user needs. School social workers will complete similar assessments of school-related services. The mayor's office will identify transportation and in-home services that the community needs.

Implementation

Target dates are set to review data and organize a plan to develop a coordinating board. Because budgets are in a no-growth/cutback mode, service gaps and overlaps are cited. Resources are realigned to establish a continuum of services from medical treatment to crisis care and outreach assistance. The coordinating board created a Web site to link volunteers to agency programs; to facilitate community awareness on poverty and homelessness; and to encourage sponsorships, donations, and resource sharing to enhance community-wide intervention.

TRSs conducted training sessions for their colleagues. They collaborated with school personnel and youth center staff to prepare transitional plans. They provided outreach programs on travel and money management. They trained volunteers on how to be leisure buddies. The committee also created a community calendar that coordinates meals, holiday socials, and a variety of cultural events and celebrations.

Evaluation

From the data gathered in the planning stage, the committee estimated the community's number of visible and "hidden" homeless (those who live with relatives or in abandoned houses), so tracking those within the system was possible. The coordinating board meets monthly to monitor resource utilization and recommend budget options. TRSs implemented a self-reporting process to monitor the effectiveness of transition plans. Client advisory groups presented input to respective service providers.

Related Considerations

"Recreational opportunities can be a means of empowerment to homeless people" (Harrington & Dawson, 1997, p. 25). As these authors note, through participation a person may redefine herself or himself without the "homeless" label. Participation in nonthreatening experiences improves quality of life while giving clients the confidence to try to escape homelessness. A TRS who encourages hope, optimism, and renewed motivation facilitates holistic well-being while promoting the spiritual aspect of leisure experiences.

When planning programs, TRSs take into consideration geographic access, welcoming attitudes of staff, clothing and equipment requirements, smoke-free and smoking areas, homeless-nonhomeless ratio and mix, methods of disseminating program information, methods to incorporate cultural sensitivity, and strategies to include clients in programming. Successful program delivery depends upon networking and volunteers (Polzer, 1995). TRSs become facilitators, educators, and advocates as they promote experiences that are integral to the solution of social issues emanating from poverty and homelessness. Information on homelessness is available on a number of Web sites including: National Coalition for the Homeless, http://www.nationalhomeless.org; U.S. Conference of Mayors, http://www.usmayors.org; U.S. Department of Housing and Urban Development, http://www.hud.gov; and National Law Center on Homelessness & Poverty, http://www.nlchp.org.

DELINQUENT AND CRIMINAL BEHAVIORS

Violence is a worldwide issue; more than 1.6 million people throughout the world lose their lives to violence each year (WHO, 2009). Further, the U.S. spends billions each year on health care, law enforcement, and lost productivity due to violence. The issues of crime, delinquency, and an ever-increasing prison population have been the focus of much concern and debate. While most people would agree that "something" should be done, there is little consensus on what constitutes the most effective response. And, with more people being placed into prisons annually in the U.S. than being released (Leavitt, 2007), public concern about safety and the debate over whether to focus resources on prevention or punishment is ongoing.

Patterns of behavior that deviate from cultural norms and threaten the welfare of others are labeled as **delinquent** when they are committed by persons under 18 years old, while offenses committed by adults are labeled as **criminal.** The criminal justice system is composed of police agencies, the judiciary, and penal systems that function at the national, state, and local levels. Data on crime are kept by two different agencies, each with its own system of collecting information. As a consequence, statistics and crime reports by type of crime may vary. The FBI's *Uniform Crime Reports* is an annual collection of crime data voluntarily submitted to the FBI by community police agencies. The Justice Department also tabulates data on crime in the form of its *National Crime Victimization Survey,* a national survey conducted via house-to-house interviews. This second data set uncovers crimes never reported to the police and, as a consequence, not recorded in the FBI's *Uniform Crime Reports.*

Of those individuals under some form of correctional supervision, the majority are on **probation** (sentence ascribed to be served in the community rather than prison) or **parole** (release of an offender whose sentence has not expired on condition of supervision). Of the male inmates in the U.S. serving time, over half are serving time for violent offenses, while the predominant offenses committed by women tend to be property crimes or drug violations; that is, nonviolent (West & Sabol, 2008). World-wide, violence is "among the leading causes of death for people aged 15–44 years . . . accounting for 14% of deaths among males and 7% of deaths among females" (WHO, 2009). Inmates in the U.S. tend to serve their time in state prisons; roughly one in every 198 U.S. residents was imprisoned (in either a federal or state prison) with a sen-tence of more than one year (West & Sabol). During the first decade of the twenty-first century, the total number of people incarcerated by federal and state authorities expe-rienced annual increases, although at a slower pace than in previous decades.

Delinquency and crime are multidimensional issues associated with the complex interaction of offender traits and environmental influences. Characteristics of males who commit half or more of the reported serious crimes include criminal parents, dys-functional families, low verbal intelligence quotients, poor school performance, sub-stance abuse, and poverty (Wilson, 1997). The social evolution of a future criminal begins with parental neglect and the youth's acceptance by aggressive, hostile class-mates at school. This results in delinquent gang behaviors that lead to friendships with people who specialize in different types of crime (Fagan, 1997). Antisocial behaviors serve as coping mechanisms for such youth. Inability to appropriately satisfy needs is manifested by getting into trouble with the law. Increasing numbers of youth are con-sidered to be "at-risk" (Sprouse & Klitzing, 2005). Youth are considered to be **at-risk** when "detrimental influences in their lives cause them to be functioning from a disad-vantaged position" (McCready, 1997, p. 31). According to the ongoing *National Youth Gang Survey of Cities, Suburban Areas, Towns, and Rural Counties,* cities are the predomi-nant location of both gangs and gang members and continually report increases in gang problems (National Youth Gang Center, 2007). While gangs offer an avenue to meet youth needs like friendship and refuge from family abuse, they place youth at risk for increased use of illicit drugs and violence.

Functioning Characteristics

People who are legal offenders tend to experience difficulty managing daily living tasks and interpersonal relations. Correlative issues include poor judgment; low motiva-tion, self-worth, and self-esteem; poor family management practices and family conflict; early and persistent antisocial behaviors; alienation and rebelliousness; substance abuse; lack of impulse control; sensation seeking; low harm avoidance; underachievement in sports; participation in negative leisure activities; and no constructive activities in free time (Hawkins, 1997; Schultz, Crompton, & Witt, 1995). Youth in today's society face a number of challenges that continue to be major health concerns—smoking, alcohol and drug use, criminal behavior, decreased physical activity and increased obesity, and dis-appearance of social norms resulting in overall poor judgment (Allen, Cox, & Cooper, 2006; Sklar, Anderson, & Autry, 2007). Consequently, these challenges manifest into problems like suicide, delinquency, and substance abuse. At-risk youth are ill-equipped to generate self-motivated, meaningful experiences and are prone to boredom: They are vulnerable to peer pressure and activities that offer immediate gratification (Sklar et al.).

People who are legal offenders tend to have difficulty managing interpersonal relationships and may exhibit antisocial behavior, rebelliousness, and lack of impulse control.

Individuals who are offenders typically respond to immediate and to externally driven desires. They tend to be less physically healthy and to have acquired fewer expressive outlets. People who have been incarcerated experience a phenomenon similar to that felt by persons with HIV/AIDS. They become stigmatized by the public and devalued by and dependent upon an institutional system that supports learned helplessness and loss of autonomy, integrity, and personal rights. Concerns for privacy, safety, security of self and personal belongings, and separation from significant others, when combined with the above factors, may create anxiety and depression. Hence, the individual who is a prisoner also may become a "prisoner" on the inside.

Purpose of Therapeutic Recreation

The goals of correctional agencies are twofold: (1) to constrain offenders to prevent them from doing harm to themselves or others; and (2) when released, at the very least, to prevent them from repeating the behaviors that caused the incarceration or, at best, to help them become productive members of society. The long-standing punishment versus rehabilitation debate stems from factors like the public's attitude toward and fear of violence, media portrayal of the justice system and exploitation of criminal acts, and the continuing evidence of high rates of **recidivism** (rate of return to prison) regardless of the dollar amounts spent on correctional alternatives. Therapeutic recreation has not escaped this controversy. When the intent of correctional intervention is viewed as punishment, recreation serves as a reward for good behavior. When the intent of sanctions is to treat, therapeutic recreation interventions become a part of the rehabilitation plan and target behaviors that diminish well-being.

TRSs promote experiences that encourage self-awareness, positive self-image, decision-making, wellness, family leadership, social interaction skills, resource awareness, management of discretionary time, stress management, coping with authority and high-risk situations like gang pressure to conform, and academic and vocational skill building. Within prison, therapeutic recreation serves as a catharsis from the realities of confinement, offers some freedom of choice in otherwise controlled environments, and provides for needed exercise and stress relief (Carter & Russell, 2005). As a form of treatment, focus is on coping skills, anger management, emotional control, enhanced thinking skills, and functional skill development (Ardovino, 2006). For those who are not imprisoned, TR services play a valuable role in preventing youth from becoming at-risk and modifying behaviors like drug abuse that contribute to criminal acts (McCready, 1997; Witt & Crompton, 1997). Youth are given the opportunity to discover healthy interests, positive role models, and strengthen leadership skills and **resiliency factors** (skills and attitudes necessary to adapt and cope with everyday life). Further, positive experiences become the "hook" to collaborative relationships and prevention programs that address non-recreative needs (Sprouse & Klitzing, 2005). Unique developmental opportunities are realized through leisure (Darling, Caldwell, & Smith, 2005). Through extracurricular and summer camp programs, youth develop resilient life skills like values orientation, humor, independence, relationships, and higher levels of aspiration (Allen et al., 2006; Darling et al.).

Delivery Settings

Programs with at-risk youth, delinquents, and offenders are found in settings like detention centers, youth camps, residential and day-treatment centers, public park and recreation departments, and state and federal prisons. In prisons, TRSs function as treatment team members on forensics' units serving prisoners who may also be substance abusers, and have cognitive impairments or mental health needs. In these settings, the TRS leads skill development classes, supervises areas like the library and gym, and coordinates with other team members like the chaplain and vocation specialist to offer prison ministry and job-training services. At the local level, TRSs collaborate with education, law enforcement, and nonprofit or government agencies to provide direct services to youth at-risk. Focus is on prevention, referral, and follow-up to enhance self-esteem, increase physical activity, and promote skill development. These protective factors help counter risk factors. Recreators and TRSs facilitate program access, provide case management and staff training, and coordinate direct services like social skills training, adventure/challenge courses, summer and extracurricular programs, sports, drug-awareness, nutrition, and academic enrichment programs.

Leadership Interaction and Intervention Considerations

Below is a list of some strategies and interventions used by TRSs when working with offenders or those at-risk of offending.

- Security and safety concerns influence both the setting and content of programs. Items used in experiences can become lethal weapons or escape tools. The person who is a candidate for **elopement** (runaway or escape) is restricted to certain areas and recreation times.

- The prison environment offers little personal freedom. A graduated privileging system is implemented to allow choice, foster self-determination, and support tolerated degrees of nonconformity and self-expression.

- Experiences like jogging, aerobics, basketball, and volleyball provide outlets to express aggression and release tension through quick movements and striking legitimate targets. Weight-lifting is a common activity in prison and jails, providing tension release.

- Animal-assisted therapy in prisons involves partnerships with animal shelters that allow prisoners to rehabilitate and care for dogs who are then adopted.

- Recreation experiences like holiday events involve clients and family members in culturally normative celebrations that promote resource awareness and tolerance—resiliency skills.

- During adventure/challenge programs, clients learn more about themselves and their interactions with others, including family members, through successful completion of initiatives (McCready, 1997; Pommier & Witt, 1995; Sklar et al., 2007). Such experiences provide immediate concrete feedback. Debriefing addresses issues like self-determination, social capital, and positive youth development.

- Parents and youth become active intervention team members; they are empowered to assume decision-making responsibilities essential to the development of leadership skills and perceptions of competence (Sprouse & Klitzing, 2005).

- Long-term interventions, continuity of services, and an individualized holistic approach are necessary since challenges youth face are ever present and positive behaviors require supportive environments and role models (Allen et al., 2006).

- Extracurricular activities are structured to address adolescent adjustment and academic issues (Darling et al., 2005). These programs help prevent problems faced by youth like experimentation with problematic activities such as drug and alcohol use during unstructured social leisure.

- To an inmate, a TRS represents an authority figure; therefore, inmates may blame the TRS for inadequacies or challenge the TRS's authority. A TRS realizes inmates have poor social and anger management skills and attempts to avoid situations in which the inmate is devalued in front of others.

- Self-esteem is enhanced when participants assume responsibility; for example, supervising equipment check-in, library use, or volunteering to repair children's toys.

Applying the Therapeutic Recreation Process

This case study presents a client, Tony, with a somewhat typical prisoner profile. The TRS working with Tony has experience with psychiatric rehabilitation and behavior management interventions and applies protocols similar to those used in chemical dependency.

Assessment

Demographic information.   The inmate, Tony, is a 25-year-old male serving time in the treatment unit of a medium security state prison for armed robbery, aggravated assault, and drug abuse violations.

History. Tony is a repeat offender who has violated parole and has an arrest record for possession of drugs. This is his second incarceration; the first was in a treatment security unit.

Present behavior. The state medical center staff has completed diagnostic work-ups and has prepared a rehabilitation plan. Staff will also use court records and assessments like the Draw-A-Person and the Minnesota Multiphasic Personality Inventory (MMPI) to project Tony's personality and self-image factors. Tony completed the ninth grade, has no employment record, and was a gang member. He has no known family.

Planning

Long-term goal. The long-term goal of Tony's TR intervention is to enhance self-determination skills.

Short-term goals. The two short-term goals are to articulate leisure preferences and to maintain emotional control during group experiences.

Objective. Tony will (1) select a cell activity and a yard activity once per month and participate in each and (2) will remain in control during at least 50% of the activity time.

Content. Tony will be enrolled in leisure education classes and daily physical activity classes that require him to select alternative fitness workouts and skills to practice. The classes also will allow him to choose between library, gym, yard, and exercise room time and will set behavioral expectations for each area.

Process. Tony will earn points by attaining personal goals in recreation. The points can be applied to canteen purchases, leadership options, and library time. TRSs will enforce rule compliance and behavioral expectations in each program area. TRSs and class members will jointly plan large group events, and a TRS will meet with Tony routinely to chart personal accomplishments.

Implementation

Tony was required to attend daily fitness sessions and weekly leisure education and skill development classes. A rehabilitation team met monthly with the inmate. A TRS charted Tony's expressed requests and preferences and noted his self-management during group activities.

Evaluation

The rehabilitation team reevaluates each inmate's rehabilitation plan semiannually and gives recommendations to the parole board; re-administration of assessment tools also occurs semiannually. Tony is serving consecutive terms and is considered to have a high potential for recidivism due to drug addiction and lack of a support system. The rehabilitation goal was to promote sobriety and social efficacy to enable transition from the treatment security unit to medium security within the state prison.

Related Considerations

The conditions present with at-risk youth, delinquents, and criminal offenders are not unlike those associated with maltreatment, substance abuse, and poverty. Individuals are embedded in situations that require long-term holistic intervention. The result of disruptive, antisocial behaviors is lack of acceptance. The negatively sanctioned activities undertaken as alternatives impact family and community members. TRSs partner with health and human service providers, the public, and participants to prevent situations like unsupervised free time that might result in delinquent or criminal acts. Supportive social structures that facilitate uninterrupted intervention are essential to community development and client well-being. Resources are available through the World Health Organization (www.who.int) and the American Correctional Association (www.aca.org).

SUMMARY

Although this chapter discussed a variety of impairments—HIV/AIDS conditions, child maltreatment, homelessness, and delinquent and criminal behaviors—they are commonly labeled "social disabilities" because individuals with these disorders display similar psychosocial behaviors. Common characteristics include low self-esteem, social incompetence, limited resource-acquisition skills, and feelings of disconnection, isolation, and for some a sense of entitlement. Common health patterns include substance abuse, sexually transmitted diseases, stress, and physical and mental impairments.

Several concerns presented in this chapter are evident worldwide, including HIV (human immunodeficiency virus) and AIDS (acquired immune deficiency syndrome). Since the first reported cases of AIDS in 1981, there is still no cure or immunization, the incidence of HIV infection continues to rise, and if AIDS develops the outcome is fatal. The prevalence of the disease is now of pandemic proportions. Violence also is a global problem and intertwined closely with child maltreatment. Children today face numerous challenges and as a consequence are more at-risk of maltreatment than in previous years. The injury inflicted during childhood may carry into adulthood and is exhibited in such characteristics as social isolation, fear of forming close relationships, and a low self-concept.

Another issue that has received attention is the increasing number of individuals who experience poverty and homelessness. These people are profoundly alone and include a broad spectrum of individuals: runaways, single-parent families, very young children, individuals who abuse drugs, veterans, and people with mental illness. Characteristics of these individuals are similar to those of others studied in this chapter: disenfranchisement, learned helplessness, dependency, stigma of stereotyping, limited political power, and lack of a comprehensive coordinated service network. The closing section of the chapter considered individuals whose social deviancy has resulted in legal sanction. Increasing numbers of at-risk youth point to the need for preventive and long-term intervention.

TRSs interact with these individuals in a number of settings. Comprehensive treatment goals address clients' health, functional needs, and quality of life issues, yet initially these concerns are mitigated by the immediacy of medical needs. As TRSs intervene, they are challenged to consider their own personal feelings and attitudes toward clients who are devalued by society.

Key Terms

abuse Act of commission or inflicting injury or allowing injury to result to a child.

asymptomatic Without clinical signs or symptoms, as with HIV infection.

at-risk youth Those whose detrimental influences cause them to function at a disadvantage.

commission Acts of abuse of children, inflicting or allowing the infliction of injury to a child.

criminal Offenses committed by adults (18 and older) that violate cultural norms or threaten welfare of others.

delinquent Offenses committed by youth (under age 18) that violate cultural norms or threaten the welfare of others.

elopement A person who runs away or escapes from legally imposed confinement.

neglect Act of omission or failure to act on behalf of a child.

omission Acts of neglect or failure to act on behalf of a child.

parole The release of a criminal offender whose sentence has not expired on condition of supervision.

probation Sentence ascribed to be served in a community rather than in a prison.

recidivism Rate of return to prison by former inmates.

resiliency factors Skills and attitudes necessary to adapt and cope with everyday life.

Study Questions

1. Describe the clinical manifestations of each of the social disabilities studied in this chapter.

2. What are the purposes of therapeutic recreation with the individuals studied in this chapter?

3. Summarize the intervention strategies and leadership interactions recommended with each population.

4. Explain the significance of "here and now" experiences with people with HIV/AIDS.

5. What are three "hidden" characteristics that affect TRSs' interactions with individuals experiencing poverty or homelessness?

6. Describe environmental factors that contribute to at-risk, delinquent, and criminal behaviors.

7. Describe the factors that contribute to social disabilities worldwide.

8. Describe what is meant by the cycle of violence.

Practical Experiences to Enhance Student Objectives

1. Visit a TRS in a state or federal correctional facility to identify the nature of intervention programs and security issues that impact service delivery (respecting his/her confidentiality).

2. Monitor the news on TV, radio, and the Internet. What forms of crime are predominately covered? What social issues appear in the media coverage? What are the similarities and differences found between U.S. and international social issues?

3. Visit a welfare agency, health and human service department, halfway house, or shelter. What observations can you make about the individuals seeking services? Analyze your personal feelings about your visits to these environments.

4. Conduct Internet searches of sites like the WHO or CDC (www.cdc.gov) to identify recommendations and resources for prevention or intervention with clients experiencing social challenges.

5. Visit with social service personnel regarding their interactions with clients who have been a part of the social services system for extended time periods. What are their needs and how can the system adjust to form networks to resolve these needs?

6. Visit a site providing prevention or intervention programs for at-risk youth. Who are the leaders, what are their qualifications, and what experiences are being provided? Contact the Search Institute (www.search-institute.org) and request information on the 40 Developmental Assets and how they are incorporated into therapeutic recreation programs.

7. Visit with professionals providing services through partnerships like those found with extracurricular experiences or adventure/challenge. What are outcomes and quality indicators of these interventions?

Children and Youth in Health-Care Settings

After reading this chapter, students will be able to

✔ Describe pediatric health-care issues and the nature of health-care settings and services experienced by children, youth, and their caregivers

✔ Identify the developmental needs of children and youth (birth to 21 years) and their responses to illness, injury, and hospitalization

✔ Describe the purpose and outcomes of therapeutic recreation in health-care settings with children and youth

✔ Identify the delivery settings in which TRSs interact with children, youth, and their caregivers

✔ Outline therapeutic recreation leadership interactions and interventions applied in the context of family-centered care, including the importance of accurate communication, recognition of cultural variables, and the roles of various health-care professionals and caregivers

✔ Identify goals of selected interventions with children and youth in pediatric health care

✔ Describe the application of the therapeutic recreation process, including consideration of programmatic factors like recreation spaces, equipment, and policies; and interactions with related health-care team and family members

Chapter 11 was revised with contributions from Dana Dempsey, MS, CTRS, and the staff of the Therapeutic Recreation Dept., Texas Scottish Rite Hospital for Children, Dallas; and Sandra K. Negley, MS, MTRS/CTRS, Expressive Therapies Dept., University of Utah Neuropsychiatric Institute, Salt Lake City.

This chapter provides an overview of therapeutic recreation in pediatric settings. Because of the special needs of children and youth, the unique characteristics of pediatric health care, and the diversity of pediatric illnesses and disabilities, therapeutic recreation for children and youth in health-care facilities merits special attention (refer to chapters 6, 7, 9, and 10 for consideration of children with physical and psychosocial issues that might be addressed in hospital settings).

INTRODUCTION

Health-care issues and hospitalization introduce significant changes to the customary lifestyle of children and youth. They face separation from parents, siblings, and peers. Children and youth must accept new routines, relinquish privacy, and undergo strange and often painful medical procedures. Hospitalized children and youth are surrounded by strangers and circumstances over which they have no control. Adolescents and young adults meet their developmental needs through recreation and leisure; thus, illness, disease, and injury interrupt development. Because peers are important, the isolation of hospitalization can be difficult (Ball & Bindler, 2008). Adolescents and young adults need outlets for stress and opportunities to experience the independence interrupted by hospitalization. With each age group, various developmental responses occur with illness, injury, or hospitalization. This chapter explores these growth stages and the role of therapeutic recreation in addressing the developmental needs of children and youth in health-care settings. The purposes of therapeutic recreation extend from assessment, diagnosis, rehabilitation, and education to helping children and youth cope and adjust to immediate and long-term pain, the consequences of accidents, and to life-ending illnesses and disabilities.

Pediatric professionals function in many different settings and treat children and youth with a wide range of illnesses, traumas, and chronic diseases and disabilities. Acutely ill children have shorter hospital stays as increased technology has facilitated caregiver ability to care for children in the home or community setting (James & Ashwill, 2007). Professionals interact with ill or injured children in their own homes, in schools, and in outpatient, inpatient, and hospice settings. Most illnesses are treated in ambulatory settings (e.g., clinics, convenient care centers), leaving hospitals with children who are acutely ill or have complex medical needs (James & Ashwill). Home nursing care is increasingly utilized as the result of cost-containment practices and availability of portable technology. This approach recognizes the ever-increasing roles played by families in the care of their children and youth. **Family-centered care** strives to support natural caregiving roles and promotes healthy patterns of living at home and in the community. Routine patterns of growth and development prevail, the stress of separation from caregiver support is reduced, and recreation continues within a familiar environment.

As the therapeutic recreation process is carried out, therapists consider how illness and injury impact the use of recreation areas and the types and quality (i.e., products containing latex) of toys and equipment used during interventions. Special consideration is given to the language therapists use as they interact with children and youth. The cultural context also influences how the therapist interacts with family members and caregivers.

This chapter will also consider changes in the health-care system that have focused and will continue to focus attention on health promotion and prevention. Because children and youth with highly complex needs are being cared for by families and caregivers in alternative settings, new roles for therapists are emerging. One challenge will remain regardless of health-care trends: the nature of therapeutic recreation with terminally ill children and youth. Therapists practicing in pediatric settings interact with a number of professional disciplines and, in some instances, these professions use play as an intervention **(Child Life Specialist).** Thus, throughout the chapter, we will consider the nature of related health-care professionals and interrelationships among team members caring for children and youth.

POPULATION OVERVIEW

Pediatric professionals in health-care settings treat children and youth with a wide range of acute, chronic, and traumatic conditions. Services are provided over the entire range of the care continuum, from emergency rooms, intensive care units, and specialized children's hospitals to rehabilitation centers, outpatient clinics, and the family home. Likewise, the therapeutic recreation process may be applied within a brief time period, perhaps a day or less, or may extend from the birth of an infant into young adulthood. Therapeutic recreation professionals are instrumental in the delivery of therapeutic interventions that prevent and mitigate undue distress, reduce time spent in the hospital, and lessen the anxieties caused by disruption in developmental processes (Jessee, 1992; Rode, 1995).

Children and youth experience different health-care issues than adults; moreover, the illness or injury that limits activity, requires medical attention, or results in a chronic condition also varies with age and development (Ball & Bindler, 2008). Leading causes of death with children under the age of one include congenital anomalies, low birth weight, respiratory distress syndrome, and pregnancy complications. For those between the ages of 1–19, unintentional injury attributed to motor vehicle crashes, drowning, fires and burns, firearms, and suffocation are primary contributors (Ball & Bindler). Medical deaths in this age range result from congenital malformations, cancer, and heart diseases. The average length of stay (LOS) among all youth (chronological age 1–18) in 2005 was 4.9 and 4.5 days respectively for males and females, with leading causes of short-term hospitalizations being injuries, poisoning, and respiratory disorders. Mental disorders contributed to hospitalizations among older youth (15–21) (Ball & Bindler; National Center for Health Statistics, 2007). Though science and life-saving technology have enabled youth to not only survive injury and illness but to return home, the high cost of today's health care sometimes places new stressors on the family.

Some children and youth are admitted to a hospital because of a sudden or unexplained onset of symptoms. This would include those with respiratory conditions, fractures, and traumatic injuries. Others enter outpatient clinics in hospitals for diagnostic procedures, such as **cardiac catheterization** (a diagnostic procedure in which a small tube is inserted in a vein of the leg or arm and threaded through the venous system to the heart). A third group enters hospitals for planned inpatient surgery, such as **reconstructive surgery** (surgery that builds up or restores body tissues that have been damaged or destroyed), or open-heart surgery. A fourth group of children and youth is admitted to the hospital to manage conditions associated with chronic illnesses, such as diabetes, **juvenile rheumatoid arthritis (JRA)** (a disease that affects the large joints of children under the age of 16), **renal disease** (a disorder that involves the kidney), or oncological diseases (leukemia or cancer, for instance).

In addition to disrupting general growth and development, illness, injury, and chronic conditions uniquely impact each child or adolescent. As the TRS initiates intervention, assessments take into consideration the holistic nature of the disruptions and the ramifications of the specific illness, injury, or chronic disability. The therapist must consider the following:

- The circumstances under which an injury was sustained are significant. Often a child/youth who was playing with a forbidden item (matches, cleaning fluid, a parent's tools) or violating the law (speeding) suffers guilt and fear of punishment if that recreation experience or act led to an accident or injury to the self or others.

- Another important factor is the effect of the treatments for the particular disease or trauma. Chemotherapy, an aspect of the treatment for various cancers, has a wide range of side effects including hair loss, nausea, and susceptibility to infection. A child or youth who has fractured a number of bones will spend lengthy periods of time in traction followed by more time in a body cast. Because treatments are painful, invasive, and result in loss of control and privacy they are significant stressors for all children and youth (Ball & Bindler, 2008).

- TRSs should also consider any temporary or permanent **disfigurement** (the loss, damage, or change to a part of the body that causes a noticeable change in physical appearance) or impairments that result from the illness. A child/youth with third-degree burns on the face will always wear the scars of that injury. A child/youth with a cardiac disease will frequently have physical and dietary restrictions that must be accepted as part of daily living. A colostomy requires adjustments to self-care routines.

- The role of the family and the caregiver system, especially the parents, in dealing with and emotionally supporting the hospitalized child/youth is also important. If the hospital is far away from home and there are other children in the family, parents may be stressed as they try to manage their home lives as well as meet the needs of a hospitalized sibling. Moreover, if parents feel they could have prevented the illness or accident, they may be harboring guilt that may manifest itself in a wide range of behaviors. Thus, separation from the primary caregiver as well as the family's coping and adaptation impacts youth development and reaction to health issues.

- A final consideration includes the various roles played by members of the health-care team in the treatment of a child/youth with a particular illness. The role each professional plays is frequently determined by the type of illness or injury the individual has. A lifelong physical impairment will usually require a great deal of coordinated input from the entire health-care team, especially the rehabilitation specialists. Care of a child who is a suspected abuse victim will likely require the investigation and intervention of the physician and social worker, as well as specialized services from psychosocial professionals. Roles of health-care professionals vary from one setting to another, just as protocols for specific illnesses vary. The TRS must be familiar with the intervention techniques and protocols of all health-care team members.

CHILDREN AND ADOLESCENTS: DEVELOPMENTAL PROCESSES AND RESPONSES TO HEALTH CARE

Children and adolescents in health-care settings range in age from newborns through adolescence into young adulthood. Illness and hospitalizations are disruptive and have the potential to negatively influence development both during and after the health-care experience (Hart, Mather, Slack, & Powell, 1992; Rode, 1995). Depending on their level of development, children and adolescents experience separation, loss of autonomy, independence, and control; fear of mutilation, bodily harm, and death; guilt, pain, fear of the unknown; and uncertainty about limits, outcomes, and how to behave (James & Ashwill, 2007; Lingnell & Dunn, 1999; Muller, Harris, Wattley, & Taylor, 1992; Rode). Additional stressors from hospitalization include stranger anxiety due to multiple personnel and new faces, fear of needles, view of hospitalization or procedures as punishment, family and caregiver anxiety and its effects on the patient, and overstimulation or sensory deprivation (Child Life Council, 1997). Although each child/youth develops and responds in an individual fashion, there are certain general characteristics of different age groups that impact their response to health care. Developmental concerns and responses of each age group are reviewed in the following sections.

The Newborn and Infant (0 to 1 Year)

The first year of life is one of rapid change. During the first 12 months of life an infant triples his or her birth weight, becomes proficient in fundamental words, and develops from a reflexive person to one with purposeful movements (crawling). The infant learns to distinguish himself/herself as separate from the mother and other caregivers, tolerates small doses of frustration, and trusts that needs will be met eventually by mother or caregivers. As the infant develops imitation, the use of symbols, repetition, and anticipation, these elements of play become part of the growth process. Play begins in a reflexive manner as the infant moves extremities or grasps objects. Next, through manipulation, the infant learns about objects and the surrounding environment. "Human interaction is the most important component of play" (James & Ashwill, 2007, p.128). Interaction with caregivers increases as the infant grasps objects, repeats movements, and pushes-pulls blocks and books.

When illness or hospitalization separates an infant from primary caretakers, separation anxiety is likely to be displayed with some form of protest, screaming, or withdrawal from medical staff. With a disruption in routines like feeding, sleeping, and playing (nearer one year), the child is likely to become fussy and irritable (Lingnell & Dunn, 1999). The strong need for comfort triggers immediate responses to pain and bodily harm. The family needs information and support to relieve their fears and uneasiness. During infancy, family and caregivers are the primary safety monitors and

With infants, play with caregivers involves grasping objects and repeating movements.

thus if an injury is the result of a fall, burn, or poisoning, for example, parental anxiety, guilt, and anger become issues addressed by the health-care team.

The Toddler (1 to 3 Years)

The toddler in a health-care setting represents a unique challenge to the pediatric staff. During these years, the child's skills are developing at a rapid rate, and the youngster needs to be able to continue this development, at least in part, while in treatment. The child's primary way of learning new skills is through repetition. Repetitious play leads to mastery of a behavior and the incorporation of that behavior into a child's repertoire. Closely related to this is the child's need for physical activity. Learning to walk is the primary physical activity of this age group; the toddler is in perpetual motion and continually wants to explore and investigate the new world that has opened up. However, a child's need for mobility becomes secondary when the need for intravenous medication, required traction, or recent surgery necessitates limitations in physical activity. This is difficult to explain successfully to a toddler! The toddler's efforts for repeated gross motor activity are frustrated, and this can result in maladaptive behavior and regression if no effort is made to help the child compensate. Further, a toddler's motor development outpaces development of judgment and perception, which increases the risk of injury (James & Ashwill, 2007).

Toddlers still have a close bond with their mothers, even though the process of separation and individuation has begun. Separation from the mother or primary caregiver remains the major stressor for toddlers (Ball & Bindler, 2008). The **egocentricity** (a psychological orientation that causes an individual to be totally self-absorbed) of

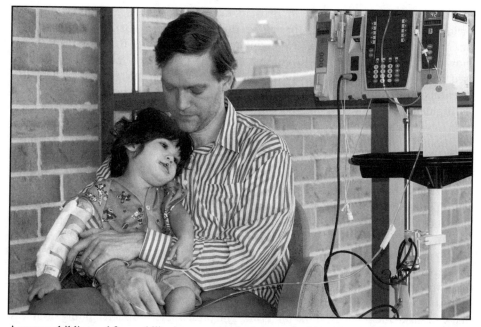

A young child's need for mobility is constrained when medical interventions like IVs, catheters, or the need to immobilize limbs impose necessary restrictions.

toddlers affects their limited understanding of separation, and their increasing awareness of cause-and-effect relationships may result in the belief that the child has caused the parent to leave or that magic caused the illness (James & Ashwill, 2007). Further, the toddler's limited cognitive development makes him or her more vulnerable to strangers, multiple team members, and the foreign environment of a health-care setting. Imagined or real fears and perceptions are alleviated by providing developmentally appropriate communication about procedures and bringing familiar toys and play objects with the toddler to the health-care setting. TRSs will notice an immediate physical response to pain and unfamiliar words and places. Therapists must give family and caregivers guidance in monitoring risky behaviors that might result in falls and accidents or in selecting playthings that could contribute to choking or latex allergies, for example.

The Preschooler (3 to 6 Years)

The preschooler in a health-care setting also has difficulty separating from the familiarity of home. This child is recognizing and developing membership in the family unit and play group. During a hospital stay, the family or familiar support group is not readily available to the child. Although the increased, exclusive attention the child might receive from a parent may be welcomed, the child may also be confused by this change in events. Before the illness, parents and siblings probably had been encouraging the child to be increasingly independent. However, the nature of the illness might require relinquishing some or all of that independence.

Preschool years are a time for new initiatives and endless projects—a time to explore the properties of new things and people around them (Ball & Bindler, 2008). Not only do preschoolers want to manipulate and create things, they also want to ask "how" and "why" questions—lots of questions. Often the medical equipment that is used with or on a child is "off limits," since manipulation may impair or alter the function of the equipment. Also, the preschooler observes many intriguing, and possibly frightening, events or items. There may be either no one available to answer the child's questions at the time, or the child may be too frightened or otherwise unable to ask about the puzzling occurrence. Often a simple explanation will precipitate a multitude of questions. Preschoolers usually interpret explanations literally and view their body as a container. As a consequence, telling a four-year-old, "You have a bug in your tummy" may conjure up visions of an insect scampering around his or her stomach. Likewise, saying "I am going to take your blood pressure" may result in the belief that once this occurs no more will be left. In this situation, increased anxiety may intensify the already present fear of body mutilation (Lingnell & Dunn, 1999).

Preschoolers are still relatively egocentric and see occurrences only from their perspective. They do not realize why, for example, parents leave the hospital when they want them to stay (Ball & Bindler, 2008). They have not reached the level of sophistication in their thought that allows them to see hospitalization as something that will make them better in the long run. The preschooler's understanding of illness is that it is a major, stressful interruption in life. A child at this age may translate this unpleasant and sometimes painful interruption as punishment (intense guilt feelings) (Ball & Bindler). In the preschooler's brief life experience, deliberately inflicted pain (a spanking, for example) might be punishment for wrongdoing. When sick or hospitalized, the child is confused, wondering what the "misdeed" was that precipitated the "punishment" of sickness and hospitalization (James & Ashwill, 2007).

Whereas not all toddlers are toilet trained, most preschool-age children have mastered the art of proper elimination. Issues of toilet training may become problematic for preschoolers because hospital routines and illness do not always allow them to continue their customary toilet habits. Bedpans and urinals may be confusing to the recently toilet-trained child. The child often needs assistance in using this equipment and may not be able to wait until help arrives. Even when toilet-training habits are reinforced, the child may well regress to the point of wetting the bed or having "an accident."

By age 5 a child has developed many motor skills and needs opportunities for practicing coordination for exercise and for release of physical energy. Just like the toddler, the preschooler may be frustrated by medically necessary physical restrictions. In addition to further development of physical skills, the preschool child needs opportunities for social interactions. Increasingly, the child is becoming an active member of peer groups (associative play) and enjoys trying out social skills as a group member (Ball & Bindler, 2008).

Whether in group play, parallel play (when children play side by side without interacting with each other), or solitary play, a preschool-aged child has the cognitive ability to engage in symbolic play and imitative play. Imagination carries the child into fantasy play with imaginary friends, which in many instances will relate to what is occurring around the child. The preschooler will spontaneously act out his own perception of events and people in the health-care setting, mixing fantasy with reality.

While this play provides professionals with valuable diagnostic information, they must be alert to the point at which the child wanders too far from reality. TRSs may help family members create positive images of health-care settings through virtual reality experiences or may facilitate stress management by practicing coping skills.

As the preschooler develops, parents find themselves on one hand encouraging initiative, and on the other setting limits to prevent injuries. This balancing act may carry over into the hospital setting, where therapists must weigh the child's natural inclination for movement against appropriate safety precautions. Other issues to which the therapist must give consideration are the introduction of gender roles and cultural expectations, such as when caregivers purchase toys or validate the appropriateness of crying.

The School-Age Child (6 to 12 Years)

The school-age child has a more sophisticated thought process and problem-solving ability with which to handle an injury or illness than does a younger child; yet, illness or hospitalization for children in this age group can be traumatic. In the health care environment, school-age children are often anxious to learn about the medical setting and the nature of illnesses and injuries; on the other hand, they must face feelings of inadequacy, loss of control, fear of pain, and the inability to be productive. School-age children strive to contribute to their environment and work to receive recognition (sense of industry). Often there is little opportunity for children to be productive or to contribute in the health-care setting. During the school-age years, a child ventures outside the family unit and has an increasing desire to spend free time with friends (Ball & Bindler, 2008). This individual is building identification with the peer group, working to find a place where he or she belongs and can be accepted. Not only does injury or hospitalization interrupt this process, it prompts concern for never being well again and causes anxiety over separation from peers (Lingnell & Dunn, 1999).

In a hospital setting, the child often must come to terms with the fact that the parent is not the person in control. The child must therefore deal with the anxiety and frustration that result when a parent cannot prevent painful procedures that are required for recovery or remission. The child's disappointment in the parent may give rise to feelings of anger or guilt, which may be compounded if the child in some way assumes blame for the illness or hospitalization. A school-age child often sets inflexible standards of right and wrong and may believe that for every unpleasant or unfortunate event, someone is at fault. When the hospital experience is perceived in this light, the child might take the blame for the hospitalization and feel responsible for the surrounding circumstances. These feelings will most likely negatively influence the child's self-esteem, which may be quite fragile during a hospital stay—particularly during an extended one.

School age is the last period when boys and girls appear physically similar (Ball & Bindler, 2008). Even so, injuries and hospitalizations can create modesty concerns. Even though they understand incisions will heal and an arm will look the same after an intravenous infusion is removed, fear of pain remains ever present at this age. For the first time, school-age children are aware of the concerns of others (like fear expressed by parents), distinguish natural from supernatural, and begin to make judg-

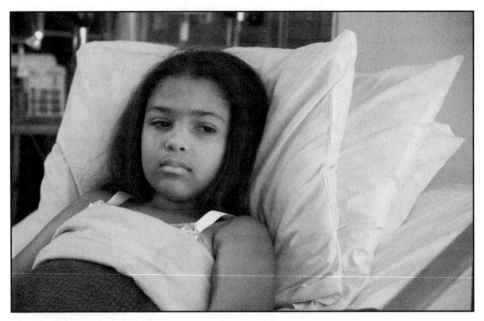

Hospitalized children often have to deal with anxiety over upcoming procedures and the frustration that comes with loss of control.

ments about acceptable behaviors versus risky behaviors. However, they still need to be reminded about the dangers in their environment because they unrealistically judge their physical capabilities.

A growing concern is the prevalence of obesity in school-age children. These children may experience psychosocial difficulties, eating disorders, sleep apnea, orthopedic problems, hypertension, and diabetes (James & Ashwill, 2007). Today's school-age children are also subject to considerably more stress than children of previous generations (James & Ashwill). Social change, demands for achievement, competitive athletics, rushed schedules, school (bullying and safety), and the media are sources of stress. Hospitalization and health-care issues result in physical inactivity and additional stress. TRSs may need to assist caregivers in locating community resources that offer safe recreation environs, physical activity, and opportunities to gain coping skills in order to manage stress. Therapists might also provide values clarification sessions to explore at-risk behaviors like substance abuse with school-age peers and their caregivers. TRSs may help caregivers support the child's links with friends to nurture the child's increasing interdependence, social competence, and physically active behaviors since peers tend to be influential role models.

Adolescence to Young Adulthood (12 to 21 Years)

The young adult is moving ever closer to independence from parents and family. Relationships with the family change during this time as the individual focuses on several important issues. One of these issues is separation from the family and independence from parental rules and values. Teenagers are usually still financially dependent on parents and in many ways are emotionally dependent as well, but they also are becoming increasingly self-sufficient. They seem to be looking at both short- and long-term goals; that is, they want immediate independence from adult-imposed restrictions and yet also have a great concern with career and life plans. During a hospitalization, adolescents and young adults frequently find they must relinquish a great deal of independence and privacy. Treatment protocols and rules may place more stringent controls on them than they would encounter at home, and hospitalization and illness may temporarily put a halt to any further bid for independence and self-determination. An adolescent may react to such a halt with ambivalence. On the one hand, the young adult may be relieved that no one is expecting a continuing move to independence. A dependent state may even be appealing for a while. On the other hand, the inability to have control over his or her life may be seen as a disruptive and unwelcome factor. Consequently, rules are broken in the adolescent's quest for self-awareness. With chronic health issues like diabetes or heart problems, professionals may rely on contracts to increase adherence to health-care protocols and rules (Ball & Bindler, 2008).

The teenager's drive for establishing an identity is a major concern during this period. Establishing independence from family values is an important part of developing an identity. Values are derived in part from the family but to a considerable degree from the peer group. This peer group may change from time to time, but input from individuals one's own age continues. The hospitalized teen is isolated from the customary peer group and may feel anxious about this separation, both in terms of needing support from the group during a difficult time and in terms of being accepted back into the group once recovery is complete (Lingnell & Dunn, 1999). Preoccupation with body image and appearance are the focus of a great deal of attention during this period. Body image is closely related to self-esteem and can significantly impact interactions with family and friends. Appearance relates directly to the peer group, since the young adult will often see appearance, as well as conformity, as criteria for group acceptance. Additional physical changes and long-term implications due to an illness or bodily injury can be difficult for the adolescent to handle. If the young adult anticipates even a temporary unattractive change in appearance, anxiety and negative behaviors—like regressing to more childlike behaviors or denying the extent of an illness or injury—may result (Lingnell & Dunn; Muller et al., 1992).

While the above concerns may create anxiety for a hospitalized teen, his or her ability to comprehend aspects of the illness and treatment is usually seen by the health-care staff as helpful. Most young adults are able to understand abstractions and can reason deductively. Nonetheless, the adolescent's cognitive level, his or her keen interest in personal health and its effects, and his or her need to assume responsibility and control make it imperative that discussions, explanations, and decision making regarding the illness and treatment include the young adult as well as the family (Lingnell & Dunn, 1999; Muller et al., 1992).

"Injuries claim more lives during adolescence than all other causes of death combined" (James & Ashwill, 2007, p. 99). Young adults often believe they are invulnerable, with little thought given to negative outcomes of their behavior (James & Ashwill). Moreover, factors like depression, "poor impulse control, poor school performance, family disorganization, conduct disorders, substance abuse, homosexuality, and recent stress" (James & Ashwill, p. 200) place adolescents at risk for suicide. One risk-taking behavior that is costly to the individual and society is teen pregnancy; the United States has one of the highest rates of any country in the Western world (James & Ashwill). Additional risky behaviors include performance-enhancing drugs, sun-tanning, body piercing, tattoos, unsound nutritional habits, and violence. As a result of these risky health behaviors, young adults experience traumatic hospitalizations, lengthy physical rehabilitation, grieving, and treatment for depression and other psychiatric issues. Health-care providers respect the need for privacy and accept that the vacillation between adult and childlike behaviors may be an attempt to cope with concerns about separation from peers, body image, and changes in physical appearance. Therapists facilitate continued development and preparation for adult life by, for example, opportunities for problem-solving, choice-making, and social engagement; assertiveness training; leisure education; and encouraging the use of computers and technology as career and educational resources.

A hospitalized child/youth of any age requires special consideration. Before providing therapeutic recreation to a child or young adult, therapists must understand the nature of the diagnosis and treatment, the demands and realities of the health-care setting, and the developmental stage of the child.

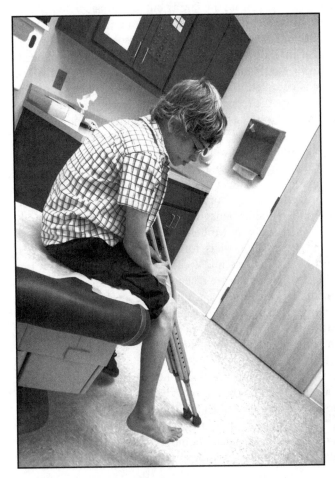

Injuries are one of the most common reasons for teens to encounter a health-care setting.

PURPOSE OF THERAPEUTIC RECREATION

Throughout the developmental period, children and youth are exposed to a wide range of health concerns and risks—from auto accidents to violence to inactivity to substance abuse. Some youth who survive injury may experience lifelong disabilities, while others face health issues as a result of acute and chronic health disorders like cancer and diabetes. The focus of therapeutic recreation interventions is to improve functional ability and independent functioning, prevent developmental delay, promote coping, enhance psychosocial functioning, prepare families and clients for healthy leisure lifestyles, and improve overall quality of life (ATRA, 2003). Specifically, youth benefit from having emotional outlets and options to mitigate stress. This enables them to regain control, privacy, and self-esteem; maintain friendships and a sense of normalcy; develop better use of free time and physical activity opportunities; and engage in supportive family interactions.

"The character of play changes as a child matures, but children at all ages play if they are able to. Play contributes to and is an expression of development" (Betz et al., 1994, p. 624). Since play and recreation are the "work" of children and youth, the therapist uses this natural language as a diagnostic tool to gain insight into coping strategies and elements in the health-care environment that cause anxiety (James & Ashwill 2007; Ball & Bindler, 2008; Henniger, 1995; Jessee, 1992; Murphy & Carr, 2000). The TRS uses various forms of play and recreation as interventions to promote health and prevent injury, as educational and rehabilitative tools in the treatment of acute and chronic needs, as avenues to assess and evaluate functioning and health status, and to facilitate transitions, discharge planning, and compliance with treatment plans.

A variety of interventions and techniques are used to accomplish specific outcomes. The scope of service of Texas Scottish Rite Hospital for Children (TSRHC) illustrates the contribution of TR services to the growth and development, leisure functioning, and health of children and youth with orthopedic problems and hidden disabilities like those described in chapters 6 and 7 (see also exhibit 11.1). Specific program goals may include opportunities to:

- Enhance self-awareness and positive self perceptions
- Develop and practice social skills to establish and maintain relationships
- Contribute to overall physical and emotional health
- Reinforce academic/career skills in a recreation and/or leisure setting
- Facilitate cognitive growth and development
- Promote motivation, self-initiation, and responsibility for participating in recreation experiences at appropriate levels of independence
- Promote inclusion and active participation in community-based programs
- Express emotions
- Provide input in program development, treatment goals, and evaluation of TR services

The use of recreation therapy as a treatment modality in the Expressive Therapies Department of the University of Utah Neuropsychiatric Institute illustrates commonalities of our professional roles among pediatric settings (see exhibit 11.2). Clientele

Exhibit 11.1   Scope of Service

Therapeutic recreation serves patients from 5-18 years of age. All therapeutic recreation services will be provided and/or supervised by a Certified Therapeutic Recreation Specialist (CTRS). Services and interventions may include:

- individualized assessment to determine leisure interests, strengths, and leisure-related needs
- development of a plan of action to address the child's needs
- prescribed activities that improve physical functioning related to recreation and leisure involvement
- leisure education focusing on personal interests, abilities, leisure-related skills and knowledge development, leisure support systems, and community leisure resources
- leisure activities that promote a healthy sense of self and perspective of self in relation to society
- leisure experiences which provide therapeutic interactions and model appropriate behavioral expressions
- community outreach programs, which promote inclusive and/or adapted recreation and leisure activities, designed to educate the general population and service providers

Reprinted with permission of the Therapeutic Recreation Department, Texas Scottish Rite Hospital for Children, Dallas, Texas.

Exhibit 11.2   Program Description

Recreation therapy as a form of active treatment intends to preserve or improve functional ability in order to enhance the client's coping skills, utilization of community integration, and overall quality of life. This outcome is accomplished through:

- integrated assessment conducted upon admission
- goals and objectives established according to assessed needs and documented on an integrated treatment plan that incorporates physical, social, intellectual, spiritual, cultural, emotional, recreation, and health and wellness needs
- psychoeducational opportunities assist patients in understanding and developing skills in values clarification, time management, feeling identification, coping skills, conflict resolution, enhancing self-esteem, leisure benefits, and leisure resource development
- recreation/social activities serve as distractions from the patient's daily schedule, or from the individual's disability
- discharge planning assists patients in understanding and maintaining appropriate coping skills, a healthy and active lifestyle, and an improved quality of life

Adapted from the Expressive Therapies Department, University of Utah Neuropsychiatric Institute, Salt Lake City, Utah.

served in this setting represent populations described in chapters 9 and 10. Interventions outlined in the scope of service include leisure education, self-esteem education, anger management, social skills, problem-solving skills, stress management/relaxation, discharge planning, pet therapy, and experiential education. The selection of specific interventions is influenced by the individual's developmental stage, nature of the illness/injury, the team's and family's intent, and resources available in the health care environment. Example cases illustrate how therapeutic recreation reaches desired outcomes in the following sections.

Normative Growth and Development

Purposefully presented, therapeutic recreation can focus on the well or healthy aspects of the child or young adult at a time when the attention of many medical professionals is directed toward the illness or injury. With an emphasis on what is right with the youth and also familiar and appropriate activities, a therapeutic recreation program provides intervention fostering normal growth and development. It may be seen not only as incorporating familiar and usual experiences into an unfamiliar environment, but as helping to prevent regression, withdrawal, or negative behaviors.

Case: A School-Age Child with Accidental Injuries

Bernie, age 7, had his first admission to the pediatric unit with fractured ribs and a fractured femur following a motor vehicle accident. His parents, also injured in the accident, were unable to visit him for the first few days. Bernie engaged in activities for only very brief periods of time. Movies were the single exception. His behavior was causing tension for the nursing staff. He shouted at any and all passersby to get him one thing or another. Several nurses had already tried curbing these negative behaviors by threatening to withdraw TV/DVD privileges for a certain amount of time during the day.

The TRS initiated and maintained daily visits but voiced frustration over not being able to provide an intervention that might help modify Bernie's behavior. When the therapist arrived at Bernie's room with Star Wars figures and suggested they "pretend" with the figures, Bernie enthusiastically agreed, stating, "Those are like mine!" He attended for 45 minutes and asked the therapist to bring the figures again. Bernie used the Star Wars figures frequently, and, as he became more accepting of the therapist spending time with him, he also was increasingly agreeable to trying other games. As his skills diversified and his ability to share feelings increased, his acting-out behaviors decreased and his relationships with the staff improved.

Emotional Adjustment and Support

Psychosocial support is part of every contact for hospitalized children and young adults. The consistency and predictability associated with the familiar nature of recreation provides support. In family-centered care, an initial TRS task is to help caregivers remain connected, cope, and support the child/youth. Staff can offer various types of recreation (e.g. anger management and conflict resolution) as opportunities for emotional outlet and release in an acceptable manner, with supportive team members on hand to help the child understand and accept these feelings and to help the family interpret the child's various reactions. For children and caregivers, the therapist provides much needed emotional support by communicating recognition of the difficult nature of hospitalization and by offering feedback about coping and managing the stress of hospitalization.

Case: A Preschooler with Leukemia

Joel, age 4, was hospitalized with a diagnosis of acute lymphocytic leukemia. He was highly anxious and fretful on admission and became distraught to the point of hysteria whenever his mother attempted to leave his sight. His mother stated that she was exhausted and frustrated by Joel's unwillingness to separate from her. The TRS began observing recreation with Joel and his mother, sitting with them and commenting about the action. She also began to talk about how difficult it is to feel okay about mom or dad leaving, even for short periods of time. Once Joel would accept the therapist in conversations, the therapist began introducing activities for the mother, Joel, and the therapist to do together. When participating, it was observed that Joel would let go of his mother for longer and longer periods of time. Eventually he was able to separate physically from his mother without becoming upset and would readily agree to her leaving as he participated with the therapist.

Social Skill Development

In an adolescent lounge setting, recreation can be used to create situations where opportunities for peer interaction are optimal. The camaraderie and support that is shared by children and young adults in the same health-care setting has a normalizing effect. The TRS can evaluate situations and use therapeutic recreation to create opportunities to practice social skills and promote a healthy sense of self in relation to society. The therapist's role includes initiating interactions and encouraging the development of relationships, both with peers and with staff, and helping to stabilize situations of interrupted friendships due to hospitalization or death of a young patient. A therapist may need to work closely with a participant, focusing on the development of communication skills when these skills are underdeveloped or inappropriate for social interactions.

Case: Adolescent with Rheumatoid Arthritis

Charlie, age 13, had multiple admissions to the hospital because of juvenile rheumatoid arthritis. Not only was hospitalization an indication that his medical status had deteriorated, to Charlie, it was a profound interruption to his life at home and his relationships with his mother and peers. His mother related that Charlie had few friends because he was always "sickly" and hardly ever attended school. Charlie agreed to come to recreation therapy only after a great deal of preparation and encouragement. Once there, he sat in silence and observed group activities. When invited by the TRS to join, he would say that he did not feel well enough. The only type of interaction he would allow was an activity on a one-to-one basis with the therapist, during which there was little verbal exchange.

The therapist continued to see Charlie on a daily basis. She talked about the difficulties of developing friendships and how hard it is to participate without previous experience. The activities she used in his room were computer games commonly used by Charlie's peers. Eventually Charlie agreed to join as the therapist's partner in a small-group game. As Charlie agreed to do this more often, the TRS gave him an increasing amount of responsibility for making decisions about therapy experiences and for interacting with the other youth. As others became comfortable with Charlie's membership in the group, they began to initiate interactions with him on the unit. As these changes were taking place, Charlie's mood and affect notably improved, as did his relationships with the nursing staff and medical staff.

Independence

Throughout childhood and adolescence, a major component of development is mastering the tasks and skills necessary to increase independence. This aspect of development is unavoidably threatened by the very nature of hospital routines and medical care. Hospital routines and rules may create a daily structure that a child or young adult is powerless to change. Concerned parents may remain nearby and make decisions the child is accustomed to making independently. The child has a need to overcome this situation of dependence and often finds this important opportunity in the therapeutic recreation program. If the child or young adult has ample opportunities to be independent and to make choices during recreation, it is far more likely that he or she will not choose issues such as eating, toilet training, or compliance with medical procedures to exert control.

Case: A School-Age Child with Gastrointestinal Disturbances

Jeanie, age 8, was admitted to the hospital for persistent diarrhea and weight loss. After two weeks of diagnostic testing, physicians could find no medical cause and called in a psychiatrist for consultation. More testing and behavioral observations followed, but revealed no helpful information. Her diet was manipulated and, at one point, she was fed through a **nasogastric tube** (a small tube that is placed through the nose and down into the stomach to introduce medications or nutritional formulas into the digestive system).

As the battery of tests and trial diets continued and the number of consulting physicians multiplied, Jeanie became increasingly withdrawn. She did, however, continue her interactions with the TRS, and her parents reported that she looked forward to the therapist's daily visit. Since she withdrew from interactions with the medical staff, it was generally agreed that this was her way of exerting some control. The therapist began to offer self-esteem and problem-solving experiences that allowed Jeanie to make choices and to have control. The medical staff and dieticians then developed a rigid diet that appeared to decrease Jeanie's episodes of diarrhea. However, five days after beginning the new diet, Jeanie refused to eat. Her medical condition was precarious, and the staff was concerned about the consequences of Jeanie's refusal to eat. At a team meeting, the TRS suggested offering creative cooking activities in which Jeanie could prepare foods that were allowed by her special diet. Through close coordination with the dietician, the therapist's time with Jeanie was centered on cooking. Jeanie would choose the foods from a special list and would then prepare them according to her diet specifications. After beginning the cooking activities, Jeanie's refusal to eat her special diet markedly declined.

Creative Expression

In the stressful environment of the hospital, a child or young adult needs outlets to cope with anxieties, uncertainties, pain, and separation. Youth may react to hospitalization with hostility, withdrawal, or noncompliance with medical treatment. Youth are in need of safe means by which they can share their perceptions and their feelings about illness, treatment, and the realities of hospitalization. Creative experiences provide outlets while encouraging expression that develops healthy coping strategies. Creative activities also can help patient's feel confident in exploring new experiences, in practicing new roles, and in mastering unfamiliar situations. Offering such activities may help in the adjustment to hospitalization and treatment and adapting to a temporary or permanent physical change.

Case: A School-Age Child with Serious Burns

Jack, age 6, had a five-month hospital stay following an accident in which he sustained second- and third-degree burns to his chest, arm, neck, and back. During the first month of his hospitalization, Jack refused to participate in any activities. Repeated trips to the operating room for skin grafts, severe infections, and poor nutritional status kept Jack in an unstable medical state. When he began to stabilize and improve, he seemed more receptive to therapeutic recreation interventions and eventually established a good rapport with the therapist. The TRS continually offered expressive activities, and Jack participated in painting and crafts. However, he never directly spoke about his accident or injury during these sessions.

During his planned admission for reconstructive surgery two months later, the therapist found that drawing was still one of Jack's favorite activities. During one session, she suggested that Jack might like to draw pictures about what it is like to get burned and to get better from a burn, to help other children understand. Jack slowly agreed. Then the TRS suggested making a book with the pictures. Jack said, "Let's start at the fire." Subsequently, he drew pictures and narrated each one, telling the story of his accident and recovery.

Diversion and Stress Management

Hospitalized children and adolescents are in need of therapeutic "time-outs" from the hospital routine. Many youth need this break in order to cope successfully with the stresses they encounter in the health-care setting. Diversion or temporary distraction becomes therapeutic when the therapist purposely offers an intervention (e.g., pet therapy) that will require the participant's complete concentration and involvement. For youth who are overwhelmed by physically or psychologically painful events—as well as for those who appear to be coping adequately—diversion, systematically offered, is an avenue to manage stress.

Case: Adolescent Hospitalized for Open-Heart Surgery

Betsy, age 15, had to be hospitalized for an extended period. For a month after open-heart surgery, her precarious cardiac condition had kept her either in intensive care or confined to her bed on the teen unit. Betsy tried hard to comply with all of her treatment and therapies but had an especially difficult time dealing with blood tests and IV insertions.

When developing a comprehensive therapeutic recreation treatment plan for Betsy, the TRS recognized the need to focus her attention on something other than her illness. Since her strength was minimal, the therapist focused on passive interventions, offering a choice of activities. Every day Betsy would select either a DVD or

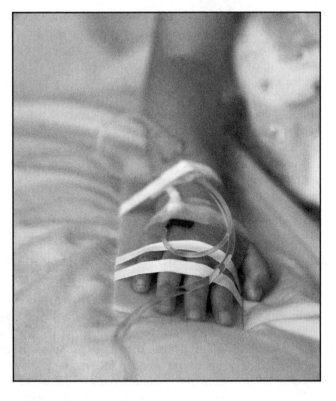

The stress associated with IV insertions and other invasive procedures can sometimes be minimized by activities designed to divert the patient's attention.

computer games. Following each session, Betsy displayed increased interest in her surroundings, engaged in conversation more easily, and seemed to better manage the invasive nature of IV insertions.

DELIVERY SETTINGS

Therapeutic recreation specialists interact with children, young adults, and their families in a number of settings, including pediatric hospitals, pediatric units within a general hospital, general hospital settings, outpatient and day facilities which may be part of a hospital or free standing, emergency and intensive care units, medical-surgical and oncology units, rehabilitation and residential (head injuries and burns) centers, psychiatric units, and community settings like home health, schools, camps, and recreation venues (ATRA, 2003). The hospital stay will continue to be "integrated into a continuum that allows children to complete therapy at home, at school, or in other community settings" (Ball & Bindler, 2008, p. 7). While the delivery systems vary and the personnel within these systems fluctuate, the family is the constant in the child's life, and as a consequence, it plays an increasingly important role in integrated health-care systems. In family-centered care, the TRS incorporates family members in the care of the child or adolescent and provides encouragement and the necessary support to facilitate their role as helpers. (For additional information on family-centered care, consult the Institute for Patient- and Family-Centered Care, http://www.ipfcc.org/faq.html.)

Although the care of children and youth continues to move from traditional hospitals to community-based settings, there is no way in which the health-care services, individually or collectively, can completely replicate the child's customary environment. Clinical settings and interventions are like visiting a foreign country where the language, culture, and activities are unfamiliar to the child and family (James & Ashwill, 2007). Characteristics of a health-care setting—elevator bells that can be heard from nearby rooms, windows that rarely can be opened, side rails on beds that snap into place at bedtime, paging operators' voices heard over the loudspeakers, "beeps" emitted from slim gray boxes carried by medical personnel, white lab coats and special uniforms worn by health-care workers, meals that arrive on trays, and medical personnel who change two and three times a day—are constant reminders of the differences between the clinical setting and the child's home.

LEADERSHIP INTERACTION
AND INTERVENTION CONSIDERATIONS

Each child develops within a unique family and culture that influence and shape his or her responses to an illness or hospitalization and communication with health-care professionals. Family members are important team members who help the child/youth cope and adapt to illness and hospitalization. Yet, a number of variables influence the manner in which the family interacts with and supports the child and health-care providers. Cultural variables impact how the TRS interacts with the patient and family. Thus, objective consideration of the cultural context and worldviews among family members and health-care providers is important to ensure sensitive and responsive interactions. Also important is the ability to establish partnerships with families and caregivers through effective communication (James & Ashwill, 2007). The child's cognitive skills and developmental level and the family's cultural context influence understanding and interpretation of medical terms and phrases; for example, "flush your IV" (interpreted as flush ivy down the toilet) or "dressing change" (interpreted as change my clothes). Thus, as the TRS implements the therapeutic recreation process, he or she considers word choices and meanings as well as the patient's and family's background and relationships.

Families and caregivers profoundly influence children and youth. Helping extended families find a role in the care and recreation of a child with an illness or disability may involve the TRS. Family members and caregivers may need support in managing their own feelings and in handling the demands of a family crisis. Assessment determines whether conditions within the family—like chronic marital discord, single parent with changing live-in partners, or dysfunction as a result of addictions—impact the family's ability to deal more effectively with a health-care experience (Betz et al., 1994; Hart et al., 1992). Families at-risk are those with multiple and repeated social, economic, legal, and health problems who view health as a primary concern only when it interferes with their daily activities. These families may literally move from one emergency room to the next rather than bring the young patient back for treatments and follow-up appointments.

The TRS uses recreation to assess family strengths and coping methods. Information about relationships and activities done together is gathered since "there is a high positive relationship between number of leisure time factors and family health" (Betz et al., 1994, p. 48). The TRS may support family relationships by, for example, intervening when working parents are unable to be present, or planning a celebration with siblings and extended family members when a treatment milestone is reached.

A TRS interacts with a mix of cultural groups with ever-increasing diversity. "Culture is among the most significant factors that influence parenthood, health, and illness" (James & Ashwill, 2007, p. 33). Culturally sensitive care requires that the TRS becomes aware of and incorporates into policy and practice recognition of cultural diversity, strengths, and individuality within and across families and health-care providers. TRSs are sensitive to the multiple ways that families perceive help-seeking behaviors, causes of diseases and illnesses, death and dying, caretaking and caregiving, and child-rearing practices. They also consider such factors as rituals and practices of extended family members, relationships with authority figures, religion, education, life views, forms and styles of communication, time and personal space issues, and permissible contact with strangers (Ball & Bindler, 2008; Child Life Council, 1997; Hart et al., 1992).

The TRS needs to examine his or her own cultural views and consider how these values may differ from those of patients and families. With this assessment, the TRS learns to interact more effectively with families. When a family's cultural values are incorporated into treatment and intervention plans, the family is more likely to comply with needed care in the home setting. For example, some cultures practice alternative therapies or celebrate certain rituals with which the TRS may not be familiar. The TRS may find that these practices and beliefs influence the family's support of selected interventions (aromatherapy) and engagements (holiday events). Consequently, the family may be less than supportive of the child's intervention plan. The more open the TRS is to understanding the values that determine family behavior and drive decisions, the more able the TRS is to accommodate the young patient and family.

As suggested in the section on developmental processes, styles and forms of communication among patients, family members, and health-care providers are critical considerations as the TRS develops intervention plans. Developmental levels and cultural systems influence the types of communication used and the understanding and interpretation of meanings given to medical terms and phrases. Also, the context in which communication takes place influences a family's ability to receive and respond to information. To illustrate, the family of a critically ill and dying child needs to receive consistent information from all team members. Message consistency instills confidence and reassures parents that overall responsibility for the care of their child remains with themselves and their chosen doctor, even as staff rotates through intensive care units.

Maintaining open lines of communication among families and health-care providers ensures that family members feel competent and confident to navigate the health-care system. For children and youth, open lines of communication between the TRS and patient helps the TRS sustain participant attention and maintain a safe environment. Both families and patients need to feel comfortable asking for assistance so they don't become overwhelmed or experience unmet emotional needs. Likewise, the TRS needs to maintain professional boundaries so he or she balances being connected in a meaningful way with establishing supportive therapeutic relationships.

The TRS's assessment determines the patient's cognitive, emotional, and language abilities and the family's cultural context and worldviews. With this information, the TRS selects terms and intervention procedures that lack ambiguity and are not culturally or emotionally laden. For example, rather than say "stretcher" (stretch who?), the therapist might say "bed with wheels." Rather than say "the doctor will put you to sleep" (my cat was put to sleep and never came back), instead "the doctor will give you medicine to help you sleep during the operation" (James & Ashwill, 2007). Terms and abbreviations like non-weight-bearing (NWB) can be simplified by suggesting that the activity take place with everyone seated at a table or by recommending aquatic interventions. For patients whose primary language is not English, therapists may use communication boards with the names of items in both languages. If physical assistance is required, one therapist may stand in front of the child to give an explanation while a second therapist assists the child from behind. The TRS communicates empathy when, for example, he or she indicates that it is okay to cry or to be upset about the loss of privacy yet affirms that the project was completed successfully. Therapists encourage listening by removing distractions like computer games or closing doors in the recreation area. They carefully monitor feedback for accuracy of information as this reduces fears and anxieties.

Goals of Selected Interventions

Several of the interventions used to support TR treatment goals and outcomes with children and youth are presented. Refer to chapter 3 for a more inclusive list of alternative interventions.

Bibliotherapy and Journaling

These creative and expressive interventions are used not only with youth but clients of all ages. The therapist uses books and journaling to engage youth in storytelling and writing to facilitate expression, coping, identifying health-care issues and concerns, providing cognitive stimulation and language development, and providing alternative interests and problem solutions. The TRS may tell a story to the child using puppets, a storybook, a felt board, or other such materials. After the TRS has told a story, then the child can model this behavior and begin telling a story by using a puppet, by writing and illustrating a book, by making a tape recording or video, using the computer, or by developing a felt-board story. When youth keep journals, feelings and thoughts are captured that help them better understand the experience while enabling them to communicate their concerns and desires orally during formal debriefing or informal conversations with staff. This process also labels experiences that are satisfying and resolve conflicts. Through journals, children and youth experience change and growth and realize factors that contribute to their self-worth. TRSs explore relationships among self-esteem, health, and interactions with others.

Community Reintegration

Community events and trips take place in outdoor areas on or near the hospital grounds; nearby locations like sports facilities, theaters, or parks; and at commercial recreation venues. A trip away from the health-care facility for any length of time must be carefully approved and coordinated with the treatment schedule, insurance carrier, and the health-care team. TRSs should obtain the necessary permissions and support from the parent(s), team, doctor, and insurance provider prior to the event. Such experiences are advisable when the consensus is that the participant and family are emotionally and physically prepared to go out into the community and the outcomes are intended to satisfy treatment objectives and explore issues related to discharge planning. Reintegration experiences are especially helpful in preparing the participant and family for returning to the home and community environment. While preparing for the event, and as the experience occurs, the patient and family can develop skills in utilizing community resources, determine their ability to manage accessibility challenges, and gauge their comfort with attitudinal responses to the illness or disability. Team members help parents become comfortable with adaptive devices and supportive needs while encouraging parents and patients to cope with real and perceived barriers. Community events also provide a welcome break from the all-too-well-known hospital routine. These "time-outs" encourage independent functioning and can also restore self-confidence and a wellness perspective.

Creative Cooking

Creative cooking may be done with an individual or in a group and may include parents or other staff, as appropriate. The TRS must take several considerations into account in planning a cooking activity: the diets of the children and youth involved, the quantity of cooking materials and facilities available, the age and number of participants, and the time required for an activity. Frequently, cooking can be offered as an activity with a participant who is unable to be involved in group experiences. The preparation can often be done at the bedside, and the food to be cooked can be carried to the oven. The most consistent benefit from creative cooking is that it can be a positive experience with food, as well as a successful experience. Many children and youth have nutritional requirements that they find troublesome or "impossible." Within the boundaries of what is required for that individual, the therapist can offer food in a positive and appealing way. By dealing with food in a nonstressful manner, creative cooking activities are an opportunity to improve a child's or teen's attitude toward eating. This is also a good opportunity to teach the individual about special dietary needs. By promoting healthy eating habits, cooking may be part of a weight management program. Additionally, clients may become more independent in preparing their own snacks and meals. Cooking also provides helpful socialization opportunities. Additional positive outcomes that result from cooking activities are the reinforcement, attention, and praise that the children and youth involved receive from the medical staff. This reinforcement and attention are always increased when those staff members are invited to share in the finished product!

Expressive and Creative Arts

Expressive and creative arts include activities such as painting and drawing; crafts or art projects; dance, drama, poetry, and other performing arts; and creative media activities that use finger paints, sand, water, bubbles, or clay. These activities may be done individually or in a group, and may be adapted to a wide variety of physical and developmental needs. Participants may focus on familiar materials or may choose to experiment with various media or projects. Experiences allow freedom and control while providing staff with the opportunity to gain insight into a youth's feelings, perceptions, and concerns. A TRS collaborating with an art therapist may discern recurrent themes significant to the participant's psychosocial or physical well-being.

Craft projects lend themselves to giving and contributing or diverting the focus from oneself to others; for example, when holiday decorations are made for the recreation area or projects result in gifts that can be given to others. Involvement in a craft project may serve as a temporary distraction and result in more comfortable dialogue otherwise not possible. Like art therapists, TRSs recognize art interventions enhance inclusion, socialization, communication, and serve as a means to project feelings, perceptions, and conflicts.

Participation with creative media provides a positive, nonpainful tactile activity. The various media can be manipulated with implements and/or participants' hands and feet. Participants experience control, self-expression, and satisfaction with minimal amounts of energy expenditure.

Leisure Education

Leisure education involves not only instruction and recreation activities, but also educating the patient and parent to opportunities, barriers, values, time management, and how leisure affects daily life balance. This involves discussing with the patient and parent alternative recreation activities—and any necessary adaptations—appropriate during hospitalization and following discharge. Ultimately, the leisure education goal with children having chronic medical conditions is to provide the child and parent with the knowledge they need for the child to actively engage in recreation and leisure activities that maintain optimal health. The TRS conducts activities, presents information, and visits with patients and family members about experiences that foster active participation. The TRS develops a written referral list of leisure opportunities and gives it to the patient and family before separation or discharge. Such planning encourages awareness of the benefits and requirements of various therapeutic recreation options while in the hospital; facilitates transition from hospital experiences to available options at home; and creates access to meaningful and beneficial leisure opportunities in the community. This type of intervention is especially important for the individual with a limited repertoire of recreation skills and for the participant who requires adaptation of activities to accommodate functional abilities.

Music Activities

Music activities range from listening to MP3 players, CDs, or a musical performer to singing, watching a DVD, playing a musical instrument, or participating in a group activity such as a dance. The outcomes of a music activity range from relaxation to acceptable and frequently familiar self-expression and motivation to continue participation. In a group activity, the individual has an opportunity for group membership and affirmation. Active involvement in a music activity provides recognition of talent and positive reinforcement from other members of the health-care team while facilitating relaxation and stress management. When music therapists are team members, the TRS may collaborate to design intervention sessions on song writing or movement with the intent of promoting communication, cognitive functioning, and social growth.

Physical Activity

Physical activity includes gross and fine motor activities, recreation, sports, and aquatics that encourage movement and active participation within the limits of what can be safely tolerated. Throwing, beating (drums, pillows), bicycle riding, marching, lawn bowling, and pushing one's wheelchair (to and from an event) are examples of gross motor activities. Gross motor activities can provide outlets to cope with intense emotions (i.e., release anger) and energy in a manner that promotes physical health.

In fine motor activities, items are constructed, piled, strung, connected, and manipulated, like the computer mouse or touch pad that controls software functions. The therapist assesses the level of difficulty of any fine motor experience to ensure the participant's safety and to consider the "frustration factor" inherent in the experience. Experiences using fine motor skills allow the participant to make decisions regarding what materials will be used and how long his or her involvement in the activity will last. These are types of developmental activities that can be used to increase the participant's concentration span by systematically increasing the duration or complexity of the activity. Problem-solving and coordination are also developmental outcomes of fine motor activities. Physical activities are frequently coordinated with occupational therapy or physical therapy to reinforce physical strengthening and conditioning, functional skill improvements, developmental play, and any rehabilitation involving the hands.

Recreation and sports may include board games, card games, video and computer games, outdoor recreation and adapted sports, and aquatic activities such as swimming, playing games in the water, or hot and cold water therapy. Recreational games and sports are therapeutic in several ways. First, they are familiar activities for youth and are readily identified as enjoyable. Second, games and sports are activities in which parents and siblings or staff and patient can participate. Third, games and sports provide opportunities for socialization. For some youth it is easier to initiate interactions while playing a game rather than through a direct discussion or encounter—becoming comfortable with another person while playing a game may aid in establishing a positive trust relationship with that person. Finally, games and sports offer physical activity and competition to youth who need opportunities to promote and maintain healthy behaviors and competitive skills in life-long activities. The practicing of familiar games and the learning of new, and possibly, adapted games can be carried over into the home, school, and community (BlazeSports or Paralympics Games) following discharge. Aquatics also offer life-time physical activity while promoting mobility, social interaction, inclusion, and stress management.

Sensory Stimulation

Objects having sensory appeal diversify the sterile hospital environment. The TRS might put up mobiles, posters, and collages on hospital walls or attach them to IV poles, bed rails, or traction bars. These materials are easily visible, brightly colored, and easy to change frequently. Sensory materials also include CDs, movies, music, and interventions that provide varied, nonpainful tactile stimulation such as snoezelen carts and pet therapy. Objects with sensory appeal spark the child's memory of familiar experiences and provide relaxation, the opportunity to be engaged with minimal movement, and distraction from pain, frustration, or boredom. Introducing nature activities can provide diversion and relaxation as well as physical activity, cognitive stimulation, creativity, personal growth, social-emotional development, and understanding of life's lessons. Horticultural therapy, outdoor recreation activities

An outdoor activity can provide diversion and relaxation as well as sensory stimulation.

like a family picnic or visit to the flower gardens or reflection pond on the health-care grounds, and individual or team initiatives require the use of the senses, address holistic health, and reunite children and youth to nature as a moral teacher (Louv, 2005).

Applying the Therapeutic Recreation Process

Casey is a 16-year-old male who was diagnosed with cystic fibrosis (CF) at 18 months of age. He has a younger sister and brother; the brother also has CF. Management of CF consists of taking enzymes, diet modification, inhalation therapy, and respiratory treatments administered at home after school and on weekends. Casey holds a part-time job and often visits with friends, thus he frequently misses meals and taking his enzymes. Respiratory treatments are sometimes missed too. Casey is aware that not following the treatment regimen can endanger his health, yet he is not willing to comply when friends are present. This is his second hospitalization this year due to infection.

Assessment

Demographic information.   Casey is 16 years old and lives with two siblings, one of whom has CF, and his mother in a large metropolitan area. His father's medical policy covers a portion of Casey's expenses.

History.   Casey was diagnosed with CF at 18 months. He has since experienced repeated bouts of pneumonia and bronchitis. He is below his age level for height and weight on growth charts and his secondary sex characteristics are delayed. His extremities are thin and he is barrel-chested. Wheezing and a dry, nonproductive cough have been present since diagnosis of CF.

Present behavior.   Casey's mother performs segmental postural drainage with inhalation therapy two times per day. He is on a high-calorie, high-protein diet, pancreatic enzyme replacement therapy, and fat-soluble vitamin supplement. He is supposed to exercise at least 30 minutes per day.

His recent hospitalization results from a respiratory infection. When he entered the hospital, Casey's cough was wet and followed by vomiting with increased coughing, dyspnea, cyanosis, and emphysema. Increased respiratory distress was caused by ineffective airway clearance due to increased pulmonary secretions. He is on bronchodilators; humidified low-flow oxygen; and IV therapy.

Planning

Long-term goal.   The long-term goal of Casey's intervention is to comply with his treatment regimen.

Short-term goals.   The two short-term goals are to maintain an oxygen saturation level of greater than 94% and to rest comfortably and engage in physical activity as energy permits.

Objective.   By discharge, Casey will comply with the team's recommendation on his daily treatment and exercise protocol by (1) writing a daily plan that includes one 30-minute exercise session and two 30-minute treatment sessions, (2) calling two friends to request their participation in his daily physical activity, (3) practicing the postural drainage routine and inhalation therapy with his mother at least four times prior to discharge, (4) meeting with the team and his parents to develop a school/work schedule that permits time for daily nutritional meals, and (5) participating in one session with his siblings on self-care and hygiene.

Content.   In a one-on-one session, the TRS will complete leisure satisfaction scales and review caloric values of various physical activities. Casey will also participate in a cooking activity in the recreation room, as well as visits and phone calls to friends. He will also visit the fitness center/health club in the hospital.

Process.   The TRS visits Casey in his private room to complete the leisure satisfaction scale, arrange a visit to the hospital fitness center/health club, and invite him to the outside recreation area for a teen cookout.

Implementation

Casey completed the satisfaction scale and the Teen Leisurescope Plus. During the teen cookout in the outdoor area, Casey assisted in food preparation and, with two other teens, used a computer software program to determine caloric values of various physical activities.

Evaluation

The TRS helps the family write a daily exercise/meal schedule and develop a computer database to record activity participation, frequency and duration, fluid intake, breathing exercises, and calorie/protein diet records. The record will be monitored when Casey returns to the outpatient clinic every 6 months for exercise testing and sputum cultures.

RELATED CONSIDERATIONS

A number of resources are necessary to deliver therapeutic recreation experiences in pediatric settings. Of primary importance are the play and recreation spaces, supplies and equipment, and operational policies and procedures. As TRSs carry out the therapeutic recreation process, they may co-treat with child life specialists; dieticians; speech, occupational, and physical therapists; as well as other health-care professionals. Therefore, an understanding of their roles is critical to ensure the team functions in an effective manner to address the needs of the young patient and his or her family. Integral members of the care team include siblings, parents, and sometimes extended family members who desire to be a part of the care process yet may need support from therapists to participate as team members. Volunteers may also enhance team effectiveness and extend program resources, thus the TRS can plan to incorporate them into interventions and monitor and reward their performance. Finally, as the TRS interacts on family-centered teams with young patients who are chronically ill and dying, strategies to manage and cope with their own grief and that of team members and families are infused into the care process.

Recreation Spaces, Equipment, and Policies

The physical facilities available to a pediatric therapeutic recreation program play an important role in setting the tone and scope of the program. Much of the health-care environment is unfamiliar to children; therefore, it should be supplemented with recreation areas that are comfortable and secure from the unknown aspects of intervention.

The size of recreation areas is important. Areas should be (1) large enough to accommodate the necessary number of children and their medical equipment, (2) accessible to all participants, and (3) appealing to children of varying ages and abilities.

The area must be accessible to the population being served and must be close enough to the unit to encourage participation. Some children/youth and their parents are anxious about going too far from their rooms. Others are not medically stable enough to travel long distances from their units. The entryways and travel routes to outside areas and recreation areas need to accommodate not only ambulatory children but also children in traction beds, wheelchairs, and with adaptive apparatus. Space must be adequate and accessible to accommodate IV poles, and indoor areas must have outlets for plugging in certain IV equipment. If there is not a separate

The outdoor play area behind a children's hospital offers opportunities for young patients to engage in physical activity.

young adult area or an adolescent lounge, it is helpful to either section off one portion of the recreation area or use a separate lounge or patient room for adolescents, decorating it in a way that appeals to the teenage population of the unit.

As play and recreation spaces are created, it is recommended that available toys and resources be suitable for all ages and developmental levels and include toys that represent real-life experiences as opposed to "make believe" toys (ambulances, computers), toys that release aggression and allow for acting out (toy medical kit, stethoscope, and syringes), and toys for creative expression and enhancement of self-concept (arts and crafts, video equipment, and library resources) (Child Life Council, 1997; Lingnell & Dunn, 1999). Another factor considered in the selection of toys and resources is the potential for allergic reactions, such as that found with latex products. Health-care professionals; children with spina bifida; those who have other allergies, asthma, or eczema; or those with conditions that involve multiple surgical procedures are at higher risk for developing latex allergy. A number of Web sites identify toll-free phone numbers for manufacturers of toys and baby products so consumers can obtain information on natural rubber content (www.latexallergyhelp.com or www.latexallergyresources.org).

Therapists also consider the benefits of outpatient recreation and play in hospital clinics. Children and youth with chronic disease or prolonged acute illness such as cancer, cystic fibrosis, spina bifida, or who have been burned or experienced traumatic injury and require ongoing medical intervention benefit from returning to activity centers where they have had trusting relationships and opportunities to reach their potential (Lingnell & Dunn, 1999). A TRS may deliver services on pediatric units and in outpatient clinics throughout the hospital.

Another concern is whether the storage areas are accessible to the recreation areas and to the staff. In order to accommodate the wide age range and varying abilities of the children and youth, a program needs a sizable amount of materials and equipment. Ideally, toys and games should be attractively displayed in a manner that invites the child or adolescent to participate and should be accessible to all youth when appropriate. Therapists may receive a call from a clinic to assess the child's leisure functioning or a physician's order to incorporate physical activity in the intervention plan through gross motor activities (bicycling or golf); thus, location of storage areas is critical to program operation.

Just as important as clearly identifying recreation areas is establishing the guidelines for appropriate use of equipment. Since children and youth with ongoing medical problems are more susceptible to infection, infection control, isolation, and cleaning policies are carefully followed. Protocols may require toys be cleaned after each session and the activity area disinfected on a regular basis and may delineate specific procedures for toys and equipment used with youth in isolation. Staff must monitor not only the use of materials but also routinely inspect and evaluate toys, games, equipment, and recreation areas to ensure the accessibility, upkeep and safety of the materials and areas. Some settings have a written policy regarding the safety and maintenance of play and recreation equipment. A policy of this nature is shown in exhibit 11.3.

Adequate and accessible storage areas facilitate program options.

Exhibit 11.3   Cleaning of Toys and Play Areas

Purpose: To provide clean toys and play environments for patients.

Toy Cleaning/Disinfection Responsibility and Frequency

A. Toys, books, games, and other play materials are checked and sorted on an ongoing basis by staff in each activity area.

B. As needed, the staff will discard worn, soiled, or otherwise undesirable items.

C. All toys distributed to inpatient rooms are placed in the "toy return" bin and are cleaned and disinfected before being returned to the shelves and made available to other patients. In the clinics, toy return bins are also available and these toys are cleaned and disinfected before being returned for use by other patients.

D. All toys which come into contact with body fluids (i.e., due to mouthing) or a child with a known or suspected infectious disease will be placed in the toy return bin or designated area and disinfected before being returned to the shelves and made available to other patients.

E. All toys in inpatient activity areas are disinfected between patients (as noted above) and at least once per month.

F. All toys in outpatient areas are disinfected between patients (as noted above) and at least once per month. Clinics with high volume/usage of toys may consider cleaning weekly.

G. All toys in treatment rooms/examination rooms will be disinfected between patients and at least weekly.

H. All mats are cleaned (disinfected) between patients.

I. Therapy balls are cleaned (disinfected) daily or more frequently as needed (i.e. if a child lies on a ball with face contact, the ball is disinfected between patients).

J. TV/VCR/video games and computers attached to carts will be disinfected by wiping with germicidal wipes between each patient. In general, these items should not be used in isolation rooms.

K. Toys in therapy closets that are used sporadically will be cleaned as needed (based on the discretion of the therapist) and after being used with any isolation patient. Items that cannot be disinfected (books, board games) are not to be used with isolation patients.

L. Carpet on the carpeted tubes/swings should be cleaned on a regular basis and whenever contaminated with body fluids.

Adapted and reprinted with permission of the Department of Therapeutic Recreation/Child Life, The Children's Hospital, Aurora, Colorado.

Health-Care Team and Family-Centered Care

You will discover that roles and responsibilities in pediatrics vary from one health-care setting to another. Responsibilities are closely related to the number of staff and their expertise. TRSs on teams will coordinate their efforts with professionals having training and credentials in medical care of children and youth. These professionals include pediatric nurses; Child Life Specialists; dieticians; and speech, occupational, and physical therapists. In some hospitals, therapeutic recreation specialists and child life specialists may be organized in one department with individual staff members having either one or both sets of credentials; in other hospitals, staff may be organized in separate child life and recreation therapy departments. A Child Life Specialist focuses on the emotional and developmental needs of children and families using age-appropriate play to reduce the stress of health-care experiences (Ball & Bindler, 2008; Child Life Council, 1997). Course work includes classes in child life, child development, and child and family studies with an internship in a child life clinical experience under a Certified Child Life Specialist.

Family-centered care may include participation of siblings and parents (Lingnell & Dunn, 1999). Siblings may feel guilty about being healthy or perceive that they did something to cause their sibling's accident or illness; they may fear the possible death of their sibling; and/or they may be angry about the additional attention being given to their sibling or frustrated by the lengthy separation from parents (Lingnell & Dunn). Involvement in therapeutic sessions promotes the continuation of developing relationships and acceptance of feelings while increasing an understanding for what their sibling is experiencing. Parents may feel helpless, vulnerable, and incompetent or guilty, especially if their actions or genetics precipitated injury or disability (cystic fibrosis). A team member may need to consciously give support to a parent to assist with adjustment to their child's illness. And, for parents, like children, engaging in recreation therapy is a routine interaction that may increase their feelings of competence and support their role as parents.

Therapists may find the team's effort is supported by volunteers with vested interests and special talents (Child Life Council, 1997). Careful attention to liability issues requires formal programs that screen, train, place, monitor, recognize, and terminate volunteers. Likewise, interns can expect strict adherence to preparatory training courses and prerequisite practical experiences.

Interaction with a dying child is one of the greatest challenges a therapist may experience. Children as young as 5 years of age may sense the seriousness of an illness (Ball & Bindler, 2008). A school-age child intuitively may know when he or she is dying and have the same fears as an adult. TRSs are encouraged to directly acknowledge impending death of a child and to help children understand the finality of death. The fact that the child will not be going home from the hospital needs to be acknowledged consistently by each member of the health-care team during his or her interactions with the child and family members. TRSs may help the child and family through the grieving process by creating and saving mementos, maintaining communication with friends outside the hospice setting, providing activities that channel feelings, and connecting parents with others in support groups. For the TRS and other members of the team, caring for dying children and youth is stressful because children and teens are supposed to live normal life spans, so their deaths are tragic. Consequently, debriefing sessions are often conducted to help team members cope with feelings of powerlessness and loss.

SUMMARY

This chapter presents an overview of children and youth with illness, injuries, chronic disabilities, and elective surgeries who experience hospitalization. Regardless of their chronological age, hospitalization disrupts growth and development and has a profound impact on the child/youth and members of the caregiving system. Family-centered care has become integral to the delivery of comprehensive services as the length-of-stay continues to decrease and treatment and rehabilitation are provided in alternative settings like outpatient clinics, private homes, schools, rehabilitation clinics, and hospice sites. Since play and recreation are a child's first teacher, experiences become avenues for family and team members to communicate and interact with youth as they navigate health-care systems. Recreation therapy improves functional ability and independent functioning, prevents developmental delays, promotes coping, enhances psychosocial functioning, prepares families and clients for healthy leisure lifestyles, and improves overall quality of life (ATRA, 2003).

Although each child or teen uniquely responds to hospitalization, general reactions and needs were identified for each age group. Infants' need for comfort triggers immediate response to discomfort, especially when routines are interrupted. Toddlers experience anxiety when separated from mothers and are easily confused by the multiple interactions with health-care team members. Preschoolers ask lots of questions, need outlets for continual physical development, and may assume they are being punished for a misdeed when they are sick or ill. A school-age child may become upset or disappointed with family members when they can't seem to control the pain being inflicted on their child. The drive for independence is interrupted when a teen or young adult becomes ill or is injured. Moreover, peer group reactions may be cause for concern when hospitalization is lengthy and permanent scars are anticipated.

The therapeutic recreation process is applied during brief (one day or less) treatment or lengthy hospitalization stays. A number of cases were presented to illustrate several general outcomes; these include normal growth and development, emotional adjustment and support, social skill development, independence, creative expression, and diversion and stress management.

Each child develops within a unique family and culture that shape his or her responses to hospitalization. As interventions are selected, the TRS considers the influence of family, culture, and communication on therapeutic interactions. Families remain the constant in the child's life, yet care-giving responsibilities are also sometimes extended to friends and neighbors. As our culture becomes more diverse, TRSs become more sensitive to the methods and beliefs families have about care-giving, child-rearing, causes of illness and disease, and death and dying. The types and forms of communication used by the TRS and team members are influenced by the patient's developmental level and the family's cultural heritage.

Related factors important to the delivery of a safe, professional program include the size of recreation areas as well as the access, storage, and transportability of equipment to recreation areas within and outside the health-care facility. Policies on space use, isolation, latex-safe environments, and infection control are critical to participant well-being and are monitored by internal and external standard-setting bodies.

Professional programs are delivered by credentialed specialists like therapeutic recreators and child life specialists who collaborate to achieve treatment objectives. Therapists may need to support parents as they take part in certain procedures and help them work through any feelings of guilt or incompetence. Volunteers and interns may play a role in TR programs, and hospitals have specific policies addressing their involvement, especially as it relates to liability and professional preparation in clinical settings. The challenge of working with dying children and youth means that TRSs must attend to their own grief while also supporting families and other team members.

Key Terms

cardiac catheterization A diagnostic procedure in which a small tube is inserted in a vein of the leg or arm and threaded through the venous system to the heart.

Child Life Specialist A credentialed professional who uses age-appropriate play to address development needs of children and their families in the hospital setting.

disfigurement The loss, damage, or change to a part of the body that causes a noticeable change in physical appearance.

egocentricity A psychological orientation that causes an individual to be totally self-absorbed.

family-centered care A philosophy of care that integrates family and caregiver values and contributions into the delivery of health-care services to children and youth.

juvenile rheumatoid arthritis (JRA) A disease that affects the large joints of children under the age of 16.

nasogastric tube A small tube that is placed through the nose and down into the stomach to introduce medications or nutritional formulas to the digestive system.

reconstructive surgery Surgery that builds up or restores body tissues that have been damaged or destroyed.

renal disease A disorder that involves the kidney.

Study Questions

1. Develop a rationale for including therapeutic recreation services in health-care agencies that serve children and adolescents with medical illnesses.

2. Identify several ramifications of a disease or injury that might affect a child's psychosocial response to treatment and rehabilitation.

3. What unique developmental issues must be considered when treating newborns and infants? Toddlers? Preschoolers? School-age children? Adolescents and young adults?

4. Give specific goals and discuss when and why you would use each of the following therapeutic interventions: bibliotherapy and journaling, community reintegration, creative cooking, expressive and creative arts, leisure education, music activities, physical activity, and sensory stimulation.

5. Describe four family and cultural influences that shape the leadership interactions of the TRS with children and youth who are hospitalized.

6. Explain the significance and issues involved in communicating with families having diverse backgrounds and with hospitalized children and youth.

Practical Experiences to Enhance Student Objectives

1. Visit or volunteer on the pediatric unit of a local hospital. Keep a log or diary of your experiences. Compare hospitalized children to children playing at a local preschool.

2. Select one childhood illness, such as cystic fibrosis, and research the nature, cause, symptoms, and treatment for this disease. What are the implications for the child's play and recreation behaviors?

3. Discuss with class members any experiences you may have had as a hospitalized child. What do you remember from the experience? Was there a recreation therapy program in your hospital?

4. Search the following Web sites and collect information on children and youth who experience hospitalizations:

   - www.childlife.org
   - www.jhu.edu
   - www.nydic.org
   - www.nichcy.org
   - www.recreationtherapy.com
   - www.safekids.org
   - www.familycenteredcare.org
   - www.tsrhc.org

The Aging Process

> ## *After reading this chapter, students will be able to:*
>
> ✔ Describe the physical, psychological, intellectual, and sociological changes accompanying the aging process
>
> ✔ Identify the lifelong, adult-onset, and traumatic illnesses and disabilities associated with aging
>
> ✔ Explain the functioning characteristics and leisure needs of aging adults who experience varying degrees of well-being
>
> ✔ Outline the settings, programs, and services appropriate to aging adults
>
> ✔ Summarize the application of the therapeutic recreation process with aging people
>
> ✔ Identify leadership and intervention considerations when implementing leisure services and therapeutic recreation with aging individuals

In this chapter we will discuss the aging process and the illnesses and disabilities experienced by aging people. The first section of this chapter introduces you to the natural consequences of the aging process and of reaching an "old" age. The second section of the chapter presents information on lifelong, adult-onset, and traumatic illnesses and disabilities experienced by aging persons.

INTRODUCTION

Aging is a universal phenomenon, yet it is uniquely individualistic. The personality and philosophy of life an individual brings to the aging process greatly influence

Chapter 12 was revised with contributions from Claire M. Foret, PhD, CTRS, University of Louisiana at Lafayette.

how he or she "ages." Aging commences with conception, follows the developmental process through childhood and adolescence, accelerates during the maturing years of life, and is most evident in the senior years when physical, psychological, intellectual, and sociological changes are vividly apparent. The global population, including the United States, "is in the midst of a profound demographic change: the rapid aging of its population" (Himes, 2008, p. 2). The demographic impact of lower birth rates, longer life spans, and aging baby boomers is unprecedented (Centers for Disease Control and Prevention, 2007). The older population is expected to continue to grow, and older people with lifelong, adult-onset, and traumatic illnesses or disabilities are living longer and are expected to continue increasing in number.

Life expectancy is increasing worldwide. "The number of people ages 85 and older is now the most rapidly growing segment . . . developing countries are experiencing the most rapid growth in people over 65" (Population Reference Bureau, 2007, p. 1). Ancient Romans lived on average 22 years, while today a global citizen can expect to live to 65, and by 2050 the average life expectancy may be nearly 100 (Morrison, 1996; Weiss, 1997). Those over 85 are expected to continue to increase at a faster rate than those 65 and older: Greater proportions of 65-year-olds are living until age 85, with more 85-year-olds living into their 90s (Himes, 2008). While increasing numbers of older people are healthier and more active and there has been a dramatic reduction in chronic disabilities in the 85 and over cohort, functional assistance needs are greater than for other cohorts and the percentage residing in long-term care facilities is higher.

Another population segment experiencing steady growth in numbers is people with lifelong disabilities, such as those with developmental disabilities: "For the first time in human experience, persons with developmental disabilities are living longer" (Minde & Friedman, 2002, Introduction, para. 1). The life expectancy of the majority of persons with developmental disabilities approaches or equals that of the general population (American Association on Intellectual and Developmental Disabilities [AAIDD], 2009). It is estimated that 600,000 to 1.6 million people with developmental disabilities are over 60 years of age, with this number expected to double by 2030 (AAIDD; Gordon, 2005). Although legislation tends to use age 60 as the basis for planning services for people with developmental disabilities, there is evidence of earlier onset of aging processes in this population segment (Boyd, 1997), and thus their need for services may occur at age 50.

With the aging population, leisure and therapeutic recreation take on many foci. Programming with aging persons who are cognitively impaired or who experience physical health problems (cardiovascular and orthopedic diseases) and psychological issues (such as depression and loneliness) aims toward active treatment/rehabilitation. Leisure experiences with those who remain within their homes and in the community assume an educational and health promotion role. One goal of leisure education with older adults is to promote the making of choices, which facilitates participation and enhances the likelihood that older adults will choose options to sustain a physically active lifestyle and, among baby boomers, foster lifelong hobbies and sports (Godbey, 2005; Ziegler, 2002). Aging people who participate in leisure activities of their own volition do so for a number of reasons: companionship, health and physical well-being, cognitive stimulation, satisfaction, adventure, and to make meaningful contributions and commitments to others—outcomes linked to spiritual well-being ("Active Recreation," 2007).

As you interact with aging people you will discover that professional roles and settings are just as diverse as program options. Students training to become Certified Park and Recreation Professionals (CPRPs) and Certified Therapeutic Recreation Specialists (CTRSs) will administer activities and programs for aging individuals in a variety of settings. The setting and the agency focus greatly influence staff composition and employment responsibilities. A student with a major in either leisure services or therapeutic recreation and a specialty in aging might, upon graduation, obtain a position with a public parks and recreation department as a senior program specialist, or in a social service program sponsored by an **area agency on aging (AAA)** (local agency through which federal funds are dispersed) as a coordinator of aging affairs, or a for-profit company with baby boomers as a tour guide/event planner, or in a skilled nursing facility (SNF), or inpatient psychiatric hospital as a therapeutic recreation specialist.

POPULATION OVERVIEW: THE AGING INDIVIDUAL

As noted earlier, aging begins with conception, progresses through developmental periods, accelerates in the middle years, and ends with death. The quality with which each individual ages varies, as does his or her interpretation of what is "old." Social, political, and economic factors have shaped our beliefs about patterns associated with the aging process. From observing our own parents and grandparents we have come to expect a period of schooling, followed by a period of work and establishing a home and family, followed by some form of retirement. However, the expectations of retiring baby boomers and the interpretation of what is "old" will be "significantly different than those of their parents and grandparents" (Arsenault & Anderson, 1998, pp. 29–30). Boomers tend to separate themselves from signs that connect them to being old; they are concerned with "youthfulness" and respond as though they were 10 years younger than their actual age (Ziegler, 2002). The older adult of the twenty-first century is healthier, better educated, willing to work, views retirement as a mid-life event, and remains dedicated to health and wellness.

The average age of the population is increasing and is expected to continue to increase in the future. A child born in 1900 had a life expectancy of 47 years; today, the majority of the children born in the United States can expect to live into their eighth decade or beyond (Gorina, Hoyert, Lentzner, & Goulding, 2005; Townsend, 2006). Additionally, the proportion of people over 85 years of age is projected to continue increasing at rates faster than any other age cohort in many countries; and, in developing countries, the elderly population is expected to grow by 140% before 2030 (Population Reference Bureau, 2007). This phenomenon is due to several factors: people are living longer because of better health care, sanitation, and lifestyles; medical advancements; declining death rates from heart disease, cancer, and stroke; a decrease in women's mortality due to childbirth, and lowered fertility levels; and the large number of baby boomers, people born from 1946 to 1964, that will be reaching the age of 65 between 2010 and 2030. Thus, those reading this text can expect to spend a much larger portion of your adult lives in old age than did your grandparents.

Active baby boomers are redefining what it means to be "old." Here a couple meets with a trainer at their health club to customize a fitness routine.

Older individuals are opting to continue to work and *age in place;* that is, continue living in their home communities alone or with a spouse, family, or relatives. However, the proportion of older adults living in family settings decreases with age (Townsend, 2006). Because the life expectancy for women is longer than men and women outnumber men at every age among the elderly, women are far more likely to live alone than men (Himes, 2008; Townsend; Voelkl & Aybar-Damali, 2008). Thus, with increasing age the proportion living with a spouse decreases while those living in institutional settings increases. Those who move or transition into institutional settings are likely to be over 85, with the relocation precipitated by a change in their health status and the quality and affordability of their living arrangements (Voelkl & Aybar-Damali).

Several factors influence the quality of the aging process and longevity, including heredity, gender, ethnicity, lifestyle, education, medical care, health status, the presence of illnesses and disabilities, and economic level. Heredity determines an individual's predisposition to certain deficiencies and diseases and his or her adaptability to living under certain conditions. The older adult population is becoming more ethnically diverse. The life expectancy of women among ethnic populations tends to be higher than that of men. Lifestyle influences the health and functional status of aging adults in several ways—the rate of decline and the quality and longevity of life are impacted positively by physical activity, proper nutrition, and healthy habits like not smoking (Topolski et al., 2006). Higher levels of formal education tend to be associated with increased longevity. Likewise, those who receive proper medical care or who do not have an illness or disability tend to outlive those who either receive inadequate medical assistance or who have lifelong, adult-onset, or traumatic illnesses and disabilities.

The economic level of the aging person influences his or her choice of living arrangements, health and personal care, and ability to lead an active life. While most older adults are relatively secure financially and the poverty rate is lower than in the previous decade, higher-than-average poverty rates are found among pockets of elderly, including those living alone, older women, and Hispanic and Black women (Administration on Aging [AOA], 2007; Papalia, Sterns, Feldman, & Camp, 2007). Expenditures for personal health costs increase with age, as does the number of days in which usual activities are restricted because of illness or injury (Townsend, 2006). Thus a decline in personal resources becomes an issue for older adults since most experience one or more chronic conditions, and require more doctor visits and longer hospital stays than other age cohorts (AOA; Voelkl & Aybar-Damali, 2008). Many adults remain active into their seventies and therefore some health-care issues evident in the old are due to lifestyle factors that may or may not accompany aging (Papalia et al.).

Physical Changes Associated with Aging

The aging process is primarily a physiological phenomenon unique to each individual. The chronological age at which observable age-related changes appear varies from individual to individual. The first sign of slower response rate and recovery may appear during the 30s, or not until the 60s. Each of us brings to the aging process a personality that influences how well we respond to the physiological changes accompanying aging. Environmental factors also influence our responses to the physical changes that accompany aging. These include diet, lifestyle, rest, pollutants, alcohol, cleanliness, temperature, exposure to sunlight, and stress. Other factors influencing physical well-being as we age include our resistance to illness, exposure to trauma, infections, past diseases, and the health practices we adopt throughout our life span (Townsend, 2006).

A number of age-related changes contribute to decline in bodily functions. Although changes in the senses are gradual, which permits adjustment and compensation, decrements in the senses influence the quality of interactions with others and the environment and the ability to process information; if losses are great enough in one of the senses, social life, independence, and enjoyable activities are curtailed and safety and mobility are affected (Papalia et al., 2007; Smith & Gove, 2005). Visual and hearing acuity losses are the most common sensory changes, with visual acuity beginning to decrease in mid-life (late 30s and early 40s). As a result of changes in the lens and retina, older adults experience difficulty shifting from far to near vision, focusing sharply on close objects, adjusting to glare, discriminating shorter light waves of color (blues, greens, and violets), and adapting to changes in light intensity; they also require greater illumination to see (Papalia et al.; Smith & Gove). Serious visual impairments may result in functional and total blindness if not treated: Cataracts, macular degeneration, and glaucoma are among the leading causes of blindness in the world and tend to appear after age 60 (Papalia et al.; Smith & Gove).

Although hearing loss is more common among aging people than visual loss, it does not result in major activity limitations. Like vision, hearing is at its best before age 25. With age, there is a dramatic decline in the ability to hear high-pitch and high-frequency sounds (more so in men than in women) and to discern background noise from foreground conversation (Papalia et al., 2007; Townsend, 2006). Taste and smell may begin to decline in middle age yet losses may not be evident until after age 70. Touch and pain sensitivity decline with age. There is a lessened ability to adjust to temperature changes and to maintain homeostasis even in unchanging environments. The ability to perceive and interpret painful stimuli changes and with the thinning of the skin, there is greater potential for infection and injury (Papalia et al.; Smith & Gove, 2005; Townsend).

The three body systems crucial to homeostasis are the musculoskeletal, cardiovascular, and respiratory systems. Age-related changes in the musculoskeletal system result in such noticeable changes as diminished height and a shortened gait with a wider base and forward lean. The reduction in muscle mass, decrease in muscle elasticity, and subsequent joint stiffening cause reduced range of motion and increase the likelihood of falls. For those age 65 or older, arthritis is the leading chronic condition

The reduction in muscle mass, decrease in muscle elasticity, and subsequent joint stiffening that accompany the aging process can increase the likelihood of falls.

that restricts one's lifestyle. Further, stress is both a contributor to and an outcome of arthritis that may escalate into depression (Payne, Mowen, & Montoro-Rodriguez, 2006). Decreases in flexibility, fine motor dexterity, motor performance, strength, balance, coordination, and endurance vary among individuals but are accelerated by nutritional deficiencies and inactivity. After exposure to intense muscle activity, the return to a state of homeostasis takes longer. Less efficient coordination, a slower reaction time, and slower information processing make driving more risky—which contributes to isolation and further inactivity.

The cardiovascular and respiratory systems provide support for the transport of nutrients and oxygen to the body (Papalia et al., 2007). With age, there is a reduction in vital capacity and the reserve capacity of the lungs; when the lungs lose elasticity, increased energy is necessary to sustain breathing capacity. Each breath becomes less effective since the ability of the lungs to exchange air with the blood system is reduced. After physical exercise, shortness of breath and fatigue may be evident. Aging also causes a reduction in heart output. The quantity of oxygen reaching the lungs decreases, the heart pumps less blood with each beat, blood decreases in total volume and increases in viscosity, and the blood vessels tend to narrow. The net effects are that blood pressure increases, the heart takes longer to recover after each beat, and there is lower blood flow to other organs. Consequently, the capacity to return to homeostasis is diminished as is the body's ability to adjust to stress (Papalia et al.). Heart conditions are the leading cause of death in developed nations. Further, decline in the cardiovascular system is the major cause for the loss of conditioning, overall energy reserve, and change in cognitive functioning (causing forgetfulness) (Townsend, 2006; Smith & Gove, 2005).

Age-related changes that occur in other bodily systems are less likely to significantly impact functioning, although reductions in, for example, kidney function may cause activity interruptions, embarrassment, or result in limited fluid intake that causes dehydration—a serious problem. Physical appearance and mobility serve as primary indicators of aging. Characteristics particularly revealing of age include loss of or wearing down of teeth, graying and loss of hair, sagging chin, wrinkled or sagging cheeks, sagging upper eyelids, drying skin, and watery-looking eyes. In general, age-related physical changes result in a decrease in the body's capacity to resist illness and disability, recover from physical exercise, and interact efficiently with others and the environment.

Psychological Changes Associated with Aging

A number of challenges test the emotions and spiritual well-being of aging adults. With age, the body responds less efficiently to stress and is at a higher risk for emotional distress. Age-related losses in physical health, perhaps decreases in social and economic resources, increased vulnerability to loneliness resulting from the loss of family members and friends, and the embarrassment associated with performing tasks that were once easily completed earlier in life necessitate emotional adjustments. A person's adjustment to this life stage is greatly influenced by his or her psychological preparedness, spiritual well-being, and perception of and attitude toward aging. People who believe they should be healthy and active tend to conform to these expectations and to realize higher levels of life and leisure satisfaction, while those who focus on their losses tend to experience lesser degrees of well-being. The key to successful aging is adaptation—compensating for losses and declines while retaining the potential for growth (Kinsella & Phillips, 2007a).

Fear, anxiety, and loss of autonomy become more prominent with the occurrence of disease, illness, pain, hospitalization, or surgery. Although the body is subject to physical or cosmetic changes, for most aging individuals the self-concept and self-image remain unchanged because they rely on preestablished ideas rather than current feedback to define their well-being (Townsend, 2006). Older adults also tend to become introspective, recognizing the need to resolve issues attributed to changing roles and perceptions. The critical issue is the ability of older adults to adapt to age-related changes and the challenges associated with managing their well-being. Although most older adults enjoy good mental health, the amount of energy consumed in adapting to changes, adjusting to role losses, and recovering from stress may result in functional impairment in life activities and cognitive decline (Papalia et al., 2007).

An individual's sense of control, competence, and freedom are important to independent functioning and psychological health (Searle et al., 1998). Aging adults who believe health problems can be prevented tend to adopt lifestyle programs that directly counter or control precipitating factors, such as lack of exercise and social isolation. Those who are intrinsically motivated tend to continue to exhibit personal control and to make decisions that support life satisfaction; for example, positive adaptations include replacing losses with new relationships and roles or retraining. Participation in leisure experiences, particularly leisure education, has been shown to contribute to life satisfaction because feelings of competence and independence result (Searle et al.).

Intellectual Changes Associated with Aging

Age-related declines in intelligence, memory, and learning are minimal, though factors that accompany the aging process have an effect on performance and expression of intelligence. Visual and hearing losses, poor physical health, social isolation, diminished financial resources, environmental interference, and residential displacement impede intellectual activities. The concept of "intelligence" is often construed to mean academic preparation; however, the knowledge accumulated from life experiences and the resulting maturity of judgment also involve intellect—although, as yet, they remain outside the parameters of formal measurement. Across the life span there appears to be a high degree of regularity in intellectual functioning (Townsend, 2006). Crystallized intelligence, the ability to learn information from experience, tends to improve through middle age and often until near the end of life, while fluid intelligence, the capacity to process novel information, tends to decline gradually from young to old adulthood (Papalia et al., 2007; Townsend). Thus, the ability to learn continues throughout life, perhaps at a slower pace due to ordinary slowing of reaction time, and is strongly influenced by factors such as interests, motivation, health, experience, and physical activity (Townsend). Further, researchers have shown that intellectual performance can improve throughout the life span with use, physical and mental exercise, and practice (Papalia et al.). Older people are generally interested in learning information that helps them in their everyday lives and enhances the quality of their lives. For the older adult,

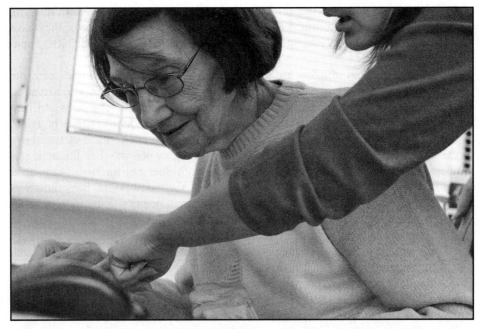

Older adults are generally interested in learning information that helps them in their everyday lives. Both formal and informal education promote higher degrees of satisfaction and enhance quality of life.

formal and informal education are forms of leisure that promote higher degrees of satisfaction and the motivation to adapt to age-related changes.

The attitude toward learning may change with age. This can be observed when older individuals base their decisions on past habits and knowledge rather than on exploration or experimentation with new ideas. Memories of the past may seem more pleasing than those of the present. Memory allows individuals to learn from encounters throughout life. The capacity of working or short-term memory (the ability to hold and process information) tends to shrink with age (Papalia et al., 2007) while long-term memory capacity (the ability to store information) does not show similar changes (Townsend, 2006). Nevertheless, with age, changes in memory of declarative information (i.e., names, facts, events) are more evident than declines in nondeclarative information like skills and procedures (Papalia et al.; Townsend). Thus, we may return to a favorite pastime of our youth and experience success (i.e., playing tennis), but might be unable to recall the name of our grade-school tennis instructor.

Sociological Changes Associated with Aging

Aging brings significant socially induced changes. In some cultures, Japan for example, the elderly are the most engaged and respected members of society, while in other industrialized countries like the U.S., stereotypes color the status and integration of aging residents, which in turn impacts living and employment options (Townsend, 2006). A disparity between "haves" and "have-nots" is apparent worldwide. In developed countries like the U.S., as well as in underdeveloped or developing countries, because adults continue to work for income to meet basic needs, they have fewer choices to achieve satisfaction (Gist, Figueiredo, & Ng-Baumhackl, 2001; Papalia et al., 2007).

The social changes of aging are influenced by an individual's attitudes and role expectations, income, relationships to and with family, employment and retirement, friendships, living environment, and physical and mental health. The costs of living and availability of social services also contribute to the sociological aspects of aging. Physical and mental health determine the degree of influence of each of the above forces. Social changes do not weigh as heavily on an aging person when financial status permits customary living patterns, physical health does not interfere with social functions, and the aging process is accepted. As the numbers of baby boomers increase, status and benefits are likely to also increase since this generation is better educated and brings greater diversity in economic resources and experiences to the political arena (Gist et al., 2001; Townsend, 2006).

The rising cost of living and escalating health-care costs make it difficult for some aging adults to afford items that contribute to quality of life. In 1982 the United States government extended to all people the opportunity to contribute to individual retirement accounts (IRAs) as well as to maintain a pension or retirement plan with the employing agency. Nevertheless, today many envision their "retirement" to be active, engaged, and working either full or part-time, relying not only on pensions and social security but also earnings and health insurance to remain socially integrated (Gist et al., 2001). Yet, even though there is a decrease in the poverty rate among older adults, a growing disparity exists between the rich and the poor; those living alone, women, and minorities are more likely to be poor (Gist et al.; AOA, 2007).

In less-developed countries people tend to live in multigenerational households, while in developed countries like the U.S. the usual household is a nuclear family—with independent living a hallmark of adult life (Papalia et al., 2007). While the number of older adults living alone increases with age, many older adults are maintaining households where grandchildren are present or adult children are returning due to divorce or economic challenges (AOA, 2007; Papalia et al.). Most older people want to live in the community and age in place. More older people are living in single-unit dwellings, often without family or friends nearby. Moreover, as life expectancy and mobility continue to increase, more older adults are less likely to have family in close proximity. While living arrangements can become a major issue among older adults, an emerging array of housing options and community support programs allow aging in place either independently or with family and friends as caregivers.

Retirement has a greater social significance than the mere cessation of gainful employment. Benefits associated with a career include friendships, meaningful social activities, independent functioning, a means to achieve self-worth and recognition, emotional support, financial security, and exposure to knowledge, resources, and leisure opportunities. The meaning of retirement is being redefined as the structure of our workforce and the nature of the workplace change. For example, the balance of professional and manufacturing jobs is changing as organizations downsize, thereby reducing the number of managers and placing higher demands for productivity on fewer employees. These changes place greater demand on employees' abilities to adapt and learn (Papalia et al., 2007). Because the Age Discrimination in Employment Acts (1967, 1978, 1986) eliminated mandatory retirement, employees may choose when to leave the workforce. Boomers are likely to remain in the workforce longer than originally anticipated due to economic issues and diminished retirement savings. Multiple career pathways may characterize the transition from work to retirement. To accommodate changes in the workforce and workplace, some may have more than one career before opting for part-time work that allows them to remain active in the labor force while pursuing leisure activities (Kinsella & Phillips, 2007b). Well-being during retirement is affected not only by physical health and income levels but also family support, relationships, and the variety of self-determined meaningful daily activities—including leisure experiences—that promote social support and participation.

Functioning Characteristics

An individual's social activity is influenced by factors such as physical and mental health, accessibility to transportation, and financial resources. For example, the slightest visual or hearing loss interferes with conversation, the heart of social interaction. Likewise, an inadequate public transportation system or inability to use a personal vehicle also affects social activity. Place of residence may or may not offer social outlets. Those residing in retirement villages or in their home communities have access to more social interactions than do those living in rural communities. Previous interests and past experiences also affect social experiences. As an illustration, those who are active in clubs and organizations during college are more likely to continue similar involvements after graduation. The same is true of aging people: those who were

Seniors residing in retirement villages or in their home communities have more opportunities for social interaction than do those living in rural communities.

eager to venture into new or untested social environments in the past are more likely to do so in the future.

Although there is little overall change in the personality as aging occurs, characteristics like resistance to change, detachment, selective attending, and concern for health and financial security may describe an older adult's emotional behavior. Because sensory awareness decreases with age, decision making and affective responses appear to be slower. A longer time is taken to react to increasingly complex situations and new or unique tasks. Aging people use such defense mechanisms as selective memory and sensory perception to cope with emotional losses. The heart of emotional character is our self-concept. Since "self" is formed during early childhood, older people tend to retain views developed earlier in life. The self is impacted by losses that contribute to identity, like the role of parent or successful employee. The degree to which the older adult turns inward may influence the impact of status and role losses and age-related changes.

As noted earlier, the impact of aging on the physical functioning of people varies greatly; no one generalization applies to all individuals. With age, the most noticeable change occurs in physical appearance. Additional changes occur in physical functioning. Speed, reaction time, and accuracy of voluntary movements decrease, and stiffening in the joints occurs. Osteoporosis causes the bones to become lighter, lose elasticity, and become more susceptible to breakage. Balance recovery and reflex response are slower and less efficient. Auditory and visual acuity decrease. Olfactory acuity (sense of smell), especially odor identification, decreases with age while **gustatory** (sense of taste) does not vary significantly with age. Touch, pain, cold and heat sensitivity tend to decline with age (Smith & Gove, 2005). The ability of the heart to respond to extra work and to maintain normal output at rest declines. Reduced **vital capacity** (the breathing capacity of the lungs measured by the amount of air that can be forcibly exhaled after a full inspiration) causes shortness of breath following activity. Progressive increase in peripheral resistance to blood flow and **systolic blood pressure** (contraction of the heart producing maximum pressure on blood vessel walls; in other words, high blood pressure) and a tendency to be anemic are also natural results of aging.

Decreased muscular activity and reduction of fluids in the gastrointestinal tract cause bladder and bowel **incontinence** (the loss of the ability to control urination and the bowels). Diminution in renal functioning results in more frequent need to urinate and increased incidences of urinary incontinence. There is a tendency toward dehydration and constipation caused by a decrease in water intake. The maintenance of body temperature is difficult. The insulating qualities in the subcutaneous tissue (skin) and the rate of metabolism decrease. Most older adults report that at least one disability affects their daily activities, while one in five over age 65 does not drive because of disability-related limitations (Voelkl & Aybar-Damali, 2008).

Intellectual functioning of aging persons is affected by their attitude toward learning and their capacity to use the sensory organs and attend to the task at hand. The mere fact of "living" enhances intellectual capacity. Yet, the world in which we live is rapidly changing. Memory of the past (stored information) is more meaningful and understandable when compared to the events of today (declarative information). The attitude toward learning determines whether "new" rather than "old" processing methods are used to solve problems. Avenues used to acquire new behavior become strained with age. Visual and auditory perceptions are less acute and effective. Therefore, learning through reading or physical exploration is limited. Furthermore, by engaging in selective listening and watching, some individuals decrease their opportunities to learn new material. Despite these limitations, lifelong learning is becoming more characteristic of today's aging adults as they tend to be more highly educated and desire to continue learning for its intrinsic value and opportunity to socialize (Papalia et al., 2007).

Purpose of Therapeutic Recreation

Therapeutic recreation experiences with aging individuals (1) promote functional independence; (2) optimize health, well-being, and life satisfaction (Nimrod, 2007; Payne et al., 2006); (3) foster feelings of control, confidence, and competence (Godbey, 2005); (4) facilitate cognitive stimulation and lifelong learning (Godbey; Ziegler, 2002); (5) serve as a vehicle for social interaction (McGuire, Boyd, & Tedrick, 1999); (6) allow for meaningful roles and contributions while adapting to leisure; and (7) permit adjustment to the changes and losses associated with the aging process. Participation is influenced by a number of variables not necessarily evident with other age cohorts. Obstacles to participation include concern for psychological and physical safety, fear of falling, embarrassment resulting from incontinence, hearing and visual deficits, loss of family and friends, low motivation to sustain participation regardless of the weather, or reliance on others for transportation, for example.

Recreative experiences are conduits to information and resources that sustain participants' self-worth, while also stimulating continued interest in and responsibility for their own well-being. Leisure experiences provide the opportunity to form relationships and interact with new-found companions and friends. Social support encourages older adults to assume meaningful roles that foster both self-worth and self-confidence: isolation and loneliness are offset by the emotional support of others (Orsega-Smith et al., 2007). Moreover, attending social functions requires the practice of self-care skills. This counters a tendency to become less attentive to personal care and hygiene.

Aging people lean toward experiences that have previously given enjoyment and satisfaction: Older adults prefer to use leisure time doing satisfying things and having satisfying relationships (Papalia et al., 2007). While the number of activities decreases with age, older individuals, especially boomers, do not see themselves as different, so they avoid experiences like "bingo at the Senior Center" that redefine them as "old." *Informal leisure* like visits with family tend to continue and result in happiness while *formal leisure,* participation in organizations, tends to decrease with age even though those engaged in serious leisure like hobbies, cultural pursuits, and educational experiences report increased happiness (Janke, Davey, & Kleiber, 2006; Papalia et al.). Psychological well-being is supported when seniors assume responsibility for and control during their participation in activities. For example, the desire and ability to lead and serve others is demonstrated with the Institutes for Learning in Retirement. These are self-funded and rely on their members to teach college-level classes and guide others in study (Arsenault & Anderson, 1998).

Aging adults lean toward experiences that have previously brought enjoyment and satisfaction.

Leisure activities encourage aging adults to remain in contact with reality and current events. They also provide an avenue to the social service network. For example, leisure education programs expose aging persons to available sources of transportation, medical care, financial management, and health and nutrition advice. A favorable attitude toward education and lifelong learning encourages successful adjustment to aging by supporting opportunities to develop coping strategies, establish new interests and contacts, create more meaningful outlets, and thus instill a sense of accomplishment (MacNeil, 1998). Desirable lifelong learning experiences are those that are personally meaningful, allow adults to control the learning process, and are taught in settings where direct learning experiences occur as, for example, with Elderhostels (Papalia et al., 2007).

Leisure education empowers seniors to make decisions about alternative uses of their time. It facilitates a more positive outlook that helps seniors rebound from losses and function better on their own volition. Today's seniors and their caregivers can access a wide range of resources and social contacts with technology. The Internet is increasingly being used for education, communication, and social and financial endeavors—especially among the boomers.

Physical activity and fitness have been found to promote functional independence, cognitive functioning, and higher levels of overall health and well-being among aging adults. The *Healthy People 2010* initiative identifies leisure time physical activity as an indicator of older adult health (CDC, 2007). The older adults become, the less likely they are to exercise: it has been reported that approximately 25% of U.S. adults do not engage in any physical activity. By age 65, 80% do not satisfy the CDC criteria of moderate activity for 30 or more minutes, five times per week; or vigorous activity for 20 minutes or more, three times per week (Godbey, Burnett-Wolle, & Chow, 2007). This inactivity has lead to obesity and overweight conditions among those 65 and over and is thought to contribute to reduced life expectancy for this segment of the older population. Progressive deterioration in the ability to perform self-care skills is seen with aging adults. "Limited functional fitness can predispose elderly persons to frailty, falls, and institutionalization" (Mobily, Mobily, Lane, & Semerjian, 1998, p. 43).

On the other hand, participation in physical activity options like swimming, golf, and outdoor pursuits has been found to stimulate the mind; to lower blood pressure, increase good (HDL) cholesterol, and reduce visits to the doctor's office and the number of medications taken; and to motivate seniors to be active and to be with other people (Eckhart & Allen, 1998; Godbey, 2005; Godbey et al., 2007; Katzenmeyer, 1997). When fitness elements like strength, endurance, coordination, and balance are improved, the risk of falls is reduced and the ease with which self-care activities are completed is improved (Mobily et al., 1998). These improvements tend to promote satisfaction with the quality of one's life. The interest created by proper exercise motivates concern for nutrition and diet control, both of which are important in aiding digestion and elimination and in countering age-related diseases. Participation in physical activity also acts as a nonpharmacologic therapy that not only reverses functional declines but enables older adults to increase their own sense of control over the aging process (Brandon, 1999; Mathieu, 1999).

Finally, the time to practice the learning that comes with living occurs during later adulthood. Volunteer programs provide opportunities for seniors to apply acquired knowledge and skills through service to others. Volunteering also is a means to develop meaningful relationships and healthy self-concepts, and is a social experience that maintains and improves intellectual capacities and encourages community service. In both developed and undeveloped countries worldwide, older adult volunteers are increasing; yet, the nature of volunteerism is changing as well-educated boomers dedicate themselves in concentrated time frames to specific tasks or assume roles as part-time paid staff members (Papalia et al., 2007; Ziegler, 2002). One form of volunteering is found with intergenerational programming. These programs bring various age cohorts together to share each other's expertise and meet social and educational needs—adults may participate in after-school programs while youth visit older adults in their homes. Intergenerational programs encourage physical activity and promote participation in activities like tai chi and yoga, which contribute to mental health and continued use of cognitive processes like concentration and short-term memory (Harper, 1999; Yan & Downing, 1998).

Delivery Settings

Several factors determine the agencies involved and services provided to aging adults. Commitments made during adulthood—for example, church selection and social club participation, financial planning, access to transportation, and available social supports—are primary influences on both place of residence and leisure alternatives. Seniors participate in programs at private clubs, multipurpose recreation centers, adult day-care sites, churches, outdoor recreation areas, in their own homes, and in planned retirement communities. The staff conducting these programs includes social workers, those with training in gerontology, recreators, and TRSs.

Leadership Interaction and Intervention Considerations

Aging adults are capable of making most, if not all, decisions about their leisure. Although the traditional preference has been for social and cultural activities near home and with family and friends, today's mature adult, like other age cohorts, "is becoming more active and adventurous, both intellectually and physically" (Riley & Stanley, 2006, p. 22). Additionally, older adults are seeking competitive sport challenges on the courts and fields in their communities (Tedrick, 2004). The baby boomers will remain dedicated to health, wellness, and exercise (Ziegler, 2002) yet they will fulfill educational, social, and recreational needs through lifelong education and instruction (Riley & Stanley). Although an interest in passive activities remains, participation in sports like swimming and golf, and outdoor pursuits like hiking and water rafting is increasing ("Active Recreation," 2007; Tedrick). Technology and media will continue to provide social and educational options—from computer clubs to virtual travel on the information superhighway (Ziegler). An increasing number of intergenerational programs partner seniors with youth to complete specific or time-limited volunteer and service-learning projects (McGuire & Hawkins, 1998; Ziegler). Value placed on spirituality takes on more significance with aging, as older adults become more contemplative and focused inward, so access to faith-based experiences is a consideration in programming for seniors. Visits to parks and participation in nature-oriented experiences like bird watching or nature walks promote inner peace and psychological well-being. The introduction of physical activity stations in parks and stress management strategies like meditation and guided imagery also promote inner harmony while enhancing physical well-being (Godbey, 2005).

Therapeutic recreation planning involves participants in the preparation and delivery of services. It also takes into consideration the age span and diversity of participants. "Currently, about 80% of older Americans are living with at least one chronic condition" (CDC, 2007, p. III). With the projected increases in life expectancy and in the size of the age cohort 85 and over, the number of individuals with functional limitations also is expected to increase more dramatically, particularly because the majority of people over age 65 do not maintain desired levels of exercise. Integration of people with various limitations or of people with age differences of as much as 25 or more years affects the focus of the program and its content and leadership. No one group of activities or schedule can meet the goals of all seniors, and leadership varies with content. With the boomers, programming length and timing will be compressed as recreation will occur in small segments, an hour here and there, throughout the week, both day and night, as boomers transition between full, seasonal, and part-time employment (Ziegler, 2002). A knowledge of assessment principles, motivational and compliance techniques, activity and task analyses, and an awareness of activity alternatives is helpful. Specific leadership techniques are outlined below.

- Enunciate clearly. Stand directly in front of participants, and make sure you gain their attention before speaking. Speak in a lower voice tone, since upper frequencies are more difficult to hear. Repeat directions to compensate for declines in working (short-term) and declarative (facts) memory.
- Individualized goal-oriented experiences are preferred as are workshop formats, rather than lengthy class sessions, with instruction shared among partici-

pants and professionals, rather than leader-driven programs (Riley & Stanley, 2006; Ziegler, 2002).

- Plan rest intervals, avoid extended periods of standing, and encourage conversation as a form of social interaction. Communication and creative experiences like art foster mental stimulation, relationships, relaxation, and lifelong learning (Riley & Stanley).

- Intersperse motivators such as refreshments, humor, reward/recognition, meaningful "traditional" experiences, and responsibility in the program. A supportive social climate, like established tennis or weight-lifting partners, tends to encourage engagement (Godbey et al., 2007). The club format is popular with, for example, computer and literary pursuits.

- Pairing intellectual activity with physical activity like studying flora and fauna while taking a hike, tends to heighten cognitive ability while fostering continued participation (Godbey et al.).

- Schedule activities with daily routines in mind. Consider weather, traffic patterns, amount of daylight remaining, transportation routes, and access to additional supportive services. With boomers, leisure will occur in brief segments, nine holes of golf rather than 18, throughout the week both day and night (Ziegler).

- Activities should allow for various energy and skill levels. Participants should feel comfortable dropping into and out of activities. Graduated reward systems, a heightened sense of self-efficacy, and social support foster participation (Orsega-Smith et al., 2007).

- Provide opportunities for sufficient practice so optimal performance levels are achieved. Pre- and post-assessments that substantiate noticeable improvements are effective motivators. More older athletes are seeking competition with appropriate degrees of challenge, and this trend is likely to continue (Tedrick, 2004).

- Schedule intergenerational activities to encourage participation with people from different age cohorts. Intergenerational programs foster harmony and increase social identity (Riley & Stanley).

- Compensate for lessened visual and auditory acuity by using contrasting colors and sizes. Auditory stimulation enhances memory, so encourage participants to use hearing during participation.

- Include such experiences as volunteering or service projects to allow participants to share their expertise. Boomers tend to volunteer for time-limited causes or specific tasks.

- A majority of those over age 65 do not meet recommended minimal levels of physical activity and many also are overweight or obese. Also, participation in formal exercise programs is short-lived. Thus, to improve health and promote physical well-being, intrinsically motivated and freely chosen experiences are necessary (Godbey et al.). An active living approach integrates physical activity into daily routines through interdisciplinary planning and design of environments that support close social networks, mastery, vicarious experiences (i.e., observations of others doing the activity), and verbal persuasion from family and friends (Orsega-Smith et al.).

- Cost analysis occurs in the planning of all programs but is most critical with aging people as their incomes may be fixed or impacted by health-care issues.
- We do not automatically improve with age. Recognize real and perceived barriers. Habits and beliefs are carried through the aging process. A person who lacked musical ability and interest as a child will probably not develop an interest as an adult.
- Plan carefully around the physical environment. Restrooms and parking lots should be close and accessible. Entries and exits should be well lighted and marked. Voice amplifiers and controls for heat, lights, humidity, and temperature should be available.
- Realize and consider the importance of feelings. Fear of crime, failure, loss of health, financial dependency, death and dying, and the physical changes associated with aging are realities for these people. Acknowledge the desire to leave something meaningful, to share a special memento, to "get things in order," to eat certain foods, or to follow a specific routine. Include spiritual activities and experiential therapies as a means to boost morale and enable older adults to cope with age-related changes and losses (Hawkins, May & Rogers, 1996).
- Leisure education helps identify leisure assets, unmet needs, and the availability of resources. It reinforces the significance of participating in exercise, social events, and adult learning. These experiences contribute to a sense of continuity and encourage the expression of habits and preferences with age.
- Lifelong learning programs promote control and independence by encouraging healthy behaviors like exercise. This, in turn, fosters a desire to remain active. Active seniors are more likely to seek out information on, for example, insurance, home health care, nutrition, legal topics, and medical services.

Applying the Therapeutic Recreation Process

Mr. and Mrs. Jones represent the growing number of adults over 50 who have devoted their energy to careers, family, and social obligations. Like many in this cohort, they were unaware of any leisure deficits until transitioning from full-time employment. For Mr. Jones, the TRS employed with the city became a conduit to community-wide resources through a cosponsored adult education program.

Assessment

Demographic information.   Mr. Jones is 68 years old. He resides with his wife in a midwestern community. His son and daughter live with their families out of state. He is a member of a local church and its Men's Club, which supports social concerns in the community.

History.   Mr. Jones, at age 62, transitioned from full-time employment to a consultant for his global logistics firm. He presently participates in golf and church-related social activities. He enjoys relatively good health, with an annual physical noting slightly high blood pressure. His physician has placed restrictions on his diet and has recommended physical activity, stress management, and adult education experiences.

Present behavior.   Mr. Jones continues to travel for his firm, golf, read, and attend business clubs and luncheons. He experiences depression and boredom. Recently Mr. Jones was elected to office in the Men's Club. He is uncomfortable doing household chores and is somewhat concerned about his future income level.

The TRS and Mr. Jones worked together to determine his needs. Mr. Jones desires to maintain his present social activities and to increase his physical activity level. He needs greater awareness of available health and leisure resources, and he needs to develop a financial management plan. Finally, Mr. Jones desires to expand his interests and become more involved in business activities. His assets are a supportive wife and church community, the presence of some leisure skills, and relatively good health.

Planning

Long-term goal.   The long-term goal of Mr. Jones' TR intervention is to increase the number of leisure options.

Short-term goal.   The short-term goal is to increase awareness of available leisure resources.

Objective.   After participating for three months in a cosponsored adult education club, Mr. Jones will identify at least three experiences offered through either his church or the park and recreation department that are of interest, accessible, and will increase his physical activity level.

Content.   Mr. Jones and the TRS will discuss experiences promoted by his firm as well as those offered through the church or the recreation department. Through internet access during adult education programs, Mr. Jones will be exposed to events, adult education options, and the community service directory, all of which will increase his resource awareness.

Process.   The TRS will administer an interest inventory; design a program incorporating leisure education, stress management, and physical activity; and help Mr. Jones consider life satisfaction factors using life review processes to support his objective. During this phase of program development, the TRS employed by the park and recreation department will make arrangements for luncheon speakers, travel logs, and interagency information fairs and will develop a plan so Mr. Jones can document his types of participation and the kinds of experiences he seems to enjoy.

Implementation

Mr. Jones participated in cosponsored functions, business meetings and travel dialogues, and programs such as golfing, family socials, walking, and a computer club. Simultaneously, he recorded the frequency and nature of his participation.

Evaluation

Mr. Jones' objective served as the primary evaluation tool. Discussion with Mr. Jones' wife and review of his personal participation record determined how successful he was in achieving his objective. Mr. Jones and the TRS developed a leisure plan through meetings with community resource persons and as a result of discussions with his wife. As Mr. Jones became more aware of available resources, the TRS encouraged him to increase his physical activity and leisure skills through adult learning opportunities.

POPULATION OVERVIEW:
AGING PERSONS WITH ILLNESSES AND DISABILITIES

Many aging adults, especially those over 65, encounter a variety of cognitive, physical, sensory, communication, emotional, and social impairments and addictions. The most frequently reported chronic conditions occurring among aging individuals include hypertension, arthritis, heart disease, cancer, diabetes, and hearing impairments (AOA, 2007; Federal Interagency Forum on Aging-Related Statistics, 2006; Smith & Gove, 2005). Detailed descriptions of these illnesses and other physical and sensory impairments with high incidence among older adults (e.g., strokes, Parkinson's disease, COPD, obesity, visual losses) are presented in chapters 6 and 7. The impact of these disorders on aging adults is discussed later in this chapter under "Leadership Interaction and Intervention Considerations." The following discussion will introduce information on disabilities unique to the aging population.

One such disability is dementia, a cognitive impairment that is manifest in organic brain syndrome and disorders like Alzheimer's disease. The incidence of Alzheimer's disease increases with age. Today it is estimated that 13% of those over 65 and nearly 50% of those over 85 years of age have Alzheimer's (Alzheimer's Association, 2008). Along with Alzheimer's disease and a number of related dementias identified in the *DSM–IV–TR* (APA, 2000), older adults also experience emotional impairments and addictions, especially depression and alcoholism, which require intervention. Older adults rely on over-the-counter drugs and prescriptions to manage health-care needs, so monitoring medication regimes becomes a professional concern as we interact with older adults.

One category of the aging population expected to experience rapid growth during the twenty-first century is individuals with developmental disabilities, including those with intellectual disabilities; by 2030 this population is expected to be several million (AAIDD, 2009). These individuals generally have similar health issues as their aging cohort yet they have minimal contact with people without disabilities, especially as family members pass; less income; fewer opportunities to make choices; and tend to decrease their activities over time (AAIDD; Sherrill, 2004; Wilhite & Keller, 1996). Persons with Down syndrome have a higher risk of developing Alzheimer's disease at an earlier age than those in the general aging population (AAIDD; Sherrill); further, these individuals also tend to experience higher rates of sensory loss, diabetes, and strokes than others with intellectual disabilities.

The aging individual with an impairment brings to the therapeutic environment secondary concerns not evident with a younger person having a similar impairment. Secondary impairments more evident among aging adults include contractures, pressure sores, respiratory (pneumonia) infections, dehydration, malnutrition, obesity, and perceived and real fear of accidents and falls. However, aging adults tend to manifest fewer signs of illness like changes in body temperature, pulse rate, and coloration than do younger people. Additionally, they tend to have a higher tolerance for pain and to limit reporting discomfort.

Illnesses and Disabilities Experienced by Aging Persons

Dementia

Dementia refers to a group of conditions with common symptom presentation that result in cognitive deficits severe enough to cause impairment in occupational and social functioning. Behavioral changes represent a decline in functioning and are evidenced by memory impairment in at least one of the following areas: aphasia (language), apraxia (motor functioning), agnosia (object identification), or executive functioning (planning, abstract thinking) (APA, 2000). Dementia may be manifest in Alzheimer's disease, vascular disease, **Pick's disease** (progressive deterioration of the brain accompanied by atrophy of the cerebral cortex), Parkinson's disease, Huntington's disease, brain injuries, HIV infection, multiple sclerosis, and other neurological conditions. Dementia as manifest in Alzheimer's disease is the most common type of dementia, representing over 50% of those with dementia and affecting more than 15 million people worldwide (Papalia et al., 2007; Porter & burlingame, 2006). It may be characterized as either early onset (age 65 or under) or late onset (after age 65). Alzheimer's disease is a progressive, irreversible neurological disorder that results in complete loss of cognitive functioning, followed by loss of all physical abilities. While common in those over age 65, Alzheimer's disease may appear in individuals still in their 40s. Although research results disagree, decline occurs over eight or more years and may extend to as many as 20 years (average is three to eight, with an outside range of 10 to 20), with death often attributed to pneumonia (APA, 2000; Porter & burlingame; Sherrill, 2004). Since Alzheimer's and Down syndrome are both genetic mutations of the twenty-first chromosome, these diseases are closely related, and a high probability exists that a person with Down syndrome will develop Alzheimer's or Alzheimer's-like dementia after the age of 50 (Gordon, 2005).

The early stages of Alzheimer's are indistinguishable from the aging process. A probable diagnosis becomes likely when the person is unable to hold a job, care for daily needs, or display reasonable judgment (e.g., disturbances in executive functioning). As the disease progresses, a general level of confusion and recent memory loss is followed by expressive and receptive aphasia, the inability to walk or sit up (apraxia), and the inability to recognize family members and their own reflection in the mirror (agnosia). When a brain tissue biopsy is conducted after death, the presence of neurofibrillary tangles, plaques, and brain atrophy confirms Alzheimer's disease.

Other types of dementia include vascular dementia (the second most common type of dementia, accounting for up to 30% of those with dementia), which is more common in males than females, with onset earlier than dementia associated with Alzheimer's disease (Alzheimer's Association, 2008; APA, 2000; Porter & burlingame, 2006). Along with the deficits cited above for dementia, vascular dementia is accompanied by cerebrovascular disease. Among individuals with Parkinson's disease, some 20–60% are reported to have dementia.

Emotional Impairments and Addictions

Depression is the most prevalent emotional impairment among older adults. Addictive use of alcohol, over-the-counter drugs, and prescribed medications is also common among aging people. These disorders may be adult-onset or lifelong, brought to the aging process from earlier years. Anxiety, insomnia, and dementia associated with addictive use of alcohol also are emotional issues experienced by older adults. With aging people, it is difficult to determine whether cognitive symptoms indicate a major depressive disorder or dementia. Depression among older adults is commonly attributed to either severe psychosocial stress, such as the loss of a spouse, or a chronic general medical condition, such as stroke, cancer, or heart disease (APA, 2000). *Reactive depression* is a likely short-term response to loss of a loved one while *clinical depression* lingers and is often associated with a stroke or Parkinson's disease. While many incidents of depression go unreported or undiagnosed, especially in men, 8–20% of older adults have depression (Papalia et al., 2007; Sherrill, 2004). In contrast to dementia, a depressive disorder can be controlled by intervention and medication. Even though depression is managed by medications and psychotherapies, it remains a serious emotional impairment among older adults since it is associated with a high rate of suicide. Unlike other age groups, older adults may complain of physical symptoms rather than mental distress or suicidal ideation, so the intent is undetected and the likelihood of death as a result of suicide is higher (Papalia et al.). Financial setbacks, loss of control and independence, social isolation, and illness accompanied by pain precipitate suicide attempts (Townsend, 2006).

Addictive use of alcohol, over-the-counter drugs, and prescribed medications among aging adults is often a response to pain, loss of social support, and for some, a continuation of the abuse from their earlier adulthood. Older adults comprise the largest group of drug consumers, and as a consequence, potential for abuse is high; and as the baby-boom cohort ages, the illicit use of alcohol and drugs (including the nonmedical use of prescription drugs) is likely to increase since this cohort has experienced heavier use earlier in life than previous generations (Papalia et al., 2007). Over-the-counter drugs that are frequently abused include laxatives, pain relievers, and cold medications. Prescription drug abuse results when, for example, medication regimes are confused or drug prescriptions from several physicians are not coordinated. Excessive use of drugs and alcohol contributes to circulatory and central nervous system disorders as well as domestic violence, family conflict, and decreased life expectancy.

Developmental Disabilities

As a result of biomedical advances and health-care improvements, the number of older adults with lifelong impairments like developmental disabilities is increasing, as is their life expectancy: Approximately 12% of all people with developmental disabilities are 65 years or older (Minde & Friedman, 2002). Early onset of aging is associated with Down syndrome and cerebral palsy (Boyd, 1997). According to one source, a very high percentage of adults with Down syndrome develop Alzheimer's disease neuropathologies after the age of 35, with a higher probability of developing Alzheimer's or Alzheimer's-like dementia after the age of 50 than the general population (Minde & Friedman). Further, with Down syndrome, symptoms of aging like diminished hearing, respiratory difficulties, and obesity-related diseases like diabetes occur earlier than in the general population (Gordon, 2005). Also, older adults with cerebral palsy may exhibit increasing rates of motor and sensory impairments (Hawkins, B. A., 1997).

Individuals with developmental disabilities tend to have few friends outside of staff and family; and, as they age, tend to lose informal caregiver support systems comprised of parents and siblings. While adults with developmental disabilities are beginning to outlive their parents, the growth in the number of older parents caring for a son or daughter with intellectual disabilities will continue as a result of increased longevities of both offspring and parents (Connolly, 1998; Fullmer, Tobin, & Smith, 1997). This trend, along with the general population explosion of older adults, has prompted study of caregiver needs and the contributions to be made by TRSs with caregivers and their older adult children.

Functioning Characteristics

The impact of an illness or disability on the aging adult, like the aging process, is unique. The reactions and coping strategies of aging people with impairments are affected by cost and access to medical care, health insurance and earnings, the onset and nature of the illness or disability, premorbid personality, lifestyle behaviors including leisure behaviors, residual abilities, the setting in which they receive treatment, motivational level, and attitudes of caregivers and professionals. The general functioning characteristics associated with dementia, emotional impairments and addictions, and aging adults with developmental disabilities as they affect therapeutic recreation are summarized in the following paragraphs.

Dementia

Cognitive impairments experienced with dementia include loss of memory, orientation, speech, and judgment. While we all experience memory changes as we age, with Alzheimer's disease, severe problems in this area impact functioning (Sherrill, 2004). Early symptoms like the inability to recall recent events or take in new information may be overlooked as signs of "normal" aging. Also in evidence early in the disease process are personality changes like the persistence of a labile affect, rigidity, apathy, anxiety, and depression: these behaviors aid in confirming the presence of the disease (Papalia et al., 2007). The ability to adapt or adjust to change or to cope with "newness" is absent (e.g., executive functioning deficits). Wandering, perseveration, and purposeless word usage are responses a TRS might receive to direct questioning or a request to walk to a designated location. As dementia progresses, silence, blank stares, a screech, a tight wrist grip, or physical resistance interferes with planned activity. By the end, the client cannot understand or use language, recognize family, walk, or swallow food and relies on others for personal care (Papalia et al.).

The losses and rate of progression are unique to each individual, yet common patterns of the illness exist (Alzheimer's Association, 2008). People with Alzheimer's may live eight years after symptoms are noticed by others, but survival ranges from three to twenty years. A seven-stage system identifies cognitive and behavioral deficits with the disease progression (Alzheimer's Association):

Stage 1. No impairment, person does not experience memory problems, and health professional does not notice evidence of symptoms.

Stage 2. Very mild decline, person may feel memory lapses are present, like locating everyday objects or forgetting familiar words, yet no signs are detected in medical exam.

Stage 3. Mild cognitive decline, difficulty maybe noticed by family or friends, memory or concentration problems may be detected during medical exam; examples include problems coming up with the right word, remembering people's names, misplacing valuable objects, increasing trouble with planning.

Stage 4.   Moderate cognitive decline, early-stage Alzheimer's, medical exam will detect problems like forgetting recent events or personal history, becoming moody and withdrawn during social experiences or mentally challenging situations, impaired ability to complete math tasks like counting backwards from 100 by 7s.

Stage 5.   Moderately severe cognitive decline or mid-stage Alzheimer's, person needs help with day-to-day activities, memory and thinking gaps; examples include the inability to recall address or phone number, confusion about what day it is or where he/she is, needs help with choosing proper clothing yet remembers significant details about self and family; is able to eat and toilet without assistance.

Stage 6.   Severe cognitive decline, moderately severe or mid-stage Alzheimer's, memory worsens, personality changes appear, help is needed with daily activities; examples include remembrance of own name but not personal history, difficulty distinguishing familiar and unfamiliar faces, requiring assistance to dress, sleeping during the day with restlessness at night, bowel and bladder incontinence, personality changes like suspiciousness (i.e., caregiver is a thief), tendency to wander (become lost).

Stage 7.   Very severe cognitive decline, severe or late-stage Alzheimer's, person does not respond to the environment, cannot carry on conversation or control movement yet may say words or phrases; needs assistance with personal care and eating, is unable to sit up and support his/her head, swallowing is impaired and muscles become rigid.

Although the losses may seem pervasive, individuals may retain ingrained behaviors and personal characteristics, like a smile or the ability to acknowledge pleasure with personal preferences like music. Even in the final stages of Alzheimer's when one author's mother could not swallow or hold her head up, she responded with a smile when her name was spoken and when soft music was played.

Emotional Impairments and Addictions

Emotional impairments like depression impact functioning in each of the other behavioral areas. While older adults show more symptoms of mood disturbances than younger individuals, they are less likely to be diagnosed and are not necessarily subject to depression as a natural consequence of aging (Papalia et al., 2007). However, later life depression affects older adults with medical conditions like heart disease, cancer, stroke, and Parkinson's (Sherrill, 2004). Also, the incidence of depression increases with age and may in part result from declining levels of physical activity (Sherrill). Symptoms like sadness, anxiety, irritability, pessimism, lowered frustration levels, lack of interest, feelings of helplessness, lack of reasoning and concentration, loss of appetite, insomnia, and fatigue are characteristic of emotional issues. Thus, depression among older adults may go undetected for a number of reasons: (1) associating symptoms with other physical illnesses, (2) older adults are less likely to say they feel depressed, and (3) symptoms may be perceived or actually overlap with the natural aging process.

In most nations the rate of suicide rises with age and is higher with men than women (Papalia et al., 2007; Townsend, 2006). Suicide often occurs in conjunction with serious depression or debilitating physical illnesses (Papalia et al.; Sherrill, 2004); family conflicts, financial issues, and increased social isolation (divorced, widowed, living alone) also are contributing factors (Townsend). Potential signs of suicide include continued depression, sudden changes in sleeping and eating patterns, unusual behaviors like giving away cherished possessions or becoming angry, personality changes, withdrawing from family or friends, and abusing drugs or alcohol (Papalia et al.).

As with emotional issues, addictions in older adults may be difficult to detect because they tend to tolerate pain and typically are not in contact with professionals who would be alert to substance use issues. Further, many older adults live alone and have few social contacts who might detect the problem (Papalia et al., 2007). Older adults, especially men, are more likely to abuse alcohol than drugs (Papalia et al.). Symptoms of substance abuse with the elderly are similar to those of other age cohorts except the effect may be more profound because of a decline in metabolism (Hawkins et al., 1996). Signs of inappropriate use of over-the-counter drugs and prescription medications include depression, pain disorders, defensiveness, changes in social behaviors and sleep patterns, and more frequent accidents, especially falls.

Developmental Disabilities

The individual with developmental disabilities has needs similar to other aging adults. They may need support in understanding and adjusting to the changes common to the aging process, like the death of a friend or the need to wear reading glasses and this may occur at an earlier age than with older adults without developmental disabilities. Also, older adults with intellectual disabilities may have similar concerns yet they tend to have less income, fewer opportunities for choice, and less knowledge of options than do older adults in the general population (AAIDD, 2009). Most individuals remain able to independently carry out the activities of daily living, the exception being those with multiple impairments; yet assistance often is necessary during such activities as banking, arranging medical appointments, shopping, and traveling (Hawkins, B. A., 1997). Health problems found with older adults with developmental disabilities include obesity, chronic skin problems, hygiene-related problems, vision and hearing loss, loss of independent mobility, tendency to fall, incontinence, and musculoskeletal conditions like chronic pain, osteoarthritis, osteoporosis, and scoliosis that worsen over time (AAIDD; Connolly, 1998; Sherrill, 2004). Those with Down syndrome may experience intensification of pre-existing conditions like hearing losses, cardiovascular problems, decreased muscle tone, ligamentous laxity, hypothyroidism, and susceptibility to infection (Boyd, 1997; Fenderson, 1998).

Older adults with developmental disabilities tend to be at a social disadvantage because they may not have experienced the common sources of social support like marriage and employment within the wider community (Boyd, 1997). They depend primarily on family members, staff, and others with disabilities for support and friendships. They face emotional challenges when relocation occurs; for example, when an aging parent is no longer capable of caregiving, the aging son or daughter is placed in an assisted living setting. As a result of transitions such as this, depression and behavioral changes may become apparent as individuals attempt to cope with declines in functional capacities as well as loss of their independence and closest friends and care-givers (Minde & Friedman, 2002; Sherrill, 2004).

Purpose of Therapeutic Recreation

Aging people with illnesses and disabilities may reside in their own homes, in long-term facilities where a continuum of care is in place, or in a number of other set-tings (e.g., assisted living with varying degrees of intervention available). When they reside in their own homes with or without family caregivers, home-health care may be provided or they may voluntarily attend programs; for example, an adult day program or an aquatic therapy class at an outpatient rehabilitation clinic. The number of pro-grams in community settings is increasing and the range of services extends from health-related to recreation participation adaptations and alternatives (Teague, McGhee, & Hawkins, 2001). Therapeutic recreation experiences promote health, choices, and independence; prevent impairment; maintain optimal physical and cog-nitive function; remediate in the instance of disablement; and serve as an avenue to access essential health information, social support (e.g., companionship), and services for the aging individual as well as the caregiver (Hawkins et al., 1996).

Aging adults with illnesses and disabilities in long-term care may be in the reha-bilitative phase of a traumatic incident (such as a CVA), or may be in a specific unit like a memory unit of a skilled-care facility as a result of chronic debilitating disorders like Parkinson's or Alzheimer's diseases. Therapy programs are designed to facilitate medical stabilization, curtail deterioration of functional capacities, maintain physical health, stimulate sensory awareness, enhance social interactions and residual abilities, and to help the elderly and their caregivers cope with death. The TRS also leads or co-leads patient and family support groups.

When aging people experience emotional impairments and addictions, TRSs intervene to promote physical health, family relations, maintenance of independence, and preservation of self-esteem. For individuals with developmental disabilities, the scope of services is also very broad. TRSs use leisure as a developmental tool and as a means to maintain friendships and inclusion options, health maintenance and under-standing, and adjustment to the aging process. Therapeutic recreation programs may include adaptation to residential relocation and replacement of work functions. Thera-pists monitor physical health and activity and use reality orientation and behavior management to structure daily routines. The TRS also provides valuable services to the aging person's caregivers. For example, therapists are conduits to needed social services and caregiver education and leisure through caregiver support groups. As a component of support groups, adult day care, respite, and in-home programs, leisure education is a necessary intervention that addresses caregiver needs like lowered life satisfaction, social isolation, and the negative consequences of life without leisure (Rogers, 1999).

Delivery Settings

The nature and philosophy of the setting greatly influence the goals of therapeutic recreation with older adults with illnesses and disabilities. Therapeutic recreation occurs in the person's home, community facilities like YMCAs and multipurpose cen-ters, special care units in hospitals, and private long-term care facilities where seniors reside permanently. A number of community settings are designed to support people in their own homes: a TRS might provide intervention in foster care, or adult day health care, for example, with "gero-psych" participants, so older persons may reside in their homes for as long as they remain safe. In a medical facility, the TRS and health-care team work with the elderly on skilled care, subacute, physical rehabilitation, and psychiatric units. When aging adults live in comprehensive long-term care facilities, TRSs may be part of the social services or recreation therapy departments. In this capacity they provide therapeutic programs to the skilled nursing, Alzheimer's, and dementia or memory units, and also to residents living on the grounds in independent living or assisted living arrangements. TRSs also provide services in hospice settings and retirement communities. Aging adults with addictions participate in inpatient and outpatient programs in settings like psychiatric units and mental-health day facilities. Individuals with developmental disabilities are involved in programs like Special Olympics, attend programs in adult foster care and assisted living centers, and participate with other residents in therapeutic activities offered in long-term care facilities.

Leadership Interaction and Intervention Considerations

With aging individuals who are ill or disabled, the TRS uses standardized interventions to prevent further deterioration and to promote the use of existing strength areas. Specific techniques include formal and informal **reality orientation (RO), attitude therapy, remotivation, resocialization, reminiscence,** and **validation therapy.** TRSs conduct or supervise formal classes, train other staff or family members to use

Reminiscing or re-experiencing past events can be an effective technique for stimulating current memory.

these techniques, and monitor informal use of these processes. An in-depth discussion of these facilitation techniques is presented in chapter 3.

For adults over 65, falls are the leading cause of deaths due to injury and the most common cause of hospital admissions for trauma (CDC, 2007). Within one year of falling, most fallers over age 80 die (Sherrill, 2004). TRSs implement strategies to screen and assess for personal risk factors like poor balance, diminished vision, medication management, and environmental risk factors like tripping hazards. TRSs use the results of functional fitness tests and assessments for fall confidence, gait, and balance, to co-treat with physical therapists during fall-prevention classes. They also conduct postural training to improve strength, agility, reaction, balance, and stability. The fear of falling is shared by older adults with and without disabilities. Thus, TRSs institute safety measures to prevent falls wherever interventions with older adults take place.

In addition to the above standardized interventions, TRSs implement strategies appropriate to specific situations like dementia, emotional impairments and addictions, and developmental disabilities.

Dementia

Aside from the structured interventions cited above, a variety of behavioral and cognitive strategies are used to counter the negative health outcomes resulting from declines associated with dementia (Buettner, 2006). A majority of those with dementia reside in the community with their caregivers. A holistic approach embraces caregivers and family members and uses non-pharmacological interventions to maintain and improve cognition and functioning, while reducing behavioral symptoms like wandering and agitation (Buettner; Penrose, 2005). The role of therapeutic recreation interventions in promoting executive functioning is evident with brain fitness activities like neurobics (Buettner, Kolanowski, & Yu, 2007; Engelman, 2006). Exercise combined with cognitively challenging activities and leisure education is a holistic approach that maintains functioning, improves health-related quality of life, and supports caregivers (Janssen, 2004; Penrose; Wang, 2008).

Useful behavioral interventions include physical guidance, prompting, cueing, visual demonstration, and hand-over-hand assistance to complete projects. Effective interventions also include physical experiences like exercise and wheelchair biking; cognitive activities like table and board games; and life roles like cooking. When these are delivered using the APIE process in small groups using individualized attention, they are effective in changing behaviors like apathy and agitation and engaging and enhancing cognitive function of older adults with dementia (Buettner et al., 2007; Buettner, Fitzsimmons, & Atav, 2006). Participation in physical activity significantly impacts the health perception of older adults (Wang, 2008). People with Alzheimer's experience psychological, physical, and social benefits like "improved gait and balance, increased sleep time, reduced depression, and reduced wandering behavior" (Penrose, 2005, p. 37).

Leisure education participation tends to improve quality of life perceptions of older adults (Janssen, 2004). A growing baby-boomer generation residing in the community increases the need for effective caregiver support groups. Leisure education with clients and caregivers in the community and long-term care settings is beneficial to both—the caregiver benefits from the time away from the care recipient while the client improves brain fitness (Buettner, 2006).

A holistic approach employs caregivers and family members in interventions to counter the declines associated with dementia. Activities like table and board games, for example, can help maintain and enhance cognitive functioning.

Experiential activities like animal-assisted therapy and gardening have been found to improve social behaviors and reduce negative behaviors like agitation that impact functioning (Buettner et al., 2006; Sellers, 2005). Also, these interventions are conduits to intergenerational engagement and positive caregiver interaction. Validation and range-of-motion activities may improve the person's involvement in day-to-day interactions and self-care. **Validation therapy** is a form of communicating with older adults who are diagnosed with dementia that emphasizes respect and empathy for the older individual (refer to chapter 3 for a description of the intervention). The TRS uses a variety of techniques with each stage to help the person remain in touch with reality and maintain self-worth (Feil, 2002).

A number of specific leadership interactions foster participant involvement (McGuire et al., 1999; Porter & burlingame, 2006):

- TRSs are alert to the side effects of medications like Aricept that treat the symptoms of Alzheimer's.

- Positive behavior change is evident with groups of six or fewer members in environments with limited stimulation; a standard routine including orientation activities to time, place, and people; and adequate daylight (without glare caused by shiny floors or metal objects).

- Information is repeated using the same words.
- Eye contact is made with participants during conversations.
- TRSs employ meaningful activities that promote functional abilities and reflect life themes of the generation.
- Task analysis is used to break down skills and present experiences in a step-by-step sequence so tasks are matched to client skills.
- Increasing physical activity levels on a daily basis promotes cognition, contributes to attention processes, and includes stretching, walking, basic exercise, target games like horseshoes, Frisbee, and dancing (Sherrill, 2004).
- Projects are completed around a table so participants model one another and maintain eye contact.
- Contrasting colors and markings are used to distinguish, for example, exits, obstacles (fire extinguishers), and transitions (between floor and furniture).
- Relaxation and stress reduction techniques reduce agitation.
- Sundowning (restless behavior that occurs with the twilight hours) is managed by, for example, leaving lights on and introducing physical activity.

Emotional Impairments and Addictions

Over-the-counter medications (sedatives and antihistamines) and prescribed medications (anticonvulsant, antidepressant, antianxiety, and antipsychotic substances) compensate for the physical pain that accompanies aging. The TRS is alert to the side effects of medication (hypotension, fatigue, depression, dizziness, urinary incontinence, photosensitivity, heat intolerance, and neuroleptic-induced Parkinsonism or ataxia) during participation. TRSs are also alert to signs of depression as it is a major predictor of suicide and elder abuse, and because it is often minimized or denied (Townsend, 2006). Manifestations of elder abuse are, in addition to depression, withdrawal, welts, evidence of hair pulling, hunger, poor hygiene, unattended physical problems, or an unexplained sexually transmitted disease (Townsend). Physical or mental impairments, inability to meet self-care needs, and needs that exceed a caretaker's ability are risk factors for elder abuse.

A number of interventions reduce negative feelings, anxiety, and stress associated with declining health. TRSs use exercise, ADL activities, leisure awareness, music therapy, validation, and reminiscence to promote self-esteem, family relations, leisure skill development, independence, and resolution of the losses contributing to depression (Teague et al., 2001). TRSs colead family and caregiver support groups that encourage communication, relaxation, and solace among group members undergoing similar experiences. Intergenerational programs and volunteering opportunities promote feelings of self-worth and the satisfaction of helping others accomplish a task. Moreover, giving clients responsibilities and a chance to use their talents during programs helps foster feelings of control and self-worth. Horticulture therapy and animal-assisted therapy also offer outlets for giving and experiencing growth.

Developmental Disabilities

TRSs are conduits to essential medical, health, and social services and to leisure companions and affordable recreation programs. Older adults with disabilities tend to live sedentary lives and have limited leisure skill repertoires. Consequently, regular physical activity is essential for promoting mobility and improved cardiovascular fitness while countering the increased risk for falls and fractures at an earlier age (Connolly, 1998). Creative arts, nutrition classes, and organized social and hobby clubs also address these needs. Leisure education provides opportunities to practice choosing leisure options and to participate in socially preferred experiences. It also enables participants to redefine their concepts of productivity to include beneficial uses of their time outside of paid work or family settings (Wilhite & Keller, 1996). With caregivers, leisure education is a way to address the constraints caused by caregiving and to promote awareness of caregiver and care recipient needs. Since people with Down syndrome are at increased risk of experiencing Alzheimer's disease neuropathologies over the age of 35, TRSs may employ the strategies discussed earlier regarding dementia while working with caregivers to establish structures, limits, and routines that reinforce maintenance of independent functioning (Minde & Friedman, 2002).

As noted in the introduction to this section of the chapter, a number of physical and sensory impairments considered in chapters 6 and 7 have high incidence rates among older adults, especially those over age 60. Leadership interaction and intervention considerations unique to older adults are summarized below for selected high-incidence impairments.

Arthritis

Most people over age 75 are affected by osteoarthritis (OA) or degenerative joint disease (DJD) in the hands and weight-bearing joints (knees, hip, and spine), while rheumatoid arthritis affects people over 50 primarily in the wrist and finger joints and is symmetrical so the same joints on the right and left side are affected (Porter & burlingame, 2006; Sherrill, 2004). With OA, cartilage deteriorates and bone ends begin to rub together. With rheumatoid arthritis, pain, stiffness, and swollen and reddened joints are evident upon waking in the morning or after excessive use. Secondary disabilities experienced are depression, pain, obesity, and impaired mobility. To prevent contractures and joint aggravation, people with arthritis monitor their posture and diet, avoid fatigue and conserve energy, do not remain in one position for extensive time periods, and participate in such nonweight-bearing activities as aquatics and sit-aerobics. Interventions promote the use of fine motor skills, generalized strengthening, ADL activities like cooking, pain and stress management, exercise and mobility, and adaptation of leisure interests to facilitate continual participation.

Parkinson's Disease

As parkinsonism progresses in people over 60, with increasing incidences in those over 70 and 80 (Sherrill, 2004), tremors spread and become more severe, slowness and poverty of movement occurs, and mobility is characterized by short, rapid, shuffling steps. Depression, decreased activity levels, falls, and general deconditioning are secondary issues (Porter & burlingame, 2006). TRSs use walking, relaxation, hand-cycles, and cool (as opposed to warm) water therapy to promote joint range of motion, as well as to develop proper breathing, muscle strength, and walking balance.

Older adults with arthritis benefit from such nonweight-bearing activities as stretching exercises from a seated position.

Hot or humid settings (warm water therapy) exacerbate stiffness and therefore are avoided. Physical leisure activity, relaxation training, and fall prevention and safety are recommended interventions (Porter & burlingame, 2006). TRSs are aware that antiparkinsonian medications may cause side effects like involuntary movements (neuroleptic-induced parkinsonism) and take precautionary measures to protect against falls or environmental obstacles.

Cardiopulmonary Impairments—Heart Attacks and Strokes

The incidence of hypertension increases with age and leads to heart attacks (the majority occur over age 65) and strokes (experienced by those 60 years and over) that impose a number of functional limitations. These limitations require lifestyle adjustments and continuous monitoring to prevent further impairment. TRSs are also alert to the psychosocial responses (denial, anxiety, depression) of the participant and caregivers. TRSs in cardiac rehabilitation are alert to the side effects of heart medication, like hypotension, urinary incontinence, and excessive bleeding (refer to chapter 7 for medication implications). Therapists also take the warning signs of heart attacks seriously (pain in the chest of two or more minutes in duration; the spread of pain to the shoulders, neck, or arms; and dizziness, fainting, sweating, nausea, or shortness of breath). Therapists use leisure and health-related education to develop awareness of alternative leisure experiences and knowledge of energy expenditures (MET) during physical exercise. Relaxation training, stress management, and self-monitoring of activity levels are addressed in health promotion classes. TRSs work with dieticians and family members to plan healthy meals, and collaborate with the cardiac rehab team to plan lifestyle adjustments and activity adaptations.

Strokes remain a major cause of adult long-term disabilities. Signs of an impending stroke include transient numbness on one side of the body, temporary blindness in one or both eyes, double vision, temporary speech difficulty, loss of strength in an arm or leg, dizziness, severe headache, or personality change (Sherrill, 2004). A person with right hemiplegia (left cerebral damage) experiences an inability to understand spoken or written language or even to produce it (aphasia). This impairs emotional expression, social interactions, and care of self. An oversensitivity to a traumatic event may lead to anxiety and depression. A TRS will discover that demonstration, modeling, and nonverbal interactions are useful leadership strategies. Stroke patients may exhibit impaired recall, recognition, and retention, and a slow, disorganized response; TRSs compensate for these impairments by using repetition, structure, and reality orientation. A person with left hemiplegia (right cerebral damage) experiences intellectual impairments that affect his or her ability to interpret visual information and orient to the surrounding environment. The person experiences difficulty in developing self-care skills because, for example, the concepts of "inside" and "outside" are not distinguishable from one another. A TRS will find words to be more effective than gestures and that the environment must be cleared of nonessential equipment or visual distractions.

Whether experiencing right or left hemiplegia, a person who has had a stroke may acknowledge briefly stated requests and is reassured with immediate feedback. Frustration and feelings of distress are psychosocial issues addressed through creative pursuits or relaxation experiences, like listening to CDs or making collages (Auerbach & Benezra, 1998). TRSs consider their physical position, as the client may not detect a person's presence to either side of the midline. TRSs require clients to demonstrate skills so they can confirm clients' actual abilities and safety management skills. Table and board games foster bilateral movements, grasping-releasing, and flexion-extension, which counter visual neglect, contractures, and shoulder subluxation. Leisure education games encourage problem-solving, word finding, and receptive and expressive language. Craft projects address such cognitive deficits as sequencing, following directions, and processing information (Auerbach & Benezra, 1998). Physical activity promotes endurance, balance, range-of-motion, use of the neglected side, and strengthening the unimpaired body parts. Because an increasing number of aging people survive strokes and live in the community, stroke support groups use a leisure education format to promote family and caregiver well-being, health, and resource awareness. Such clubs encourage social contacts among caregivers and continued participation through the modification and adaptation of previous leisure interests.

Cancer
The risk of a cancer diagnosis increases with age, especially after 55 (Porter & burlingame, 2006). Cancer management with older adults is not unlike cancer treatment with other age groups. Difficulty arises when an individual does not respond to signs of a tumor in a timely fashion, as older individuals are more tolerant of pain. Also, it is easier for an aging person to dismiss the reporting of pain by attributing it to other causes, like arthritis. A further complication of cancer among aging people is that individuals' premorbid health conditions influence their tolerance of surgical, radiation, and chemotherapy treatments. Generalized weakness after extended periods of bed rest results in longer recovery periods.

Pain management is an issue that affects TRS-client interactions. Treatment goals include increasing strength, joint function, ambulation, and psychological adjustment to cosmetic changes. TRSs promote active daily lifestyles and support clients in managing their grief, depression, and end of life issues, i.e., reminiscence with caregivers. TRSs provide diversionary bedside activities and cognitive stimulation through expressive and creative arts and animal assisted therapy.

Sensory Impairments

A natural and widespread consequence of aging and advanced age is sensory impairments. Decreases in sensitivity and acuity may first be noticed during an individual's 40s. After age 65, serious hearing and visual losses may be experienced. **Presbycusis**, or "old hearing," is a gradual decline in the ability to hear certain sounds, commencing with those in the high-frequency range (high pitched smoke alarm). Tinnitus (a persistent ringing or buzzing in the ears) increases with increasing age and results in hearing loss (Papalia et al., 2007). Presbycusis also describes "old vision," which results from the loss of acuity as the eye becomes less fluid. With age, most people become farsighted, require more light without glare for reading and more time to adjust to changing amounts of light, and experience decline in depth perception and perception of certain colors. Diseases that affect vision among older adults include diabetes, **glaucoma** (pathologically high intraocular pressure that causes pressure on the iris and results in blindness), **macular degeneration** (leading cause of blindness for those over 55—pigmentation change in the retina; a gray shadow is seen in the center of vision), and **cataracts** (degenerative opacity of the lens causing obstruction of light rays to the retina). Both glaucoma and cataracts are manageable with surgery, medication, laser treatments, or eye drops if treated early; although with glaucoma, there are few symptoms or early warnings other than gradual loss of peripheral vision (Papalia et al.). The proprioception sense is also affected by age; as vestibular structures degenerate, dizziness and vertigo are experienced.

Although not always noticeable to an observer, sensory decline affects participants' adaptations to environmental stimuli, limits intellectual and social experiences, and impairs mobility. A slower response rate, inattentiveness, and resistance to new activity settings are reflective of these losses. TRSs use color contrasts, control noise levels, demonstrations, and adjust voice volume and physical position to compensate for clients' sensory deficits. Exercise and training as well as continued vigilance help prevent falls. TRSs aid clients as they use adaptive devices (e.g., books on tape or magnifying glasses) in social and leisure experiences.

Applying the Therapeutic Recreation Process

In the following case, Mrs. Smith characterizes a typical resident, and the techniques presented are typical of those used in long-term care settings. The TRS supervises paraprofessionals involved in the facility's therapeutic recreation programs.

Assessment

Demographic information.   Mrs. Smith is a widow of chronological age 75. She has resided for two years in a private facility having a continuum of services. Her two children and her grandchildren visit monthly. She has been transferred from her assisted living apartment to an intermediate care unit. She frequently receives notes and visits from community social club members, although as her memory and health decline, these visits have become fewer in number.

History.   Medical records reveal prescriptions for antidepressants, diabetes mellitus, and hypertension. Following her husband's death and a year prior to admission, Mrs. Smith suffered a mild CVA.

Present behavior.   When admitted, Mrs. Smith was meticulous with her self-care and was willing to maintain social contacts and initiate communication. However, she now has a flat affect and needs assistance in ADL. She is aware of her response level when reprimanded. She complains to nursing personnel about food service and room care. She resists participation in the facility's programs. Depression and mood swings are apparent. Her diabetes requires continual monitoring as her eyesight is declining and circulation is very poor in her lower extremities.

Planning

Long-term goal.   The long-term goal of Mrs. Smith's therapeutic recreation program is to improve her ADL skills.

Short-term goal.   The short-term goal is to demonstrate basic self-care.

Objective.   Mrs. Smith will complete all self-care skills before attending and during participation in daily therapeutic recreation experiences.

Content.   The TRS will cooperate with the nursing staff and occupational therapist to assure that Mrs. Smith completes ADL tasks before leaving her room to attend programs. Also, during sessions, the TRS, when appropriate, will require Mrs. Smith to use the restroom and wash her hands.

Process.   The TRS will display an attitude of kind firmness toward the resident. Also, the TRS will use techniques of informal or unstructured RO, resocialization, reminiscence, and validation.

Implementation

Mrs. Smith was scheduled to attend therapeutic recreation daily. The TRS preceded her attendance at the program with a brief room visitation. These visits were gradually eliminated and replaced by a question or appropriate comment about Mrs. Smith's attire when she arrived at the program.

Evaluation

The TRS recorded on Mrs. Smith's chart the status of demonstrated self-care and appearance per visit. Progress notes also documented the number of times Mrs. Smith was unprepared to attend or came to an activity without completing self-care tasks. The TRS also completed sections F (Preferences for Customary Routine and Activities) and O (Special Treatments and Procedures) of the Minimum Data Set (MDS). The TRS documented the number of days Mrs. Smith attended at least 15 minutes or more of recreation therapy in section O, and the preferred activity settings and preferences in section F of the MDS. The TRS shared this information during staff meetings with the occupational therapist and nursing staff.

RELATED CONSIDERATIONS

The biological and physiological changes that occur with age necessitate programming precautions. One consideration is the degree of clients' residual vision. Direct nonfluorescent lights help illuminate the subject more clearly than many forms of soft lighting. Distinctive color contrasts, such as black on white or yellow, also are helpful. Large block print is easier for clients to read than is script. Magnifying glasses also are effective visual aids. TRSs should also consider the degree of residual hearing maintained by clients. When clients wear hearing aids or use assisted listening devices like hearing amplifiers, TRSs may be called upon to operate the devices. Keep in mind that hearing aids may or may not compensate for all hearing losses.

Aging people often experience bowel and bladder incontinence or are unable to urinate or defecate. The aging body system often does not generate needed fluids. On the other hand, sometimes loss of muscle control causes more frequent use of the facilities. Therefore, restrooms must be located near the primary program area and TRSs should encourage liquid intake.

The helping process encompasses life and death, and this is perhaps nowhere more apparent than with aging people. As individuals and as professionals, how we feel about life and death affects how we interact with aging adults. As the TRS interacts with elderly clients, the complex relationships between health, functioning, and the quality of life and death are experienced. In hospice settings, for example, TRSs may use recreation experiences to enable clients to address their fears, escape the stress of terminality (even though only temporary), work through unfinished business, and reach spiritual or inner peace (DeMong, 1997). (Additional information is available from the National Hospice and Palliative Care Organization at www.nhpco.org.) TRSs also help caregivers affirm their roles by conducting parallel programs for caregivers and their care recipients and promoting increased awareness of personal and community resources to augment leisure experiences for both (Bedini & Guinan, 1996).

Government regulations, standards of third-party payers, and guidelines of regulatory bodies affect programming for the elderly. These standards (summarized below) influence fiscal and personnel management, documentation, program operation, and participants' rights. The 1935 Social Security Act provided benefits for industrial and commercial workers. In 1940 the first benefits were paid. Presently, coverage is available to most workers over age 62. The Supplemental Security Income (SSI) program became effective under the 1974 Social Security Act Amendments. This program guarantees a monthly income—adjusted for cost-of-living increases—to individuals with a demonstrated need. Those who are eligible include individuals who are elderly, blind, disabled, or have low incomes. This program covers housing costs, day care, home care, transportation, counseling, nutrition, and health needs.

In 1965 the Social Security Act was amended to include the Medicare program. Medicare (Part A, Hospital Insurance and Part B, Medical Insurance) provides hospital, home health care, hospice, outpatient hospital care, skilled nursing care, and physician's care for those over 65 and for those with certain disabilities. All persons over 65, those with end-stage renal disease, or those who have certain disabilities are eligible for services under this insurance program, which is funded by workers' and employers' contributions. Medicare does not cover the cost of long-term custodial care in nursing homes. In 2003 the Medicare Prescription Drug Improvement and Modernization Act permitted everyone with Medicare to enroll in an insurance plan to cover drug costs commencing in 2006. Private companies also provide coverage, so individuals must select a plan and pay monthly premiums. Medicaid is a federal assistance program administered through the states that pays for most medical needs for persons of any age who have been declared eligible. Medicaid pays for physicians' services, hospital care, medications, supplies, and long-term care in a nursing home or an adult care home, but not in assisted living. When long-term care is required (as with Alzheimer's) and caregivers have depleted their assets, Medicaid is available to pay the difference between income and cost of care.

With a focus on quality care at reduced costs, the Balanced Budget Act of 1997 (Public Law 105-33) reduced Medicare and Medicaid spending, established a **prospective payment system (PPS)** (reimbursement at a predetermined set rate based on Medicare regulations) for reimbursement in some service areas, and set up managed care options for Medicaid beneficiaries. The overall outcome of this act was a shift from service coverage based on reasonable cost to reimbursement for services essential to treatment of a specific person or population based on a federal rate that is adjusted according to the case mix. The CMS (Centers for Medicare and Medicaid Services) uses a **resource utilization group (RUG)** system to classify patients and determine payment based on the intensity of resources used and also sets caps on the length of therapy services.

The CMS Omnibus Budget Reconciliation Act (OBRA) of 1987 (which became effective October 1, 1990), required states to assess and report outcomes to CMS for long-term facilities whose residents were receiving monies from Medicare or Medicaid. Each resident is to be assessed using the **Minimum Data Set (MDS 3.0, revised 2009)**, an assessment, reimbursement, quality improvement tool. Assessment occurs at specified intervals commencing five days after admission and when change occurs in services rendered. The MDS 3.0 Section F (Preferences for Customary Routine and Activities) and Section O (Special Treatments and Procedures) require documentation of activity preferences and documented outcomes attributed to recreation therapy. Recreation therapy consists of physician ordered treatment that includes frequency, duration and scope of treatment; is provided by qualified CTRSs; and satisfies the definition for active treatment. Data collected on Section O are reported to CMS via online computer information/retrieval systems. Such data are used to calculate case mix rates for reimbursements directly to service providers.

The Older Americans Act of 1965, amended 15 times since and due for reauthorization in 2011, created the Administration on Aging (AOA, www.aoa.gov). The administration oversees a variety of programs including nutrition centers, low-cost transportation, day-care centers, and the services offered through the local Area Agency on Aging (AAA). Recent amendments created the National Family Caregiver Support program that provides information, training, counseling, and respite care to assist family and others with frail, ill, and disabled older adults; awarded grants to states to detect elder abuse; required AOA and AAAs to plan comprehensive systems of home and community-based services to help elders with long-term care needs remain in their homes; and funded Aging and Disability Resource Centers (ADRCs) to assist older adults with disabilities in accessing information and long-term care options.

The TRS working with aging adults may access information from a variety of sources: organizations devoted to aging issues, health and human service agencies serving persons with developmental disabilities, public park and recreation senior centers, and private organizations that manage assisted living and home health-care operations. Funding resources and information on, for example, legislation, transportation, and medication are available through agencies like the AAA and on a number of Web sites; for example, the National Institutes of Health (www.nih.gov), National Institute on Aging (www.nia.nih.gov), and the Centers for Medicare & Medicaid Services (CMS, www.cms.hhs.gov). With updated contacts and materials, the TRS becomes an advocate for comprehensive planning and management among the diverse networks associated with aging populations.

SUMMARY

Longer life spans, a large cohort of aging baby boomers, and a growing segment of people ages 85 and older are contributing to an increasing population of older adults worldwide. The aging population is a heterogeneous group. Several factors, both external to and within each person, determine the influence of the aging process. These same factors determine the extent to which aging persons direct their own leisure experiences or require the assistance of TRSs. The ability of an aging individual to adjust to changing times is contingent on his or her health status, personality, previous life experiences, and social support system (including finances, transportation, housing, medical care, and leisure).

Two types of clients were considered in this chapter: those who are basically healthy and those with illnesses and disabilities. Individuals who are aging well use therapeutic recreation resources available to adults living in the mainstream. Their needs are served by leisure education experiences and activities that optimize health; promote lifelong learning; foster meaningful roles, control, competence, functional independence and social interaction; and permit adjustment to the aging process. Such opportunities are provided by leisure professionals (including therapeutic recreation specialists). Individuals with illnesses and disabilities interact with TRSs in the health-care and social-service systems, as well as in their own homes. The intent of intervention with such individuals is to assess, treat/rehabilitate, promote health and functional well-being, serve as a conduit to essential services, ensure a continuum of care, and support caregivers.

A primary goal of leisure is to enable the aging person to adjust effectively to natural growth processes and the changes that accompany aging. Aging adults are encouraged to continue those experiences that counter the declines in functioning ability, while recognizing that the natural consequences of the aging process create certain needs. If you plan to enter into helping relationships with aging people, give special consideration to your own feelings about living and dying and to your personal viewpoint on the aging process. Practical experiences with the elderly will dispel myths about aging; for example, you will learn that chronological age is not the primary indicator of the aging process.

Key Terms

area agency on aging (AAA) A local agency through which federal programs are administered in a state.

attitude therapy A form of behavior modification used by therapeutic recreation staff to reinforce desirable behaviors and to eliminate undesirable behaviors.

cataracts Degenerative opacity of the ocular lens causing obstruction of light rays to the retina. The most common visual problem associated with aging. If left untreated, results in loss of central, followed by peripheral, vision.

dementia A disorder characterized by multiple cognitive deficits—including memory impairment and disturbances in aphasia (language), apraxia (motor functioning), agnosia (object identification), or executive functioning (planning, abstract thinking)—severe enough to impact an individual's social and occupational functioning.

glaucoma Pathologically high intraocular pressure that causes pressure on the iris and results in blindness. Treated with eye drops and laser surgery.

gustatory Having to do with the sense of taste.

incontinence The loss of ability to control the bladder and/or the bowels.

macular degeneration Pigmentation change in the retina; a gray shadow is seen in the center of vision.

minimum data set (MDS) 3.0 revised 2009 An assessment, reimbursement, quality improvement tool used with Medicare or Medicaid recipients, with data reported through online information/retrieval systems to CMS.

Pick's disease Progressive deterioration of the brain accompanied by atrophy of the cerebral cortex.

presbycusis Term used to describe "old hearing or vision" associated with hearing losses in high frequency range and loss of visual acuity as people age.

prospective payment system (PPS) Reimbursement at a predetermined rate based on Medicare regulations managed by CMS; data from the MDS is used to calculate the case mix rates.

reality orientation (RO) An intervention technique used with the elderly to make them aware of the present, especially with regard to time, day, their location, name, and activity in which they are participating.

reminiscence An intervention technique in which re-experiencing of past events is used to stimulate current memory.

remotivation An intervention technique that is used following the completion of formal RO classes to encourage people to become interested in activities of everyday life.

resocialization An intervention technique using structured group programs to increase people's awareness of experiences and choices in the community.

resource utilization group (RUG) A system used to classify people and determine payment according to the intensity of resources used; managed by CMS.

systolic blood pressure Contraction of the heart producing maximum pressure on blood vessel walls.

validation therapy A form of communication with older adults that uses a variety of techniques influenced by the life stage of the adult in order to show respect and empathy during interactions.

vital capacity The breathing capacity of the lungs measured by the amount of air that can be forcibly exhaled after a full inspiration.

Study Questions

1. List at least three changes that accompany the aging process in each of the following areas: physical, psychological, intellectual, and sociological.

2. Identify at least one lifelong and two adult-onset disabilities and describe for each functioning characteristics impacting leisure opportunities for the aging individual.

3. Compare the focus of leisure with a "traditional" senior, a baby boomer, and an individual with dementia.

4. List at least three leadership considerations and three therapeutic interventions that could be implemented with both well-aging people and aging people with disabilities.

5. Consider the two case studies in this chapter. Identify additional (a) program goals; (b) participants' needs met by the programs; (c) leadership and intervention techniques used in the programs; and (d) special service delivery considerations.

Practical Experiences to Enhance Student Objectives

1. Interview people your parents' age and your grandparents' age. Ask them to describe their leisure activities, the factors that influence their quality of life and leisure patterns, and how participation in leisure activities contributes to their health and well-being. Compare the information gathered during the interviews and summarize the role of leisure through the life span.

2. Visit a person living in an assisted living complex and one who lives in a skilled care unit. Discuss with each their preparation for life as an older adult. Compare your conversations.

3. Visit a local social security office and collect pamphlets on Medicare, Medicaid, and SSI regulations. Conduct Internet searches through professional organizations to acquire resources (www.alz.org; www.asaging.org; www.ncoa.org).

4. Visit or interview someone who has lived in or worked in a hospice. Discuss the aging person's view of time, sense of the life cycle, life fulfillment, and relationship of leisure to quality of life.

5. Participate in a class discussion on leisure professionals' roles in clients' living and dying. What are the responsibilities of the professional and how can a student prepare to meet these responsibilities? Search the Internet for resources and services offered by hospice organizations.

References

Abikoff, H. B., & Hechtman, L. (1996). Multimodal therapy and stimulants in the treatment of children with attention-deficit hyperactivity disorder. In E. D. Hibbs & P. S. Jensen (Eds.), *Psychosocial treatments for child and adolescent disorders: Empirically based strategies for clinical practice* (pp. 341–369). Washington, DC: American Psychological Association.

Acello, B. (2003). Handling an unwelcome comeback: Postpolio syndrome. *Nursing, 33*(11), 32hn1–32hn5.

Ackerman, S. J. (1999). Examining epilepsy. *NCRR Reporter, 23*(2), 5–7.

Active Recreation Tops Lifestyle Desires for Older Baby Boomers, Senior Citizens. (2007). Retrieved March 2, 2009, from http://seniorjournal.com/NEWS/Features/2007/7-04-13-ActiveRecreation.htm.

Adler, M. (1991). *Desires, right and wrong: The ethics of enough.* New York: Macmillan.

Administration on Aging (AOA). (2007). *A profile of older Americans: 2007.* Washington, DC: U.S. Department of Health and Human Services.

Aiken, L. H. (2003). Achieving an interdisciplinary workforce in health care. *New England Journal of Medicine, 348*(2), 164–166.

Allen, L. R., Cox, J., & Cooper, N. L. (2006). The impact of a summer day camp on the resiliency of disadvantaged youths. *Leisure Today/Journal of Physical Education, Recreation & Dance, 77*(1), 17–23.

Alloy, L. B., Acocella, J., & Bootzin, R. R. (1996). *Abnormal psychology: Current perspectives* (7th ed.). New York: McGraw Hill.

Allsop, J. A., & Dattilo, J. (2000). Therapeutic use of T'ai Chi Ch'uan. In J. Dattilo (Ed.), *Facilitation techniques in therapeutic recreation* (pp. 245–272). State College, PA: Venture Publishing.

Alzheimer's Association. (2008). *Basics of Alzheimer's disease: What it is and what you can do.* Chicago, IL: Author.

American Academy of Pediatrics, Child Life Council and Committee on Hospital Care. (2006). Child life services. *Pediatrics, 118*(4), 1757–1763.

American Alliance for Health, Physical Education, Recreation, and Dance. (1988). *Physical best.* Reston, VA: Author.

American Association on Intellectual and Developmental Disabilities. (2008). *Frequently asked questions on intellectual disability and the AAIDD definition.* Retrieved June 20, 2008, from http://aamr.org/Policies/faq_intellectual_disability.shtml

American Association on Intellectual and Developmental Disabilities (AAIDD). (2009). Aging: Older adults and their aging caregivers. Retrieved March 1, 2009, from http://www.aaidd.org/content_181.cfm.

American Medical Association. (2006). *Health professions career and education directory 2006–2007.* Chicago, IL: Author.

American Psychiatric Association. (2000). *Diagnostic and statistical manual of mental disorders* (4th ed., text revision). Washington, DC: Author.

American Society of Group Psychotherapy & Psychodrama (ASGPP) (2006). *Psychodrama.* Retrieved July 27, 2007, from http://asgpp.org/pdrama1.htm

American Therapeutic Recreation Association. (2000). *Standards for the practice of therapeutic recreation and self-assessment guide* (2nd ed.). Alexandria, VA: Author.

American Therapeutic Recreation Association. (2001). *Code of ethics.* Retrieved December 12, 2007, from http://www.atra-tr.org/ethics.html

American Therapeutic Recreation Association. (2003). *Recreational therapy: A viable option in health and rehabilitation treatment services to prevention* (2nd ed.). Alexandria, VA: Author.

American Therapeutic Recreation Association. (2006). *Statement on diversity.* Retrieved November 17, 2007, from http://www.atra-tr.org/about.htm

American Therapeutic Recreation Association. (n.d.). *ATRA research agenda approved August, 2004.* Alexandria, VA: Author.

Anderson, S. C., & Stewart, W. (1980). Therapeutic recreation education survey. *Therapeutic Recreation Journal, 14*(3), 4.

Annand, V., & Powers, P. (1991). The benefits of therapeutic recreation in pediatrics. In C. P. Coyle, W. B. Kinney, B. Riley, & J. W. Shank (Eds.), *Benefits of therapeutic recreation: A consensus view* (pp. 205–233). Ravensdale, WA: Idyll Arbor.

Anzueto, A. (2006). Clinical course of chronic obstructive pulmonary disease: Review of therapeutic interventions. *The American Journal of Medicine, 119*(10A), S46–S53.

Ardovino, P. S. (2006). Trends and issues in therapeutic recreation programs in Wisconsin's correctional and forensic institutions. *American Journal of Recreation Therapy, 5*(4), 11–18.

Ardovino, P. S., Todd, B. K., & Navar, N. H. (2002). The Leisure Lifestyle Center: "It's been awesome for me." *Parks & Recreation, 37*(5), 40–46.

Armstrong, M., & Lauzen, S. (1994). *Community integration program* (2nd ed.). Ravensdale, WA: Idyll Arbor.

Aronow, W. S. (2007). Management of peripheral arterial disease in the elderly. *Geriatrics, 62*(1), 19–25.

Arsenault, N., & Anderson, G. (1998). New learning horizons for older adults. *Leisure Today/ Journal of Physical Education, Recreation & Dance, 69*(3), 27–31.

Ashton-Shaeffer, C., & Constant, A. (2005). Why do older adults garden? *Activities, Adaptation & Aging, 30*(2), 1–18.

Ashton-Shaeffer, C., Sheldon, M., & Johnson, D. E. (1995). The social caterpillar and the wallflower: Two case studies of adolescents with disabilities in transition. *Therapeutic Recreation Journal, 29*(4), 324–336.

Auerbach, J., & Benezra, A. (1998). Therapeutic recreation and the rehabilitation of the stroke patient. In W. Sife (Ed.), *After stroke: Enhancing quality of life* (pp. 123–128). New York: The Haworth Press.

Austin, D. R. (1997). *Therapeutic recreation processes and techniques* (3rd ed.). Champaign, IL: Sagamore Publishing.

Austin, D. R. (1998). The health protection/health promotion model. *Therapeutic Recreation Journal, 32*, 109–117.

Austin, D. R. (2000). *Therapeutic recreation processes and techniques* (4th ed.). Champaign, IL: Sagamore Publishing.

Austin, D. R. (2002). A call for training in physical activity. In D. R. Austin, J. Dattilo, & B. P. McCormick (Eds.), *Conceptual foundations for therapeutic recreation* (pp. 225–234). State College, PA: Venture Publishing.

Austin, D. R. (2002a). A third revolution in therapeutic recreation? In D. R. Austin, J. Dattilo, & B. P. McCormick (Eds.), *Conceptual foundations for therapeutic recreation* (pp. 273–287). State College, PA: Venture Publishing.

Austin, D. R. (2002b). Conceptual models in therapeutic recreation. In D. R. Austin, J. Dattilo, & B. P. McCormick (Eds.), *Conceptual foundations for therapeutic recreation* (pp.1–30). State College, PA: Venture Publishing.

Austin, D. R. (2002c). Professionalism. In D. R. Austin, J. Dattilo, & B. P. McCormick (Eds.), *Conceptual foundations for therapeutic recreation* (pp. 265–271). State College, PA: Venture Publishing.

Austin, D. R. (2004). Therapeutic recreation: A long past but a brief history. *Palaestra, 20*(1), 37–42.

Austin, D. R. (2009). *Therapeutic recreation processes and techniques* (6th ed.). Champaign, IL: Sagamore Publishing.

Austin, D. R., & Crawford, M. E. (2001). *Therapeutic recreation: An introduction* (3rd ed.). Boston: Allyn and Bacon.

Austin, D. R., Dattilo, J., & McCormick, B. P. (2002). *Conceptual foundations for therapeutic recreation*. State College, PA: Venture Publishing.

Austin, E. N., Johnston, Y. A. M., & Morgan, L. L. (2006). Community gardening in a Senior Center: A therapeutic intervention to improve the health of older adults. *Therapeutic Recreation Journal, 40*(1), 48–56.

Austin, J. K., Dunn, D. W., & Price, M. J. (2009). Health and safety considerations. In D. R. Austin (Ed.), *Therapeutic recreation: Processes and techniques* (6th ed., pp. 451–489). Champaign, IL: Sagamore Publishing.

Avedon, E. M. (1974). *Therapeutic recreation service: An applied behavior science approach*. Englewood Cliffs, NJ: Prentice Hall.

Avert. (2008). *Worldwide HIV & AIDS Statistics*. Retrieved July 1, 2008, from http://www.avert.org/worldstats.htm.

Balady, G. J., Williams, M. A., Ades, P. A., Bittner, V., Comoss, P., Foody, J. A. M., et al. (2007). Core components of cardiac rehabilitation/secondary prevention programs: 2007 update. *Journal of Cardiopulmonary Rehabilitation and Prevention, 27*(3), 121–129.

Baldwin, C. K., Hutchinson, S. L., & Magnuson, D. R. (2004). Program theory: A framework for theory-driven programming and evaluation. *Therapeutic Recreation Journal, 38*(1), 16–31.

Ball, E. L. (1968). Academic preparation for therapeutic recreation personnel. *Therapeutic Recreation Journal, 2*(4), 13–19.

Ball, E. L. (1969). Excellence in the therapeutic recreation profession. *Recreation in Treatment Centers, 6*, 9–12.

Ball, J. W., & Bindler, R. C. (2008). *Pediatric nursing: Caring for children* (4th ed.). Upper Saddle River, NJ: Pearson Education.

Barkin, R. L., Lubenow, T. R., Bruehl, S., Husfeldt, B., Ivankovich, O., & Barkin, S. J. (1996). Management of chronic pain part II. *Disease-a-month, 42*(8), 457–507.

Barletta, A-R., & Loy, D. P. (2006). The experience of participation in Challenger Little League through the eyes of a child with a physical disability. *American Journal of Recreation Therapy, 5*(3), 6–12.

Bartels, M. N., Whiteson, J. H., Alba, A. S., & Kim, H. (2006). Cardiopulmonary rehabilitation and cancer rehabilitation. *Archives of Physical Medicine and Rehabilitation, 87*(Suppl 1), S46–S56.

Basco, M. R., & Rush, A. J. (1996). *Cognitive-behavioral therapy for bipolar disorder*. New York: Guilford Press.

Basting, A. D. (2006). Arts in dementia care: "This is not the end . . . it's the end of this chapter." *Generations, 30*(1), 16–20.

Beaudouin, N. M., & Keller, M. J. (1994). Aquatic-solutions: A continuum of services for individuals with physical disabilities in the community. *Therapeutic Recreation Journal, 28*(4), 193–202.

Beck, P. (1982). The successful interventions in nursing homes: The therapeutic effects of cognitive activity. *The Gerontologist, 22,* 383–389.

Bedini, L. A. (1991). Modern day "freaks"? The exploitation of people with disabilities. *Therapeutic Recreation Journal, 25*(4), 61–70.

Bedini, L. A., & Guinan, D. M. (1996). The leisure of caregivers of older adults: Implications for CTRS's in nontraditional settings. *Therapeutic Recreation Journal, 30*(4), 274–288.

Beland, K. (2007). Boosting social and emotional competence. *Educational Leadership, 64*(7), 68–71.

Bent, L. M., Johnson, K., Klaas, S., Rathsam, S., & Schottler, J. (2003). An upward slope: Therapeutic recreation and downhill skiing. *Parks & Recreation, 38*(4), 58–62.

Berg, S., & Van Puymbroeck, M. (2005). Research update: Under-represented groups need physical activity. *Parks & Recreation, 40*(7), 24–29.

Berger, B. G., & Owen, D. R. (1988). Stress reduction and mood enhancement in four exercise modes: Swimming, body conditioning, hatha yoga, and fencing. *Research Quarterly for Exercise and Sport, 59*(2), 148–159.

Berlin, B., Moul, D. E., LePage, J. P., Mogge, N. L., & Sellers, D. G., Jr. (2003). The effect of aquatic therapy interventions on patients with depression: A comparison study. *Annual in Therapeutic Recreation, 12,* 7–13.

Berryman, D. L. (1971). *Recommended standards with evaluative criteria for recreation services in residential institutions.* New York: New York University, School of Education.

Betz, C. L., Hunsberger, M., & Wright, S. (1994). *Family-centered nursing care of children* (2nd ed.). Philadelphia: W. B. Saunders.

Beukema, M. J. (1977). *Physical confidence therapy.* Grand Rapids, MI: Pine Rest Christian Hospital.

Bintzler, S. (2006). Research update: Water works wonders. *Parks & Recreation, 41*(11), 26–31.

Blair, D. K., & Coyle, C. (2005). An examination of multicultural competencies of entry level Certified Therapeutic Recreation Specialists. *Therapeutic Recreation Journal, 39*(2), 139–157.

Blakely, T. L., & Dattilo, J. (1993). An exploratory study of leisure motivation patterns of adults with alcohol and drug addictions. *Therapeutic Recreation Journal, 27*(4), 230–238.

Blinded military members and veterans to participate in national sports festival. (2008). *Journal of Visual Impairment & Blindness, 102*(4), 246.

Bocarro, J., & Sable, J. (2003). Finding the right P.A.T.H.: Exploring familial relationships and the role of a community TR program in the initial years after a spinal cord injury. *Therapeutic Recreation Journal, 37*(1), 58–72.

Bole, R. K., Costa, B. R., & Frey, J. B. (2007). The impact of animal-assisted therapy on patient ambulation: A feasibility study. *American Journal of Recreation Therapy, 6*(3), 7–19.

Bonadies, V. (2004). A yoga therapy program for AIDS-related pain and anxiety: Implications for therapeutic recreation. *Therapeutic Recreation Journal, 38*(2), 148–166.

Borduin, C. M., Mann, B. J., Cone, L. T., Henggeler, S. W., Fucci, B. R., Blaske, D. M., & Williams, R. A. (1995). Multisystemic treatment of serious juvenile offenders: Long-term prevention of criminality and violence. *Journal of Consulting and Clinical Psychology, 63,* 539–578.

Boyd, R. (1997). Older adults with developmental disabilities: A brief examination of current knowledge. *Activities, Adaptation & Aging, 21*(3), 7–27.

Brammer, L. M., & MacDonald, G. (2003). *The helping relationship: Process and skills* (8th ed.). Boston: Allyn & Bacon.

Brandon, L. J. (1999). Promoting physically active lifestyles in older adults. *Journal of Physical Education, Recreation & Dance, 70*(6), 34–37.

Braswell, H. (2006). Fun size fitness gyms begin to target a new group of clients . . . children. *Parks & Recreation, 41*(10), 60–65.

Bray, S., Barrowclough, C., & Lobban, F. (2007). The social problem-solving abilities of people with borderline personality disorder. *Behaviour Research and Therapy, 45*(6), 1409–1417.

Brieger, G. H. (1976). Medicine and surgery. In *Dictionary of American history* (rev. ed., vol. 4, pp. 295–299). New York: Charles Scribner's Sons.

Brill, N. I., & Levine, J. (2005). *Working with people: The helping process* (8th ed.). Upper Saddle River, NJ: Pearson Education.

Broach, E., & Dattilo, J. (2000). Aquatic therapy. In J. Dattilo (Ed.), *Facilitation techniques in therapeutic recreation* (pp. 65–98). State College, PA: Venture Publishing.

Broach, E., & Dattilo, J. (2003). The effect of aquatic therapy on strength of adults with multiple sclerosis. *Therapeutic Recreation Journal, 37*(3), 224–239.

Broach, E., Dattilo, J., & Deavours, M. (2000). Assistive technology. In J. Dattilo (Ed.), *Facilitation techniques in therapeutic recreation* (pp. 99–132). State College, PA: Venture Publishing.

Broach, E., Dattilo, J., & Loy, D. (2000). Therapeutic use of exercise. In J. Dattilo (Ed.), *Facilitation techniques in therapeutic recreation* (pp. 355–384). State College, PA: Venture Publishing.

Broach, E., Dattilo, J., & McKenney, A. (2007). Effects of aquatic therapy on perceived fun or enjoyment experiences of participants with multiple sclerosis. *Therapeutic Recreation Journal, 41*(3), 179–200.

Broida, J. K. (2006). Marketing new approaches for therapeutic recreation. In M. J. Carter & G. S. O'Morrow, *Effective management in therapeutic recreation service* (2nd ed. pp. 157–165). State College, PA: Venture Publishing.

Broida, J. K., & Germann, C. (1999). Enhancing accessibility through virtual environments. *Parks & Recreation, 34*(5), 94–97.

Brooks, P. M. (2006). The burden of musculoskeletal disease—a global perspective. *Clinical Rheumatology, 25*, 778–781.

Brownlee, S., & Dattilo, J. (2002). Therapeutic massage as a therapeutic recreation facilitation technique. *Therapeutic Recreation Journal, 36*(4), 369–381.

Buettner, L. L. (2006). Peace of mind: A pilot community-based program for older adults with memory loss. *American Journal of Recreation Therapy, 5*(3), 42–48.

Buettner, L. L., & Fitzsimmons, S. (2007). Introduction to evidence based recreation therapy. *Annual in Therapeutic Recreation, 15,* 12–19.

Buettner, L. L., Fitzsimmons, S., & Atav, A. S. (2006). Predicting outcomes of therapeutic recreation intervention for older adults with dementia and behavioral symptoms. *Therapeutic Recreation Journal, 40*(1), 33–47.

Buettner, L. L., Kolanowski, A., & Yu, F. (2007). Cognitive program area. *American Journal of Recreation Therapy, 6*(1), 25–30.

Bullock, C. C., Mahon, M. J., & Killingsworth, C. L. (2010). *Introduction to recreation services for people with disabilities: A person-centered approach* (3rd ed.). Champaign, IL: Sagamore Publishing.

Burgess, A., Kunik, M. E., & Stanley, M. (2005). Chronic obstructive pulmonary disease: Assessing and treating psychological issues in patients with COPD. *Geriatrics, 60*(12), 18–21.

Burlingame, H. (2007). Exercising their right to play: Calorie-counters say playground adventures keep kids fit. *Parks & Recreation, 42*(12), 34–37.

burlingame, j. (1998). Customer service. In F. Brasile, T. K. Skalko, & j. burlingame (Eds.), *Perspectives in recreational therapy: Issues of a dynamic profession* (pp. 249–264). Ravensdale, WA: Idyll Arbor.

burlingame, j., & Blaschko, T. M. (2010). *Assessment tools for recreational therapy and related fields* (4th ed.). Ravensdale, WA: Idyll Arbor.

Bushnell, J. (1997). Eating disorders. *Mental health in New Zealand: From a public health perspective.* Wellington, New Zealand: Ministry of Health.

Caldwell, L. L. (Ed.). (2000). Special issue on youth and leisure [Special issue]. *Journal of Park and Recreation Administration*, 18(1).

Caldwell, L. L., Baldwin, C. K., Walls, T., & Smith, E. (2004). Preliminary effects of a leisure education program to promote healthy use of free time among middle school adolescents. *Journal of Leisure Research, 36*(3), 310–335.

Caldwell, L. L., Dattilo, J., Kleiber, D. A., & Lee, Y. (1994/95). Perceptions of therapeutic recreation among people with spinal cord injury. *Annual in therapeutic recreation, 5,* 13–26.

Callaghan, P. (2004). Exercise: A neglected intervention in mental health? *Journal of Psychiatric & Mental Health Nursing, 11*(4), 476–483.

Caperchione, C., & Mummery, K. (2006). The utilization of group process strategies as an intervention tool for the promotion of health-related physical activity in older adults. *Activities, Adaptation & Aging, 30*(4), 29–45.

Caroleo, O. (1999). The impact of a therapeutic recreation program on the use of coping strategies among people with AIDS. *Annual in Therapeutic Recreation, 8,* 22–32.

Carruthers, C. (1993). Leisure and alcohol expectancies. *Journal of Leisure Research, 25*(3), 229–244.

Carruthers, C. (1999). Pathological gambling: Implications for therapeutic recreation practice. *Therapeutic Recreation Journal, 33*(4), 287–303.

Carruthers, C. P. (1997/98). Therapeutic recreation efficacy research agenda. *Annual in therapeutic recreation, 7,* 29–41.

Carruthers, C. P., & Hood, C. D. (1994). Alcohol use in leisure. *Journal of Leisurability 21*(1), 3–12.

Carruthers, C., & Hood, C. (2007). Building a life of meaning through therapeutic recreation: The leisure and well-being model, part I. *Therapeutic Recreation Journal, 41*(4), 276–297.

Carter, M. J. (1981). Registration of therapeutic recreators: Standards from 1956 to present. *Therapeutic Recreation Journal, 15*(2), 17–22.

Carter, M. J. (1983). Therapeutic recreation credentialing: Its history, issues and future. In G. Hitzhusen (Ed.), *Expanding horizons in therapeutic recreation* (pp. 193–208). Columbia: University of Missouri.

Carter, M. J. (1998). Increased professionalism: An experience from the United States. *Journal of Leisurability, 25*(2), 20–25.

Carter, M. J. (1999). Serving a brave new world. *The Millennium Vision: Exploring the Future of Parks and Recreation, Parks & Recreation, 34* (Suppl.), 20–25.

Carter, M. J., & Folkerth, J. E. (1989). The evolution of the National Council for Therapeutic Recreation Certification, Inc. In D. Compton (Ed.), *Issues in therapeutic recreation: A profession in transition* (pp. 505–510). Champaign, IL: Sagamore Publishing.

Carter, M. J., & Folkerth, J. E. (Eds.). (2006). *Therapeutic recreation education: Challenges and changes.* Ashburn, VA: National Recreation and Park Association.

Carter, M. J., & Foret, C. M. (1994). Building transition bridges for the disabled. *Parks & Recreation, 29*(4), 78–83.

Carter, M. J., & James, A. (1979). Continuing professional development program for therapeutic recreators. *Therapeutic Recreation Journal, 13*(3), 12–15.

Carter, M. J., & LeConey, S. P. (2004). *Therapeutic recreation in the community: An inclusive approach* (2nd ed.). Champaign, IL: Sagamore Publishing.

Carter, M. J., Nezey, I. O., Wenzel, K., & Foret, C. (1999). Leisure education with caregiver support groups. *Activities, Adaptation & Aging, 24*(2), 67–81.

Carter, M. J., & O'Morrow, G. S. (2006). *Effective management in therapeutic recreation service* (2nd ed.). State College, PA: Venture Publishing.

Carter, M. J., & Russell, K. J. (2005). What is the perceived worth of recreation? Results from a county jail study. *Corrections Today, 67*(3), 80–83, 91.

Carter, M. J., Washington, S. J., Witman, J., & Beck, T. M. (1994). Privileging: The right to practice. *Schole, 9,* 13–20.

Castillo, R. J. (1997). *Culture and mental illness: A client-centered approach.* Pacific Grove, CA: Brooks/Cole.

Center for the Health Professions. (1998, Winter). Changing health care system demands new leaders. *Front & Center, 2*(3), 1, 4.

Center for Neurological Diseases/Rocky Mountain Multiple Sclerosis Center. (1998). *Multiple sclerosis handbook.* Englewood, CO: Author.

Centers for Disease Control and Prevention and The Merck Company Foundation. (2007). *The state of aging and health in America 2007: Executive summary.* Whitehouse Station, NJ: The Merck Company Foundation.

Centers for Disease Control and Prevention. (2008a). *About autism.* Retrieved June 19, 2008, from http://www.cdc.gov/ncbddd/autism/

Centers for Disease Control and Prevention. (2008b). *CFS: Basic facts.* Retrieved June 18, 2008, from http://www.cdc.gov/print.do?url=http://www.cdc.gov/cfs/cfsbasicfacts.htm

Centers for Disease Control and Prevention. (2008c). Physical activity and health. Retrieved March 9, 2010, from http://www.cdc.gov/physicalactivity/everyone/health/index.html

Centers for Disease Control and Prevention. 2009. *Trends in Tuberculosis, 2008.* Fact Sheet. Retrieved from www.cdc.gov/tb/publications/factsheets/statistics/TBTrends.htm

Centers for Disease Control and Prevention. 2010. *U.S. Obesity trends, by state, 1985–2009.* Retrieved from www.cdc.gov/obesity/data/trends.html#state

Chakrabarty, S., & Zoorob, R. (2007). Fibromyalgia. *American Family Physician, 76*(2), 247–254.

Chang, B., Wu, A. W., Hansel, N. N., & Diette, G. B. (2004). Quality of life in tuberculosis: A review of the English language literature. *Quality of Life Research, 13*(10), 1633–1642.

Cheek, D., Jensen, L., & Smith, M. (2004). Preventing and treating heart disease in women. *Nurse Practitioner, 29* (Supplement), 4–8.

Child Life Council. (1997). *Guidelines for the development of child life programs* (2nd ed.). Rockville, MD: Author.

Child Welfare Information Gateway. (2008). *What is child abuse and neglect?* Factsheet. Retrieved February 8, 2009, from http://www.childwelfare.gov/pubs/factsheets/whatiscan.cfm.

Christian, B. J., & D'Auria, J. P. (2006). Building life skills for children with cystic fibrosis: Effectiveness of an intervention. *Nursing Research, 55*(5), 300–307.

Cleveland Clinic. (2007). *Dissociative identity disorder (multiple personality disorder).* Retrieved November 20, 2007, from http://www.clevelandclinic.org/health/health-info/docs/3700/3782.asp?index=9792

Cockerham, S. (2002). Beyond OTP: Why wilderness programs do work and are safe. *Journal of Therapeutic Wilderness Camping, 2*(2), 12–16.

CoCo-Ripp, J. A. (2005). Including people who are deaf in recreation. *Parks & Recreation, 40*(2), 26–33.

Colberg, S. R. (2000). Practical management of type 1 diabetes during exercise. *Journal of Physical Education, Recreation & Dance, 71*(2), 24–27, 35.

Coleman, D., & Iso-Ahola, S. E. (1993). Leisure and health: The role of social support and self-determination. *Journal of Leisure Research, 25*(2), 111–128.

Coleman, J. C. (1980). *The nature of adolescence.* London: Methuen.

Compton, D. M., & Iso-Ahola, S. E. (Eds.). (1994). *Leisure & mental health.* Park City, UT: Family Development Resources.

Conn, J. (2007). The 'other' category. *Modern Healthcare, 37*(15), 30–31.

Connolly, B. H. (1998). General effects of aging on persons with developmental disabilities. *Topics in Geriatric Rehabilitation, 13*(3), 1–18.

Conroy, M., Fincham, F., & Agard-Evans, C. (1988). Can they do anything? Ten single subject studies of the engagement level of hospitalized demented patients. *British Journal of Occupational Therapy, 51,* 129–132.

Cooley, W. C. (2004). Providing a primary care medical home for children and youth with cerebral palsy. *Pediatrics, 114*(4), 1106–1113.

Corcoran, K., Fischer, J., & Barlow, D. H. (1994). *Measures for clinical practice: A source book* (2nd ed.). New York: Free Press.

Corson, M. (2002). Challenge to change: The benefits of adventure therapy for youth and families. *American Journal of Recreation Therapy, 1*(1), 33–39.

Cory, L., Dattilo, J., & Williams, R. (2006). Effects of a leisure education program on social knowledge and skills of youth with cognitive disabilities. *Therapeutic Recreation Journal, 40*(3), 144–164.

Cousins, N. (1989). *Head first: The biology of hope and healing power of the human spirit.* New York: Penguin Books.

Cowden, J. E., & Eason, R. L. (1991). Legislative terminology affecting adapted physical education. *Journal of Physical Education, Recreation & Dance, 62*(6), 34.

Cox, C. L., & Dobbins, V. (1970). Before the merger: The National Association of Recreational Therapists (1953–1967). *Therapeutic Recreation Journal, 4*(1), 3–8.

Coyle, C. P., Boyd, R., Kinney, W. B., & Shank, J. W. (1998). The changing nature of therapeutic recreation: Maintaining consistency in the face of change. *Parks & Recreation, 33*(5), 56–63.

Coyle, C. P., & Kinney, W. B. (1990). A comparison of leisure and gambling motives of compulsive gamblers. *Therapeutic Recreation Journal, 24*(1), 32–39.

Coyle, C. P., Kinney, W. B., Riley, B., & Shank, J. W. (Eds.). (1991). *Benefits of therapeutic recreation: A consensus view.* Ravensdale, WA: Idyll Arbor.

Coyle, C. P., Shank, J. W., Kinney, W. B., & Hutchins, D. A. (1993). Psychosocial functioning and changes in leisure lifestyle among individuals with chronic secondary health problems related to spinal cord injury. *Therapeutic Recreation Journal, 27*(4), 239–252.

Coyne, P., & Fullerton, A. (2004). *Supporting individuals with autism spectrum disorder in recreation.* Champaign, IL: Sagamore Publishing.

Crawford, M. E. (2001). Organization and formation of the profession. In D. R. Austin and M. E. Crawford (Eds.), *Therapeutic recreation: An introduction* (3rd ed., pp. 22–44). Boston: Allyn & Bacon.

Crawford, M. E., & Mendell, R. (1987). *Therapeutic recreation and adapted physical activities for mentally retarded individuals.* Englewood Cliffs, NJ: Prentice Hall.

Crews, L. (2007). Around the bend. *American Fitness, 25*(3), 25–27.

Crisp, A. (2006). Anorexia nervosa in males: Similarities and differences to anorexia nervosa in females. *European Eating Disorders Review, 14*(3), 163–167.

Crompton, J. L. (1999). *Financing and acquiring park and recreation resources.* Champaign, IL: Human Kinetics.

Dail, P. W. (1992). Recreation as socialization for the homeless: An argument for inclusion. *Leisure Today / Journal of Physical Education, Recreation & Dance, 63*(4), 37–40.

Dailey, S. J. (2000). *Spiritual wellness: How to address the spiritual needs of people in long-term care settings.* Columbia: University of Missouri Curators.

Dansky, K. H., & Brannon, D. (1996). Using TQM to improve management of home health aides. *Journal of Nursing Administration, 26*(12), 43–49.

Darling, N., Caldwell, L. L., & Smith, R. (2005). Participation in school-based extracurricular activities and adolescent adjustment. *Journal of Leisure Research, 37*(1), 51–76.

Dattilo, J. (Ed.) (2000). *Facilitation techniques in therapeutic recreation.* State College, PA: Venture Publishing.

Dattilo, J. (2002a). *Inclusive leisure services: Responding to the rights of people with disabilities* (2nd ed.). State College, PA: Venture Publishing.

Dattilo, J. (2002b). Perceptions of a leisure education program by youth with mental retardation. *Annual in Therapeutic Recreation, 11,* 55–65.

Dattilo, J. (2008). *Leisure education program planning: A systematic approach* (3rd ed.). State College, PA: Venture Publishing.

Dattilo, J., Born, E., & Cory, L. (2000). Therapeutic use of animals. In J. Dattilo (Ed.), *Facilitation techniques in therapeutic recreation* (pp. 327–353). State College, PA: Venture Publishing.

Dattilo, J., & Guerin, N. (2001). Mental retardation. In D. R. Austin & M. E. Crawford (Eds.), *Therapeutic recreation: An introduction* (3rd ed., pp. 130–156). Boston: Allyn & Bacon.

Dattilo, J., Kleiber, D., & Williams, R. (1998). Self-determination and enjoyment enhancement: A psychologically based service delivery model for therapeutic recreation. *Therapeutic Recreation Journal, 32*(4), 258–271.

Dattilo, J., & Williams, R. (2000). Leisure education. In J. Dattilo (Ed.), *Facilitation techniques in therapeutic recreation* (pp. 165–190). State College, PA: Venture Publishing.

Dattilo, J., Williams, R., & Cory, L. (2003). Effects of computerized leisure education on knowledge of social skills of youth with intellectual disabilities. *Therapeutic Recreation Journal, 37*(2), 142–155.

Davidson, J. R. T., & Foa, E. B. (Eds.). (1993). *Post traumatic stress disorder: DSM-IV and beyond.* Washington, DC: American Psychiatric Press.

Davison, G. C., & Neale, J. M. (1990). *Abnormal psychology* (5th ed.). New York: John Wiley & Sons.

Davison, G. C., & Neale, J. M. (2001). *Abnormal psychology* (8th ed.). New York: John Wiley & Sons.

de Vries, H. A. (1987). Tension reduction with exercise. In W. P. Morgan & S. E. Goldston (Eds.), *Exercise and mental health* (pp. 99–104). Washington, DC: Hemisphere Publishing.

DeGraaf, D. (1997). Adapting equipment and activities for creative programming. In G. Hitzhusen & L. Thomas (Eds.), *Expanding horizons in therapeutic recreation* (vol. 17, pp. 183–192). Columbia: Curators of University of Missouri.

DeGraaf, D., Tilley, C., & Neal, L. (2001). *Servant leadership characteristics in organizational life.* Indianapolis, IN: The Greenleaf Center for Servant-Leadership.

Dehn, D. (1995). *Leisure step up, healthy choices.* Ravensdale, WA: Idyll Arbor.

DeMong, S. A. (1997). Provision of recreational activities in hospices in the United States. *The Hospice Journal, 12*(4), 57–67.

DeRosa, S. (2003). Communicable diseases in the recreation community. How do you include HIV-positive participants in public sports? *Parks & Recreation, 38*(1), 64–66.

DeSalvatore, G., & Roseman, D. (1986). The parent-child activity group: Using activities to work with children and their families in residential treatment. *Child Care Quarterly, 15*(4), 213–222.

DeSalvatore, H. G. (1989). Therapeutic recreators as family therapists: Working with families on a children's psychiatric unit. *Therapeutic Recreation Journal, 23*(2), 23–29.

Devine, M. A. (Ed.). (2004). *Trends in therapeutic recreation: Ideas, concepts, and applications.* Ashburn, VA: National Recreation and Park Association.

Devine, M. A. (2008). Person-first philosophy in therapeutic recreation. In T. Robertson & T. Long (Eds.), *Foundations of therapeutic recreation* (pp. 51–76). Champaign, IL: Human Kinetics.

Devine, M. A., & Dattilo, J. (2000). Expressive arts as therapeutic media. In J. Dattilo (Ed.), *Facilitation techniques in therapeutic recreation* (pp. 133–164). State College, PA: Venture Publishing.

Dickason, J. G., & London, P. H. (2001). Pediatric play. In D. R. Austin & M. E. Crawford (Eds.), *Therapeutic recreation: An introduction* (3rd ed., pp. 255–268). Boston: Allyn & Bacon.

Dieser, R. B. (2005/2006). Explaining the mosaic certification framework to an American audience. *Annual in Therapeutic Recreation, 14,* 42–55.

Dieser, R. B., & Peregoy, J. J. (1999). A multicultural critique of three therapeutic recreation service models. *Annual in Therapeutic Recreation, 8,* 56–69.

Dieser, R. B., & Ruddell, E. (2002). Effects of attribution retraining during therapeutic recreation on attributions and explanatory styles of adolescents with depression. *Therapeutic Recreation Journal, 36*(1), 35–47.

Dieser, R. B., & Voight, A. (1998). Therapeutic recreation and relapse prevention intervention, *Parks & Recreation, 33*(5), 78–83.

Disley, B. (1997). An overview of mental health in New Zealand. *Mental health in New Zealand: From a public health perspective.* Wellington, New Zealand: Ministry of Health.

DiStefano, A. F., Huebner, K. M., Garber, M., & Smith, A. J. (2006). Community services, needs, and resources in visual impairment: A 21st century public health perspective. *Journal of Visual Impairment & Blindness, 100* (Special Supplement), 793–805.

Dixon, W. A. (2000). Problem-solving appraisal and depression: Evidence for a recovery model. *Journal of Counseling & Development, 78*(1), 87–91.

Dossey, L. (1993). *Healing words: The power of prayer and the practice of medicine.* San Francisco: HarperCollins.

Drake, R. D., & Sederer, L. I. (1986). The adverse effects of intensive treatment of chronic schizophrenia. *Comprehensive Psychiatry, 27,* 313–326.

Drexler, K. (2009). Case history: Use of the Nintendo Wii™ to increase fine motor dexterity post cerebral vascular accident. *American Journal of Recreational therapy, 8*(3), 41–46.

Dubow, J. S., & Kelly, J. P. (2003). Epilepsy in sports and recreation. *Sports Medicine, 33*(7), 499–516.

Dunn, J. M., & Leitschuh, C. A. (2006). *Special physical education* (8th ed.). Dubuque, IA: Kendall/Hunt.

Durall, J. K. (1997). Encountering child abuse at camp. *Camping Magazine, 70*(6), 31–34.

Earle, R. B. (1997). Helping to prevent child abuse and future criminal consequences: Hawaii healthy start. In J. J. Sullivan & J. L. Victor (Eds.), *Criminal justice 97 / 98* (21st ed., pp. 67–75). Guilford, CT: Dushkin/McGraw-Hill.

Easterbrooks, S. R., & Scheetz, N. A. (2004). Applying critical thinking skills to character education and values clarification with students who are deaf or hard of hearing. *American Annals of the Deaf, 149*(3), 255–263.

Eckhart, A. S., & Allen, L. (1998). Benefits-based programming: Improving the health of seniors. *Parks & Recreation, 33*(7), 21–25.

Edwards, T. J., & Poff, R. A. (2008). Recreation professionals can help prevent childhood obesity. *Parks & Recreation, 43*(3), 22–26.

Egan, G. (2002). *The skilled helper: A problem-management and opportunity-development approach to helping* (7th ed.). Pacific Grove, CA: Brooks/Cole.

Ellis, A. (1984). Rational-emotive therapy. In R. J. Corsini (Ed.), *Current psychotherapies* (3rd ed.). Itasca, IL: Peacock Press.

Ellison, C. W., & Smith, J. (1991). Toward an integrative measure of health and well-being. *Journal of Psychology and Theology, 19*(1), 35–48.

Engelman, M. (2006). *Attainment's aerobics of the mind: Mental fitness programming for older adults* (Rev. ed.). Verona, WI: Attainment Company.

Esquenazi, A. (2004). Amputation and prosthetic restoration. From surgery to community reintegration. *Disability & Rehabilitation, 26* (14/15), 831–836.

Evans, C. C., Sherer, M., Nick, T. G., Nakase-Richardson, R., & Yablon, S. A. (2005). Early impaired self-awareness, depression, and subjective well-being following traumatic brain injury. *Journal of Head Trauma Rehabilitation, 20*(6), 488–500.

Everett, W. G. (1918). *Moral values: A study of the principles of conduct.* New York: Henry Holt.

Ewert, A. W. (1983). *Outdoor adventure and self-concept: A research analysis.* Eugene, OR: Center for Leisure Studies.

Ewert, A. W. (1988). Reduction of trait anxiety through participation in Outward Bound. *Leisure Studies, 10,* 107–117.

Ewert, A., Voight, A., & Harnishfeger, B. (2002). An overview of therapeutic outdoor programming. In D. R. Austin, J. Dattilo, & B. P. McCormick (Eds.), *Conceptual foundations for therapeutic recreation* (pp. 133–150). State College, PA: Venture Publishing.

Facon, B., & Darge, T. M. (1996). Evaluation of toy validation on engagement in a leisure activity of two children with profound multiple handicaps. *Psychological Reports, 79*(1), 203–210.

Fagan, P. F. (1997). Disintegration of the family is the real root cause of violent crime. In J. J. Sullivan & J. L. Victor (Eds.), *Criminal justice 97 / 98* (21st ed., pp. 28–34). Guilford, CT: Dushkin/McGraw-Hill.

Federal Interagency Forum on Aging Related Statistics. (2006). *Older Americans update 2006: Key indicators of well-being.* Washington, DC: U.S. GPO.

Feil, N. (2002). *The validation break through: Simple techniques for communicating with people with "Alzheimer's-type dementia"* (2nd ed.). Baltimore: Health Professions Press.

Fenderson, C. B. (1998). Down syndrome and aging: Implications for rehabilitation. *Topics in Geriatric Rehabilitation, 13*(4), 39–51.

Fink, P. J. (2005). Dissociative disorders. *Clinical Psychiatry News, 33*(12), 12.

Fischer, E. A., & Coddington, D. C. (1998). Integrated health care: Passing fad or lasting legacy? *Healthcare Financial Management, 52*(1), 42–48.

Fox, M. H., & Rowland, J. L. (2007). Disaster preparedness and response for persons with mobility impairments: Results from the University of Kansas nobody left behind study. *Journal of Disability Policy Studies, 17*(4), 196–205.

Frankl, V. (1963). *Man's search for meaning.* New York: Washington Square.

Frick, D. M., & Spears, L. C. (Eds.). (1996). *Robert K. Greenleaf on becoming a servant-leader.* San Francisco: Jossey-Bass.

Fristad, M., Goldberg-Arnold, J. S., & Gavazzi, S. (2002). Multifamily psychoeducation groups for families of children with bipolar disorder. *Bipolar Disorders, 4*(4), 254–262.

Frye, V. (1962). Historical sketch of recreation in the medical setting. *Recreation in Treatment Centers, 1*, 40–43.

Frye, V., & Peters, M. (1972). *Therapeutic recreation: Its theory, philosophy, and practice.* Harrisburg, PA: Stackpole Books.

Fullmer, E. M., Tobin, S. S., & Smith, G. C. (1997). The effects of offspring gender on older mothers caring for their sons and daughters with mental retardation. *The Gerontologist, 37*(6), 795–803.

Gambling with the Good Life. (2006). *Statistics.* Retrieved November 20, 2007, from http://www.gamblingwiththegoodlife.com/statistics.htm

Garcia, M., Jemal, A., Ward, E. M., Center, M. M., Hao, Y., Siegel, R. L., et al. (2007). *Global cancer facts & figures 2007.* Atlanta: American Cancer Society.

Garnick, D. W., Horgan, C. M., & Chalk, M. (2006). Performance measures for alcohol and other drug services. *Alcohol Research & Health, 29*(1), 19–26.

Garralda, M. E., & Chalder, T. (2005). Practitioner review: Chronic fatigue syndrome in childhood. *Journal of Child Psychology and Psychiatry, 46*(11), 1143–1151.

Gartner, J., Larson, D. B., & Allen, G. D. (1991). Religious commitment and mental health: A review of the empirical literature. *Journal of Psychology and Theology, 19*(1), 6–25.

Gass, M. A. (1993). *Adventure therapy: Therapeutic applications of adventure programming.* Dubuque, IA: Kendall/Hunt.

Gay Men's Health Crisis (GMHC). (2007). Women's Institute. Retrieved July 15, 2008, from http://www.gmhc.org/programs/womens_institute.html.

Germ, P. A., & Schleien, S. J. (1997). Inclusive community leisure services: Responsibilities of key players. *Therapeutic Recreation Journal, 31*(1), 22–37.

Getz, D. A., & Austin, D. R. (2001). Key competencies in multicultural education for entry-level therapeutic recreation professionals. *Annual in Therapeutic Recreation, 10*, 23–31.

Getz, D., Hironaka-Juteau, J., & Melcher, S. (2005). *Diversity: Case studies in healthcare.* Alexandria, VA: American Therapeutic Recreation Association.

Gevirtz, C. (2006). Managing postpolio syndrome pain. *Nursing, 36*(12), 17.

Gist, J., Figueiredo, C., & Ng-Baumhackl, M. (2001). *Beyond 50: A report to the nation on economic security.* Washington, DC: American Association of Retired Persons.

Glanzman, M. M., & Blum, N. J. (2007). Attention deficits and hyperactivity. In M. D. Batshaw, L. Pellogrino, & N. J. Roizen (Eds.), *Children with disabilities* (6th ed., pp. 345–365). Baltimore, MD: Paul H. Brookes.

Glass, J. S., & Myers, J. E. (2001). Combining the old and the new to help adolescents: Individual psychology and adventure-based counseling. *Journal of Mental Health Counseling, 23*(2), 104–114.

Godbey, G., (2005). Providing more for older adults. *Parks & Recreation, 40*(10), 76–81.

Godbey, G., Burnett-Wolle, S., & Chow, H-W. (2007). New ideas for promoting physical activity among middle age and older adults. *Journal of Physical Education, Recreation, and Dance, 78*(7), 22–26.

Gold-Steinberg, S., & Logan, D. (1999). Integrating play therapy in the treatment of children with obsessive-compulsive disorder. *American Journal of Orthopsychiatry, 69,* 495–503.

Goode, W. J. (1957). Community within a community: The professions. *American Sociological Review, 22* (7), 194–200. In R. P. Reynolds and G. S. O'Morrow (Eds.), *Problems, issues & concepts in therapeutic recreation.* Englewood Cliffs, NJ: Prentice Hall, 1985.

Goodman, G., & Williams, C. M. (2007). Interventions for increasing the academic engagement of students with autism spectrum disorders in inclusive classrooms. *Teaching Exceptional Children, 39*(6), 53–61.

Goodwin, R. D., & Pine, D. (2002). Respiratory disease and panic attacks among adults in the United States. *Chest, 122,* 645–650.

Gordon, R. (2005). The developmentally disabled are aging too. Retrieved March 2, 2009, from http://www.nsnn.com/developmentally_disabled_are_agi.htm.

Gorina Y., Hoyert, D., Lentzner, H., & Goulding, M. (2005, October). Trends in causes of death among older persons in the United States. *Aging Trends, 6.* Hyattsville, MD: National Center for Health Statistics.

Gostin, L. O. (2004). *The AIDS pandemic: Complacency, injustice, unfilled expectations.* Raleigh: The North Carolina Press.

Gray, D., & Greben, S. (1974). Future perspectives in recreation. *Parks and Recreation, 9*(7), 26–35.

Greenleaf, R. K. (1977). *Servant leadership: A journey into the nature of legitimate power and greatness.* New York: Paulist Press.

Griest, J. H. (1987). Exercise intervention with depressed outpatients. In W. P. Morgan & S. E. Goldston (Eds.), *Exercise and mental health* (pp. 117–121). Washington, DC: Hemisphere Publishing.

Griffin, J. (2005). Recreation therapy for adult survivors of childhood abuse: Challenges to professional perspectives and the evolution of a leisure education group. *Therapeutic Recreation Journal, 39*(3), 207–228.

Grimaldi, P. L. (1998). Risk adjustment for health status. *Nursing Management, 29*(3), 18, 20–21.

Groff, D., & Dattilo, J. (2000). Adventure therapy. In J. Dattilo (Ed.), *Facilitation techniques in therapeutic recreation* (pp. 13–39). State College, PA: Venture Publishing.

Grossman, A. H. (1997). Concern, compassion, and community: Facing the daunting worldwide challenges of HIV/AIDS. *Therapeutic Recreation Journal, 31*(2), 121–129.

Grossman, A. H., & Caroleo, O. (2001). HIV disease. In D. R. Austin & M. E. Crawford (Eds.), *Therapeutic recreation: An introduction* (3rd ed., pp. 297–317). Boston: Allyn and Bacon.

Grote, K. A., & Hasel, M. A. (1998). *Guidelines for internships in therapeutic recreation.* Hattiesburg, MS: American Therapeutic Recreation Association.

Grote, K. A., Hasel, M. A., Krider, R., & Mortensen, D. M. (1995). *Behavioral health protocols for recreational therapy.* Ravensdale, WA: Idyll Arbor.

Gulick, E. E. (1997). Correlates of quality of life among persons with multiple sclerosis. *Nursing Research, 46*(6), 305–311.

Gunn, S. L., & Peterson, C. A. (1978). *Therapeutic recreation program design: Principles and procedures.* Englewood Cliffs, NJ: Prentice-Hall.

Hain, N., Dattilo, J., & Loy, D. (2000). Therapeutic use of play. In J. Dattilo (Ed.), *Facilitation techniques in therapeutic recreation* (pp. 409–437). State College, PA: Venture Publishing.

Hansel, N. N., Wu, A. W., Chang, B., & Diette, G. B. (2004). Quality of life in tuberculosis: Patient and provider perspectives. *Quality of Life Research, 13*(3), 639–652.

Hare, R. D., Harpur, T. J., Hakstian, A. R., Forth, A. E., Hart, S. D., & Newman, J. P. (1990). The revised psychopathy checklist: Reliability and factor structure. *Psychological Assessment, 2*(3), 338–341.

Harrington, M., & Dawson, D. (1997). Recreation as empowerment for homeless people living in shelters. *Journal of Leisurability, 24*(1), 17–29.

Hart, K. (1984). Values programming in family recreation. *Journal of Health, Physical Education, Recreation & Dance, 55,* 8–10.

Hart, R., Mather, P. L., Slack, J. F., & Powell, M. A. (1992). *Therapeutic play activities for hospitalized children.* St. Louis, MO: Mosby/Year Book.

Harvard Medical School. (2001). *Alcohol use and abuse.* Boston: Harvard Health Publications.

Haun, P. (1965). Prescribed recreation. *Recreation in Treatment Centers, 4,* 25–27.

Hawkins, B. A. (1997). Health, fitness, and quality of life for older adults with developmental disabilities. *Activities, Adaptation & Aging, 21*(3), 29–35.

Hawkins, B. A. (2001). Autism. In D. R. Austin & M. E. Crawford (Eds.), *Therapeutic recreation: An introduction* (3rd ed., pp. 113–129). Boston: Allyn & Bacon.

Hawkins, B. A., May, M. E., & Rogers, N. B. (1996). *Therapeutic activity intervention with the elderly: Foundations & practices.* State College, PA: Venture Publishing.

Hawkins, J. D. (1997). Controlling crime before it happens: Risk-focused prevention. In J. J. Sullivan & J. L. Victor (Eds.), *Criminal justice 97/98* (21st ed., pp. 167–172). Guilford, CT: Dushkin/McGraw-Hill.

Haworth, N. A., & MacDonald, E. M. (1946). *Theory of occupational therapy.* Baltimore: Williams & Wilkins.

Heintzman, P. (1997). Putting some spirit into recreation services for people with disabilities. *Journal of Leisurability, 24*(2), 22–30.

Heintzman, P. (1999). Spiritual wellness: Theoretical links and leisure. *Journal of Leisurability, 26*(2), 21–32.

Henggeler, S. W., Schoenwald, S. D., Borduin, C. M., Rowland, M. D., & Cunningham, P. B. (1998). *Multisystematic treatment of antisocial behavior in children and adolescents.* New York: Guilford.

Henniger, M. L. (1995). Play: Antidote for childhood stress. *Early Child Development and Care, 105,* 7–12.

Herson, J. (2007). The coming osteoporosis epidemic. *Futurist, 41*(2), 31–35.

Hill, C. S., Cleeland, C. S., & Gutstein, H. B. (2001). Effective pain treatment in cancer patients. In R. E. Lenhard, Jr., R. T. Osteen, & T. Gansler (Eds.), *The American Cancer Society's clinical oncology* (pp. 765–810). Atlanta: American Cancer Society.

Hillman, W. A. (1970). Therapeutic recreation as a profession: A status report. *Therapeutic Recreation Annual, 7,* 1–4.

Himes, C. L. (2008). Elderly Americans. In H. Cox (Ed.), *Aging 07/08* (20th ed., pp. 2–6). Dubuque, IA: McGraw-Hill.

Hitt, D., Kitchner, N. J., & Bisson, J. I. (2004). *Mental health practice: Developments in treating post traumatic stress disorder using a cognitive-behavioral therapy model.* London: Royal College of Nursing.

Ho, B. C., Black, D. W., & Andreasen, N. C. (2003). Schizophrenia and other psychotic disorders. In R. E. Hales & S. C. Yudofsky (Eds.), *The American psychiatric publishing textbook of clinical psychiatry* (4th ed., pp. 379–438). Washington, DC: American Psychiatric Publishing.

Hodge, D. R. (2005). Spiritual assessment in marital and family therapy: A methodological framework for selecting from among six qualitative assessment tools. *Journal of Marital and Family Therapy, 31*(4), 341–356.

Hodges, S. (2003). Borderline personality disorder and posttraumatic stress disorder: Time for integration? *Journal of Counseling & Development, 81*(4), 409–417.

Hood, C. D., & Carruthers, C. P. (2002). Coping skills therapy as an underlying framework for therapeutic recreation services. *Therapeutic Recreation Journal, 36*(2), 137–153.

Hood, C., & Carruthers, C. (2007). Enhancing leisure experience and developing resources: The leisure and well-being model, part II. *Therapeutic Recreation Journal, 41*(4), 298–325.

Howard, D., Browning, C., & Lee, Y. (2007). The International Classification of Functioning, Disability, and Health: Therapeutic recreation code sets and salient diagnostic core sets. *Therapeutic Recreation Journal, 41*(1), 61–81.

Howard, D., Russoniello, C., & Rogers, D. (2004). *Healthy People 2010* and therapeutic recreation: Professional opportunities to promote public health. *Therapeutic Recreation Journal, 38*(2), 116–132.

Hubbard, P. A., Broome, M. E., & Antia, L. A. (2005). Pain, coping, and disability in adolescents and young adults with cystic fibrosis: A web-based study. *Pediatric Nursing, 31*(2), 82–86.

Hunt, M. (2007). Borderline personality disorder across the lifespan [Electronic version]. *Journal of Women and Aging, 19*(1–2), 173–191.

Hunter, D. J. (1996). The changing roles of health care personnel in health and health care management. *Social Science and Medicine, 43*(5), 799–808.

Huovinen, E., Kaprio, J., & Koskenvuo, M. (2003). Factors associated to lifestyle and risk of adult onset asthma. *Respiratory Medicine, 97*(3), 273–280.

Hutchins, D. A. (2005/2006). Competencies required for effective clinical supervision during the therapeutic recreation internship. *Annual in Therapeutic Recreation, 14*, 114–130.

Hutchinson, P., & Lord, J. (1979). *Recreation integration: Issues and alternatives in leisure services and community involvement.* Ottawa, Ontario: Leisurability Publications.

Hutchinson, S. L., LeBlanc, A., & Booth, R. (2002). "Perpetual problem-solving": An ethnographic study of clinical reasoning in a therapeutic recreation setting. *Therapeutic Recreation Journal, 36*(1), 18–34.

Insalaco, D., Ozkurt, E., & Santiago, D. (2007). The perceptions of students in the allied health professions towards stroke rehabilitation teams and the SLP's role. *Journal of Communication Disorders, 40*(3), 196–214.

Ipson, N., Mahoney, E. M., & Adams, J. H. (2005). Public relations, marketing, and customer service. In B. van der Smissen, M. Moiseichik, & V. J. Hartenburg (Eds.), *Management of park and recreation agencies* (2nd ed., pp. 341–398). Ashburn, VA: National Recreation and Park Association.

Iso-Ahola, S. E. (1980). *The social psychology of recreation and leisure.* Dubuque, IA: Wm. C. Brown.

Iso-Ahola, S. E., & Weissinger, E. (1984). Leisure and well-being: Is there a connection? *Parks and Recreation, 18*(6), 40–44.

Jahoda, M. (1958). *Current concepts of positive mental health.* New York: Basic Books.

Jakobsson, U., & Hallberg, I. R. (2002). Pain and quality of life among older people with rheumatoid arthritis and/or osteoarthritis: A literature review. *Journal of Clinical Nursing, 11*(4), 430–443.

James, A. (1998). The conceptual development of recreational therapy. In F. Brasile, T. K. Skalko, and j. burlingame (Eds.), *Perspectives in recreational therapy: Issues of a dynamic profession* (pp. 7–38). Ravensdale, WA: Idyll Arbor.

James, D. J., & Glaze, L. E. (2006). *Bureau of Justice Statistics special report: Mental health problems of prison and jail inmates.* Washington, DC: U.S. Department of Justice.

James, M. R., & Crawford, M. E. (2001). Convulsive disorders. In D. R. Austin & M. E. Crawford (Eds.), *Therapeutic recreation: An introduction* (3rd ed., pp. 280–296). Boston: Allyn and Bacon.

James, S. R., & Ashwill, J. W. (2007). *Nursing care of children: Principles & practices* (3rd ed.). St. Louis, MO: Saunders Elsevier.

Janke, M., Davey, A., & Kleiber, D. (2006). Modeling change in older adults' leisure activities. *Leisure Sciences, 28*(3), 285–303.

Jansma, P., & French, R. (1994). *Special physical education: Physical activity, sports, and recreation* (2nd ed.). Englewood Cliffs, NJ: Prentice Hall.

Janssen, M. (2004). The effects of leisure education on quality of life in older adults. *Therapeutic Recreation Journal, 38*(3), 275–288.

Jencks, C. (1994). *The homeless.* Cambridge, MA: Harvard University Press.

Jennings, B. (2006). The ordeal of reminding traumatic brain injury and the goals of care. *Hastings Center Report, 36*(2), 29–37.

Jessee, P. O. (1992). Nurses, children, and play. *Issues in Comprehensive Pediatric Nursing, 15*(4), 261–269.

Jewell, D. L. (1999). *Confronting child maltreatment through recreation* (2nd ed.). Springfield, IL: Charles C. Thomas.

Jimenez, C. C., Corcoran, M. H., Crawley, J. T., Hornsby, G., Peer, K. S., & Philbin, R. D., et al. (2007). National Athletic Trainers Association position statement: Management of the athlete with Type I diabetes mellitus. *Journal of Athletic Training, 42*(4), 536–545.

Johnson, D., & Ashton-Shaeffer, C. (2003). Virtual buddies: Using computer-mediated communication in therapeutic recreation. *Parks & Recreation, 38*(3), 76–79.

Johnson, J. (1995). Learning disabilities: The impact on social competencies of adults. *Journal of Leisurability, 22*(3), 4–13.

Johnson, K. A., Bland, M. K., & Rathsam, S. M. (2002). Taking root: The development of a hospital garden. *Parks & Recreation, 37*(1), 60–64.

Joint Commission on Accreditation of Healthcare Organizations. (2005). *Comprehensive accreditation manual for hospitals: The official handbook.* Oakbrook Terrace, IL: Joint Commission Resources.

Jones, C. D., Lowe, L. A., & Risler, E. A. (2004). The effectiveness of wilderness adventure therapy programs for young people involved in the juvenile justice system. *Residential Treatment for Children and Youth, 22*(2), 53–62.

Jones, D. B., & Anderson, L. S. (2004). The status of clinical supervision in therapeutic recreation: A national study. *Therapeutic Recreation Journal, 38*(4), 329–347.

Jordan, D. J., DeGraaf, D. G., & DeGraaf, K. H. (2005). *Programming for parks, recreation, and leisure services: A servant leadership approach* (2nd ed.). State College, PA: Venture Publishing.

Kagan, R. J. (2000). Evaluation and treatment of thermal injuries. *Dermatology Nursing, 12*(5), 334–350.

Kaiser, R., & Robinson, K. (2005). Risk management. In B. van der Smissen, M. Moiseichik, & V. J. Hartenburg (Eds.), *Management of park and recreation agencies* (2nd ed., pp. 593–616). Ashburn, VA: National Recreation and Park Association.

Kamphaus, R. W., & Frick, P. J. (1996). *Clinical assessment of child and adolescent personality and behavior.* Boston: Allyn and Bacon.

Kaptian, J. (2003). Blazing new trails: Adventure therapy for adolescents with eating disorders. *American Journal of Recreation Therapy, 2*(3), 41–48.

Karande, S. (2006). Autism: A review for family physicians. *Indian Journal of Medical Sciences, 60*(5), 205–215.

Kaslow, N. J., & Thompson, M. P. (1998). Applying the criteria for empirically supported treatments to studies of psychosocial interventions for child and adolescent depression. *Journal of Clinical Child Psychology, 27,* 146–155.

Katzenmeyer, C. (1997). Active options for seniors. *Parks & Recreation, 32*(10), 62–65.

Kaur, H., Hyder, M. L., & Poston, W. S. C. (2003). Childhood overweight—an expanding problem. *Treatments in Endocrinology, 2*(6), 375–388.

Keogh-Hoss, M. A., Powell, L., & Sable, J. (2006). Health care trends: Implications for therapeutic recreation. In M. J. Carter & J. E. Folkerth (Eds.), *Therapeutic recreation education: Challenges and changes* (pp. 107–128). Ashburn, VA: National Recreation and Park Association.

King, S. J., Yang, H., & Malkin, M. J. (2006). Perceived biopsychosocial benefits and leisure satisfaction from participation in an Arthritis Foundation Aquatic Program. *American Journal of Recreation Therapy, 5*(1), 40–48.

Kingma, M. (1998). Marketing and nursing in a competitive environment. *International Nursing Review, 45*(2), 45–50.

Kinnaman, K. (2007). Patient safety and quality improvement act of 2005. *Orthopaedic Nursing, 26*(1), 14–16.

Kinney, J. S., & Kinney, W. B. (2001). Psychiatry and mental health. In D. R. Austin & M. E. Crawford (Eds.), *Therapeutic recreation: An introduction* (3rd ed., pp. 57–76). Boston: Allyn & Bacon.

Kinney, J. S., Kinney, T., & Witman, J. (2004). Therapeutic recreation modalities and facilitation techniques: A national study. *Annual in Therapeutic Recreation, 13*, 59–79.

Kinney, J. S., Warren, L., Kinney, T., & Witman, J. (1999). Use of therapeutic modalities and facilitation techniques by therapeutic recreation specialists in the Northeastern United States. *Annual in therapeutic recreation, 8*, 1–11.

Kinney, T., & Witman, J. (Eds.). (1997). *Guidelines for competency assessment and curriculum planning in therapeutic recreation: A tool for self-evaluation.* Hattiesburg, MS: American Therapeutic Recreation Association.

Kinsella, K., & Phillips, D. R. (2007a). Successful aging. In H. Cox (Ed.), *Aging 06/07* (19th ed., pp. 40–41). Dubuque, IA: McGraw Hill Contemporary Learning Series.

Kinsella, K., & Phillips, D. R. (2007b). Work, retirement, and well-being. In H. Cox (Ed.), *Aging 06/07* (19th ed., pp. 118–120). Dubuque, IA: McGraw Hill Contemporary Learning Series.

Klerman, G. L. (1988). Depression and related disorders of mood (affective disorders). In A. M. Nicholi, Jr. (Ed.), *The new Harvard guide to psychiatry* (pp. 309–336). Cambridge, MA: Belknap Press.

Klitzing, S. W. (1993). Homelessness: The tragedy continues. In G. L. Hitzhusen & L. T. Jackson, (Eds.), *Expanding horizons in therapeutic recreation* (vol. 15, pp. 168–181). Columbia: Curators of the University of Missouri.

Klitzing, S. W. (2004). Women living in a homeless shelter: Stress, coping and leisure. *Journal of Leisure Research, 36*(4), 483–512.

Klitzing, S. W., & Wachter, C. J. (2005). Benchmarks for the delivery of inclusive community recreation services for people with disabilities. *Therapeutic Recreation Journal, 39*(1), 63–77.

Klomek, A. B., Marrocco, F., Kleinman, M., Schonfeld, I. S., & Gould, M. S. (2007). Bullying, depression, and suicidality in adolescents [Electronic version]. *Journal of the American Academy of Child & Adolescent Psychiatry, 46*(1), 40–49.

Kloseck, M., Crilly, R. G., & Hutchinson-Troyer, L. (2001). Measuring therapeutic recreation: Further testing of the Leisure Competence Measure. *Therapeutic Recreation Journal, 35*(1), 31–42.

Knapp, R. F., & Hartsoe, C. E. (1979). *Play for America: The National Recreation Association 1906–1965.* Arlington, VA: National Park and Recreation Association.

Knight, C. (2006). Groups for individuals with traumatic histories: Practice considerations for social workers. *Social Work, 51*(1), 20–30.

Koch, W. (2007, February 28). HUD gets new view of who's homeless: Study a "huge leap" in understanding problem, chief says. *USA Today,* p. A1.

Kraus, R. (1983). *Therapeutic recreation service: Principles and practices* (3rd ed.). Philadelphia: W. B. Saunders.

Krigger, K. W. (2006). Cerebral palsy: An overview. *American Family Physician, 73*(1), 91–100.

Krug, E. G., Dahlberg, L. L., & Mercy, J. A. (2002). *World report on violence and health.* Geneva, Switzerland: World Health Organization.

Kunstler, R. (1993). Serving the homeless through recreation programs. *Parks & Recreation, 28*(8), 16–22, 73.

Kunstler, R. (2001). Substance abuse. In D. R. Austin & M. E. Crawford (Eds.), *Therapeutic recreation: An introduction* (3rd ed., pp. 94–112). Boston: Allyn & Bacon.

Kunstler, R., Greenblatt, F., & Moreno, N. (2004). Aromatherapy and hand massage: Therapeutic recreation interventions for pain management. *Therapeutic Recreation Journal, 38*(2), 133–147.

Kurt, O., & Tekin-Iftar, E. (2008). A comparison of constant time delay and simultaneous prompting with embedded instruction on teaching leisure skills to children with autism. *Topics in Early Childhood Special Education, 28*(1), 53–64.

Kurylo, M. F., Elliott, T. R., & Shewchuk, R. M. (2001). FOCUS on the family caregiver: A problem-solving training intervention. *Journal of Counseling & Development, 79*(3), 275–281.

Lancioni, G. E., Singh, N. N., O'Reilly, M. F., LaMartire, M. L., Stasolla, F., Smaldone, A., & Oliva, D. (2006). Microswitch-based programs as therapeutic recreation interventions for students with profound multiple disabilities. *American Journal of Recreation Therapy, 5*(2), 15–20.

Lancioni, G. E., Singh, N. N., O'Reilly, M. F., Oliva, D., & Basili, G. (2005). An overview of research on increasing indices of happiness of people with severe/profound intellectual and multiple disabilities. *Disability and Rehabilitation, 27*(3), 83–93.

Langelaan, M., deBoer, M. R., vanNispen, R. M. A., Wouters, B., Moll, A. C., & vanRens, G. H. (2007). Impact of visual impairment on quality of life: A comparison with quality of life in the general population and with other chronic conditions. *Ophthalmic Epidemiology, 14*(3), 119–126.

Langlois, J. A., Rutland-Brown, W., & Wald, M. M. (2006). The epidemiology and impact of traumatic brain injury. *Journal of Head Trauma Rehabilitation, 21*(5), 375–378.

Latimer, A. E., Martin Ginis, K. A., & Hicks, A. L. (2005). Buffering the effects of stress on well-being among individuals with spinal cord injury: A potential role for exercise. *Therapeutic Recreation Journal, 39*(2), 131–138.

Lawson, L. M., Coyle, C. P., & Ashton-Shaeffer, C. (2001). *Therapeutic recreation in special education: An idea for the future.* Alexandria, VA: American Therapeutic Recreation Association.

Leavitt, P. (2007, June 28). U.S. prison population grew 2.8% last year. *USA Today*, p. 9A.

LeConey, S., Devine, M. A., Bunker, H., & Montgomery, S. (2000). Utilizing the therapeutic recreation process in community settings: The case of Sue. *Parks & Recreation, 35*(5), 70–77.

Lee, B., Godbey, G., & Sawyer, S. (2003). Research update: SeniorNet, v. 2.0. *Parks & Recreation, 38*(10), 22–27.

Lee, H. L., Tan, H. K., Ma, H. I., Tsai, C. Y., & Liu, Y. K. (2006). Effectiveness of a work-related stress management program in patients with chronic schizophrenia. *The American Journal of Occupational Therapy, 60*(4), 435–441.

Lee, S. H., Ahn, S. C., Lee, Y. J., Choi, T. K., Yook, K. H., & Suh, S. Y. (2007). Effectiveness of meditation-based stress management program as an adjunct to pharmacotherapy in patients with anxiety disorder. *Journal of Psychosomatic Research, 62*(2), 189–195.

Lee, Y., & McCormick, B. (2002). Toward evidence-based therapeutic recreation practice. In D. R. Austin, J. Dattilo, & B. P. McCormick (Eds.), *Conceptual foundations for therapeutic recreation* (pp. 165–183). State College, PA: Venture Publishing.

Lee, Y., & McCormick, B. (2004). Subjective well-being of people with spinal cord injury: Does leisure contribute? *Journal of Rehabilitation, 70*(3), 5–12.

Lee, Y., McCormick, B., & Perkins, S. (2000). Are you an outcome engineer? Therapeutic recreation practice in the third millennium. *Parks & Recreation, 35*(5), 64–68.

Lee, Y., & Skalko, T. K. (1996). Multicultural sensitivity: An innovative mind-set in therapeutic recreation practice. *Parks & Recreation, 31*(5), 50–53.

Leeth, L. (2004). Are you fiscally fit? *Nursing Management, 35*(4), 42–47.

Lehmann, C. (2003). Combined therapies produce better bipolar outcomes. *Psychiatric News, 38*(6), 36. Retrieved March 31, 2007, from http://pn.psychiatryonline.org/cgi/content/full/38/6/36

Lenhard, R. E. Jr., & Osteen, R. T. (2001). General approach to cancer patients. In R. E. Lenhard, Jr., R. T. Osteen, & T. Gansler (Eds.), *The American Cancer Society's clinical oncology* (pp. 149–229). Atlanta: American Cancer Society.

Levine, G. R. (2001). Neuromuscular disorders. In D. R. Austin & M. E. Crawford (Eds.), *Therapeutic recreation: An introduction* (3rd ed., pp. 190–219). Boston: Allyn and Bacon.

Levinson, D. J. (1978). *The seasons of a man's life*. New York: Knopf.

Levy-Dweck, S. (2005). HIV/AIDS fifty and older: A hidden and growing population. *Journal of Gerontological Social Work, 46*(2), 37–50.

Lewis, J. A. (2006). Recreational therapy intervention following stroke: Community reintegration. *American Journal of Recreation Therapy, 5*(3), 26–30.

Li, R. K. K. (1981). Activity therapy and leisure counseling for the schizophrenic population. *Therapeutic Recreation Journal, 15*(4), 44–49.

Lieberman, L. J., & MacVicar, J. M. (2003). Play and recreational habits of youths who are deaf-blind. *Journal of Visual Impairment & Blindness, 97*(12), 755–768.

Limburg, C. E. (2007). Screening, prevention, detection and treatment of cancer-therapy-induced bone loss in patients with breast cancer. *Oncology Nursing Forum, 34*(1), 55–61.

Lingnell, L., & Dunn, L. (1999). Group play wholeness and healing for the hospitalized child. In D. S. Sweeney & L. E. Homeyer (Eds.), *The handbook of group play therapy: How to do it, how it works, whom it's best for* (pp. 359–374). San Francisco: Jossey-Bass.

Litner, B., & Ostiguy, L. (2000). Understanding attention deficit hyperactivity disorder: Strategies and consideration for inclusion of youth in leisure services. *Journal of Leisurability, 27*(2), 11–18.

Lloyd, L. F., Malkin, M. J., & Poppen, R. (1997). Development of a leisure planning training package for persons with traumatic brain injury. In G. L. Hitzhusen & L. Thomas (Eds.), *Expanding horizons in therapeutic recreation* (vol. 17, pp. 167–182). Columbia: Curators of University of Missouri.

Lochner, C., Mogotsi, M., du Toit, P., Kaminer, D., Niehaus, D., & Stein, D. (2003). Quality of life in anxiety disorders: A comparison of obsessive-compulsive disorder, social anxiety disorder, and panic disorder. *Psychopathology, 36*(5), 255–262.

Lofthouse, N., Fristad, M., & Splaingard, M. (2007). Parent and child reports of sleep problems associated with early-onset bipolar spectrum disorders [Electronic version]. *Journal of Family Psychology, 21*(1), 114–123.

Long, T. (2008). Therapeutic recreation and mental health. In T. Robertson & T. Long (Eds.), *Foundations of therapeutic recreation* (pp. 145–163). Champaign, IL: Human Kinetics.

Long-term risks of tardive dyskinesia. (1993). *The Menninger Letter, 1*(12), 6.

Lonn, E., & Grewal, J. (2006). Drug therapies in the secondary prevention of cardiovascular diseases: Successes, shortcomings and future directions. *Current Vascular Pharmacology, 4*(3), 253–268.

Lord, M. A. (1997). Leisure's role in enhancing social competencies of individuals with developmental disabilities. *Parks & Recreation, 32*(4), 35–36, 38–40.

Louv, R. (2005). *Last child in the woods: Saving our children from nature-deficit disorder*. Chapel Hill, NC: Algonquin Books of Chapel Hill.

Lynch, C. J. (2006). Exercise: A treatment intervention for dysthymia in the geriatric population. *American Journal of Recreation Therapy, 5*(2), 27–36.

Mackenzie, D. (2006). Stem cells reverse muscular dystrophy. *New Scientist, 192*(2578), 12.

MacLean, J. R. (1963). Therapeutic recreation curriculums. *Recreation in Treatment Centers, 2*, 23–29.

MacNeil, R. D. (1998). Leisure, lifelong learning, and older adults: A conceptual overview. *Leisure Today/Journal of Physical Education, Recreation & Dance 69*(2), 26–28.

Malkin, M. J., Coyle, C. P., & Carruthers, C. (1998). Efficacy research in recreational therapy. In F. Brasile, T. K. Skalko, & j. burlingame (Eds.), *Perspectives in recreational therapy: Issues of a dynamic profession* (pp. 141–164). Ravensdale, WA: Idyll Arbor.

Malkin, M. J., & Howe, C. Z. (Eds.). (1993). *Research in therapeutic recreation: Concepts and methods.* State College, PA: Venture Publishing.

Malkin, M. J., Phillips, R. W., & Chumbler, J. A. (1991). The family lab: An interdisciplinary family leisure education program. *Annual in Therapeutic Recreation, 2,* 25–36.

Malkin, M. J., Voss, M. C., Teaff, J. D., & Benshoff, J. J. (1993/94). Activity & recreational therapy services in substance abuse treatment programs. *Annual in Therapeutic Recreation, 4,* 40–50.

Malley S., & Dattilo, J. (2000). Stress management. In J. Dattilo (Ed.), *Facilitation techniques in therapeutic recreation* (pp. 215–244). State College, PA: Venture Publishing.

Manning, A. (2007, November 12). Diabetes "revolution" is cutting both ways. *USA Today,* 1a-2a.

Martin, D. G. (2010). *Counseling and therapy skills* (3rd ed.). Long Grove, IL: Waveland Press.

Martin, D., & Wilhite, B. (2003). Understanding meaning: A writing intervention to explore the personal relevance of recreation and leisure participation. *American Journal of Recreation Therapy, 2*(1), 49–55.

Martinsen, E. (2005). Exercise and depression [Electronic version]. *International Journal of Sport and Exercise Psychology, 3*(4), 469–483.

Maslow, A. H. (1968). *Toward a psychology of being.* New York: Van Nostrand-Reinhold.

Mathieu, M. A. (1999). The Surgeon General's report and leisure services for older adults. *Journal of Physical Education, Recreation & Dance, 70*(3), 28–31.

Mayo Foundation for Medical Education and Research. (2007). *Antisocial personality disorder.* Retrieved August 2, 2007, from http://mayoclinic.com/print/antisocial-personality-disorder/DS00829

McArdle, P. (May, 2007). Comments on NICE guidelines for "depression in children and young people." *Child and Adolescent Mental Health, 12*(2), 66–69.

McAuliffe-Fogarty, A. H., Ramsing, R., & Hill, E. (2007). Medical specialty camps for youth with diabetes. *Child and Adolescent Psychiatric Clinics of North America, 16,* 887–908.

McAvoy, L., Smith, J. G., & Rynders, J. E. (2006). Outdoor adventure programming for individuals with cognitive disabilities who present serious accommodation challenges. *Therapeutic Recreation Journal, 40*(3), 182–199.

McConnell, S., Jacka, F. N., Williams, L. J., Dodd, S., & Berk, M. (2005). The relationship between depression and cardiovascular disease. *International Journal of Psychiatry in Clinical Practice, 9*(3), 157–167.

McCormick, B. P. (2002). Healthcare in America: An overview. In D. R. Austin, J. Dattilo, & B. P. McCormick (Eds.), *Conceptual foundations for therapeutic recreation* (pp. 185–206). State College, PA: Venture Publishing.

McCormick, B. P., & Darnsteadt, J. (1999). Quality and performance improvement: Implications for therapeutic recreation. *Annual in therapeutic recreation, 8,* 70–80.

McCormick, B. P., & Funderburk, J. (2000). Therapeutic recreation outcomes in mental health practice. *Annual in Therapeutic Recreation, 9,* 9–19.

McCready, K. (1997). At-risk youth and leisure: An ecological perspective. *Journal of Leisurability, 24*(2), 31–36.

McFarlane, N. (2007, November/December). Managing MS-related fatigue. *American Therapeutic Recreation Association Newsletter, 23*(6), 12–13.

McFarlane, N., Hoss, M. A. K., Jacobson, J. M., & James, A. (1998). *Finding the path: Ethics in action.* Hattiesburg, MS: American Therapeutic Recreation Association.

McGuire, F. A., Boyd, R. K., & Tedrick, R. E. (1999). *Leisure and aging: Ulyssean living in later life* (2nd ed.). Champaign, IL: Sagamore.

McGuire, F. A., & Hawkins, M. O. (1998). Introduction to intergenerational programs. *Activities, Adaptation & Aging, 23*(1), 1–9.

McKenney, A. (2002). Moving beyond values clarification: A cognitive-developmental approach to challenging the free-time choices of children and youth with emotional and behavioral disorders. *Annual in Therapeutic Recreation, 11,* 67–76.

McKenney, A., Dattilo, J., Cory, L., & Williams, R. (2004). Effects of computerized therapeutic recreation program on knowledge of social skills of male youth with emotional and behavioral disorders. *Annual in Therapeutic Recreation, 13,* 12–23.

McKnight, B., McDaniel, S., & Ehmann, V. (2006). Staffing and scheduling try point incentives for employee reward and recognition. *Nursing Management, 37*(12), 42–45.

Meister, T., & Pedlar, A. (1992). Leisure patterns and needs of adult survivors of childhood sexual abuse. *Leisure Today/Journal of Physical Education, Recreation & Dance, 63*(4), 52–55.

Melcher, S. (1999). *Introduction to writing goals and objectives: A manual for recreation therapy students and entry-level professionals.* State College, PA: Venture Publishing.

Menninger, W. C. (1948). Recreation and mental health. *Recreation, 41*(9), 17.

Merskey, H., and Bogduk, N. (Eds.). (1994). *Classification of chronic pain* (2nd ed.). Seattle: IASP Press, 209–214.

Metitieri, T., Zanetti, O., Geroldi, C., Frisoni, G. B., deLeo, D., Dello Buono, M., et al. (2001). Reality orientation therapy to delay outcomes of progression in patients with dementia: A retrospective study. *Clinical Rehabilitation, 15*(5), 471–478.

Meyer, L. E. (1977). A view of therapeutic recreation: Its foundation, objectives and challenges. In G. C. Zaso (Ed.), *Therapeutic recreation dialogues in development: Concepts and action.* Durham: University of New Hampshire, School of Health Studies, Recreation, and Dance and Parks Program.

Meyer, L. E. (1980a). Philosophy and curriculum. In D. R. Austin (Ed.), *Directions in health, physical education, and recreation. Therapeutic recreation curriculum: Philosophy, strategy, and concepts* (Monograph No. 1, pp. 9–12). Bloomington: Indiana University School of Health, Physical Education, and Recreation.

Meyer, L. E. (1980b). Philosophical alternatives and the professionalization of therapeutic recreation (NTRS Report of Philosophical Statement Task Force, May 1980). Arlington, VA: National Recreation and Park Association.

Miller, D., & Jake, L. (2001). *Eating disorders: Providing effective recreational therapy interventions.* Ravensdale, WA: Idyll Arbor.

Miller, K. D., Schleien, S. J., Brooke, P., Frisoli, A. M., & Brooks III, W. T. (2005). Community for all: The therapeutic recreation practitioner's role in inclusive volunteering. *Therapeutic Recreation Journal, 39*(1), 18–31.

Miller, K. E. (2004). Therapy options for post-traumatic stress disorder [Electronic version]. *American Family Physician, 69*(9), 2239.

Minde, J. H., & Friedman, A. R. (2002). The graying of disabled America. Retrieved March 2, 2009, from http://www.nsnn.com/graying_of_disabled_american.htm.

Mitchell, D. A., & Lassiter, S. L. (2006). Addressing health care disparities and increasing workforce diversity: The next step for the dental, medical, and public health professions. *American Journal of Public Health, 96*(12), 2093–2097.

Mitchell, H. J., & Hillman, W. (1969). The municipal recreation department and recreation services for the mentally retarded. *Therapeutic Recreation Journal, 3*(4), 32–40.

Mitsubishi Electric America Foundation. (n.d.). *Paths to Inclusion.* [Brochure]. Arlington, VA: Author.

Mitty, E. (2007). Hastings Center special report: The ethics of using QI methods to improve health care quality and safety. *Journal of Nursing Care Quality, 22*(2), 97–101.

Mobily, K. E. (1999). New horizons in models of practice in therapeutic recreation. *Therapeutic Recreation Journal, 33*(3), 174–192.

Mobily, K. E., & MacNeil, R. D. (2002). *Therapeutic recreation and the nature of disabilities.* State College, PA: Venture Publishing.

Mobily, K. E., Mobily, P. R., Lane, B. K., & Semerjian, T. Z. (1998). Using progressive resistance training as an intervention with older adults. *Therapeutic Recreation Journal, 32*(1), 42–53.

Mobily, K. E., Mobily, P. R., Lessard, K. A., & Berkenpas, M. S. (2000). Case comparison of response to aquatic exercise: Acute versus chronic conditions. *Therapeutic Recreation Journal, 34*(2), 103–119.

Mobily, K. E., Mobily, P. R., Raimondi, R. M., Walter, K. L., & Rubenstein, L. M. (2004). Strength training and falls among older adults: A community-based TR intervention. *Annual in Therapeutic Recreation, 13,* 1–11.

Mobily, K. E., & Ostiguy, L. J. (2004). *Introduction to therapeutic recreation: U.S. and Canadian perspectives.* State College, PA: Venture Publishing.

Mobily, K. E., & Verburg, M. D. (2001). Aquatic therapy in community-based therapeutic recreation: Pain management in a case of fibromyalgia. *Therapeutic Recreation Journal, 35*(1), 57–69.

Moore, E. R., & Coyle, C. P. (2007). Using poetry in therapeutic recreation interventions with a focus on applications in behavioral healthcare. *American Journal of Recreation Therapy, 6*(3), 35–47.

Morrison, L. (1996). Crisis or comfort? It's your retirement choice. *Parks & Recreation, 31*(3), 88–96.

Mueller, D. R., & Roder, V. (2005). Social skills training in recreational rehabilitation of schizophrenia patients. *American Journal of Recreation Therapy, 4*(3), 11–19.

Mueser, K. T., & Liberman, R. P. (1995). Behavior therapy in practice. In B. Bongar & L. E. Beutler (Eds.), *Comprehensive textbook of psychotherapy: Theory and practice* (pp. 84–110). New York: Oxford University Press.

Muller, D. J., Harris, P. J., Wattley, L. A., & Taylor, J. (1992). *Nursing children psychology: Research and practice* (2nd ed.). London: Chapman & Hall.

Mundy, J. (1997). Developing anger and aggression control in youth in recreation and park systems. *Parks & Recreation, 32*(3), 62–69.

Mundy, J. (1998). *Leisure education, theory and practice* (2nd ed.). Champaign, IL: Sagamore Publishing.

Murphy, E., & Carr, A. (2000). Pediatric pain problems. In A. Carr (Ed.), *What works for children and adolescents? A critical review of psychological interventions with children, adolescents, and their families* (pp. 258–279). London: Taylor & Francis.

Murphy, N. A., & Carbone, P. S. (2008). Promoting the participation of children with disabilities in sports, recreation, and physical activities. *Pediatrics, 121*(5), 1057–1061.

Myer, D. G. (1986). *Psychology.* New York: Worth.

National Center for Health Statistics. (2007). *Health, United States, 2007 with chartbook on trends in the health of Americans.* Hyattsville, MD: U.S. Department of Health and Human Services.

National Center on Family Homelessness. (2008). *America's homeless children.* Retrieved November 8, 2008, from http://www.familyhomelessness.org/pdf/fact_children.pdf.

National Coalition for the Homeless. (2008). *How many people experience homelessness?* NCH fact sheet #2. Retrieved November 9, 2008, from http://www.nationalhomeless.org/publications/facts/How_Many.pdf.

National Council for Therapeutic Recreation Certification (NCTRC). (1997). *Updated NCTRC exam content outline: Supplement to the NCTRC candidate bulletin.* Thiells, NY: Author.

National Council for Therapeutic Recreation Certification. (2007a). *2007 NCTRC job analysis report: NCTRC report on the international job analysis of Certified Therapeutic Recreation Specialists.* New City, NY: Author.

National Council for Therapeutic Recreation Certification. (2007b). *NCTRC position paper on the legal regulation of the practice of recreation therapy.* Retrieved April 10, 2007, from http://www.nctrc.org/documents/NCTRCLegalRecognitionPaper.doc

National Council for Therapeutic Recreation Certification. (2009). *Recreation therapy: CTRS profile* [Brochure]. New City, NY: Author.

National Dissemination Center for Children with Disabilities. (2004). *Spina bifida fact sheet 12 (FS12).* Retrieved February 14, 2007, from http://www.nichcy.org/pubs/factshe/fs12txt.htm.

National Institute of Allergy & Infectious Diseases (NIAID). (November, 2003). *HIV infection in infants and children*. Retrieved July 6, 2008, from http://www.thebody.com/content/art6573.html.

National Institute of Mental Health (NIMH). (2000). *Child and adolescent bipolar disorder: An update from the National Institute of Mental Health*. Retrieved November 20, 2007, from http://www.nimh.nih.gov/health/publications/child-and-adolescent-bipolar-disorders/summary.shtml

National Institute of Mental Health (NIMH). (2006 revised). *The numbers count: Mental disorders in America*. Retrieved July 16, 2007, from http://www.nimh.nih.gov/health/publications/the-numbers-count-mental-disorders-in-america.shtml

National Institute of Neurological Disorders and Stroke (NINDS). (2001). *Pain: Hope through research*. Retrieved June 7, 2008, from http://www.ninds.nih.gov/disorders/chronic_pain/detail_chronic_pain.htm?css=print

National Institute of Neurological Disorders and Stroke. (2005). *Asperger syndrome fact sheet*. Retrieved June 19, 2008, from http://www.ninds.nih.gov/disorders/asperger/detail_asperger.htm?css=print

National Institute of Neurological Disorders and Stroke. (2006). *Autism fact sheet*. Retrieved June 19, 2008, from http://www.ninds.nih.gov/disorders/autism/detail_autism.htm

National Jewish Medical and Research Center. (1995). *Understanding asthma*. Denver, CO: Author.

National Law Center on Homelessness & Poverty (NLCHP). (2008). *Homelessness & poverty in America*. Retrieved December 3, 2008, from http://www.nlchp.org/hapia.cfm.

National Therapeutic Recreation Society (NTRS). (1997). *NTRS internship standards and guidelines for therapeutic recreation*. Arlington, VA: Author.

National Therapeutic Recreation Society. (2001). *NTRS code of ethics and interpretive guidelines*. Retrieved December 12, 2007, from http://www.nrpa.org/content/default.aspx?documentId=867

National Therapeutic Recreation Society. (2003). *Standards of practice for a continuum of care in therapeutic recreation*. Retrieved December 3, 2007, from http://www.nrpa.org/content/default.aspx?documentId=1446

National Youth Gang Center. (2007). *National youth gang survey analysis*. Retrieved February 14, 2009, from http://www.iir.com/nygc/nygsa/prevalence_of_youth_gang_problems.htm.

Naugle, K., Stopka, C., & Brennan, J. (2007). Common medical conditions in athletes with spina bifida. *Athletic Therapy Today, 12*(1), 18–20.

Neulinger, J. (1976). The need for and the implications of a psychological conception of leisure. *The Ontario Psychologist, 8*(June), 15.

Neulinger, J. (1981). *To leisure: An introduction*. Boston: Allyn and Bacon.

Nicholson, M. (2004). Caring for war veterans—victims or heroes? *Kaitaki: Nursing New Zealand*. Wellington: New Zealand Nurses Organization.

Nickel, R. E., & Desch, L. W. (2000). *The physician's guide to caring for children with disabilities and chronic conditions*. Baltimore, MD: Paul H. Brookes Publishing.

Nijs, J., Paul, L., & Wallman, K. (2008). Chronic fatigue syndrome: An approach combining self-management with graded exercise to avoid exacerbations. *Journal of Rehabilitation Medicine, 40*(4), 241–247.

Nimrod, G. (2007). Retirees' leisure: Activities, benefits, and their contribution to life satisfaction. *Leisure Sciences, 26*(1), 65–80.

Nisbett, N., Brown-Welty, S., & O'Keefe, C. (2002). A study of ethics education within therapeutic recreation curriculum. *Therapeutic Recreation Journal, 36*(3), 282–295.

Nosek, L. J. (2004). Globalization's costs to healthcare. How can we pay the bill? *Nursing Administration Quarterly, 28*(2), 116–121.

O'Brien, K., Nixon, S., Tynan, A., & Glazier, R. H. (2006). Aerobic exercise interventions for people living with HIV/AIDS: Implications for practice, education, and research. *Physiotherapy Canada, 58*(2), 114–129.

O'Keefe, C. (2005). Grounding the therapeutic recreation process in an ethic of care. In C. Sylvester (Ed.), *Philosophy of therapeutic recreation ideas and issues* (vol. III, pp. 73–83). Ashburn, VA: NTRS/National Recreation and Park Association.

O'Morrow, G. S. (1980). *Therapeutic recreation: A helping profession* (2nd ed.). Reston, VA: Reston Publishing.

O'Morrow, G. S. (1991). *National Therapeutic Recreation Society: 25th anniversary, a historical perspective 1966–1991*. Alexandria, VA: National Recreation and Park Association.

O'Morrow, G. S., & Reynolds, R. P. (1989). *Therapeutic recreation: A helping profession* (3rd ed.). Englewood Cliffs, NJ: Prentice Hall.

O'Reilly, M. F., Lancioni, G. E., Sigafoos, J., Green, V. A., Ma, Chia-Hui, & O'Donoghue, D. (2004). A further comparison of external control and problem-solving interventions to teach social skills to adults with intellectual disabilities. *Behavioral Interventions, 19*(1), 173–186.

Oei, T. P. S., & Browne, A. (2006). Components of group processes: Have they contributed to the outcome of mood and anxiety disorder patients in a group cognitive-behavior therapy program? *American Journal of Psychotherapy, 60*(1), 53–70.

Okun, B. F., & Kantrowitz, R. E. (2008). *Effective helping: Interviewing and counseling techniques* (7th ed.). Belmont, CA: Thomson Brooks/Cole.

Oltman, P. K., Norback, J., & Rosenfeld, M. (1989). A national study of the profession of therapeutic recreation specialist. *Therapeutic Recreation Journal, 23*(2), 48–58.

Olusanya, B. O., & Roberts, A. A. (2006). Physician education on infant hearing loss in a developing country. *Pediatric Rehabilitation, 9*(4), 373–377.

Orsega-Smith, E. M., Mowen, A. J., Payne, L. L., & Godbey, G. C. (2004). The interaction of stress and park use on psycho-physiological health in older adults. *Journal of Leisure Research, 36*(2), 232–256.

Orsega-Smith, E. M., Payne, L. L., Mowen, A. J., Ho, C-H., & Godbey, G. C. (2007). The role of social support and self-efficacy in shaping the leisure time physical activity of older adults. *Journal of Leisure Research, 39*(4), 705–727.

Palmier, R. L. (2005). Is it myasthenia gravis or Guillain-Barré syndrome? *Nursing, 35*(12), 32hn1–32hn4.

Pang, M. Y. C., Eng, J. J., Dawson, A. S., McKay, H. A., & Harris, J. E. (2005). A community-based fitness and mobility exercise program for older adults with chronic stroke: A randomized controlled trial. *Journal of the American Geriatrics Society, 53*(10), 1667–1674.

Papalia, D. E., Sterns, H. L., Feldman, R. D., & Camp, C. J. (2007). *Adult development and aging* (3rd ed.). New York: McGraw-Hill.

Passmore, T. R. J. (2007). *Coverage of recreational therapy: The rules and regulations*. Alexandria, VA: American Therapeutic Recreation Association.

Passmore, T., & Lane, S. (2006). Exercise as treatment for depression: A therapeutic recreation intervention. *American Journal of Recreation Therapy, 5*(3), 31–41.

Patterson, I. (2004). Snoezelen as a casual leisure activity for people with a developmental disability. *Therapeutic Recreation Journal, 38*(3), 289–300.

Paul, G. L., & Menditto, A. A. (1992). Effectiveness of inpatient treatment programs for mentally ill adults in public psychiatric facilities. *Applied and Preventive Psychology: Current Scientific Perspectives, 1*, 41–63.

Payne, L. L., Mowen, A. J., & Montoro-Rodriguez, J. (2006). The role of leisure style in maintaining the health of older adults with arthritis. *Journal of Leisure Research, 38*(1), 20–45.

Pearce, W. J., & Pezzot-Pearce, T. D. (1997). *Psychotherapy of abused and neglected children.* New York: Guilford.

Pederson, P. (Ed.). (1998). *Multicultural counseling competencies: Individual and organizational development.* Thousand Oaks, CA: Sage Publications.

Peniston, L. C. (1995). When kids have trouble playing the game. *Parks & Recreation, 30*(3), 58–62.

Peniston, L. C. (1999). Learning disabilities in campers. *Camping Magazine, 72*(1), 32–34, 36–37.

Penrose, F. K. (2005). Can exercise affect cognitive functioning in Alzheimer's disease? A review of the literature. *Activities, Adaptation & Aging, 29*(4), 15–40.

Peterson, C. (1984). A matter of priorities and loyalties. *Therapeutic Recreation Journal, 18*(3), 11–16.

Pollock, N., Stewart, D., Law, M., Sahagian-Whalen, S., Harvey, S., & Toal, C. (1997). The meaning of play for young people with physical disabilities. *Canadian Journal of Occupational Therapy, 64*(1), 25–31.

Polzer, C. (1995). How to program to the homeless. *Parks & Recreation, 30*(3), 53–56.

Pomeroy, J. (1969). The San Francisco Recreation Center for the Handicapped: A brief description. *Therapeutic Recreation Journal, 3*(4), 15–19.

Pommier, J. H., & Witt P. A. (1995). Evaluation of an Outward Bound school plus family training program for the juvenile status offender. *Therapeutic Recreation Journal, 29*(2), 86–103.

Population Reference Bureau. (2007, October). *Today's research on aging.* Washington, DC: Author.

• Porter, H. R., & burlingame, j. (2006). *Recreational therapy handbook of practice: ICF-based diagnosis and treatment.* Enumclaw, WA: Idyll Arbor.

Porter, H. R., & Van Puymbroeck, M. (2007). Utilization of the International Classification of Functioning, Disability, and Health within therapeutic recreation practice. *Therapeutic Recreation Journal, 41*(1), 47–60.

Porter-O'Grady, T. (2003). Of hubris and hope: Transforming nursing for a new age. *Nursing Economics, 21*(2), 59–64.

Post-traumatic stress disorder. (2004). *British Medical Journal, 328*(7440), 624.

Powell, J. S. J. (2002). Why am I afraid to tell you who I am? In R. Purtilo & A. Haddad, *Health professional and patient interaction* (6th ed.). Philadelphia: W. B. Saunders.

Preparing students for today's global economy. (2007). *Presidency, 10*(1), 9.

Purtilo, R. (1999). *Ethical dimensions in the health professions* (3rd ed.). Philadelphia: W. B. Saunders.

Purtilo, R., & Haddad, A. (2002). *Health professional and patient interaction* (6th ed.). Philadelphia: W. B. Saunders.

Ragheb, M. G. (1993). Leisure and perceived wellness. *Leisure Sciences, 15*, 13–24.

Raschke, D. B., Dedrick, C. V. L., Heston, M. L., & Farris, M. (1996). Everyone can play, adapting the Candyland board game. *Teaching Exceptional Children, 28*(4), 28–33.

Rathsam, S. (2002). Puppy uppers. *Parks & Recreation, 37*(11), 58–62.

Ratner, J., & Griffiths, T. J. (1995). Exercise-induced asthma and indoor swimming. *Parks & Recreation, 30*(7), 46–51.

Reeve, J. (2006). Group psychotherapy with children on an inpatient unit: The MEGA group model. *Journal of Child & Adolescent Psychiatric Nursing, 19*(1), 3–12.

Regan, K. J., Banks, G. K., & Beran, R. G. (1993). Therapeutic recreation programmes for children with epilepsy. *Seizure, 2*(3), 195–200.

Reid, D., & Campbell, K. (2006). The use of virtual reality with children with cerebral palsy: A pilot randomized trial. *Therapeutic Recreation Journal, 40*(4), 255–268.

Remien, R. H., & Rabkin, J. G. (2001). Psychological aspects of living with HIV disease. *Western Journal of Medicine, 175*(5), 332–335.

Revheim, N., & Marcopulos, B. A. (2006). Group treatment approaches to address cognitive deficits. *Psychiatric Rehabilitation Journal, 30* (1), 38–45.

Reynolds, R. P., & O'Morrow, G. S. (1985). *Problems, issues & concepts in therapeutic recreation.* Englewood Cliffs, NJ: Prentice Hall.

Richeson, N. E., & McCullough, W. T. (2002). An evidence-based animal-assisted therapy protocol and flow sheet for the geriatric recreation therapy practice. *American Journal of Recreation Therapy, 1*(1), 25–29.

Richeson, N. E., & McCullough, W. T. (2003). A therapeutic recreation intervention using animal-assisted therapy: Effects on the subjective well-being of older adults. *Annual in Therapeutic Recreation, 12,* 1–6.

Richeson, N. E., Croteau, K. A., Jones, D. B., & Farmer, B. C. (2006). Effect of a pedometer-based intervention on the physical performance and mobility-related self-efficacy of community-dwelling older adults: An interdisciplinary preventive health care intervention. *Therapeutic Recreation Journal, 40*(1), 18–32.

Ries, A. L., Bauldoff, G. S., Carlin, B. W., Casaburi, R., Emery, C. F., Mahler, D. A., et al. (2007). Pulmonary rehabilitation: Joint ACCP/AACVPR evidence-based clinical practice guidelines. *Chest Supplement, 131*(5), 4S-42S.

Riley, B. (Ed.). (1991). *Quality management applications for therapeutic recreation.* State College, PA: Venture Publishing.

Riley, B. (Ed.). (2000). Outcome measurement in therapeutic recreation [Special issue]. *Annual in Therapeutic Recreation, 9.*

Riley, B., & Connolly, P. (1997). Statistical results of the NCTRC certification exam: The first five years. *Therapeutic Recreation Journal, 31*(1), 38–52.

Riley, B., & Connolly, P. (2007). A profile of Certified Therapeutic Recreation Specialist practitioners. *Therapeutic Recreation Journal, 41*(1), 29–46.

Riley, B., & Skalko, T. K. (1998). The evolution of therapeutic recreation. *Parks & Recreation, 33*(5), 64–71.

Riley, K., & Stanley, M. A. (2006). Research update: Art programs for older adults. *Parks & Recreation, 41*(2), 22–27.

Robertson, B. J. (2000). Leisure education as a rehabilitative tool for youth in incarceration settings. *Journal of Leisurability, 27*(2), 27–34.

Robertson, T., & Long, T. (Eds.). (2008). *Foundations of therapeutic recreation perceptions, philosophies, and practices for the 21st century.* Champaign, IL: Human Kinetics.

Rode, D. C. (1995). Building bridges within the culture of pediatric medicine: The interface of art therapy and child life programming. *Art Therapy: Journal of the American Art Therapy Association, 12*(2), 104–110.

Rogers, C. (1951). *Client-centered therapy.* Boston: Houghton Mifflin.

Rogers, D., Lee, Y., & Yang, H. (2007). Adolescents with spinal cord injury: Indicators and suggestions for recreational therapy practice. *American Journal of Recreation Therapy, 6*(1), 13–24.

Rogers, N. B. (1999). Caring for those who care: Achieving family caregiver wellness through social support programs. *Activities, Adaptation & Aging, 24*(1), 1–12.

Roland, C. C., & Havens, M. (1981). *An introduction to adventure: A sequential approach to challenging activities with persons who are disabled.* Loretto, MN: Vineland National Center.

Rooney, J. (2004). Oh, those aching joints. *Nursing, 34*(11), 58–64.

Rosenberger, R. S., Sneh, Y., Phipps, T. T., & Gurvitch, R. (2005). A spatial analysis of linkages between health care expenditures, physical inactivity, obesity and recreation supply. *Journal of Leisure Research, 37*(2), 216–235.

Roth, A. J., & Massie, M. J. (2001). Psychiatric complications in cancer patients. In R. E. Lenhard, Jr., R. T. Osteen, & T. Gansler (Eds.), *The American Cancer Society's clinical oncology* (pp. 837–851). Atlanta: American Cancer Society.

Roth, B. E. (1997). The current health care environment and stages of market development. *Gastroenterology Clinics of North America, 26*(4), 715–724.

Rothwell, E., Piatt, J., & Mattingly, K. (2006). Social competence: Evaluation of an outpatient recreation therapy treatment program for children with behavioral disorders. *Therapeutic Recreation Journal, 40*(4), 241–254.

Rowe, M. (2007). Virtual way to confront fears. *Nursing Standard, 21*(22), 29.

Russoniello, C. V. (1991). *An exploratory study of physiological and psychological changes in alcoholic patients after recreation therapy treatments.* Paper presented at the Benefits of Therapeutic Recreation in Rehabilitation Conference, Lafayette Hill, PA.

Ruzek, J. I., Brymer, M. J., Jacobs, A. K., Layne, C. M., Vernberg, E. M., & Watson, P. J. (2007). Psychological first aid [Electronic version]. *Journal of Mental Health Counseling, 29*(1), 17–49.

Ryall, R. (1974). Delinquency: The problem for treatment. *Social Work Today, 15*, 98–104.

Sable, J., & Bocarro, J. (2004). Transitioning back to health: Participants' perspective of project PATH. *Therapeutic Recreation Journal, 38*(2), 206–224.

Sadock, B. J., & Sadock, V. A. (2003). *Kaplan & Sadock's synopsis of psychiatry* (9th ed.). Philadelphia: Lippincott Williams &Wilkins.

Sausser, C., & Dattilo, J. (2000). Therapeutic horseback riding. In J. Dattilo (Ed.), *Facilitation techniques in therapeutic recreation* (pp. 273–301). State College, PA: Venture Publishing.

Scalise, D. (2006). Clinical communication and patient safety. *Hospitals & Health Networks/AHA, 80*(8), 49–54.

Scanlon, W. J. (2006). The future of Medicare hospital payment. *Health Affairs, 25*(1), 70–80.

Scherer, Y. K., & Shimmel, S. (1996). Using self-efficacy theory to educate patients with chronic obstructive pulmonary disease. *Rehabilitation Nursing, 21*(5), 262–266.

Schleien, S. J., Fahnestock, M. K., & Miller, K. D. (2001). Severe multiple disabilities. In D. R. Austin & M. E. Crawford (Eds.), *Therapeutic recreation: An introduction* (3rd ed., pp. 156–189). Boston: Allyn & Bacon.

Schleien, S. J., Germ, P. A., & McAvoy, L. H. (1996). Inclusive community leisure services: Recommended professional practices and barriers encountered. *Therapeutic Recreation Journal, 30*(4), 260–273.

Schleien, S. J., Green, F. P., & Stone, C. F. (2003). Making friends within inclusive community recreation programs. *American Journal of Recreation Therapy, 2*(1), 7–16.

Schleien, S. J., & Ray, M. T. (1997). Leisure education for a quality transition to adulthood. *Journal of Vocational Rehabilitation, 8*(2), 155–169.

Schleien, S. J., Ray, M. T., & Green, F. P. (1997). *Community recreation and people with disabilities: Strategies for inclusion* (2nd ed.). Baltimore: Paul H. Brookes Publishing.

Schneider, M. A. (2000). In response to deinstitutionalization: Farm communities as a housing alternative for individuals with autism. *Journal of Leisurability, 27*(1), 10–17.

Scholl, K. G., Dieser, R. B., & Davison, A. (2005). Together we play: An ecological approach to inclusive recreation. *Therapeutic Recreation Journal, 39*(4), 229–311.

Schönherr, M. C., Groothoff, J. W., Mulder, G. A., & Eisma, W. H. (2005). Participation and satisfaction after spinal cord injury: Results of a vocational and leisure outcome study. *Spinal Cord, 43*(4), 241–248.

Schultz, L. E., Crompton, J. L., & Witt, P. A. (1995). A national profile of the status of public recreation services for at-risk children and youth. *Journal of Park and Recreation Administration, 13*(3), 1–25.

Schwalm-Lopez, M., & MacNeil, R. D. (2005). Chronic fatigue syndrome: Implications for the therapeutic recreation profession. *American Journal of Recreation Therapy, 4*(3), 32–40.

Schwartz, S. (2000). *Abnormal psychology: A discovery approach.* Mountain View, CA: Mayfield.

Searle, M. S., Mahon, M. J., Iso-Ahola, S. E., Sdrolias, H. A., & vanDyck, J. (1998). Examining the long-term effects of leisure education on a sense of independence and psychological well-being among the elderly. *Journal of Leisure Research, 30*(3), 331–340.

Seibert, M. L. (1991). Keynote. In C. P. Coyle, W. B. Kinney, B. Riley, & J. W. Shank (Eds.), *Benefits of therapeutic recreation: A consensus view* (pp. 5–15). Ravensdale, WA: Idyll Arbor.

Sellers, D. M. (2005). The evaluation of an animal assisted therapy intervention for elders with dementia in long-term care. *Activities, Adaptation & Aging, 30*(1), 61–77.

Sellew, G., & Ebel, M. E., Sr. (1955). *A history of nursing* (3rd ed.). St. Louis: C. V. Mosby.

Sessoms, H. D., & Orthner, D. K. (1992). Parks and recreation and our growing invisible populations. *Parks & Recreation, 27*(8), 62–65.

Shank, J., & Coyle C. (2002). *Therapeutic recreation in health promotion and rehabilitation.* State College, PA: Venture Publishing.

Shank, J. W., Coyle, C. P., Boyd, R., & Kinney, W. B. (1996). A classification scheme for therapeutic recreation research grounded in the rehabilitative sciences. *Therapeutic Recreation Journal, 30*(3), 179–196.

Sheehan, T. (1993). Outcome measures and therapeutic recreation. In G. Hitzhusen & L. T. Jackson (Eds.), *Expanding horizons in therapeutic recreation* (vol. 15, pp. 129–142). Columbia: Curators of University of Missouri.

Sheldon, K., & Dattilo, J. (2000). Therapeutic reminiscence. In J. Dattilo (Ed.), *Facilitation techniques in therapeutic recreation* (pp. 303–326). State College, PA: Venture Publishing.

Sherrill, C. (2004). *Adapted physical activity, recreation and sport: Cross disciplinary and lifespan* (6th ed.). Boston: McGraw Hill.

Sigafoos, J., Tucker, M., Bushell, H., & Webber, Y. (1997). A practical strategy to increase participation and reduce challenging behavior during leisure skills programming. *Mental Retardation, 35*(3), 198–208.

Sigerist, H. E. (1933). *The great doctors.* New York: W. W. Norton.

Sime, W. E. (1987). Exercise in the treatment and prevention of depression. In W. P. Morgan & S. E. Goldston (Eds.), *Exercise and mental health* (pp. 145–154). Washington, DC: Hemisphere.

Simon, J. M. (1996). Chronic pain syndrome: Nursing assessment and intervention. *Rehabilitation Nursing, 21*(1), 13–19.

Singh, M. K., & Patel, J. (2005). *Chronic pain syndrome.* Retrieved June 7, 2008, from http://www.emedicine.com/pmr/topic32.htm

Sitlington, P. L. (1996). Transition to living: The neglected component of transition programming for individuals with learning disabilities. *Journal of Learning Disabilities, 29*(1), 31–39, 52.

Skalko, T. K. (1998). Reimbursement. In F. Brasile, T. K. Skalko, & j. burlingame (Eds.), *Perspectives in recreational therapy: Issues of a dynamic profession* (pp. 447–462). Ravensdale, WA: Idyll Arbor.

Skalko, T., Van Andel, G., & DeSalvatore, G. (1991). The benefits of therapeutic recreation in psychiatry. In C. Coyle, W. B. Kinney, B. Riley, & J. W. Shank (Eds.), *Benefits of therapeutic recreation: A consensus view* (pp. 289–337). Ravensdale, WA: Idyll Arbor.

Skinner, B. F. (1953). *Science and human behavior.* New York: Macmillan.

Sklar, S. L., Anderson, S. C., & Autry, C. E. (2007). Positive youth development: A wilderness intervention. *Therapeutic Recreation Journal, 41*(3), 223–243.

Sklar, S. L., & Autry, C. E. (2008). Youth development and therapeutic recreation. In T. Robertson & T. Long (Eds.), *Foundations of therapeutic recreation* (pp. 165–183). Champaign, IL: Human Kinetics.

Slawta, J. (2006). Be a fit kid: Promoting healthful lifestyles in adolescents with special needs. *American Journal of Recreation Therapy, 5*(1), 7–17.

Smith, G. B. (2003). Nursing care of patients with HIV disease and AIDS. In L. S. Williams & P. D. Hopper (Eds.), *Understanding medical surgical nursing* (2nd ed., pp. 1008–1025). Philadelphia: F. A. Davis Company.

Smith, R. W., Austin, D. R., & Kennedy, D. W. (2001). *Inclusive and special recreation opportunities for persons with disabilities* (4th ed.). Boston: McGraw Hill.

Smith, R. W., Austin, D. R., Kennedy, D. W., Lee, Y., & Hutchison, P. (2005). *Inclusive and special recreation opportunities for persons with disabilities.* (5th ed.). Boston: McGraw Hill.

Smith, S., & Gove, J. E. (2005). *Physical changes of aging.* Gainesville: University of Florida Press.

Smith, T. E. C., Polloway, E. A., Patton, J. R., & Dowdy, C. A. (2008). *Teaching students with special needs in inclusive settings* (5th ed.). Boston: Pearson Education.

Sorensen, B., & Luken, K. (1999). Improving functional outcomes with recreation therapy. *The Case Manager, 10*(5), 48–52.

Spears, L. (1998). Introduction. In L. S. Spears (Ed.), *The power of servant leadership* (pp. 1–15). San Francisco: Berrett-Koehler Publishers.

Sprouse, J. K. S., & Klitzing, S. W. (2005). Youth at risk: Recreation and prevention. *Parks & Recreation, 40*(1), 16–21.

Stein, D. J. (2002). Obsessive-compulsive disorder. *The Lancet, 360*(9330), 397–405.

Stein, T. A. (1970). Therapeutic recreation education: 1969 survey. *Therapeutic Recreation Journal, 4*(2), 4–7.

Stein, T. A., & Sessoms, H. D. (Eds.). (1973). *Recreation and special populations*. Boston: Holbrook Press.

Stevens, B., Kagan, S., Yamada, J., Epstein, I., Beamer, M., Bilodeau, M., & Baruchel, S. (2004). Brief report adventure therapy for adolescents with cancer. *Pediatric Blood & Cancer, 43*(3), 278–284.

Stevens-Ratchford, R., & Krause, A. (2004). Visually impaired older adults and home-based leisure activities: The effects of person-environment congruence. *Journal of Visual Impairment & Blindness, 98*(1), 14–27.

Stone, C. F. (2003). Exploring cultural competencies of Certified Therapeutic Recreation Specialists: Implications for education and training. *Therapeutic Recreation Journal, 37*(2), 156–174.

Stone, K. (2007, November/December). Therapeutic recreation and the Autism Society of North Carolina. *American Therapeutic Recreation Association Newsletter, 23*(6), 17–18.

Strock, M. (2007). *Autism spectrum disorders, pervasive developmental disorders with addendum January 2007*. Bethesda, MD: Department of Health and Human Services. National Institutes of Health.

Stumbo, N. J. (1994/95). Assessment of social skills for therapeutic recreation intervention. *Annual in Therapeutic Recreation, 5*, 68–82.

Stumbo, N. J. (1995). Social skills instruction through commercially available resources. *Therapeutic Recreation Journal, 29*(1), 30–55.

Stumbo, N. J. (1996). A proposed accountability model for therapeutic recreation services. *Therapeutic Recreation Journal, 30*(4), 246–259.

Stumbo, N. J. (2002a). *Client assessment in therapeutic recreation services*. State College, PA: Venture Publishing.

Stumbo, N. J. (2002b). *Leisure education II: More activities and resources* (2nd ed.). State College, PA: Venture Publishing.

Stumbo, N. J. (2003a). The importance of evidence-based practice in therapeutic recreation. In N. J. Stumbo (Ed.), *Client outcomes in therapeutic recreation services* (pp. 25–48). State College, PA: Venture Publishing.

Stumbo, N. J. (2003b). Outcomes, accountability and therapeutic recreation. In N. J. Stumbo (Ed.), *Client outcomes in therapeutic recreation services* (pp. 1–24). State College, PA: Venture Publishing.

Stumbo, N. J. (2006a). An evidence-based approach to providing physical activity and cognitive-behavioral therapy to older adults with pain. *American Journal of Recreation Therapy, 5*(3), 13–25.

Stumbo, N. J. (2006b). Unique issues in pain management for older adults. *American Journal of Recreation Therapy, 5*(2), 37–46.

Stumbo, N. J. (Ed.). (2003). *Client outcomes in therapeutic recreation services*. State College, PA: Venture Publishing.

Stumbo, N. J., & Bloom, C. W. (1990). The implications of traumatic brain injury for therapeutic recreation services in rehabilitation settings. *Therapeutic Recreation Journal, 24*(3), 64–79.

Stumbo, N. J., Carter, M. J., & Kim, J. (2004). 2003 national therapeutic recreation curriculum study part B: University, faculty, student, and placement characteristics. *Therapeutic Recreation Journal, 38*(1), 53–71.

Stumbo, N. J., Pegg, S., & Lord, E. (2007). Physical activity and older individuals: Benefits, barriers, and interventions. *American Journal of Recreation Therapy, 6*(4), 7–18.

Stumbo, N. J., & Peterson, C. A. (1998). The leisure ability model. *Therapeutic Recreation Journal, 32*(2), 82–95.

Stumbo, N. J., & Peterson, C. A. (2009). *Therapeutic recreation program design: Principles and procedures* (5th ed.). San Francisco: Pearson Benjamin Cummings.

Summers, L. (1962). The American Red Cross program of recreation in military hospitals: A retrospective view. *Recreation in Treatment Centers, 1*, 18–22.

Sweet, R. A., Mulsant, B. H., Gupta, B., Rifai, A. H., & Pasternak, R. E., et al. (1995). Duration of neuroleptic treatment and prevalence of tardive dyskinesia in late life. *Archives of General Psychiatry, 52*, 478–486.

Sylvester, C. (1987). Therapeutic recreation and the end of leisure. In C. Sylvester (Ed.), *Philosophy of therapeutic recreation: Ideas and issues* (vol. 1, pp. 76–89). Alexandria, VA: National Recreation and Park Association.

Sylvester, C. (2002). Ethics and the quest for professionalism. *Therapeutic Recreation Journal, 36*(4), 314–334.

Sylvester, C. (Ed.). (2005). *Philosophy of therapeutic recreation: Ideas and issues* (vol. III). Ashburn, VA: National Therapeutic Recreation Society.

Sylvester, C., Voelkl, J. E., & Ellis, G. D. (2001). *Therapeutic recreation programming: Theory and practice.* State College, PA: Venture Publishing.

Tasiemski, T., Kennedy, P., & Gardner, B. P. (2006). Examining the continuity at recreation engagement in individuals with spinal cord injuries. *Therapeutic Recreation Journal, 40*(2), 77–93.

Taylor, G. (2006). Vision, mission, philosophy, and objectives. In M. J. Carter & G. S. O'Morrow, *Effective management in therapeutic recreation service* (2nd ed., pp. 49–57). State College, PA: Venture Publishing.

Taylor, G. P. (1985). *Therapeutic recreation for children in shelters for domestic violence.* Unpublished master's thesis, Central Michigan University, Mt. Pleasant, MI.

Teague, M. L., McGhee, V. L., & Hawkins, B. A. (2001). Geriatric practice. In D. R. Austin & M. E. Crawford (Eds.), *Therapeutic recreation: An introduction* (3rd ed., pp. 233–254). Boston: Allyn & Bacon.

Tedrick, T. (2004). Research update: Seniors set sights on staying competitive. *Parks & Recreation, 39*(8), 28–33.

Thomas, H., Feyz, M., LeBlanc, J., Brosseau, J., Champoux, M-C., Christopher, A., et al. (2003). North Star Project, reality orientation in an acute care setting for patients with traumatic brain injuries. *Journal of Head Trauma Rehabilitation, 18*(3), 292–302.

Thompson, G. T. (1996). Structuring your department to manage coverage and third-party reimbursement. In D. Wagner, B. Kennedy, & A. Prichard (Eds.), *Recreational therapy: The next generation of reimbursement* (pp. 1–18). Hattiesburg, MS: American Therapeutic Recreation Association.

Thorndike, E. L. (1935). *The psychology of wants, interests and attitudes.* New York: Appleton-Century.

Thorp, D. M., Stahmer, A. C., & Schreibman, L. (1995). Effects of sociodramatic play training on children with autism. *Journal of Autism and Developmental Disorders, 25*(3), 265–282.

Topolski, T. D., LoGerfo, J., Patrick, D. L., Williams, B., Walwick, J., & Patrick, M. B. (2006, October). The rapid assessment of physical activity (RAPA) among older adults. *Preventing Chronic Disease, 3*(4), 1–8.

Townsend, M. C. (2006). *Psychiatric mental health nursing: Concepts of care in evidence-based practice* (5th ed.). Philadelphia: F. A. Davis.

Trader, B. R., & MacKinnon, J. (1998). Start with the arts to encourage confident and enthusiastic learners. *Parks & Recreation, 33*(5), 94–98.

Treatment challenges in bipolar disorder: Pharmaceutical and psychological interventions sponsored by Janssen-Cilag. (2006). *Bipolar Disorders, 8* (Suppl. 1), 1–68.

Tsai, E., & Fung, L. (2005). Perceived constraints to leisure time physical activity participation of students with hearing impairment. *Therapeutic Recreation Journal, 39*(3), 192–206.

Tummers, N., & Hendrick, F. (2004). Older adults say yes to yoga. *Parks & Recreation, 39*(3), 54–60.

Turkus, J. A., & Kahler, J. A. (2006). Therapeutic interventions in the treatment of dissociative disorders [Electronic version]. *The Psychiatric Clinics of North America, 29*(1), 245–262.

U.S. Conference of Mayors. (2008). Hunger and homelessness survey, a status report on hunger and homelessness in America's cities. Retrieved February 12, 2009, from http://www.usmayors.org/pressreleases/documents/hungerhomelessnessreport_121208.pdf.

U.S. Department of Health & Human Services (USDHHS). (1996). *Physical activity and health: A report of the Surgeon General.* Atlanta: Centers for Disease Control and Prevention.

U.S. Department of Health and Human Services. (2000). *Healthy people 2010* (Conference ed.). Washington, DC: Author.

U.S. Department of Health and Human Services. (2007). *Leading health indicators touch everyone.* Retrieved February 6, 2007, from http://www.healthypeople.gov/LHI/Touch_fact.htm

Van Andel, G. E. (1981). Professional standards: Improving the quality of services. *Therapeutic Recreation Journal, 15*(4), 23–30.

Van Andel, G. E. (1998). TR service delivery and TR outcome models. *Therapeutic Recreation Journal, 32*(3), 180–193.

Van Bourgondien, M. E., & Schopler, E. (1996). Intervention for adults with autism. *Journal of Rehabilitation, 62*(1), 65–71.

van der Smissen, B., Moiseichik, M., & Hartenburg, V. J. (Eds.). (2005). *Management of park and recreation agencies* (2nd ed.). Ashburn, VA: National Recreation and Park Association.

Van Puymbroeck, M., & Ashton-Shaeffer, C. (2007). The meanings of leisure for individuals waiting for a heart transplant: Implications for recreational therapy interventions. *Annual in Therapeutic Recreation, 15,* 20–34.

Van Puymbroeck, M., & Wahba, A. (2007). Ethical issues in cross-cultural health research in the United States: Implications for recreation therapy. *Annual in Therapeutic Recreation, 15,* 85–95.

Veenstra, J., Brasile, F., & Stewart, M. (2003). Perceived benefits of aquatic therapy for multiple sclerosis participants. *American Journal of Recreation Therapy, 2*(1), 33–48.

Velting, O. N., Setzer, N. J, & Albano, A. M. (2004). Update on and advances in assessment and cognitive-behavioral treatment of anxiety in children and adolescents. *Professional Psychology: Research and Practice, 35*(1), 42–54.

Voelkl, J. E., & Aybar-Damali, B. (2008). Aging and the life span. In T. Robertson & T. Long (Eds.), *Foundations of therapeutic recreation: Perceptions, philosophies, and practices for the 21st century* (pp.185–196). Champaign, IL: Human Kinetics.

Vogel, L. C., Hickey, K. J., Klaas, S. J., & Anderson, C. J. (2004). Unique issues in pediatric spinal cord injury. *Orthopaedic Nursing, 23*(5), 300–308.

Wachtel, R. (2003). Implementing recreation and leisure for the young child with health in mind. In M. Bender & C. A. Baglin (Eds.), *Implementing recreation and leisure opportunities for infants and toddlers with disabilities* (pp. 55–60). Champaign, IL: Sagamore Publishing.

Wachter, C. J. (1994). The influence of communication mode on the leisure behavior of adults who are deaf. *Therapeutic Recreation Journal, 28*(4), 213–220.

Waite, P. J., & Tatchell, T. (2005). The perceived health benefits of community service-learning: Reminiscence therapy's impact on novice practitioners. *College Student Journal, 39*(1), 104–116.

Wall, M. E., & Gast, D. L. (1997). Caregivers' use of constant time delay to teach leisure skills to adolescents or young adults with moderate or severe intellectual disabilities. *Education and Training in Mental Retardation and Developmental Disabilities, 32*(4), 340–356.

Wallis, C. (1983, June 6). Stress: Can we cope? *Time,* 48–54.

Wallis, C. (1996, June 24). Faith & Healing. *Time,* 58–62.

Walsh, J. (2002). Project adventure's programs for youth at risk: A developing continuum. *Zip Lines: The Voice for Adventure Education, 44,* 18–21.

Wang, Y. (2008). Physical activities and health-related quality of life in older adults: Findings from the BRFSS 2000. *Annual in Therapeutic Recreation, 16,* 102–113.

Ward, J. (1995). Homeless people and recreation needs. *Journal of Leisurability, 22*(1), 3–9.

Warden, D. (2006). Military TBI during Iraq and Afghanistan wars. *Journal of Head Trauma Rehabilitation, 21*(5), 398–402.

Watson, J. B. (1913). Psychology as the behaviorist views it. *Psychological Review, 20,* 158–177.

Weckworth, C. F. (1964). Research on current recreational practices in treatment centers. *Recreation in Treatment Centers, 3,* 64–67.

Wegner, D., & Jarvi, C. K. (2005). Planning for strategic management. In B. van der Smissen, M. Moiseichik, & V. J. Hartenburg (Eds.), *Management of park and recreation agencies* (2nd ed., pp. 103–124). Ashburn, VA: National Recreation and Park Association.

Weiss, R. (1997). Aging—New answers to old questions. *National Geographic, 192*(5), 2–31.

Welsh, R., Burcham, B., DeMoss, K., Martin, C., & Milich, R. (1997). *Attention deficit hyperactivity disorder diagnosis and management: A training program for teachers.* Frankfurt: Kentucky Department of Education.

Wenzel, K. (1999). Technology partnerships and therapeutic recreation. *Parks & Recreation, 34*(5), 72–76.

Wenzel, K. C. (2006). Working effectively with management. In M. J. Carter, & G. S. O'Morrow. *Effective management in therapeutic recreation service* (2nd ed. pp. 91–99). State College, PA: Venture Publishing.

Werhan, P. O., & Groff, D. G. (2005). Research update: The wilderness therapy trail. *Parks & Recreation, 40*(11), 24–29.

West, D., Quigley, A., & Kay, J. (2006). MEMENTO: A digital-physical scrapbook for memory sharing. *Personal and Ubiquitous Computing, 11*(4), 313–328.

West, H. C., & Sabol, W. J. (2008). *Prisoners in 2007.* Retrieved February 14, 2009, from http://www.ojp.usdoj.gov/bjs/pub/pdf/p07.pdf.

West, R. E., Kinney, T., & Witman, J. (Eds.). (2008). *Guidelines for competency assessment and curriculum planning for recreational therapy practice.* Hattiesburg, MS: American Therapeutic Recreation Association.

Whelan, L. (2006). Competency assessment of nursing staff. *Orthopaedic Nursing, 25*(3), 198–202.

Whitman, B. Y., & Munkel, W. (1991). Multiple personality disorder: A risk indicator, diagnostic marker, and psychiatric outcome for severe child abuse. *Clinical Pediatrics, 30*(7), 422–428.

Wichrowski, M., Whiteson, J., Haas, F., Mola, A., & Rey, M. J. (2005). Effects of horticultural therapy on mood and heart rate in patients participating in an inpatient cardiopulmonary rehabilitation program. *Journal of Cardiopulmonary Rehabilitation, 25*(5), 270–274.

Widmer, M. A., & Ellis, G. D. (1998). The Aristotelian good life model: Integration of values into therapeutic recreation service delivery. *Therapeutic Recreation Journal, 32*(4), 290–302.

Wikström, B-M. (2005). Communicating via expressive arts: The natural medium of self-expression for hospitalized children. *Pediatric Nursing, 31*(6), 480–485.

Wilhite, B. C., & Keller, M. J. (1996). Integration, productivity, and independence among adults with developmental disabilities: Implications for therapeutic recreation. *Therapeutic Recreation Journal, 30*(1), 64–78.

Wilhite, B. C., Keller, M. J., & Caldwell, L. (1999). Optimizing lifelong health and well-being: A health enhancing model of therapeutic recreation. *Therapeutic Recreation Journal, 33*(2), 98–108.

Wilhite, B. C., Keller, M. J., Collins, J. R. Jr., & Jacobson, S. (2003). A research agenda for therapeutic recreation revisited. *Therapeutic Recreation Journal, 37*(3), 207–223.

Wilhite, B. C., Keller, M. J., Gaudet, G., & Buettner, L. L. (1999). The efficacy of sensory stimulation with older adults with dementia-related cognitive impairments. *Annual in Therapeutic Recreation, 8,* 43–55.

Williams, B. (2000). The treatment of adolescent populations: An institutional vs. a wilderness setting. *Journal of Child and Adolescent Group Therapy, 10*(1), 47–56.

Williams, B. K., & Knight, S. M. (1994). *Health for life: Wellness and the art of living.* Pacific Grove, CA: Brooks/Cole.

Williams, R. (2002). Humor as a therapeutic recreation intervention. *Parks & Recreation, 37*(5), 48–53.

Williams, R., & Dattilo, J. (1997). Effects of leisure education on self-determination, social interaction, and positive affect of young adults with mental retardation. *Therapeutic Recreation Journal, 31*(4), 244–258.

Williams, R., & Dattilo, J. (2000). Therapeutic use of humor. In J. Dattilo (Ed.), *Facilitation techniques in therapeutic recreation* (pp. 385–407). State College, PA: Venture Publishing.

Wilson, J. Q. (1997). What to do about crime. In J. J. Sullivan & J. L. Victor (Eds.), *Criminal justice 97/98* (21st ed., pp. 14–24). Guilford, CT: Dushkin/McGraw-Hill.

Witman, J. (1994). Demonstrating treatment outcomes in therapeutic recreation. *Parks & Recreation, 29*(4), 84–89.

Witman, J., & Batchelder, K. (1992). Implications of brief treatment for therapeutic recreation. In B. H. Hitzhusen & L. T. Jackson (Eds.), *Expanding horizons in therapeutic recreation* (vol. 14, pp. 273–287). Columbia: University of Missouri.

Witman, J. P., & Preskenis, K. (1996). Adventure programming with an individual who has multiple personality disorder: A case history. *Therapeutic Recreation Journal, 30*(4), 289–296.

Witmer, J. M., & Sweeney, T. J. (1992). A holistic model for wellness and prevention over the life span. *Journal of Counseling & Development, 71*, 140–148.

Witt, P. A., & Baker, D. (1997). Developing after-school programs for youth in high risk environments. *Journal of Physical Education, Recreation & Dance, 68*(9), 18–20.

Witt, P. A., & Caldwell, L. L. (2005). Recreation and youth development. State College, PA: Venture Publishing Inc.

Witt, P. A., & Crompton, J. L. (1997). The at-risk youth recreation project. *Parks & Recreation, 32*(1), 54–61.

Witt, P. A., & Crompton, J. L. (Eds.). (1996). Recreation programs that work for at-risk youth: The challenge of shaping the future. State College, PA: Venture Publishing Inc.

Wojciechowski, E., & Cichowski, K. (2007). A case review: Designing a new patient education system. *Internet Journal of Advanced Nursing Practice, 8*(2), 2–26.

Wolfe, B. D., Dattilo, J., & Gast, D. L. (2003). Effects of a token economy system within the context of cooperative games on social behaviors of adolescents with emotional and behavioral disorders. *Therapeutic Recreation Journal, 37*(2), 124–141.

Wolffe, J. B. (1957). *Recreation, medicine and the humanities.* Chapel Hill: University of North Carolina, Third Southern Regional Institute on Hospital Recreation.

Wood, R. T., & Griffiths, M. D. (2007). A qualitative investigation of problem gambling as an escape-based coping strategy [Electronic version]. *Psychology & Psychotherapy: Theory, Research & Practice, 80*(1), 107–125.

Woolf, A. D., & Pfleger, B. (2003). Burden of major musculoskeletal conditions. *Bulletin of the World Health Organization, 81*(9), 646–656.

World Health Organization (WHO). (2001). *Mental health problems: The undefined and hidden burden.* Retrieved on November 26, 2007, from http://www.who.int/mediacentre/factsheet/fs218/en/index.html

World Health Organization. (2003). *ICF checklist.* Retrieved April 13, 2009, from http://www.who.int/classifications/icf/training/icfchecklist.pdf

World Health Organization. (2005). *The World Health Organization announces first-ever international forum on community mental health services.* Retrieved July 16, 2007, from http://www.who.int/mediacenter/news/release2005/pr21/en/index.html

World Health Organization. (2009). *Violence.* Retrieved February 14, 2009, from http://www.who.int/violence_injury_prevention/violence/en/.

World Health Organization. (2010a). *New action plan lays the foundation for tuberculosis elimination.* News Release, Oct. 13, 2010. Retrieved from www.who.int/medicentre/news/releases/2010/tb_20101013/3n/index.html

World Health Organization. (2010b). *Tobacco.* Fact Sheet 339. Retrieved October 26, 2010, from www.who.int/mediacentre/factsheets/fs339/en/index.html

Wozencroft, A. J., Voelkl, J. E., & McGuire, F. A. (2006). Professionalism in recreation therapy. *American Journal of Recreation Therapy, 5*(2), 21–26.

Wyller, V. B. (2007). The chronic fatigue syndrome—an update. *Acta Neurologica Scandinavica, 115* (Suppl. 187), 7–14.

Yang, S., Telama, R., Viikari, J., & Raitakari, O. T. (2006). Risk of obesity in relation to physical activity tracking from youth to adulthood. *Medicine & Science in Sports & Exercise, 38*(5), 919–925.

Young, J. M., & McNicoll, P. (1998). Against all odds: Positive life experiences of people with advanced amyotrophic lateral sclerosis. *Health & Social Work, 23*(1), 35–43.

Zabriskie, R. B. (2003). Research into practice: Methodology insight measurement basics: A must for therapeutic recreation professionals today. *Therapeutic Recreation Journal, 37*(4), 330–338.

Zabriskie, R. B., & Ferguson, D. D. (2004). A national study of therapeutic recreation field work and internships. *Annual in Therapeutic Recreation, 13,* 24–37.

Zabriskie, R. B., Lundberg, N. R., & Groff, D. G. (2005). Quality of life and identity: The benefits of a community-based therapeutic recreation and adaptive sports program. *Therapeutic Recreation Journal, 39*(3), 176–191.

Ziegler, J. (2002). Re-creating retirement: How will baby boomers reshape leisure in their 60s? *Parks & Recreation, 37*(10), 56–61.

Zijlstra, H. P., & Vlaskamp, C. (2005). Leisure provision for persons with profound intellectual and multiple disabilities: Quality time or killing time? *Journal of Intellectual Disability Research, 49*(6), 434–448.

Name Index

Subject Index